Accident Reconstruction Science

Fourth Edition

Alan J. Watts, Ph.D.

Lawyers & Judges Publishing Company, Inc.
Tucson, Arizona

Lawyers & Judges Publishing Company, Inc.

P.O. Box 30040 • Tucson, AZ 85751-0040
(800) 209-7109 • FAX (800) 330-8795
e-mail: sales@lawyersandjudges.com
www.lawyersandjudges.com

Library of Congress Cataloging-in-Publication Data

Watts, Alan J.
Accident reconstruction science / Alan J. Watts. -- 4th ed.
p. cm.
Rev. ed. of: Low speed automobile accidents : accident reconstruction and occupant kinematics, dynamics, and biomechanics. 3rd ed. c2003.
Includes bibliographical references and index.
ISBN-13: 978-1-936360-03-1 (hbk. : alk. paper)
ISBN-10: 1-936360-03-9 (hbk. : alk. paper)
1. Traffic accident investigation--United States. 2. Traffic accidents--United States. 3. Liability for traffic accidents--United States. 4. Evidence, Expert--United States. I. Watts, Alan J. Low speed automobile accidents. II. Title.
HV8079.55.W37 2011
363.12'565--dc23

2011032832

Printed in the United States of America
10 9 8 7 6 5 4 3 2 1

Contents

Preface

The third edition of this book, called *Low Speed Automobile Accidents*, was apparently fairly well received. Why not a more general book that covered higher speed events? This was easier said than done. First, as the *Low Speed* book grew (from the first edition in 1996 at 270 pages, to the third edition in 2003 at 870 pages) it progressively contained more data that was not strictly relevant to only low speeds (closing speed of say less than 20 mph). Second, some other very good books were published (*Accident Analysis and Reconstruction Techniques*, ref 113, by the father-son team of Raymond Brach and Matthew Brach). Third, what new could be said?

As the Brach's noted, many existing texts were either summaries of equations (but with little explanation), or examples of how specific problems had been solved. A more technical approach was needed. But having read the Brach's book (which we thoroughly recommend) it became apparent that perhaps their book was a little too technical: wonderful for physicists and engineers but perhaps beyond the grasp of some others.

Any author of a book on accident reconstruction faces the dilemma: who is the anticipated audience? This can range from legal and insurance professionals to others already involved in the subject, including engineers, scientists, private practitioners (who are well-versed in the relevant physical logic) and police officers (who frequently have limited prior training in physics and mathematics). Finally, the book must convey knowledge that can be presented in a manner that a typical jury can understand, should the analysis be needed in a courtroom. Most jurors have limited backgrounds in either science or mathematics, so it behooves the expert explaining the analysis to summarize the data in a simplified, yet accurate, way.

Unfortunately, *physics is physics*, which presents a problem: how to cover certain topics which have already been written about? The answer is to re-present some data but to add new topics. Since each author has his own unique viewpoint, this can allow some readers to suddenly "see the light." Having done some grammar school mentoring many years ago it was discovered that merely rewording a problem (with perhaps some analogies) suddenly converted a blank stare into comprehension.

Accordingly, some of this work carries over material from the previous edition, but extra topics have been added. These include the "sideswipe" collision, more details on rollovers, calculations of collision timing and accelerations and a discussion on whether measuring vehicle crush by breaking the latter into multiple zones (instead of using a simple average) *really* produces a more accurate solution. Time is devoted to the issue of the "heavy versus light vehicle" problem, with discussion of vehicle size versus weight. We apologize for the repetition, but it appears some potential readers thought the previous edition was *only* about low speed accidents, whereas (in reality) much of it applied to many higher speed collision crashes too.

Since giving concrete examples is always useful, especially in graphical form, we have included many illustrations derived with the Mathcad computer program. This is a general purpose mathematics, physics, and engineering code used by many scientists and engineers. (There are other mathematics-based programs with similar capabilities, for example SMath Studio which can be downloaded free from the Internet. While SMath is not as flexible as Mathcad it can nevertheless perform many of the calculations indicated in this book.) The Mathcad code is *not* a "black box" program, where the user has to assume the "inner workings" are what the program authors claim they are (since line-by-line inspection of source code is not always possible). Instead, the code is used in the same manner as a hand calculator (e.g., an HP48GX): the analyst starts with a "clean sheet" and must input all the necessary equations and input parameters, and then asks the code to compute the answers. The important point here is that Mathcad is *not* an accident reconstruction code. Unlike a hand calculator, Mathcad can compute hundreds of calculations within seconds (on a modern computer) and allows the results to be presented in graphical form (which is frequently far more useful and instructive than reading tabular data). Better yet, once the basic calculations are done the code allows almost any parameter to be plotted versus another, since all the necessary interpolations are immediately done.

The important point about using Mathcad is that the user (or anyone else) can actually review the equations used for analysis. The program is its own "source code" and nothing is hidden.

We also give the reader examples of how generic collision analysis can be done, showing which parameters are important and indicating which ones have very little effect on the final answers (simultaneously indicating the overall supposed accuracy of many accident reconstruction solutions). The issue of "large versus small" collisions is illustrated, showing how some assumptions (the same crush always implies the same *delta-v*) are not strictly true.

Note, this book covers accident *reconstruction* rather than *investigation*. The latter involves such things as carefully studying the scene (tire marks, damaged items, details of the road (slope, camber, curvature, etc.) and identifying debris fields). Also included are studies of the scrapes on vehicles which undergo rollovers, since such scrapes can indicate how the vehicle rolled (number of quarter-turns and changes in direction). There are many good books on this topic. *Reconstruction* is the act of understanding the physics and engineering aspects of the problem and applying the correct mathematical techniques to arrive at solutions.

Finally, like most others we still use the term *accidents* although the modern trend is to call them what they usually are: (dumb) *crashes*. Rarely is a crash due to a sudden failure of a vehicle component; most are due to dumb behavior by a driver (including drinking, eating, being drunk, putting on makeup and using a cell phone). Even the recent problems with "runaway" cars (Toyota) the government has at best concluded the throttle was sticking to or under the floor mats. But the simple solution was to put the car into neutral. The engine may "race" and suffer damage, but the brakes and steering should still work. However, do not use the ignition key to switch off the engine: on most modern cars this will lock the steering!

The first edition of the *Low Speed* book was written to enable analysts to address the issues of collisions where vehicle damage is small. These collisions involve many disputes concerning occupant injuries, especially of the whiplash variety. However, this fourth edition covers all speed ranges. For high-speed cases there is relatively little argument over injuries. Accordingly, we have renamed this fourth edition and have also removed the section on biomechanics and occupant responses. However, we retain all the biomechanical references to help those who wish to independently study the literature. Biomechanics may be reintroduced in future editions.

We have chosen to place all references at the end of the book. Many of the references can be considered as background data. But when we cite a specific reference we indicate the number, even if the order seems illogical.

We hope this book proves useful.

Chapter 1

Introduction

Synopsis

1.1 Understanding the Physics

In the 15 years since we wrote the first edition of the "Low Speed" book (1996) there have been significant improvements in the field of Accident Reconstruction (AR). This includes the development of several computer codes which also include the ability to perform animations. Animations can be wonderful additions to explain "what happened" to the jury, assuming the judge allows them. The question arises: how many analysts (expert witnesses) actually understand what these various codes are solving?

Although the purveyors of these codes give training lessons on the proper use (inputting data and interpreting the outputs) how often do they explain the underlying physics and equations? As anybody in the computer world knows, even "respected" codes can occasionally have their foibles. Consider the "never-ending" updates provided by a major developer to their PC operating software. Why? Because they sell you a "beta" version of the software, which they then attempt to make into the "alpha" version it should have been in the first place. This is a bit like buying a three-wheel car with the promise "we'll supply the fourth wheel free of charge later"!

An "extreme" case of problems occurred when one of our computers (using *Existing*) crashed due to an automatic update. The update put the computer into an "endless loop." Apparently, the only real solution was to re-install the *Existing* software (which, of course, did not come as a separate item with the computer). But with the ever-advancing improvements in software (and the dropping of prices) it became easier to buy a new computer (using *Better)* than simply buy a version of the older operating software (and then have the *pleasure* of re-installing everything else, assuming you had the original programs, and all the files stored on a backup hard drive).

While working on government programs we occasionally tried to solve an unusual unique problem that the government-developed code wasn't properly designed to handle: the output was "garbage" (recognizable since we understood the physics). However, we had the luxury of picking up the phone and explaining the problem to the code developers (and, yes, we knew their names and phone numbers). They rapidly discovered the code-error and sent us a corrected version that worked well. This interaction is rarely possible with many "proprietary" code developers. Also, the "problem" can only be appreciated by someone well versed in the physics involved.

It is rare for the proprietary code purveyors to give access to "source code" which would allow the user to check every line of code. But, even if the user had access how many could immediately spot an error in the physics/engineering? Not many AR analysts are computer programmers, and even fewer are physicists or engineers. Even "help" files or operating manuals rarely give the underlying physics.

For all these reasons it behooves the AR analysts to actually know the *scientific theory* behind the calculations. "Blindly" using a computer code is a dangerous path to follow.

This book is an attempt to explain the *science* behind accident reconstruction.

1.2 Accuracy

There are many books that explain "standard error analysis." Here, we mean the overall accuracy that can be expected for a solution of a collision "in the field" (i.e., not a check on specially designed crash tests where we know the input and output before even attempting to confirm calculations). Put bluntly, we are wary of any solution that claims accuracy to better than about 5 percent, and many are credible to only 10 percent. The reasons are plentiful. These include:

1. Uncertainties in the true post-impact motions and directions of the vehicles involved.
2. Uncertainties in the effective drag factors (especially for spinning vehicles and curved paths).
3. Uncertainties in the definition of "crush."
4. Uncertainties in the appropriate crush factors (for example, the A, B and G terms used in the CRASH3 methodology, or the corresponding R, a and vL terms for the POD approach)(see later).
5. Uncertainties in the degree of offset that causes vehicle spin.
6. Uncertainties in true vehicle weight (unknown cargo) and radius of gyration (unknown weight distribution including cargo).

7. Uncertainties in friction between vehicles which undergo sideswipes, or friction with the ground that cause rollovers.

All these issues are discussed later in this book. We include the problems with the crush-energy approach of CRASH3 and why it gives poor solutions for low speed impacts, and give the POD model, which is an attempt to improve the low speed cases. Both algorithms converge for the higher speed cases where it is well accepted that CRASH3 yields meaningful solutions. Thus the examples we give for use of POD (using Mathcad) cover the entire range of low speed (negligible crush damage) to high speed (lots of crush damage). We also explain how POD can be used "as if" CRASH3 by giving the conversions of the latter parameters to those employed in the former.

1.3 Terminology

As scientists we are bemused at the use of certain terms. For example, the unit "G" is frequently used to mean gravity at the surface of the earth. However, in science capital G is used for the Universal Gravitational Constant, which is the term used to describe the gravitational attraction between bodies (sun-earth, earth-moon, etc.). When describing gravity at the earth's surface the correct term is g, which is *almost* constant throughout the world (and equal to roughly 32.2 ft/s/s). Many people do not seem to understand that the term "weight" is actually a force (gravity pulling a vehicle downward) or that the term "lbs-force" is a redundancy. Should we use CG (center of gravity) or CM (center of mass)? While most people use CG the correct term is CM. Why? Because the rules for collisions are true even in outer space, where there is zero gravity, and where we should use mass instead of weight. Should we use mph for speed and ft/s for velocity? Answer: no! Both sets of units apply to either case because the *distinction* between speed and velocity is that the former is a scalar (no direction implied) while the latter is a vector (with direction implied). See Appendix A.

A vector can always be resolved into two components at two angles to the original. This clearly applies to velocities and momenta. The angles need *not* be orthogonal so long as the components sum to the original. But energy is a scalar, so does this mean we cannot also have components? Components *can* be derived but only if along orthogonal axes. This follows because of the Pythagoras theorem. With vectors the cosine law can be applied with *any* included angle, but for energy the included angle must be 90 degrees, which reduces the cosine law to Pythagoras and allows the "squares" of velocities (hence energies) to be added.

1.4 A Matter of Perspective

Let the y-axis represent velocity while the x-axis gives time. Consider a simple central impact of vehicle 1 (mass m1, velocity v1) into vehicle 2 (mass m2, velocity v2).

Start with v2 = 0. This represents a collision into a "stopped" vehicle. A plot of response shows vehicle 1 slowing while vehicle 2 accelerates. The vehicles reach a common speed vcom. Conservation of linear momentum then shows delta-v1/delta-v2 = - m2/m1.

Now "shift the zero" of velocity so both initial values add a common positive value. We still have delta-v1/delta-v2 = - m2/m1.

If, instead, we shift the starting velocities by a common negative quantity, the velocity changes maintain the same relationship.

What does this demonstrate? It shows that the *response* does not depend on the so-called initial absolute velocities. Indeed, there is *no* such thing as "absolute" velocity. The "stopped" vehicle in the first example is only considered stopped relative to the "local world" (e.g., the roadway). In reality the earth is moving due to spin about the north-south axis, and the earth is moving relative to the sun, etc.

The value of energy loss is given by the product of "effective" mass (m1m2/(m1 + m2)) and the "closing velocity" (squared). But closing velocity is simply (v1 – v2), and this remains constant, regardless of the so-called "absolute" initial values. Thus, again "shifting the zero" of velocities has no effect.

We mention this because there are times when "redrawing the zero" can make the overall response easier to understand.

Chapter 2

General Material Loading Responses

Synopsis

2.1 Energy and Force

In order to understand the response of vehicles during a collision it is necessary to first understand the generic response of materials to the application of loads. Whenever two bodies collide, forces will be generated between them which cause a deceleration of one body and an acceleration of the other. Newton's laws state that, at any instant, the forces must be identical at either side of the colliding surfaces. A *force* is a vector quantity, having both magnitude and direction. Thus, although the forces may vary with time and direction throughout the impact while the bodies remain in contact, they must also be equal in magnitude and opposite in direction at all time. This condition immediately satisfies the requirement of conservation of momentum, because the reduction in one body's momentum is replaced by an identical increase in momentum of the other body. The overall averaged direction of the force acting on each of the two bodies defines the principal directions of force. Except for at very low speeds, the interaction of the vehicles with a third body (e.g., a road surface) is negligible during the impact.

The energy of the interaction must also be conserved. Initially, the moving bodies have motion and mass, and thus kinetic energy. After the impact, at least one body may still have motion and thus kinetic energy. This energy may involve both linear and rotational components. Except for the idealized case of a perfectly elastic collision, the total kinetic energy of both bodies after the impact will be less than that before the impact. Some energy will have been consumed, but because total energy must be conserved, this means that the lost energy has been transformed into some other form. The major consumer of this energy is irreversible geometrical changes in the bodies, which is the crush damage. Other minor absorbers of energy include the generation of heat, sound and light.

A body can suffer from two types of forces, purely external and internal. Consider two equal forces acting on opposite sides of a body and in opposite directions. The net external force is zero and so the net acceleration of the body is also zero. However, the body is subject either to compression or tension. If the two forces are not equal, then the situation can be treated as if they are the result of two forces which do balance and a remaining force which is unbalanced. For example, if 1,000 pounds of force pushes on the left of the body while only 800 pounds of force pushes back on the right of the body, this is equivalent to a compression of 800 pounds and an acceleration force of 200 pounds to the right. This is illustrated in Figure 2.1. Because a moving body has inertia, when it collides with a second body, force is applied to the second body and the first one slows. The side of the first body opposite the collision sustains no force, but a net force acts on the body to produce the deceleration. As a result, stress waves travel through the body and cause portions of it to be subjected to local stresses and forces, which cause localized compressions, tensions or both. Because of the difference in forces impinging on each side of the object, it suffers a force gradient, with the highest force at the point of the impact, and zero at the other end.

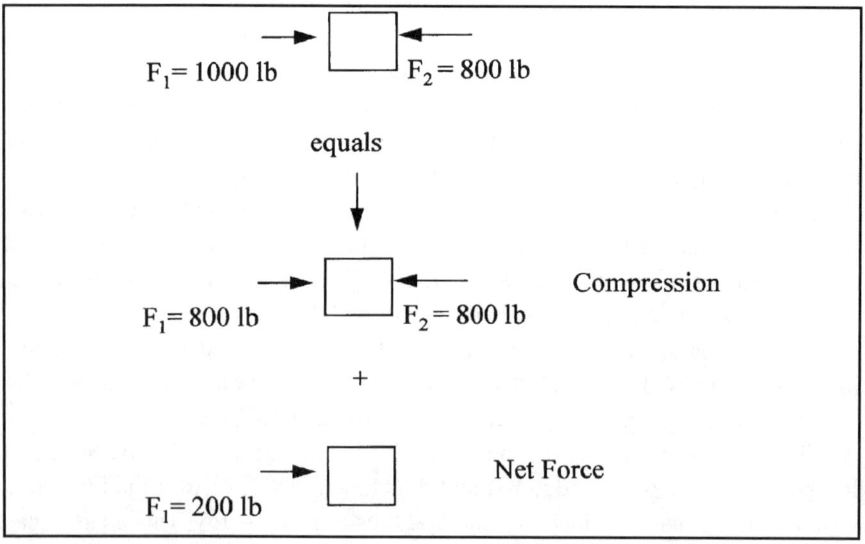

Figure 2.1 *Force logic*

The response of the body is elastic for low forces. Sudden impact at one end of the body causes elastic stress waves to travel along the body. These waves move very fast, having a speed (commonly called the speed of sound in the material) determined by the square-root of the ratio of the elastic (Young's) modulus to the material density. Typical wave speeds for car materials are about 3×10^5 cm/s to 5×10^5 cm/sec, or about 9,843 ft/s to 16,404 ft/s. Note that these speeds are about ten times the speed of sound in normal atmospheric air (about 1,050 ft/s). For a typical car length of about 15 feet, the elastic wave takes only about 1.5 milliseconds to travel the entire length of the car. Since a typical car crash lasts about 0.1 to 0.2 second, this means that the elastic wave travels at least sixty-seven times the length of the car (about thirty-three reverberations) during the time of first contact to the time of final disengagement.

Higher forces cause *plastic flow*. The effective modulus becomes much smaller. Consequently, the associated wave motion (the plastic wave) travels much slower, and is moving only a little faster than the actual collapsing impact surface of the vehicle relative to the remainder of the car. This difference in speeds versus time defines the actual thickness of the plastically crushed region. Thus, a two-wave structure develops, namely a small-amplitude elastic wave and a larger-amplitude plastic wave. The small-amplitude elastic wave slows down the uncrushed part of the vehicle, while the larger-amplitude plastic wave is responsible for the permanent crush next to the impacted portion of the vehicle. This two-wave effect is shown in Figure 2.2.

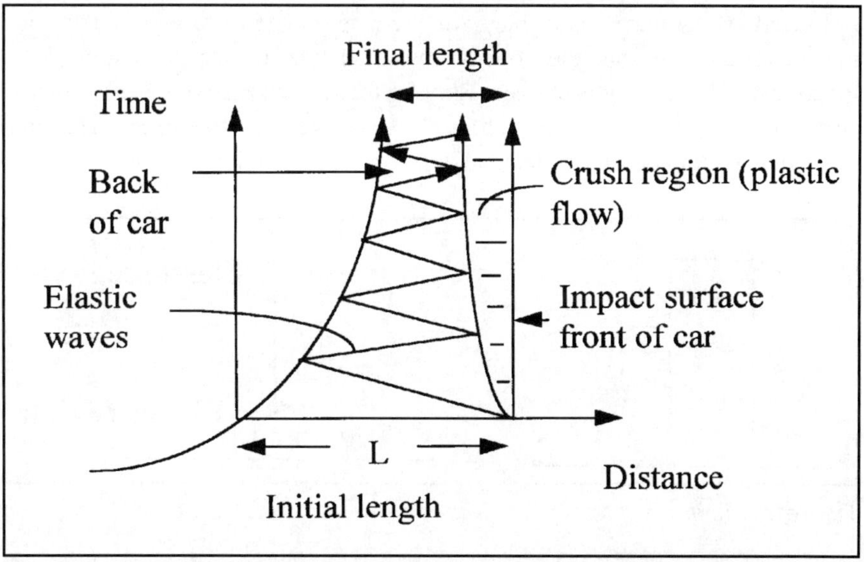

***Figure 2.2** Rigid barrier impact*

This dynamic behavior produces results which differ from normal static behavior. For static loading, it is always the weakest portion of the vehicle which first starts to collapse because the entire structure is subject to the same load. However, under dynamic loading, the traveling waves invariably cause crush damage next to the region of impact, even if the weakest part of the vehicle is farther back.

Indeed, in the world of the hydrodynamicist there is a test called the Taylor rod test. A uniform right-cylindrical rod of material strikes a rigid wall with the axis of the rod perpendicular to the plane surface of the wall. With sufficient speed, the colliding end of the rod develops a mushroom shape, with the end splayed outward and shortened. This well-understood phenomenon is a classic test for any newly written hydrodynamics computer code, since failure of the code to properly predict the rod's behavior is a sure sign of coding error. Figure 2.3 shows the Taylor test.

2.2 Responses to Force

There are four basic response modes for a body when subjected to external force: elastic, plastic, viscoelastic, and brittle (and combinations thereof).

A. Elastic Response

A body is said to behave elastically if the deformation induced during the application of a force is completely recovered when the load is removed, and the energy absorbed (more properly, stored) by the body during deformation is also recovered. Many materials display a linear response of force versus deflection in the elastic regime, and the slope of this line defines the elastic modulus. (See Figure 2.4.) However, it is not necessary for the response to be linear in order to be elastic. The simplest example of the elastic body is a perfect spring. The loading and unloading paths are identical on a force-deformation plot.

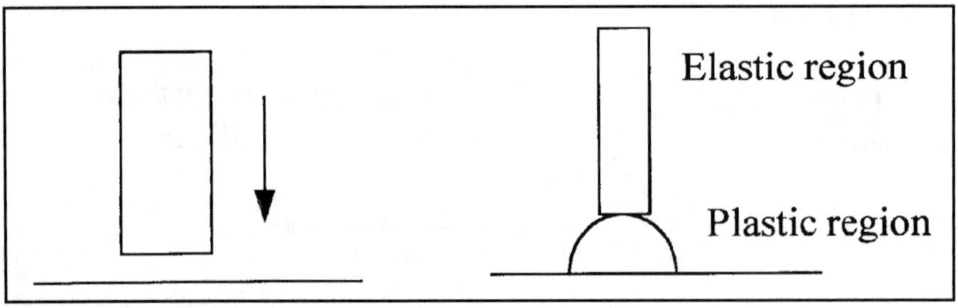

Figure 2.3 *Taylor rod test*

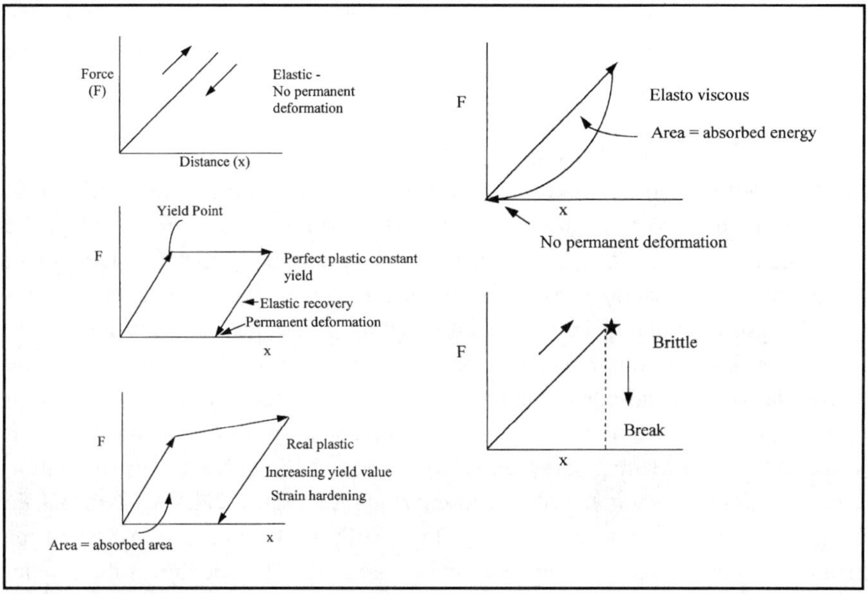

Figure 2.4 *Material modes of response*

B. Plastic Response

If a body deforms under a load and does not recover its initial geometry upon release of the load, it is said to have undergone plastic flow. This results in a loading path that differs from the unloading path, and a force-deformation plot indicates a parallelogram-type of loop. (See Figure 2.4.) Because energy absorbed is the product of a force times the motion in the direction of the force, it follows that the body must have permanently stored (i.e., absorbed) some of the applied energy in the form of plastic deformation. A body undergoing perfect plastic flow is one in which the force to initiate plastic flow is a fixed limit, such that once exceeded the body continues to plastically deform until the load is removed. In reality, very few materials (except very pure metals) are capable of this; instead, they exhibit *strain-hardening* in which the force required to continue plastic flow continues to increase with the increase in deformation. To a first approximation, this increase in force is roughly linear as compared to the deformation. Thus, unless the applied force increases, the degree of deformation is limited. Ultimately, for a sufficiently large force the body will rupture. Until that point is reached, the body will absorb energy and fail to recover its initial geometry.

Note that so-called plastic materials (generically known as polymers; e.g., Bakelite, polythene or polyethelene, thermoplastics and thermosets) rarely behave in a plastic manner, and most tend to be brittle. Their name comes from the fact that most such materials are frequently extruded into their final form when hot and uncured, and this extrusion represents a plastic flow. To help avoid the confusion between plastic behavior and plastic material, this book will adopt the convention of using the word Plastic (capital P) to describe a plastic material.

C. Viscoelastic Response

If a body deforms under load such that it recovers its geometry upon release of the load, but does so by following a different unloading path, then it displays the phenomenon of *viscoelastic response*. Here, the initial geometry is recovered, but the body permanently absorbs some of the applied energy. This energy frequently appears in the form of heat, although the associated temperature rise for a one-shot compression is usually quite low. Examples of this behavior include many elastomers, the spring-and-shock-absorber system on vehicles, several bumper systems, and, of course, the tires. The condition of having a return path different from the loading path again creates a loop in the force-deformation plot, and this loop represents the absorbed energy. (See Figure 2.4.) As with plastic flow, this looping behavior constitutes the condition of *hysteresis*. Vehicle tires heat up with use because of the continual cyclic flexing that occurs as the contact point with the road causes flattening and rebounding of the tires. Each cycle dissipates a small amount of energy within the rubber because of the viscous behavior. Thus, the tire slowly heats up until the heat losses balance the energy dissipation. Because underinflated tires flex more than properly inflated ones, they heat up faster, and the rubber degrades faster.

D. Brittle Response

A material is said to behave in a brittle manner if it ruptures with negligible plastic flow, such as when glass breaks. Thus, up to the point of rupture the response is almost purely elastic, but beyond this condition the material suddenly breaks. Clearly, such response indicates a go/no-go situation for interpretation of energy absorption. If the body in question does not break, then an upper limit on absorbed energy is implied whereas, if failure does occur, a lower limit on energy absorption is implied.

Real materials frequently display combinations of all four responses to varying degrees. Most steels used for vehicle construction display primarily elastic and plastic responses. Viscous behavior reveals itself only for conditions of very high rates of deformation (known as strain-rate hardening, which is important for strong shock waves) or for hot metal approaching the melting point (not usually relevant for vehicle collisions). Figure 2.4 indicates the four major modes of response. Typical vehicle steel is elastic until the force exceeds the yield point. Thereafter, plastic flow occurs and continued deformation requires an increase in force. Upon release of the force, there is an elastic recovery, but also a permanent geometry change resulting in a plastic offset. This offset constitutes the vehicle crush observed after the impact. Materials such as fiberglass and ordinary or toughened window glasses usually display brittle responses, whereas laminated windshields display a mixture of brittle and plastic responses.

2.3 Other Definitions

A. Stress

If the net applied force is divided by the perpendicular cross sectional area that the force acts upon, the resulting quantity is called the *normal stress*. If the force acts in the plane of the area, it is called the *shear stress*. Figure 2.5 illustrates the meanings of stress.

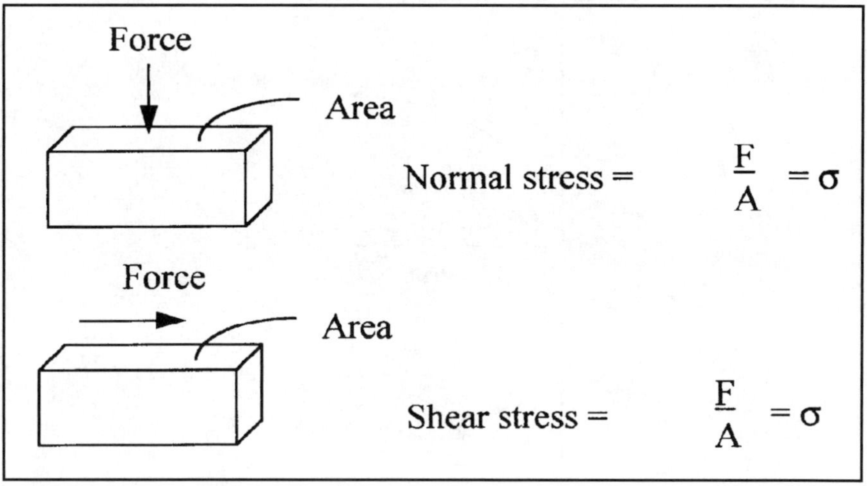

Figure 2.5 *Stress definitions*

B. Strain

When a body deforms it develops *strain*. The strain is defined as the fractional change in geometry per initial geometry, and is thus dimensionless. Thus linear strain is the fractional decrease (or increase) in length per initial length. The integral of the stress versus strain gives a measure of the energy absorbed by the body. Specifically, this quantity is the energy per unit volume. If the cross-sectional area is known, and the initial geometry length is known, then since stress × area = force, and strain × length = deformation, the area under the force versus deformation plot gives the total absorbed energy. If a shear motion is induced the strain is a shear one and is a measure of the twisting angle, and is also dimensionless.

Modulus is simply the ratio of the stress to the strain, and thus has units of stress. For a solid able to accept long-lived shears, the stress can be different in three mutually perpendicular directions. However, for a fluid, such shears cannot be maintained, and only short-lived viscous shears can exist during material flow. Consequently, the stress is normally forced to be the same in all directions. For this case, the stress is known as the *pressure*.

Note that the modulus must always be a positive quantity (an increase in strain must be accompanied by an increase in stress); otherwise, material instability occurs, as shown in Figure 2.6. Thus, for a negative modulus the material would "run away," because increasing strain would require a lower balancing stress. For a fixed, applied stress the material would simply continue straining until rupture occurred. Also, since sound speed is proportional to the square root of the modulus, a negative modulus would imply an imaginary wave speed.

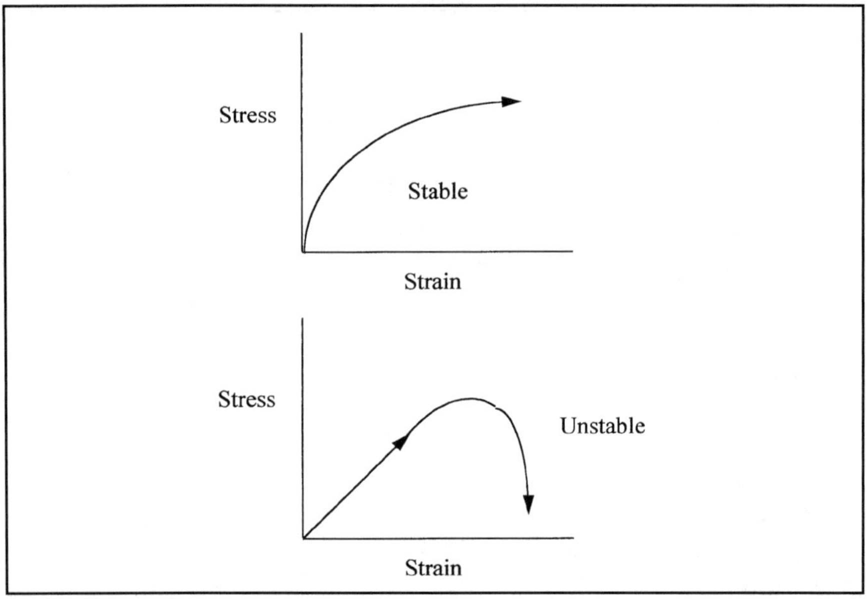

Figure 2.6 *Stress versus strain options*

The remarks in the preceding paragraph refer to true stress and true strain (as used by physicists) rather than engineering stress and strain. For small values, there is no distinction, but for large strains and stresses the two definitions differ. The engineering definitions of stress and strain both refer to the original cross-sectional area and length, respectively. True stress and strain refer to the locally changing values of area and length. These distinctions are introduced to help explain an apparent anomaly, namely the stretching of a thin wire or rod, as it is well known that runaway stretching does occur once a certain load is exceeded. However, this happens because of the "necking" that occurs, which actually reduces the local cross-sectional area, as seen in Figure 2.7. Thus, the modulus appears to have become negative. In reality, the actual true stress at the necking region is still increasing, so the real modulus is positive. The necking behavior is really a structural effect rather than a material effect.

2.4 Sign Convention

For those who read physics and engineering textbooks, it should also be noted that the two professions disagree on sign convention. For the engineer, a compression is considered negative while a tension is considered positive. This occurs because an engineer considers it natural to first pull (or stretch) a material. However, the same engineers consider a gas pressure (such as steam pressure) to be positive. This switch can cause numerical confusion if a material changes state, and goes from being a solid to a gas. This is, however, a rare consideration for most engineering applications (not many engineering conditions involve this effect). Physicists, however, are used to dealing with a more generic class of problems, where state changes are common. Consequently, physicists define pressure and compression both as positive, while tension is considered negative. This automatically avoids the problem of sign switching during phase changes. The only difference is in the sign used to describe the properties. This explanation is given merely to help those readers of standard texts who may become thoroughly confused by the difference between engineering's and physics' definitions.

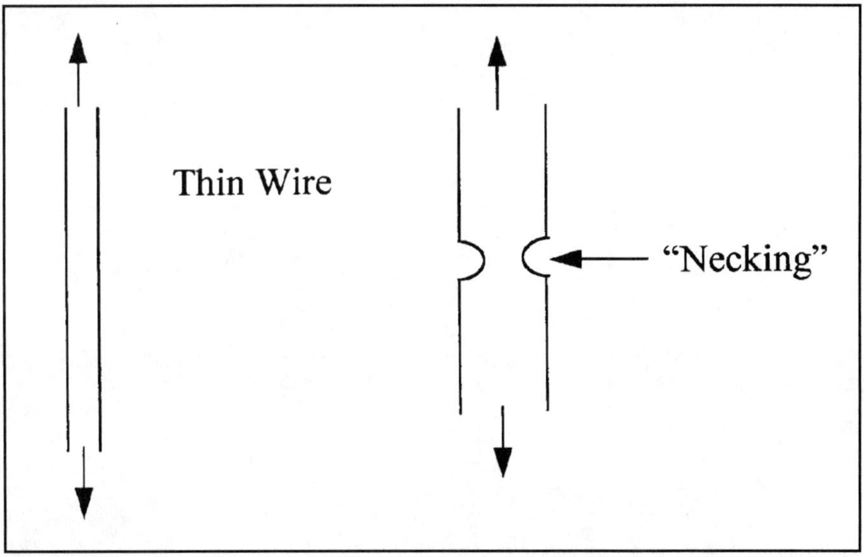

Figure 2.7 *Structural necking effect*

Chapter 3

Vehicle Crush Response for Low-Speed Impacts into Rigid Barriers

Synopsis

3.1 The Bumper Response

Bumpers were first applied to railroad cars, mostly to protect the cargo rather than the car. Later, they were applied to road vehicles mostly to protect the vehicle rather than the passengers. This inversion of logic arose because railroad cars are inherently strong, while most road vehicles are generally weak since the weight must be kept low to allow for acceptable performance with limited engine sizes. The railroad bumpers were not intended to handle high-speed collisions (such as train-into-train) but were intended to handle the lower speed differential motions between the cars caused by the loose coupling systems used. Thus damage to the cars was not the concern; limiting the induced accelerations to the cargo was the issue. Such bumper systems work very well at low speeds. Unfortunately, the automobile manufacturers seem to have lost this piece of insight. In their quest to minimize bumper performance (mostly to save weight) they seem to have forgotten that at low speeds bumpers actually protect the "cargo" of the cars: the passengers. Instead, car manufacturers concentrate on designing the vehicle itself to collapse somewhat like a bumper, which is necessary for higher-speed collisions. However, this results in unnecessary repair expense even for low-speed collisions.

It is important to realize that a bumper works by virtue of energy considerations, rather than simple consideration of forces or momentum. A given vehicle will start to suffer permanent damage if the applied force exceeds a certain value, F_0. Thus a bumper must be capable of containing the energy of a moving vehicle while simultaneously keeping the peak force below the value F_0. A bumper must be capable of either storing or absorbing energy to avoid structural damage. The only real difference between these two approaches is that the storage method involves a significant bounce after initial compression, while the absorbing method minimizes the bounce. Note that a plastically responding bumper cannot recover. Consequently, such a bumper is a one-shot device of limited use, and is thus not used in practice except for cheap pick-up bumpers, which are usually connected directly to the frame horns. While the latter allow for limited elastic response, most of the energy is consumed by permanent plastic bending of the bumper.

The simplest version of a bumper is a spring. Upon impact, the spring will compress and the force increases. Because the force acts in the direction of compression energy is stored in the spring. For a perfect, linear spring, this energy is simply $E = 1/2 \times F \times d$, where F is the built-up force and d is the compression motion amplitude. With F in pounds and d in feet, the energy is in pounds-foot.

If a vehicle has no bumper, the elastic range of response will be very limited. Although a real vehicle is not a simple, solid chunk of material, its behavior will still mimic that of a solid, albeit a porous one. The amplitude of elastic deformation for the underframe of the vehicle is only about 0.07 to 0.12 inch for a solid car. This can be readily explained. Modern cars are designed to have controlled collapsible front and rear ends, which protects the passenger compartment by absorbing energy before large loads reach this compartment. (Note that the concept that the passenger compartment is "strong" is actually wrong. It is the protective energy-absorbing nature of the front or back of the vehicle which makes the compartment appear strong; for side impacts directly into the passenger compartment, its weakness becomes apparent.)

Collapsible front and rear ends allow a "gentle" crush that limits the accelerations or decelerations experienced by the passengers. The collapsible front part of the vehicle is typically about 36 to 60 inches long. Automobile steel reaches its elastic limit for about 0.2 percent strain, thus the motion is about 0.07 to 0.12 inches. Even if the total fifteen-foot length of a typical car were involved, the decrease in length for 0.2 percent strain is only 0.36 inch. These values would apply exactly if the vehicle were a simple solid piece of steel. In reality, since the vehicle is a structure which can buckle as well as suffer linear compression, the true linear motion is larger, but still quite limited, being about 0.5 inch. This limited deformation results also in limited energy absorption. Thus the elastic region of response is easily exceeded, and initiation of permanent frame damage can occur for very low impact speeds (about 1 mph for a collision into a rigid barrier). For the soft side and upper panels, damage can initiate even more easily.

These very low speeds can be understood by equating the vehicle's kinetic energy with the stored elastic energy. Thus,

$$(w/2g)v^2 = (1/2)F_0D \text{ or } v^2 = (F_0/w)gD = 12R_0gD \ (D \text{ in feet}) = R_0g\,D \ (D \text{ in inches})$$

where $12R_0$ is the strength-per-weight, g is 32.2 ft/s^2 and D is the amplitude of motion. For $D = 0.07$ inch, and $R_0 = 0.6$, $v = 0.79$ mph. Even for $D = 0.36$ inch, $v = 1.8$ mph.

Older cars (and most existing pick-ups, vans and trucks) were built with an independent chassis, with the remainder of the car panels, engine and transmission attached to it. Such a chassis gives a rigid frame, but also adds weight to the vehicle. Most modern cars no longer use independent chassis construction. Instead, most cars use the unibody or monocoque construction. Here the frame is an integral part of the overall bodywork, consisting of strengthened regions made by forming box sections, and so forth. This includes the sills under the doors. Some cars also employ subframes which are small remnants of the old chassis logic used for specific sections of the vehicle (e.g., engine attachment). These newer techniques are more expensive, and thus only suitable for mass production work. However, they allow for lighter vehicles, and thus improved performance and fuel consumption.

In addition to the underframe, vehicles also employ vertical frames called the A, B, and C frames. The A frame is the section containing the front door hinges, windshield and firewall. The B frame is the one that contains the front door latches, and the C frame contains the rear window and back door locks. Some vehicles (such as station wagons) have a D frame containing the rear end of the vehicle.

These various frames give the vehicles their rigidity and strength. It takes high forces to cause damage. However, because of the limited elastic strain capacity of structural steels, the frames do not allow for much energy absorption before plastic deformation occurs. This is the purpose of the bumper.

The bumper is intended to minimize any permanent structural plastic damage in a collision. For example, most good cars are fitted with 5-mph bumpers, although many trucks and pick-ups come only with cheaper 2.5-mph bumpers. The meaning of a 5-mph bumper is that a collision at no greater than about 5 mph into a rigid barrier will not cause any permanent body damage, in particular, to the lights, and so forth. Instead, only superficial scrapes and dents on the bumper should occur (note that the speed capability of bumpers is not a precise quantity). This means that the bumper assembly must be capable of absorbing the kinetic energy of the car. Since the force, F_0, at which permanent damage initiates is fixed for a given vehicle, the only method available for increasing energy absorption is to allow for a significant bumper deformation amplitude. Further, since the energy increases in relation to the square of the vehicle's speed, the necessary bumper amplitude also increases in relation to the square of the speed. Thus a 5-mph bumper requires four times the amplitude of a 2.5-mph one. These points are shown in Figure 3.1. This effect explains the outcry from the car manufacturers when bumper limits were legislated, since a large bumper costs more to implement and is heavier (which counters attempts to improve fuel economy, a further government requirement). Note that the bumper response also allows a go/no-go analysis, because if there is no permanent damage to a vehicle then the energy involved must be less than the corresponding damage limit, and vice versa.

With a fixed, maximum-allowed force for a given vehicle, the necessity to increase the bumper amplitude to increase the speed capability also means that the corresponding spring constant is smaller, and the spring becomes softer. This reduces the acceleration imposed on the vehicle, and thus on the passengers. Provided the upper limit of the bumper is not reached, the passengers suffer a smaller jolt. Put another way, for a fixed impact speed into a rigid barrier, the higher the bumper limit the better it is for the passengers. A softer spring also

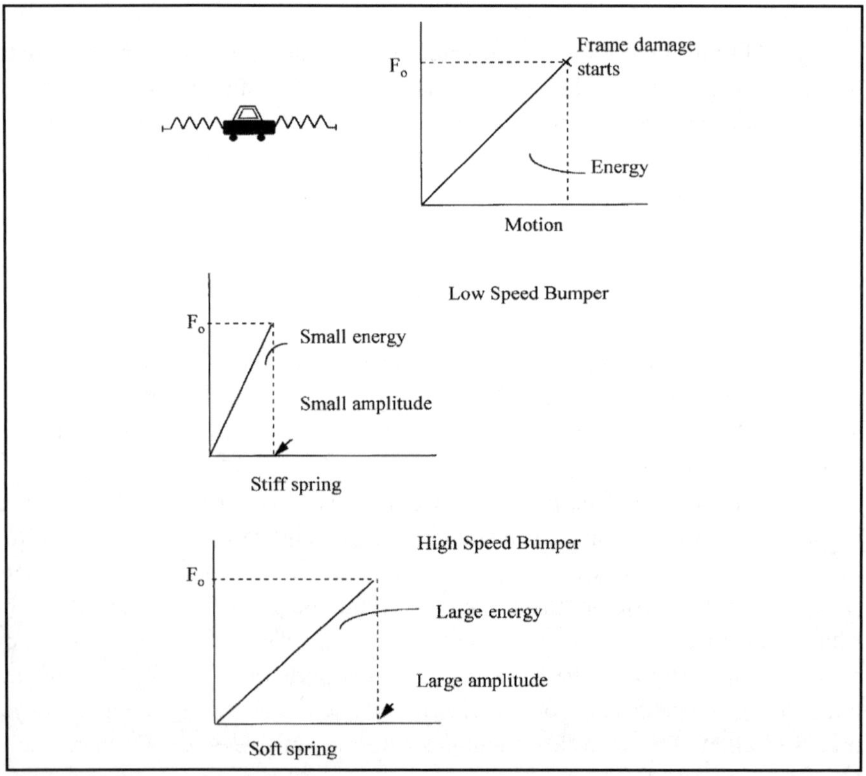

Figure 3.1 *Bumper logic*

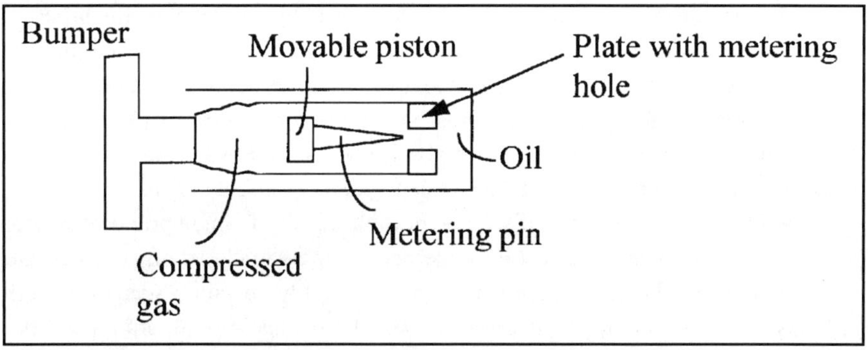

Figure 3.2 *Typical isolation*

implies a lower oscillation frequency, and therefore a longer period for the compression and rebound. This increase in time allows a passenger more time to react by applying his muscles, which again usually makes the situation better and helps avoid injury.

Why not use high-speed bumpers? The answer is that such a bumper would protrude significantly beyond the car proper (making it ugly, and thus unwanted by the customer), would weigh far more (worsening fuel economy and compromising corporate average fuel economy (CAFE) requirements), and would cost far more (raising the price of the vehicle). Conversely, by using cheaper bumpers the cost of repairing the damage from low-speed accidents increases and the passengers are less well protected.

Note that bumpers are frequently tested using a swinging log-like pendulum, in addition to driving the vehicle into a rigid barrier. Likewise, rear-end damage is frequently tested by hitting a stationary vehicle with a moving concrete "car."

Modern bumpers do not act as simple springs. Instead, they employ some form of internal damping mechanism. There are two major types of bumpers: the isolated version and the Plastic version. The isolated bumper uses rigid metal bumpers that are attached to the vehicle frame by isolators. These isolators are small piston-in-cylinder devices. Figure 3.2 shows a typical isolator. The outer portion, nearest the bumper, is a cylinder containing high-pressure nitrogen gas. This acts as a spring. The inner portion is a cylinder containing oil. Between these sections are two pistons. One is a floating piston, which separates the gas from the oil and acts as a movable barrier. The other is a piston with a small hole and a metering pin and is within the section containing the oil. As the bumper compresses, the piston with the metering hole is driven back into the oil, which in turn flows through the hole toward the floating piston. Simultaneously, the volume containing the gas is compressed. The oil flow develops a viscous force which adds to the gas force during the compression. When the bumper relaxes, the gas pressure forces the bumper back to its original position. Now the oil flows in the opposite direction through the hole. Consequently, the gas force and the oil force now compete with each other to give a smaller net force, so the bumper moves out more slowly than it compressed. The two-way flow of the oil causes fluid damping and permanent energy absorption (which heats the oil slightly). Thus, the bumper rebounds with less violence than a perfect spring.

The Plastic bumper is usually made of high-density foamed polyurethane or polystyrene and attached to a rigid plate next to the vehicle frame. An alternative version uses Plastic in the form of an open-cell honeycomb structure. Both versions have similar mechanical response. These Plastic bumpers should not be confused with the rubberized-Plastic covering which many new cars use to hide metal bumpers. The latter system is mostly cosmetic. Here, we are discussing bumpers which are truly made of a Plastic material. The polyurethane has a natural elastoviscous response and small plastic response, which acts like a spring coupled with a fluid damper. Thus, once again the bumper relaxes back outwards slower than it initially compressed, and again absorbs some energy by slightly heating the Plastic. Be careful with the confusion between the bumper being made of a Plastic material, and its mechanical response which is mostly elastoviscous and not plastic.

Regardless of type, all bumpers must store or absorb the initial kinetic energy of the vehicle while slowing it down. Upon subsequent relaxation, the degree of bounce simply depends on the degree of energy absorption during the complete cycle. Both types of bumpers should return to their initial positions provided that the speed-limit capability is not exceeded. However, for high-impact speeds the isolators frequently need replacing even if the bumper itself is mostly undamaged. This is because the viscous force of the oil flow increases with impact speed. Ultimately this force can become large enough to cause permanent frame damage because the isolator no longer isolates, but instead acts as a rigid rod transferring load to the frame. To avoid this, at high forces the metering pin is designed to "punch out" a larger hole in the piston. This allows easier oil flow and reduces the force. However, because this constitutes internal damage the isolator must be replaced.

The isolators sometimes leave telltale scrapes when compressed. These can sometimes be measured to estimate the degree of compression. However, this can be unreliable for several reasons. The production of a scrape is really a result of poor precision of the piston in the cylinder and poor lubrication. If the isolator were better made and lubricated, it would behave like the piston in a cylinder in a car's engine. There would be negligible scraping or scoring. Thus the scrape marks are due to frictional drag acting on paint, or on dirty or rusted metal. However, the scrapes are also only capable of giving information concerning the minimum motion of the bumper. This is because a loose fit of the piston in the cylinder readily allows canting when the piston is mostly out of the cylinder. But as the piston moves into the cylinder the degree of canting decreases, the piston more accurately aligns with the cylinder, and the propensity of the scrapes to occur decreases. If a piston seizes then the scrape is minimized, and the isolator does not isolate. Hence such scrapes invariably give only minimum motion data.

Experiments have been done (ref 15) to calibrate isolator piston motions versus impact speeds. To guarantee an observable scrape the pistons were spray-painted with a white paint. Unfortunately, this information is of limited use to an investigator in the field, since real cars do not have this paint and some isolators leave no scrape marks at all (hence the need for the paint). Further, it was noticed that the observable length of the piston in the outward position did not always indicate the true maximum possible piston motion before bottoming occurred. Many isolators bottomed with smaller net motions. The fractional bottoming varies from about 50 percent to 90 percent, depending on design. Most such isolators (ref 15) have maximum possible amplitudes in the range of 40 millimeter (1.57 inches) to 80 millimeters (3.15 inches), with many about 57 millimeters (2.24 inches). The bottom line is that even impact speeds near the limit of the bumper's capability can leave small scrapes or none at all, fooling the investigator into believing the impact was at a lower speed than it actually was.

If the scrapes *do* indicate the true isolator motion then the maximum effective barrier impact speed can be approximated by

$$v_{max} = (\text{observed scrape amplitude/maximum possible piston motion}) \times v_{bumper\ limit}$$

provided we have a pseudo-linear springlike bumper response. Of course, to perform this calculation the maximum possible piston motion must also be known for the isolator in question.

Note that isolators behave differently when loaded in a static manner. At very low speeds of compression the oil flows readily without much force. Hence, the isolator response is due only to the gas compression. For a rapid dynamic collision, however, the oil force increases significantly and the isolator is much stiffer, presupposing dynamic impacts.

Similarly, many of the Plastic bumpers can completely compress and rebound without showing any obvious signs of damage afterward. Indeed, the only indication of the bumper being overdriven is actual frame damage! The exception is for strong local loadings, where some small degree of imprint is seen. Such localized loadings include collisions with license plate holders, overriders, edges of other bumpers and, of course, collisions with narrow objects such as poles.

These imprints occur because the polyurethane has a weak plastic response in addition to its elastoviscous response.

3.2 Vehicle Crush Characteristics

Consider the effect of a sudden application of force to a vehicle through the bumper, a result of an impact. We will consider first the case of a full frontal impact, such that the entire bumper is uniformly loaded. Initially, the bumper begins to move back in the direction of the vehicle, increasing its force with amplitude of motion. This increase is linear for a simple spring response, and pseudo-linear for most real bumpers. Eventually, the bumper bottoms out, and any increase in force is transmitted to the vehicle frame behind as a load capable of initiating permanent deformation. This deformation initially consists of localized plastic yielding where the bumper joins the frame. With a further increase in load, buckling of the main body parts constituting the frame occurs, and portions of this frame start to develop plastic hinges, where concentrated stresses cause strong localized plastic flow. The frame begins onto collapse on itself like a bellows. As the frame collapses, other parts are driven into plastic flow. These parts include non-frame body panels which proceed to bend and buckle by virtue of being attached to the frame sections. Thus the vehicle progressively collapses and absorbs part of the impact energy by plastic flow. Eventually, the force peaks, and thereafter decreases back to zero. This peak force occurs at the time of maximum engagement of the vehicle and the second body. This means that it occurs when the deformation amplitude becomes a maximum for both bodies. This condition is the one where the maximum loss in kinetic energy occurs. As the force decreases, part of the contained energy is released in the form of recovered elastic energy. Most of this recovery is due to the spring-back of the bumper, but a small portion is also due to the natural elastic rebound of the vehicle's structure. Finally, the force returns to zero and the vehicle is left with a permanent deformation but also suffers a bounce away from the other body.

These effects can be illustrated by Figure 3.3, which shows a force-deformation plot of typical behavior. The initial steep linear portion, OA, is the elastic bumper response. At the point A the bumper motion reaches its limit (amplitude x_0) and the main body frame proceeds to collapse, following the path AB. At B the collapse stops (maximum deformation x_{max}) and the recovery is elastic along path BC. Thus there is a permanent deformation of OC (deformation x_{final}), but a maximum deformation of OB. This is the basis of the POD model.

As the frame collapses, the absorbed energy increases with deformation amplitude. Let us define a dimensionless quantity, R, as the ratio of energy (foot-pounds) per incremental crush of deformation (inches) per weight of vehicle (pounds). Thus, R is a *specific rigidity* (rigidity per weight). If the vehicle's col-

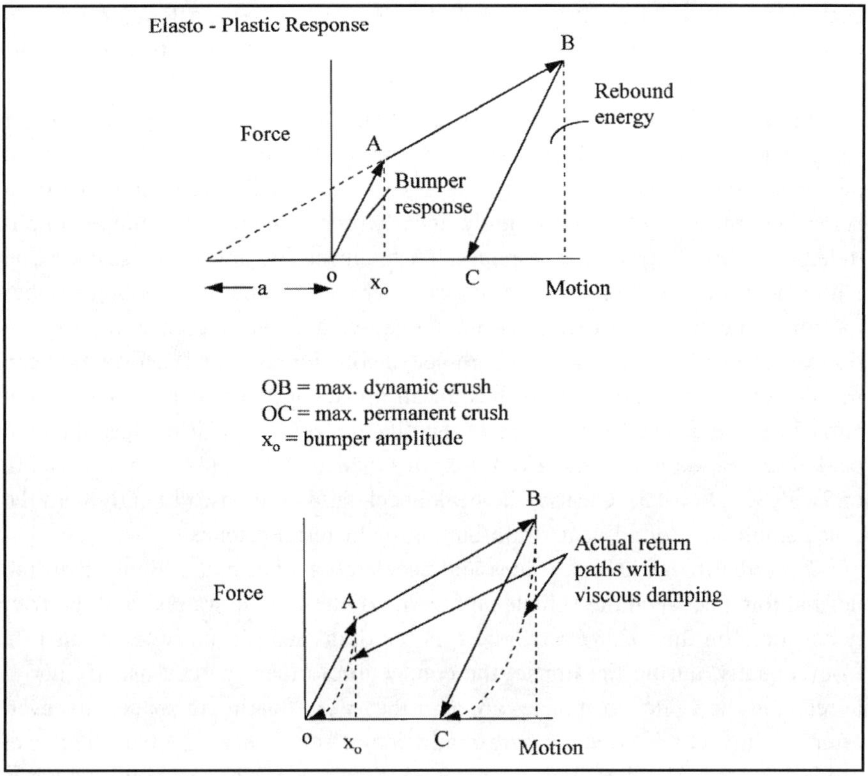

***Figure 3.3** Vehicle crush response*

lapse was simple plastic beyond the point A, then the value of R would be a constant. However, because of the strain-hardening behavior, forming the slope AB, the value of R increases with deformation amplitude such that $R = R_0(1 + x/a)$, where R_0 is the initial value for incipient crush, x is the local crush and the quantity a describes the slope of the strain hardening section, as indicated in Figure 3.3. In reality, the section AB is not truly linear. Indeed, a detailed study would show that the required crush force oscillates with the degree of crush because of variations in local strength, but on average gradually increases with continued crush. However, within the uncertainties and limited experimental data for vehicle crushing, a presumption of simple linearity is reasonable, at least for small degrees of crush which do not cause an incursion into the passenger compartment.

From the definition of R, the force required to initiate body crush is just $F_0 = 12R_0w$, where w is the vehicle weight, and the factor of 12 arises because the energy is measured in foot-pounds while the deformation is measured in inches. Because force divided by mass is acceleration, we immediately determine that acceleration is equal to $12R_0$ in units of g, where g is the acceleration of gravity (32.2 ft/s^2). Typically, many vehicles have values for R_0 (for structural frame damage) in the range 0.5 to 1.0. For example, for a 3,000-pound car with R_0 = 0.6, the force to initiate crush would be about 21,600 pounds. At the bumper limit, where permanent crush starts, the acceleration experienced by the rigid passenger compartment is in the range of 6 g's to 12 g's. Before the bumper limit is reached, the acceleration is roughly linearly proportional to the bumper amplitude, for a simple springlike response. Thus, during the impact the acceleration climbs very quickly from zero to the value $12R_0$ as the bumper motion reaches its limit. Thereafter, further deformation causes a slower increase in acceleration versus crush. However, for a high-speed collision, the total deformation can become quite large (about 25 inches for an impact at about 35 mph into a rigid barrier). For example, if the value of the quantity a is about 10 inches, then the peak acceleration becomes $12R_0(1 + 25/10)$, which is $42R_0$ (42 g's for R_0 = 1.0, or 21 g's for R_0 = 0.5). Clearly, the peak acceleration increases linearly with the crush amplitude, for a linear strain-hardening material response.

Note that these impact forces and accelerations are much higher than the normal force between the vehicle and the road (the vehicle weight) and the frictional force on the road (Fw, where F is the drag factor, usually less than 1.0). Consequently, during the impact the connection to the road can usually be ignored, and the vehicle responses are as if they were floating in space. However, after the impact the effects of tire-road friction come back into play. This can produce different effects. For example, consider a car traveling south which is hit sideways in the rear by a car travelling west. The result is to give the first car's center of mass a new heading, which is southwest, while inducing counterclockwise rotation. If the tire-road friction is very small, as on ice, these motions continue. However, if the wheels are not locked, so that friction applies only sideways to the wheels, then both the lateral motion and the rotation will rapidly cease, and the car can now continue on a new heading, which may be southeast. This is indicated in Figure 3.4.

The issue of road friction becomes progressively more important as the impact reduces in severity. To illustrate, note that the typical tire-road friction is rarely much above 0.8 (except for special soft-rubber racing tires), so the maximum frictional force on the vehicle is about $0.8w$. However, at the bumper limit the force acting on a vehicle is $12R_0w$. Even for a low R_0 value of about 0.5, this represents about 6-g acceleration. For a linear bumper force-deflection response, this means that the peak bumper force is proportional to the change in speed of the vehicle, measured as delta-v, or Δv. These two forces become equal when

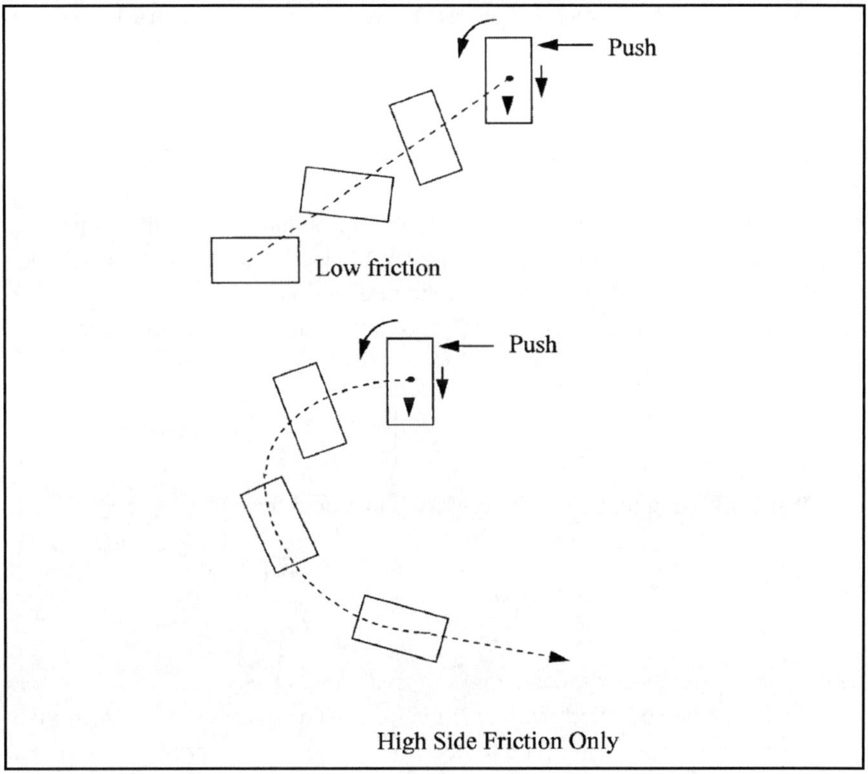

Figure 3.4 *Time/road effects*

$$delta\text{-}v = \Delta v = \left(\frac{0.8w}{12R_0 w}\right) v_L \tag{3.1}$$

where v_L is the bumper's limit speed. Thus, for $R_0 = 0.5$, and $v_L = 5$ mph, we equate the forces for a delta-*v* of about 0.67 mph. For lower bumper speed limits and/or higher R_0 values, the corresponding delta-*v* is even smaller. These low speeds represent the case in which, for a stationary target vehicle, the impact is just at the limit where the car will start to be pushed against its own brakes. For lower impact speeds the car will simply rock on its suspension without net motion. Such small changes in speed are not normally associated with passenger injury. Thus, at speeds of interest it is usually true that the effect of tire-road friction can be mostly ignored for responses during the impact, especially for through-the-bumper collisions. For a soft-body impact (to a fender or middle of an unstrengthened door) the effective value of v_L is quite low, about 1 mph. Now the delta-*v* can be even lower, implying that tire-road friction can be important for incipient damage to such soft parts. However, passenger injury is very improbable at these very low speeds.

If the vehicle hits a rigid barrier, then:

$$E_{in} = 6R_0 w\left(\frac{x_0 + a}{a}\right)\left[\frac{x_{final}^2}{a} + 2x_{final} + \left(\frac{a}{x_0 + a}\right)x_0\right] = \frac{wv_{in}^2}{2g} \tag{3.2}$$

with w in pounds; x_{final}, x_0 and a in feet; E_{in} in foot-pounds; and v_{in} in feet per second. This represents the area under the plot of Figure 3.3, and is thus the vehicle's initial energy measured up to the maximum deflection.

If $a \gg x_0$, we have $(x_0 + a)/a \to 1.0$, and thus Equation 3.2 approximates to

$$E_{in} = 6R_0 w\left[\frac{x_{final}^2}{a} + 2x_{final} + \frac{v_L^2}{12R_0 g}\right] \text{with} \frac{v_L^2}{12R_0 g} = x_0 \text{ (see below)} \tag{3.3}$$

and thus, converting units, we can rewrite Equation 3.3 as

$$v_{in}^2 = R_0 g\left[\frac{x_{final}^2}{a} + 2x_{final} + \frac{v_L^2}{R_0 g}\right] \tag{3.4}$$

with v_{in} and v_L in feet per second, and x_{final} and a in inches.

Here v_L is the so-called bumper limit speed. The quantity $v_L^2/(12R_0 g)$ gives the maximum bumper amplitude (x_0 feet) before permanent crushing commences (i.e., we equate $wv_L^2/(2g)$ with the triangular area OAx_0). For $R_0 = 1.0$, and $v_L = 7.335$ ft/s (5 mph), this amplitude is about 0.139 foot or 1.67 inches, whereas, for $R_0 = 0.5$, the amplitude is about 3.34 inches. Thus the bumper amplitude is small, and the condition $a \gg x_0$ is easily satisfied, since a is usually greater than 10 inches. Note that as $x_{final} \to 0.0$, so $v_{in} \to v_L$, as expected. The terms E_{in} and v_{in} represent the input energy and velocity, respectively. The necessary distinction between input energy and absorbed energy will be discussed below.

We see that the equations involve three terms, namely a constant one, a term linear in crush amplitude and a term dependent on the square of the crush amplitude. For $x_{final} \ll 2a$ and $2x_{final} \gg x_0$ Equation 3.4 approximates to

$$v_{in}^2 = 2R_0 g x_{final} \quad \text{or} \quad v_{in} = (2R_0 g)^{1/2} x_{final}^{1/2} \tag{3.5}$$

(v in ft/s and x_{final} in inches) which implies a square-root response for velocity versus crush, and a linear relationship of energy versus crush. Note the correspondence between Equation 3.5 and the well-known one for skid distances, namely

$$v_{in}^2 = 2Fgs \tag{3.6}$$

where F is the coefficient of friction (or drag factor) and s is the skid distance (feet).

When $2a < x_{final}$ the result approximates to

$$v_{in}^2 = \left(\frac{R_0 g x_{final}^2}{a} \right) \quad \text{or} \quad v_{in} = \left(\frac{R_0 g}{a} \right)^{1/2} x_{final} \tag{3.7}$$

which implies a linear response of velocity versus crush depth and a square-law relationship of energy versus crush.

Figure 3.5 illustrates the behavior of Equation 3.4, giving the collision velocity versus permanent crush for an impact into a rigid barrier. We see that there is a lower velocity limit necessary to induce permanent damage, an initial square-root behavior for velocity versus crush at the lower speeds, and a trend toward a linear plot at the higher speeds. It should be emphasized, however, that these equations are only good approximations up to a certain speed at impact. The reason is that ultimately the vehicle's crush will be sufficient for various hard or soft points to be involved.

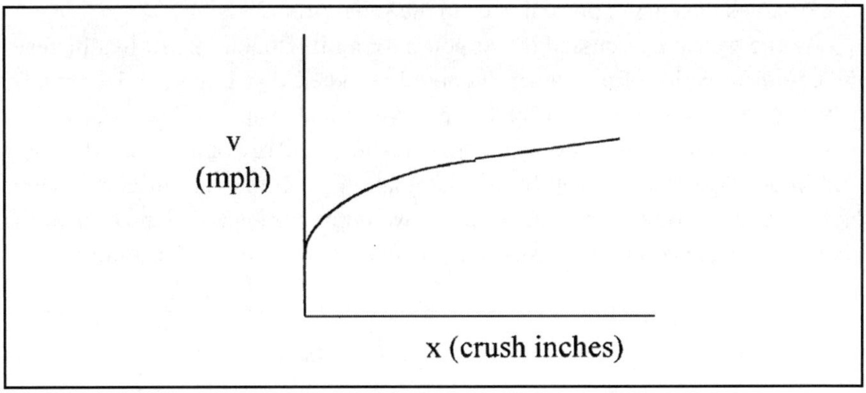

Figure 3.5 *Rigid barrier impact*

For example, for excessive frontal crush eventually the collapse will involve pushing the engine and transmission assembly back and distortion of the A frame. Thus, beyond this point the vehicle changes its rigidity (this is equivalent to suddenly changing the value of a), and Equation 3.4 will thereafter incorrectly predict the velocity at impact. Specifically, the so-called "rigid" passenger compartment is frequently softer than the front of the vehicle. In particular, experiments indicate (ref 16) that the compartment behaves almost as a material with a constant yield strength (no strain-hardening). This results in a trend toward more crush versus increase in impact speed, or conversely, a lower implied speed for a given observed crush, which occurred at the higher impact speeds. The result is that a further kink occurs on the velocity-crush plot at the about 30- to 35-mph barrier impact speed, and the plot once again tends toward a square-root behavior. This point is discussed in reference 16.

Modern cars are designed to allow the engine-transmission assembly to shear off the vehicle frame and submarine under the passenger compartment. This minimizes the transferred force and consequential passenger compartment acceleration, and prevents them from being propelled through the firewall. This makes it safer, especially for a front wheel drive vehicle. However, for a front-engine/rear-wheel-drive vehicle, this behavior can ultimately introduce another problem, that of the drive shaft digging into the road and causing the vehicle to pole vault over the contact point on the road.

Figure 3.6 indicates the effects of varying the R_0 and a parameters. To ensure that a given observed crush occurs for a given impact speed (i.e., the curve passes through a known point) these two parameters must be adjusted together, and a decrease in one implies a decrease in the other. It can be seen that for low values of both parameters the curve rapidly approximates to a straight line, whereas for larger values the curve approximates to the square-root law.

While we have discussed the response for a full-frontal impact that involves the complete width of a bumper, it should be noted that Equation 3.2 actually applies to any component of a vehicle, provided that the appropriate values of R_0, a and v_L are known. In this way, the total absorbed energy of a damaged vehicle can, in principle, be deduced from a summation of all the various components. However, this is rarely done and to do so would require detailed analysis of the response of each component, which is possible, but very time-consuming.

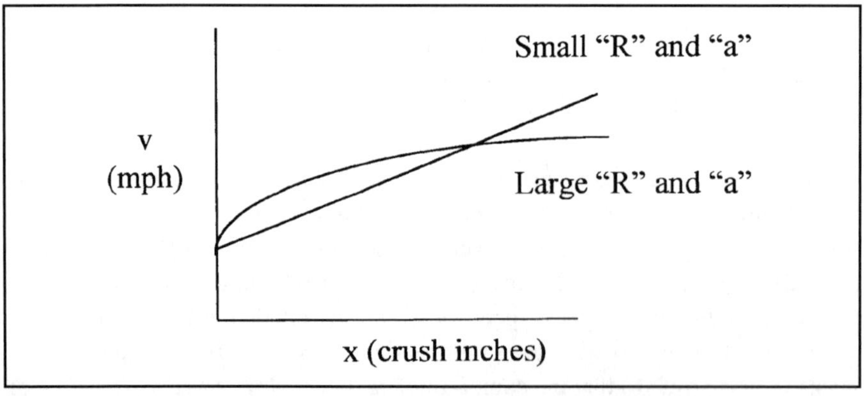

Figure 3.6 *Crush characteristics for variable R and a parameters*

3.3 The Difference between Input and Absorbed Energy

Equation 3.2 above refers to the input energy of the vehicle, which is directly given by its impact speed. If we assume that the force relief follows an elastic path parallel to the initial bumper-frame loading path, the recovered energy is given by

$$E_{rec} = \left(\frac{wv_L^2}{2g}\right)\left(1+\frac{x_{final}}{a}\right) = E_{bumper}\left(1+\frac{x_{final}}{a}\right) \tag{3.8}$$

where E_{bumper} is the energy (foot-pounds) to initially bottom-out the bumper.

Thus, the actual absorbed energy is approximately given by

$$E_{ab} = 6R_0w\left[\frac{x_{final}^2}{a} + 2x_{final} + \frac{v_L^2}{12R_0g}\right] - E_{rec} \tag{3.9}$$

or

$$E_{ab} = 6R_0w\left[\frac{x_{final}^2}{a} + 2x_{final} + \frac{v_L^2}{12R_0g}\right] - E_{rec} \tag{3.10}$$

or

$$E_{ab} = 6R_0w\left[\left(\frac{x_{final}^2}{a}\right)\left(1-\frac{v_L^2}{12R_0ga}\right) + 2x_{final}\left(1+\frac{v_L^2}{12R_0ga}\right)\right] \tag{3.11}$$

with x_{final} and a in feet. This distinction in energies becomes progressively more important as the impact's severity decreases, and can frequently be ignored for high-impact speeds.

However, because most real bumper systems involve some degree of viscous damping, the actual recovered energy is usually only a fraction, f, of the perfect-spring value given above. This effect is discussed later. Thus Equation 3.11 is really a lower limit for absorbed energy.

Note that because Equations 3.2 and 3.11 contain both a quadratic term and a linear term for crush then a plot of $E^{1/2}$ relative to crush will not be a straight line unless the square term dominates the linear term. Thus, straight-line behavior is not appropriate at low speeds.

Chapter 4

Crush Responses in Two-Vehicle, Low-Speed Collisions

4.1 In-Line Collisions

In general, collisions occur between two vehicles each with finite mass and crush capabilities. When a car collides with a rigid barrier, no significant energy is absorbed by the barrier, either in the form of crush damage or as induced motion. For the two-vehicle impact, however, energy is transferred from the bullet vehicle to the target vehicle, both in the form of damage and motion. It can then be shown that the closing speed v_c of the vehicles is given by

$$v_c^2 = 2E_D g \frac{(w_1 + w_2)}{\left[w_1 w_2 \left(1 - e^2\right)\right]} \tag{4.1}$$

in which the w's are the two vehicles' weights and E_D is the total absorbed energy for damage to both vehicles. The quantity e is the coefficient of restitution, which is the ratio of the difference in vehicle speeds after impact to the difference in speeds before the impact. It is a measure of the collision's elasticity, and is dimensionless.

Thus,

$$e = \frac{(v_2' - v_1')}{(v_1 - v_2)} = -\frac{(v_1' - v_2')}{(v_1 - v_2)} \tag{4.2}$$

where unprimed quantities are before the impact, and primed quantities are after the impact. Note the inversion in the order of speeds (1 versus 2). This occurs because the bounce associated with recovered energy is in the opposite direction to its initial motion. Mathematically, a ratio should always be defined with the numerator and denominator listed in the same order. Thus e is usually a negative number, as stated in the second part of Equation 4.2. However, many texts automatically invert the order to give a positive quantity, leading to unnecessary confusion, applying e in equations as if it were a positive quantity. The only solution to this problem is to be very careful to make sure that any use of e is done in a consistent manner. Throughout this book we use the mathematical version of e, which is usually negative. Of course, for Equation 4.1 the use of the square of e means that the sign of e is immaterial. However, the equations for post-impact speeds, given below, need the proper signs.

Following the second edition of this book, I was criticized for defining a "peculiar negative" restitution. However, this is how Newton defined it. Further, Professor Damask (a well-known physicist) also defined it this way (see Chapter 1 of reference 17). The point is that the equation for restitution is inherently negative. But because normally the bounce is in the reverse sense of direction the result is the product of two negative quantities. Hence usually the numerical value is considered positive. However, there are cases where the sign of restitution changes. A classic case occurs for strongly offset impacts (perpendicular impact on the nose of a vehicle) in which the bullet can end up moving both faster than the target and in the same direction (see Appendix A). The glancing blow also qualifies.

For a very elastic collision (no permanently absorbed energy), the value of e becomes –1.0, whereas, for a very plastic collision (the maximum possible energy is absorbed) the value becomes 0.0. Thus all "normal" vehicle collisions must have values in the range $0.0 > e > -1.0$.

Note that Equation 4.1 is usually applied for the case of a colinear impact between vehicles, or one that does not also induce rotations of either vehicle. If rotations are induced then the rotational kinetic energy must be taken into account. For this case the solution must include all forms of energy and the vehicle's initial speeds, which are then deduced independently by noting the maximum loss in initial kinetic energies. However, it can be shown that this is merely the same as using Equation 4.1 but with *effective weights*. These effective weights are discussed later where we address vehicle rotations.

For standard rigid-barrier crash tests, the norm is to evaluate the final crush in relation to the known vehicle input kinetic energy, rather than the actual absorbed energy. High-speed films of such impacts clearly show the recovered energy in the form of a bounce, and the vehicle is always found away from the barrier. However, this bounce is usually ignored in the definition of the energy associated with the corresponding degree of permanent crush. This is not an issue until one attempts to use Equation 4.1 which requires the absorbed energy. Thus, the *input* energy should be associated with the maximum dynamic crush (which is temporary, and only measurable with devices such as high-speed films) while the *absorbed* energy should be associated with the permanent crush.

An interesting example of double dipping can arise if these distinctions are not appreciated. Consider the following test case. A vehicle hits a rigid wall and then bounces back with the brakes fully locked, thus leaving skidmarks. The vehicle crush is noted. To deduce the vehicle's initial speed at impact, one has two choices. Either the standard permanent crush versus input energy can be used by itself, or the energy deduced from the bounce's skidmarks is added to the actual absorbed energy for the crush. What is not allowed is to add the skid energy and the input crash energy, because the latter already includes the bounce energy.

Note that these arguments presuppose that vehicle damage is due to a bumper-to-bumper impact, where the major thrust is through the bumper and thus into the strong underframe of the vehicle. However, sometimes non-bumper collisions occur. An example is when a car runs into the rear of a high four-wheeler with a bumper higher than that of the car. An alternative example is when a car is rapidly braking and adopts the nose-down, tail-up posture. If two cars are braking, the nose of the second car can easily submarine under the tail of the first one.

Whenever the impact does not involve a bumper, large amounts of upper body damage can be caused. This involves remarkably little energy, since the upper body panels are quite weak, and the crash does not involve the major vehicle frame. Thus the damage is really cosmetic, and often costs a lot to repair, but involves very little energy absorption compared to a through-the-bumper thrust. Similar upper-body damage can be produced by a person wielding a hammer or baseball bat. For these reasons the standard energy approach cannot be used unless the real strength of the panels is known, and attention should be concentrated on any observed bumper or frame damage. As a general rule, the effective value of R for soft-panel hits and for vehicle-side hits is about one-half, or less, of the value for direct bumper or frame impacts.

That vehicles really do bounce is demonstrated by inspection of the individual NHTSA reports, such as those generated by NCAP (New Car Assessment Program). For example, the test of the 1994 Ford Probe two-door model (ref 4) involves a standard frontal impact at 35 mph. The vehicle was found two feet (distance, *s*) away from the barrier after the test. The front section of the car crumpled back enough to grab the two front wheels, preventing rotation and causing the car to act as if the front brakes were being strongly applied. Assuming a friction coefficient (*F*) of about 0.7 acting on the frontal weight fraction (*fw*) of about 0.6 (no back-wheel braking), this implies a bounce at a speed of

$$v_{bounce} = (2\,F(fw)gs)^{1/2} = (2 \times 0.7 \times 0.6 \times 32.2 \times 2.0)^{1/2} = 7.36 \text{ ft/s} = 5.0 \text{ mph.}$$

The car collided with a barrier which contained thirty-six load cells that give the force-versus-time history of the crash. The integral of this force-time data gives the net change in the vehicle momentum. This value was observed to be about 5,730 lb-s. However, the vehicle weight was 3,178 pounds, and at 35 mph (51.3 ft/s) this represents an input momentum of 5,068 lb-s. Thus, the net change was calculated as 5,730/5,068 = 1.13 times larger than the input momentum. This implies a reverse bounce of about 4.6 mph, consistent with the estimate above. Thus $e = -5/35 = -0.14$ for this high-speed case. The same data is also obtained directly by integrating the deceleration-versus-time recording of the accelerometers attached to the rear-seat cross-members, which gives the velocity versus time. Practically all of the various cars tested (at the standard NCAP speed of 35 mph) indicate an initial rebound in the speed range of 5 to 7 mph.

4.2 Post-Impact Speeds

Consider vehicle 1 colliding with vehicle 2 at speed v_0, with vehicle 2 initially standing stationary. The two speeds after impact are

$$v_2' = \left[\frac{w_1}{w_1 + w_2}\right](1 - e)v_0 \tag{4.3}$$

and

$$v_1' = \left[\frac{(w_1 + ew_2)}{(w_1 + w_2)}\right]v_0. \tag{4.4}$$

Thus the final speeds depend on both the weights and the value of *e* (remember;

e is really negative for typical vehicle crashes). For a perfectly elastic collision $e = -1.0$. We obtain

$$v_2' = \left[\frac{2w_1}{(w_1 + w_2)}\right] v_0 \tag{4.5}$$

and

$$v_1' = \left[\frac{(w_1 - w_2)}{(w_1 + w_2)}\right] v_0. \tag{4.6}$$

If $w_1 < w_2$, this states that the bullet vehicle bounces in the reverse direction (i.e., v_1' becomes negative), since the numerator is clearly negative. For a plastic collision ($e = 0.0$) both v_1' and v_2' become equal (the vehicles stick together) at

$$v_1' = v_2' = \left[\frac{w_1}{(w_1 + w_2)}\right] v_0. \tag{4.7}$$

Real collisions lie somewhere between these extremes. In terms of the individual delta-*v*'s seen by the bullet and the target, Equation 4.1 becomes

$$(\text{delta-}v_1)^2 = \Delta v_1^2 = \frac{2E_D g w_2 (1-e)^2}{\left[w_1 (w_1 + w_2)(1 - e^2)\right]} \tag{4.8}$$

$$(\text{delta-}v_2)^2 = \Delta v_2^2 = \frac{2E_D g w_1 (1-e)^2}{\left[w_2 (w_1 + w_2)(1 - e^2)\right]} \tag{4.9}$$

Note that $(\text{delta-}v_1)/(\text{delta-}v_2) = w_2/w_1$, as required by the law of conservation of linear momentum. Note that these delta-*v*'s are the important ones for consideration of personal injury.

Although the above example applied for a stationary target, the various delta-*v*'s apply for any initial target speed. Thus Equation 4.1 gives the differential closing speed between the two vehicles, and Equations 4.3 through 4.9 give the differential speeds after the collision, all relative to the true initial target speed. Thus the entire process of vehicle speed changes can be adjusted up or down linearly with the initial target speed, since this is merely a consequence of conservation of momentum. Note that this is one of the few cases where velocities can be directly added, because most other cases involve additions of energy (e.g., when adding the effects of both crush and skid effects).

4.3 Coefficient of Restitution

We see that to use Equations 4.1, 4.3, 4.4, 4.8 and 4.9 we always require the value of *e*. However, this value is rarely quoted. Instead, many reconstructionists use rules such as "*e* is large for low impact speeds and small for high impact speeds." While this statement is generally true, it is useless for numerical purposes. Thus, a more rigorous method is needed to define the value. Although empirical equations exist for predicting values of *e*, these are usually little more than curves that are fitted to data, and rarely have much theoretical (and, hence, physical) basis. Such curve fits can be misleading, because they rarely apply over the entire range of speeds with any reliability. These fits frequently lead to asymptotes, such as the bumper speed limit, which fail to agree with known experimental facts. One such fit for *e* is given by Wood (ref 17). However, he cautions that it only applies for differential impact speeds above about 5 mph. Since the latter is comparable with the bumper response limit, his equation is clearly of limited use for low-speed collisions.

Indeed, the usual attempt to reduce all vehicular impact responses to simple curve fits invariably results in doubtful results for interpretation of low speed collisions. Such curve fits are couched in terms of regression coefficients with quotes of standard deviations. However, when these standard deviations are several mph (which they usually are) the fits become meaningless for analysis of low-speed collisions, although they are usable for higher speeds. This is because for high speeds interpolation is used within the database, whereas for low speeds extrapolation is required. The latter is always a dangerous exercise if the data are not based on a good theoretical understanding of the physical behavior. Only those enamored with statistical analysis are content with such approaches, since these approaches have little to do with physics, engineering or reality!

A classic example of this problem is the use of an equation such as the following: v (mph) = 1.3 x_{max} – 6 (inches), which is quoted in the *Accident Reconstruction Journal* (example, see page 8 of the July/August, 1995 edition). When x_{max} drops to zero this equation states that the vehicle is moving away from the barrier at 6 mph! Although such fits are reasonable for significant crush damage, they clearly fail to work at low speeds. This equation does not apply for a crush below 6/1.3 = 4.6 inches. Of course, ARJ writers are aware of this issue, and do not claim that such equations are meaningful for low-speed impacts.

Since e = (delta-bounce velocity)/(delta-input velocity) then e^2 = (bounce energy)/(input energy). Thus, the effective value of *e* can be deduced by considering the recovered energy versus the initial input energy. The recovered energy of each vehicle is given by Equation 3.8, for a simple spring-bumper response. Thus by summing the total recovered energies and dividing by the total input energy, the value of *e* is determined. As a simple example, for a rigid-barrier impact, and a perfect-spring response, we have

$$e^2 = \frac{\left\{\frac{wv_L^2}{2g}\right\}\left[1+\frac{x_{final}}{a}\right]}{\left(\frac{wv_{in}^2}{2g}\right)} = \left(\frac{v_L^2}{v_{in}^2}\right)\left(1+\frac{x_{final}}{a}\right) \tag{4.10}$$

thus,

$$e = \left(\frac{v_L}{v_{in}}\right)\left(1+\frac{x_{final}}{a}\right)^{\frac{1}{2}} \text{ (absolute value).} \tag{4.11}$$

Thus the value of e gradually increases slightly with increasing vehicle damage, but decreases even faster with increasing impact speed. Also, note that the speed differential after impact is given by

$$(v_2' - v_1') = -(v_1' - v_2') = -ev_{in} = -v_L\left[1+\frac{x_{final}}{a}\right]^{\frac{1}{2}}. \tag{4.12}$$

Since the quantity $[1 + x_{final}/a]^{1/2}$ changes only relatively slowly with impact speed, the post-impact differential speed also changes only slowly with the impact speed, and is almost a constant value. This effect has been observed for many vehicle collisions (ref 2). Equation 4.12 explains the observed bounces off the rigid barrier for the NCAP tests.

Clearly, Equation 4.1 is insensitive to the exact value of e, provided the latter is small. Thus, the solution is quite accurate for higher-speed impacts, and an assumption of $e \rightarrow 0.0$ will yield reasonable results, and Equation 4.7 will roughly apply. However, Equation 4.1 is very sensitive to the value of e when the latter approaches the value –1.0, as are Equations 4.3 and 4.4. This applies for the case of a low speed impact. It should be noted that, while reconstruction schools like Northwestern University Traffic Institute (NUTI) do explain the meaning of restitution, they never actually use it in any equation. This is because such schools really teach only the effects of the higher speed impacts. Indeed, NUTI states "in very low-velocity impacts, however, restitution may have to be considered."

However, as mentioned earlier, most modern bumpers involve some degree of internal energy absorption owing to the use of viscous responses. This means that a download factor of f is appropriate. Thus, $e \rightarrow fe$, where f is less than 1.0. The previous description assumed that $e = -1.0$ provided the bumper limit speed was not exceeded. Experimental data show that e is generally somewhat less than –1.0 when the bumper limit is reached. Since viscous response usually causes forces proportional to speed, the simplest modification is of the form

$$f = \left(1 - \frac{pv}{v_L}\right) \tag{4.13}$$

where v is the impact speed (less than the bumper limit) and v_L is the bumper limit speed, and p is a simple number less than 1.0. Experiments suggest that p is about 0.3 to 0.5. Thus, at the bumper limit, $e = 0.7$ to 0.5 for many cars. For higher impact speeds the plastic deformation effects give the rapid drop in e mentioned before. So for impacts exceeding the bumper limits the value of e given by Equation 4.11 should be multiplied by about 0.7 to 0.5.

It should be noted that even the rigid barriers generally use a facing sheet of 0.75 inches of plywood. Unfortunately, it is well known that wood itself displays significant plastic and viscous response (if you hammer on wood it will dent and only slowly recover). Further, this thickness of wood is not negligible compared to the amplitude of bumper motion, although it is small compared to the total crush for a 35-mph impact. Consequently, the observed bounce from the barrier is frequently a measure of both the bumper response and of the properties of the wood, rather than simply of the bumper assembly itself, and so misleading apparent low values of e can be inferred for low-speed impacts. Unfortunately, very few low-speed barrier tests have been done without the plywood.

The reason for using the 0.75-inch sheet of plywood is to protect the rigid barrier. Although the barrier is made with a front surface of steel, after enough collisions the steel will suffer damage. Because the barrier is large and heavy, repair would be expensive. Hence the plywood is used as a sacrificial bumper, which is inexpensive to replace. The fact that the plywood needs to be replaced is proof that it suffers permanent damage, that is due to plastic and viscous deformation.

Another reason for confusion with regard to low-speed values of e concerns failure to conserve momentum in experimental car-to-car tests. Equation 4.10 applies only to a single vehicle hitting a rigid barrier. For two vehicles colliding above the critical speeds defined below, we must add the two elastic energies for both vehicles. For example, Szabo and Welcher (ref 18) performed collisions using Ford Escorts for both bullets and targets. Tests were done with initial bullet speeds of 5 mph (2.23 m/s), 10 mph (4.47 m/s) and 15 mph (6.71 m/s) into stationary targets. Yet their own data indicated that at the common velocity the total momentum was only about 85 percent of the initial, and no discussion of the missing 15 percent is given. No braking was employed. Further, the measurements indicated that about 65 percent of the initial kinetic energy was absorbed for the two higher speeds. (For a totally plastic collinear collision of two identical bodies the maximum possible energy loss can only be 50 percent. To lose more implies an imaginary value of e. Some other mechanism is clearly removing both linear momentum and energy. This makes the true value of e difficult to determine.)

Lastly, Szabo and Welcher's measurements of vehicle accelerations frequently displayed double humps. These accelerometers were mounted at the vehicle's centers of mass. This two-peak behavior was almost certainly a consequence of beating between the pseudo-spring response of car-on-bumper and the natural oscillation behavior of the car's structure. Such beating can easily give an erroneous response, because the measured result will vary from position to position in the car. The only way to avoid it is to use many differently located accelerometers and to average their responses. Better still, if the intent is to measure bumper response then the bumpers should be mounted on a very rigid body so that only the bumper behavior is measured rather than the combined response of the bumper and car.

Finally, it should be noted that very few so-called in-line collisions are truly so. Many of the NCAP crashes indicate some form of yawing and pitching. High-speed video frequently shows that the rear wheels lift up off the ground during the impact. This implies that the bumper thrust must be acting somewhat below the vehicle's center of mass (CM). The resulting pitching rotation implies some of the initial vehicle energy has been converted into rotational energy. The same applies to any yawing. However, the pitching effect is small since the car only rises a few inches, whereas the 35-mph initial speed is the equivalent of a 41-foot drop under gravity.

It is sometimes mistakenly thought that conservation of momentum can be demonstrated by good repeatability of experiments. However, this merely demonstrates precision, not accuracy. The latter term relates to the correct answer, whereas the former only relates to repeatability, even if the answer is wrong each time. For example, a well-machined ruler may always give a length of 12.001 inches, or 11.999 inches, when measuring one foot, because of a systematic error caused by temperature effects (the ruler shrank or elongated).

The only real way to prove conservation of momentum between colliding vehicles is to perform an inverted test. Consider an impact between vehicles A and B. There is a decrease in velocity for A (–delta-v_A) and an increase in velocity for B (+delta-v_B) which are determined purely by the weight ratio. Now reverse the experiment, and hit A with B. This will again give two delta-v' values, but now the ratio is inverted. If the product of the two sets of delta-v's equals unity, momentum is being conserved. Thus

$$-\text{delta-}v_A / \text{delta-}v_B = w_B / w_A \text{ and } -\text{delta-}v'_B / \text{delta-}v'_A = w_A / w_B$$

and thus

$$(-\text{delta-}v_A / \text{delta-}v_B)\,(-\text{delta-}v_B' / \text{delta-}v_A') = (w_B / w_A)\,(w_A / w_B) = 1.0$$

There have been several reports of simulated low-speed car crashes in which the data clearly implies that momentum is not being conserved, because there have been cases that actually involved these inverted crashes. Unfortunately, the authors of these papers failed to note their problem. This makes the experimental data somewhat suspect, particularly where estimates of coefficient of restitution are being given. The values of e for such tests vary wildly for many of these low-speed crashes, and have even been calculated to locally increase with increasing speed. This is physically impossible unless the cars have some form of hidden internal energy source! The coefficient of restitution can only decrease as impact speeds increase. This is due to either greater viscous damping or greater plastic flow. Thus, great care must be taken with regard to some of the published data.

The failure to conserve momentum sometimes has an obvious cause, such as drivers applying brakes during impact. In these cases momentum is being transferred to the road. This effect is greatest when very low speeds (below about 3 mph) are involved. However, many of the tests do not involve braking. For these cases the missing momentum is less easy to explain. Part of the problem may relate to the time over which the data is measured. There is always some rocking motion of a car on its suspension when struck, and this motion involves a natural oscillation period. Unless the data is recorded over a time equal to several such oscillations (which dampen), it is possible to catch the data during an oscillation and record an unexpected answer. Unfortunately, few authors give enough experimental data to allow for a simple evaluation of such effects.

Similar oddities have been noticed in the detailed NCAP reports. For example, the load cells on the rigid barrier occasionally read tensions. Since nothing can pull on these cells, this is not possible. The errant tensile readings probably arise from induced oscillations in the barrier and the cells themselves (dynamic overshoot). However, oscillations in the rigid barrier prove that it is not really rigid.

4.4 Critical Damage Speed

Because different vehicles have different crush characteristics, it is necessary to include these facts in order to determine the minimum critical impact energy that barely causes vehicle damage for a two-vehicle collision. One vehicle will be weaker than the other, and thus the general rule is that one vehicle will start to suffer damage at a first critical limit while the other is still within the bumper limit. Note that here the bumper limit may not actually involve a bumper;

instead any threshold limit that describes the onset of permanent damage can be construed to represent a bumper. However, above a second critical limit, both vehicles will suffer damage. Thus, there is a window of limits. Consider a bullet vehicle hitting a stationary target vehicle. It can then be shown that the first limit is given by

$$v_{crit,1}^2 = \left[\frac{(w_1 + w_2)}{w_1}\right] v_{L2}^2 \left[1 + \left(\frac{w_2}{w_1}\right)\left(\frac{R_2}{R_1}\right)^2\left(\frac{v_{L1}}{v_{L2}}\right)^2\right] \tag{4.14}$$

where the v_L values apply to each bumper limit, and R values apply to each vehicle. There are several options. In all cases vehicle 1 is the stronger one, which is usually the heavier one.

1. For the rigid barrier case we set w_1 and R_1 to very large values (i.e., the barrier is both massive and strong). The solution is simply $v_{crit,1} = v_{L2}$, as expected from the definition of the barrier bumper speed.
2. For $w_1 = w_2$, but a large value of R_1, we obtain $v_{crit,1}{}^2 = 2v_{L2}{}^2$. Thus, the critical speed is 1.414 × the bumper limit speed. This situation represents a collision with a similar body weight which is very strong and cannot crush (e.g., a concrete "car" on wheels), has no bumper, or both. Note that this condition applies to some of the NHTSA and IIHS tests, where such a concrete "car" is indeed used to test for rear-end and side collision damage (the vehicle is actually a very rigid-frame of steel on wheels).
3. For two identical vehicles, we obtain $v_{crit,1}{}^2 = 4v_{L2}{}^2 = 4v_{L1}{}^2$. Thus, the critical speed is twice the bumper limit speed.

Note that for a very rigid second body but with a weight different from the subject car, the critical speed for bumper damage depends only on weights and the car bumper limit. This is merely a variant on case 2, and essentially removes the square-bracket portions of Equation 4.14. This is the situation that applies to the pendulum test that is frequently used to test bumper responses, and regularly used by organizations such as Consumers Union to check for car response. For instance, by knowing the ratio of weights for the vehicle and pendulum, the drop height can be adjusted to give the necessary impact speed that corresponds to a rigid-barrier crash at 5 mph. Consumers Union regularly does this test to simulate a 5-mph barrier impact, and then note the degree of induced damage. Those vehicles with 5-mph bumpers display zero damage, whereas those with weaker bumpers indicate damage. Although the amount of damage may be quite small, the cost of repair can easily reach $1,000.

Equation 4.14 is based on the logic that vehicle 2 (the weaker one) has just absorbed enough energy to exceed its bumper limit, and has thus just reached its damage force ($F_{0,2}$), while vehicle 1 is only absorbing a fraction of its bumper limit energy and has not yet reached its own damage force limit. The force is equal in magnitude for both vehicles.

Equation 4.14 has built-in symmetry. To appreciate this, consider two vehicles which are identical *except* for their bumper speed limits. Let $v_{L,1} = 5$ mph and $v_{L,2} = 2.5$ mph. We also have $(w_1 + w_2)/w_1 = 2.0$, $(w_2/w_1) = 1.0$ and $(R_2/R_1) = 1.0$. Substitution into Equation 4.14 then gives $v_{crit,1} = 7.91$ mph as the first critical speed for damage to either car. However, if we switch cars and invert the bumper limits, we obtain the same answer. This is to be expected. The critical closing speed must be independent of which vehicle has what properties, because it is a mutual answer.

The second critical limit is given by

$$v_{crit,2}^2 = \left[\frac{(w_1 + w_2)}{w_1}\right]\left\{v_{L2}^2 + \left(\frac{w_1}{w_2}\right)v_{L1}^2 + \left[\frac{12ga_2(R_1w_1 - R_2w_2)^2}{R_2w_2w_2}\right] + \left(\frac{24ga_2}{w_2}\right)(R_1w_1 - R_2w_2)\right\} \tag{4.15}$$

This limit is seen to depend on the a value of the weaker vehicle. This is because when the stronger vehicle just reaches its damage force value the weaker vehicle is already partway along its crush curve. As with Equation 4.14, if the two vehicles are identical, $v_{crit,2} = 2v_{L,1} = 2v_{L,2}$ and so forth

When these facts are combined with Equation 4.1 it is possible to derive the following equation giving the differential closing speed for a two-vehicle collision that involves damage to only one vehicle:

$$v_{close}^2 = \left[\frac{(w_1 + w_2)}{w_1}\right]v_{L2}^2\left[1 + \left(\frac{w_2}{w_1}\right)\left(\frac{R_2}{R_1}\right)^2\left(\frac{v_{L1}}{v_{L2}}\right)^2\right] + \frac{2gE_D(w_1 + w_2)}{(w_1w_2)}. \tag{4.16}$$

Note that for high-speed collisions the second term in Equation 4.16 is much larger than the first term because of the large value of E_D. For these cases the first term can be ignored. This reduces Equation 4.16 to the same as Equation 4.1, but with $e = 0.0$.

In view of all the above, it should be obvious that it is *not* possible to deduce the vehicle impact speeds merely by looking at the vehicle damage. The degree of damage merely allows one to calculate the absorbed energies, then it is necessary to use Equation 4.16 with the vehicle weights, R values and bumper limit speeds, in order to compute a speed. Finally, this speed is not absolute, but is instead the differential speed between the two vehicles. To establish absolute speeds other information is required, such as knowledge of the post-impact skidmark lengths.

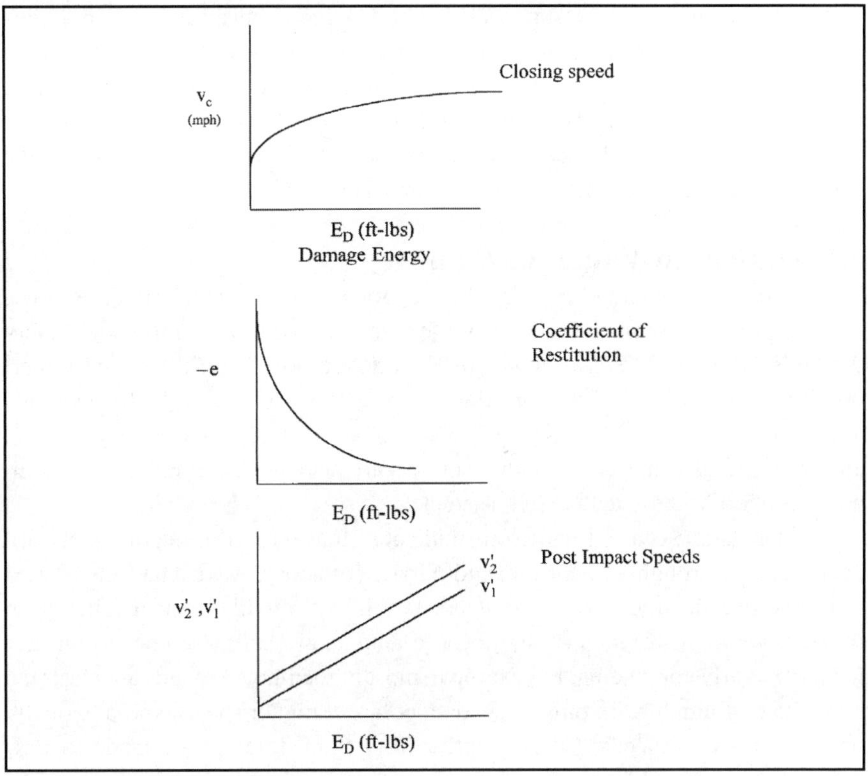

Figure 4.1 *Two-vehicle responses*

To prove this latter point, consider a simple case of the bullet vehicle moving at 20 mph striking a target at zero mph. Are these the two speeds? Answer: No! An equally good answer is that the two speeds are 920 mph and 900 mph. Why? Because the vehicles are on a rotating planet and are moving around its north-south axis at about 900 mph. This simple, if perhaps, nonsensical, example illustrates very clearly that the only velocity derived from an energy-of-crush analysis is the *differential* speed.

Examples of applying this logic to the two-vehicle bumper-to-bumper impact are given in Figures 4.1a, b and c. The independent variable is the total absorbed crush energy. Figure 4.1a gives the differential closing speed of the bullet vehicle versus the target as the crush energy increases, with the speed increasing from the lower critical speed at crush energy of zero. Figure 4.1b shows the corresponding behavior for the coefficient of restitution. As the crush energy increases, the value of *e* rapidly decreases. Finally, Figure 4.1c shows the post-impact vehicle speeds. Note how the difference between these post-impact speeds is almost constant.

The foregoing logic presupposes that both vehicles have springlike bumpers which return to their initial state after impact. This ensures that $e = -(1 - p)$ at the bumper limits. For real bumpers the effective value of e is lower than –1.0 as the bumper limit speed is approached. However, this does not influence the definition of the critical speeds; it merely alters the post-impact speeds of the vehicles, causing the differential to be somewhat smaller.

4.5 Numerical Values of *R* and *a*

There are several sources of data which characterize the actual crush response of many cars. These include data from the National Highway Traffic and Safety Administration (NHTSA, as quoted by Expert Autostats™, ref 19), from Limpert (ref 2), from Noon (ref 20), from the Northwestern University Traffic Institute (data from Severy, ref 21, and the CRASH3 model, ref 22), from Severy (ref 23), and from Lundstrom (ref 24). Other sources are also available (ref 25). Unfortunately, not all of these data are consistent.

Older data (Severy, Lundstrom) indicated that the crush depth versus impact speed was roughly linear for rigid-barrier collisions. Also, data from Severy indicated that the under-seat peak deceleration was roughly a linear function of impact speed. However, scrutiny of these data show that these conclusions are not particularly convincing. For example, most of the impact speeds are clustered about 25 to 40 mph, with only a few data points at higher speeds and practically no data at lower speeds. Consequently, almost any line can be made to pass through the points. This linear approach is the one adopted by NUTI (using the CRASH3 model). This approach implies low values for both the R and a terms. This then implies low initial vehicle accelerations at incipient crush but with very rapid increases in acceleration as crush depth increases (see also Chapter 5).

However, data from Expert Autostats™ and Noon imply an almost constant crush strength versus crush depth. Wood (ref 17) also assumes a step function of constant crush strength regions per step versus crush. This implies a multipart square-root dependence of velocity versus crush depth, and thus large values of R and a. Finally, Limpert gives empirical fits to data which again imply a rough square-root behavior.

It should be noted that all these various fits pass close to each other for impact speeds near 30 to 35 mph. This is hardly surprising, however, because this is where the majority of the data exist. However, only NUTI gives results which imply the existence of bumpers, with most other data asymptoting to zero speed at zero crush. This is clearly wrong. Unfortunately, the CRASH3 data frequently predict zero crush at speeds greater than 5 mph, which is also incorrect (unless it is proven that a specific vehicle has unusually good bumpers).

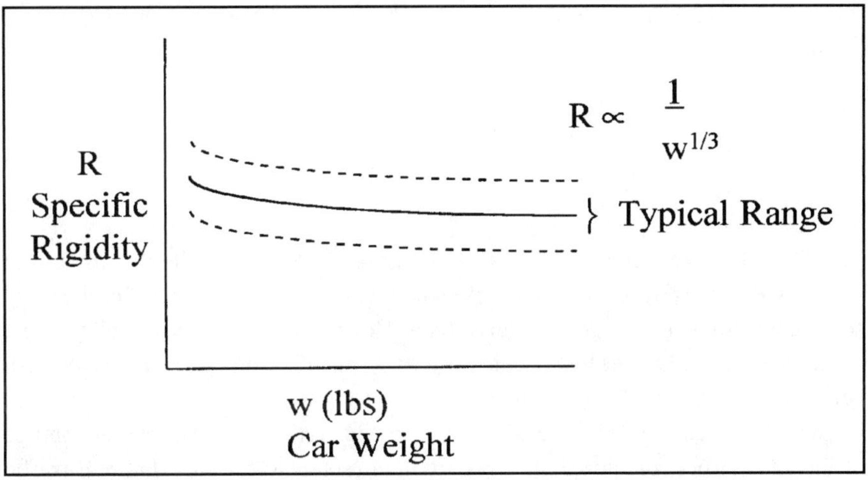

Figure 4.2 *Rigidity versus weight*

The data from both Noon and Limpert support a well-known fact, namely that for impacts into rigid barriers, larger cars suffer greater crush depths. Wood also notes a similar effect. The reason is simple: larger cars have longer hoods and can therefore be designed to have greater crush depths for a given impact speed. This is in accordance with simple physics. Consequently, larger cars give lower decelerations to the occupants, and are therefore safer for the passengers. This effect gives R values which decrease as the vehicle weights increase. However, the crush force (i.e., $F = 12Rw$) increases with vehicle weight. Thus, larger cars are stronger than small cars. This results in a second effect: in a collision between a large car and a small one, the larger car always "wins" in that the crush depth is smaller for the large car than for the small car. Further, owing to the weight ratio, the large car suffers a smaller deceleration than does the small car. Again, larger cars are safer. Figure 4.2 illustrates the data from Noon. Wood states that the crush strength tends to be proportioned to the vehicle mass to the two-thirds power, while the crush depth itself is proportioned to the one-third power of the vehicle mass. This essentially agrees with the Noon and Limpert data. Note that, when normalized versus vehicle mass, a force proportional to the two-thirds power of mass implies a power law for force-per-weight (R) which is the inverse of the one-third power of mass. Thus Wood's data again indicates that as the vehicle weight increases so the value of R decreases (with roughly a $1/w^{1/3}$ law). Thus for an increase in weight of a factor of 2.0, the value of R decreases by about 1.26, while the actual crush force increases by about 1.59. Likewise, for a given speed, the crush depth increases by about 1.26 for a rigid-barrier impact.

Using these approximations we can rewrite Equation 4.14 by noting that the ratio $(R_2/R_1)^2 = (w_1/w_2)^{2/3}$. Thus the product $(w_2/w_1)(R_2/R_1)^2 = (w_2/w_1)^{1/3}$. Hence, we obtain

$$v_{crit,1}^2 = \left[\frac{(w_1 + w_2)}{w_1}\right] v_{L2}^2 \left[1 + \left(\frac{w_2}{w_1}\right)^{1/3} \left(\frac{v_{L1}}{v_{L2}}\right)^2\right]. \quad (4.17)$$

This effect of large car versus small car explains part of the dilemma with the NCAP car crash results. A simple study of the raw NCAP data implies that small cars can be just as good as large ones. However, the data only applies to the fixed speed rigid barrier tests, which are the equivalent of a mirror image crash between two identical cars with identical speeds. Real life frequently involves impacts between cars of different size, and thus only then does the advantage of larger cars become apparent. The problem relates to the fact that real traffic involves a spread in vehicle weights. If all vehicles were of the same weight then the NCAP results would directly relate to real accident crashworthiness.

This large versus small behavior is at the root of NHTSA's dilemma with regard to how to explain the meaning of its NCAP test results. Frequently, a one-star large car can actually be safer than a five-star small car, for the average mixed-weight crash. However, to state this in plain English NHTSA would encourage car buyers to always purchase large cars. Because large (heavy) cars consume more fuel, this would worsen the overall fuel consumption for the U.S. as a whole. The predicament for NHTSA would then be that this response would fly in the face of another government ruling, the CAFE, which forces the auto-

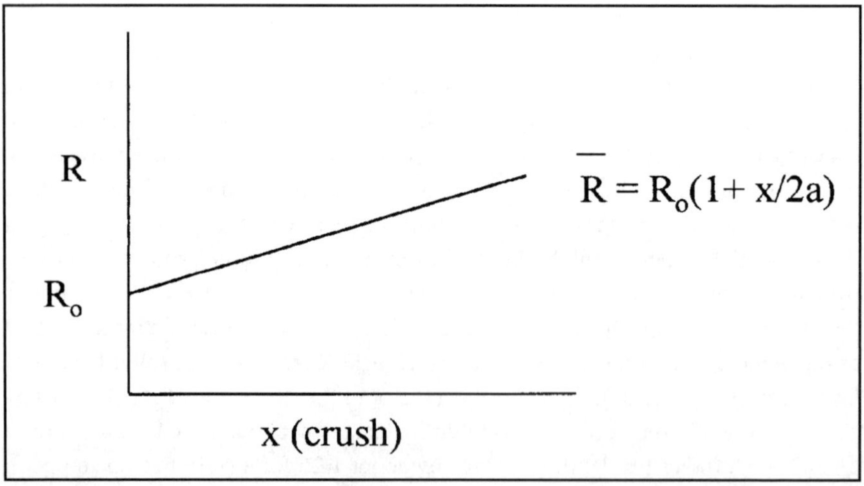

Figure 4.3 *Vehicle rigidity versus crush*

mobile manufacturers to ensure that their average fleet of vehicles (by sales volume) maintains a certain overall fuel economy. We have previously pointed out that using different materials can improve the strength-to-weight ratios, thereby allowing lighter strong cars. Unfortunately, these aerospace techniques, such as using high-strength aluminum alloys (such as 7075) are much more expensive. Thus, the consumer would balk at the resulting cost.

The Noon data really give the average values for R over speed ranges of 20 to 40 mph. Thus, we must reinterpret in order to obtain R_0 and a. Figure 4.3 illustrates how this can be done. The correspondence is simply $R_{ave} = R_0(1 + x/2a)$. By comparing the options versus the data from Limpert and others the effective values can be deduced.

4.6 Contact Time

A vehicle crash occurs in a very short time. Treating the system as a mass-on-spring, the contact time is one-half the natural period of oscillation. This oscillation frequency is given by

$$\varpi^2 = \frac{K}{m} = \frac{Kg}{w} = (2\pi)^2 f^2 = \frac{(2\pi)^2}{T^2} \tag{4.18}$$

where ϖ is the angular frequency (radians/s), K is the spring rate (force per unit motion, pounds per foot), m is the mass, w is the weight, f is the frequency (Hz, or cycles per second), $\pi = 3.1416$, and T is the period. In the elastic regime the value of K is given by the incipient crush force ($12R_0w$) divided by the bumper amplitude ($x_0 = v_L^2/(12R_0g)$, see Chapter 3(a)). Thus, we obtain

$$\varpi = 2\pi f = \frac{2\pi}{T} = \frac{12R_0 g}{V_L}. \tag{4.19}$$

Thus,

$$T = \frac{2\pi v_L}{12R_0 g}. \tag{4.20}$$

For the rigid-barrier case, an elastic collision involves a contact time given by one half of the period

$$t_{contact} = \frac{\pi v_L}{12R_0 g}. \tag{4.21}$$

For $v_L = 7.335$ ft/s, and $R_0 = 1.0$, this is about 0.06 second, and even for a low R_0 value of 0.5 the time is only 0.12 second.

The rigid barrier case assumes that the second body is infinitely massive.

For a two-vehicle collision, the contact time is one-half the period for the coupled pair. To compute this we use the reduced effective spring rate and reduced weight for the pair. The reduced spring rate and weight are given by

$$K_{red} = \frac{K_1 K_2}{(K_1 + K_2)} \text{ and } w_{red} = \frac{w_1 w_2}{(w_1 + w_2)}, \text{ respectively.} \tag{4.22}$$

Note that reduced values involve the ratio of product over sum. This is similar to the rule for parallel resistances in electrical circuits. This gives

$$t_{contact} = \left(\frac{\pi}{12 R_{01} R_{02} g} \right) \left[\frac{\left(R_{01}^2 w_1 v_{L2}^2 + R_{02}^2 w_2 v_{L1}^2 \right)}{(w_1 + w_2)} \right]^{1/2}. \tag{4.23}$$

When the two vehicles are identical, this gives the same answer as for the rigid barrier case.

For a plastic deformation the total contact time increases, but is still rarely much more than 0.1 to 0.2 second for most cases. These very short contact times are faster than a human response time necessary to innervate the muscles (typically 0.1 to 0.2 second), which explains the inability of the occupants to immediately fight the induced motions by application of their muscles. Thus their body parts tend to flop around like a rag doll. These effects are important for considerations of occupant kinematics. The exact contact time for the plastic case is given by using the effective spring constants for the plastic flow region of Figure 3.3, line AB. This slope is simply $K = 12R_0 w/a$ for each vehicle. Then we obtain

$$t_{contact} = \left(\frac{\pi}{2} \right) \left\{ \frac{R_{01} w_1 a_2 + R_{02} w_2 a_1}{\left[12 g R_{01} R_{02} (w_1 + w_2) \right]} \right\}^{1/2}. \tag{4.24}$$

If the two vehicles are identical we obtain $t_{contact} = \pi/2 \cdot \{a/(12R_0 g)\}^{1/2}$, which is also the answer for the rigid-barrier impact. For Equation 4.24 the value of a is in units of feet. Note the leading factor of 1/2 in Equation 4.24. This arises because the plastic contact time represents only one-quarter (.25) of a period, since it only applies during the loading part of the motion. This assumes moderate plastic deformation where the initial elastic response is overshadowed by the plastic response (otherwise during the loading phase we have a mixture of elastic and plastic responses). For the unloading response we again have pseudo-elastic behavior, but also only for .25 period. Thus Equation 4.24 really describes the stopping time before any bounce. Note that a measurement of this time gives the ratio (a/R_0) for the rigid-barrier impact, which can be compared with the values deduced from the velocity-crush data. The total contact time for a crash is simply the sum of the plastic quarter-period (if crush damage occurs) and the elastic quarter-period. Setting a = 10 inches = 0.833 foot, and using $R_0 = 0.5$, the rigid barrier stopping time becomes 0.103 second, while for $R_0 = 1.0$ the time is 0.073 second.

Inspection of the detailed NCAP reports indicate that many vehicles stop in about 0.08 second, and disengage from the rigid barrier after about 0.14 second, in approximate agreement with these predictions. Plots of the speed versus time for these crashes also demonstrate that the responses are very similar to a damped half-cycle harmonic motion. Figure 4.4 illustrates typical speed versus time behavior for both low-speeds and high-speeds.

4.7 Distance Moved during Impact

It is important to realize that a stationary target moves very little during a low-speed impact. For an impact which just reaches the target bumper limit, the distance moved by the target while the bullet and target reach their common speed is only $(\pi/2 - 1)x_0 = 0.57x_0$, where x_0 is the bumper amplitude. The total distance moved by the target until vehicle separation is $\pi x_0 = 3.14\ x_0$. The value of x_0 =

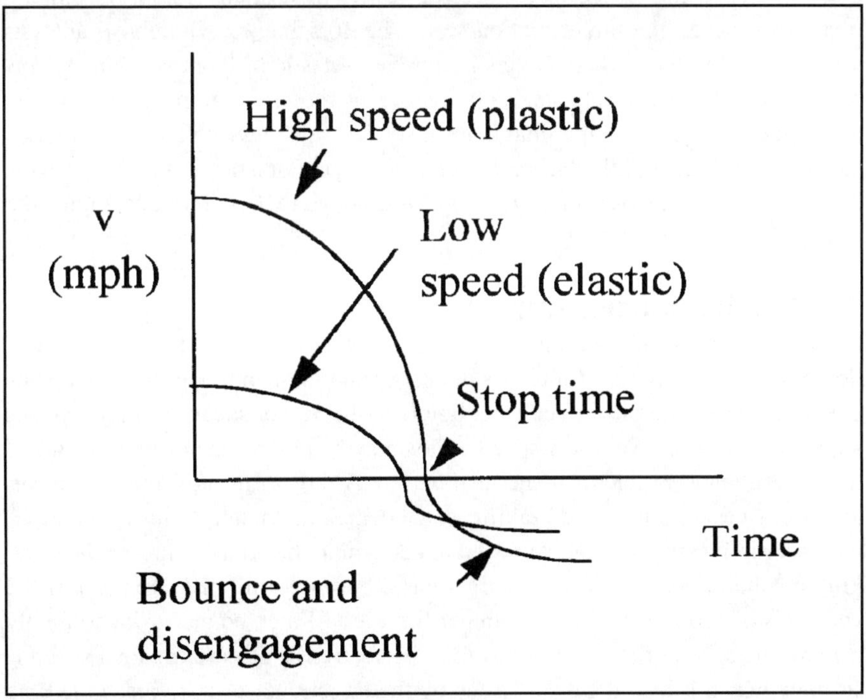

Figure 4.4 Rigid barrier speed versus time

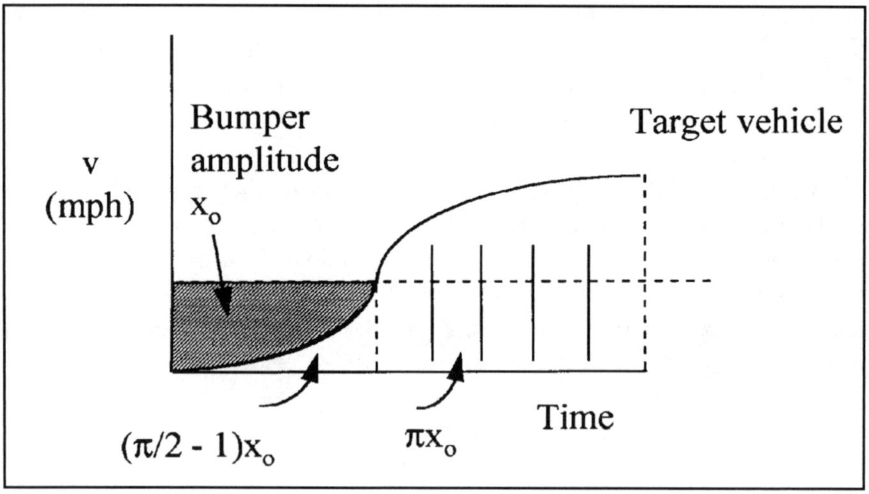

Figure 4.5 *Motion of target*

$v_L^2/(R_0 g)$ in inches with the speed in ft/s. For v_L = 5 mph = 7.335 ft/s and R_0 = 0.5 the bumper amplitude is only 3.34 inches. Thus as the vehicles approach their common speed the target only moves about 1.9 inches, and when the vehicles finally disengage the target motion would be 10.5 inches. The above analysis assumes the bumper assembly acts in a pseudo-elastic fashion, and ignores any braking by the target vehicle. With significant rebound damping, the time to disengage increases, but the final bounce speed is also less, so the target motion usually decreases slightly during the rebound stage. For a target which is moving at initial speed v_0 the quantity $v_0 t_{contact}$ must be added to these motions. Figure 4.5 illustrates these effects.

4.8 Braking during Impact

Because an impact takes a finite time and involves a finite motion, the application of braking involves a finite loss of energy and momentum to the road during the collision. While this effect is negligible at the higher speeds, it may produce significant effects at very low speeds. This may be partly the reason for some of the experimental problems mentioned before. Although most of the staged car-to-car crashes have not used braking, some degree of friction is always present.

A simplification can be employed to determine the effect of pre-applied braking for the target. Suppose the target has a bumper limit of 5 mph (v_L). If the vehicle is hit from rest up to its bumper limit it will then bounce away to finally achieve the speed of $(1 - e)v_L$. Thus for a perfectly elastic case the final speed is 10 mph, which is also the delta-v seen by the target. However, to reach the time of disengagement takes a one-half period ($T/2$), as given in Equation 4.21. If during this time the brakes apply a drag factor of f, then the vehicle speed will be reduced by approximately delta-v = $fgT/2$. This is only approximate since it ignores the fact that the target does not start moving until after the bumper force exceeds the frictional force, as described before. Thus, this correction is an overestimation. Substituting for $T/2$ we obtain delta-v = $f\pi v_L/(12R_0)$. For $v_L = 5$ mph and $R_0 = 0.5$, delta-v = 2.68f mph. Thus with hard braking ($f = 0.75$), delta-v = 1.96 mph. Hence the true peak speed reached by the target is now only 10 – 1.96 = 8.04 mph. This is the equivalent of $e = -0.607$. If, instead, $f = 0.4$, the peak speed is about 10 – 1.04 = 8.95 mph, implying an effective $e = -0.79$. Even for $f = 0.1$, the effective value of e becomes –0.946. This effect helps explain why measured values for e are always below –1.0, even for a highly elastic inherent bumper response.

Note that since delta-v is mostly determined by the half-period ($T/2$), which is not dependent on amplitude for an elastic system, the degradation in apparent e becomes greater as the speeds decrease. Thus, for a push to 3 mph (the common speed of both vehicles) and elastic bounce to 6 mph, the delta-v of 2.68f mph now reduces the peak speed to only 3.99 mph, for $f = 0.75$, and the effective value of e is –0.33, even for a truly elastic bumper response. This simple logic states that the car hardly moves if the initial induced common speed is below about 2.68 × 0.75 = 2 mph, for hard braking. This is again a low value similar to that quoted before.

Note that when the target has its brakes applied it effectively increases its apparent weight at low speeds. This causes the bullet to slow more than it otherwise would. Thus, the target sees a reduced overall delta-v while the bullet sees an increased delta-v. However, these effects are occurring at such low speeds that personal injury is unlikely, unless the person has a predisposition to injury.

The above assumed that the frictional drag was f. However, this is the effective value since we are dealing with a two-vehicle impact. The effective value of drag is only equal to that of the target if both bullet and target have the same friction. Hence, the proper value to use is given by

$$f_{average} = (f_{bullet} w_{bullet} + f_{target} w_{target})/(w_{bullet} + w_{target}).$$

Thus, if the bullet is heavy and does not apply its brakes, the effective value of f is small, even for strong braking of the target.

4.9 The Engineer's Box

While Figure 4.2 shows the gradual decrease in R with increase in vehicle weight, it also indicates a remarkably small spread in R values for a given weight. This can be explained by considering the "engineer's box." The engineer invariably finds himself struggling to satisfy several conflicting requirements. As a result, he finds he is in a box that limits his options. For example, he must minimize the weight to give good fuel mileage, ensure sufficient body rigidity to prevent body flex on rough roads, design the crush characteristics consistent with the vehicle's not crushing too much or too little, and do this at a reasonable cost.

The net result is that two different engineers will tend to produce very similar designs in terms of crush characteristics for a given vehicle weight. This explains Wood's observation that most vehicles have remarkably similar strength and crush properties when normalized to the weights, regardless of maker or designer. However, a superior strength-to-weight car can be designed by using specialty metals, such as titanium and special aluminum alloy (as do very specialized car makers such as Bugatti), but the cost of the car then becomes prohibitive. The sheet metal panels can be replaced by fiberglass, but fiberglass is brittle and absorbs less energy than structural steel. Thus, this effect must be offset by redesigning the remainder of the vehicle. Note that this brittle response for fiberglass (and many other Plastics) explains why the frame of a car is not made with such materials. The car would crack in half rather than provide the gentle ride down associated with plastic deformation in metals.

The observed small spread in R values implies that exact numbers for a given vehicle are usually not necessary, unless high accuracy is intended in a given analysis. The uncertainties associated with using average behavior can generally be held to less than ±10 percent for speed predictions. Indeed, larger uncertainties can be attributed to unknowns in the exact conditions of an incomplete impact (one involving the bumper only partially). Lastly, the actual measurement and determination of the crush depth itself is often ambiguous, since it is rare for the observed surfaces to move in a clean linear manner. Instead, the once-simple surface is frequently corrugated and folded in odd ways. In this respect, low-speed impacts are actually simpler, because the small degree of damage usually involves a pushed-in bumper which is still basically straight.

Note that for litigation purposes it is rarely necessary to require very high accuracy in the computations. This is because court battles are usually of the form "was the speed greater than that necessary to…(exceed the speed limit, cause the injury, etc.)," and determining who was at fault. This rarely requires estimates with several significant figures, and such estimates would be meaningless for many cases owing to uncertainties elsewhere (exact drag factor on the road, weight of vehicle plus payload, bone breaking strength, etc.).

4.10 Rule of Thumb: The "One-mph-per-Inch-Crush" Rule

An approximation rule frequently quoted is that each incremental inch of crush represents about one mph of equivalent barrier speed for a full-frontal collision. Can this be explained? Yes. Consider that when a car crashes the graph of velocity versus time is essentially a damped sinusoid, and the time to stop (t_{stop}) is effectively a quarter-period, where T is the period. Then it can be shown that the initial velocity (v) and the amplitude of motion (x, the crush) are related by $v = \omega x$, where $\omega = 2\pi f = 2\pi/T = \pi/(2t_{stop})$, where f is the frequency (Hz) and ω is the angular rate (radians/s). Since a typical crash causes the vehicle to stop in about 0.08 seconds (ignoring any bounce), we obtain $\omega = 19.6$ radians/s. Thus we get v (ft/s) $= 19.6x$ (feet), or v (mph) $= 19.6/(12 \times 1.467)x$ (inches) $= 1.12x$ (inches). Thus the numerical multiplier is a directly related to the inverse the stopping time, and is close to the value of 1.0. This rule is only appropriate for the higher speeds, when bumper response can be ignored.

4.11 Incomplete and Side Impacts

If an impact does not involve the full width of a bumper, it is called an incomplete impact. Clearly, this will give an asymmetric crush damage profile. For the same mean depth of crush, the volume of metal involved in the crush is necessarily less than that for the full bumper case, and the energy absorbed is also less. The issue is how to correctly interpret this effect. The CRASH3 model assumes that the damage energy should be apportioned in a linear manner as a function of damage width, and thus volume. This logic assumes that the vehicle is comprised of totally independent small parts, such that each part crushes independently of its neighbor. Clearly, this is not strictly correct since these parts have cross-connections. A simple example is the bending of a cantilever beam. When a load is applied to the free end of the beam, maximum amplitude of motion occurs at that end. But there is a stress distribution along the entire beam, and the maximum stresses occur at the clamped end. Indeed, the maximum absorbed energy occurs at the clamped end. Thus when plastic flow occurs it is at the clamped end, although the maximum observed permanent shift is at the free end. In a similar manner, crushing the right of a vehicle necessarily applies loads to the left side.

The concept that energy is proportional to the volume of damage would be correct for an isotropic homogeneous body such as a simple block of steel, where the strength and moduli are the same in all directions. However, a real car does not behave this way. Consequently, for an oblique or incomplete impact, it is necessary to resolve the forces and deformations into orthogonal ones along the vehicle's longitudinal axis and perpendicular to this axis, and to sum the independent energies. Nevertheless, the use of the volume concept is reasonable for first-order analysis. Thus, if the damage profile extends only across a fraction, f, of the car's width, the corresponding energy and force terms are also a fraction f of the values for a full-width deformation, at least to first order. However, Wood has pointed out that for typical car structures, the internal stresses tend to average out regardless of the exact details of initial loading. This fact is the simplest explanation for why the "*f* value" logic works.

A classic application of this logic is for a collision in which only one-half of the bumper is contacted. For full compression of this one half, this implies only one half of the stored energy compared to a full bumper impact. Because kinetic energy is proportional to the square of speed, this implies that the effective bumper speed limit is only $(1/2)^{1/2} = 0.717$ the normal value. Thus a 5-mph bumper acts as if it were a 3.54-mph one. This then is the value to set v_L to for use in Equations 4.14, 4.16 and 4.17.

The offset crash is receiving special attention these days since it is a very common type of crash, and is not presently part of the government testing requirements. The IIHS in particular has been studying this problem since this type of crash frequently involves significant injuries to the legs of the driver, even though the deceleration experienced by the driver is actually less than for a full-bumper impact at the same speed. To understand the issue, consider the case of a half impact, where the crash involves only one half of the bumper's width. At a given speed the fixed energy is absorbed by approximately one half the car width, thereby making the absorption of energy twice the full-bumper value in terms of energy-per-volume. This is the equivalent to increasing the effective crash speed (i.e., equivalent barrier speed) by a factor $2^{1/2} = 1.414$ as far as depth of crush is concerned for the impacted half. This produces a crush significantly larger than for the full-bumper case on the impacted half, thereby explaining the leg injuries.

For example, at 30 to 35 mph with a springlike crush response (i.e., the strain-hardening response given by Equation 3.2, a full-bumper crush of 24 inches may become about 34 inches on the impacted half. This will convert a crush that does not reach the occupant compartment into one that encroaches into the passenger compartment and causes leg injuries, especially for the driver's side where the foot pedals are located. However, the net retarding force is lower, thus giving a lower net deceleration of the vehicle. This is because although the greater crush implies a larger force-per-width, the peak crushing force only increases by about $2^{1/2} = 1.414$, while the width is only one-half the full vehicle width. Thus, the actual total force is only $2^{1/2}/2 = 0.717$ of the value for the full-bumper case. This argument ignores the fact that an offset collision also induces rotations of the vehicle, which actually reduces the net energy loss. Some of the lost energy is converted into rotational energy instead of crush energy. Thus, the deceleration experienced by the driver is actually less than the factor given above, and the degree of crush is also less. Nevertheless, the amount of crush is larger than for the full-bumper case, and can lead to significant leg injury.

For a side impact on a vehicle there can be considerable uncertainty in the crush response. A major reason is that, unlike a full-front or full-rear impact, the strength of the side of most vehicles varies significantly from point to point. Whereas the side frames (A, B and C) and wheel-axle assemblies are hard points, the sides of fenders and the middle of doors tend to be much softer. Thus the effective strength depends on where and how the vehicle is struck, which depends on such factors as whether the bumper of the bullet vehicle straddled the vertical frames of the target one. On average, the *R* value for such soft structure responses are usually in the range of about 0.2 to 0.5, versus the range 0.5 to 1.0 for bumper-frame response.

However, although these effects make accuracy of interpretation of a side impact worse than for a frontal or rear one, Newton's third law can be usefully employed. Suppose the bullet vehicle itself has a full-frontal impact with the front side portion of another vehicle. Since the frontal collision can be reasonably interpreted, the absorbed energy and maximum force can be deduced for the bullet vehicle. Then, Newton's law states that the maximum force acting on the target is also that for the bullet. Since the two vehicles' crush depths can be measured, an estimate of the absorbed energy for the target can be made. From this, the total absorbed energy is derived, and although the value for the target is less certain than for the bullet, the total has an intermediate accuracy which can still yield useful interpretation. In essence, this approach is one in which a calibrated vehicle is used to calibrate the other vehicle. This logic has been invoked by Hull (ref 26), and Wood.

4.12 Partial or Sideswipe Impacts

Many vehicle collisions involve sideswipes, where one vehicle effectively runs along the side of the other. This type of collision is peculiar in that it involves a positive coefficient of restitution. For a normal impact the difference in speeds first decreases to zero (at which point both vehicles have the same speed) and then increases again by an amount that depends on the degree of elastic bounce. Since this process reverses the order of speeds (i.e., the target is now faster than the bullet) we are dealing with a negative coefficient of restitution, as explained before. However, for the sideswipe, the centers of mass (CMs) of the two vehicles generally do not reach a common speed, and the impact finishes with the bullet still moving faster than the target. Thus, the ratio of speed difference post-impact to pre-impact is positive.

Note that this type of impact involves far less vehicle damage than for the normal type. Also, it generally induces significant rotations of the vehicles. If one vehicle (target) approaches slowly from the side and hits the side door of a faster moving vehicle (bullet) at a high angle (e.g., near 90 degrees between vehicles) the result is to induce a rapid rotation of the target but a slower rotation of the

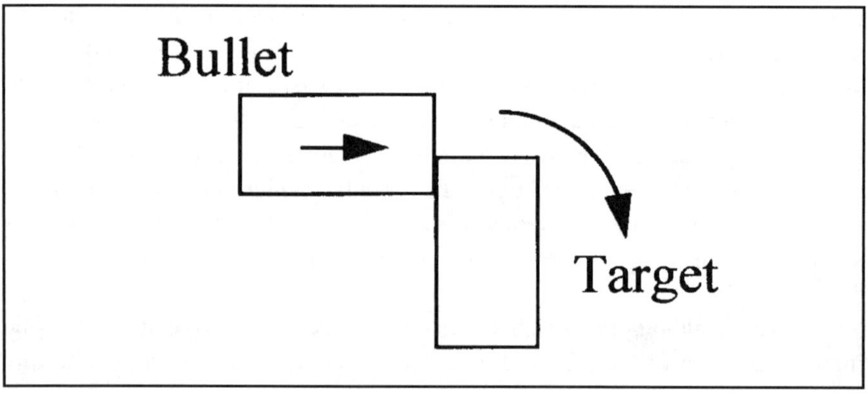

Figure 4.6 *"End hit" on target—rapid target rotation*

bullet. A similar effect occurs if the bullet vehicle perpendicularly strikes the far end of the target. See Figure 4.6. Further, the transferred linear momentum to the target is also quite low, as is the corresponding speed change, while the angular momentum and energy are significant. These effects occur because, for the high-speed bullet, the impact force is directed almost through the bullet vehicle's CM inducing little rotation. For the target, the impact was effectively along the front surface, and thus the force is directed almost perpendicular to the vehicle's axis. Hence, the torque arm is a maximum and can cause very rapid rotation.

Note also that this same effect frequently occurs for an impact between a car and a pedestrian. Here, a low frontal hood and bumper can cause the pedestrian's body to be both accelerated forward and to suffer a rotation (feet upward). The result can be that the pedestrian is thrown onto the car's hood. However, while the result is accurate, the mechanism is wrong. In reality, the pedestrian's body (center of mass) achieves a speed less than that of the car, and thus we have a positive coefficient of restitution. The car actually drives under the rotating pedestrian's body, causing the latter to go onto the hood. For high speeds the pedestrian can actually go completely over the car, because the car is able to completely drive under the body. The differential speed of the car versus the pedestrian implies a kinetic energy for the pedestrian, as if the pedestrian were moving rapidly at a stationary vehicle. Likewise, the rotation also implies energy. When the sum of these energies is large enough, the pedestrian can climb against gravity and go completely over the vehicle, including cartwheeling. For an excellent description of the myriad ways in which pedestrians can interact with vehicles see the book and video by Eubanks (ref 27).

4.13 Induced Rotations

If a vehicle impact does not involve a force which passes directly through its center of mass (CM) (a non-centered impact), then rotations are induced. The angular rotational rate is given by

$$\varpi = (\text{radians / s}) = \frac{Ftr}{I} \quad (4.25)$$

where F is the applied force, t is the time of application, and r is the effective torque-arm, and I is the moment of inertia about the vehicle's CM, or about a fixed axis. Note that one radian is $180/\pi = 57.3$ degrees. Since $P = Ft$ is the induced momentum change, and v_{CM} (change) $= P/m = Pg/w$, and $v_{rot} = r\omega$, the rotation has velocities superimposed on the linear motion changes. Here, v_{rot} is the induced rotational velocity of the pushed part relative to the CM axis of rotation. The moment of inertia of the body can be written as $I = mk^2 = (w/g)k^2$, where k is known as the radius of gyration. For a car rotating about its own CM, the value of k is approximately given by $k^2 = L^2/12$, where L is the car length (obviously the true value can be obtained for a given vehicle, such as the quotes from Expert Autostats [ref 19]). It can then be shown that the net speed of the car's CM motion is given by

$$v_{CM} = \frac{v_{hit}}{\left(1 + \left(\frac{r}{k}\right)2\right)} \text{ or } v_{hit} - v_{CM} = v_{CM}\left(\frac{r}{k}\right)^2 \quad (4.26)$$

where v_{hit} is the local common induced hit speed at the distance r from the vehicle CM. The hit speed is the common speed for both vehicles that occurs at the point of contact. The act of imparting rotation as well as linear motion of the CM means that the vehicle has two forms of kinetic energy, namely linear and rotational. The linear part is simply

$$E_{lin} = \left(\frac{w}{2g}\right) v_{CM}2 \quad (4.27)$$

while the rotational energy is

$$E_{rot} = \frac{I\varpi^2}{2} = \left(\frac{w}{2g}\right)k^2\varpi^2 = \left(\frac{w}{2g}\right)\left(\frac{k}{r}\right)^2 v_{rot}^2. \quad (4.28)$$

Thus the total energy is

$$E_{rot} = \left(\frac{w}{2g}\right)\left[v_{CM}^2 + k^2\varpi^2\right] = \left(\frac{w_{eff}}{2g}\right)v_{CM}^2 \quad (4.29)$$

or

$$E_{tot} = \left(\frac{w}{2g}\right)\frac{v_{hit}^2}{\left(1+\left(\frac{r}{k}\right)^2\right)} = \left(\frac{w_{eff}}{2g}\right)v_{hit}^2 \qquad (4.30)$$

where w_{eff} is the effective weight of the vehicle which gives the same total kinetic energy. Thus a rotating body acts as if its weight is changed, such that

$$w_{eff} = w\left[1+\left(\frac{k}{r}\right)^2\left(\frac{v_{rot}}{v_{CM}}\right)^2\right] = w\left[1+\left(\frac{r}{k}\right)2\right] \qquad (4.31)$$

if we refer to the CM's velocity, and

$$w_{eff} = \frac{w}{\left[1+\left(\frac{r}{k}\right)^2\right]} \qquad (4.32)$$

if we refer to the velocity (v_{hit}). Equation 4.32 is the more useful version.

Thus, when $r = 0.0$ (i.e., we have a centered hit with the thrust passing through the vehicle's CM), the effective weight is just the true value, whereas, for a significant value of torque-arm, r, the effective weight of the target decreases significantly as seen by the bullet vehicle. This means that the common value v_{hit} is higher than otherwise expected, as if the struck vehicle was lighter. However, the corresponding value of the target vehicle center of mass velocity, v_{CM}, is lower by the factor $1 + (r/k)^2$. Thus, the struck vehicle can develop significant rotation but have a relatively small induced change in its CM motion.

As an example, suppose the bullet (1) has an initial speed v_1 and hits the target (2) at 90 degrees to the target's front end. Let the initial speed of the target be zero. Assume the bullet sees a thrust through its CM and so does not spin. For the target, however, $k^2 = L^2/12$ (roughly), and $r = L/2$ or $r^2 = L^2/4$, assuming the target CM is at the midpoint of its long axis. Thus the factor $(1 + (r/k)^2) = 1 + 3 = 4$. Then the common hit speed is given by

$$v_{hit} = \frac{w_1}{\left(w_1 + \frac{w_2}{4}\right)}v_1 \qquad (4.33)$$

while the actual target CM's speed is given by

$$v_{CM,2} = \frac{v_{hit}}{4} = \left(\frac{1}{4}\right)\left[\frac{w_1}{\left(w_1 + \frac{w_2}{4}\right)}\right]v_1 \qquad (4.34)$$

and the rotation speed is

$$v_{rot,2} = v_{CM,2}\left(\frac{r}{k}\right)^2 = 3v_{CM,2} = \left(\frac{3}{4}\right)\left[\frac{w_1}{\left(w_1 + \frac{w_2}{4}\right)}\right]v_1. \qquad (4.35)$$

The rotation rate is

$$\varpi = \frac{v_{rot}}{r} = \frac{2v_{rot}}{L} = \left(\frac{3}{2L}\right)\left[w_1 + \frac{w_2}{4}\right]v_1 \text{ radians / sec.} \qquad (4.36)$$

These quotes ignore any vehicle bounce. This is usually reasonably valid since most such collisions involve the soft, non-bumper impacts where the coefficient of restitution is usually small.

As an example, if w_1 = 3,000 pounds and w_2 = 4,000 pounds, and L_2 = 14 feet, we obtain

$$v_{hit} = 0.75v_1,\ v_{CM,2} = 0.1875v_1, \text{ and } v_{rot,2} = 0.5625v_1 \text{ and } \omega_2 = 0.08v_1.$$

Compare these values with the normal central-impact common speed of v_{hit} = $0.42857v_1$ and zero rotation. If v_1 = 44 ft/s (30 mph) we obtain

$$v_{hit} = 22.5 \text{ mph},\ v_{CM,2} = 5.625 \text{ mph},\ v_{rot,2} = 16.88 \text{ mph},$$
$$\text{and } \omega_2 = 3.54 \text{ rad/s} = 202 \text{ deg/s}.$$

For a simple centered impact, we would have $v_{hit} = v_{common} = v_{CM,2}$ = 12.86 mph, and zero rotation. If both vehicles have non-centered impacts, the same treatment is applied to each vehicle. Thus, we establish the values of *r* and *k* per vehicle. Figures 4.7 and 4.8 illustrate the overall logic.

The true definition of moment of inertia for a rectangular prismatic body about any axis perpendicular to one of the body's plane surfaces is

$$I = m\left(\frac{L^2 + W^2}{12}\right) + mQ^2 \qquad (4.37)$$

where *L* is the length, *W* is the width, and *Q* is any offset between the CM of the vehicle and the axis about which the vehicle is rotating, with the latter perpendicular to both *L* and *W* for a yaw spin. $Q = 0.0$ if the vehicle spins about its own CM. This equation assumes that the vehicle acts as if it has uniform density. Because a real car is not uniformly dense, and tends to have its mass closer to the center, the effective value of $L^2 + W^2$ is actually quite close, numerically, to the value L^2. This explains the previous approximation. Note that Limpert also gives an approximation, namely $k^2 = (L \times \text{WB})/7.76$, where WB is the wheelbase. Nu-

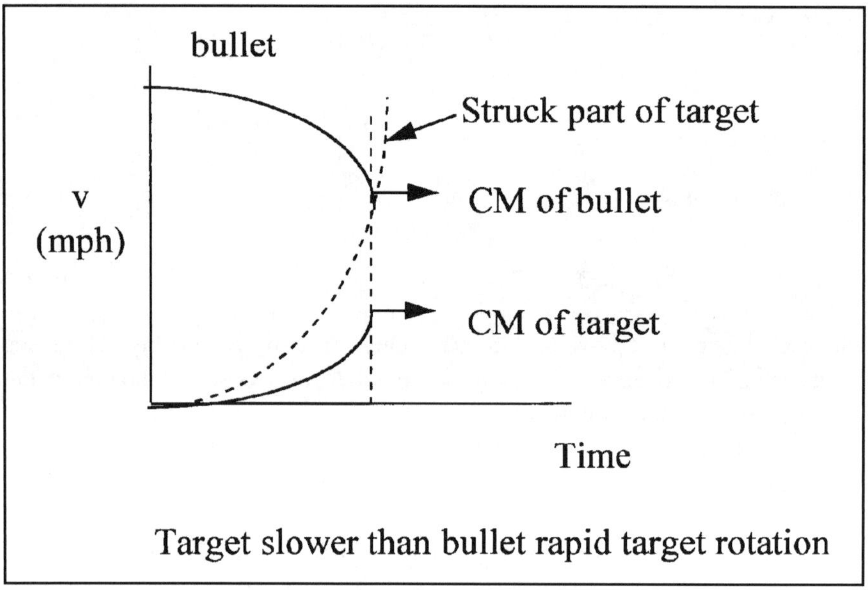

Figure 4.7 *Velocity-time for "end hit"*

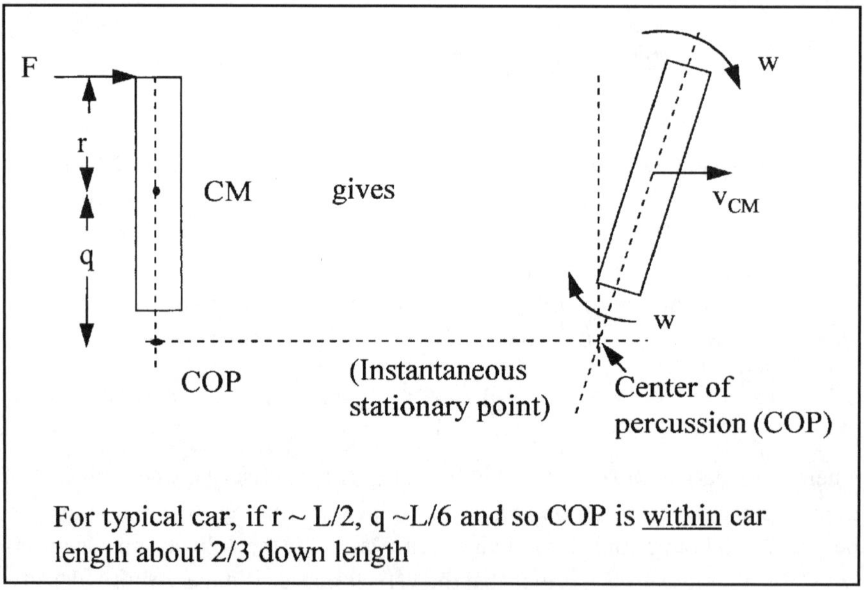

Figure 4.8 *Rotation about the center of percussion*

merically this is similar to $L^2/12$ for many cars. However, this approximation is only good for vehicles (such as a car) which are not designed to carry a significant payload. With pick-ups and vans the approximation is much worse because of the larger difference between an empty and loaded vehicle. When empty, the mass is closer to the vehicle front and the value of the radius of gyration (k^2) is usually less than $L^2/12$, whereas for a heavily loaded vehicle with weight toward the back the value of k^2 can be larger than $L^2/12$. For such cases it is advisable to obtain a proper estimate of the moment of inertia in order to obtain k^2.

The combination of linear CM motion and rotation causes a point away from the impact region to achieve an instantaneous speed of zero. This point is known as the center of percussion (COP), illustrated in Figure 4.8. It lies on the side of the vehicle's CM opposite the strike point on the longitudinal axis at the distance $q = k^2/r$, from the CM. Thus for the previous example, $k^2 = L^2/12$ and $r = L/2$, hence $q = L/6$ from the CM away from the impact point. Thus the total distance from the impact point is $L/2 + L/6 = (2/3)L$. For many cars this is roughly the position of the rear axle. Because of the action of the differential this is a preferred rotation point, since it minimizes any tendency for side motion tire scuffing. Hence, many cars apparently rotate about their rear axle when hit sideways at the front. Note that as $r \to 0.0$ so $q \to \infty$. Thus, the COP moves a large distance away from the vehicle. A central hit can be viewed as one with very slow rotation occurring about an axis at infinity.

Such rotational effects are also important for the study of the motions of the vehicle's occupants. Note that these rotational effects also apply for the case of the sideswipe. In particular, note that the rotation rate is a function of the imparted momentum change, the moment of inertia and the torque arm, whereas, the linear-induced change in speed is a function of only the momentum change and the weight. Thus a knowledge of the rotation rate gives data on the corresponding linear motion, since the two are directly related. If the principal direction of force and torque-arm are known there is a fixed relationship between the induced rotation rate and the induced change in linear momentum (CM speed).

The off-center side hit is easily recognized. It produces minimal net target motion but with large rotation, and small apparent crush damage.

4.14 Movie Theatrics

It is unfortunate, but many movies demonstrate both real physics and false physics; which is shown seems to depend on what particular aspect the producer wishes to illustrate. Movies are intended to be spectacular, so a producer frequently embellishes facts in order to make the movie more interesting. This is distressing, because many court jurors watch these movies and may not appreciate the difference between reality and special effects. This then behooves the expert witness to adequately explain the difference and convince the triers of fact of the physical realities.

Examples of false behavior include he four following misrepresentations.

1. The vehicle nearly always burns or explodes in a crash. This is nonsense. Government regulations apply to the issue of fuel leakage and spark-ignition of fuel, and vehicle manufacturers must design their products to minimize such burns and explosions. Indeed, despite the notoriety of side collisions on some side-tanked GMC trucks and the rear-end impacts on the Ford Pintos, the reality is that very few actual explosions occurred. Indeed, one TV company wishing to illustrate the problem with the GMC trucks got itself into legal trouble when it was disclosed that it had used small explosives in order to guarantee a fuel-tank-impact explosion!
2. In a rear-end impact with a parked, stationary target car, the bullet vehicle can jump up over the target, usually with an induced roll, so as to land on its roof. This is also nonsense. The trick to making this happen is to use asymmetric ramps hidden behind the target car. No normal crash involves this absurd behavior.
3. A vehicle can successfully jump across a missing piece of road (bridge, etc.). A classic example of this nonsense is seen in the movie *Speed*, where a city bus apparently jumps a gap in an almost-finished piece of new interstate highway. Not only is the road height the same at both sides of the gap, but the bus mysteriously adopts a nose-up position while landing on the far side of the gap. This effect was again produced only with the use of special ramps (carefully hidden from the camera!) on the approach side of the gap. Under real conditions the front of a vehicle will immediately start to rotate with a downward acceleration as soon as the front wheels leave the road and the back wheels are still on the road. Once the back wheels leave the road the rotational acceleration stops, and the vehicle now moves downward under gravity but with a fixed forward rotation. Thus only if the second side of the road is sufficiently lower than the first can the vehicle avoid plowing front-first into the wall on the second side. The vehicle can never adopt the nose-up attitude without special ramps, or an inclined approach side to the gap. See Figure 4.9.
4. A high-speed crash can nearly always be suffered without bodily injury even for occupants who do not wear seatbelts or have vehicles without airbags. This is most unlikely in real life, yet many movies imply that the occupants can invariably walk away from serious crashes (including rollovers) without a scratch!

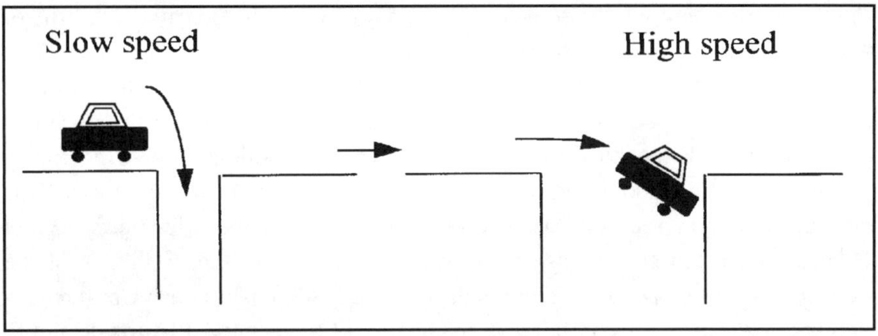

Figure 4.9 *Real behavior on jumping a gap*

On the other hand, many movies also show real physics. In particular, *Speed* demonstrated very nicely the effect of the frontal sideswipe. Here, the same city bus was shown sideswiping the fronts of stationary cars, including police cars. The movie realistically illustrated how these police cars moved very little (CM motion), but suffered rapid rotations so as to rapidly swing out of the way of the bus, with the latter barely slowing in the process (because of the huge ratio of bus weight to the effective "reduced" car weight).

4.15 Payload Considerations

Payload is any weight in excess of the curb weight of the vehicle. It includes occupants, shopping bags, tools, and camper shells. How should payload be treated with regard to momentum and energy calculations? Provided the payload remains attached to the vehicle, and can undergo only limited differential motion versus the vehicle, it should always be included as part of the total weight for momentum calculations. This is because the payload momentum has nowhere else to go. (However, see below.) Shifts in the payload will produce small shifts in the net CM but otherwise have negligible effect. However, for energy calculations the treatment depends on how rigidly the payload is attached to the vehicle.

For example, a camper shell is normally fastened in a rigid manner to the pick-up truck. Consequently, its kinetic energy is directly transferred to the vehicle and thus helps contribute to any crush of that vehicle. This does not apply for any movable, or loosely-coupled, payload. For moveable payloads, differential motions occur, and the kinetic energy of the payload is usually dissipated within the vehicle, and does not contribute significantly to the vehicle crush. As a simple example, consider a loose tool box in the trunk. With a violent sudden stop of the vehicle, the tool box will continue forward within the trunk. Its kinetic energy will be dissipated by some frictional drag on the trunk carpet, but most will go into the sudden thump into the structure at the back of the rear seats.

Consequently, there will be some degree of damage within the trunk and little of the energy ends up causing additional vehicle crush.

The same effect occurs for the occupants. If an occupant were immobilized within a plaster cast which was rigidly fixed to the vehicle, two things apply. First, there would be no differential body segment motions and so no injury (ignoring movements of internal organs such as the brain, heart, and liver). This explains why very securely fastened occupants tend not to suffer injury except at very high crash speeds, as was proven by Col. John Stapp (USAF), of the well-known rocket sled tests and resulting annual Stapp Car Crash Conferences sponsored by SAE (ref 28). Second, the energy of the occupant is transferred to the car to increase the car's crush. However, in the absence of such a rigid cast the occupant will move relative to the vehicle, and there will be differential body segment motions. The occupant runs into either the steering wheel or dash, or is stopped by the seatbelts or an airbag. Thus we have an internal impact. However, here the occupant's initial kinetic energy is dissipated by stretching the belts, deforming the steering wheel or dash, or by producing personal injury. Indeed, it is precisely because the occupant's energy does not simply transfer to the vehicle that injury can occur, or there would be no source for the injury mechanism, all of which involve sudden energy absorption by the human body.

This internal impact is the meaning of the second collision with regard to the definition of crashworthiness. Because the vehicle is very heavy relative to an occupant (typically about twenty times the weight), the moving occupant's momentum is transferred to the vehicle but very little of the energy is transferred. In fact, Equation 4.1 applies. For the human body the coefficient of restitution is small (a lot of the human body is elastoviscous). Rewriting Equation 4.1 we obtain

$$E_D = \left[\frac{w_1 w_2}{(w_1 + w_2)}\right]\left[\frac{(1 - e^2)}{2g}\right] v_c^2 \tag{4.38}$$

where E_D is the absorbed energy, and v_c is the closing speed (person versus car). If "1" is the vehicle and "2" is the occupant, then since the vehicle is so heavy compared to the occupant, Equation 4.38 approximates to

$$E_D = \left(\frac{w_2}{2g}\right)(1 - e^2) v_c^2 = \left(\frac{w_2}{2g}\right) v_c^2 \tag{4.39}$$

because e is also small. Thus, almost the entire initial kinetic energy of the occupant is dissipated within the crash between the occupant and the vehicle, and little is left over to contribute to the other impact between the vehicle and the original hard body (another car, etc.). For a 20-to-1 car-to-occupant weight ratio, and a value of e of 0.2, about 0.91 (91 percent) of the occupant's energy does not get transferred to the overall vehicle to contribute to the car's crush. Thus, in general the payload is not part of the weight of the vehicle for purposes of energy-of-crush calculations, unless the payload can be considered rigidly attached to the vehicle, and is unable to dissipate its kinetic energy within the vehicle.

However, an unrestrained payload can also sometimes cause problems even with conservation of momentum. For example, consider a pick-up truck weighing 3,000 pounds hitting an identical target truck. Let the bullet have a 1,000 pounds payload at the rear of the bed, and let this payload be on rollers (small friction). If the impact speed was 10 mph we would ordinarily compute the common speed as (3,000 + 1,000)/(3,000 + 1,000 + 3,000) × 10 mph = 5.71 mph. But this applies only for a rigidly mounted payload. For the unrestrained payload, the initial impact is the same as for two equal-mass vehicles, in which case the common speed is 5.0 mph. The vehicles will subsequently bounce apart and disengage. Let the coefficient of restitution be 0.6. Then the target will reach 8.0 mph, while the bullet will slow to 2.0 mph. This typically takes about 0.14 second. During this time the bullet has an average speed of about (10 + 2)/2 = 6 mph and moves about 1.23 feet. However, the payload continues at 10 mph and thus moves 2.05 feet. Thus, the payload moves a differential distance down the truck bed of about 0.82 foot = 9.9 inches. Clearly, for a long truck bed this motion can be less than that needed to reach the truck cab region. Thus, the payload was not part of the momentum calculation for the initial truck-to-truck impact, and it behaved as a separate third body. Given sufficient time, the payload will eventually catch up to the cab. It is at this time that the momentum of the payload comes back into play. Now conservation of momentum requires the bullet vehicle and its payload to come to a new common speed. This will be given by v = (1,000 pounds × 10 mph + 3,000 pounds × 2.0 mph)/(4,000 pounds) = 4.0 mph. Thus, the bullet suffers a sudden forward jolt. However, this occurs after the two trucks have disengaged, and thus does not contribute to the original truck-to-truck collision. See Figure 4.10.

4.16 Sensitivity Analysis

Thus far, all the equations give the implication that for known input parameter values precise calculations can be performed. In reality this is nonsense, because all the input values are rarely known. Excepting constants like g (note that even g varies slightly from place to place on the Earth, but the change is small) all other parameters invariably have uncertainties associated with them. Simple examples include real drag coefficient of friction, true skidmark length, and true total vehicle weight. If a payload is added to a vehicle at its center of mass the total weight will increase, but there is negligible change in the radius of gyration. However, if the payload is not at the vehicle's CM then there is an increase in both the weight and the radius of gyration. Such effects are rarely known accurately. Thus, all actual calculations must involve uncertainties.

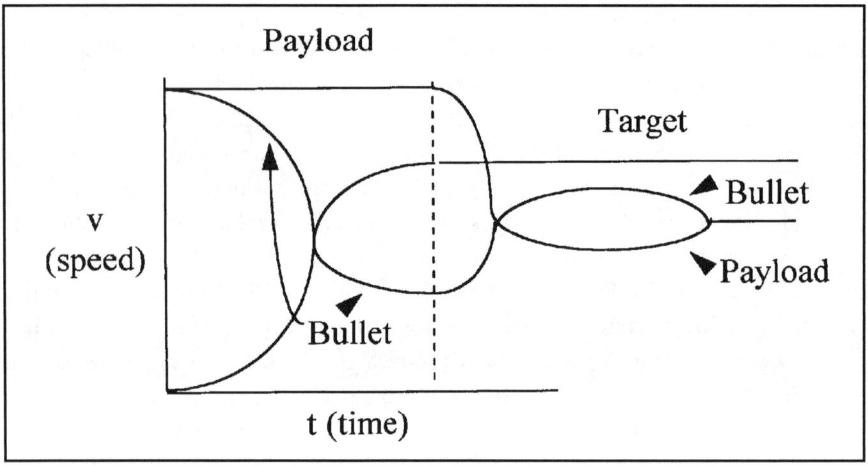

Figure 4.10 *Loose payload effects*

A simple approach to this problem would be to merely rework the equation(s) using credible extremes in the individual parameter values. However, since it is unlikely that all uncertainties are high or low simultaneously, this approach usually gives too large a range in possibilities. In general, there is a tendency for the uncertainties to somewhat cancel each other. There are several mathematical techniques for handling this problem. We will limit our discussion here to a well-known one, namely the log-differential technique.

To apply this technique we perform the following maneuvers. First, write the equation. Then rewrite it in logarithmic form. Finally, differentiate the log version of the equation. Now insert the credible uncertainties to achieve a credible estimate of the overall fractional error.

First, a reminder of the rules for logarithms:

$$\log(abc) = \log(a) + \log(b) + \log(c) \text{ and } \log\left(\frac{a}{b}\right) = \log(a) - \log(b) \text{ and } \log(a^n) = n\log(a) \quad (4.40)$$

The differential of a log is simply $d(\log(a))/da = \Delta a/a$.

Take the simple equation for speed from skid, $v^2 = 2fgs$. In log form this becomes

$$2\log(v) = \log(2) + \log(f) + \log(g) + \log(s) \quad (4.41)$$

Differentiating,

$$\frac{2\Delta v}{v} = 0 + \frac{\Delta f}{f} + 0 + \frac{\Delta s}{s}. \quad (4.42)$$

Note how the differentials of the constants (2 and *g*) are both zero, since there is no uncertainty.

Rewriting,

$$\frac{\Delta v}{v} = \left(\frac{1}{2}\right)\left[\frac{\Delta f}{f} + \frac{\Delta s}{s}\right]. \tag{4.43}$$

As an example, suppose the value for friction is between 0.6 and 0.8, with a mean of 0.7. The fractional uncertainty is about ± 0.1/0.7 = ± 0.143. Suppose the skid mark is between 38 feet and 42 feet, with a mean of 40 feet. The fractional uncertainty is about ± 2/40 = ± 0.05. Then the overall fractional uncertainty in the velocity is ± (1/2)[0.143 + 0.05] = ± 0.096 (± 9.6 percent). Then the average calculated speed of 42.5 ft/s = 28.9 mph has an uncertainty of ± 2.79 mph. Thus the credible range of speed is between 26.1 and 31.7 mph. The same values are obtained by direct substitution of the extremes into the original skid equation.

Note how Equation 4.43 states that the fractional error in v is only one-half that of the fractional error in either f or s. This is because the skid equation involves a square-root of speed versus skid. Thus any equation which involves an nth-root of a quantity has only a $(1/n)$ fractional error versus the fractional error in the parameters within the equation.

Equation 4.43 involves two fractional errors. To account for the fact that such errors can compete with each other (move in opposite directions) we can apply the RMS (root-mean-square) logic for random errors to obtain an even more credible estimation of the final fractional error in speed. This simply states

$$\left(\frac{\Delta v}{v}\right)^2 = \left(\frac{1}{2}\right)^2\left[\left(\frac{\Delta f}{f}\right)^2 + \left(\frac{\Delta s}{s}\right)^2\right]. \tag{4.44}$$

For the above example this gives $\Delta v/v = 0.076$ (7.6 percent). If there is only one parameter with uncertainty (such as f) *then the RMS value is identical to the log-differential value.*

Chapter 5

Computer Modeling Methods

Synopsis

5.1 Introduction

Many low-speed accidents, such as a simple rear-ender, involve in-line collisions. For such collisions the standard momentum calculation cannot give unique solutions. This is because when the momentum vectors (pre-impact and post-impact) align with each other there is insufficient data for a solution, with more variables than equations to solve them. Hence the emphasis on energy-of-crush solutions. However, the standard versions of the latter also usually give errors at low speeds, mostly because they were not written for low-speed applications.

5.2 The CRASH3 Program

Many accident reconstructionists do energy-of-crush analysis by using the CRASH3 program, which was developed by CALSPAN (ref 22), or variations of the same logic. This is the model used by NUTI and many others. Unfortunately, there are logical errors in this method, and thus in any computer program based on it. Since the following involves a seemingly harsh critique of CRASH3, a little history is needed.

It should be noted that CRASH3 was not initially written for the purpose of reconstructing a specific crash. Instead, it was written for NHTSA to interpret classes of accidents, and sometime later CRASH3 was released to the public domain. Unfortunately, it immediately began to be used to solve specific accidents, apparently without much understanding of its limitations.

The model assumes that vehicles crush as if behaving as a dissipative spring, with a linear increase in crush force versus the degree of crush. This linear part of the logic is reasonable, and agrees with the model given earlier. However, the reason given for it is incorrect; in reality it occurs because of the strain-hardening of metal, as mentioned before. Further, this plastic response occurs after the elastic behavior, which itself involves a much stiffer force-crush curve (see Figure 3.3, line OA). Thus there should be an obvious kink in the force-deformation plot when the yield point is reached. The only time this kink will not appear is when the slope of the bumper's compression response happens to be identical to the crush stiffness slope of the vehicle. However, this is unlikely, since it would require very soft bumpers.

The CRASH3 model assumes that the extension of the force-crush plot to the left of the zero crush point represents the elastic response of the vehicle (see Figure 5.1). This is also incorrect; it merely represents the mathematical extension of the curve and has no physical meaning. The true elastic and plastic behaviors are as given in Figure 3.3, which clearly shows the kink. The CRASH3 model uses only two measured parameters, namely A (pounds/inch) and B (pounds/inch^2), and a derived parameter, G (pounds). These are parameters per unit width (W, inches or feet) of the vehicle. Thus, each should be multiplied by the width in order to obtain the total values for the vehicle. The value of AW gives the incipient crush strength (force, pounds), the value BW gives the linear increase in strength versus crush (force per incremental crush, pounds/inch), and the value GW supposedly gives the elastic energy to initiate crush (lbs-ft). Note that $G = A^2/(2B)$.

The implied elastic flexing of the vehicle before any permanent crush is simply A/B (inches). Likewise, the implied critical speed for collision into a fixed rigid barrier is given by

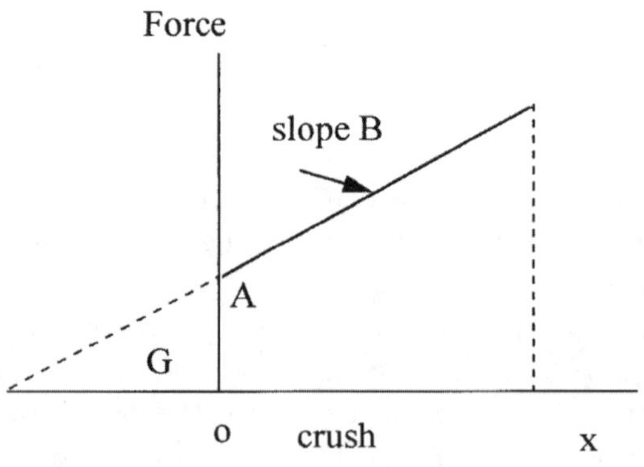

A = incipient crush force per width
B = incremental force per width
G = extension area per width

Figure 5.1 *CRASH 3 force-crush logic*

$$v_{crit}^2 = \frac{2gGW}{w} \text{ (ft / s)}^2 \tag{5.1}$$

where w is the vehicle weight (pounds), and W is the car width (feet).

A quick look at some of the numbers used in the CRASH3 model immediately reveals some irregularities, and even total absurdities. Consider a 1977 Ford Thunderbird. This vehicle has a length of 215.5 inches, a width of 78.5 inches, and a weight of 3,907 pounds. Then, for the rear end of the Thunderbird (a class-4 stiffness category vehicle), the numbers, using $A/B = C$, imply a value of about 27 inches and a critical speed of about 15.7 mph! This critical speed is obviously considerably higher than any real bumper limit. Here, C is equivalent to our a term. For the *front* of this vehicle we have a C value of 10.5 inches (not quite so absurd as the rear-end value, but still well in excess of the true bumper amplitude), and the critical speed is about 9.7 mph. Similar oddities arise for practically every other listed vehicle and struck vehicle surface. Even for frontal impacts into rigid barriers, the elastic flexing turns out to be no smaller than about 5.7 inches, and as large as 10.5 inches. Yet real bumpers have an amplitude of only about 3 inches since this is how far they extend beyond the bodywork. Of course, the A value merely gives the incipient force to cause damage, while the B value is merely a description of the strain-hardening slope. The two have nothing to do with each other, because the yield strength and the strain hardening slope are not related, and hence nothing to do with G or the true bumper amplitude.

Using the above values for the Ford Thunderbird, we can also derive the effective R values. Thus, for the front, $R_0 = AW/(12w) = 356$ (lb/in) $\times$ 78.5 (inches) /(12 $\times$ 3,907 (pounds)) = 0.596. The rear value is almost identical. So, at the instant of incipient frame crush, the vehicle passenger compartment sees a peak deceleration of about $12 \times 0.596\ g = 7.15\ g$'s. For a total crush of about 20 inches, the R value becomes $R_0(1 + x_{crush}/C) = R_0(1 + x_{crush}(B/A)) = 0.596 \times (1 + 20/10.5) = 1.734$, and the peak deceleration is now 20.81 g's.

The problem with the CRASH3 model is that it was not based on known engineering concepts. Instead it was developed empirically on the basis that, experimentally, the data describing impact velocity versus crush depth implied a straight line. Close scrutiny of such data, however, reveals that this was more wishful thinking than anything else, and was forced by very few (and sometimes only one) data points for the higher speeds. (Note: standard accepted engineering and scientific practice demands that multiple data points must be obtained before any credence can be given to experimental data). Removal of the high-speed points immediately allows for a nonlinear curve fit, as given empirically by Limpert and Noon. This behavior for the higher speeds is simply an example of the sudden changes in stiffness of the vehicle due to engagement with characteristic points such as the engine, a frame, or passenger compartment. If sufficient data points existed, it would be found that the velocity-versus-crush plot suddenly becomes steeper above a certain high speed where engine engagement occurs, and then less steep above another speed where the passenger compartment starts to collapse. However, with only widely-spaced data, the appearance can be of an intermediate, and steep, pseudo-straight line. To correctly handle these changes in higher-speed stiffness it is necessary to employ additional parameters in the equations.

By assuming the linear velocity-crush relationship and assuming that G represents the elastic energy, the logic of the CRASH3 model forces a constrained group of values of A, B and G which frequently give odd implied bumper behavior, and *always* yield straight line data for velocity versus crush, which is hardly surprising, since this was presumed going into the analysis.

Note, however, that the CRASH3 model involves the same kinds of terms as does the modified model given before: a constant term, one dependent on a linear relationship versus crush, and one dependent on the square of the crush. Only the individual constants in the equation change. For this reason, the CRASH3 model does give good values for the intermediate equivalent barrier impact speeds (e.g., about 20 to 50 mph), as seen in Figure 5.2, where all the models are very close. However, at the low incipient crush speeds, CRASH3 gives poorer predictions and generally overestimates the impact speeds for a given level of crush. Compare this with the data of Noon and Limpert, however, whose curve fits ignore the existence of bumpers. However, neither Noon nor Limpert claim their approaches are suitable for low speeds, and Limpert specifically warns not to expect good data below about 15 to 20 mph equivalent barrier speeds using his empirical curve fits.

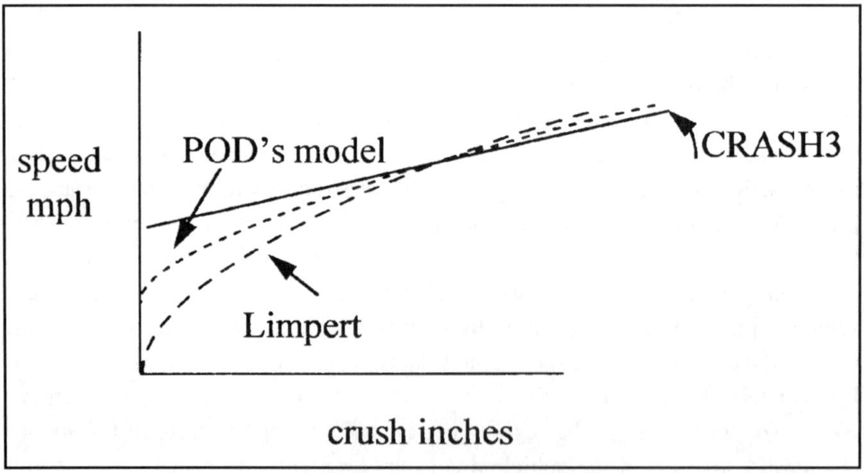

Figure 5.2 *Comparison of speed crash models*

Comparing the CRASH3 model with the POD model, we find that the equivalents are $A = 12R_0w/W$ (W in inches), $B = 12R_0w/(aW)$ (both a and W in inches), and $G = (w/2gW)v_L^2$ (with W in feet), and $a = A/B = C$. CRASH3 sets $G = A^2/(2B)$.

Note that the real difference is that for our model we do *not* equate $G = A^2/(2B)$. This is the key to avoiding the problem of locking the A, B, and G parameters together in a forced fashion. In order for CRASH3 to avoid unrealistically large values of G, the value of A must be kept small, while B is large. However, this is equivalent to giving small R_0 and a values. It was pointed out before that small values of these two parameters automatically lead to the straight line response for velocity versus crush. The problems occur because CRASH3 has only *two* parameters, which attempt to be compatible also with the bumper response. For our model, there are *three* free parameters, and the bumper response is set independently of the other two. A really true model would use at least four independent parameters, but the experimental data are usually too sparse to justify this for modeling purposes.

Note also that the CRASH3 model does not define any coefficient of restitution. In fact, CRASH3 is unable to define such a quantity for the same reason that it wrongly predicts low-speed behavior: namely, the logic of the G parameter, and the missing kink in the force-crush plot. Since the model assumes that the elastic energy is the integral under the extension of the force-crush plot to the left of the zero crush point (without the kink), then any attempt to invoke elastic recovery would immediately force the model to retrace its crush path and end up with *zero* crush. What CRASH3 really does is to assume vertical jumps for the initial loading (zero force to incipient crush) and final unloading (maximum force back to zero). Since this implies no associated displacements, there are also no associated changes in energy. The elastic energy needed to reach crushing is then independently added to the model in an inconsistent manner. These problems vanish when using our more realistic model.

While the CRASH3 model directly uses energy arguments to deduce collision conditions, there are also simplistic velocity-versus-crush models. The latter are only appropriate for full frontal or rear impacts, and cannot be used for partial and sideswipe impacts. One such model is that presented by Campbell (ref 29). Again, this model assumes a linear relationship of the form $v = b_0 + b_1x$, where b_0 is the incipient damage speed, b_1 is the slope of the velocity-crush line, and x is the inches of crush. This model strictly describes impacts into rigid barriers. The energy for a crush can be deduced by using the equivalent barrier speed (EBS) equation. Thus, we merely equate

$$E_D = \left(\frac{w}{2g}\right)v_{barrier}^2 = \left(\frac{w}{2g}\right)(EBS)^2 = \left(\frac{w}{2g}\right)\left[b_0^2 + 2b_0b_1x + b_1^2x^2\right] \quad (5.2)$$

where the barrier speed is from Campbell's equation. However, note that, as with CRASH3, there is no restitution and no distinction between input energy and absorbed energy. Thus, both the CRASH3 and Campbell approach work well only for higher speeds.

To actually use CRASH3, the damage region is divided into several (usually five) equal sections. Thus, there are six measurements of crush; two end ones and four inner ones. Each section defines a mean crush depth, and the CRASH3 equation is applied to each section to obtain the section energy. Then all the energy terms are summed to obtain the total crush energy. This approach explains why the vehicle strength is given in terms of unit width of damage.

For an impact which is not perpendicular to a vehicle surface, a correction factor is employed. This factor is $1 + \tan^2\theta$, where θ is the off-normal angle of the thrust. This approach works reasonably well, provided that the angle never exceeds 45 degrees. For higher angles the solution should be viewed as a collision on an orthogonal surface. Thus, a 70-degree impact on the front is really a 20-degree impact using side-impact strength values. Note that, strictly speaking, the term $\tan^2\theta$ should actually be $\tan\theta\tan\alpha$, where α is the approach angle for the effective closing velocity vector of the two vehicles, and θ is the direction of the principal direction of force (PDOF) versus the vehicle's longitudinal axis (see ref 17); however, the distinction is small and well within the other uncertainties. The logic of the correction factor is that for an angled thrust the true deformation motion is larger than the apparent value perpendicular to the surface by the factor $1/\cos\theta$. Since the force also increases with deformation for a springlike response, this also implies that the corresponding energy increases by $1/\cos^2\theta$ which is the same as $1 + \tan^2\theta$.

Because CRASH3 has the same general terms as our derived crush equation (a constant, a term linear in crush and a term dependent on the square of the crush) then it also asymptotically approaches the simpler linear-only terms for very small crush, appropriate for low-speed crashes. Indeed, the velocity-crush equation of Campbell also produces the familiar three terms if it is rewritten in terms of input energy versus crush, as given in Equation 5.2.

To actually use CRASH3, the following equation is used for a five-segment damage region,

$$E = \frac{W}{5}\begin{bmatrix} 5G + \frac{A}{2}\left(C_1 + 2C_2 + 2C_3 + 2C_4 + 2C_5 + 2C_6\right) + \\ \frac{B}{6}\begin{pmatrix} C_1^2 + 2C_2^2 + 2C_3^2 + 2C_4^2 + 2C_5^2 + 2C_6^2 + C_1C_2 + \\ C_2C_3 + C_3C_4 + C_5C_6 \end{pmatrix} \end{bmatrix}\left(1 + \tan^2\theta\right) \quad (5.3)$$

where the individual C values are the x_{crush} values (inches), and W is the damage-zone width. This equation is merely a trapezius treatment for the five segments and six crush depths.

For a one-zone full-bumper determination of energy, CRASH3 gives the simple equation

$$E = W\left[\left(\frac{A^2}{2B}\right) + Ax_{crush} + \left(\frac{B}{2}\right)x_{crush}^2\right]. \tag{5.4}$$

5.3 Multiple Hits on a Vehicle

Occasionally a given vehicle may suffer more than one impact on the same part, such as two sequential hits on its front bumper. If the first impact is totally elastic (within the bumper limit), there will be no effect on the response for any subsequent impact. However, if the first impact exceeds the bumper limit then the crush response is modified for any second impact. The result is determined by the force-crush plot shown in Figure 5.3. Consider the crush path OABC. For a second impact, the new loop will be CBDE, where D is a new maximum deformation, and E is the new final crush. Thus, the major effect of a prior plastic crush is to increase the effective value of F_0 (i.e., give the path CB instead of OA). There is no change in the slope of the strain-hardening portion, namely AB (and, correspondingly, BD). In the language of CRASH3, this is the same as saying that the *A* parameter increases, but the *B* parameter stays constant.

This logic merely states that the elastic paths are retraceable, and that multiple sequential impacts merely open up the plastic loop. Thus, the overall sum of crush damage is directly related to the total plastic absorbed energy for *all*

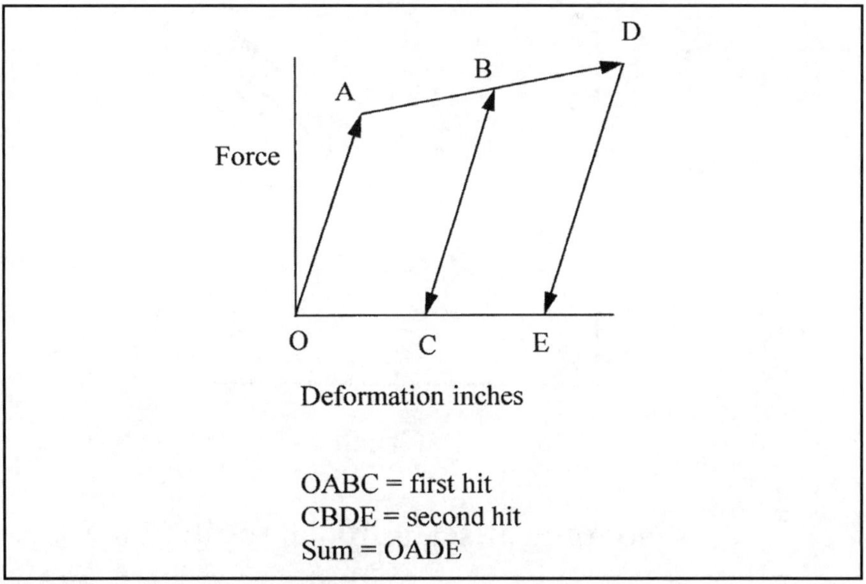

Figure 5.3 *Multiple vehicle hits*

the impacts. Indeed, this summed energy approach has been used as a way of increasing the database using a single vehicle and multiple impacts over a range of impact speeds (ref 16).

5.4 Issues to Watch Out For

Another code frequently used is SMAC and as its derivatives. SMAC is a forward simulation code, meaning that, given some initial conditions, SMAC predicts the resultant vehicle motions. It does this by computing the mutual forces between the vehicles and then tracking, as a function of time, the ensuing results. However, to compute these mutual vehicle collision forces SMAC uses an algorithm even less scientific than CRASH3, assuming a purely linear force-crush relationship without any initial force offset. In short, it completely ignores the existence of bumpers and ignores the concept of a required minimum force to initiate permanent crush damage. Further, although SMAC tries to include restitution, it does so by applying a correction that has nothing to do with physics or engineering, and is simply a mathematical "fudge" (see Figure 5.4). There have been papers describing methods for trying to make SMAC and CRASH3 agree with each other (ref 30). However, since the two algorithms differ with respect to the initial force offset, there is no way such efforts can ever succeed except over small ranges of options. This is a simple mathematical consequence of the form of the two algorithms. To allow the two algorithms to agree, they must both have

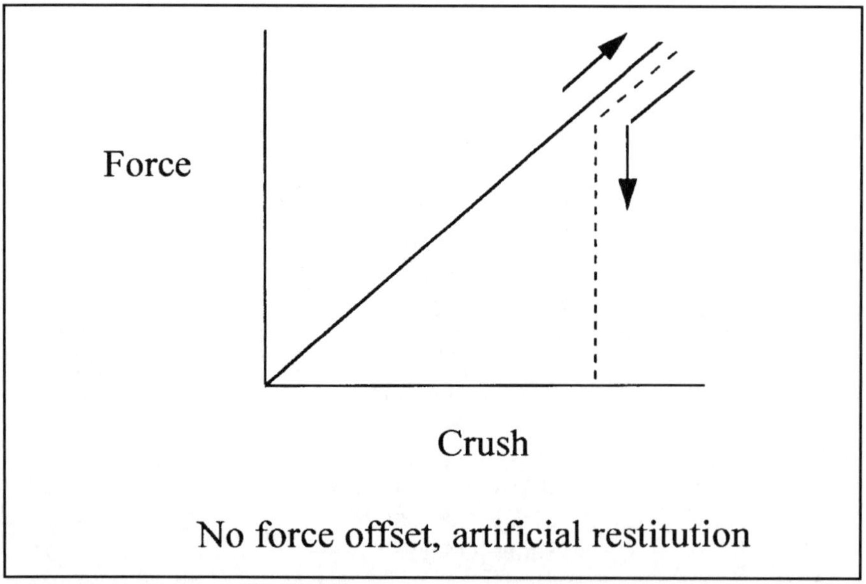

Figure 5.4 *SMAC force-crush logic*

the same form. Despite our previous statements concerning CRASH3, the fact remains that its form is fundamentally correct (we merely disagree on the interpretation of certain parameters). As with CRASH3, the major errors in a SMAC analysis occur for low-speed impacts. Both algorithms give respectable solutions for the higher speed collisions. Thus, to solve the discrepancies between the codes, it is SMAC that needs redefining to be more like CRASH3. Better still, *both* codes should be rewritten to agree with reality.

It must be appreciated that, although computer programs are wonderful labor-saving devices, they are limited by what their authors are willing or able to program into them. It takes a lot of testing and debugging for a programmer to identify every potential pitfall in a program. Most commercial programmers do not have the luxury of spending a lot of time finding these pitfalls. So, it is inevitable that the relatively inexpensive reconstruction codes that are available will have some inaccuracies. In general, such codes can be expected to perform 95 to 99 percent of all calculations without a problem. It is the remainder that give trouble. Only a user with considerable scientific/engineering expertise can be expected to immediately recognize the pitfalls one may encounter when using such codes. Thus, second looks are advisable to ensure the code's output makes sense.

The authors of this book are well-seasoned scientists and engineers who have worked many years on behalf of various government (US and UK) scientific and engineering agencies. This includes developing and working with very powerful codes developed at national laboratories, such as Sandia National Laboratories-Albuquerque (SNLA). These codes are very good and exceedingly complex (many require workstations, such as the Sun, or even Cray supercomputers, to run). Consequently, they usually include a few errors when first written. The authors of these codes are painfully aware of the possibility of such problems. Indeed, they usually invite users of these codes to inform them of such errors, to allow the programmers to correct them. Indeed, SNLA always puts a disclaimer on their reports and codes to the effect that they may not necessarily represent the final opinions of the labs, and may contain errors.

This problem of complex codes having errors has led to a standard joke in the PC world. When a new version of a working code is released, one should always wait a few months for the bugs to be found and corrected before buying.

Bottom line: Always use physics and engineering to crosscheck any code before accepting its answer.

Chapter 6

Energetics of Collisions

Synopsis

6.1 The Energetics of a Collision

For an in-line collision, there are four different energies to consider. These are

1. the initial input energy, which is the sum of the two vehicles' kinetic energies before the crash;
2. the final output energy, which is the sum of the two vehicles' kinetic energy after the crash;
3. the intermediate lost energy, which is the change (loss) in total kinetic energy which occurs when the two vehicles reach a common speed; and
4. the final absorbed energy, which is the total kinetic energy taken out of the system when the vehicles finally part company, and is thus the overall difference between input and output. This absorbed energy itself has two components, namely viscous energy and plastic energy. The distinction is very important for low-speed crashes. Failure to properly distinguish these two types of absorbed energy can easily lead to errors of interpretation, especially for the multiple-hit experiment in which a single vehicle is subjected to multiple sequential low-speed hits in order to simulate a single higher-speed hit (see later).

Let the bullet be (1) with weight w_1 and initial speed v_1. Let the target be (2) with weight w_2 and initial speed v_2. Thus the closing speed is $v_{close} = v_1 - v_2$. The input energy is simply

$$E_{in} = \frac{w_1}{2g}v_1^2 + \frac{w_2}{2g}v_2^2. \tag{6.1}$$

By conservation of momentum, the common speed is given by

$$v_{com} = \frac{(w_1 v_1 + w_2 v_2)}{w_1 + w_2}. \tag{6.2}$$

Note that Equation 6.2 does not contain any g terms since they merely cancel out. At the common speed the new total kinetic energy is given by

$$E_{com} = \left(\frac{w_1 + w_2}{2g}\right) v_{com}^2 = (w_1 + w_2)\left\{\frac{(w_1 v_1 + w_2 v_2)}{(w_1 + w_2)}\right\}^2 \left(\frac{1}{2g}\right). \tag{6.3}$$

Subtracting Equation 6.3 from Equation 6.1 gives the lost energy. Rearranging terms we get

$$E_{loss} = \frac{(w_1 w_2)}{(w_1 + w_2)} \frac{(v_1 - v_2)^2}{2g} = \frac{w_1 w_2}{(w_1 + w_2)} \frac{v_{close}^2}{2g}. \tag{6.4}$$

Equation 6.4 applies on the assumption that only the two vehicles were involved in the collision and ignores third bodies such as any interaction with the road surface through braking. Thus, Equation 6.4 will not accurately apply for very low closing speeds (below about 3 mph), but otherwise applies to all simple in-line collisions. Friction with the road surface will involve both a loss in total momentum and a loss in total energy. This effect is easily identified by simple inspection of low-speed car-to-car crash tests, since it gives the appearance that the laws of both conservation of momentum and of energy are being violated.

The many published papers on such low-speed tests (frequently published by SAE) usually give sufficient data (weights and pre- and post-impact speeds) for the reader to perform an independent assessment of these effects. What is most surprising is that the authors of these papers seem not to have done these cross-checks themselves! We find very little discussion of the "missing" momentum and energy. For example, one recent paper (ref 31) contains several tests where the total momentum has dropped to about 0.45 of its input value when comparing conditions after and before! This is a factor of over two to one. Of interest is the fact that, although the momentum loss generally became smaller as the impact speeds increased, this was not always the case.

Equation 6.4 is most important. Note that the equation contains the weights, the closing speed, and the acceleration due to gravity. It does *not* contain any information concerning the structure of the two bodies. The equation describes the maximum loss in energy. This maximum loss occurs at the instant of maximum two-body engagement, and thus maximum localized deformation of the two vehicles. It thus describes the compressive stage of the crash before any rebound occurs. This equation applies to both perfectly elastic and perfectly plastic conditions. *It matters not one iota whether the cars have perfect springs for bumpers, nor whether they have energy-absorbing bumpers, nor whether any permanent crush was induced to either vehicle, nor whether they both act like putty.*

Equation 6.4 can be rewritten to give

$$v_{close}^2 = \frac{2gE_{loss}\left(w_1 + w_2\right)}{w_1 w_2}. \tag{6.5}$$

Thus the actual closing speed is defined by only the weights, g and the value of E_{loss}. It is the art of defining E_{loss} that can cause trouble. Note that Equation 6.5 can only give the closing speed, which is $v_1 - v_2$. It does not give any absolute speeds for v_1 or v_2. These latter must be obtained by independent means (such as skidmark lengths).

Car crashes nearly always involve some degree of bounce, or rebound. The exception is when the two vehicles somehow become interlocked (bumpers lock together, etc.). At high speeds (i.e., closing speeds above 30 mph) the coefficient of restitution, e, is small and can often be ignored. At the lower closing speeds e is larger and must be included in any analysis. The definition of e is

$$e = \frac{\left(v_2' - v_1'\right)}{\left(v_1 - v_2\right)} = -\frac{\left(v_1' - v_2'\right)}{\left(v_1 - v_2\right)} \tag{6.6}$$

where unprimed speeds are pre-impact and primed speeds are post-impact. Note that this implies e is negative if we adopt the mathematical convention of both numerator and denominator being listed in the same order. After vehicle disengagement the final total energy is given by

$$E_{final} = \frac{w_1}{2g} v_1'^2 + \frac{w_2}{2g} v_2'^2. \tag{6.7}$$

Using Equations 6.5, 6.6 and 6.7 it can then be shown that

$$E_{absorb} = E_{loss}\left(1 - e^2\right). \tag{6.8}$$

Figure 6.1 shows the velocity versus time behavior for a simple in-line collision.

Figure 6.2 shows the corresponding behavior for kinetic energy. We see that the total kinetic energy drops to a minimum at the common speed (hence the maximum value of E_{loss}) and then increases with the rebound. For a perfectly elastic rebound, the final energy is equal to the initial energy, the value of e is unity (strictly $e = -1.0$), and thus the absorbed energy is zero. E_{absorb} is obtained from the experimental test results. Likewise, the value of e can also be obtained from the test. Use of Equation 6.8 then allows for a determination of E_{loss}. Consequently we can rewrite Equation 6.5 to obtain

$$v_{close}^2 = \frac{2gE_{absorb}\left(w_1 + w_2\right)}{w_1 w_2\left(1 - e^2\right)}. \tag{6.9}$$

Equation 6.9 is the most commonly used version of these equations for establishing the closing speed for an in-line two-car crash. Unfortunately, since experimental values are used to define both E_{absorb} and e, this can give problems. These problems arise at the low speeds for which road interaction must be accounted. Thus, if road friction is important the observed value of E_{absorb} will be too large, and the observed value of e will be too small. Unless some form of understood correction can be applied the use of Equation 6.9 becomes suspect. However, the value of v_{close} is itself known for the low-speed car crash tests. We

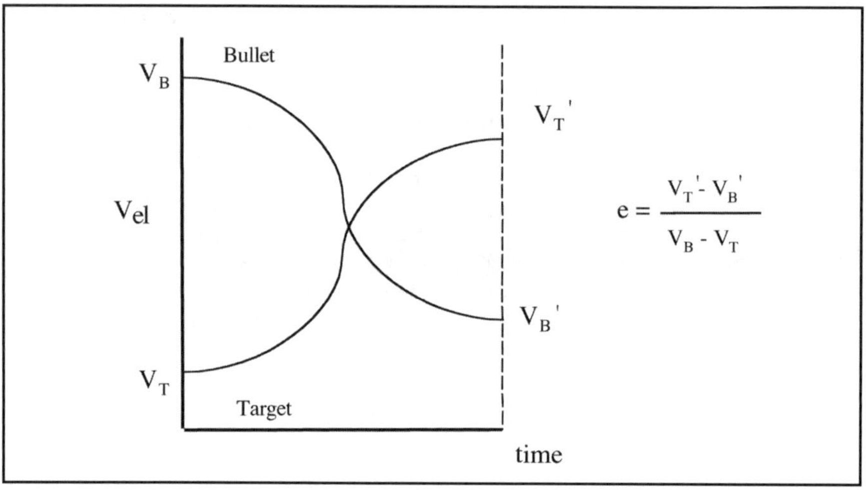

Figure 6.1 *Velocity versus time*

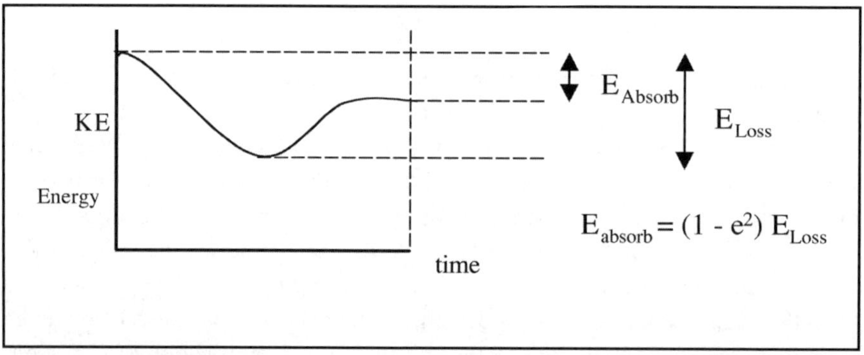

Figure 6.2 *Kinetic energy versus time*

thus rapidly obtain a conundrum in terms of properly determining E_{absorb} and e. This is because the three terms (speed, energy and rebound) will not give self-consistent answers.

As an example, consider test A2 of reference 31. This involved a bullet (1990 Ford F150 pick-up, weight of 3,652 pounds,) and a target (1993 Ford E250 van, weight of 4,917 pounds) with the bullet's initial speed at 3.74 ft/s (2.55 mph = 4.1 km/h) and the target stationary. The observed speed changes were $v_{bul} = -3.74$ ft/s (the pick-up just stopped) and $v_{tar} = +1.82$ ft/s. The change in momentum for the bullet was 3,652 × 3.74/32.2 = 424.2 lb-secs. The change for the target was 4,917 × 1.82/32.2 = 277.9 lb-secs. This implies that the output momentum was only about 0.66 of the input momentum. The apparent coefficient of restitution was 0.49.

However, the input kinetic energy was about E_{input} = 793 ft-lbs while the output kinetic energy was about E_{final} = 253 ft-lbs. This implies an overall absorption of E_{absorb} = 540 ft-lbs. But, if momentum was conserved the common speed would be v_{com} = 1.59 ft/s, the common-speed energy would be E_{com} = 336 ft-lbs and the maximum lost energy would be E_{loss} = 457 ft-lbs. Thus the actual test lost more energy than it should and lost momentum.

Since $E_{absorb} = E_{loss}(1 - e^2)$ we have a problem. To relate E_{absorb} to E_{loss} we require an imaginary value of e (i.e., a square-root of a negative number), because the absorbed energy is larger than the lost energy. If we use Equation 6.9 to calculate the original impact speed, using the measured values of E_{absorb} and e, we calculate v_{close} = 4.67 ft/s = 3.18 mph = 5.13 km/h. But the measured impact speed was only 4.1 km/h. Conversely, if we use Equation 6.5 and use the expected value of E_{loss} we get an impact speed of 3.74 ft/s = 2.55 mph = 4.1 km/h. This is the actual measurement. Clearly something is wrong, and no reliance can be put on the measured value of restitution. This test was very clearly strongly dominated by road interactions. The observed restitution was more a measurement of tire friction than of the true vehicle bounce.

This same paper also attempted to relate a representative coefficient of restitution (called e_{rep}) to the square-root of absorbed energy. The chosen fit was a straight line, with e_{rep} decreasing as $\sqrt{E_{absorb}}$ increased. However, this immediately gives an absurd prediction: for sufficiently large values of absorbed energy the value of e_{rep} will first become zero and then change sign. Thus for hard hits the collision would *generate excess speed differential!*

Finally, the authors of this same paper attempted to perform the multiple hit assessment. However, they did not (indeed *could* not) distinguish between viscous losses (if any) and plastic losses, nor frictional losses. They also incorrectly summed their energies. The equation they used was

$$\Delta v_1 = \left\{ \frac{1+e}{1+\dfrac{m_1}{m_2}} \right\} \sqrt{\frac{2\Sigma E\left(m_1+m_2\right)}{\left(1-e^2\right)m_1 m_2}} \tag{6.10}$$

where delta-v is the equivalent-induced, summed impact speed change for the target, and where $\sum E$ is the summed total plastic energy for each crash and e is the observed restitution per crash. However, the correct equation should be

$$\Delta v_1 = \left\{ \frac{1+e}{1+\dfrac{m_1}{m_2}} \right\} \sqrt{\frac{2\left(m_1+m_2\right)}{m_1 m_2}\left[\Sigma \frac{E_i}{\left(1-e_i^2\right)}\right]} \tag{6.11}$$

where E_i and e_i are the individual values per impact, whereas e is the value for the last impact. Thus the term $1 - e^2$ should be part of the summation for E, rather than outside this summation.

The above cited paper is merely one of the more recent ones; several others contain such oddities.

All low-speed tests done which clearly fail to conserve momentum (and this is true of the majority of such published tests) must be corrected in order to adequately determine the correct parameters. A simple attitude of "well, this is real life, isn't it?" will not work. The reason is simple; if the experiments were done with no braking then how would the results change with braking (and vice versa)? It is impossible to account for various braking conditions unless the data can first be corrected for zero road effects. For example, even if the test is considered representative of a real crash on a level, dry asphalt road, what would be the result for a crash on glare-ice? We have yet to see these corrections done in a truly self-consistent manner, although some authors have at least tried to account for these effects (ref 32). This has usually been done by introducing an Ft term, where F is the frictional force and t is the time period for vehicle contact. However, even here there is a problem because the value of F is usually assumed to be the same for both vehicles. But because we are dealing with independent tire frictions for each vehicle this may not be true. Each car-to-road (and thus road-to-car) force has to obey Newton's third law, but that does not mean that each car sees the same total force.

The reality is that by including interactions with the earth we are now dealing with a three-body problem. Such problems are not directly solvable. Solutions are obtained by successive approximations. (Ask anyone who has tried to solve the orbital dynamics of a satellite, where the influence of an oblate earth, the moon, the sun and rarified air-drag must be included; these effects all account for why real satellites are given small hydrazine rockets to allow for updated "station-keeping.") Further explanations of these effects are given in Section 11.6.

For example, using Equation 6.4 it is easy to show that the value of E_{loss} is a maximum of 50 percent when the vehicle weights are equal. Then for a moving bullet into a stationary target it can be shown that the maximum value of E_{loss} is simply one-half of the bullet's original kinetic energy. Yet many of the published experiments have implied energy losses of more than 50 percent. This clearly demonstrates losses due to road friction or other sources.

A related issue is induced vertical bounce in vehicles. The mere fact that a vehicle may develop a pitching motion when struck does not alter its net weight (hence force) on the ground unless one vehicle literally lifts the other off the ground (severe under-ride). For the latter case there is weight transfer between the vehicles rather than just between the axles of a given vehicle. Thus from considerations of wheel friction the weight transfer is only important if the front wheels have different friction compared to the rear wheels. Even this factor is only important for a vehicle which rapidly stops in a very short distance, such that the entire stop involves only a partial-period of pitching. For a longer-lived motion the vehicle will oscillate and thus average out the pitching.

However, what does matter with induced pitching is the energy absorption within the shock-absorbers of the suspension. The oscillation will force these dampers to absorb some of the imparted energy. Unfortunately, any such pitching is specific to the vehicles involved. It depends on relative bumper heights and centers-of-mass (CMs). There is no generic method for handling this effect.

The above discussion of corrections may seem a little tortuous. Consider that Newton's third law has been well-proven and accepted by all physicists and engineers for about 300 years. What may not be so obvious is that this same law immediately implies the law of conservation of momentum. Momentum change is simply force × time-interval. Since Newton's law states that both bodies have the same force (but equal and opposite) and the bodies are in contact for the same time, momentum conservation follows. To really know the low-speed impact behavior of two cars we should hang them on pendulum strings (the "sky hook" approach) in the same manner as the Newton's Cradle. This would remove the extraneous road interactions. Then comparison of the pendulum answers versus the on-road answers would give the road effect (rolling friction, braking, car in gear, vehicle pitching, etc.). It is precisely because on-road tests are not unique that the need to understand the corrections arises. Otherwise the tests give results only pertinent to those specific tests.

6.2 The Critical Speeds

We previously defined two critical speeds for an in-line collision. The lower critical speed defined the upper closing speed which would cause zero permanent damage to either vehicle. The upper critical speed gave the minimum closing speed required to cause some permanent damage to both vehicles. How were these obtained? The answer is to establish the maximum energy loss during the compressive phase of the collision, and then apply Equation 6.5.

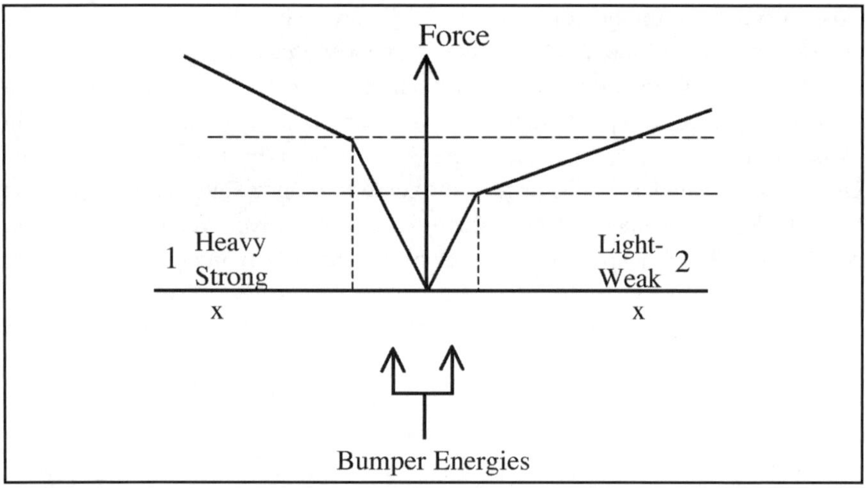

Figure 6.3 *Force versus compression*

Consider Figure 6.3. This is a mirror-image diagram of applied force to each vehicle versus deformation of each. This same figure has been published before by Ishikawa (figure 2 of his paper, ref 33). Note carefully: this figure is *not* the one associated with the CRASH3 model. The assumption is that either vehicle first undergoes a pseudo-elastic compression during the bumper's stroking. Upon reaching a certain maximum force, each vehicle then proceeds to start permanent plastic crushing. The maximum force before plastic crush occurs is given by $F = 12Rw$, where R is the specific rigidity (strength [force, pounds] per weight [pounds], thus a dimensionless number) and w is the weight for each vehicle. These forces define the kinks seen on each plot. Thus the model is a simple elasto-plastic one for vehicle response during the compression phase. Implied in this model is the concept that the area under each initial triangle (zero force to the kink) is a measure of the energy stored by the vehicle which accounts for the bumper limit. Thus, for a vehicle with a so-called 5-mph bumper (7.335 ft/s) this triangle of energy must equal the vehicle energy corresponding to the bumper speed, since this is the meaning of the bumper limit for a full-width barrier crash (no induced damage to the vehicle, but maybe some to the bumper).

Equating energies, we have

$$\frac{w}{2g}v_L^2 = 0.5(12Rw)x_0 \tag{6.12}$$

where v_L is the bumper speed limit and x_0 is the maximum stroke of the bumper (*not* necessarily just the isolator) before bottoming. Note that Equation 6.12 also yields

$$v_L^2 = 12Rgx_0\left(x_0 \text{ in feet}\right) \quad \text{or} \quad v_L^2 = Rgx_0\left(x_0 \text{ in inches}\right) \tag{6.13}$$

During vehicle engagement forces will build up on each vehicle. Newton's third law states that these forces are equal and opposite for the two vehicles. Thus, as time and engagement proceeds up to the point of maximum engagement, this common force increases to a maximum. To avoid permanent damage to either vehicle this force must remain below the lower kink (i.e., the weaker vehicle). At this point, the triangle for the weaker vehicle represents the bumper energy of that vehicle. We define the stronger (heavier) vehicle as (1) and the weaker (lighter) vehicle as (2).

However, at this same force the figure clearly demonstrates that the stronger vehicle has not yet exhausted its own bumper limit since, for this vehicle, the force is only partway up its curve to its own kink. Note that this balancing act is based on force, not on the bumper speeds. The stronger vehicle is only partway up its bumper curve regardless of the actual bumper speed capability. The weaker vehicle crushes first even if it has the higher bumper speed. It is relative strength (force) that determines which vehicle first crushes. The bumper speeds merely determine when (i.e., at what closing speed) this occurs.

For a linear force-deformation behavior of the bumper, the area under the triangle is proportional to the square of the peak force (this is simple well-known geometry for a triangle). Then, if the bumper energy for vehicle 1 is $(w_1/(2g))v_{L1}{}^2$ the actual stored energy of vehicle 1 for the kink force of vehicle 2 is simply

$$E_1 = \left(\frac{12R_2w_2}{12R_1w_1}\right)^2\left(\frac{w_1}{2g}\right)v_{L1}^2 = \left(\frac{R_2}{R_1}\right)^2\left(\frac{w_2}{w_1}\right)^2\left(\frac{w_1}{2g}\right)v_{L1}^2 \tag{6.14}$$

while that for vehicle 2 is simply

$$E_2 = \left(\frac{w_2}{2g}\right)v_{L2}^2. \tag{6.15}$$

We now add these energies and equate them to the total loss of energy, E_{loss}. Doing this, and rearranging terms, and using Equation 6.5, we obtain

$$v_{critl}^2 = \left(\frac{w_1 + w_2}{w_1}\right)\left[1 + \left(\frac{w_2}{w_1}\right)\left(\frac{R_2}{R_1}\right)^2\left(\frac{v_{L1}}{v_{L2}}\right)^2\right]v_{L2}^2. \tag{6.16}$$

This is our previously derived equation for the lower critical speed (a closing speed, of course).

An alternative simplified approach can also be used. Simply consider Equation 6.14 as being

$$E_1 = \alpha\left(\frac{w_1}{2g}\right)v_{L1}^2 \tag{6.17}$$

where α is a fraction that is less than 1.0. Then we have

$$E_{Total} = \alpha\left(\frac{w_1}{2g}\right)v_{L1}^2 + \left(\frac{w_2}{2g}\right)v_{L2}^2. \tag{6.18}$$

We now substitute Equation 6.18 into Equation 6.5 to obtain

$$v_{crit}^2 = \left(\frac{w_1 + w_2}{w_1}\right)\left[1 + \alpha\left(\frac{w_1}{w_2}\right)\left(\frac{v_{L1}}{v_{L2}}\right)^2\right]v_{L2}^2. \tag{6.19}$$

We now simply recognize that for our linear-triangle approach we have

$$\alpha = \left(\frac{R_2 w_2}{R_1 w_1}\right)^2. \tag{6.20}$$

Direct substitution of this factor into Equation 6.19 yields Equation 6.16.

Equation 6.16 assumes full-bumper impacts. If the impact is only partial, such as the left front half of the bullet hitting the right rear half of the target, we need to amend the bumper limit speeds. We use the same logic as CRASH3, and assume that for a fractional contact of F times the full-bumper width the allowable maximum input energy is also only a fraction F before inducement of body/frame damage. This means $v_{L,effective}^2 = F v_L^2$. Thus Equation 6.16 still applies, but we substitute $v_{L,eff} = F^{1/2} v_L$ for each vehicle. Thus for a partial hit on a vehicle, a 5-mph bumper behaves as a 3.54-mph one.

To derive the upper critical speed we merely allow the common force to increase until it equals the value $F = 12\,R_1 w_1$, which is the strong vehicle's kink. For this case, the weaker vehicle 2 has clearly started along its crush path. Thus we now add the total bumper energy for vehicle 1 to the total bumper energy of vehicle 2, and add the energy consumed by vehicle 2 for the corresponding degree of maximum deformation. The latter clearly involves the slope of the crush path for vehicle 2, and thus includes the a_2 term. Again, by equating this total compressive energy with the total loss energy, E_{loss}, and by using Equation 6.5, the equation for the upper critical speed is derived, as given below. We leave this as an exercise for the reader.

$$v_{crit2}^2 = \left[\frac{w_1 + w_2}{w_1}\right]\left\{v_{L2}^2 + \left(\frac{w_1}{w_2}\right)v_{L2}^2 + \left[\frac{12ga_2\left(R_1w_1 - R_2w_2\right)^2}{R_2w_2w_2}\right] + \left(\frac{24ga_2}{w_2}\right)\left(R_1w_1 - R_2w_2\right)\right\} \tag{6.21}$$

For a partial impact we again use the effective bumper speeds and also use effective *R* values by defining $R_{eff} = FR$.

We hope that the reader now understands the previous comment concerning the fact that the value of E_{loss}, as related in Equation 6.5, does not depend on structure. It depends only on maximum compression. Thus it has nothing to do with such things as energy-absorbing bumpers. This energy-absorption for bumpers determines the degree of rebound (i.e., the coefficient of restitution) but *not* the initial compression behavior, except in as much as the bumper may not obey a pseudo-linear compression versus force (see below).

6.3 Example: Two-Car Crash Effects

We may exercise these critical speeds to illustrate the response for a crash between two different vehicles. What follows is merely a generic example. Vehicle 1 is the bullet hitting a stationary vehicle 2, the target. Following Wood's rule we assume $R = (3{,}000/w)^{1/3} \times 0.6$ for each vehicle, $a = 0.5$ feet, and $v_L = 5$ mph. We now start with both vehicles at 3,000 pounds each and then systematically increase the weight of the bullet while reducing that of the target. For each weight combination we compute the values of lower and upper critical speed. We also compute the corresponding incipient crush forces, and the corresponding peak accelerations. The results show a dramatic effect as the difference in vehicles becomes ever larger. For large weight disparity the smaller vehicle suffers tremendously compared to the large vehicle. These effects must be kept in mind whenever we try to reconstruct a case such as a Chevrolet Suburban hitting a Geo Metro. *The results amply demonstrate why the NCAP "Star" quoting approach is so thoroughly misleading*. Incipient crush forces are simply $F = 12Rw$ for each vehicle. However, the force for vehicle 2 at the incipient crush force for vehicle 1 (i.e., at v_{crit2}) is

$$F = 12R_1w_1 = 12R_2w_2\left[1 + \frac{x_2}{a_2}\right]. \tag{6.22}$$

Thus

$$x_2 = a_2\left[\left(\frac{R_1w_1}{R_2w_2}\right) - 1\right]. \tag{6.23}$$

This allows the crush on vehicle 2 to be determined when at the upper critical speed. For Tables 6.1 and 6.2 we kept $a = 0.5$ foot as a constant. Again following Wood's rule, a more accurate approach would be to use $a = 0.5(w/3{,}000)^{1/3}$ feet (i.e., large cars tend to crush more for a given barrier-impact speed). While this would change the absolute numbers, it would not change the overall behavior.

Table 6.1
Critical Speeds and Forces

w_1 pounds	w_2 pounds	(w_1/w_2)	R_1 —	R_2 —	v_{crit1} pounds	v_{crit2} pounds	Peak F_1 pounds	Peak F_2 pounds
3,000	3,000	1.000	0.6	0.6	10.0	10.0	21,600	21,600
3,200	2,800	1.143	0.587	0.614	9.58	10.98	22,541	20,630
3,500	2,500	1.400	0.570	0.638	9.01	12.58	23,940	19,140
4,000	2,000	2.000	0.545	0.687	8.20	15.90	26,160	16,488
4,500	1,500	3.000	0.524	0.756	7.51	20.84	28,296	13,608
5,000	1,000	5.000	0.506	0.865	6.89	29.73	30,360	10,380

Table 6.2
Accelerations at the Critical Speeds

At Lower Critical				At Higher Critical		Crush at v_{crit2}		
w_1 pounds	w_2 pounds	(w_1/w_2)	$accel_1$ g's	$accel_2$ g's	$accel_1$ g's	$accel_2$ g's	x_1 inches inches	x_2
3,000	3,000	1.000	−7.20	+7.20	−7.20	+7.20	0.00	0.00
3,200	2,800	1.143	−6.45	+7.37	−7.04	+8.05	0.00	0.56
3,500	2,500	1.400	−5.47	+7.66	−6.84	+9.58	0.00	1.50
4,000	2,000	2.000	−4.12	+8.24	−6.54	+13.08	0.00	3.52
4,500	1,500	3.000	−3.02	+9.07	−6.29	+18.86	0.00	6.48
5,000	1,000	5.000	−2.08	+10.38	−6.07	+30.36	0.00	11.55

Note the dramatic effects for a weight ratio of (say) 2.00. The lower critical speed (no damage to the small vehicle) has fallen from 10 mph to 8.20 mph, while the upper critical speed (where damage starts for the larger vehicle) has risen from 10 mph to 15.90 mph. Likewise, at the lower critical speed (8.20 mph) the small vehicle suffers a peak acceleration of +8.24 g's (increasing speed) while the large vehicle sees only a peak acceleration (deceleration) of –4.12 g's. At the upper critical speed (15.90 mph) the small vehicle suffers +13.08 g's while the large vehicle suffers only –6.54 g's. Simultaneously, at the upper critical speed the small vehicle suffers 3.52 inches of crush. We see the effects become considerably worse as the weight ratio increases.

This explains why the occupants of the larger vehicle rarely complain or suffer injury versus those in the small vehicle. Also, the large vehicle suffers zero damage up to v_{crit2}. No wonder the NCAP results are so misleading!

6.4 Relative Energy Absorption

When the two vehicles reach the common speed, each has stored or absorbed some energy. At the first critical speed the ratio of these energies is given by Equations 6.14 and 6.15. Thus the ratio of maximum energy losses is given by

$$\frac{E_1}{E_2} = \left(\frac{R_2}{R_1}\right)^2 \left(\frac{w_2}{w_1}\right)^2 \left(\frac{w_1}{2g}\right)\left(\frac{2g}{w_2}\right)\left(\frac{v_{L1}}{v_{L2}}\right)^2 = \left(\frac{R_2}{R_1}\right)^2 \left(\frac{w_2}{w_1}\right)\left(\frac{v_{L1}}{v_{L2}}\right)^2. \tag{6.24}$$

Using Wood's rule of R proportional to $(1/w)^{1/3}$, this then gives

$$\frac{E_1}{E_2} = \left(\frac{w_2}{w_1}\right)^{\frac{1}{3}} \left(\frac{v_{L1}}{v_{L2}}\right)^2. \tag{6.25}$$

Note that if both vehicles have identical bumper speed capability this states that the lighter vehicle stores more energy than the heavier one. At higher speeds it remains true that the lighter vehicle stores more energy than the heavier one. At very high speeds the ratio approximates to the inverse of the vehicle weights.

The latter effect can be easily shown. Consider two vehicles approaching each other with equal momentum. The net momentum is zero. Let the collision be perfectly plastic with no rebound, so the vehicles both simply stop next to each other. Since each vehicle completely stops then each must absorb its original kinetic energy and convert into crush energy. However, kinetic energy is simply (momentum)^2/(2 × mass). Thus, for identical initial (but opposite) momenta each vehicle must absorb energy in inverse proportion to its mass, or weight.

Chapter 7

Bumper Behavior

Synopsis

7.1 Energy-Absorbing Bumpers

The previous logic for establishing the two critical speeds assumed a linear compression versus force behavior. What do real bumpers actually do? The Plastic bumpers leave no evidence of compression unless over-driven. To actually determine a Plastic bumper response to dynamic impacts (the only ones important for a car crash!), it would be necessary to perform dynamic measurements of the bumper response. This could be done by using high-speed cameras, stress (force) gauges or displacement gauges versus time. To date, no independent group has done this for Plastic bumpers, although Chrysler Corporation has published a paper describing some barrier tests on reconstituted Plastic bumpers (ref 34). This paper indicated a roughly linear load-versus-deformation relationship (with a small degree of "stiffening") and gave a peak load of about 24,270 pounds when mounted on a body of weight 3,593 pounds. This implies an effective R value of about 0.56. The peak amplitude of deformation (the stroke) was about 2.5 inches. This implies a bumper speed of at least 4.6 mph. Thus, at present the limited data forces us to assume a pseudo-linear compression.

However, measurements have been done for those bumpers which use isolators. A little background is necessary. These isolators are combined springs and viscous-oil dashpots. The spring portion may be a real spring (as often used by Chrysler Corporation) or may be compressed nitrogen gas (as used by most other car manufacturers). The dashpot is an in-line piston-and-cylinder containing oil which is forced to move viscously past a piston. As the oil is forced from one side of the piston to the other, it moves a floating piston on the other side of which is the spring or gas. Since the other side of the spring or gas is itself moving in with the bumper, this causes simultaneous compression of the spring or gas. The in-line geometry looks like a Maxwell (M) damper. However, the behavior is really a Kelvin-Voigt (KV) damper. The KV damper is one where the dashpot effectively acts as though it is in parallel with the spring rather than in series with it.

Because the actual geometry of the damper looks like a series one it can be difficult to realize that the behavior is really that of a KV damper. A little logic helps to explain this. Suppose the oil was very viscous (such as thick treacle). The dashpot would behave as a solid rod and would be very difficult to compress. However, without oil flow to the floating piston within the device there is no way of compressing the spring or gas. The entire isolator would act as a solid rod and fail to isolate! This "rigidizing" is the response of a rigid dashpot which is parallel to a spring. Thus we have a KV response. For a Maxwell series arrangement a really viscous dashpot will rigidize the dashpot but still allow compression of the spring portion. In reality the isolator behaves in exactly the same way as the suspension spring and shock-absorber system on the car. Of course, here the shock-absorber is obviously in parallel with the springs. Figure 7.1 illustrates the difference between a Maxwell damper arrangement and the Kelvin-Voigt one.

The term "shock-absorbers" is a misnomer. They do not actually absorb shocks. What they do is dampen motions. The damper adds a force to that of the spring during compression, and then subtracts from the spring force during rebound. This behavior generates a hysteresis loop in the force-deflection plane (compressive force higher than release force). This loop represents absorbed energy which becomes heat in the oil. Since this heat is itself lost by virtue of conduction, convection and/or radiation, then this absorbed energy is transient and

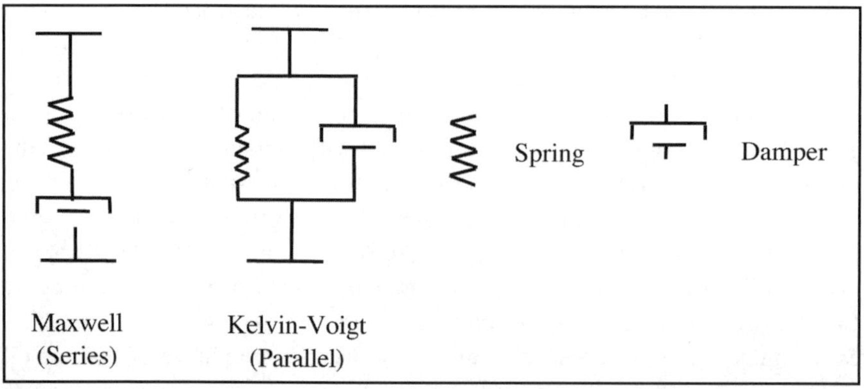

Figure 7.1 *Damper types*

produces no permanent effects. This is unlike plastic flow where the absorbed energy is permanent owing to the permanent nature of the deformation.

So why call them shock absorbers? The answer may be that during compression (an upward motion of the wheels versus the bodywork) the damper increases the net force since it adds to the spring force. Without the damper the spring can move farther. Thus for large amplitude the spring assembly can "bottom." This always involves an uncomfortable thump (or shock), and is usually handled by using hard rubber pads on the spring stops. With the dampers the net amplitude is reduced. Hence the probability of the suspension bottoming is less. Thus we remove the thump and apparently absorb the shock. In reality, all the damper actually did was make the spring act more stiffly during the compression.

Having said all this, what are the actual experimental measurements for isolators? The answer is that for most experiments the stroke (amplitude of motion) is very closely a linear one versus impact speed (ref 35) during the compressive phase. This is the classical response for a springlike system. Damping, if not too large, merely reduces the peak amplitude and decreases the period of oscillation, during the initial compression phase (i.e., the first quarter-period), but increases the period during the rebound phase (second quarter-period). It does not significantly modify the linear relationship between stroke and impact speed. To quote, "If it looks like a duck, waddles like a duck and quacks like a duck, then it probably is a duck." So, because the experiments indicate an essentially linear response of stroke versus speed, then the isolator behaves as if it is a linear spring; this is its functional response. Figure 7.2 shows the deflection versus time for a damped-spring system, while Figure 7.3 shows velocity versus time. In these two figures we show four cases, corresponding to $e = 1.0$ (no damping), $e = 0.71$, $e = 0.58$ and $e = 0.32$. All cases represent an initial speed of 5 mph (7.335 ft/s). The undamped case has a quarter-period of 0.05 second and a peak compression amplitude of 0.23 foot. For this case the second-quarter is symmetric, and the total half-period is 0.1 second (time to recover to zero deflection). With increasing damping, we note that

1. the peak amplitude decreases (down to 0.15 foot for $e = 0.32$),
2. the first quarter-period decreases (down to about 0.04 second for $e = 0.32$), and
3. the first quarter-period still looks like a sinusoid.

Factors 1 through 3 are typical of a stiffer spring. But, also note that the second quarter-period becomes progressively asymmetric, and this period increases such that the total time of recovery to zero deflection increases to about 0.105 second, while the second quarter period is itself about 0.105 – 0.04 = 0.065 sec-

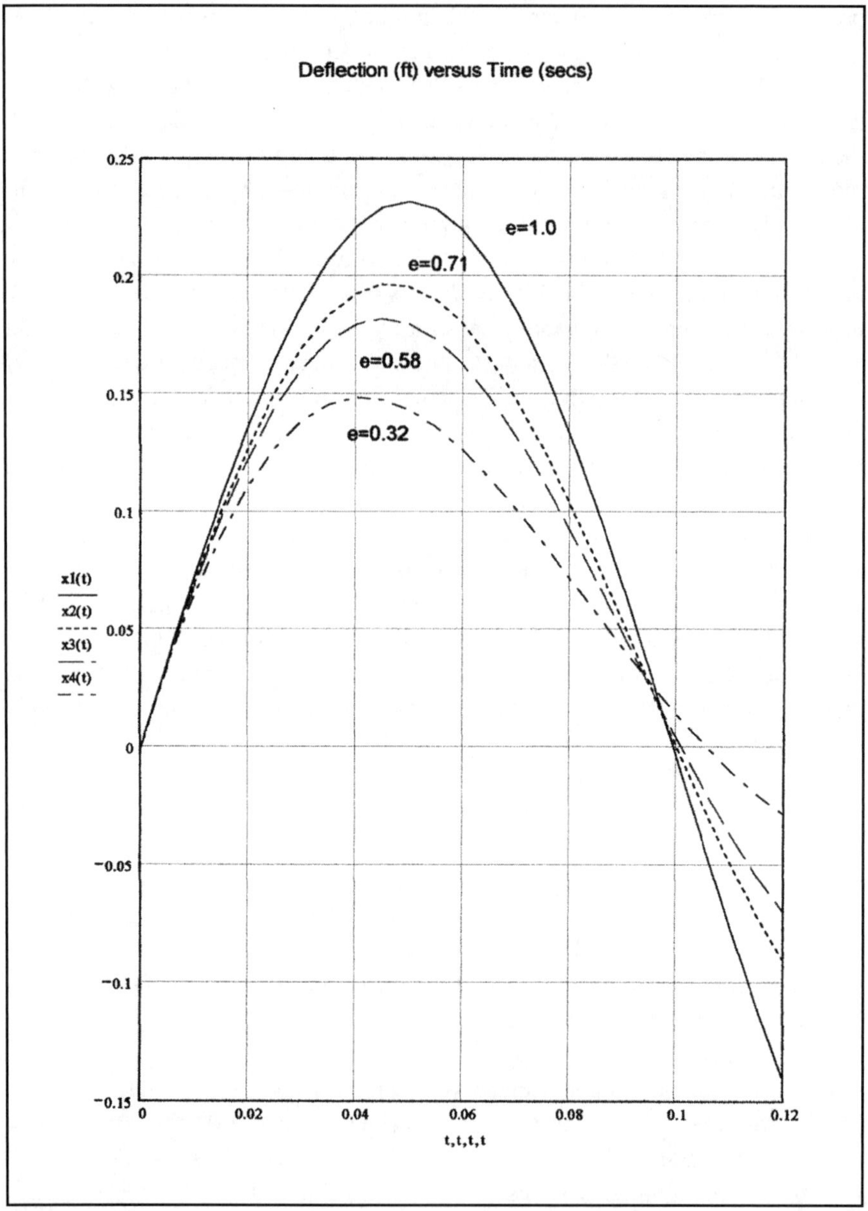

Figure 7.2 *Deflection versus time*

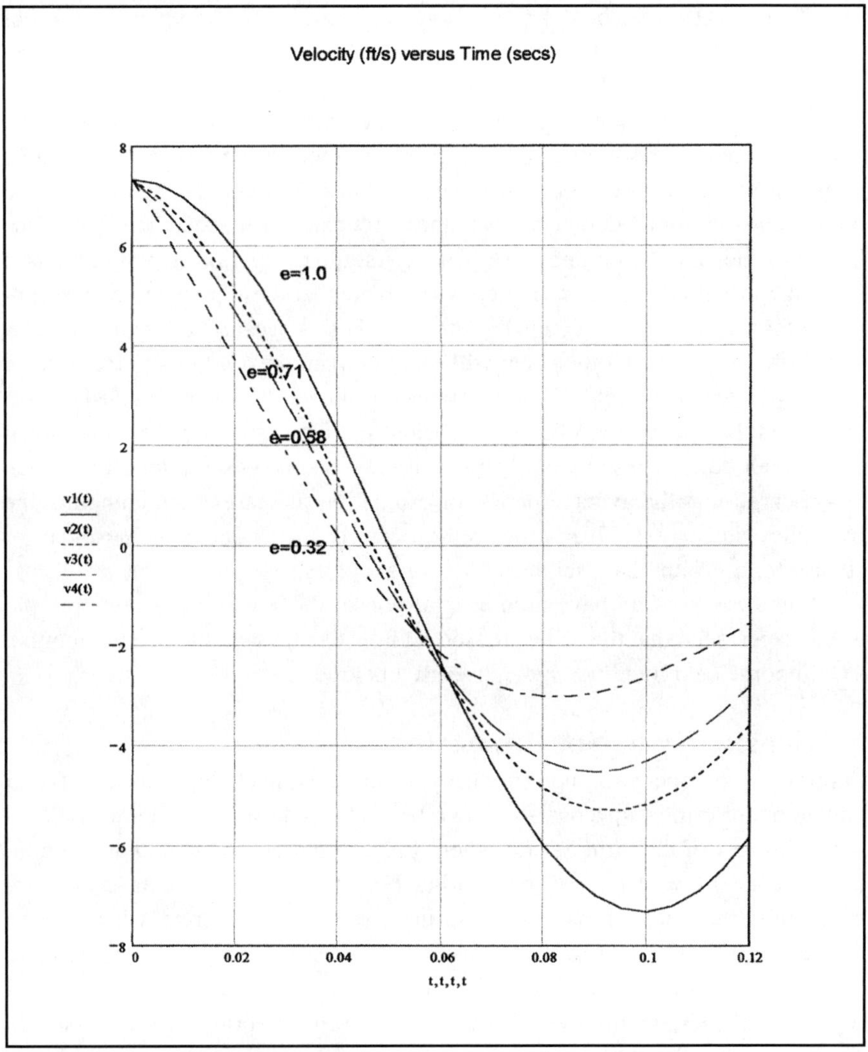

Figure 7.3 *Velocity versus time*

ond. Thus time out is about 1.625 as long as time in. This is typical of a softer spring. Since the amplitude "out" is the same as "in," the rebound speed is clearly less than the input speed. This is more obvious in the velocity plot.

These calculations were done for a damper with a linear response such that damping force is proportional to local speed (the most common type of hydraulic damper). We see that the plots confirm the stiff in and soft out behavior described before, and that for moderate damping the result changes the total half-cycle time by very little, and the compressive phase (first quarter-period) simply acts as if we had a modified, higher spring constant. Note that these plots are only meaningful for the range of deflection back to zero. This is because unless the vehicles somehow lock to each other they will part company beyond this point, and we can only have a half-cycle of mutual contact. If the vehicles were bonded to each other, and the bumpers worked in extension the same as in compression (which they do not do), the result would be a continued damped oscillation. It will then be observed that the average period of oscillation increases with damping (the frequency decreases). This is the well-known result for damped sinusoidal response for a system that oscillates for several cycles.

Some isolators do have nonlinear response: those that use a metering pin with a taper, such that the orifice for the oil flow changes with the piston motion. The importance of nonlinearity is discussed below.

7.2 Sensitivity to Non-Linearity

Suppose the bumper stroking is *not* truly linear. How much does this modify our equations for critical speeds? As shown below, very little. Consider a force-deformation law of the form $F = kx^n$ where k is a spring-constant and n is an exponent. For $n = 1.0$ we have the linear spring. For nonunity value we have a nonlinear spring. If n is greater than 1.0 the spring is said to be stiffening, whereas for n less than 1.0 the spring is said to be softening. These effects are shown in Figure 7.4. Regardless of the power law the area under the force-deformation curve still represents the energy involved. Whereas for the linear spring behavior the area (hence energy) was proportional to the square of the peak force, for a nonlinear spring the result is

$$F = kx^n \text{ and thus } E = \frac{k}{(n+1)} x^{n+1}. \tag{7.1}$$

Thus,

$$E = F^{\left(1+\frac{1}{n}\right)} / \left[k^{\frac{1}{n}} \right] \left(\frac{1}{1+n} \right). \tag{7.2}$$

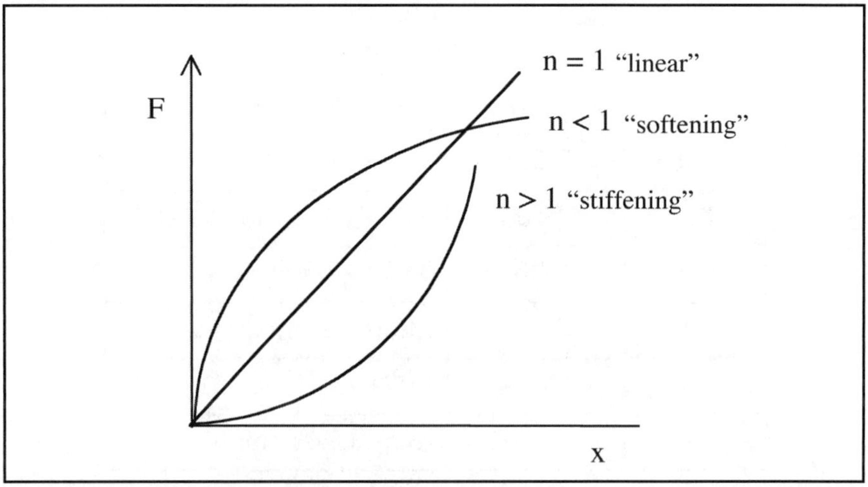

Figure 7.4 *Spring force versus compression*

So the energy is proportional to the peak force raised to the $1 + 1/n$ power. We now merely substitute this rule in place of the square law. The result is

$$v_{crit}^2 = \left(\frac{w_1 + w_2}{w_1}\right)\left[1 + \left(\frac{w_2}{w_1}\right)^{\frac{1}{n}}\left(\frac{R_2}{R_1}\right)^{1+\frac{1}{n}}\left(\frac{v_{L1}}{v_{L2}}\right)^2\right] v_{L2}^2. \qquad (7.3)$$

We see that only the weight ratio and the R ratio terms within the bracketed terms have altered. Let us now use the data provided by Wood, namely that the R values scale with $(1/w)^{1/3}$. First note that for identical vehicles $w_2/w_1 = 1.0$ and $R_2/R_1 = 1.0$. Since $1.0^n = 1.0$ regardless of the value of n, we obtain an "uninteresting" result. So instead, choose a "large disparity" case, such as $w_1 = 4{,}000$ pounds and $w_2 = 2{,}000$ pounds. Thus $R_2/R_1 = 2^{1/3} = 1.26$. Also, let both vehicles have 5-mph bumpers. Table 7.1 indicates how the answer for critical speed changes with the assumed value of the exponent n.

We see that even for drastic changes, such as $n = 0.5$ (a square-root law) or $n = 2.0$ (a square law) the change in calculated value for critical speed is less than 9.0 percent. This is less than uncertainties in the real value of the bumper limit speed. The latter are not precision quantities; a nominal 5.0-mph bumper may actually bottom at 4.5 mph or 5.5 mph.

We conclude that the stroking behavior of bumpers needs to be *significantly* nonlinear in order to prevent our previous equation from working well. Since the published experimental data for isolator stroking indicate a very close approximation to true linear response, Equation 6.16 is considered accurate to within a few percent. Likewise, although the true force-deflection curves for the Plastic bumpers have not yet been determined accurately, their response would need to be considerably nonlinear in order to significantly modify Equation 6.16.

Table 7.1
Sensitivity to Nonlinearity

n	$v_{critical}$ mph	Ratio relative to n=10
0.4	7.238	0.882 (12% low)
0.5	7.500	0.914 (8.6% low)
0.8	8.001	0.975 (2.5% low)
1.0	8.202	1.000 (original answer)
1.4	8.454	1.031 (3.1% high)
2.0	8.661	1.056 (5.6% high)

Note that if the true stroking behavior is a "sinusoidal snake" about a linear line (i.e., the actual response oscillates about a linear line), then it can be shown that the error-from-linear is less than the estimates given above. This follows simply because such an oscillation always stays close to the linear approximation.

Finally, to our knowledge, Equations 6.16 and 6.21 are the only ones that attempt to determine critical speeds. All other techniques involve studying isolator stroking. However, because most manufacturers are slowly moving away from using isolators and instead are using Plastic bumpers (which leave no calibrating marks) this technique is going to be ever less useful. Perhaps the makers could be convinced to provide calibrators on their bumpers? A simple device like the push-rod tire-pressure gauge would be useful.

7.3 Preload Effects and Isolator Friction

Experiments show that real isolators do not start stroking until after some initial force is applied (usually in the range of from hundreds of pounds to about 1,000 pounds). This can be explained by two effects. First, friction occurs within the system as a result of the seals necessary to contain the compressed gas and the oil. Second, the gas (or real spring) is stored under compression even when the isolator is fully out. This is to guarantee full recovery of the bumper system after a non-damaging impact. However, this nonstroking effect is observed for finite impact speeds into rigid barriers, usually below one mph. Clearly, the vehicle has finite energy which is being stored somewhere. Energy is simply force × motion. Thus for finite energy and finite force there must be an associated finite motion. Since the isolator itself is not stroking something else must be. There are two potential sources of this "something else." One possible source is the bumper

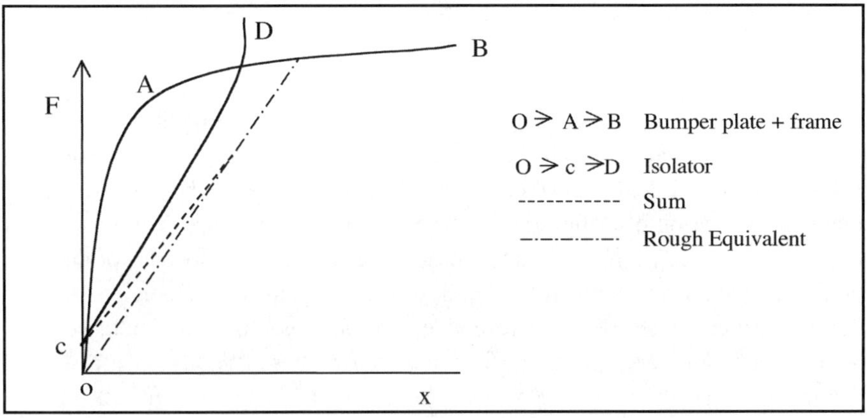

Figure 7.5 *Bumper and isolator force–compression behavior*

plate itself. For instance, many bumpers are not flat-fronted but instead have a bow to them. During early compression the bumper can flex and start to remove this bow. The second possible source is actual elastic (nondamaging) flexing of the car frame to which the isolators are attached.

Regardless of what is flexing, it is the overall combination of the three components of bumper-plate, isolator and vehicle-frame that determines the bumper's net response. Attempts to determine an impact speed based on a very small apparent stroking of an isolator will be inaccurate, since the additional flexing is not well-characterized.

The real behavior of a bumper assembly (meaning the combination of bumper-plate, isolator and vehicle-frame) is shown in Figure 7.5. The bumper-plate and vehicle-frame can be combined to give the response shown as OAB. This is an elastic response for OA followed by a plastic response AB. The isolator response is curve CD. Point C is the threshold force where stroking first starts. Point D is the force where the isolator bottoms. The overall combined response is obtained by simply adding the displacements for any given force; this gives the dashed line. To a first approximation the net behavior is the dash-dot line, which is the functional pseudo-linear response.

Different cars have different isolator and frame responses. Consequently, for a two-car impact it is possible to again construct a mirror-image diagram of force-deflection. This is shown in Figure 7.6. As with Figure 6.3, we again have multiple kinks. These kinks imply mini critical speeds. In ascending order of equivalent closing speed these are

1. the speed where one isolator starts stroking,
2. the speed where the other isolator starts stroking,

3. the speed where one isolator bottoms, and
4. the speed where the other isolator bottoms.

These four mini critical speeds are in addition to the two that were previously defined (for actual vehicle damage). Since the kinks depend on the specific vehicles, so will these mini critical speeds. This immediately explains the experimental observation of differences between car-to-barrier impacts and car-to-car impacts. This occurs for the same reason that the critical speeds for induced permanent damage depend on the details of the two vehicles. Equation 6.16 gives the first critical speed somewhere between 5 mph and 10 mph if both vehicles have 5-mph bumpers. Exactly where the answer lies depends on the vehicle weight ratio and the ratio of *R* values. An impact between an eighteen-wheeler and a small car will give about 5 mph, whereas, an impact between two similar vehicles gives about 10 mph. Similarly, the mini critical speeds will depend on the individual threshold forces and energies for isolator stroking (this is equivalent to defining new *R* values and new v_L values).

Should we bother with these mini critical speeds? In principle the answer is yes. However, to do so would require careful calibration of the entire bumper assembly (not just the isolator response) for all vehicles. Further, all these critical speeds will be low. Thus attempting to assess these speeds will probably not be worthwhile, unless the expert wishes to interpret a car crash using only isolator piston motions. The problem is that these same reasons for the differences between car-to-car and car-to-barrier responses also give rise to errors in isolator interpretations.

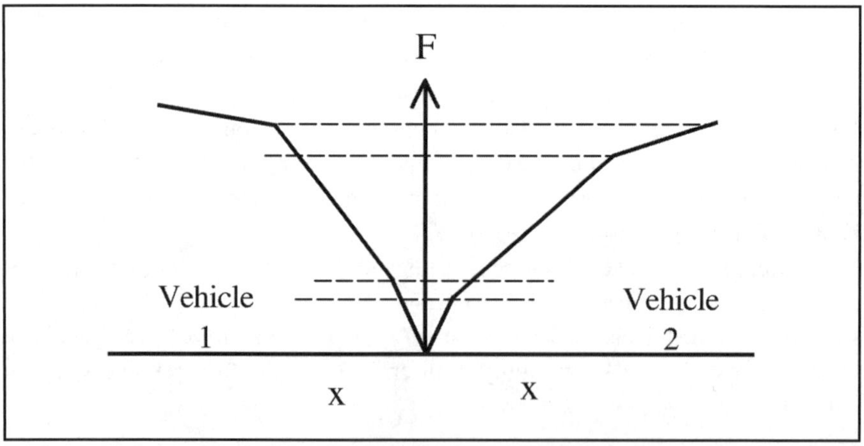

Figure 7.6 *Bumper/isolator thresholds for vehicle-to-vehicle*

7.4 Isolator Aging

Isolators are not designed to leave stroking marks. Indeed, some leave none at all even if fully stroked. The marks are entirely by accident and due to scraping on paint, rust or dirt. However, the rust and dirt are there in the first place only because the isolator is typically open to the environment. This brings up an important issue: How rapidly do these isolators age? For example, will a stroke mark caused by an accident in 1990 still be visible in 1997? If a vehicle suffers several impacts before the investigator studies the car, how do we know which marks belong to which impact? The problem is that all the testing of isolators have involved immediate inspection after a known impact. To unambiguously identify a given impact with a subsequent stroking the experimenters have usually painted the isolators with a white snow paint before each impact. This is fine for testing, but not very useful for in-field investigations. Finally, to our knowledge no one has studied the aging effect.

This issue arose during a court case. A rear-end collision occurred in 1992 between a small car with a Plastic rear bumper and large one with an isolator front bumper. No damage was induced in either vehicle. However, the isolator was not inspected until 1995 (of course, there was "nothing to inspect" with the Plastic bumper). This inspection identified a small one-eighth-inch scrape on one isolator. This scrape was remarkably clean and shiny for a supposedly three-year old hit (hardly any rusting or additional dirt accumulation). However, the photographs also revealed very faint signs of a one-inch scrape on the other isolator. This mark was difficult to unambiguously discern owing to the post-motion rusting. Which mark represented the court case? The small scrape indicated a closing speed of less than 2.5 mph, whereas the larger scrape indicated a closing speed of at least 7.5 mph. The first answer would not imply personal injury, whereas, the second answer could. Put bluntly, no one (neither expert) could rigorously answer the question; it became pure opinion, meaning mostly guesswork. Indeed, since no one has scientifically studied these aging effects there would be no basis on which to even try to claim experience.

7.5 Viscous Behavior of Plastic Bumpers

It is useful to understand exactly why these bumpers can act in a viscous manner. The answer is that they are made of high-density foams which contain air within the pores. If the pores are closed cell (i.e., they do not interconnect) then rapid compression of the foam causes adiabatic heating of the air (the same reason hand air-pumps get hot with use). However, this heat is then transferred to the foam walls. Upon re-expansion adiabatic cooling occurs which now tries to extract heat from the walls. The net result is to induce hysteresis and this causes damping. For an open-cell foam the air is actually pumped between the cells in a viscous manner. Although the viscosity of air is very low compared to that for oil the huge numbers of little cells and orifices gives a significant overall damping effect.

This behavior must be distinguished from actual plastic collapse of the cells. The latter occurs for higher forces, and leaves the Plastic foam in a state of permanent compaction (crush).

7.6 Transmission of Bumper Force

It may not be obvious how little pieces of foamed Plastic can possibly absorb the energy of a barrier-equivalent impact at 5 mph. After all, such Plastic is not very strong. This Plastic is very much like the Plastic packaging used for boxing such items as TV sets (it even looks the same). The secret lies in a fundamental difference in the manner of transmitting the force to the car as compared to that for the isolator approach. With the isolators, the entire bumper force is transmitted to the car by the two isolators only; thus we have concentrated loading. While the speed capability is determined by the stroking amplitude, the actual strength of the isolators is a function of their diameter; thus large cars have large-diameter isolators.

With the Plastic bumpers the Plastic is backed by a steel plate next to the car structure and the entire facial surface area is used to transmit the force. For example, for a 3,000-pound car with $R = 0.6$, the peak force before structural damage is $F = 12Rw = 21{,}600$ pounds. However, such a car is typically about 72 inches wide and has a bumper about 5 inches tall (top to bottom). Thus the presented area is about 360 square inches and the mean pressure acting on the Plastic foam is only $P = 21{,}600/360$ psi $= 60$ psi. This is only 4.1 atmospheres, and can easily be handled. For the isolators, however, each one would have to handle 10,800 pounds. If the isolator diameter is two inches the cross-sectional area is only 3.14 square inches, and the pressure is 3,438 psi. Thus the isolator has to be built strongly and is made of thick-walled steel.

7.7 Static versus Dynamic Isolator Forces

Frequently, measurements are made of the static force-deflection for isolators. However, this data is not useful for dynamic vehicle impacts. It might be useful if we have a case of one vehicle gently pushing another (as when aiding a disabled car by pushing it to a garage). The only time the static response is identical to the dynamic response is when we have a perfect spring. Since, by definition, isolators absorb energy and involve damping, the static response is forced to be different from the dynamic one. In essence, the viscous oil force adds to any spring force during compression and subtracts from the spring force during rebound. It is this difference that causes energy absorption. Thus, to understand the initial compressive impact response (which always determines maximum compression and thus any crush) we need to know the dynamic force-deflection response. The only real effect of damping is to make the isolator stiffer during dynamic compression.

It is easy to show why the static response is inappropriate. Using the published literature for static behavior it is possible to perform an integration of force versus isolator deflection. This represents the stored energy. It is then found that this static data always implies a maximum equivalent barrier speed which is much lower than the actual bumper limit. Use of dynamic data cures this problem. Like it or not, a barrier impact at the bumper limit (no damage) has to dispense its kinetic energy into the bumper assembly. So the integrated energy for the bumper stroking must equate with the initial car kinetic energy. Note: we are referring to the bumper, not just the isolator.

7.8 Bumper Stroking versus Delta-*v*: Restitution for Car-to-Car Impacts

It used to be normal to quote vehicle responses in terms of the EBS (equivalent barrier speed). However, we have noticed a recent trend to report results in terms of the net delta-*v*, which is the net change in vehicle speed. Thus, isolator stroking is usually quoted in this form. However, it is not clear why the authors are doing this. The reality is that the maximum isolator stroke is only a function of the maximum EBS; any rebound is separate. The value of net speed change is simply $\Delta v = (1 - e)\text{EBS}$ for a barrier impact (with e negative). The authors seem to be trying to link potential occupant injury to the measured isolator stroking. The problem is that this only works for a barrier impact.

The catch is that for a car-to-car impact the effective coefficient of restitution is different from the individual values for car-to-barrier impacts. Hence any direct link to injury is immediately falsified. This is related directly to the point made before concerning the mini critical speeds. A simple measurement of an isolator stroke amplitude does not give a unique answer for the impact severity (although sometimes it is a good answer).

Suppose we have vehicle (1) hitting a rigid barrier with parameters w_1, and e_1. Now have vehicle (2) hit a barrier with parameters w_2 and e_2. What happens if the vehicles hit each other?

This can be solved by considering the situation within the reference frame of the net CM (center of mass) for both vehicles. To understand this let (1) be traveling to the right at v_1 while (2) is traveling to the left at v_2. Let $v_2 = -(w_1/w_2)v_1$. Then the total momentum is zero and we are in the CM frame of reference. Let the vehicles rebound off each other with speeds v_1' and v_2'. To maintain zero net momentum we also have $v_2' = -(w_1/w_2)v_1'$. We also have $e_{cc} = (v_2' - v_1')/(v_1 - v_2)$.

For individual barrier impacts the input energies are simply $E_1 = v_1^2 w_1/(2g)$ and $E_2 = v_2^2 w_2/(2g)$. However, the output energies are $e_1^2 E_1$ and $e_2^2 E_2$, respectively. If we now compare the net returned output energies versus the net original input energies we can define e_{cc}, which is the mutual coefficient of restitution. Doing this we get

$$e_{cc}^2 = \frac{\left(w_1 e_2^2 + w_2 e_1^2\right)}{\left(w_1 + w_2\right)}. \tag{7.4}$$

This is also equivalent to

$$e_{cc}^2 = 1 + \frac{w_1\left(e_2^2 - 1\right) + w_2\left(e_1^2 - 1\right)}{\left(w_1 + w_2\right)}. \tag{7.5}$$

This latter version has been quoted by Siegmund (ref 36).

Using Equation 7.4, it is easy to show that individual barrier restitution values are not the same as the mutual car-to-car value. For example, let $w_1 = 4{,}000$ pounds and $e_1 = 0.5$, while $w_2 = 2{,}000$ pounds and $e_2 = 0.7$. Then $e_{cc} = 0.64$. Note that as the weight ratio w_1/w_2 becomes larger so the value of e_{cc} becomes closer to the value of the lighter vehicle barrier value, e_2, and vice versa.

Chapter 8

Integrated Hits and Other Effects

Synopsis

8.1 Absorbed Energy (Again) and the Multiple-Hit Logic

When a bumper compresses and re-expands, some energy is absorbed. This is why they are called "energy absorbing" and why they can reduce the rebound relative to a pure spring. They cannot alter the common speed condition, however, because the latter is driven by the law of conservation of momentum. This is why energy-absorbing bumpers have no effect on our Equation 6.16. By reducing the rebound, they also reduce the overall net change in speed (known as the delta-v). This helps minimize injury to occupants, since such injury is usually associated with the sudden total speed change which occurs very rapidly (for slower-speed, longer-lived changes it is the acceleration that determines injury).

However, the viscous energy absorption of bumpers is transient. There is no permanent effect. This is important for the interpretation of the multiple-hit testing. The logic behind such multiple hits is that the absorbed energy per hit can be integrated over several hits. This then gives the same effect as one stronger hit. In principle, this allows one vehicle to be studied over a speed range. However, care must be exercised with this logic. It only applies to the integration of plastically absorbed energy (i.e., associated with permanent damage). It does not apply to viscous energy absorption. Hence it is necessary to know which energy absorption mode is being applied.

To illustrate, suppose our car has a 5-mph bumper. We perform a 3-mph impact with a rigid barrier. What is the damage? The answer should be zero. Now repeat this 3-mph impact 100 times. What is the damage? The answer should still be zero. Yet each such impact absorbed some energy. But none of this absorbed energy was permanent; it was all transient viscous heating. Indeed, the whole point of having energy-absorbing isolators (or Plastic bumpers) is to allow multiple low-speed impacts without needing to replace the bumper, because such bumpers are supposed to recover for each such hit and be ready for another.

Suppose we now perform a 6-mph impact. This will give some small permanent damage. Repeating such 6-mph impacts will now start to integrate the plastic portion of the absorbed energy. However, the bumper itself may still be operational per impact. So some of the absorbed energy is still viscous. This portion does not integrate. So to correctly add up the absorbed energy from the multiple impacts, we can only use the plastic energy.

This is where relying on experimental values of restitution (e) gives immediate trouble. Attempts are frequently made to infer the energy loss by using Equation 6.8. But the experimental value of e is a combined value, being partly due to viscous rebound and partly due to plastic crush. Unless we determine the proportions of each component, the equivalent closing speed will be wrong. In fact it will be too high. Use of our previous model for crush solves the issue. This is so because our model treated actual plastic crush (and the associated energy absorption) independently of the bumper response. This is why so much emphasis was given to the distinctions between input energy and plastically absorbed energy, and why our equation for closing speed is given by the sum-of-squares of the critical speed and the true absorbed energy speed. Thus we write

$$v_{close}^2 = v_{critical}^2 + \frac{2gE_{absorb}\left(w_1 + w_2\right)}{w_1 w_2} \tag{8.1}$$

where E_{absorb} is given by our model in Figure 3.3. From this model we obtain

$$E_{absorb} = F\left[6Rw\left(\frac{x^2}{a} + 2x + \frac{v_L^2}{12Rg}\right) - \frac{wv_L^2}{2g}\left(1 + \frac{x}{a}\right)\right] \tag{8.2}$$

where F is the fractional width of damage, equal to 1.0 for a full-width bumper impact, and x is the permanent crush. Note how as x drops to zero so the entire value of E_{absorb} becomes zero. This is to be distinguished from E_{input} which can still be finite (as for just at or below the bumper limit). Also, any viscous energy absorption which occurs solely within the bumper assembly is likewise ignored. Equation 8.2 describes the plastic absorbed energy not the viscous absorbed energy. Note that these distinctions are not made in the CRASH3 algorithm. To sum energies for multiple-hit testing it is our defined plastic $E_{absorbed}$ that must be used and not the apparent values obtained by considering the experimental value of e. However, since the plastic energy absorption rapidly dominates the viscous term with increasing plastic permanent vehicle damage, the distinction becomes moot for higher closing speeds. This explains the observation that the summed energy logic works well only above a certain minimum speed (ref 31), which is itself higher than the bumper speed even for simple barrier impacts.

To illustrate the summed energy approach for multiple barrier hits we note that if Equation 8.2 is rewritten in terms of equivalent barrier speed (EBS) we obtain (for $F = 1.0$)

$$v_{impact}^2 = 12Rg\left(\frac{x^2}{a} + 2x + \frac{v_L^2}{12Rg}\right) - v_L^2\left(\frac{x}{a}\right). \tag{8.3}$$

Thus when $x \rightarrow 0.0$, so $v_{impact} \rightarrow v_L$, as expected. To compute the "equivalent single impact" for several lower-speed impacts we must take into account that each successive degree of permanent crush stiffens the car for each subsequent impact (this is known as strain hardening). This means that the value of R must be updated after each impact. This is because any form of permanent crush moves the new starting point farther up the force-deflection curve. This was shown in Figure 5.3.

For the first impact above the bumper limit we use Equation 8.3 to solve for the induced crush, x_1 and use the initial value R_1. For the second impact we must update R to get R_2. This is done by using

$$R_{new} = R_{old}\left(1 + \frac{x}{a}\right) \tag{8.4}$$

We now reuse Equation 8.3 with R_2 to re-solve for x_2. This process is repeated for each impact. It will be observed that for sequential identical barrier speeds the incremental values of crush actually decrease, although the total integrated crush increases. Finally, when we have determined the total crush for all the impacts, we re-solve Equation 8.3, but using the original value for R. This gives the equivalent single impact speed which would cause the same total crush. As an example, let our car have $R = 0.6$ initially, and $a = 0.5$ feet, and $v_L = 5$ mph (7.335 ft/s). Consider ten repeated barrier impacts, all at 8 mph (11.74 ft/s). Table 8.1 shows the results.

As a simple cross-check, note that since energy is proportional to v^2, we anticipate the result to be given by $v^2_{equiv} = 10 \times (8^2 - 5^2) = 390$ (mph)^2. Thus v_{equiv} = 19.75 mph. This is the same answer as for the above table (within 0.7 percent), at least within sequential rounding errors.

As the impact speed increases from the lower critical speed to the upper critical speed a small correction should be added to Equation 8.1 in order to account

Table 8.1

Hit #	v_{impact} mph	Incremental Crush		Total Crush		*R* value	Equiv Speed	
——		feet	inches	feet	inches	——	ft/s	mph
1	8.0	0.189	2.272	0.189	2.272	0.600	11.74	8.0
2	8.0	0.136	1.632	0.272	3.904	0.827	13.6	9.27
3	8.0	0.121	1.452	0.393	5.356	0.926	16.29	11.10
4	8.0	0.104	1.249	0.497	5.965	1.072	18.58	12.67
5	8.0	0.093	1.116	0.590	7.081	1.197	20.62	14.06
6	8.0	0.085	1.019	0.675	8.100	1.308	22.48	15.33
7	8.0	0.079	0.944	0.754	9.044	1.410	24.21	16.50
8	8.0	0.074	0.840	0.828	9.932	1.504	25.82	17.60
9	8.0	0.069	0.833	0.897	10.76	1.594	27.32	18.62
10	8.0	0.066	0.792	0.963	11.55	1.676	28.75	19.60

for the increasing absorption of energy within the heavy vehicle bumper. This correction is

$$E_{corr} = \left(\frac{v - v_{crit1}}{v_{crit2} - v_{crit1}}\right)^2 \left(\frac{w_1 v_{L1}^2}{2g}\right)\left[1 - \left(\frac{R_2 w_2}{R_1 w_1}\right)\right] \tag{8.5}$$

for v between v_{crit1} and v_{crit2}. Once above v_{crit2} the correction is simply

$$E_{corr} = \left(\frac{w_1 v_{L1}^2}{2g}\right)\left[1 - \left(\frac{R_2 w_2}{R_1 w_1}\right)^2\right]. \tag{8.6}$$

These corrections are usually small. Ignoring them tends to decrease the calculated closing impact speed (thus being conservative) by less than 10 percent over a small speed range. This is usually less than about 1 mph change.

8.2 Front-to-Front versus Front-to-Rear Impacts

It is sometimes observed that even for identical cars there is a difference between a front-to-front impact and a front-to-rear one. This effect has been observed with the ubiquitous 1981–1985 Ford Escort (a vehicle which seems to have been studied to death). The effect can be explained by noting that the rear of the vehicle is weaker than the front. Although both the front and rear bumpers are supposedly rated for 5 mph they have different isolators (ref 35). Those on the front have a maximum stroke of about 57 millimeters (2.24 inches). However, those on the rear have a maximum stroke of about 64 millimeters (2.5 inches).

Consider Equation 6.13. For the same bumper speed capability this states that the larger the amplitude for the bumper (the isolator stroke) the lower the rigidity factor, R. Thus, the implied R values are $RF = 0.746$ for the front and $RR = 0.668$ for the rear. Now substitute these figures into Equation 6.16. For either a front-to-front *or* a rear-to-rear impact we obtain a critical closing speed of 10 mph. This is because of symmetry, with the R values equal (both front or both rear).

However, for a front-to-rear impact we obtain a critical closing speed of only 9.49 mph. Further, it is the weaker rear end that first suffers damage. If we use our previously quoted equation for the upper critical speed, and use $a_2 = 0.5$ feet, we obtain a closing speed of 11.39 mph. Thus the rear of an Escort starts to suffer crush at a closing speed of about 9.49 mph, but the front starts crushing at 11.39 mph, and this is from an impact between two identical vehicles.

Using Equations 6.22 and 6.23 for the force balance with the above R values and weights of 2,200 pounds for each car, we can solve to obtain the plastically induced rear-end damage. This is about 0.7 inch. Thus we have almost one inch of crush on the rear of the target vehicle before any damage occurs on the front of the bullet.

8.3 Bumper Speed Limits

Before 1983, car bumpers (not those on trucks, vans or SUVs) had to be capable of allowing for an equivalent full-width, rigid-barrier impact of 5 mph minimum without associated permanent vehicle damage. Under pressure from the car manufacturers (mostly to reduce weight and thus more readily comply with the CAFE rules) the government allowed a relaxation to a new rule of the limit of 2.5 mph minimum. There is nothing to prevent a car maker from using a higher limit. We have been startled to find that some accident reconstruction experts have taken the new rule to mean that all cars built after 1983 now have 2.5-mph bumpers.

This is wrong.

While some of the smaller, less expensive, cars have used lower speed bumpers (usually of the Plastic variety), many of the larger, more expensive cars have retained higher speed bumpers. According to an article in *Automotive Engineering* (published by SAE, May, 1995, authors P. Dellock and T. Sweder [both of Ford Motor Company], ref 37), Ford Motor Company has maintained nominal 5-mph bumpers for their cars. To quote them, "The major competitors in the MPV market (Aerostar, Chrysler's minivans, Toyota Previa, GM APVs, and Mazda MPV) have, at best, 4-km/h [2.5 mph] systems. All Ford cars and most passenger vehicles have 8-km/h [5.0 mph] bumper systems." [Note: this article concerned the newly-designed bumper for the Ford Windstar, which does have 5-mph bumpers, thus making it somewhat unique for a van.] Of course, now that 5 mph is a factor of 2 larger than the requirement, there is probably less emphasis on accurately ensuring a 5-mph performance. Thus, the bumper may actually only provide protection at (perhaps) 4 to 4.5 mph rather than a minimum of 5 mph.

For example, on modern Ford cars the following "bumper quality" label will be found.

> This vehicle is equipped with bumper systems that can withstand a frontal barrier impact speed of 5 miles per hour and a rear barrier impact speed of 5 miles per hour with no more damage than allowed by the Federal Bumper Standard. The Federal Bumper Standard allows damage to the bumpers and attaching hardware and specifies barrier tests to be conducted at 2.5 miles per hour.

What does this mean? It means that such bumpers can (and do) suffer damage as prescribed by the government, but that they do so at 5 mph rather than at the minimum government-defined speed of only 2.5 mph. However, there should be no damage to the vehicle itself.

Many modern cars are "bumper tested" by organizations such as Consumers Union. The latter frequently use a hydraulic thumper and perform four hits, two to the front and two to the rear, first at 2.5 mph and then at 5 mph. Many cars pass these tests with no trouble. However, some cars sustain induced damage. The costs of estimated repair can range from a low of $150 (refurbishing of outer Plastic covers) to over $1,000. The modern rule requires protection of the car, but not necessarily for the bumper itself. Typically, the cost of replacement of a full bumper assembly is about $400 to $600, that of individual isolators (if used) is about $50 to $70. Thus, repair costs of less than $400 usually imply only a damaged bumper. Costs of $1,000 or more imply some actual vehicle damage. However, it should be noted that the cost of body repair escalates very rapidly. Thus, even a $1,000 bill still only represents a small degree of damage. Merely dropping the bumper performance from 5 mph to 4 mph (in a 5-mph test) can readily cause such damage.

IIHS also performs bumper tests. It includes rear impacts into poles at 5 mph. It is these pole impacts (and other localized impacts) that cause problems. Note there is no regulation for a pole impact. It is because the pole impacts frequently do cause damage that the reputation of modern Plastic bumpers is poor. However, most cars can still survive a full-width barrier impact at 5 mph without vehicle damage. The bumper may suffer damage, but many cars do not even have this problem. These effects can be seen in the IIHS *Status Report*, such as that for Vol. 28, No. 3, March 1993 (ref 38).

A simple example of the fact that modern bumpers may not be exactly 5-mph ones is revealed when these bumper tests cause no damage to one bumper (e.g., the front) but cause some damage to the other (rear, or vice versa). There is also the issue of how close the actual bumper test was to 5 mph (both Consumer's Union and IIHS are frequently silent on this issue, and leave the reader to merely assume they did the test correctly).

For example, the Honda Accord DX suffered zero (financial) damage for both a full-front and a full rear 5-mph barrier impact. The rear pole impact damage cost $224. This was damage to only the bumper. For the Ford Tempo GL, the front and rear barrier impacts cost $48 and $56 to repair. This is typical of repainting. For the rear pole impact, however, the cost was $1,373, which implies vehicular damage to the bodywork. The reason for this poor response in localized impacts is discussed in Section 9.2, "Beam Bending."

However, some of these tests done for IIHS make little sense. For instance, data presented by NTS (National Technical Services, ref 39) indicate that some cars suffer less damage (even zero) for a rear-end impact at 5 mph into a pole than when the same car suffers finite rear-end damage for a full-width barrier impact at 5 mph. This is difficult to accept since a pole impact is localized, whereas the barrier impact is distributed. It would make sense if the central section of the rear bumper was somehow more resilient than the entire bumper. However, a geometry capable of doing this is hard to understand, because even the full-width barrier impact must also use this resilient portion of the bumper. We suspect the odd results are more an illustration of either problems with measurements of induced damage, or an indication that the full-width impacts were, in reality, not normal (i.e., skewed with more load on one side than the other), or that the measured speed was wrong.

To appreciate the expected degree of damage for a bumper limit less than 5 mph, when tested in a 5-mph barrier test, we again use Equation 8.3. First, we must determine the paired values of R and a which correctly predict a known high-speed barrier impact, such as an NCAP one. For example, let our test car have $R = 0.6$, and let the "NCAP condition" correspond to $v_{impact} = 35$ mph (51.35 ft/s) with crush, $x = 24$ inches (2.00 foot). Now choose an assumed bumper limit speed, v_L. We now solve Equation 8.3 for each v_L to obtain the a value. If the bumper limit is 5 mph (7.335 ft/s) we get $a = 0.495$ foot, for a 4-mph bumper (5.868 ft/s) $a = 0.513$ foot, for a 2.5 mph bumper (3.668 ft/s) $a = 0.531$ foot, and for no bumper $a = 0.542$ foot.

If the car truly has a 5-mph bumper the vehicle damage for a 5-mph barrier impact should be zero. However, if the bumper is really only a 4-mph one, the damage becomes 0.0464 foot = 0.557 inch. If the bumper is only a 2.5-mph one, the damage becomes 0.0849 foot = 1.019 inches, while for no bumper the damage is 0.1057 foot = 1.269 inches. We see that the difference between a 5-mph bumper and a 2.5-mph one amounts to about one inch of permanent damage in a 5-mph barrier impact. Unfortunately, even one inch of body or frame damage gets to be expensive to repair. However, this same one inch rarely disables the vehicle; the car is frequently still drivable. This explains why so many owners choose not to repair their vehicles with such damage. The repair cost can frequently be comparable to any insurance deductible.

It should also be appreciated that many MY (Model Year) changes are frequently nothing more than cosmetic. Unless a significant redesign is involved it will make no financial sense for a car maker to invest in the new tooling and other costs (through subcontractors) of providing a new bumper to an existing car. Many cars, such as the Dodge Diplomat, were continued essentially unaltered through 1983 until the model was dropped (in 1989 for the Diplomat). During this period, the car's weight actually increased slightly. There is no logical reason for a change in the bumper design for an already-existing car. The typical design time for a new car is also about four years (newer ones are getting quicker, with some down to the thirty-month range). It is unlikely that a car designed in 1982, intended for the market in 1986, would have its bumper redesigned merely because the law allowed it to be.

As pointed out before, the potential capability of a bumper is mostly determined by its possible amplitude of motion (the stroke). When this amplitude exceeds about 2 to 2.5 inches, the typical car bumper can handle about 5 mph. A quick inspection of cars reveals that most do have this capability. The big exceptions are the pick-ups, vans and SUVs. Here it is frequently observed that the bumper can rarely move much more than an inch before contact with the bodywork occurs. Of course, there are no present government rules for these bumpers. Indeed, a pick-up can be purchased without *any* rear bumpers! A typical pick-up or SUV bumper handles only about 2.5 mph for a full-width barrier impact. Recent films from the IIHS (shown on the *Dateline* TV show) have shown how poor the bumpers usually are on the so-called rough-and-tough SUVs.

So why do low-quality pick-up bumpers seem to do so well in a truck-to-car crash? The answer is again given by Equation 6.16. Usually, the truck is stronger than the car, so the car damages first. Further, many trucks have bumpers which are higher than those on cars. In such a case, the truck bumper contacts the softer parts of the typical car. Again, the car is damaged first and little damage occurs to the truck. We find it intriguing that there are government regulations for the heights of car bumpers, but not for truck or SUV bumpers. The latter vehicles are classified as commercial which explains why they have precious few rules. [It also explains why the present fad for SUVs and pick-up trucks exists. If the same CAFE rules and safety rules were applied to SUVs and pick-ups, they would rapidly vanish since they rarely satisfy either set of rules. Also, as explained in *AutoWeek*, September 1, 1997, the profit margin on trucks is huge compared to that on cars. No wonder the industry loves to promote them!] This is somewhat odd, because even eighteen-wheelers frequently have low bumpers which actually mate with those of cars.

8.4 Damage: Car-to-Car versus Car-to-Barrier

Of course, bumper standards are defined unrealistically, mostly in terms of a flat-fronted vertical rigid barrier (or moving barrier). This is rarely representative of any real car crash. We even note that for a single car, the rear bumper is sometimes higher than the front one. This is a most peculiar arrangement, because when cars are involved in rear-enders it is frequent for at least one car (sometimes both) to be strongly braking and adopting the nose-down, tail-up attitude. This makes the low-front/high-rear geometry totally absurd, since it merely exacerbates the tendency of submarining. The only cure is to guarantee a relatively deep bumper in terms of its vertical fascial height (top of bumper to bottom).

For the barrier impact the test is invariably done without braking into a flat wall. At low speeds there is negligible pitching of the vehicle, and the bumper's impact surface is easily defined. Unfortunately, these conditions do not apply to the typical car-to-car crash.

Many car bumpers have a bow to them. In addition, most have a profiled shape (sculptured, if you will) when viewed sideways. Add to this the braking nose-dive and it readily becomes apparent why the interaction of bumpers in a car-to-car hit can be different from the typical car-to-barrier test. Whereas a barrier hit may involve a thrust almost purely horizontal, the car-to-car hit can be noticeably non-horizontal, and involves a vertical component. The vertical component can cause a twist of the bumper which does not occur in a barrier hit. Without knowing the exact position of the two bumpers, this can give odd results. Also, when a heavy vehicle rear-ends a light one it is quite common for the heavy one to push down the rear end of the other one and to then demolish the soft rear vertical structure of the light vehicle. This regularly happens when a Suburban rear-ends a small car, even when the Suburban has over-riders on its front bumper (to extend the bumper's vertical height).

Note that all such effects can produce a problem with actual vehicle-to-vehicle testing: namely, that all such results have the propensity to be unique to the actual test performed, and may not represent the generic, or typical result. Without performing a huge matrix of tests (all options for vehicle-to-vehicle and all impact speeds of interest) this situation is unavoidable. However, it should act as a caution to those who put too much faith into limited experimental tests versus theory.

These various effects cause trouble when defining damage. For a flat barrier a bumper may survive a 5-mph hit totally unscathed. Yet the same 5-mph impact may cause bumper damage for a vehicle-to-vehicle hit, since bumper twisting and so forth may occur. For these reasons, the previous cost quotes of damage must be viewed very cautiously. The costs listed by the repair estimate can only be used to help support a level of damage. It is rare that the costs directly indicate the damage. To emphasize this, note that an appraiser will usually list everything that might have been damaged, even if some components are actually in good working order (this frequently happens with the isolators, when the appraiser sees a stroke mark and assumes that the isolator may be damaged). The appraiser is merely playing it safe. He usually represents an insurance company. While the insurance company has no wish to overpay for damage, it likewise does not wish to give itself a potential lawsuit by not properly repairing the vehicle (imagine a subsequent claim for damages in a later accident because a bumper collapsed too easily because of the failure of the appraiser to replace it!).

8.5 Bumper-to-Bumper versus Bumper-to-Soft-Bodywork

When a pick-up or SUV rear-ends a small car, two events can occur. Sometimes the bumpers mate and we have the simple bumper-to-bumper impact. Other times the SUV bumper is too high and the collision involves the SUV bumper hitting the car above the car bumper, and thus into the soft bodywork (vertical valence, side quarter panels, rear lights and the trunk). Common sense tells us the latter impact will produce the greater car crush. However, does it produce the greater injury potential for the car occupant?

Consider a 4,000-pound SUV (vehicle 1) hitting a stationary 2,500-pound car (vehicle 2) with a closing speed of 10 mph (14.67 ft/s). For the SUV assume $R_1 = 0.7(3{,}000/w_1)^{1/3} = 0.636$, and $a_1 = 0.5(w_1/3{,}000)^{1/3} = 0.55$ foot, and $v_{L1}=$ 3.668 ft/s (2.5 mph). For the car assume $R_2 = 0.6(3{,}000/w_2)^{1/3} = 0.638$, and $a_2 =$ $0.5(w_2/3{,}000)^{1/3} = 0.47$ foot, and $v_{L2} = 7.335$ ft/s (5.0 mph). These latter car values are for a bumper-to-frame impact. For a soft-bodywork impact, assume $R^* = 0.3$, $a^* = 0.3$ ft, and $v_L^* = 2.0$ ft/s. These latter * values are engineering estimates since such soft-body parameters are rarely measured or quoted. The meaning of the bumper speed for the soft-body is the maximum barrier speed which produces no permanent damage, when we use a sculptured barrier that allows the bumper to move into a recess and allow only impact above the bumper.

To solve these two impact options we perform the following steps.

1. Compute the lower and upper critical speeds (Equations 6.16 and 6.21),
2. compute the maximum absorbed energy (Equation 8.1),
3. compute the crush (Equation 8.2),

4. compute the maximum force (Equation 6.22) and hence vehicle accelerations,
5. compute the coefficient of restitution,
6. compute the two vehicle delta-v's, and
7. compute the relative time scale for the impacts.

A. Case A: Bumper-to-Bumper

For this case we obtain

$$v_{critical}\text{(lower)} = 10.06 \text{ ft/s} = 6.86 \text{ mph and}$$

$$v_{critical}\text{(upper)} = 20.33 \text{ ft/s} = 13.86 \text{ mph.}$$

Thus our 10-mph impact is within the window and we expect damage to the rear of the car but no damage to the front of the SUV.

The absorbed energy is $E = 2{,}724$ ft-lbs, the permanent crush is 0.132 foot = 1.58 inches, and the peak force is 24,499 pounds. So the peak acceleration of the car is 9.8 g's, while that for the SUV is –6.12 g's. The coefficient of restitution is $e = 0.7v_{crit}\text{(lower)}/v_{close} = 0.48$. Hence our delta-$v$'s are

$$\Delta v_{car} = 13.36 \text{ ft/s} = 9.11 \text{ mph and } \Delta v_{SUV} = -8.35 \text{ ft/s} = -5.69 \text{ mph.}$$

To compute the time scale of the impact we use $F_{average}\Delta t = m\Delta v = (w/g)\Delta v$, and assume the average force is about 1/2 × peak force.

For the bumper-to-bumper impact we get $\Delta t = 0.085$ second.

B. Case B: Bumper-to-Soft-Bodywork

Here we repeat all the above calculations but use the * parameters for the car.

We get

$$v_{critical}{}^{*}\text{(lower)} = 3.09 \text{ ft/s} = 2.1 \text{ mph and}$$

$$v_{critical}{}^{*}\text{(upper)} = 25.2 \text{ ft/s} = 17.18 \text{ mph.}$$

Thus, the impact is again within the window and only the car is damaged. Note how the upper critical speed increased, making it even less possible to damage the SUV.

The absorbed energy is $E^{*} = 4{,}913$ ft-lbs, the permanent crush is $x^{*} = 0.36$ foot = 4.27 inches, the peak force is $F^{*} = 19{,}668$ pounds and the peak acceleration for the car is 7.87^{*} g's while that for the SUV is -4.92^{*} g's.

The coefficient of restitution is $e^* = 0.147$, and the two vehicle delta-v's are

$$\Delta v_{car}{}^* = 10.36 \text{ ft/s} = 7.06 \text{ mph and } \Delta v_{SUV}{}^* = -6.48 \text{ ft/s} = -4.41 \text{ mph.}$$

The timescale is $\Delta t^* = 0.082$ second.

Note that for both case A and case B, the common speed achieved is 9.03 ft/s = 6.15 mph.

C. Discussion

For both types of crash the large, heavy SUV suffers no damage. Also, the delta-v of the SUV is low (5.69 mph or 4.41 mph) and is a frontal impact. Hence the probability of occupant injury in the SUV is low. For the small car, the degree of crush damage varies from about 1.6 inches to 4.3 inches. However, the larger degree of damage is associated with the smaller car's delta-v (7.06 mph versus 9.1 mph), and with a smaller peak acceleration (7.87 *g*'s versus 9.8 *g*'s), although the timescale is similar for each case.

This situation confounds the common wisdom, where the usual assumption is that the smaller the vehicle damage, the less likely any occupant injury! We see that common sense approaches are anything but reliable.

8.6 Aggressivity of Trucks and SUVs

There have been many discussions concerning the fact that pick-ups and SUVs tend to be aggressive with regard to impacts with cars. The example above illustrates why this is so. Even with the typical low-quality SUV bumper, the heavier and stronger vehicle usually wins when it collides with a typical car, and the SUV occupants rarely suffer injuries in low-speed impacts.

A classic problem is the issue of the SUV hitting a smaller car's door. The quandary is whether the door should be made rigid or soft? The above example illustrates the responses. For the rigid door the critical speed is increased, so the crush energy is decreased. Hence the door crush is reduced. However, the trade-off is a higher side acceleration for the car and occupant and a larger overall delta-v for the car's sideways motion. For this rigid-door case the occupant tends to suffer a worse side whiplash, with his head undergoing lateral motion (toward the SUV). However, if the door is soft the peak side acceleration and delta-v for the car can be reduced, thereby improving the whiplash situation. The snag is that we trade a smaller sideways motion for the occupant for a much larger side crush for the door itself. Because the initial gap between the door and the occupant is usually small, this means the door can directly collide with the side of the occupant. So we lessen the whiplash and instead suffer injury to the shoulders, upper arms, chest and pelvis. Nice choice!

Can trucks and SUVs be made less aggressive for lower-speed impacts? The answer is yes, and the solution is relatively simple. Just replace the lower-quality, rigidly mounted SUV bumpers with more car-like bumpers. The typical truck bumper is little more than an extension to the frame, and thus tends to act as a battering ram. If such bumpers were replaced with higher-speed, larger-stroking, energy-absorbing car bumpers the aggressivity would be reduced. It would also be better for the SUV and its occupants for low-speed impacts. Isn't this why we use such bumpers on cars in the first place? Wake up, NHTSA! Worrying about the weight and cost of such bumpers is a total farce. Pick-ups and SUVs haven't been satisfying CAFE requirements for several years anyway (why is the government not dealing with this?), and the profit on trucks and SUVs is already large. So why not try to add safety for a change? Isn't that supposed to be NHTSA's job?

Why would this work? As explained before, a higher-speed bumper must involve a longer stroke capability. This then implies a softer spring response. Such a bumper stores more energy for a given peak impact force. Considering the critical speed calculation, we immediately see that (all other factors equal) raising the value of bumper speed for the SUV raises the critical speed for the two-vehicle impact. This means that for a fixed closing speed the car crush energy must decrease, so the car crush is less. For two fixed vehicle weights and a fixed closing speed the maximum lost energy (occurring when the vehicles reach their common speed) is also fixed. By using high-speed softer SUV bumpers a greater fraction of this energy is stored by its bumper, so less remains to cause crush to the car.

However, by shifting energy into the SUV bumper (and thus away from the car) we also decrease the peak mutual force and, therefore, the peak acceleration. Only one problem remains: since the critical speed increased so did the coefficient of restitution, so the overall delta-v of the car may be high. This is cured by incorporating a high degree of viscous damping into the SUV bumper (even more than for typical car bumpers).

None of this is rocket science and is well within the engineering capabilities of the car makers (but, apparently, not within the priorities of either the makers or of NHTSA). While such changes in bumpers will do little for high-speed crashes, they could significantly improve the situation for low-speed cases. This improvement is not only for the poor car occupant, but also applies to the SUV occupants.

Since the publication of the second edition of this book, we have learned that at least one manufacturer has attempted to address these issues. Apparently, Ford has used a front bumper on its mammoth Excursion SUV which is really a bumper-within-a-bumper. Supposedly, there is a soft bumper within a hard bumper which helps ameliorate the aggressive behavior at low impact speeds. However, there are no published data to illustrate how well this actually works. But at least someone is paying attention (so kudos to Ford)!

Chapter 9

Interesting Mechanical Models

Synopsis

9.1 Internal Damage

Sometimes a crash gives only limited external vehicle damage such as a two-inch crush. Yet there may be damage to other components under the hood, such as the air-conditioner compressor or radiator. Since the compressor is farther back than the external crush region it can be difficult to associate damage to it with the crash. However, such effects do occur: they are a consequence of transferred inertial forces. A common observation for rear-ended pick-ups is to see impact damage at the rear of the cab, even though the cab is at least six feet away from the rear bumper. The explanation is that the truck bed is usually made with a small gap between itself and the cab. Upon the sudden rear-end thrust, the entire bed can be sprung forward, resulting in an impact with the cab.

The following experience for an author illustrates such effects. The driver once owned an old 1939 Austin 8. This was the old type of model with headlights mounted on side fenders, which were not integral with the hood (or "bonnet"). This car had a solid front axle and even used solid-rod brakes. One day the car slid on mud and proceeded to gently drift off the road and onto the level grass siding. Unfortunately, this level grass slowly converted itself into a ditch and the car ground to a halt with the solid front axle bottoming on the crest (one front wheel still on the road the other dropping into the ditch). The car stopped with no external frontal damage; but steam was exiting the hood and there was a large hole in the radiator. It was a perfect match to the fan-blades on the in-line engine! The engine was still running and the fan-blades were still in good condition, and the engine was sitting just where it normally did. So what happened? Answer: with the sudden stop, the engine had shot forward on its mounts sufficiently for the fan-blades to hit the radiator, and then had rebounded to its normal position. This was the author's first introduction to internal damage modes. He was not amused!

9.2 Beam Bending

The topic of bending beams (or rods) is important for understanding such effects as the permanent bending of bumpers, the possibility of lumbar thrusts on an occupant due to a hidden rod within a seat, the bending of steering wheels for forceful impact with the driver's head or chest, the inward bending of doors and the overall deformation of vehicles.

We will start with the simple cantilever. See Figure 9.1. Consider a uniform beam (or rod) with length L. For a beam, let the dimension along the direction of force be a, while that across the force be b. Thus any applied force acts on the surface Lb through the thickness a. Let the applied external force be F, acting at the free end, L, away from the clamp point. Let the clamp be to the left of the beam. We will ignore gravitational forces. There will be a constant shear force F acting through any cross-section (area ab) to the left of the applied force. The corresponding bending moment (BM) is the integral of this shear along the length of the beam. Thus BM is a maximum at the clamp, with a value BM = FL.

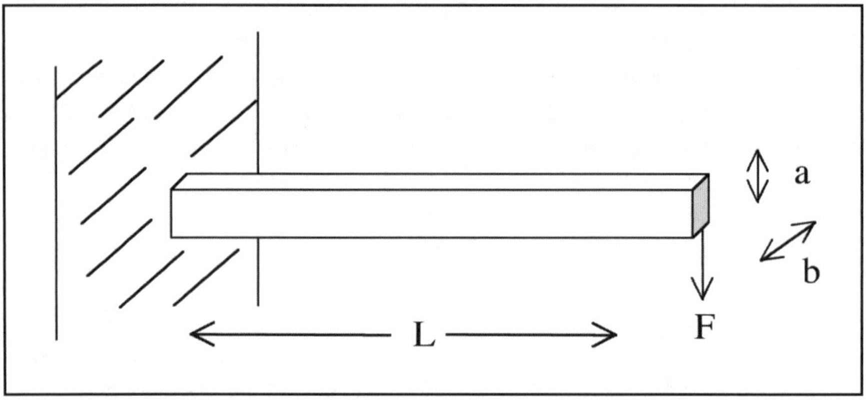

Figure 9.1 *Simple end-loaded cantilever*

The beam will bend and have an outer (convex) surface in tension and an inner (concave) surface in compression. This stress gradient passes through zero stress at the midplane, known as the null plane (we consider here only a simple uniform material, not specialized laminated composites). This gradient of stress produces an inner BM which balances the external BM. It can then be shown that

$$BM = FL = \frac{\sigma a^2 b}{6} = \frac{\sigma 4\left(\frac{a}{2}\right)^2\left(\frac{b}{2}\right)}{3} \qquad (9.1)$$

where s is the peak surface stress, (equal but opposite for compression and tension), and $a/2$ and $b/2$ are simply the half thickness and half width, respectively. The corresponding equation for a rod is simply

$$BM = \frac{\pi}{4}\sigma r_0^3 \quad \text{(solid rod) or} \quad BM = \frac{\pi}{4}\sigma \frac{\left(r_0^4 - r_1^4\right)}{r_0} \quad \text{(hollow rod)} \tag{9.2}$$

where r_0 is the outer rod radius and r_1 is the inner rod radius (thus wall thickness is $r_0 - r_i$). Provided the surface stress, a, remains below the yield stress, Y, the beam (or rod) remains elastic and recovers after removal of the external force, F.

Consider now a simple beam which is supported at two points a distance L apart. Let a concentrated load be applied at the middle (e.g., as for a central pole hit). We have what is known as a three-point bending situation, with the applied force, F, being balanced by two half-forces of $F/2$ each at the supports. See Figure 9.2. It can now be shown that the peak BM occurs under the applied load and has the value $BM = FL/4$ (i.e., half-force times half-distance). If the applied force is asymmetrical, at the position aL from one support and (1–a)L from the other, the peak bending moment is given by $BM = FL$a(1–a).

Suppose the beam represents a "metal" bumper-plate and the two supports are the isolators. Each isolator can withstand a peak force of $F = 6Rw$ before the bumper bottoms. We can now determine whether the bumper-plate will suffer permanent plastic deformation before the car suffers damage. To avoid bumper damage before vehicle damage, we require

$$6Rw \leq \frac{Ya^2b4}{6L} \leq \frac{2Ya^2b}{3L}. \tag{9.3}$$

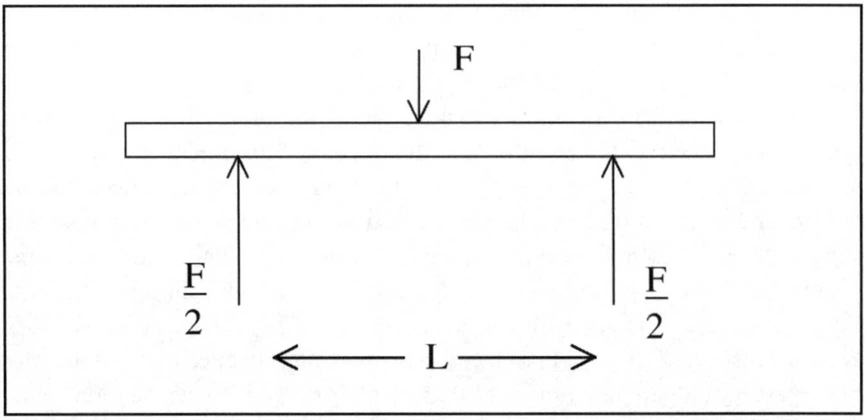

Figure 9.2 *Three-point loading of beam*

Thus, the isolators are bottomed before the bumper-plate itself suffers plastic damage. For a beam with sufficient through thickness, a, the bumper could satisfy this condition. By "through thickness" we mean the effective thickness a along the axis of the vehicle, whereas b represents the vertical height of the bumper (top to bottom).

To illustrate, let $R = 0.6$, $w = 3{,}000$ pounds, $L = 5$ feet $= 60$ inches, $b = 6$ inches, and $Y = 2.5$ kbar = 250 MPa = 2,500 atmospheres = 36,750 psi (typical steel). What value of a is required? Substituting into Equation 9.1 yields $a = 2.1$ inches. Thus, a bumper-plate with an effective through-thickness of 2.1 inches will not suffer permanent damage before the car itself does. In essence, such a bumper is able to redistribute the applied load across itself to the two isolators. Of course, having only two contact points with the vehicle frame the bumper must have some such capability. This example is simplified. In reality, real bumpers are rarely flat plates, instead most have a C-section consisting of a vertical end-face (the struck surface) and a top and bottom horizontal face. For this geometry most of the bending strength is actually provided by the two horizontal plates. Naturally, use of a higher-yield-strength metal can allow for even thinner bumpers.

Conversely, if Equation 9.3 is not satisfied, then the bumper itself will suffer permanent plastic damage before the car does. This is frequently seen on pick-up bumpers, where the bumper adopts localized permanent bending even though there may be no actual damage to the vehicle.

Now we can examine the fundamental difference between the modern Plastic bumpers and the older metal-beam variety. Whereas the metal bumpers could have significant bending resistance the Plastic ones usually have very low resistance to bending. Thus, for localized impacts the Plastic bumpers tend to suffer localized indents, which are seen everyday. It is this inability for the Plastic bumpers to redistribute a localized load across the bumper that accounts for the notoriety of these bumpers when handling localized impacts. With full-width impacts this bending is not significant; hence, the bumpers can perform well.

These comments apply mostly to the external portions of the Plastic bumper (i.e., the outer fascia skin and the inner foam core). This explains why indents are frequently observed for strong localized loadings, such as from license-plate holders and so forth. If the backing plate next to the vehicle structure proper is sufficiently rigid then even a Plastic bumper can redistribute loads across the width of the vehicle. Indeed, the development of such a high yield strength backing plate was the issue in the May, 1995, *Automotive Engineering* article (ref 40). Ford had discovered a way of producing a relatively thin-walled plate with a very high plastic yield-strength (about 11.0 kbar [161,700 psi] versus the more usual 2.5 kbar [36,750 psi]) that was used for the Windstar van.

Returning to Equation 9.1 we see that the bending moment is proportional to the quotient (a^2b/L). However, the volume (hence weight) is proportional to *abL*. Thus the bending moment is proportional to (a/L^2)(volume). Hence a rigid beam at fixed total weight requires maximizing the ratio of a/L^2. Likewise, for a given *L*, rigidity is proportional to *a*(*ab*), and so increases with increasing a for a fixed product *ab*. This explains the ability of I-beams, which are tall and thin, to handle bending loads acting through the tall direction.

Such beam behavior also explains how an engineer can make a car structure both stiff and collapsible. These attributes appear at first sight to be contradictions. However, the stiffness for normal driving loads is primarily vertical, whereas, the collapsibility for crash purposes is mostly horizontal (specifically, front-to-back). Thus, designing the frame rails to act like I-beams vertically but as easy-to-bend-and-buckle beams horizontally becomes a physical reality. A good example of how this is done in practice is described in ref 40.

9.3 The Soda-Can Model

Sometimes the crushing of a car has been likened to the collapse of a thin-walled soda-can subject to an axial load. Under such conditions the can will first compress elastically. Beyond a certain loading the can starts to suffer elastic buckling (this is simple Euler buckling), and the thin wall starts to flex sideways. With a relatively small increment in loading the wall motion becomes unstable, and "concertina" folds develop (part of the wall moves inward and part moves outward). With increasing strain these folds start to exceed the plastic yield strength and the can collapses axially upon itself with the well-known ripples in the side wall.

Such instability usually occurs at almost constant load. Increasing the input severity (hence energy) merely causes extra collapse, but induces very little increase in the associated force. Thus the effective plastic modulus is almost zero. A plot of the applied force versus deformation shows an initial linear elastic rise (Hookean response) followed by a plateau of almost constant force. Thus the soda-can behaves as a perfectly elastic and perfectly plastic body, at least until a large degree of collapse (whereupon the collapse is sufficient for the material to bottom on itself since its folds can not get out of each other's way). Only for very large collapse does the force again increase.

Does this model work well for explaining car crush? The answer is usually no. The reason is related to Newton's third law. When two bodies collide, each is subject to the same force (but in opposite directions). If one (or both) bodies display a plateau of force we immediately have a problem. As the mutual force increases it will eventually reach the plateau of the weaker body. Beyond this point the mutual force becomes locked to this plateau value. Hence, an increase in impact severity (more energy) does not increase this mutual force, it merely increases the degree of crush suffered by the weaker body. Unfortunately, this same process predicts zero crush for the stronger body.

Both the CRASH3 model and our own POD model imply the existence of the two critical speeds, discussed before. However, once above the upper critical speed both models assume that both vehicles will suffer crush. This is in accordance with everyday experience. Both models can do this because they both assume that during crush the necessary crush force increases with increasing deformation (this is due to the B term in CRASH3 and the a term the POD model). Thus a balance in force with both vehicles suffering crush is possible. With the soda-can model, this cannot happen unless the weaker vehicle suffers severe collapse (when its crush force again increases), while the stronger vehicle suffers no collapse.

Referring to our Equation 6.21 we immediately see the problem. A plateau in crush force implies zero-slope and thus an infinite value for the a_2 term. Thus, the upper critical speed also becomes infinite, and the larger (stronger) vehicle never suffers crush! This clearly does not agree with everyday observations.

Chapter 10

Comparisons between the CRASH3 and the POD Models

10.1 The Values of *R* and *a*, and the CRASH3 Equivalents *A* and *B*

Our POD model, using parameters *R* and *a* may confuse those who are used to the CRASH3 model with its parameters *A* and *B*. We will here illustrate how to convert from one model to the other, and illustrate the differences between these models.

We first define the equivalent terms. For incipient crush strength for a full-width barrier impact these are

$$F = 12Rw = AW \quad \text{or} \quad R = \frac{AW}{12w} \quad \text{or} \quad A = \frac{12Rw}{W} \tag{10.1}$$

where w is weight (pounds) and W is width (inches). The stiffening of the vehicle is given by

$$F(x) = 12Rw\left(1 + \frac{x}{a}\right) = AW + BWx. \tag{10.2}$$

Hence, differentiating:

$$\frac{dF}{dx} = \frac{12Rw}{a} = BW \quad \text{so} \quad R = \frac{aBW}{12w} \quad \text{or} \quad a = \frac{12Rw}{BW} \quad \text{or} \quad B = \frac{12Rw}{aW}. \tag{10.3}$$

Note also

$$a = \frac{A}{B} \tag{10.4}$$

For a one-zone full-width barrier impact, CRASH3 gives the energy as

$$E = W\left[Ax + \frac{B}{2}x^2 + \frac{A^2}{2B}\right] = W\left[\frac{B}{2}x^2 + Ax + G\right] \text{ where } G = A^2/(2B). \tag{10.5}$$

But this equals the input energy

$$E = \frac{w}{2g}v_{impact}^2. \tag{10.6}$$

Thus equating Equations 10.5 and 10.6 we obtain

$$v_{impact}^2 = \frac{gW}{w}\left[Bx^2 + 2Ax + 2G\right]. \tag{10.7}$$

Now substitute into 10.7 using 10.1 and 10.3 to get

$$v_{impact}^2 = 12Rg\left[\frac{x^2}{a} + 2x + a\right]. \tag{10.8}$$

Note that Equation 10.8 is identical to the standard CRASH3 model. We have merely rewritten it in terms of the parameters R and a.

Compare Equation 10.5 with our previously defined version for energy given by Equation 8.2 and compare 10.8 versus 8.3. In particular, we repeat Equation 8.3 to give

$$v_{impact}^2 = 12Rg\left(\frac{x^2}{a} + 2x + \frac{v_L^2}{12Rg}\right) - v_L^2\left(\frac{x}{a}\right). \tag{10.9}$$

Note carefully how both Equations 10.8 and 10.9 have the same basic form. The fundamental difference lies in the low-speed condition where $x \to 0.0$ (no crush). For the CRASH3 model, Equation 10.8, this gives

$$v_{impact}^2 = v_L^2 = 12Rga. \tag{10.10}$$

Thus the apparent bumper limit speed depends on the product Ra (compare with Equation 6.13: the quantity $a = A/B$, and is simply the equivalent bumper stroke). Conversely, for Equation 10.9 when the crush becomes zero

$$v_{impact}^2 = v_L^2 = v_L^2. \tag{10.11}$$

For our model the limiting impact speed simply becomes the defined bumper speed, and is independent of either *R* or *a*. This difference is because our model employs three parameters (*R*, *a* and v_L), whereas CRASH3 only employs two parameters (*A* and *B*).

The immediate consequence of the two-parameter fit for CRASH3 is that the parameters *A* and *B* (hence *R* and *a*) become locked to the assumed value of the bumper speed capability. This, of course, makes no sense. Why not? Because *A* and *B* are supposed to be descriptors of the vehicle's body and frame, not the bumper! [See the original definition of CRASH3]. If this statement is not immediately obvious consider the following. A car manufacturer can put any desired bumper on a given vehicle provided it satisfies the government regulations. Thus, having designed and built the car itself, the maker can independently choose whether to use a 2.5-mph bumper or a 5-mph one, or even a higher-speed one. The point being made is that the bumper is independent of the car proper. In reality the maker is mostly unlikely to employ a high-speed bumper (i.e., a lot better than 5 mph) simply because such a bumper costs more, weighs more, sticks out more (ugly) and is not required by law.

To show how *R* and *a* vary with the assumed bumper speed we will choose the well-known Ford Escort (1991–1995 version). This vehicle has w = 2,250 pounds, W = 66 inches, v_L = 5 mph = 7.335 ft/s. It also has an isolator stroke capacity of 57 millimeters = 2.24 inches. Using Equation 6.13 we derive $R = 0.746$.

Table 10.1
Parameter Search: CRASH3 Model

R —	***a*** feet	***A*** lb/inch	***B*** lb/inch²	**Bumper limit mph**
0.2	0.091	81.8	74.9	1.81
0.25	0.117	102.3	72.8	2.29
0.3	0.145	123	70.5	2.79
0.4	0.206	164	66.2	3.85
0.5	0.278	205	61.3	4.99
0.6	0.364	245	56.2	6.26
0.7	0.470	286	50.8	7.69
0.75	0.534	307	47.9	8.48
0.8	0.609	327	44.8	9.35
0.9	0.813	368	37.7	11.46
1.0	1.246	409	27.4	14.96

From Equation 10.1 this implies A = 305.2 lb/inch (width), and incipient crush force is F = 20,140 pounds, giving a peak acceleration at incipient crush of 8.95 g's.

To identify the A and B (or R and a), we need (at least) two data points. The upper point is frequently the observed NCAP crush condition. For this Escort, v_{impact} = 35 mph = 51.35 ft/s, and a crush of about 20 inches (1.67 feet). We now select a value for R and solve for the value a. We repeat this for a series of R values. Table 10.1 shows the results. Simultaneously, we may use Equation 10.10 to calculate the implied bumper limit. We first use the CRASH3 Equation 10.8.

We see that as R (thus A) increases so a also increases, B decreases, and the implied bumper limit also increases. To match with a 2.5-mph bumper we have (approximately) R = 0.275 and A = 112.6 lb/in, and a = 0.131 foot (1.57 inches) and B = 71.7 lb/in^2. To match a 5-mph bumper we have R = 0.5 (A = 205 lb/in) and a = 0.278 foot (3.34 inches) (B = 61.3 lb/in^2).

This habit of the A and B (hence R and a) parameters changing with the assumed low-speed bumper behavior has been quoted before. In particular, Malmsbury (ref 32) gives a plot (his figure 14) showing these variations as a function of the impact speed. The mere fact that they change at all indicates something is wrong with the model. To be consistent with most measurements of others it is necessary to adopt values of about A = 302 lb/in and B = 47 lb/in^2, as given by the standard CRASH3 Category 1 data (ref 21). However, inspection of our table then gives a bumper limit of about 8.5 mph. Conversely, fits by Neptune Engineering (ref 41) which assume a roughly 5-mph limit are A = 183 lb/in and B = 60 lb/in^2. These options are also seen in our table.

However, there are other problems. For example, if we try to relate the 2.5-mph case to the expected bumper-stroking, we find that the implied isolator stroke is about 38.6 millimeters (using Equation 6.14 and R = 0.275) while the actual measurement is 57 millimeters. Also, the implied maximum acceleration at incipient crushing is only about 3.3 g's. Conversely, if we fit to the 5-mph case, the implied isolator stroke is about 84.9 millimeters (versus 57 millimeters)(R = 0.5) and the implied peak acceleration is about 6.0 g's. Clearly, these fits are not consistent.

However, if instead we solve using our Equation 10.9 we get the following values for a 5-mph bumper limit given in Table 10.2.

If we assume a 2.5-mph bumper, we obtain Table 10.3.

By comparing Tables 10.2 and 10.3 we observe an important point: namely a very small dependence of the parameters on the assumed bumper limit. For example, consider the * data for R = 0.75. We see that for a 5-mph bumper a = 0.445 foot, whereas, for a 2.5-mph bumper a = 0.475 foot (a change of only 7 percent). Likewise, for the fixed value A = 307 lb/in, the value of B changes from

Table 10.2
Parameter Search: POD Model 5-mph Bumper

R —	***a*** feet	***A*** lb/in	***B*** lb/in²	**Bumper limit mph**
0.2	0.054	81.8	126.3	5.0
0.25	0.079	102.3	107.9	5.0
0.3	0.106	123	96.5	5.0
0.4	0.165	164	82.6	5.0
0.5	0.232	205	73.4	5.0
0.6	0.308	245	66.4	5.0
0.7	0.396	286	60.3	5.0
0.75*	0.445*	307*	57.5*	5.0*
0.8	0.498	327	54.8	5.0
0.9	0.619	368	49.6	5.0
1.0	0.764	409	44.6	5.0

Table 10.3
Parameter Search: POD Model 2.5-mph Bumper

R —	***a*** feet	***A*** lb/in	***B*** lb/in²	**Bumper limit mph**
0.2	0.082	81.8	83.1	2.5
0.25	0.107	102.3	79.7	2.5
0.3	0.135	123	75.8	2.5
0.4	0.194	164	70.3	2.5
0.5	0.261	205	65.4	2.5
0.6	0.338	245	60.5	2.5
0.7	0.426	286	56.0	2.5
0.75*	0.475*	307*	53.8*	2.5*
0.8	0.528	327	51.7	2.5
0.9	0.648	368	47.3	2.5
1.0	0.792	409	43.0	2.5

57.5 lb/in^2 to 53.8 lb/in^2 (again a change of only 7 percent). This insensitivity to bumper limits is what should happen, since A and B (or R and a) are supposed to describe the vehicle frame crush response rather than the bumper. CRASH3 only invokes a bumper response when the erroneous assumption built-in to the G-term is used.

We may also ask how the predicted NCAP crush varies with fitted parameters. To answer this, we use the paired values of R and a from Table 10.2, (5 mph) and re-solve for the NCAP crush for bumper speeds of 2.5 mph and zero (no bumper).

We note that the predicted values of the NCAP 35-mph crush vary only slightly as a function of the assumed bumper speed (even for no bumper!). In particular, for the * values we see that what was a fit to an NCAP crush of 20 inches with a 5-mph bumper now becomes a prediction of 19.5 inches for a bumper limit of 2.5 mph and 19.4 inches for no bumper at all. Thus, we have an error of only 0.6 inch for a bumper limit changing from 5 mph to zero. However, as pointed out by Varat (ref 42), this is usually within the accuracy with which different organizations actually measure crush, where differences of up to 2.3 inches have been noted. We also note that the smallest deviations in predicted crush occur for the larger values of R and a (large A and small B). This again best fits the observed peak accelerations when incipient crushing occurs, and also best fits the isolator-stroking with a 5-mph bumper limit.

We believe that the above considerations illustrate the advantage of the POD model, since the latter gives far less sensitivity to assumptions of bumper behavior. To help confirm this we now show, in Table 10.5, the predicted barrier speed-versus-permanent crush for the CRASH3 model versus the POD model.

Table 10.4
Predicted NCAP Crush Values, POD Model

R —	*a* ft	*A* lb/in	*B* lb/in^2	Crush inches	Bumper limit mph
0.3	0.145	123	70.5	18.1	2.5
0.5	0.232	205	73.5	19.1	2.5
0.75*	0.445*	307*	57.5*	19.5*	2.5*
1.0	0.764	409	44.6	19.8	2.5
0.3	0.145	123	70.5	17.4	0.0
0.5	0.232	205	73.5	18.8	0.0
0.75*	0.445*	307*	57.5*	19.4*	0.0*
1.0	0.764	409	44.6	19.7	0.0

Note how the largest differences occur for the small levels of crush. Beyond about 6.0 inches of crush the various speeds agree within about 1.5 mph, which itself is equivalent to about a 1.0-inch change in measured crush. Of course, the speeds only differ by 2.5 mph even at zero crush.

Figure 10.1 shows the results of Table 10.5. We see that the two CRASH3 plots are essentially straight lines and converge slowly to the common case at the NCAP point. However, the two POD plots rapidly converge to a common line after only a small degree of crush. Thereafter, the POD answers are independent of assumed bumper behavior, and very similar to the 5-mph CRASH3 line.

However, note how the two CRASH3 plots cross over as they pass through the NCAP point. This immediately demonstrates the *illogical* nature of CRASH3, since it means that the vehicle with the better bumper is now giving the larger overall crush. For collision speeds less than the NCAP one, CRASH3 is logical (but numerically wrong) in that it predicts less permanent crush for the better bumper, but for higher speeds it inverts the prediction! The POD model does not suffer from this illogical behavior.

Table 10.5
Crush versus Speed Model Comparisons

Crush inches	CRASH3				POD Model			
	R=0.275 A=112.6 a=0.131 B=71.7 v_L=2.5 mph		R=0.5 A=205 a=0.278 B=61.3 v_L=5.0 mph		R=0.75 A=307 a=0.475 B=53.8 v_L=2.5 mph		R=0.75 A=307 lb/in a=0.445 feet B=57.5 lb/in² v_L=5.0 mph	
	Speed mph	Accel *g's*	Speed mph	Accel *g's*	Speed mph	Accel *g's*	Speed mph	Accel *g's*
0.0	2.5	3.3	5.0	6.0	2.5	9.0	5.0	9.0
1.0	4.16	5.39	6.49	7.8	5.43	10.6	6.69	10.7
2.0	5.79	7.51	8.00	9.6	7.55	12.2	8.31	12.4
3.0	7.40	9.6	9.49	11.4	9.38	13.7	9.86	14.1
4.0	9.01	11.7	10.98	13.2	11.09	15.3	11.38	15.7
5.0	10.64	13.8	12.49	15.0	12.74	16.9	12.90	17.4
6.0	12.25	15.9	13.98	16.8	14.33	18.5	14.40	19.1
10.0	18.72	24.3	19.97	24.0	20.41	24.8	20.31	25.8
15.0	26.81	34.8	27.46	33.0	27.74	32.7	27.65	34.3
20.0	34.91	45.3	34.95	42.0	34.94	40.6	34.95	42.7
24.0	41.37	53.7	40.94	49.2	40.65	46.9	40.76	49.4

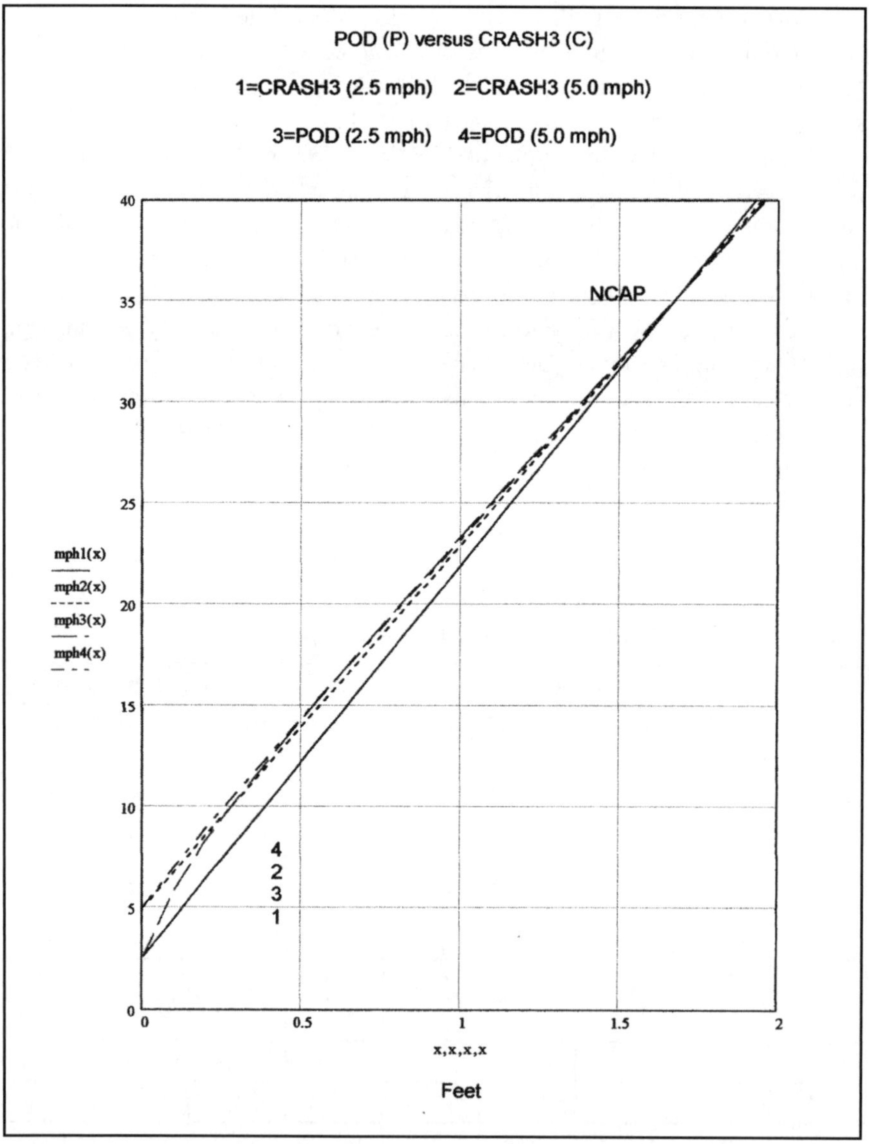

Figure 10.1 *POD versus CRASH3*

10.2 Updates for CRASH3 and SLAM

The originator of CRASH3 and SLAM (McHenry) has recently suggested updates for these models in order to allow incorporation of restitution effects (ref 43). To do this, additional parameters are invoked which relate the recovery phase of a vehicle crush to the maximum compressive loading. The presently suggested modifications do not give self-consistent answers, however. This problem is correctly discussed by Neptune (ref 43), who gives a critique of the McHenry paper (immediately following the latter).

There are several fundamental problems with the McHenry approach. First, his new suggested model requires at least four parameters in order to function mathematically. However, this implies a requirement for a large experimental database, because few of the existing crash tests provide the necessary information. This means that Occam's Razor is being ignored. Second, the modifications are being added as if the CRASH3 and SLAM models described the actual compression-release paths for vehicular material crush behavior; they do not.

10.3 Occam's Razor

Occam's (or Ockham's) Razor is named after William of Ockham (1285–1349) who is credited with first suggesting it. Occam's Razor is very simple: *If there are two ways of explaining a situation, always start with the simpler explanation and adopt complexity only if it proves necessary.* This suggestion has been standard procedure for scientists, philosophers and engineers for centuries. So what's the point being made?

Consider that CRASH3 really has only two parameters, A and B, with the G term already defined by these two parameters (so it is not an independent third parameter). With only two parameters this is Occam's Razor in action. To improve the model (make it more realistic) we should add as few extra parameters as possible. This is precisely what POD has done in its existing update, as described before. For our model we use three parameters, namely R, a and v_L, where R and a are the equivalents to A and B. The extra parameter is the bumper-limit speed which is v_L. Using these three parameters the new model can logically account for both low-speed bumper response and incipient vehicle crush, and provide a mechanism for restitution. Further, the extra parameter is already being studied and defined as part of the low-speed bumper crash tests, so no additional tests are required.

10.4 Paths and Loci

Whenever a material or structure changes its state (i.e., changes its stress, density/volume or temperature), it is common practice to plot the variations to illustrate the paths for these changes. Examples include a plot of pressure versus volume for a gas. If the compression or expansion is done at constant temperature, these plots are called isotherms. If done without allowing energy to enter or leave the system the plots are called *adiabats* (or *isentropes*). Rapidly compressing a gas such that energy cannot escape (by thermal conduction) causes the gas to heat adiabatically. Rapid expansion causes a cooling. This explains the heating of hand pumps and is the basis for refrigerators. (First compress a gas, making it hot. Then allow the heat to dissipate via a radiator mounted outside the fridge, while keeping the gas compressed, so the gas returns to ambient temperature. Then allow the gas to pass inside the fridge via pipes. Let the gas now rapidly expand. The consequential cooling will drain the heat out of the inside of the fridge as the gas once more returns to ambient temperature. Recycle back to the pump outside the fridge and repeat.) Likewise, if a material or structure is compressed or relieved, the plot can show the path of elastic compression followed by plastic flow, followed by elastic release. Mechanical engineers regularly plot such elastoplastic loops for materials and structures. The important point is that such plots illustrate the local response. These are the actual paths of behavior.

However, it is also possible to plot what are known as end points. An example is a plot linking the maximum stress with the maximum densification, such as occurs in shock waves. In a shock the material locally changes state along a path known as the *Rayleigh line*. The slope of this line gives the shock wave's speed. If a higher-stress shock is induced a new Rayleigh line is obtained with a steeper slope which gives a higher shock speed (the higher the shock stress, the faster the shock wave's speed). Thus, different shocks give different Rayleigh lines. However, each shock produces an end point, namely the peak stress and peak densification produced. If these end points are plotted we have a locus, which is known as the material Hugoniot. This locus correctly describes the end points but it does not describe an actual path for the material response. See Figure 10.2.

A similar effect can occur for an elastoplastic response for a material or structure. For example, our previous Figure 3.4 describes the path for a vehicle undergoing compression and release, linking the local force with the local deformation. Such a plot shows the initial elastic path, the following plastic path and then the elastic recovery. Included is the distinction between the transient

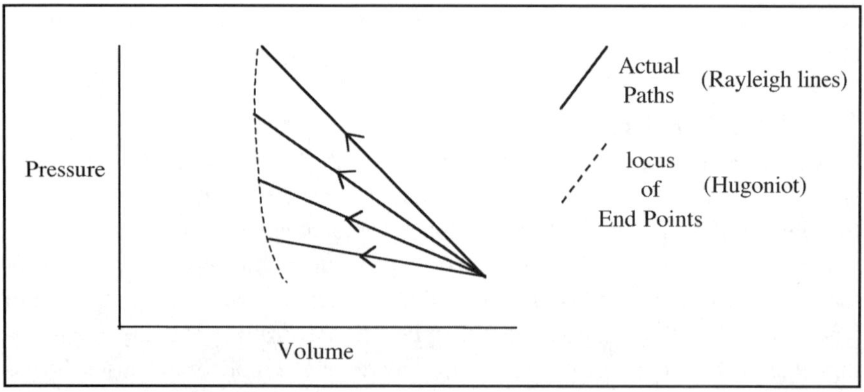

Figure 10.2 *Paths versus locus logic*

maximum deformation and the final permanent deformation. Suppose, however, we replot the data to link the peak load to the final deformation. The resulting plot becomes a locus rather than a path. Figure 10.3 shows these effects. It should be obvious that CRASH3 is really such a locus and not a path, since it links the compressive loads to the final deformation. All we have done is shift the crush plot data to the left. This immediately explains why the CRASH3 plot shows vertical portions such as that for zero load to incipient crush and peak load recovery to zero with final deformation. The very fact that the CRASH3 plot is a locus explains why this model has never been capable of explaining bumpers and restitution. The model has lost its value by first reducing the data to a locus instead of using a more realistic path.

It should also be obvious that by replotting the data as a locus we lose all information concerning the initial and final elastic slopes which exist in the path model. This missing information cannot be readily recovered, because an infinite number of possible elastic path slopes will give the same or similar locus. This is why the G-term in CRASH3 does not represent the bumper energy, and is merely a graphical extension of the load versus final deformation locus (and therefore represents precisely nothing).

Unfortunately, the suggested updates of McHenry are attempts to add to a locus model rather than to a path model. The result is to produce an apparent path response which fails to describe a real elastoplastic behavior. We are unaware of any real elastoplastic material or structure which behaves the way indicated in the new suggested CRASH3 or SLAM models. Both of these models still assume a vertical load recovery, but now there is an added triangle for restitution. While similar paths can be observed for a system which involves friction and strong viscosity, they are not observed for normal elastoplastic behavior, which is what

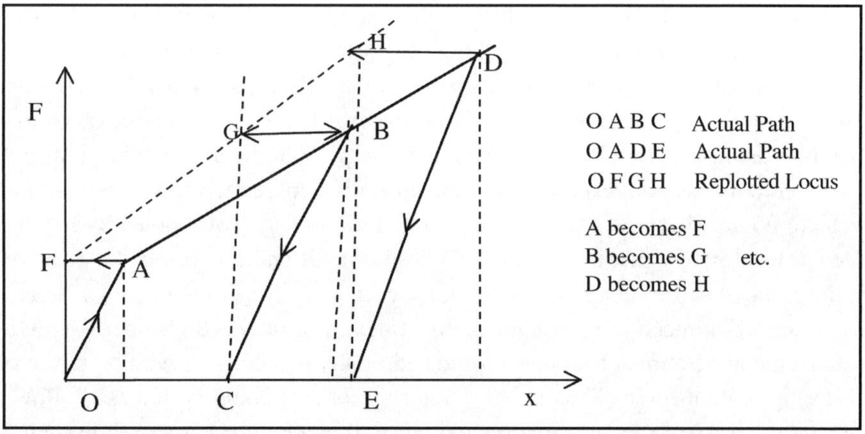

Figure 10.3 *Conversion of paths into a locus*

a vehicle crush is about (the only viscous portion being the bumper isolators). A vertical plot of load versus deformation implies an infinitely elastic rigid body (i.e., an infinite modulus), which no real vehicle is. Further, it implies zero restitution (like putty). Thus adding a slope to the release phase while still having a vertical plot is a contradiction. We both have and don't have restitution simultaneously (the point made by Neptune).

Perhaps the following simple model illustrates the problem. Consider a block of material on a horizontal surface with friction. Attach a spring to the block. Now push on the free end of the spring. As the spring compresses the force will increase, but the block does not move. Eventually, the force overcomes the friction and now the block moves at roughly constant force (and the spring will maintain constant compression). Now release the spring force back to zero. The spring will re-expand but the block does not move. If we plot the load versus the motion of the free end of the spring we obtain an elastic slope at the beginning and end of the cycle. However, if we plot the motion of the block we obtain vertical shifts at the beginning and end of the cycle. But only the spring compression and re-expansion represent deformation. The block motion represents rigid body motio*n* and is not deformation. When describing vehicle deformation we mean changes in the total length of the vehicle, we do not mean net shifts of the vehicle versus the ground.

The example above would be similar to a CRASH3 plot with $B = 0.0$. Plotting the local force versus local deformation would give the initial and final elastic slopes, as per the free end of our spring. Plotting the force versus final deformation would give the vertical initial and final slopes, as per the motion of our block. CRASH3 thus plots the block motion rather than the spring motion.

Sometimes we have seen the vertical-drop of force followed by the recovery described as if this were a real mechanism. Suppose I push on an elastoplastic cushion mounted on a rigid wall, and then suddenly withdraw my hand. The contact force (hand-to-cushion) will rapidly drop to zero with negligible cushion expansion, and the cushion will recover more slowly than my hand is moving. However, this is not an impact condition. Instead, I cause the withdrawal of my hand by using my muscles. Thus we have a retraction effect which has nothing to do with the cushion response. There is no equivalent retraction mechanism for vehicle bodies. Impacts can only cause separation of the two bodies by having a common force which pushes the two bodies apart and this implies a positive finite slope of force versus deformation for each body. To simulate the CRASH3 logic we would need the mechanical equivalent to a ratchet and timer. Using a ratchet the maximum deformation could be initially locked. This would give zero restoring mutual force. Then using a timer the ratchet could be released allowing the recovery of the deformation and generating a mutual force. While such a contrivance could be made this is hardly a valid description of a typical vehicle structure.

Also forgotten when using accelerometers in vehicles is the fact that the effective position of the accelerometer changes with any deformation (whether elastic, plastic or a combination thereof). Thus, an accelerometer which is initially positioned at the vehicle center-of-mass (CM) is no longer at the CM as soon as deformation occurs. This can immediately give odd responses, such as the value of acceleration oscillating and even locally dropping to zero. We have seen suggestions that this represents the true behavior of the vehicle's CM, and therefore implies the crush strength of the vehicle somehow suddenly became zero before increasing again. That is wrong; it merely indicates the response of the accelerometer at its new position (and includes structural vibrations) and does not describe the actual CM behavior.

If the shifting position is not obvious, consider the following. Start with a uniform structure 100 inches long and put the accelerometer at 50 inches from the back. Now crush the first 50 inches into only 30 inches (new total length is 80 inches). There is no change in the total mass (or weight), but the CM has moved from 50 inches ahead of the back of the structure to a position only 45 inches from the back. Thus, the accelerometer is no longer at the position of the new CM, and has moved forward by 5 inches, relatively. This result is easily proven by taking moments about the back of the structure. Dividing the structure into two halves, we initially have $M/2$ at 25 inches and $M/2$ at 75 inches from the back (two half-masses and corresponding positions of their individual CMs). Thus

$$ML = (M/2)(25 + 75) = (M/2)100.$$

Hence, $L = 50$ inches is the initial CM position from the back.

But in the deformed state, we have the rear half-mass still at 25 inches from the back, while the front half-mass is now at $(50 + 30/2) = 65$ inches from the back. Thus,

$$ML = (M/2)(25 + 65) = (M/2)90.$$

Hence, $L = 45$ inches is the new CM position from the back.

A little thought should make it obvious that the CM position only remains the CM's position for the case of a uniformly deformed body. Thus if our structure is uniformly crushed to a new length of 50 inches the new position of the CM will be 25 inches from the back. Although the CM moved relative to the outside world (this is in the Eulerian reference frame) it did not move relative to the mass of the structure (this is in the Lagrangian reference frame) because it still has half the mass to either side with a new uniform deformation. For the latter case the acceleration measured for an accelerometer initially positioned at the CM is the actual CM response. However, when dealing with stress waves (elastic or plastic) the structure is not uniformly deformed at any one instance. The latter is what happens during vehicular impacts.

Chapter 11

Proper Solutions to Various Problems

Synopsis

11.1 Solving the Equations

Several of the equations, such as 10.5, 10.7, 10.8 and 10.9, involve squared quantities, such as the crush depth. When solved as is, the calculation is simple. However, frequently we need to solve in reverse; we may know the absorbed energy and wish to find the corresponding crush depth. Ordinarily, we would need to rewrite the equation; this will yield quadratics. A simple way to handle such cases is to use any hand calculator or PC which has a program to solve equations. For example, this author regularly uses an HP48GX hand calculator. This has the capability of allowing the user to first write in the equation and then solve for any unknown in any order needed. The user simply enters all known values into their respective parameter fields and then puts the cursor onto the unknown parameter and hits solve. Thus, there is no need for the user to rewrite the equations, and such equations can be solved in any order desired provided there is only one unknown. Several of the previous tables were derived in only minutes by such means.

Indeed, use of such a hand calculator can even allow real-time calculations in a deposition or at trial, and allow for a quote of the full equation. If an opposing attorney starts asking what-if questions, the expert can rapidly produce the answers, and need not engage in hand waving or logic. This is very useful for demonstrating that exact vehicle weights are rarely important, and so on. This author has also discovered that doing a real-time calculation in front of the judge and jury has a very sobering effect. The jury rapidly decides who really knows his job (very important if the opposing expert "can't remember" the equation, or claims to need to "go home and re-check"—which he or she obviously cannot do while in court). A typical jury also gets tired of hearing "in my experience," or "I've done a thousand cases." Actually proving the point by a calculation tends to get their attention (and keeps them awake, which judges sometimes appreciate).

11.2 How Not to Solve a Problem

We have occasionally been depressed to find some experts blithely ignoring the laws of physics. It gets even worse when the same expert has correctly quoted the proper equation only a few pages back in his book! The following error has been quoted in a textbook by one expert, and has been used in an arbitration by another expert.

Problem: Let a moving bullet (1) strike a stationary target (2) both suffering a central-force impact (this is as simple as it gets). Let 1 have a 5-mph bumper, while 2 has a 3-mph one. The question is: What is the maximum speed of impact to just avoid damage to either vehicle? This, of course, is simply our lower critical speed.

Horror! The "answer" given was to add the two bumper energies (i.e., the sum of the two terms $wv_L^2/(2g)$) and to then equate this total energy with the incoming bullet to get the impact speed. Thus the solution given was

$$\frac{w_1}{2g}v_{hit}^2 = \frac{w_1}{2g}v_{L1}^2 + \frac{w_2}{2g}v_{L2}^2 \tag{11.1}$$

where w is weight and v_L is bumper speed.

So what is wrong? Two things. First, this solution does not take into account that the target has finite weight and so gains speed and energy. Thus, an energy term is missing. Second, this solution implicitly assumes that both bumpers bottom at the same time. This is only true if both vehicles have identical incipient crush strengths, which is rarely true except for the mirror-image collision. The explanation behind all two-body collisions is Newton's third law (without which all else fails). Hence the answer is flatly wrong. These experts seem to have forgotten not only the third law but also the conservation laws of both linear momentum and of energy, which have to apply simultaneously.

Another common error is the assumption that a given observed degree of damage (say to the back of a rear-ended car) can by itself allow for an estimate of the corresponding delta-v of that vehicle. That this is nonsense can be shown in two different ways, as follows.

First use the critical-speed logic and assume two cars of equal weight with equal strengths ($w_B = w_T$, and $R_B = R_T$). However, let the target have 2.5-mph bumpers while the bullet has 5.0-mph bumpers. Since the cars are equally strong they will both start to suffer incipient damage at the same time. However, the critical speed ay which this happens is about 7.91 mph. Thus, the common speed is about 3.95 mph. For a non-damaging collision the restitution is moderately high. Assume that $e = 0.5$. Then the delta-v of each car becomes ± 5.93 mph (+ for the target and – for the bullet).

However, if each car was independently driven into a rigid barrier we have maximum closing speeds of either 2.5 mph or 5.0 mph, and corresponding possible delta-v's of about 3.75 mph (target) and about 7.50 mph (bullet) (for the same assumed restitution, which is itself a false assumption). Thus the mutual collision yields one delta-v higher than for a barrier hit and one lower than for a barrier hit, but not equal to a barrier hit. If we merely looked at the rear of the target with the 2.5-mph bumper we would think the delta-v was about 3.75 mph, whereas in reality it is about 5.93 mph. This is an error of about 58 percent!

The second way to illustrate the problem is to use the well-known equation

$$\Delta v_T = \sqrt{\frac{2g\left(E_B + E_T\right)w_B\left(1+e\right)}{\left(w_B + w_T\right)w_T\left(1-e\right)}}. \tag{11.2}$$

Note that this equation requires knowledge of both E_B and E_T, and a value of the mutual coefficient of restitution for the car-to-car crash. The two values of E require knowledge of both car responses. Hence, it is impossible to determine the delta-v of the target merely by eyeballing the rear-end damage and trying to couple it with either a barrier hit or even a different vehicle-to-vehicle hit.

Despite this, there are some "soothsayer experts" out there who quite unabashedly claim to be able to do this! And even get quite adamant about it!

The equation above is a generic one that applies to all two-body, in-line impacts. Indeed, this equation is taught at the standard reconstruction schools, including Northwestern University Traffic Institute. The only difference is that the equation is usually applied for higher-speed crashes, so $e \rightarrow 0.0$ in these courses (which is reasonable for such cases). We find it "strange" that experts who have actually been certified by the Traffic Institute seem not to think that this equation also applies to low-speed crashes (but with finite e). No one would or should attempt to solve a high-speed crash by using data from only one vehicle, yet for low-speed crashes some experts seem to think the rules have changed. Sorry; physics is physics.

11.3 Experiments versus Theory: Balderdash, Dishonesty and Junk Science

Practically all higher-speed accidents are solved by using theory. This is not surprising because any attempt to replicate the accident entirely by experiment would be both very expensive and potentially dangerous. Theory includes energy losses through skidding and vehicle crush, and the use of the momentum laws for linear and rotational motions. The knowledge (database) which allows skid and crush effects to be used comes from many other tests performed over the years.

For low-speed accidents the skidmarks may be absent and the database for bumper behavior and crush response is more limited. Performing low-speed crashes is relatively safe. Consequently, there is a tendency to try to solve a specific collision by performing an experimental test. There is nothing wrong with this provided the correct test is performed. Unfortunately, we have seen many cases where this was not done, and where totally false conclusions were drawn.

Experiments have one enormous potential advantage: Provided they are done properly there is no need to understand why the vehicles responded the way they did. The response simply needs to be properly recorded. Thus, provided the experimenter is correctly trained in the use of the recording equipment (such as speed traps, optical decoders, high-speed video, accelerometers, load cells, etc.), there is no need for a thorough grounding in either physics or mechanical engineering. Analyzing it with theory, however, does require a good knowledge of these subjects.

What is the correct experiment? Answer: the one which properly reproduces all aspects of the accident to be solved, not just part of it. Thus, the experiment must reproduce the correct level of damage to both vehicles. This is the point made in the previous section. Since the latter is most unlikely to occur on the first test it is easy to see that, while safe, such tests are expensive. The test may need to be repeated many times before the correct answer is obtained, and the vehicles must either be replaced or repaired after each wrong test result if any damage occurs. This creates an enormous incentive to not do the job properly.

For a single experiment, the correct approach is to use two exemplar vehicles and to keep repeating the rear-end crash until all the damage seen in the subject accident is reproduced. However, it is also possible to use two separate experiments (such as two barrier tests) although we are now forced to relate these separate experiments to the subject crash through theory. The only experiment that avoids theory is the exemplar-into-exemplar test.

As another example of this problem consider the case of a small car (e.g., a Ford Mustang) rear-ending a pick-up (e.g., a Ford Ranger). Let there be a small amount of damage to the rear of the pick-up. Since cars are typically weaker than pick-ups, there will be more damage to the front of the car. Suppose we now try to experimentally test by performing barrier hits (whether stationary or moving). This could involve driving the Ranger backwards into a barrier and driving the Mustang forward into a barrier. Suppose, after repeated tries, we identify the two barrier speeds which correctly reproduce the damage on each vehicle, and we simultaneously measure the net delta-v for each such test (thus we determine the bounce, or coefficient of restitution). The barrier speeds are the EBS values, while each value of overall speed change is simply delta-$v = (1 + e)$EBS (with e positive).

Assume that for the Ranger the weight is 2,800 pounds and we reproduce the rear-end damage with a delta-v_R = 4 mph (5.868 ft/s) and a restitution of e_R = 0.2. This means the EBS_R = 4/(1.2) = 3.33 mph (4.89 ft/s). So we exceeded the typical 2.5-mph pick-up bumper limit thereby explaining the damage. The corresponding net absorbed energy is $E_R = (1 - e_R^2)(w_R/(2g))\text{EBS}_\text{R}^2$ = 998 ft-lbs.

Assume that for the Mustang the weight is 2,600 pounds and we reproduce the frontal damage with a delta-v_M = 8 mph (11.74 ft/s) and a restitution of e_M = 0.5. This means the EBS_M = 8/(1.5) = 5.33 mph (7.824 ft/s). So we also exceeded the typical car bumper limit of 5 mph explaining the damage. The corresponding absorbed energy is $E_M = (1 - e_M^2)(w_M/(2g))\text{EBS}_\text{M}^2$ = 1,853 ft-lbs.

We next need the *mutual* coefficient of restitution, e_{cc} (car-car). This is given by

$$e_{cc} = \sqrt{\frac{w_R e_M^2 + w_M e_R^2}{w_R + w_M}} \quad \text{and thus } e_{cc} = 0.386.$$

Now we use Equation 11.12 to obtain the delta-v_R. To do so we add the two absorbed energies and use the mutual restitution. This gives delta-v_R = 5.75 mph (8.44 ft/s). Likewise we obtain delta-v_M = –6.2 mph (9.1 ft/s).

Note carefully, these answers are not the same as the values observed for either barrier test. In fact, both of the individual barrier answers are wrong, even though both barrier tests correctly replicated the damage for each vehicle. This can be very confusing. The correct answers lie between the individual barrier values. In particular, the ratios of *true* delta-v's (for the actual two-vehicle crash) versus those observed in the individual barrier tests are (5.75 mph/4.00 mph) = 1.44 for the Ranger, and (6.2 mph/8.0 mph) = 0.77 for the Mustang. The only time this situation does not occur is when both vehicles are identical (including front versus rear). For this mirror image case the two independent barrier tests will give the same answers, which will also be the same answer as for the subject crash (i.e., the three sets of answers converge). However, this situation is a rarity.

These effects are summarized in Table 11.1 (Mustang into Ranger) and Table 11.2 (the mirror-image crash of a Mustang into a Mustang).

Table 11.1
Different Vehicles

		Barrier hits	Car-to-Pick-up Crash	
	Mustang	**Ranger**	**Mustang/ Ranger**	
delta-v	8.00 mph	4.00 mph	6.20 mph	5.75 mph
Restitution	0.5	0.2	0.386	0.386
EBS	5.33 mph	3.33 mph	8.62 mph	0.00 mph
Abs energy	1,853 ft-lbs	998 ft-lbs	2,851 ft-lbs total	
Closing speed	5.33 mph	3.33 mph each	8.62 mph mutual	
"Apparent" answers based on the individual barrier hits.				
delta-v	4.31 mph	4.00 mph	(if based on Ranger barrier hit)	
delta-v	8.00 mph	7.43 mph	(if based on Mustang barrier hit)	

Note how we get two different options, and neither represents the actual crash!

Table 11.2
Identical Vehicles

	Barrier hits		Car-to-Car Crash	
	Mustang	**Mustang**	**Mustang/Mustang**	
delta-v	8.00 mph	8.00 mph	8.00 mph	8.00 mph
Restitution	0.5	0.5	0.5	0.5
EBS	5.33 mph	5.33 mph	5.33 mph	5.33 mph
Abs energy	1,853 ft-lbs	1,853 ft-lbs	3,706 ft-lbs total	
Closing speed	5.33 mph	5.33 mph each	10.66 mph mutual	
"Apparent" answers based on the individual barrier hits.				
delta-v	8.00 mph	8.00 mph (if based on the first Mustang barrier hit)		
delta-v	8.00 mph	8.00 mph (if based on the other Mustang barrier hit)		

Note how we get only one option, and all answers are the same!

11.4 Component Testing versus Systems Testing

We have met so-called experts who believe that merely testing one of the vehicles will give the answer for a crash. They refer to this as "component" testing. This is fine and dandy, but apparently these experts have never been introduced to the world of "systems" testing. As any real expert knows, the response of the complete package (i.e., the system) can readily give different answers. This bugaboo is well known in the electronics world. Each individual component may work wonderfully by itself, but when all the components are put together the system responds differently. This results from mutual interactions, and should come as no great surprise to the educated reader. Indeed, we have already given an example of this when discussing bumper isolators. We pointed out that isolators require minimum forces to exceed preloads in order to start stroking, yet failure to stroke can involve a finite barrier speed. The explanation for this conundrum was that the barrier impact involved a system (bumper fascia, isolator and car frame) whereas studies of only the isolator was a component test.

Another example of muddled thinking occurs when the expert does only one rear-end experiment and also modifies the geometry. For instance, the expert takes an exemplar rear bumper from the Ranger and mounts it to a modified Ford F-250 frame. This gives an even worse problem, because part of the bumper response involves the coupling to the vehicle's frame. Real frames do flex and twist at low speed (just watch a pick-up "twang" when rear-ended), even if there is no permanent effect, and this partially accounts for the overall energy absorbed or stored. Since an F-250 has a much stronger and wider frame than a Ranger, we can not expect the same behavior.

Consider what happens when our "expert" claims to solve the crash by testing only the rear end of the Ranger, as in the case above. Lo and behold, he determines that the damage corresponds to a delta-v of 4.0 mph. Now our expert computes backward to establish both the closing speed and the delta-v of the other vehicle. To do this he uses

$$v_{close} = \left(\frac{w_R + w_M}{w_M}\right)\left(\frac{\Delta v_R}{1+e_R}\right) \quad \text{and} \quad \Delta v_M = \frac{w_R \Delta v_R}{w_M}. \tag{11.3}$$

Of course, this means we are ignoring the behavior of the front of the Mustang, and we are using the restitution of the Ranger's barrier hit rather than the mutual value for vehicle-to-vehicle. Thus the answers derived are just plain *wrong*. There are no ifs, buts or maybes about this subject! Why did this "expert" not do the frontal barrier test on the Mustang? Would he even know what to do with the data if he did? (After all, he would get two different answers).

Why is this so important? The answer is that in order to establish the possibility of any whiplash injury we must first establish the correct speed changes, especially for the target which is rear-ended (since this occupant is usually injured more easily than the bullet occupant). We see that both the process of eyeballing the rear-end damage and even doing a rear-end component test will invariably give the wrong answer. Worse, whenever the "expert" divines the delta-v for the target in this manner, he is starting the entire analysis with the required final answer. This simply means that all other calculations (such as v_{close} and the bullet delta-v) are not only wrong, but totally redundant.

We are forced to a distasteful conclusion. Either the expert does not know how to properly do testing and analysis, or he is deliberately ignoring parts of the problem. He is, therefore, either not an expert, or he is dishonest. This is to be distinguished from simple mathematical errors or the need to estimate various parameters which may be poorly defined. We are discussing scientific method, not numerical screw-ups.

Unfortunately, these examples also illustrate the issue of junk science. The courts are supposed to prevent this by virtue of either the *Frye* or *Daubert* rulings. This is clearly not working very well.

11.5 Angular Momentum (AM)

Many accident reconstruction courses regularly teach the conservation laws of energy (E) and linear momentum (LM). Few seem to teach the rules for angular momentum (AM).

At first sight AM can appear confusing. For example, in common with E and LM, AM must also be conserved during any two-body impact. There are examples that do not intuitively seem to do so. Perhaps the most obvious is the example given before, the side impact of a stationary target on its front by a bullet, such that the bullet experiences a central-force hit with no induced rotation. The bullet simply continues moving along its original straight path but with reduced speed. However, the target experiences a non-central hit. The target CM develops motion parallel to that of the bullet (but at low speed), while the target also develops spin. At first sight we appear to have invented AM out of thin air, since there was no obvious rotation before impact, yet we have rotation after impact. How are we conserving AM?

To understand this, we note that AM is merely the product of a linear momentum and the perpendicular offset to an arbitrary axis. Thus, for a mass m moving at velocity v, the AM is simply mvr, where r is the offset between a chosen axis point and perpendicular to the velocity. Since v is a vector (having both magnitude and direction) and r is a vector, then AM is also a vector. Specifically, the AM is a vector given by the cross-product, and actually defines a vector which points along the chosen axis. For a vehicle moving in the plane of a horizontal road, this axis is perpendicular to the road surface. Because the vector can point up or down, we need a sign convention to systematically handle the situation.

The concept of an arbitrary choice for the axis together with the need for a sign convention is not new. A little thought will reveal that the same arguments apply to both the conservation of energy and linear momentum (although this fact may sometimes get lost in the expert's mind). Consider the conversion of potential energy (PE) to kinetic energy (KE), as when a car rolls down a hill. The conservation law merely requires that the change in the PE be equal (and opposite) to the change in the KE. It matters not one bit how one defines the zero of energy.

Likewise, for linear momentum, it is the changes which must balance. For example, is a stopped car on a road really stopped? Only with respect to the road. As was previously pointed out, because of Earth's rotation about its north-south axis, the actual speed could be about 900 mph at a latitude of about 35 degrees. But, Earth also moves in its orbit around the Sun at about 18.5 miles per second! And the solar system moves within the galaxy, and the galaxy moves within the universe ("and bigger fleas have little fleas, and so on, *ad infinitum*" as the saying goes). In short, there is no true zero, or constant (except for the apparent constant, the speed of light). This is the whole point of Einstein's theory of relativity; everything is relative. Even poor Einstein gets misquoted. Consider the well-known equation $E = mc^2$. This relates the effective mass to the contained mass-energy through the speed of light (c). However, the equation should be $\Delta E = \Delta mc^2$, since it applies to changes in apparent mass and energy.

If we choose our axis to be such that a velocity vector passes through the axis, then AM = 0.0 relative to that axis. To determine our sign, we can merely consider the instantaneous motion to be above or below the axis (i.e., as when drawing the situation on a sheet of paper, with the axis being a point on the paper since it is directed either into or out of the paper). Thus, if a vehicle motion is above our chosen axis it will look as if the instantaneous motion is part of an arc with clockwise motion. For motion below the axis, the rotation is counterclockwise. We arbitrarily define clockwise as positive, and vice versa. Again, it does not matter how we define it, so long as we remain consistent throughout the analysis. This is no different from defining right-going as positive for LM solutions. See Figure 11.1.

Rotation or revolution? If a body spins about its own CM, we usually refer to this as a rotation. If the body moves about a displaced axis (away from the body) we call it revolution. It does not matter; both involve AM.

Back to our example, as discussed in Section 4.13.

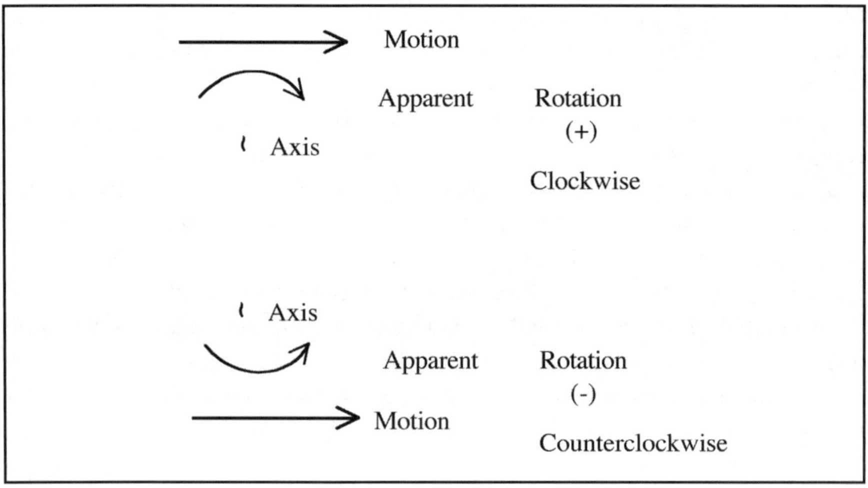

Figure 11.1 *Sign convention for induced motion*

If we define the impact speed of the bullet (B) as v_0, the frontal-nose impact gives the following for the common-speed (ignore rebound) at the point of contact

$$v_{hit} = \frac{w_B v_0}{\left(w_b + \dfrac{w_T}{\gamma} \right)} \tag{11.4}$$

where T refers to target. The quantity γ is given by

$$\gamma = 1 + \left(\frac{r}{k} \right)^2 \tag{11.5}$$

where r is the offset torque-arm for the impact on the target, and k is the radius of gyration of the target, both about its own CM. This effect of modifying the weight was discussed previously.

The induced speed for the target CM is given by

$$v_{CM,T} = \frac{v_{hit}}{\gamma} \tag{11.6}$$

while the induced rotation rate (spin) is given by

$$\omega = \frac{\left(v_{hit} - v_{CM,T} \right)}{r}. \tag{11.7}$$

Last, we note that the moment of inertia for the target is given by

$$I = \left(\frac{w_T}{g} \right) k^2 \tag{11.8}$$

We are now ready to solve the problem in terms of angular momentum. We will do so by using three different options.

A. Option A

To simplify the math we will assume the target is a simple uniform rectangular prism, and that $\gamma = 1 + (L/2)^2/(L^2/12) = 1 + 3 = 4$, since $r = L/2$ and $k^2 = L^2/12$.

Choose the reference axis as the mid-longitudinal axis point at the nose of the target. This will lie on the CM's motion of the bullet. Because the bullet moves along a straight path through this axis both before and after impact, the bullet has zero AM. Hence the input AM = 0.0.

The impact causes the target CM to move parallel to the bullet path, but below it by the distance $r = L/2$, where L is the length of our target (assumed a regular prism for this example). This introduces a negative AM given by

$$-AM_{CM} = \left(\frac{w_T}{g}\right) v_{CM} \left(\frac{L}{2}\right) = \left(\frac{w_T}{g}\right)\left[\frac{v_{hit}}{\gamma}\right]\left(\frac{L}{2}\right) = \left(\frac{w_T}{g}\right)\left[\frac{w_B v_0}{w_T + \left(\dfrac{w_T}{\gamma}\right)}\right]\left(\frac{L}{2}\right)\left(\frac{1}{\gamma}\right). \tag{11.9}$$

However, the spin of the target about its CM is clockwise (hence positive) and has an AM of

$$AM = I\omega = \left(\frac{w_T}{g}\right) k^2 \omega = \left(\frac{w_T}{g}\right)\left(\frac{L^2}{12}\right)\left[\frac{2(v_{hit} - v_{CM})}{L}\right]. \tag{11.10}$$

Substituting for v_{hit} and v_{CM} to relate to v_0 through the term, we find that the total AM is simply zero (i.e., add 11.9 and 11.10).

Thus, the CM's motion gives

$$AM_{CM} = -\left(\frac{w_T}{g}\right) v_{hit} \left(\frac{L}{8}\right) \tag{11.11}$$

while the spin's motion gives

$$AM_{spin} = +\left(\frac{w_T}{g}\right) v_{hit} \left(\frac{L}{8}\right). \tag{11.12}$$

Thus, input = output, and angular momentum is conserved.

B. Option B

For this case we choose the axis to be at the initial position of the CM of the target. Hence the bullet has $r = L/2$ for its motion. Before impact the bullet has a positive AM. This merely decreases after impact. The target undergoes two motions. The CM motion passes through our new axis; hence, it contributes zero to the AM. However, the spin of the target also contributes a positive AM. Before impact the total AM is simply

$$AM_{input} = \left(\frac{w_B}{g}\right) v_0 \left(\frac{L}{2}\right). \tag{11.13}$$

After impact the bullet has an AM given by

$$AM_{out} = \left(\frac{w_B}{g}\right) v_{hit} \left(\frac{L}{2}\right). \tag{11.14}$$

The target has only the spin with an AM given by

$$AM_{spin} = I\omega = \left(\frac{w_T}{g}\right)\left(\frac{L}{8}\right)\left[\frac{w_B v_0}{w_b + \left(\frac{w_T}{4}\right)}\right]. \tag{11.15}$$

Substituting, the total AM after impact is Equation 11.14 + 11.15

$$AM_{out_{total}} = \left(\frac{w_B}{g}\right) v_0 \left(\frac{L}{2}\right). \tag{11.16}$$

Once again, input = output, and angular momentum is conserved.

C. Option C

For this case, we choose the axis to be at the initial position of the far end of the target's longitudinal axis. Thus for the bullet $r = L$. For the target, the CM has $r = L/2$. The before- and after-impact values for the bullet's AM are positive. Likewise, the target's CM motion involves a positive value of AM. Lastly, the target's spin is also a positive value.

The pre-impact AM for the bullet is given by

$$AM_{input} = \left(\frac{w_B}{g}\right) v_0 L \tag{11.17}$$

while the post-impact AM is given by

$$AM_{input} = \left(\frac{w_B}{g}\right) v_{hit} L + I\omega + \left(\frac{w_T}{g}\right) v_{CM} \left(\frac{L}{2}\right) \tag{11.18}$$

which is the bullet's AM, the target's spin about its own axis and the target's AM for its CM motion.

By substitution and inspection, we again find that input = output, and angular momentum is conserved.

The important point about these three options is as follows: Although each option had different values for the absolute angular momentum, in all three cases the angular momentum was conserved. Absolute values are not important; conservation is.

11.6 Submarine Collision Logic

There are three basic types of rear-end, in-line collision. These are simple bumper-to-bumper, the partial underride (in which the bumpers first contact but then the bullet bumper moves down and under the target rear bumper, allowing the latter to cause damage to the grill, headlights and front of the hood for the bullet), and the "true submarine" hit.

For the latter, a rear-end crash involves a small vehicle driving completely under the rear of a larger one, as often happens with a small car and a higher pick-up. Such collisions rarely involve bumper-to-bumper impacts. Instead, it is common for the hood of the car to directly engage with the under-frame of the pick-up (or the bottom of the pick-up's rear bumper). This gives an impressive scrape on the car's hood which can easily be 3 feet long. However, such hood scraping usually involves a relatively low force, since hoods are not very strong. The low force induces low vehicle accelerations. Consequently, the effects of vehicle braking become unusually important.

Let the mutual force between the vehicles be F, while the differential motion (the hood scrape) is Δx. Let the bullet's weight be w_B, while the target's weight is w_T. Let the braking accelerations be a_B and a_T, both in units of g. We can now define the net accelerations of the bullet and target as

$$\text{bullet: } A_B = (-a_B - F/w_B)g \tag{11.19}$$

and

$$\text{target: } A_T = (F/w_T - a_T)g. \tag{11.20}$$

Such collisions rarely involve much bounce, because the hood scrape is primarily frictional. Thus the common speed is given by

$$v_{com} = v_B + A_B t = v_T + A_T t. \tag{11.21}$$

Thus

$$v_{close} = v_B - v_T = (A_T - A_B)t \text{ or } t = v_{close}/(A_T - A_B) \tag{11.22}$$

The corresponding distances moved by the bullet and target are

$$x_B = v_B t + (1/2)A_B t^2 \text{ and } x_T = v_T t + (1/2)A_T t^2 \quad (11.23)$$

Thus

$$\Delta x = (v_B - v_T)t + (A_B - A_T)t^2/2. \quad (11.24)$$

Substituting,

$$\Delta x = v_{close}{}^2/[2(A_T - A_B)] \quad (11.25)$$

or

$$v_{close}{}^2 = 2(A_T - A_B)\Delta x. \quad (11.26)$$

This last equation should be familiar (compare with the skid equation).

Substituting for the net accelerations we now get

$$v_{close}{}^2 = 2g\Delta x[F/w_T - a_T + a_B + F/w_B] \quad (11.27)$$

or

$$v_{close}{}^2 = 2gF\Delta x(w_B + w_T)/(w_B w_T) + 2g\Delta x(a_B - a_T). \quad (11.28)$$

However, $F\Delta x = E_D$ = absorbed damage energy (the "lost" energy).

Thus,

$$v_{close}{}^2 = 2gE_D(w_B + w_T)/(w_B w_T) + 2g\Delta x(a_B - a_T). \quad (11.29)$$

The first term in Equation 11.29 is the familiar energy solution for a collision. The second term is new, and accounts for the existing vehicle braking.

For a normal bumper-to-bumper impact the differential distance moved by the vehicles is small (bumper compressions at low speeds), thus Δx is small (typically inches). Likewise, the braking accelerations are normally small compared to the induced accelerations caused by the larger mutual force (F). With the submarine collision, however, these factors can change dramatically.

11.7 Special Cases

1. Let neither vehicle be braking. Then $a_B = a_T = 0.0$. In this case we get only the energy solution.

2. Let only the target be braking. This is typical of many real-life crashes, and includes some of the volunteer rear-ender experiments. Thus a_B = 0.0. In this case we get

$$v_{close}^2 = 2gE_D(w_B + w_T)/(w_Bw_T) - 2g\Delta xa_T. \quad (11.30)$$

Since a_T is a positive quantity in this equation (the appropriate sign being in the equation), this predicts a smaller closing speed than for energy alone.

3. Let only the bullet be braking. Thus $a_T = 0.0$. In this case we get

$$v_{close}^2 = 2gE_D(w_B + w_T)/(w_Bw_T) + 2g\Delta xa_B. \quad (11.31)$$

Since a_B is a positive quantity, this predicts a larger closing speed than for energy alone.

4. Let the braking accelerations be identical for both vehicles (equal magnitudes, even though the bullet is decelerating and the target is accelerating). The result is to again give only the energy solution.

Figure 11.2 illustrates these effects.

Suppose, however, the mutual contact force is very low such that F/w_T is less than a_T. This implies that an initially stationary target will not move, because the braking force is sufficiently large to defeat the mutual push (the target can not go backward). This is equivalent to setting the term $F/w_T - a_T = 0.0$. (However, this special case does not apply to a moving target, since for the latter case we are allowed a net deceleration for the target). Returning to Equation 11.27 we now have

$$v_{close}^2 = 2g\Delta x[F/w_B + a_B] = (2gE_D/w_B)[1 + (a_Bw_B/F)]. \quad (11.32)$$

We see that if $a_Bw_B/F \rightarrow 0.0$ (i.e., small braking and/or large mutual stopping force), then the above result is the same as for the bullet hitting a rigid barrier. Thus the target appears to have changed its weight to infinity. However, for finite bullet braking and/or low mutual force, the closing speed is larger than for a barrier impact, for the same degree of induced damage (E_D).

As an example of these effects consider the following. Let the bullet weigh 2,000 pounds and brake at –0.7 *g* (heavy braking). Let the target weigh 4,000 pounds and have braking at –0.2 *g* (foot lightly on the brake, as if pausing at a stop sign). Let the mutual force be 2,500 pounds and the hood scrape be $\Delta x = 3.0$ feet. Then E_D = 7,500 ft-lbs.

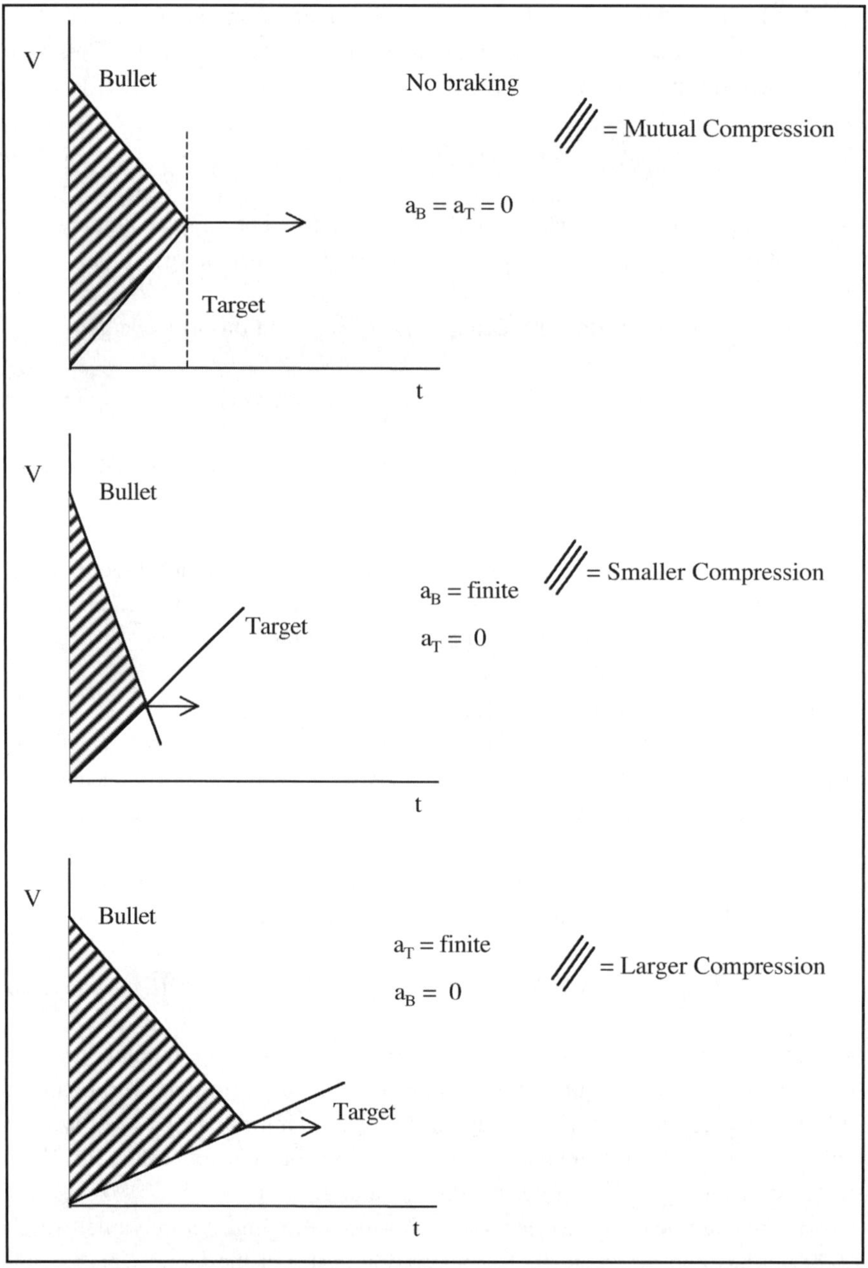

Figure 11.2 *Velocity versus time with braking options*

The net deceleration for the bullet is $A_B = -0.7\ g - (2{,}500/2{,}000)\ g = -1.95\ g$'s.
The net acceleration for the target is $A_T = (2{,}500/4{,}000)g - 0.2\ g = 0.425\ g$'s.
Hence $A_T - A_B = 2.375\ g$'s.

Then

$$v_{close}^{\ 2} = 2(A_T - A_B)\Delta x = 458.85\ (\text{ft/s})^2$$

or

$$v_{close} = 21.42\ \text{ft/s} = 14.6\ \text{mph}.$$

The time of contact (no bounce) is $t = v_{close}/(A_T - A_B) = 0.28$ second.

This is considerably longer than for the usual bumper-to-bumper impact, and explains why such submarine hits tend to be less violent.

For an initially stationary target, the induced speed increase (Δv) is given by

$$\text{delta-}v_T = A_T t = 3.833\ \text{ft/s} = 2.613\ \text{mph}$$

while the change for the bullet is given by

$$\text{delta-}v_B = -A_B t = -17.588\ \text{ft/s} = -11.989\ \text{mph}.$$

Note how the ratio of these speed changes is about 4.588, whereas, the expected ratio based on vehicle weights would be 2.000. This large difference results from the effect of the vehicles braking together with the relatively low mutual force due to contact.

Without any braking, the closing speed for the same E_D would be

$$v_{close} = 19.03\ \text{ft/s} = 12.97\ \text{mph}$$

and the common speed (no bounce) would be

$$v_{common} = \text{delta-}v_T = 6.343\ \text{ft/s} = 4.324\ \text{mph},$$

while

$$\text{delta-}v_B = -12\ 687\ \text{ft/s} = -8.648\ \text{mph}.$$

These latter speed changes are in a ratio of 2.0, as normally expected.

We see that for a given degree of damage (the energy for hood scraping), in this example, braking increases the initial closing speed but decreases the resulting delta-v for the target, while it increases the delta-v for the bullet.

The net result of such submarine hits is to reduce the potential for causing injury to the occupant of the rear-ended high vehicle. Indeed, in the event that the force is insufficient to actually produce any net motion for the rear-ended vehicle, the latter can only rock on its suspension. It may also be lifted slightly at the rear. Either way, the potential for injury of the rear-ended vehicle's occupant is then low. By "low" we mean compared to the bumper-to-bumper impact which involves the same amount of lost energy (E_D).

To confirm the latter, suppose we reconsider the above example but make it behave more like the standard bumper-to-bumper impact. To do this, we increase the mutual force by a factor of ten (hence F = 25,000 pounds) and reduce the differential motion by a factor of ten (hence x = 0.3 foot), thereby keeping E_D constant, at 7,500 ft-lbs. Now the net accelerations are

$$\text{bullet: } A_B = -0.7\ g - 12.5\ g\text{'s} = -13.2\ g\text{'s and}$$
$$\text{target: } A_T = -0.2\ g + 6.25\ g\text{'s} = 6.05\ g\text{'s.}$$

Thus $(A_T - A_B) = 19.25\ g$'s.

The closing speed is $v_{close}{}^2 = 371.9\ (\text{ft/s})^2$. Hence v_{close} = 19.285 ft/s = 13.146 mph. The time to reach the common speed is t = 0.031 second.

Then, delta-v_T = 6.06 ft/s = 4.13 mph, and delta-v_B = –13.18 ft/s = –8.98 mph.

The ratio of speed changes is now 2.175, much closer to the value 2.0 expected from the weights. We see that for the "high-F, low-delta-x" condition the results are rapidly approaching the energy only solution, and the effect of braking is much smaller.

The submarine collision also gives a good example of the problems encountered in experimental vehicle-to-vehicle tests where friction is significant, and helps highlight the issue of the three-body problem mentioned earlier. In this context, friction also includes unrecoverable energy losses due to induced vertical motions of the vehicles.

Consider Figures 11.3a, b and c. Figure 11.3a shows the speed-time relationship for no braking of either vehicle, from first contact to the common speed, assuming the target is initially stationary. (These figures are simplified, and we use straight lines for speed changes rather than the more realistic curved paths, but without loss of generality). The loop OABC is the distance moved by the bullet, while the triangular loop OBC is the distance moved by the target, both in order to achieve the common speed (at B). Thus the difference loop (triangle) OABO

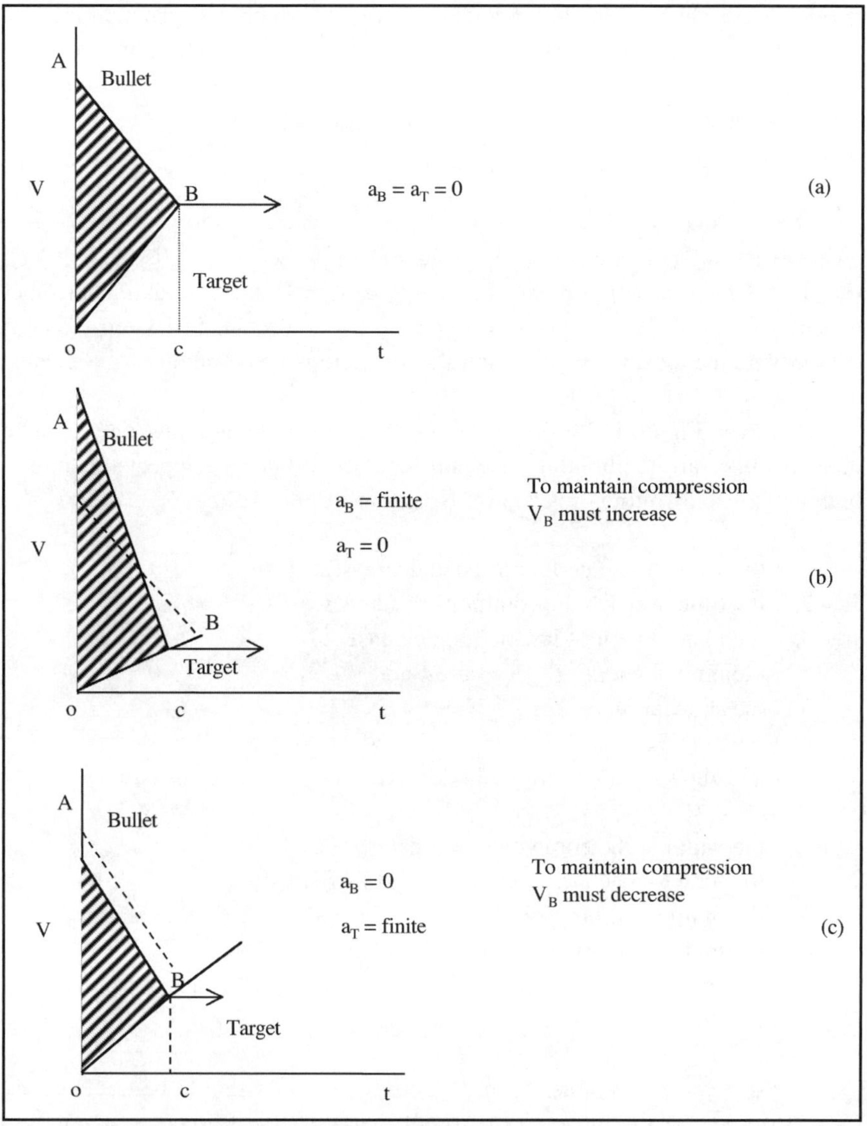

Figure 11.3 *Effects of braking for fixed total compression*

gives the overshoot of the bullet versus the target, which is the mutual interaction (compression of bumpers, maximum dynamic crush or both). This overshoot involves the mutual lost/stored energy E_M. In turn, this energy determines the degree of restitution. In general, the energetics give

$$\frac{w_B v_0^2}{2g} = \frac{(w_B + w_T) v_{Common}^2}{2g} + E_M + E_B \tag{11.33}$$

where B is bullet, T is target, v_0 is initial closing speed, v_{Common} is the common speed, and E_B is any non-recovered energy absorbed due to braking (or other forms of friction). For the no-braking (or no friction) case, E_B is zero. Thus, if we measure the closing and common speeds there is no ambiguity for the value of E_M.

However, Figure 11.3b shows the result for the bullet braking (only), where the solid lines are the braking case and the dashed lines are repeats of the no-braking case shown for convenience. Note that for this case

1. the value of the common speed decreases,
2. the time to reach the common speed decreases,
3. the mutual loop of interaction decreases,
4. the mutual energy E_M decreases, and
5. the shortfall in energy is given by E_B.

Figure 11.3c shows the result for a braking target (only). For this case

1. the value of the common speed decreases,
2. the time to reach the common speed increases,
3. the mutual loop increases,
4. the mutual energy E_M increases, *and*
5. the remaining energy E_B is finite, but usually less than for bullet-only braking.

The difference in points (5) in the above two cases should be obvious, because in order for the bullet to overshoot the target the former always moves farther than the latter, allowing for more dissipation of braking energy (at least for similar braking forces).

However, suppose our experimental test measures the closing speed and the common speed but does not also accurately measure the braking of both vehicles. Then we have more terms to solve than factors with which we can calculate. For this reason we do not get unique values of E_M or E_B. Since E_M determines restitution, *e*, we also do not get unique values for restitution. These effects help explain the observed spread in coefficients of restitution, and the corresponding spread in observed values of vehicle delta-v's, and even the observed spread in the corresponding degree of damage associated with these delta-v's.

For measured values of closing speed and common speed, the sum of E_M and E_B is fixed. But only E_M determines the true restitution. As illustrated above, the same combination of closing speed and common speed can involve different apportionments of E_M and E_B. The experimental measurement of low-speed collisions is actually more complicated than it appears, and unless every pertinent factor is recorded the results will involve the uncertainties and spreads in parameters described above.

11.8 The Influence of Restitution on Multicar Impacts

Suppose there is a line of stopped cars. This could be due to an incident farther ahead on a busy road. Each subsequent car pulls up a short distance behind the one in front. Upon stopping each driver relaxes the pressure on the brake. Now let another car crash into the rear vehicle. If the spacing between the stopped cars is small and each driver is applying only a low level of braking (merely holding the car in place), then it becomes possible for the initial rear-end crash to propagate a pulse down the line. Each vehicle in turn receives first a rear-end hit followed by a subsequent frontal impact until the front vehicle is reached. This behavior is a damped version of the Newton's cradle. The damping has two major sources. The first is the damping inherent in the bumper impacts and is the usual coefficient of restitution, e. The second results from energy losses as the cars fight tire friction and close up the initial gaps.

For a simple two-vehicle collision, the relationship between the initial closing speed (at contact) and the resulting induced delta-v for the target is

$$v_T = [w_B/(w_B + w_T)](1 + e)v_{close} \ (e \text{ positive}) \qquad (11.34)$$

where B = bullet and T = target.

This can be rewritten to give

$$v_{close} = [v_T/(1 + e)][(w_B+w_T)/w_B]. \qquad (11.35)$$

If the energy lost due to closing the gaps is included, then the initial bullet vehicle speed prior to crossing the gap is given by

$$v_{initial}^2 = v_{close}^2 + 2fgx \qquad (11.36)$$

where f is the drag factor and x is the intervehicle gap. This initial speed is the output target speed for any previous impact. Thus, if the sudden speed increase for the front vehicle is known then Equation 11.36 can be used sequentially to backtrack to the original impact speed of the last vehicle.

If e is small the effect of ignoring restitution is also small for a two-vehicle impact. For example, if $e = 0.1$, the difference is 10 percent for Δv_T versus v_{close}. However, if the entire crash scene involves several sequential impacts we must be very careful to properly include the values of e for each impact. The reason is that for N impacts the error integrates as $(1 + e)^N$. To illustrate, for $e = 0.1$ and $N = 7$, the value of $(1 + e)^N = 1.95$. What was only a 10 percent error for an individual two-vehicle impact has grown to a serious 95 percent error for seven sequential impacts. Ignoring e for each impact would result in a 2:1 error in the relationship between the initial closing speed for the last vehicle and the resulting induced speed change for the vehicle at the front of the line. This assumes that the gap-crossing losses in energy were also small.

The problem arises because if all vehicles are stopped except for the last one, and a pulse propagates sufficient to cause a significant delta-v for the first vehicle, then the usual condition is that the first impact (at the rear of the line) is at a significant speed. (This need not be true, however, if any of the other vehicles are still moving when hit; see below.) Consequently, the first hit can involve significant vehicular damage and involve a low value of restitution. However, each subsequent impact is of ever-lower intensity, so the coefficient of restitution is steadily increasing as the pulse propagates to the front of the line.

To illustrate the problem consider the following simplified case. First, assume that the energy losses due to the gap-crossings are very small. Second, assume all vehicles are of similar weight. This will give a 2:1 ratio of input speed to output speed for each collision, ignoring restitution. Let there be seven vehicles, and thus six hits. Let the front car suffer a delta-v of 5 mph. If we assume $e = 0.0$ for all impacts the implied initial speed of the last car is $5 \times 2^6 = 320$ mph! However, suppose the restitution per impact is (measured from front to back): 0.7, 0.6, 0.5, 0.4, 0.3, 0.2, respectively. This sequential change is in accordance with the decreasing severity of impacts, working from the rear of the line to the front. Then the 320 mph answer should be reduced by the factor K, where

$$K = (1+e_1)(1+e_2)(1+e_3)(1+e_4)(1+e_5)(1+e_6).$$

Thus,

$$K = (1.7)(1.6)(1.5)(1.4)(1.3)(1.2) = 8.91.$$

Our answer of 320 mph now becomes only 35.9 mph. An impossibly absurd value for the end vehicle has suddenly become credible." This is merely an example, but it illustrates why meaningful values of restitution must be included in the analysis of any multiple-vehicle pileup.

The more general case involves vehicles which may be moving when hit. Let v_B be the initial bullet speed at impact, while v_T is the initial target speed. Let v_B' be the bullet speed after the impact, while v_T' is the corresponding speed for the target.

Then

$$v_T' = [w_B/(w_B + w_T)](1 + e)(v_B - v_T) + v_T \text{ (}e\text{ positive)} \tag{11.37}$$

where, of course, $v_B - v_T = v_{close}$.

Then

$$v_B = [(w_B + w_T)/w_B][1/(1 + e)][v_T' - v_T] + v_T. \tag{11.38}$$

Suppose we now define

$$e = kv_{crit}/v_{close} \tag{11.39}$$

where k is a value less than 1.0, and v_{crit} is the first critical speed to first cause damage to the weaker vehicle.

Then Equation 11.38 can be rewritten to give

$$v_B = [(w_B + w_T)/w_B]v_T' - (w_T/w_B)v_T - kv_{crit}. \tag{11.40}$$

Equation 11.40 allows the input bullet speed for a given impact to be derived in terms of the initial and final speeds of the target, and the critical speed for impact. We previously suggested that $k = 0.7$ gave a good average fit to experimental data. Note that for a stationary target and zero restitution, Equation 11.40 reduces to

$$v_B = [(w_B + w_T)/w_B]v_T'. \tag{11.41}$$

However, this answer is nearly always wrong, because both initial target motion and restitution will reduce the implied original bullet speed. These effects rapidly escalate for the multiple-car pileup. Failure to include the second and third terms in 11.40 will inevitably result in totally absurd values for the calculated speed of the incoming bullet.

Chapter 12

Rollovers and Side Trips

Synopsis

12.1 Background

Rollovers and trips have always been contentious, and are frequently associated with significant injuries, often because occupants were not wearing their seatbelts or the vehicle roof collapsed. However, they have become more publicized because of the Firestone tire/Ford Explorer debacle which aired on TV for several months in congressional hearings. While the issue of rollovers has been simmering in the background for many years, this debacle (with Ford and Firestone each blaming the other for the events and injuries) has caused the issue to suddenly take front stage. Indeed, while groups had been suggesting some form of "rollover rating" for many years, it was not until 2001 that NHTSA started to provide them. These are in the well-known form of stars, with five stars implying a low propensity for a vehicle to roll (less than 10 percent), and one star implying a higher propensity (greater than 40 percent). These ratings refer to the propensity to roll *after* an event has occurred which could lead to a rollover; they do not indicate the propensity to get into trouble before emergency-type maneuvers. However, these ratings are based solely on the Static Stability Index (SSI), and many argue that this index is misleading. Reality shows that vehicles can roll more readily than implied by the SSI, where SSI is nothing other than the ratio of the half-track width ($T/2$) to the CM (center of mass, or gravity) height (h). Thus $SSI = T/2h$. Unfortunately, the SSI is directly applicable only to a rigid body and does not include many other factors described below.

Historically, cars have relatively high SSI ratings, with values in the range of 1.2–1.7. Pick-ups and vans have lower values in the range 0.8–1.1. Heavy trucks (including eighteen-wheelers) have always had low values in the range 0.4–0.6. Pick-ups, vans and heavy trucks used to be only commercial vehicles, but over time pick-ups and vans have been converted, become far more popular, and their numbers have vastly increased (much to the pleasure of the manufacturers, since the profit margin is very high as compared to cars). Many SUVs are nothing other than pick-ups with extra bodywork and internal seating. Example: the Bronco II was simply the Ranger pick-up with bodywork, which then became the Explorer. But adding extra weight on the upper portion (roof, glass and seating) merely worsened the rollover problem. Only some of the more recent (and sometimes expensive) versions of SUVs are designed to behave like cars (with lowered unibody construction, four-wheel independent suspension, etc.).

Because heavy trucks are inherently dangerous and their design cannot easily be revised, the cure has been the use of a special driver's license (the CDL, or commercial driver's license). This at least guarantees that the drivers appreciate the very poor handling of these trucks. But no one has yet suggested a special license for SUVs, despite their poor handling, as compared to cars, and inexperienced drivers with merely a car (class D) license can drive them. Likewise, many off-road vehicles exist, and no one has suggested that these vehicles should be towed to and from the place of intended use, as people do with a boat. Instead, these vehicles are regularly driven on the highways and hardly ever get used off the road (serious off-road vehicles, like the Land Rover and Range Rover, come with pneumatic height adjustment and are driven slowly when off-road). Even worse, although there are laws specifying what the manufacturers can make for road use, no one stops owners from modifying the vehicles after purchase. Hence we see the converted pick-ups standing eight feet tall on elevated struts and with huge tires (monster trucks) merrily driving down our streets—a rollover waiting to happen. Such vehicles are also dangerous because of their absurdly high bumpers which allow bumper strikes above typical car hoods and trunks, and directly into the passenger compartment.

The vehicle manufacturers always argue that rollovers are driver error, and will point out that any vehicle can be made to suffer a sideways trip under the appropriate conditions. This is true. Forgotten (or ignored) is the fact that almost all accidents are due to driver error (very few are due to an outright mechanical failure). Over the years the government and manufacturers have steadily introduced safety features (bumpers, crush zones, seatbelts, airbags, head restraints, door bars, etc.) to protect the driver. But little will be done to ameliorate the rollover problem unless public pressure influences sales.

A PBS TV program (February 2002) on rollovers revealed that certain designs get changed according to the manufacturer's own engineer's recommendations, and only after notoriety occurs. The new 2002 Explorer is two inches wider (as recommended by the engineers) and now has independent rear suspension. I'll let the reader decide if this was because of the notoriety (denied by Ford) or done solely to allow more passenger space. Of course, rollover problems can occur with any manufacturer's vehicle, not just Ford's. Mercedes Benz had a surprise not too long ago when one of their earlier SUVs rolled in full public view (although MB very rapidly redesigned the vehicle to cure this), and the CJ5 and CJ7 Jeeps and the Chevrolet Blazer had reputations for rollover too. This author owns two Fords, a 1997 Contour and a 2001 Ranger, and the Contour handles very much like a European vehicle (not surprising since it's based on the European-Ford's Mondeo chassis, which is also used for the smaller Jaguar model X). The Ranger is a two-wheel drive, extended-cab Edge model, and is much taller than the Contour (both roof and door sills). This author doesn't drive the Ranger the same way he does the Contour.

The problem is that too few drivers seem to appreciate the differences in handling. To be sure, the Ranger comes with warnings in its handbook to the effect that it could roll much more easily than a standard car, but the "more" is never quantified. But such warnings are of little use because even if the purchaser conscientiously reads and digests these warnings, there is usually a significant time lag between buying the vehicle and suddenly being confronted with an emergency maneuver that could cause a possible rollover. Until the emergency occurs, the driver gets used to the handling and thinks everything is okay; the driver usually doesn't push the limits of handling. But when those limits are reached, the driver is suddenly surprised by the rollover response. Let's face it; drivers do not practice rollovers. After all, I have only once actually activated the ABS on my Contour, and that was at low speed on an icy road. The pulsation of the brake pedal and the thunderous racket from the ABS system came as a surprise, even though I am a physicist and know this is what happens! Warnings do not work; vehicle redesign does.

Even more recently (April 17, 2002), a CBS's *60 Minutes II* discussed the rollover propensity of so-called "fifteen-passenger" vans, which include the Chevrolet Express 3500, the Dodge Ram Wagon B350 and the Ford Econoline E350. This TV program was in response to a NHTSA advisory issued on April 15, 2002, which itself was a repeat warning of an advisory dated April 2001. NHTSA stressed the fact that such vehicles can suddenly go from an "understeer" to an "oversteer" condition and suffer rollover when heavily loaded (ten or more occupants) but not when lightly loaded (driver only).

An issue that needs addressing is roof strength, which is especially important for sideways trips, where the subsequent hits on the ground can be significant. The present regulations are quite timid: no more than five inches of crush for a force equal to only 1.5 times the vehicle weight applied to certain areas of the frontal roof. If a vehicle with weight w is dropped through a height h, and then crushes a further distance d with a force of $1.5 \times$ weight, we have $w(h + d) = 1.5wd$. Hence $h = 0.5d$. In other words, the present roof strength regulation corresponds to an upside-down vehicle drop of only inches. The real problem is cost. Merely adding extra steel to the roof members (including the A, B and C frames) simply pushes the overall CM even higher. One solution is greater strength with minimum weight, but this requires expensive techniques and materials. Most vehicles do not have the equivalent of rollover bars. Roof crush is primarily a problem for occupants who are not ejected and remain firmly in their seats with their seatbelts tightly fastened.

The irony is that the belted occupant is unable to move out of the way, and thus becomes a sitting duck if the roof collapses above him. Conversely, for an unbelted occupant it matters little whether the roof collapses into the occupant's head or the occupant dives into the roof.

In 2008, IIHS provided statistical data illustrating that higher roof strengths *do* actually reduce rollover deaths. Since then NHTSA has also concluded that higher roof strength is valuable, and has issued a new rule for a strength-to-weight requirement of 3-to-1 for vehicles starting in 2013 (FMVSS 216). Further, the previous rule only applied to vehicles up to 6,000 lbs (loaded weight or GVWR), with no regulation for heavier vehicles. The new rule applies to vehicles up to 6,000 lbs GVWR, and the old rule of 1.5-to-1 now applies to vehicles from 6,000 lbs up to 10,000 lbs GVWR. However, the Institute has declared that only vehicles with a strength-to-weight ratio of at least 4-to-1 will qualify for their *Top Safety Pick* category. Despite many years of "it's not necessary," or "it's not easy to do," the manufacturers are suddenly providing vehicles that have much higher roof strengths, sometimes better than IIHS stipulates, and *before* the NHTSA rules begin to apply. It would appear that the car manufacturers are more concerned with satisfying the IIHS requirements (which help sell vehicles) than with satisfying NHTSA regulations (which, as always, are "behind the power curve").

To illustrate the problem with weak roofs, a case was studied in which an extended-cab pick-up slid sideways (passenger-side first) into a traffic light island. Upon hitting the curb the pick-up started to roll but also climbed the curb. Before even undergoing a quarter-turn roll the roof collided with a strong traffic light pole, near the B-pillar of the pick-up, on the passenger side. The roof collapsed down onto the driver and killed him. The pole did not breakaway at its base, indicating the impact was not severe, yet the roof collapsed over about one-half of the vehicle's width. The driver (sole occupant) motion would have been to his right and upward. He thus moved into the downward collapsing roof, even though he was wearing his three-point seatbelt. Without the severe roof collapse this driver would have probably survived.

To illustrate the problems of rollovers we can quote from NHTSA (April 2001):

> We limit our discussion here to light vehicles, which consist of (1) passenger cars and (2) multipurpose passenger vehicles and light trucks under 4,536 kilograms (10,000 lbs) gross vehicle weight rating (collectively, "light trucks").
>
> According to the 1999 Fatality Analysis Reporting System (FARS), 10,142 people were killed as occupants in light vehicle rollovers, including 8,345 killed in single-vehicle rollovers. Eighty percent of the people who died in single-vehicle rollovers were not using a seat belt, and 64 percent were ejected from the vehicle (including 53 percent who were completely ejected). FARS shows that 55 percent of light vehicle occupant fatalities in single-vehicle crashes involved rollover. The proportion differs greatly by vehicle type; 46 percent of passenger car occupant fatalities in single-vehicle crashes involved rollover, compared to 63 percent for pick-up trucks, 60 percent for vans, and 78 percent for sport utility vehicles (SUVs).

12.2 Types of Rollover

There are two fundamental types of rollover, often called the "turn" rollover and the "trip" rollover, and an intermediate case we can call "sideslip." Rollovers can occur whenever the lateral acceleration exceeds a critical value that depends on vehicle geometry, tire side flexion, suspension leaning, tire-road surface friction, and any initial lean of the road surface away from true horizontal. If this critical value condition is exceeded gradually, we have a simple rollover (the turn type). If the threshold is exceeded rapidly (as with a true "curb hit"), we can have a more dramatic side flip (the trip version). It should be noted that the corresponding induced sideways roll speed can itself be quite low, even if the vehicle's original speed was high. For this reason, consideration of rollovers is appropriate in this book, which includes low-speed accidents.

A brief description of sideways tripping is in Appendix A. Here, we will more fully consider the various mechanisms, and will include consideration of potential occupant kinematics.

The turn (or simple) rollover occurs when a vehicle attempts to corner too rapidly; the trip occurs because of an abrupt stopping of sideways motion, as with a curb hit. The intermediate sideslip case is one in which the vehicle has started moving sideways, because of the back end's swinging out, and begins to roll while still sliding sideways (so this stage is friction-dominated, and for pure side motion the vehicle is actually skidding even if the brakes are not applied), and then encounters a very rapid stopping of the leading wheels (so this second stage is impulsive, as with the curb hit). Because during the first stage the vehicle is continuously losing energy through friction, this stage may exhaust the energy necessary to complete the rollover. This has to be traded against the fact that the stage-one roll has also lowered the energy requirement for the second stage.

On the other hand, for a pure turn rollover, the vehicle keeps moving along its circular arc on the road up to the point of actually tipping over, and the tip is perpendicular to the arc motion.

A. Cornering Rollover (Turn)

1. Centripetal and centrifugal rotational effects

In order for a vehicle to change its heading there must be side forces acting through the vehicle's CM. The net force is the *centripetal* (center-seeking) force which points inward toward the center of rotation. This net force is due to tire friction on the road surface, and is given by the product of vehicle mass and centripetal acceleration, where the latter is simply (v^2/r), where v is the local CM's speed and r the radius of the turn.

Consider a rear view of a vehicle turning left. The tire-road forces are aiming to the left, but are below the CM of the vehicle. Let the net force be F_0. We may replace this single force with three forces, each with scalar magnitude F_0, by drawing two extra forces, F_1 and F_2, acting in opposite horizontal directions at the CM. Thus F_1 aims to the left through the CM and F_2 aims to the right through the CM. Because $F_1 = F_0 = -F_2$ the total force does not change. However, we may now visualize these three forces as being an actual centripetal force F_1 acting through the CM *and* a simultaneous couple of value $(-F_2h) = (+F_0h)$ which tries to rotate the vehicle to the right about the contact point with the road. Note that the force F_2, which is aiming to the right, is the explanation of the familiar centrifugal force that an occupant feels, and which tries to move the occupant to the right while the vehicle moves to the left. This force is merely a reaction to the centripetal force (Newton's third law). It can also be thought of as a lack of the centripetal force which is needed to ensure the occupant actually follows the curved path. While the vehicle is turning, the occupant tries to continue moving along the tangential path he started with until some form of restraint (seatbelt or side of vehicle) applies the necessary lateral force.

The "subtlety" of centrifugal (center-fleeing) versus centripetal (center-seeking) forces seems to be a never-ending source of confusion. Consider a person whirling a stone in a circular arc with a piece of string between the stone and the hand (as with a slingshot). The force necessary to cause this circular motion is the centripetal one, and is acting on the stone and aims at the hand. However, this force is applied through the string and causes the person to feel a tug on the hand. This tug is outward and is the centrifugal force. The two forces are equal and opposite, and exist because the string itself reaches a state of new fixed length (an extension). Being under a new static load, the string maintains its length and merely suffers an internal tension, a direct consequence of Newton's third law. If the string breaks, or the person lets go, both forces suddenly collapse. The person no longer feels the tug and the stone suddenly moves in a straight line (ignoring gravity) which is a tangent to its circular motion at the instant the force disappeared.

A similar situation occurs if the object is inside of a rotating body (which is why centrifuges work). A classic example is the circus "wall of death" in which a person steps inside of a cylindrical body (initially with a vertical spin axis) that then starts to rotate. If the person is initially away from the wall, he will try to move on a tangential motion which will force him toward the wall. When the person reaches the wall, the spinning cylinder will now apply an inward force to the him in order to keep him moving in the circular arc (assuming no openings in the wall). But the person will experience a "push" into the wall. Again, the inward force is centripetal, the outward is centrifugal. For a sufficiently fast spin, the acceleration can be larger than that due to gravity. This means that even if the rotation changes to one about a horizontal axis, the person will not drop away from the wall, but will remain pinned against the wall.

This effect is very important for explaining an occupant's motions within a rapidly spinning vehicle. For example, for a six-feet-wide vehicle which spins about its own center line through the CM, the occupant will be about three feet away from the axis when against the door. For a centripetal acceleration of g = 32.2 ft/s^2, the spin rate need only exceed ω= 3.28 radians/s = 188 degrees/s (since $v^2/r = r\omega^2$). This also represents a low tangential spin speed of about 6.7 mph for the occupant.

2. Tire forces and direction

To produce a side force, a tire must actually be moving with a sideslip angle, which is the difference between the local heading of the tire-wheel combination and the actual motion of the tire on the ground (i.e., the tire is scuffing on the road surface, but not necessarily leaving any marks). The side force initially linearly increases with slip angle, but then starts to level off at larger angles. It is also a function of vertical force (vehicle weight), type of tire (radial tires giving larger side forces than bias tires for the same slip angle), tire wall height and air pressure. To perform a low-speed turn, the necessary side force is low because the required centripetal acceleration is low. Consequently, the slip angles are also small. This means the wheels simply follow the tracking set by the Ackerman steering geometry. Ackerman steering produces the observed effect of the inner front wheel turning through a larger angle than the outer front wheel, and is needed to prevent excessive scrub and tire wear. Thus, the center of rotation lies along an extension of the rear axle (for cars without four-wheel steering), while each of the two front wheels are perpendicular to the lines joining the wheels to the common center of the turn. Since the centripetal force acts through the CM and aims somewhat rearward to the center of rotation, this means there is a forward component of centrifugal force which tries to make the front of the vehicle move down while the rear lifts (similar to braking). In combination with the lateral component of force this, explains the observed tendency of the vehicle's outer front region to dip during lower-speed cornering.

An alternative viewpoint is that when the wheels follow the Ackerman steering, the radial lines from the center of the turn to the various wheels are larger for the front wheels (especially the outer one) than for the rear wheels. Since the entire vehicle is turning at a constant rate, ω, then the accelerations must be larger for the front wheels than for the rear wheels. This again gives an overall net force which dips the front outer body.

Note that if the rear tires have negligible side friction (as on ice), the side forces due to the front tires will try to induce a "yaw spin" of the vehicle (about a vertical axis). This is because these frontal forces are ahead of the CM. A similar situation can occur if the rear wheels are deliberately locked by applying the handbrake (only) while the car has started its turn. This is because the "friction circle" logic then removes the ability to develop the normal side force for the rear tires. This explains the well-known trick of getting a car to rapidly swing round and point the other way. To do this, we get the car up to speed, start to steer, and simultaneously apply the handbrake (and hope we don't induce a rollover!). It is also the source of racing drivers doing "doughnuts" (they merely overspin the rear wheels with a powerful engine). This again reduces the rear tire side force capability while maintaining the front tire side forces.

These last effects may also be related to the fact that vehicles that are short or have short wheelbases (the two usually scale with each other) tend to suffer rollover more often. Although very little is usually discussed with regard to length, a short vehicle has a smaller yaw moment of inertia. This means there is a greater chance of the vehicle rapidly becoming sideways to its motion. For example, if a vehicle is entering a curve and the driver applies hard braking, then without ABS the rear wheels may lock before the front ones do. This can cause the rear end of the vehicle to swing out (as with oversteer) and become sideways to the net circular motion. If the driver then suddenly releases the brakes, the tire side friction suddenly increases and rollover may start. The smaller the yaw inertia, the quicker this can occur, thereby minimizing the probability that the driver can correct the problem. Moving sideways is also more likely to cause tire de-beading. When this happens the outer wheels may rapidly drop to the road surface and it then becomes possible for the wheel rim to dig into the road (producing a gouge). This then converts a simple roll into a trip. Whether ABS cures such problems has yet to be shown.

As vehicle speed increases and the required centripetal force increases so the tire slip angles increase. Now both front and rear tires are moving with a side slip. For the front wheels, the slip is as for a vehicle understeering (the wheels point sideways by more than the actual motion) while for the rear wheels the slip is as for a vehicle oversteering (the wheel motion is outboard of the wheel headings). The result is that the center of rotation is no longer along an extension of the rear axle but moves ahead of the rear axle, by an amount that depends on local tire friction and vehicle weight distribution and steering geometry (king-pin angles, camber settings, etc.). For similar tire frictions, the center of rotation tends to move to a spot somewhat midway between the front and rear axles. Higher-speed cornering usually implies a larger turning radius and hence smaller steering angles, so high speeds usually put the center of rotation close to the midpoint of the wheel base. The result is that the centripetal force acting through the CM is also approximately perpendicular to the long axis of the vehicle. For vehicles which tend to oversteer, the rotation center moves forward and the net centrifugal force acts with a backward component, while a tendency to understeer gives the opposite effect—a forward centrifugal component. These effects determine which of the innermost wheels first lift. It is rare for both inner wheels to start lifting at the same instant.

The issue with the "fifteen-passenger" vans is that, when fully loaded, their CM not only rises versus the curb weight but also moves toward the rear. This apparently causes the vehicles to suddenly adopt an oversteer response (the rear end swings out) at large lateral accelerations and rapidly puts these vehicles into a sideways stance, thereby encouraging a rollover.

For many cars, the occupant's CM is low and usually close to the height of the vehicle's CM. However, for many pick-ups, vans and SUVs this is not true. Instead, the seated occupant's CM is usually above the vehicle's CM, as is any additional payload (luggage, etc.). This means that the actual rollover propensity is worsened by the addition of occupants and luggage, a fact rarely appreciated, and the curb weight SSI is too large. NHTSA does not include this fact in their ratings. Any attempt to use a roof rack would be very ill-advised.

3. True dynamics versus accident reconstruction

In order to accurately analyze a rollover, it would be necessary to have knowledge of the real dynamic response of a given vehicle, or to properly reproduce the rollover experimentally (a somewhat dangerous exercise; those shown on TV usually involve outriggers to prevent complete rolls). Only the design engineers will have the necessary details and computer codes (the car manufacturers don't usually release all this vehicle data for fear of liability issues). Consequently, any attempt to analyze a rollover, after the event, must necessarily involve some approximations. Thus, the theory given below is best regarded as first-order only. To complicate the issue, the details of payload (occupants and luggage) are rarely known with precision. Even the design engineer, with his full knowledge of vehicle response and access to an appropriate computer codes, would have to approximate the effects of payload.

To help illustrate how difficult it can be to correctly analyze a rollover, NHTSA admitted in their 1999 Research Note "Passenger Vehicles in Untripped Rollovers" that, of 267 cases originally coded as "untripped," some 190 were arguable. In particular, Calspan Corporation disagreed with the original coding in 160 cases. Great care has to be taken with the interpretation of gouges, tire marks and impact marks on the roadway, and with crush evidence from the vehicle, in order to be sure the correct type of rollover is determined, and that the induced motions are correct.

Presently, the statistics show that turn rollovers are about 7.5 percent of all rollovers, trip rollovers are about 47.5 percent, "other" are about 39.5 percent and "unknown" are about 5.5 percent (NASS data for 1992–1996). As can be seen, there is plenty of room for improvement in analysis and interpretation.

4. The roll

As the side force increases so there is a transfer of weight towards the outer wheels. Let the vertical tire forces be F_{out} and F_{in} for the outer and inner wheels, respectively, where we ignore differences between front and rear axles. But we must also have $F_{out} + F_{in} = W$, where W is the total vehicle weight. Applying moments about the outer tire's contact point we now get

$$F_{in}T + \frac{Wv^2}{gr} = W\frac{T}{2} \quad \text{or} \quad F_{in} = \frac{W}{2} - \frac{Wv^2h}{grT} \tag{12.1}$$

where T is the track width (sometimes called tread width, which most people reserve for the actual contact width of the tires) and h is the CM height above the road. Then we have

$$F_{in} = \frac{W}{2}\left(1 - \frac{v^2 2h}{grT}\right) \quad \text{and} \quad F_{out} = \frac{W}{2}\left(1 + \frac{v^2 2h}{grT}\right). \tag{12.2}$$

Hence F_{in} drops to zero, and F_{out} rises to W, when

$$\frac{T}{2h} = \frac{v^2}{gr} \text{ which is the SSI.} \tag{12.3}$$

This merely states that the SSI is equal to the lateral acceleration, in units of g, at the instant the inner wheels start to lift. This logic applies to a rigid body and assumes no local shifts in the CM due to tire motion or suspension.

Defining the diagonal between the CM and the outer tire contact as R, we have

$$h = R\sin\theta_0 \quad \text{and} \quad T/2 = R\cos\theta_0 \quad \text{or} \quad \frac{T}{2h} = \frac{1}{\tan\theta_0} = SSI \tag{12.4}$$

where θ_0 is the initial angle for the CM height versus the contact point, measured up from the road surface.

At the instant when the inner wheel lifts off, the net turning torque is given by

$$\Gamma = mgR\left(\frac{v^2}{rg}\sin\theta_0 - \cos\theta_0\right) = I\ddot{\theta} = m\left(K_{CM}^2 + R^2\right)\ddot{\theta} \tag{12.5}$$

where m is mass, I is the moment of inertia about the rotation point (tire/road contact point), K_{CM} is the radius of gyration about the vehicle CM and $\ddot{\theta}$ is the induced angular rotation rate (radians/s^2). Thus we have

$$\ddot{\theta} = \frac{gR}{\left(K_{CM}^2 + R^2\right)}\left(\frac{v^2}{rg}\sin\theta_0 - \cos\theta_0\right). \tag{12.6}$$

Now, approximately (only), (true values should be used, if known; see below),

$$K_{CM}^2 = \frac{WID^2 + H^2}{12} \quad \text{and} \quad R^2 = \frac{WID^2 + H^2}{4}$$

where WID is the vehicle width (roughly equal to the track), and H is the vehicle height. So we have

$$K_{rot}^2 = \frac{WID^2 + H^2}{3}$$

Then we get

$$\ddot{\theta} = \frac{gR}{K_{rot}^2}\left(\frac{v^2}{rg}\sin\theta_0 - \cos\theta_0\right). \tag{12.7}$$

For a given value of lateral acceleration (v^2/rg) the induced rotational angular acceleration is proportional to (R/K_{rot}^2), and thus inversely proportional to a length. But both R and K_{rot} are functions of the lateral (width-height) dimensions of the vehicle. Thus a vehicle which is wider or taller will undergo a smaller angular acceleration than a vehicle which is squat and narrow. This then gives a longer time to develop a given net angular motion, and thus more time for the driver to potentially correct the rollover. However, a typical driver may still fail to react properly in sufficient time to prevent the CM from rising to a point directly above the contact point (TDC, or top-dead-center), beyond which gravity causes the roll to continue. Only experts (e.g., stunt drivers) learn how to drive on just the two outer wheels without either crashing back down onto all four wheels or completing the roll.

The start of rotation requires the lateral acceleration to just exceed $1/\tan\theta_0 = SSI$. For most cars the SSI is significantly larger than 1.0. On normal flat roads the limiting side acceleration is limited by the tire-road friction. Since the latter is usually smaller than 1.0, rollover is not expected, and side sliding only should occur. Rewriting the previous equation,

$$\ddot{\theta} = \frac{gR}{K_{rot}^2}(\mu\sin\theta_0 - \cos\theta_0) \text{ or } \ddot{\theta} = \frac{gR\sin\theta_0}{K_{rot}^2}(\mu - SSI) \tag{12.8}$$

$$\text{or } \ddot{\theta} = \frac{gh}{K_{rot}^2}(\mu - SSI) \tag{12.9}$$

where the upper lateral acceleration is limited by the side tire friction, μ, and h is the local value of the CM height. Note how the weight of the vehicle does not enter into Equations 12.6 though 12.9.

However, several factors can allow the tire's friction limit to effectively be exceeded. In other words, the local true value of SSI may decrease to below the real value of friction. First, if the road itself has a cross-slope (of $\tan\delta$) this increases the value of θ_0 by $\pm\delta$, where "+" implies a downward slope in the direction of the roll (down to the right in our example of a left turning vehicle), and "–" is an upward slope. Banking a curved road thus helps prevent a rollover because it tilts the vehicle towards the center of the turn. Tire flex will also effectively increase θ_0 because the tire's side wall only flexes inward. This has only a small effect on the CM height, but a more direct effect on the lateral torque arm, reducing the latter value to ($T/2 - s$), where s is the side shift for the foot print of the tire. Tires with stiff and short side walls minimize this effect (as per high performance cars). A sudden tire blowout or deflation (perhaps due to debeading) will also cause the wheel to drop to its rim. This again increases the initial angle, especially since the tire most likely to suffer this problem is the highly loaded outer tire. Since many pick-ups and SUVs have large tires with tall side walls these tire mishaps have a greater effect than for the usual car.

For example, the Ford Ranger has tires designated P235/75R15. This means the tire's tread width is 235 millimeters (9.25 inches) and has tire wall height of 75 percent of the width, which is thus 6.94 inches. For a track of about 70 inches this means that a sudden deflation of both tires on one side would tilt the vehicle by about $\tan\theta = 6.94/70 = 0.099$, so $\theta = 5.7$ degrees. Of course, it would be rare for two tires to deflate simultaneously, but even one will cause a tilt of about 3 degrees.

It is the combination of tire and vehicle response that helps determine if or when a rollover occurs. This explains the Firestone/Ford controversy: was it the tires, was it the vehicle, or was it a lousy combination? Further, the vehicle must already be subject to a significant lateral acceleration when the tire fails, or the driver must "wrongly" respond by suddenly steering. In 1982 this author was driving a Ford F-150 pick-up, with camper shell, when the right rear tire lost its tread (you guessed it; it was a Firestone!). But the vehicle was traveling straight at the time (at about 60 mph) and there were no stability problems. Despite the noise of the tread peeling off the vehicle was calmly slowed and steered over onto the shoulder with no trouble.

Another factor worsening the ability to start rollover is the induced body-lean due to the suspension. Many trucks and SUVs have lean rates of 5–8 degrees per *g* of lateral acceleration. Cars tend to have lower lean rates (less than 4 degrees/*g*). Some cars with active suspension (electronically controlled dampers and anti-roll bars) have very low lean rates of below 2 degrees/*g*. An example is the new BMW 7 series. Unfortunately, such vehicles are rare because they are so expensive. Body-lean has the effect of increasing the initial value of θ_0. Since SSI is inversely proportional to $\tan\theta_0$, anything that reduces this angle improves stability, and vice versa.

These various considerations are most strongly driven by the angle simply because the variations in R and K_{rot} are usually smaller.

Finally, there is the issue of transient cornering. This occurs when the lateral acceleration changes quickly. This can be due to a rapid continued change in the steering (tightening into the curve), or can occur during oscillatory steering (slalom maneuvers, or merely rapid lane changes), or may be due to a rapid increase in the tire-ground friction. For example, if a vehicle is turning a corner with brakes applied and the brakes are suddenly released, the maximum side friction can suddenly increase. The suspension causes a natural oscillation frequency for side body motions. For most cars this is about 1.7 Hz, whereas for pick-ups and SUVs it is usually about 1.4 Hz, and for eighteen-wheelers is about 0.9 Hz. These frequencies are those for which the required lateral acceleration to initiate a roll decreases to a minimum, which has a resonance effect. Gillespie (ref 111) shows how the normal SSI value of about 1.4 for a car can drop to only about 1.0 for a 1.0 Hz frequency and to 0.5 if the frequency of steering oscillation is about 1.7 Hz. This latter value implies that a friction value of only 0.5 could initiate rollover even on a level, flat road. For a typical SUV the normal value of about 1.0 can drop to about 0.7 at 1.0 Hz and to 0.35 at 1.4 Hz, whereas for the heavy truck the value drops from about 0.3 to about 0.25 at 0.5 Hz and to about 0.1 at 0.9 Hz.

Performing a sufficiently rapid oscillatory maneuver, to cause rollover, is more difficult for a car than for a SUV or heavy truck. For example, a simple lane change, which is a half-cycle motion, typically takes the time

$$t = 0.45\sqrt{\frac{L}{a}} \tag{12.10}$$

where L is the total side motion, and a is the mean side acceleration (units of g). Most drivers would not use a side acceleration of more than about 0.7 g (this represents an emergency maneuver close to the frictional limit of the tires). Then $L = 3.46\,t^2$ is the maximum side motion for 0.7 g. For a frequency of 1.0 Hz the half-cycle time is 0.5 second, so the value of L is about 0.86 foot (or 10.4 inches). Clearly, this represents a mere wiggle on the road. Nevertheless, because SUVs usually start with a lower SSI than cars the transient threshold can be reached more easily.

In their November 26, 2001, edition, *AutoWeek* reported a rollover with the new Jeep Liberty. This occurred during a slalom maneuver at about 40 mph (58.7 ft/s) while negotiating cones spaced seventy feet apart. No one else has yet replicated this rollover. The Jeep is six feet wide, so to "just avoid" the cones, the vehicle must move laterally by this six feet (L) to undergo a half-cycle over the seventy feet (x). We may now write

$$x = 0.45v\sqrt{\frac{L}{a}} \quad \text{or} \quad a = 0.2025\left(\frac{v}{x}\right)^2 L \tag{12.11}$$

to achieve the mean lateral acceleration in units of g. Substituting, we obtain $a = 0.854\ g$. This is clearly a high value close to the friction limit. Note how the acceleration decreases with increasing x. Most testers use $x = 100$ feet, so the acceleration is usually lower. The half-cycle period is about 1.193 seconds, implying a frequency of about 0.42 Hz.

Transient cornering allows the body-lean to overshoot the corresponding

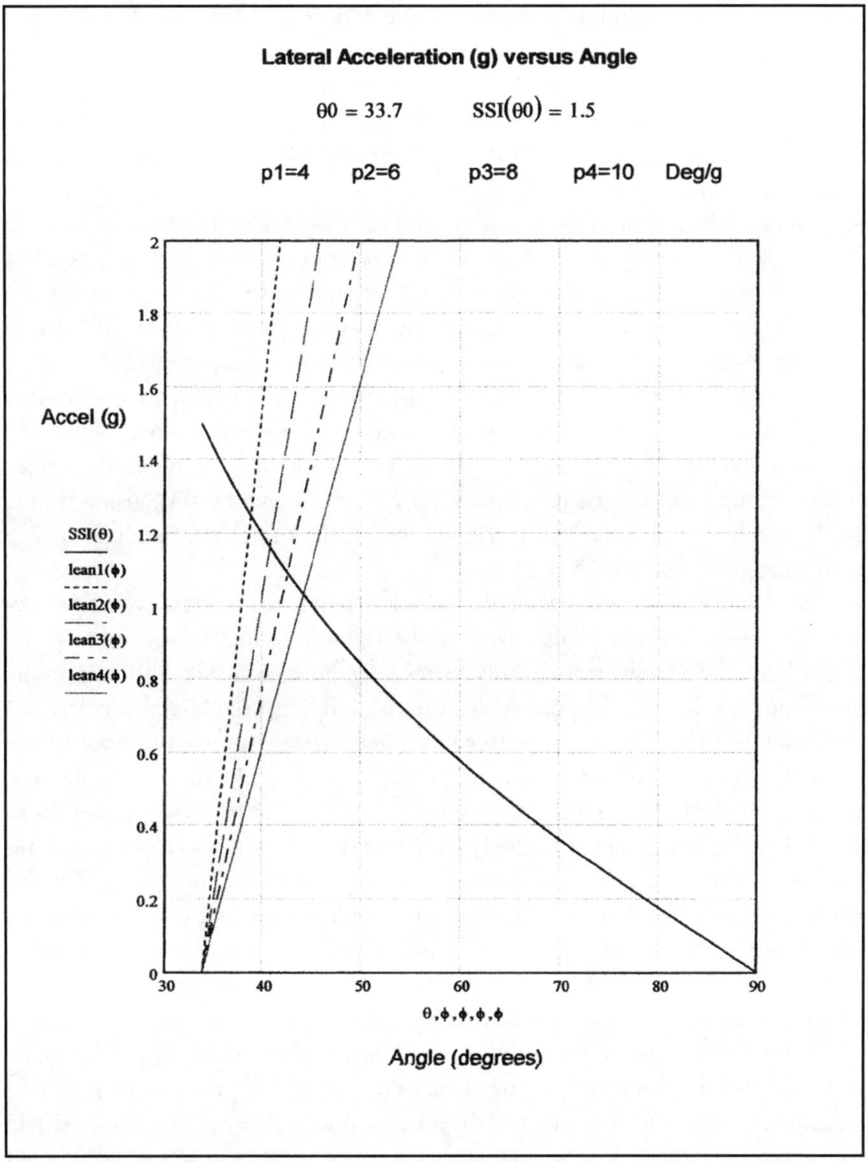
Lateral Acceleration (g) versus Angle
θ0 = 33.7
SSI(θ0) = 1.5
p1=4
p2=6
p3=8
p4=10
Deg/g
Accel (g)
SSI(θ)
lean1(ϕ)
lean2(ϕ)
lean3(ϕ)
lean4(ϕ)
2
1.8
1.6
1.4
1.2
1
0.8
0.6
0.4
0.2
0
30
40
50
60
70
80
90
θ,ϕ,ϕ,ϕ,ϕ
Angle (degrees)

Figure 12.1

static value. With negligible damping the overshoot could be up to a factor of 2.0. However, with damping and a less-than-step steer, the overshoot may be only α percent. Suppose the static body-lean rate is p degrees/g. Then the effective rate may be $(1 + \alpha)p$ degrees/g. To compute the limiting value of lateral acceleration to initiate rollover (inner wheel lift-off) we can plot the acceleration to maintain balance as a function of the tilt angle, θ. This is the angle with induced roll. This gives a line which drops from the initial value of SSI (at θ_0) to zero when $\theta = 90$ degrees, and is simply the plot of lateral acceleration versus $(1/\tan\theta)$. Against this plot we draw the line $acc = (1 + \alpha)p(\theta - \theta_0)$. Here, $(\theta - \theta_0)$ is the tilt beyond the initial condition. Where the two lines intercept gives the effective SSI. These effects are shown in Figure 12.1.

For example, if $SSI_0 = 1.5$, and the suspension lean (with any overshoot) is 6 degrees per g of lateral acceleration, the actual point where rollover will commence is about 1.16 g's of lateral acceleration and an angle of about 41 degrees (measured up from the road). Likewise, if $SSI_0 = 0.8$ and the suspension lean is 10 degrees per g of lateral acceleration, the rollover threshold is about 0.63 g with an angle of about 57.5 degrees.

We see that very stiff-suspension vehicles (performance cars) have an effective SSI close to the static value, while soft-suspension vehicles (off-roaders) can have effective SSI values noticeably lower than the static value. To interpret the plots note that for zero suspension lean for a rigid body, the lateral acceleration can climb to the value of SSI_0 without the inner wheels lifting. But once lifting starts the system is unstable, and the required side acceleration to maintain a given angle decreases. Thus, any region above the SSI plot is unstable. With suspension lean the angle of the body increases steadily with increasing acceleration, but the inner wheels do not yet lift. Lifting starts when the rising lean line intercepts the falling SSI line. This logic is simplified because usually one inner wheel starts to lift before the other. When this happens there is a new suspension lean rate which is lower than the first. The result is a kink in the rising lean plot which causes an intercept with the SSI curve at a lower value.

Why did we refer to off-roaders as soft-suspension vehicles? Because suspension is not needed merely to make the ride comfortable, it is essential to guarantee that all four wheels remain on the ground. A truly "suspension-less" vehicle would waddle along a road as a variable-leg tripod if the road were anything but perfectly flat and smooth, unless we rely on flexing in the frame (which ensures lousy handling). To help keep all wheels on very rough ground the vehicle needs to have large amplitude suspension capability, and this implies soft suspension. Otherwise the vehicle would forever have one wheel off the ground and traction would be lost unless the lifted wheel is locked so as to transfer the drive to the remaining grounded wheels, and steering would be difficult. But, to handle off-road situations we also require high ground clearance to prevent bottoming, and to also handle the large suspension motions. Off-road driving is sensibly done at only low speeds on rough ground, but the combination of high CM and soft suspension makes rollover more likely for higher speeds on highways.

5. Rotation rate

Equations 12.7 and 12.8 are based on pseudo-static forces acting on the vehicle, and give the induced angular acceleration rate. Does the induced centrifugal force acting through the CM modify this angular rate? The answer is no. The "short" proof relies on the fact that the induced centrifugal force (v_{CM}^2/R) is acting directly through both the CM and the rotation point on the ground. Hence, the force is perpendicular to the induced rotational motion and cannot apply any torque capable of altering the rotation. The "long" answer can be proven by considering the components of the centrifugal force, as shown below.

When the vehicle's CM is moving at v_{CM} at radius R from the contact point, the radially outward force has two components. One is a vertical one which is proportional to the sine of the angle between the CM and the road (θ). This provides a torque (or couple) which acts on the torque-arm of $T/2$. The other is horizontal and proportional to the cosine of the angle, and acts on the torque-arm h. The first torque acts in a clockwise direction and thus tries to add to the torque due to the side tire forces. But the second torque is counterclockwise (for tilt less than TDC) and tries to subtract from the rotation.

Defining h and $T/2$ in terms of R we have for the clockwise torque

$$\Gamma = \frac{mv_{CM}^2}{R}\sin\theta\frac{T}{2} = \frac{mv_{CM}^2}{R}(\sin\theta)R\cos\theta = mv_{CM}^2\sin\theta\cos\theta \qquad (12.12)$$

while for counterclockwise torque we have

$$\Gamma = \frac{mv_{CM}^2}{R}\cos\theta h = \frac{mv_{CM}^2}{R}(\cos\theta)R\sin\theta = mv_{CM}^2\sin\theta\cos\theta \qquad (12.13)$$

and clearly these two torques cancel. However, the vertical component of centrifugal force acts to reduce the effective weight of the vehicle (see later).

To appreciate the rate with which rolling occurs we model a simple vehicle. We choose the width to be 6 feet, the height to be 5.5 feet, and the CM to be two feet above the ground. The track width is assumed similar to the vehicle's width (for simplicity only, of course). Such a vehicle has $SSI = 1.5$, which would normally be considered stable vehicle with a five-star rating, and implies that a friction of 1.5 would be needed to start a roll on a flat level road. We here ignore the effects of suspension body lean and so forth.

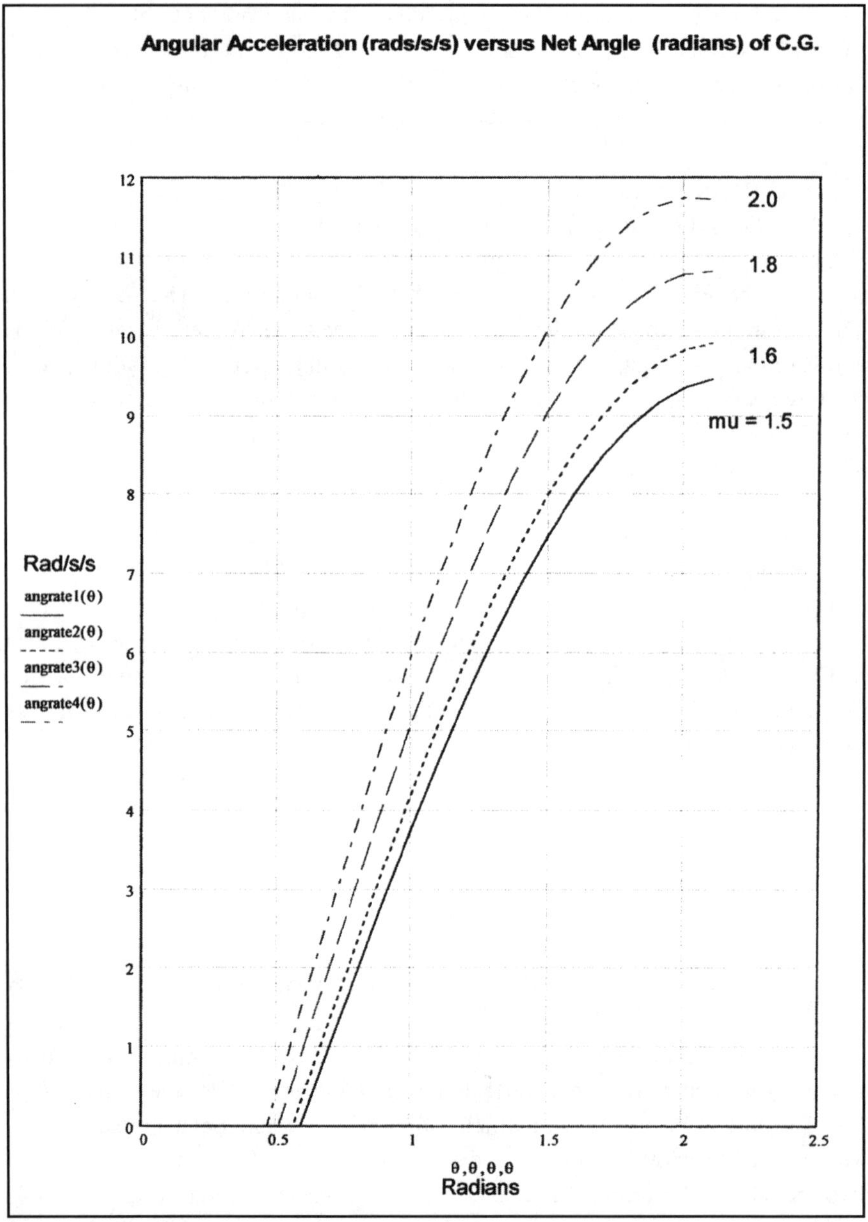
Angular Acceleration (rads/s/s) versus Net Angle (radians) of C.G.
12
11
10
9
8
7
6
5
4
3
2
1
0
0
0.5
1
1.5
2
2.5
2.0
1.8
1.6
mu = 1.5
Rad/s/s
angrate1(θ)
angrate2(θ)
angrate3(θ)
angrate4(θ)
θ,θ,θ,θ
Radians

Figure 12.2

For this model we have $R = 3.606$ feet, $K_{CM} = 2.35$ feet, $K_{rot} = 4.699$ feet and $Q = 4.61$ feet, where Q is the diagonal from the CM to a roof edge.

Figure 12.2 shows that for this given geometry and side friction the induced angular acceleration is initially roughly linear with rolled angle until the vehicle reaches TDC (90 degrees), whereupon the rate slows down as the vehicle drops over onto its side. Figure 12.3 then shows that the induced tangential speed of the vehicle's CM also increases roughly linearly with angle, at least for moderate effective friction. Note that for friction at, or just beyond the critical value, the induced CM rotational speed is only about 7 mph when the vehicle reaches TDC, and only about 10.5 mph when it finally falls on its leading side. This speed is superimposed on the actual horizontal speed of the vehicle for a side-sliding motion. For our left-turning vehicle, the collision side is the passenger side. Even for

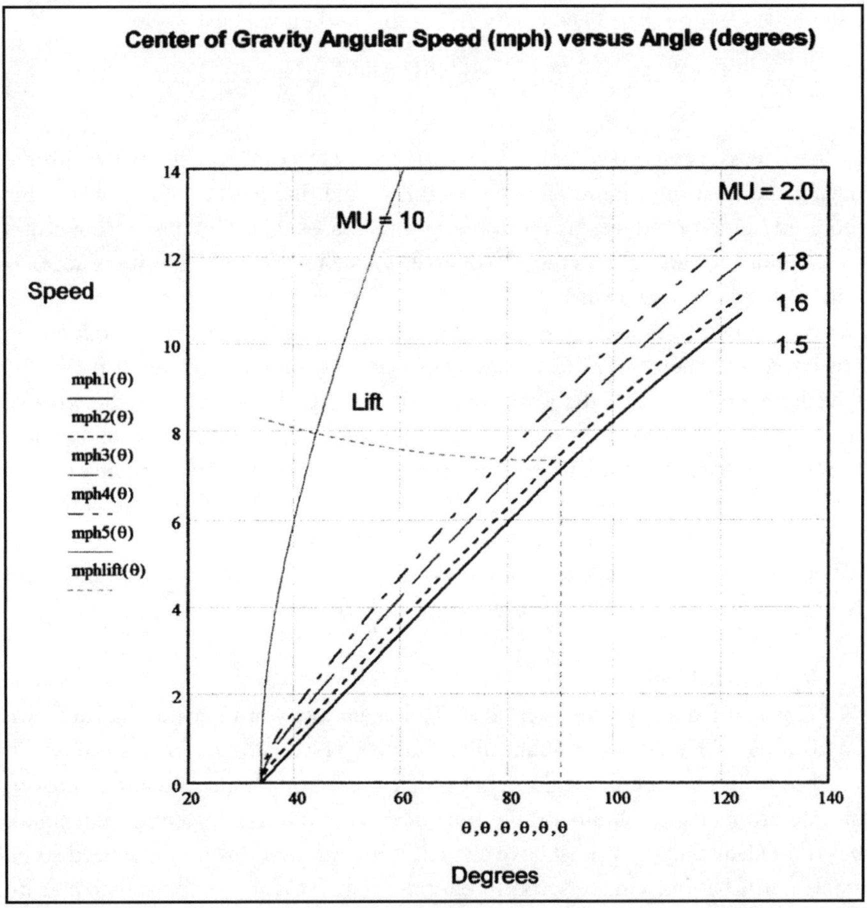

Figure 12.3

an increased friction of 2.0 these speeds only become about 9 mph and 12.5 mph, respectively. Only for much higher friction (e.g., about 10), which implies some type of ground-furrowing is occurring (a trip is developing), are higher speeds induced.

6. Contact-point lift-off

Does the vehicle contact point (tire-road) ever lift off the ground during a simple roll? To answer this we compute the possible vertical lift against gravity which can exceed the rising CM because of the circular-arc motion for a pure roll. For a given induced angle of roll and corresponding CM's velocity (tangent to the diagonal R), we calculate the locally-induced roll vertical speed and compare with the "remaining" rise of the CM. If the tangential CM roll velocity is v (ft/s) at an angle of θ, then the vertical component is $v\cos\theta$ while the remaining rise of the CM to reach TDC is $H = R(1 - \sin\theta)$. Then we have

$$v_{lift} = \frac{\sqrt{2gR(1-\sin\theta)}}{\cos\theta} \tag{12.14}$$

as the necessary speed to cause the initial contact point to lift off the ground during the rotation. Figure 12.3 shows this as the line marked "lift," where the required velocity reduces as the roll angle increases. Clearly, this lift condition only applies for angles less then 90 degrees, since beyond that gravity is accelerating the vehicle downward.

We see that for friction equal to the critical limit of 1.5 the two curves do not intercept. Therefore, lift-off does not occur (we ignore the small lift of the wheels that can occur if the lower bodywork is slightly outboard of the wheels, which gives a sudden shift in the rotation point from the tire-road to bodywork-road). Even for moderate increases in friction (e.g., 2.0) the intercept only occurs for angles very close to 90 degrees (79 degrees on the plot). Therefore, although contact point lift-off can occur it is quite minor. Only for high friction does lift-off occur at lower roll angles, at about 44 degrees and 8 mph for a friction of 10. But this situation is rapidly approaching a sudden trip.

7. Time of roll

How long does the rollover take? This is an awkward question because we are dealing with a situation of unstable balance. The analogy is with a rod which we start truly vertical. Since this is a balance condition the time to fall is forever, or indeterminate. To obtain a finite time of fall the rod must either have a small, but finite, lean angle, or must have a small initial motion. In short, we need some small perturbation. Once the perturbation exists we can compute the time by integration. This is done by using a small angle-step and computing the result-

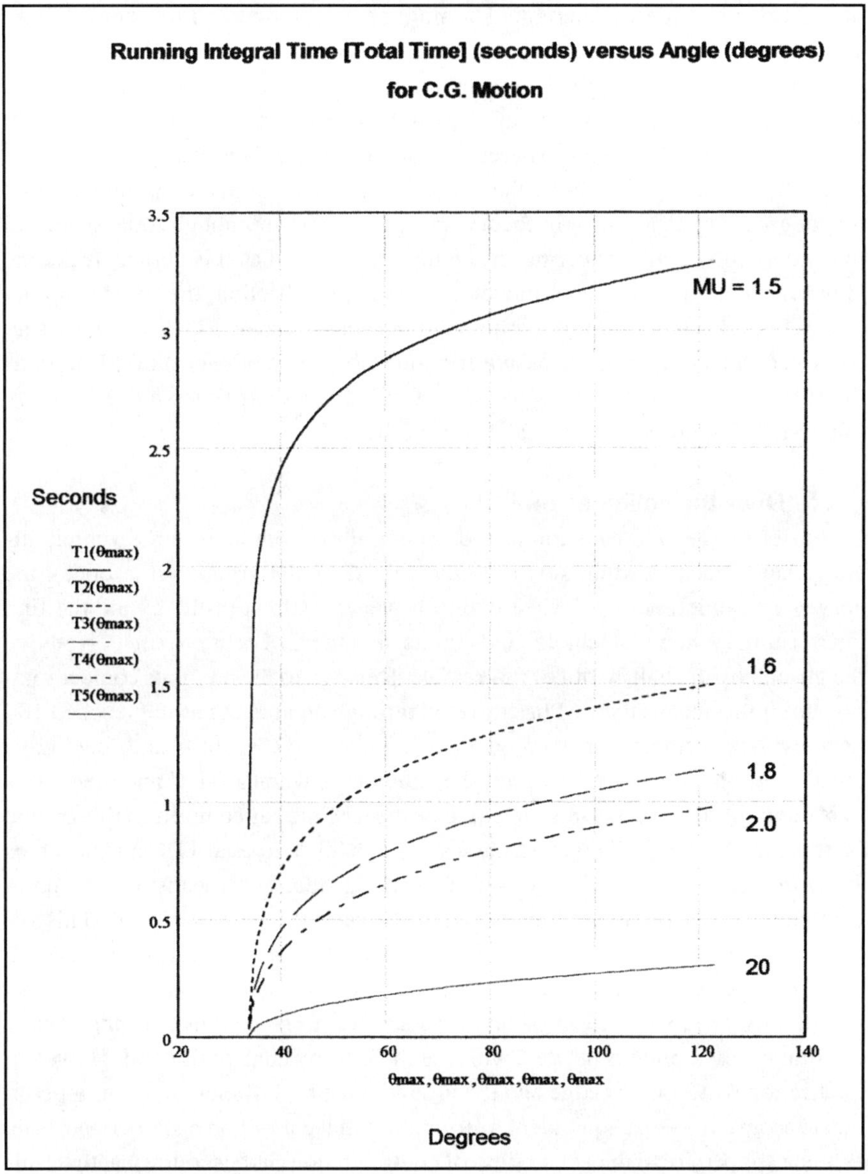

Running Integral Time [Total Time] (seconds) versus Angle (degrees)
for C.G. Motion
Seconds
T1(θmax)
T2(θmax)
T3(θmax)
T4(θmax)
T5(θmax)
MU = 1.5
1.6
1.8
2.0
20
3.5
3
2.5
2
1.5
1
0.5
0
20
40
60
80
100
120
140
θmax , θmax , θmax , θmax , θmax
Degrees

Figure 12.4

ing motions and speeds, thereby obtaining the corresponding time-steps. Figure 12.4 shows the results for an angle step of 1.0 degree. Performing the integration with this angle-step is equivalent to an initial perturbation of 1.0 degree. The plot shows that for a friction of 1.5 (the critical value to start rolling) the time to roll to TDC is about 3.1 seconds, whereas to complete the roll onto the passenger side takes about 3.25 seconds. Note the "long" time needed to rotate through the first few degrees (vertical plot). In theory, this gives a driver enough time to control the situation by countersteering, if the driver actually has this choice available. However, note that, for even moderate increases in friction, the timing rapidly drops. For a friction of 2.0 the times are 0.8 second to reach TDC and 0.95 second to complete the roll. Excessive friction (a trip-type of event) of 20 shortens the times to only 0.25 second to reach TDC. Such short times make it nearly impossible for a driver to react and control the roll.

8. Does the roll continue?

After the vehicle lands on its side does rolling continue? If the vehicle literally lands on its leading side (i.e., the side slaps the ground all at once), the answer is "sometimes no." Most eighteen-wheelers do not roll beyond the first quarter turn. When the vehicle lands on its side the CM is approximately above the ground by the half-width of the vehicle. Relative to the previous contact rotation point this means the CM has traveled through an arc but has not reached 180 degrees. For example, for the model chosen here the CM starts at 2 feet above the ground, rises to about 3.61 feet (the value of *R*) when at TDC and then drops to a height of three feet. Thus the angle of the CM measured up from the ground increases from $\theta_0 = 33.7$ degrees, passes through 90 degrees at TDC and becomes 123.7 degrees when the vehicle is on its leading side. This means the CM has a component of its velocity which is directed toward the roof as it lands. This velocity is $v_{CM}\cos\theta_0$. The vehicle would be expected to merely slide on its leading side since the vehicle has this component of speed but also still has its initial road speed. However, some form of bounce may occur. To continue rolling, a new fulcrum or pivot point is needed, which is the leading edge of the roof. However, the friction between this edge and the ground must be sufficient to act as a pivot, otherwise we have the equivalent of trying to induce a roll on a slippery surface. While a slippery road may cause loss of control, it does not encourage actual rollover; the rollover inevitably occurs after the vehicle leaves the road and enters dirt, or hits the curb at the edge of the road.

It must be remembered that our vehicle has a pseudo-rectangular cross-section and is not a simple cylinder, although most vehicles have a tapered upper body and a convex roof. Hence continued rolling requires sequential lifting and dropping of the CM. To cause this a vertical force is needed which requires sufficient from ground contact. If the friction is very small, as it is with ice, the roof edge could simply slide out and forward relative to the roll motion, in which case the roll does not continue. Once the vehicle is on its side we must redefine the h and $T/2$ parameters. The new h is the half-width = 3.0 feet, while the new equivalent to $T/2$ is the now horizontal distance from the CM to the roof, which is about 3.5 feet. Hence we have a new R which is Q = 4.61 feet and a new θ_0 = 40.6 degrees, so the new SSI = 1.17. Although this new SSI implies it is easier for the second-quarter roll than for the first, we now have a different pivot condition. Instead of high-friction rubber-to-road we have lower-friction metal-to-road. Whereas the former can exceed 0.8 the latter is usually about 0.4.

But if the leading roof edge can somehow dig into the surface, or become distorted because of crush, or the vehicle did suffer some form of contact point lift-off (thereby spinning in the air about its own CM), then the vehicle may continue the roll. This is because landing on the ground increases the effective normal force and so increases the effective value of friction. To continue the roll, the CM must be lifted again. This time the CM must rise sufficiently for it to be above the new contact point, which is now the leading roof edge. For negligible crush, this new diagonal (Q) is the distance between the roof's edge and the CM. For our model, this distance is about Q = 4.61 feet.

Thus to continue to roll the CM must be lifted again by about 1.61 feet (when the total CM angle becomes about 164.3 degrees), whereupon it can land on its roof, at which point the CM has again dropped to a height of about 3.5 feet above the ground. At this point, the CM has reached 213.7 degrees, which is 180 + 33.7 degrees. Ignoring any crush energy, this means that to achieve a rollover onto the roof or beyond, the induced roll energy must be sufficient to raise the CM though the highest point of 4.61 feet from its initial value of two feet. Without energy losses, the vehicle would just keep rolling beyond this state, since it already has the energy to raise the CM to its highest necessary point. In practice there are energy losses each time there is bodywork-to-ground contact (friction and crush), and these losses determine just how many quarter-turns the vehicle experiences before it finally settles down. For a vehicle moving sideways that does roll, the total number of quarter-turns can be considerable, allowing for multiple complete 360 degree rotations with sufficiently high initial speed.

9. Sensitivity to unknowns in R and K_{rot}

The values of R and K_{rot} are rarely known accurately, especially if payload effects are uncertain. We need to know how sensitive the analysis can be to such unknowns. To help illustrate this we consider a vehicle with a rectangular cross-section as with our previous model. The ratio of importance is (R/K^2_{rot}). Since weight is not important, we choose any convenient value.

Let width (W) be 6 feet, height (H) be 5 feet and weight (w) be 1,000 pounds. Let the vehicle have uniform density. Then the CM is 2.5 feet above the ground and R = 3.905 feet and θ_0 = 39.8 degrees.

The moment of inertia about the vehicle's CM is given by

$$I = \frac{w}{g}\left(\frac{W^2 + H^2}{12}\right) = \frac{w}{g}K_{CM}^2. \tag{12.15}$$

Thus, K^2_{CM}= 5.083 (feet)^2. But for the inertia about the rotation point on the ground

$$I = \frac{w}{g}\left(K_{CM}^2 + R^2\right) = \frac{w}{g}K_{rot}^2. \tag{12.16}$$

Thus, K^2_{rot} = 20.331 (feet)^2.

Now let us split the vehicle horizontally at the midpoint, and allow the total weight to be redistributed. This gives us two rectangles, one on top of the other. For each rectangle we have

$$K_{CM}^2 = \frac{w^2 + \left(\frac{H}{2}\right)^2}{12} \tag{12.17}$$

so K^2_{CM} = 3.5208 (feet)^2. But the two rectangles have different values of R. For the upper region

$$R_U^2 = \left(\frac{W}{2}\right)^2 + \left(\frac{3H}{4}\right)^2 \text{ and } K_{rot,U}^2 = K_{CM}^2 + R_U^2 \tag{12.18}$$

while for the lower region we have

$$R_L^2 = \left(\frac{W}{2}\right)^2 + \left(\frac{H}{4}\right)^2 \text{ and } K_{rot,L}^2 = K_{CM}^2 + R_L^2. \tag{12.19}$$

Substituting, we get R_U = 4.8023 feet, R_L = 3.2500 feet, $K^2_{rot,U}$ = 26.583 (feet)^2 and $K^2_{rot,L}$ = 14.083 (feet)^2.

Now, to obtain the net values of R and $K^2_{ro}t$, we must now add the component parts by biasing according to weight distribution.

First we weight the CM heights to get

$$h_U = 0.75Hw_U \text{ and } h_L = 0.25Hw_L \tag{12.20}$$

and then get $h_{av} = (h_U + h_L)/(w_U + w_L)$, and then define

$$R_{net} = \sqrt{h^2 av + \left(\frac{W}{2}\right)^2}.. \tag{12.21}$$

Next we weight the radius of gyration to get

$$K^2_{rot} = (w_U K^2_{rot,U} + w_L K^2_{rot,L}) / (w_U + w_L). \tag{12.22}$$

Example a. Bottom heavy

Let w_L = 700 pounds and w_U = 300 pounds. Then by substitution we get, h_{CM} = 2.000 feet, R_{net} = 3.6056 feet, and K^2_{rot} = 17.833 (feet)^2. Also, θ_0 = 33.7 degrees. Thus, (R/K^2_{rot}) = 0.20218 (feet)$^{-1}$.

Example b. Top heavy

Let w_L = 300 pounds and w_U = 700 pounds. Then we get, h_{CM} = 3.000 feet, R_{net} = 4.2426 feet, and K^2_{rot} = 22.833 (feet)^2. Also θ_0= 45.0 degrees. Thus, (R/K^2_{rot}) = 0.18581 (feet)$^{-1}$.

Example c. Uniform weight

Here $w_U = w_L$ = 500 pounds. Then we get, h_{CM} = 2.5 feet, R = 3.905 feet, K^2_{rot} = 20.333 (feet)^2. So θ_0 = 39.806 degrees. Thus, (R/K^2_{rot}) = 0.19205 (feet)$^{-1}$.

Thus for this rather extreme variation in weight redistribution we see that the ratio of the (R/K^2_{rot}) terms is about (0.18581/0.20218) = 0.919 for top-heavy-to-bottom-heavy. Comparing this ratio versus the uniform option we have 0.9675 for top-heavy-to-uniform and about 1.0527 for bottom-heavy-to-uniform. Thus, all these ratios are within 10 percent, even for the extreme case.

Finally, if we include the sinθ factor (e.g., as per Equation 12.8), we can assess the ratios of the terms $(R/K^2_{rot})\sin\theta$. This gives the ratios of about 0.9124 for bottom-heavy-to-uniform, about 1.0686 for top-heavy-to-uniform, and about 1.1712 for top-heavy-to-bottom-heavy. Now the ratios are within 17 percent, even for the extreme case.

These relatively small errors explain why an analysis of a rollover is possible even though the true vehicle details are not known precisely.

10. Conclusions for a simple turn roll

The above calculations indicate that a simple turning roll can have timings of order 2.0 seconds or less and involve roll tangential CM speeds of less than 12 mph when the roll is completed (vehicle on its side), and is unlikely to experience any significant lift-off at the tire-road contact point. However, this ignores the actual speed and motion of the vehicle while the roll occurs. For example, let the initial speed be 30 mph (44 ft/s). To achieve a lateral acceleration of 1.5 g's, the radius of curvature of the turn is about 40 feet. This is a small radius, only about twice the minimum turn radius of the vehicle. Note: most vehicles can turn with a minimum radius between about 17 feet and 25 feet. For a higher speed the radius increases with the square of the speed. Now, if the vehicle starts rolling and takes about 1.0 second to roll, the vehicle will have moved about 44 feet unless braking was involved. But, a speed of 44 ft/s with a radius of 40 feet implies a turning rate for the turn of about 1.1 radians/s = 63 degrees/s. Thus in the same 1.0 second the vehicle changes its heading by 63 degrees. This means that when rolling is complete (the vehicle is on its passenger side) the CM hits the ground at about 7–12 mph, but is also still moving at 30 mph with a new heading about 63 degrees different from the initial value.

During these motions the effective weight of the vehicle also drops as the roll approaches TDC (see Section 12.2A6). This is because the roll is dynamic rather than pseudo-static, and the increasing roll speed is producing upward lift because of the induced centrifugal force, so the effective frictional force (centripetal) also decreases. Thus the vehicle no longer follows the original turn and moves with an increasing effective-turn radius. Consequently, the actual change in heading can be less than the above calculation, unless the rear-end is swinging around. The result can be a vehicle which is on its side and sliding with a roof-first component of motion. This is obviously a potential problem if the vehicle then collides with a stationary object such as a tree, since this may induce significant roof crush.

It is also important to note that the turn rollover analysis, thus far, has concentrated on forces and turning torques. We have ignored the vehicle's actual speed and time of force application. These two factors are important for a vehicle which ends up sliding sideways because friction may itself prevent the roll. To explain, suppose the initial side speed is very low, such as 5 mph (7.335 ft/s). With a friction of 1.5, the distance to stop is only about 0.56 foot, and the time to stop is about 0.15 second. When the leading wheels come to a stop, we effectively have a new form of a trip because the rotation now occurs about a fixed contact point on the ground. Even though the lateral forces were large enough to start a roll, the timing and energy are too small to continue the roll.

If the initial side speed is larger (e.g., 30 mph, or 44 ft/s), the time to stop is about 0.91 second and, as the wheels stop, the vehicle has already gained sufficient roll energy to continue the roll. In fact, any case in which the time to stop is greater than the time to roll to TDC guarantees the roll will occur, and higher initial speeds simply allow for more quarter turns.

There is yet another subtlety. The induced rotation causes a centrifugal lift that decreases the effective weight of the vehicle during the roll, especially as it approaches the TDC condition. With a reduction in the vertical weight there is a corresponding reduction in the horizontal frictional force, because the true friction itself does not change. Note carefully that Equations 12.6 through 12.9 do not contain the vehicle's weight. What does this mean? As the vehicle tips, so the frictional loss in energy becomes less than it would be for a fixed vehicle weight and sideways motion on the road. This means the vehicle loses less energy and thus slows less than frictional arguments would suggest. The missing lost energy is actually going into the rotational energy. Clearly, for complete lift there is no further road contact, and all the remaining energy is going into the rotation or flight (ignoring air-drag effects).

B. The Curb Impact Trip Condition

Tripping occurs for any sufficiently abrupt slowing of vehicle's side motion. The classic case is a direct sideways slide into a curb. Variations can include a vehicle which leaves the road while still on its four wheels and then enters dirt and rapidly starts furrowing, or a vehicle whose front wheel hits a curb, causing the vehicle to yaw rapidly and then the rear wheel hits the curb, or merely a vehicle moving sideways on a surface with very rapidly increasing friction.

As shown for turn-rolling, a very high side friction gives an impulsive force to the outer wheels and the vehicle enters a roll state very quickly. The distinction between the turning roll and the trip roll is that for the former the vehicle is being rotationally accelerated during the entire period of first inner-wheel lift to reaching TDC and beyond, whereas for the latter the rotation state is achieved almost instantaneously after the trip starts and before any significant angular motion. The overall response is then primarily dependent on energy considerations.

A subtlety must first be discussed. When a moving body is suddenly stopped at one end of its geometry, a rotation is induced. But what determines the rotation point? For example, when a car is struck sideways at its front end by another vehicle, the car rotates in the plane of the road, but about a vertical axis through its own CM (a yaw motion). So, if a side-moving car is struck at the leading wheels by a curb, should it also rotate about an axis through the CM? If this happened, the CM of the vehicle would not rise. However, this situation requires that the leading wheels proceed to rotate downwards and drop to the maximum depth of R below the CM height. This can only happen if there is empty space immediately ahead of the curb. So such motion could occur if there was a deep gutter just ahead of the curb, and the vehicle jumped this gutter with negligible fall under gravity before hitting the curb. This would be a less common situation, but should it apply the induced roll is faster because the inertia is lower, and the vehicle does not rise. Instead it rotates onto its leading edge very quickly.

The more common situation is where there is no equivalent gutter and the roadway continues up to the curb. Unless the ground next to the curb is very soft the attempted downward rotation of the leading wheels is prevented. This induces a large vertical force in addition to the large horizontal force. It is this vertical force which lifts the vehicle and causes the roll to occur about a lowered axis, namely the one at the tire-curb contact. Thus the vehicle CM does rise, but the inertia is larger so the roll rate is lower. In reality the rising CM is a direct consequence of the fact that the vehicle has a finite width (it is not a hypothetical thin rod) which means the CM is displaced horizontally away from the curb at the instant of curb strike. However, even here we must be careful. Suppose early side-sliding with friction started a roll before the curb is reached. If the CM has already reached TDC we are back to the equivalent of the gutter situation. Now the curb strike will rapidly increase the roll speed but it will not cause any further rise in the CM.

To allow the roll to lift the CM to TDC we need sufficient sideways energy to lift the CM by the amount $R(1 - \sin\theta_0)$. This implies that

$$v_{side} = \sqrt{2gR(1-\sin\theta_0)} \tag{12.23}$$

gives the minimum velocity. This also ignores any energy lost through tire, wheel or axle damage, all of which increase the threshold. If we fail to reach this threshold the vehicle rises but stops before TDC and crashes back down onto its wheels. For slightly above the threshold the vehicle completes its roll onto its leading side. This threshold can be quite low. For our model the value is about 6.93 mph (10.17 ft/s). As the vehicle starts to rise the initial horizontal linear kinetic energy is rapidly converted into rotational energy about the contact point. Thus

$$\frac{1}{2}I_{rot}\omega^2 = \frac{1}{2}mv_{side}^2 - mgh \tag{12.24}$$

where h is the lift of the CM, from which we get the initial rotational rate (at $h = 0$)

$$\omega_0 = \frac{v_{side}}{K_{rot}} \text{ and the initial tangential CM speed becomes } v_{CM} = \frac{R}{K_{rot}}v_{side}. \tag{12.25}$$

For our model this gives $v_{CM} = 0.772v_{side}$. So to just roll, the new CM speed is about 5.35 mph and starts at the angle $\theta_0 = 33.7$ degrees from the vertical. The initial vertical speed is the cosine component which is $0.832v_{CM} = 4.45$ mph, while the new horizontal speed is the sine component which is $0.555v_{CM} = 2.97$ mph. As the vehicle falls onto its side the kinetic energy again increases and the CM speed becomes 3.27 mph, with $\theta = 123.7$ degrees and $\omega = 1.33$ radians/s. We see that these speeds are all quite low.

Provided the initial side speed remains below a second threshold the contact point does not lift, and the vehicle rolls in a perfect circular arc. This second threshold is reached when the induced vertical speed becomes large enough to cause the CM to rise by more than the circular arc. Thus we have

$$(v_{CM}\cos\theta_0)^2 = 2gR(1-\sin\theta_0) \tag{12.26}$$

which is about v_{CM} = 8.33 mph (12.22 ft/s) for our model. The corresponding initial side speed is then about v_{side} = 10.8 mph. Note that this is the same logic as was used for the turn-roll calculation of contact point lift-off, except here we use the initial angle only rather than need to track the result versus the induced roll. Once above this second threshold the contact point starts to rise, and the motion of the CM is no longer a simple circular arc.

Because the CM rapidly achieves a new velocity and angle at the start of the roll we may consider the implied parabolic trajectory motion it would follow if treated as a point mass. If the parabolic path is below the circular arc than lift-off does not occur. The vehicle crashes onto its leading side. Beyond this threshold lift-off of the contact point starts, at which instant there is no further force from the roadway. However, if only moderately above this second threshold the vehicle will crash down onto its leading roof edge.

With increasing initial side speed a third threshold is reached. Here, the contact point lift-off is significant and the CM itself rises sufficiently to allow enough rotation of the vehicle to allow a crash onto the trailing roof edge. The equation that roughly gives this situation is given in Appendix A. For our model, the initial side speed to allow this is about 15 mph.

Note that until contact point lift-off occurs the rotation is about this contact region. But once contact is lost the spin is now about the axis through the CM of the vehicle. However, because there are no new external forces (ignoring air drag, etc.) the spin rate remains constant. The rotational inertia has decreased, so the spin energy must also decrease. The so-called lost energy goes into the parabolic flight.

Figure 12.5 show several of these effects. (For all Figures 12.5 to 12.8 the right wheel-road contact is 0.0 feet on the horizontal scale.) Note how for a sufficiently large initial side speed the vehicle not only follows a significant parabolic trajectory, it also can rotate several times while in the air. Indeed, Figures 12.6 and 12.7 show the paths of the four corners (two roof edges and two bottom edges, or wheels) as cycloidal paths, illustrating the interesting looping behavior, for an initial side speed of 25 mph. The driver and passenger motions are also shown (see below).

An interesting point during such flights is that the horizontal distance moved for a given angle of roll is independent of the speed, and depends only on vehicle geometry. To understand why this is so we note that the spin rate (ω) is proportional to the initial side speed as is the induced horizontal speed of the CM. So for a given horizontal distance the time decreases but the spin rate increases as side speed increases. Net rotated angle is simply $\theta = \omega x/y$, which is constant for constant x. For our model the vehicle will be upside down whenever the lateral horizontal motion for the CM is about 6.3 feet. A higher initial side speed simply allows for (a) a greater vertical rise, (b) a greater horizontal flight, and (c) more quarter-turns before hitting the ground again.

All of the above quoted equations and figures for Section B have assumed the energy approach to rollover analysis. However, as explained in Appendix A, many analysts use the angular momentum approach. The only change to note is that the initial sideways velocity is different. If v_0 is the sideways speed for the energy solution, and v_{00} that for the angular momentum solution, the two are related by:

$$v00 = \left(\frac{K}{h} \right) v0$$

where K is the vehicle moment of inertia about the contact point of tire and road, and h is the initial vehicle CM height.

12.3 The Side Slide Case

Inspection of the plots for angular speed versus angle, and time versus angle, illustrates that as friction (μ) increases so the time (t) to guarantee "just toppling" (reaching TDC) decreases while the angle also decreases. This is probably considered obvious, and occurs because the spin-up is quicker. Hence we gain the necessary kinetic energy of rotation to allow a quarter-turn roll in a shorter time and at a lower angle. However, what is not so obvious is that the product μt also decreases. This has the effect of lowering the required initial sideways speed to induce rolling.

We assume the vehicle starts at v_0 (sideways) and the leading wheels slow to zero, and then the vehicle continues rotating (but slowing) until TDC is reached. At the instant the wheels stop the friction vanishes and now the *achieved* rotational energy just equals the *required* potential energy to reach TDC, with the two forms of energy trading with each other. But the vehicle is skidding all the time the wheels are moving, so how far does the vehicle move?

If we introduce the gravity term, g, we realize the term $\mu t g$ is a measure of velocity change, and this allows us to determine the initial minimum velocity and gives the distance over which the wheels move.

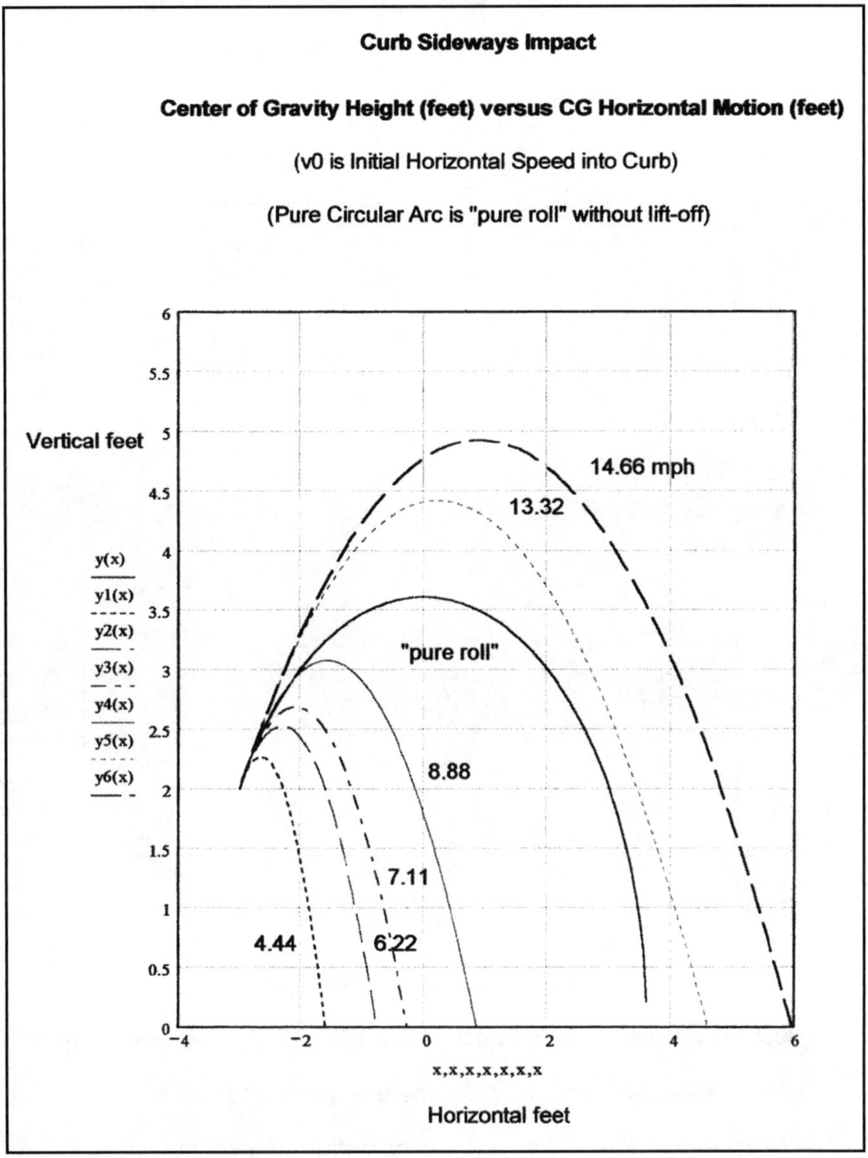
Curb Sideways Impact
Center of Gravity Height (feet) versus CG Horizontal Motion (feet)
(v0 is Initial Horizontal Speed into Curb)
(Pure Circular Arc is "pure roll" without lift-off)
Vertical feet
y(x)
y1(x)
y2(x)
y3(x)
y4(x)
y5(x)
y6(x)
14.66 mph
13.32
"pure roll"
8.88
7.11
6.22
4.44
x,x,x,x,x,x,x
Horizontal feet

Figure 12.5

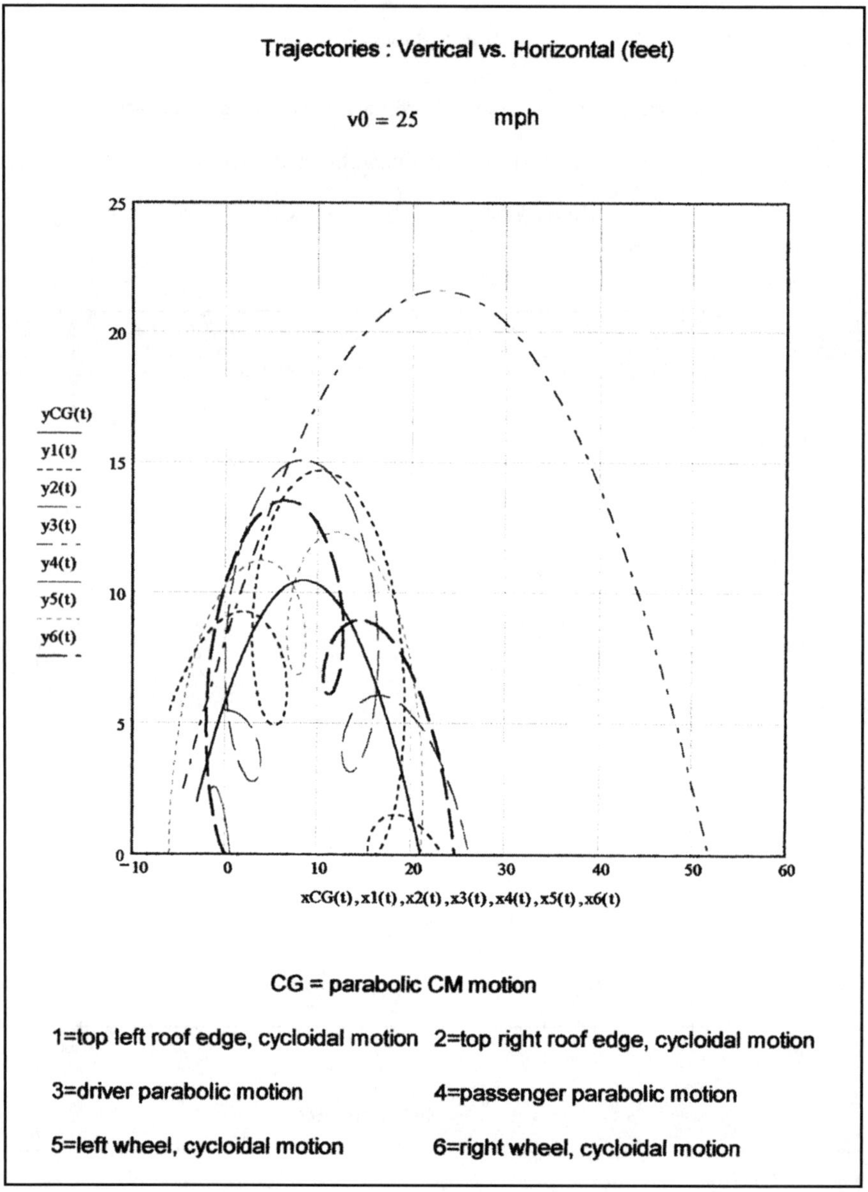
Trajectories : Vertical vs. Horizontal (feet)
v0 = 25 mph
yCG(t)
y1(t)
y2(t)
y3(t)
y4(t)
y5(t)
y6(t)
25
20
15
10
5
0
−10
0
10
20
30
40
50
60
xCG(t), x1(t), x2(t), x3(t), x4(t), x5(t), x6(t)
CG = parabolic CM motion
1=top left roof edge, cycloidal motion
2=top right roof edge, cycloidal motion
3=driver parabolic motion
4=passenger parabolic motion
5=left wheel, cycloidal motion
6=right wheel, cycloidal motion

Figure 12.6

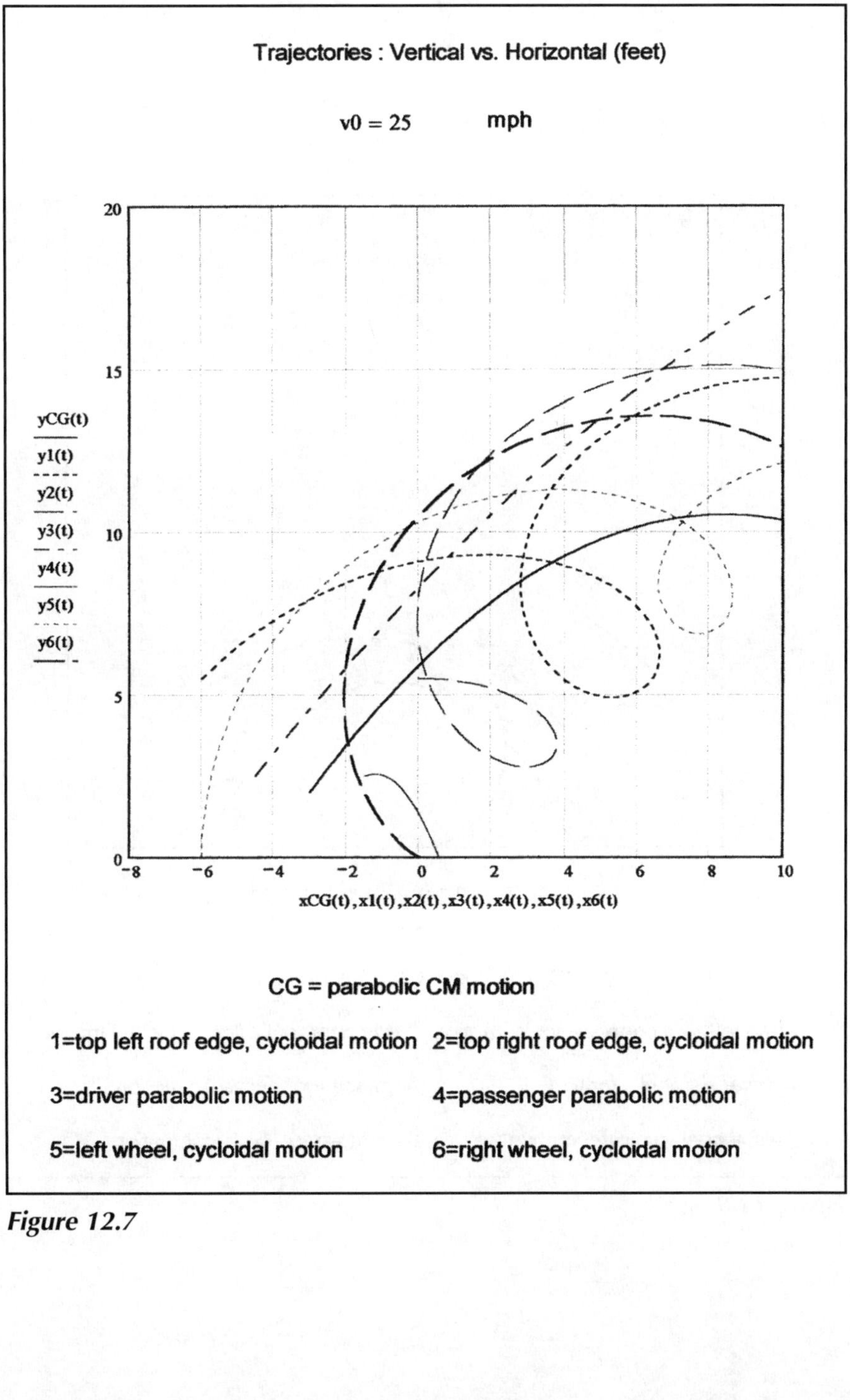
Trajectories : Vertical vs. Horizontal (feet)
v0 = 25 mph
20
15
10
5
0
yCG(t)
y1(t)
y2(t)
y3(t)
y4(t)
y5(t)
y6(t)
−8
−6
−4
−2
0
2
4
6
8
10
xCG(t), x1(t), x2(t), x3(t), x4(t), x5(t), x6(t)
CG = parabolic CM motion
1=top left roof edge, cycloidal motion
2=top right roof edge, cycloidal motion
3=driver parabolic motion
4=passenger parabolic motion
5=left wheel, cycloidal motion
6=right wheel, cycloidal motion

Figure 12.7

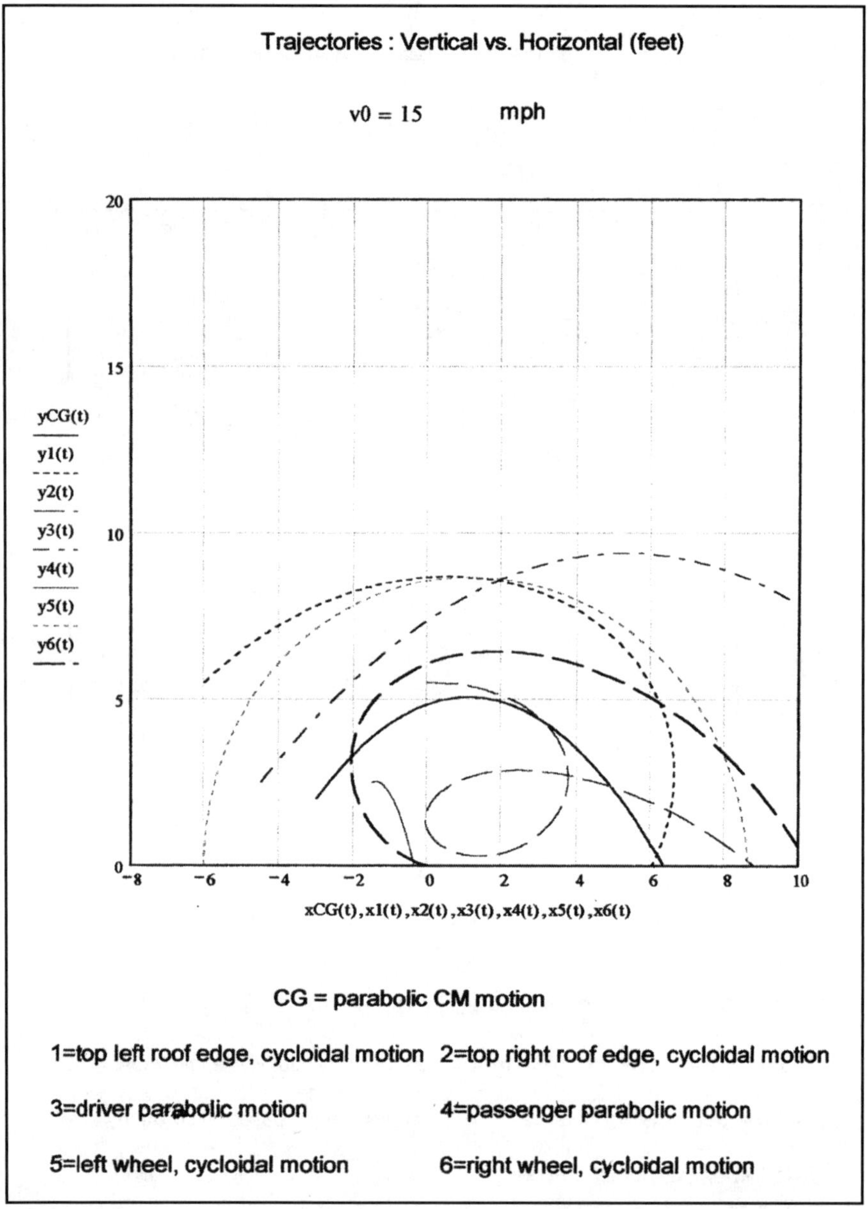
Trajectories : Vertical vs. Horizontal (feet)
v0 = 15 mph
yCG(t)
y1(t)
y2(t)
y3(t)
y4(t)
y5(t)
y6(t)
xCG(t), x1(t), x2(t), x3(t), x4(t), x5(t), x6(t)
CG = parabolic CM motion
1=top left roof edge, cycloidal motion
2=top right roof edge, cycloidal motion
3=driver parabolic motion
4=passenger parabolic motion
5=left wheel, cycloidal motion
6=right wheel, cycloidal motion

Figure 12.8

This problem has been studied by Cooperrider (ref 117) who gives the following relationship for μ versus t:

$$\mu = D + \sqrt{C + BA / t^2} \tag{12.27}$$

where $D = T/4h$, $C = (T/4h)^2$, $B = 2(k^2 + R^2)/(gh)$ and

$$A = \sqrt{\left(\frac{T}{2h}\right)^2 + 1} - 1 \tag{12.28}$$

Here, T is the track width, h is the initial height of the CM, R is the radial distance between the CM and the contact point of rotation (the leading wheels), and k is the vehicle radius of gyration about a horizontal axis through the CM.

When t is large the equation reduces to $\mu = T/2h$ which is the minimum friction needed to just cause rollover. However, as t becomes small, the equation reduces to

$$\mu t = \sqrt{BA} \tag{12.29}$$

And including g we obtain for the initial sliding velocity

$$v_0 = \left(\frac{K}{h}\right)\sqrt{2g(R-h)} \tag{12.30}$$

where

$$K = \sqrt{k^2 + R^2} \tag{12.31}$$

and is the total radius of gyration for rotation about the leading wheel(s) contact with the ground.

This value of v_0 is the same value that is derived by assuming the "momentum" approach to rollover (see Appendix A), assuming a sudden curb strike, and can be renamed vCRITICAL.

The implied side-slide distance is then given by

$$Dist(\mu) = v_0^2 / 2g\mu = 0.5\mu g t^2 \tag{12.32}$$

The following plots show the relationships between μ, t, v_0 and distance.

We see that as μ increases from $T/2h$ to a very large value so t decreases. Simultaneously, the value of vCRITICAL decreases to a fixed value while the skid distance decreases to zero.

How is this data useful? Suppose we have a vehicle which has undergone a single quarter-turn roll, and has skidmarks of length, dist, leading up to the rollover. By knowing the geometric values for the vehicle (T, h, R and k) we can read the calculated plot of distance versus vCRIT, which then gives the value of μ, which then also gives the corresponding value of t.

Example: let the skid distance be 20 feet. The plots then give a critical initial speed of about 33 mph. For this speed the plots give t of about 0.6 secs, while we also get μ of about 2.0. If instead the skid length is only 5 feet, vCRIT is about 21 mph, the time is about 0.3 secs and the friction is about 3.0. Finally, if the skid distance reduces to zero, vCRIT is about 15 mph (the curb-strike value) while the time approximates zero and the friction is very high.

We may also approximate the condition that allows for the vehicle to become airborne (to "fly"). The airborne condition occurs when the implied rise against gravity for the vehicle CM exceeds the rise needed to complete the roll and reach TDC. The modified equation becomes

$$\mu\mu(t) = D + \sqrt{C + BA\frac{E^2}{t^2}} \tag{12.33}$$

where $E = 2.K / T$.

As before for large t, this reduces to $\mu\mu = T/2h$, and implies "flying" occurs very close to TDC (i.e., the net angle between the CM and the horizontal is essentially 90 degrees). However, for very short timing, where $\mu\mu$ is large the implied velocity to start "flying" is given by

$$\text{vFLY} = E.\text{vCRIT} \tag{12.34}$$

The plots show the relationships between vFLY, t, $\mu\mu$, and Dist. Here Dist is the length of tire marks before the airborne condition is reached. Clues that "flying" occurred are given by a noticeable gap between the end of the tire marks and the position of first ground impact for the vehicle.

The overall logic is as follows. First assume a value of side friction and vary the initial side speed. For low speed (below vCRIT) the sliding will stop and the vehicle will rise but the angular rate will be insufficient to cause rollover, and the vehicle crashes back down on its wheels. As the speed increases above the critical value the sliding will guarantee rollover, but there will be no actual airborne motion. When the speed exceeds vFLY the sliding will stop but the vehicle now becomes airborne and may continue rolling beyond the first quarter-turn.

For higher speeds the total number of quarter-turns increases and the net distance to stop increases. Based purely on empirical studies the average "effective" friction beyond the first condition of going airborne (or first subsequent ground impact) has been found to be in the range 0.4 – 0.6. To date, no one has explained this value. This effective friction is a mixture of true friction during ground impacts and the "zero" friction that occurs during flight between ground impacts. More recently it has been shown that the effective friction may itself decrease with overall post-airborne motion (Rose and Beauchamp, ref 116).

When the initial friction is only slightly larger than $T/2h$ the vertical height achieved when going airborne is small because the flight phase occurs close to the TDC condition, which means the angle of launch (measured up from the horizontal) is small. But for much larger friction the vehicle can rise much more dramatically because flight occurs at a higher speed and the angle of launch becomes larger.

Rollover Cooperrider (modified)

$T := 6.0 \qquad h := 2.0 \qquad H := 5.5 \qquad W := 6.0 \qquad g := 32.2$

$$k := \sqrt{\frac{(W^2 + H^2)}{12}} \qquad R := \sqrt{\left(h^2 + \frac{T^2}{4}\right)}$$

$$A := \sqrt{\left(\frac{T}{2 \cdot h}\right)^2 + 1} - 1 \qquad B := 2 \cdot \frac{(k^2 + R^2)}{g \cdot h} \qquad C := \left(\frac{T}{4 \cdot h}\right)^2 \qquad D := \left(\frac{T}{4 \cdot h}\right)$$

$A = 0.803 \qquad B = 0.575 \qquad C = 0.563 \qquad D = 0.75$

$t := 0.001, 0.002 .. 3.0 \qquad R = 3.606 \qquad K := \sqrt{k^2 + R^2} \qquad K = 4.304$

$$\mu(t) := D + \sqrt{C + B \cdot \frac{A}{t^2}} \qquad vcrit := \left(\frac{K}{h}\right) \cdot \frac{\sqrt{2 \cdot g \cdot (R - h)}}{1.467}$$

Momentum equation

Cooperrider et al equation

$vcrit = 14.915$ **mph**

$$\Lambda := \frac{T}{2 \cdot h}$$

$\Lambda = 1.5$ **Static Stability Index**

$$E := 2 \cdot \frac{K}{T} \qquad E = 1.435$$

$t := 0.001, 0.002 .. 3.0$

$$\mu\mu(t) := D + \sqrt{C + B \cdot A \cdot \frac{E^2}{t^2}} \qquad vfly := E \cdot vcrit$$

$vfly := E \cdot vcrit \qquad vfly = 21.396$ **mph**

μ versus time (secs) for "Just Topple" and "Just Fly"

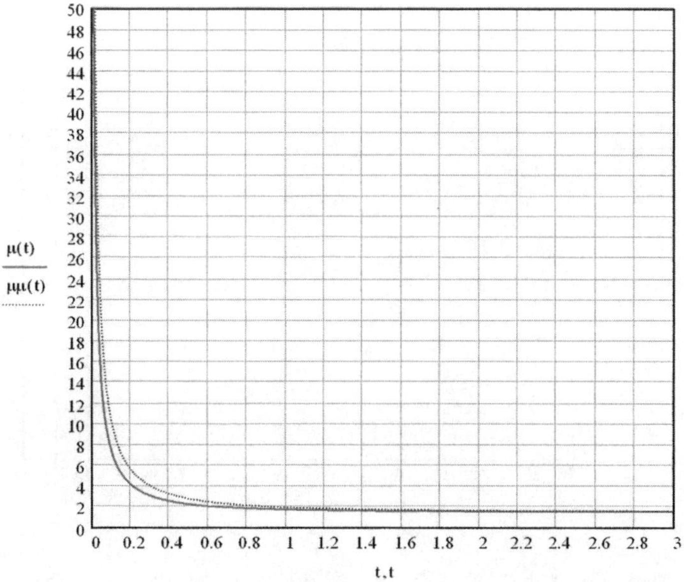

$$vCRIT(t) := \mu(t) \cdot g \cdot \frac{t}{1.467} \quad \text{mph} \qquad vcrit = 14.915 \quad \text{mph}$$

$$vFLY(t) := \mu\mu(t) \cdot g \cdot \frac{t}{1.467} \qquad vfly = 21.396$$

vCRIT and vFLY (mph) versus time (secs) to "Just Topple" and "Just Fly"

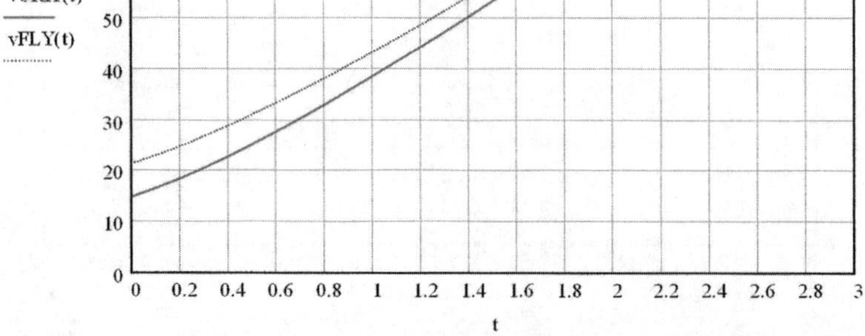

vCRIT and vFLY (mph) versus μ to "Just Topple" or "Just FLY"

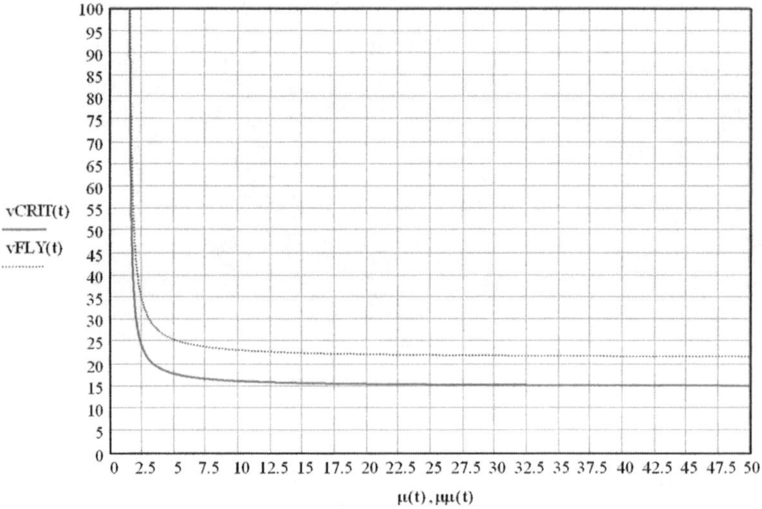

$\text{dist}(t) := 0.5 \cdot g \cdot \mu(t) \cdot t^2$ ft $\text{Dist}(t) := 0.5 \cdot g \cdot \mu\mu(t) \cdot t^2$

Slide Distance (ft), and vCRIT and vFLY (mph) versus μ to "Just Topple" or "Just FLY"

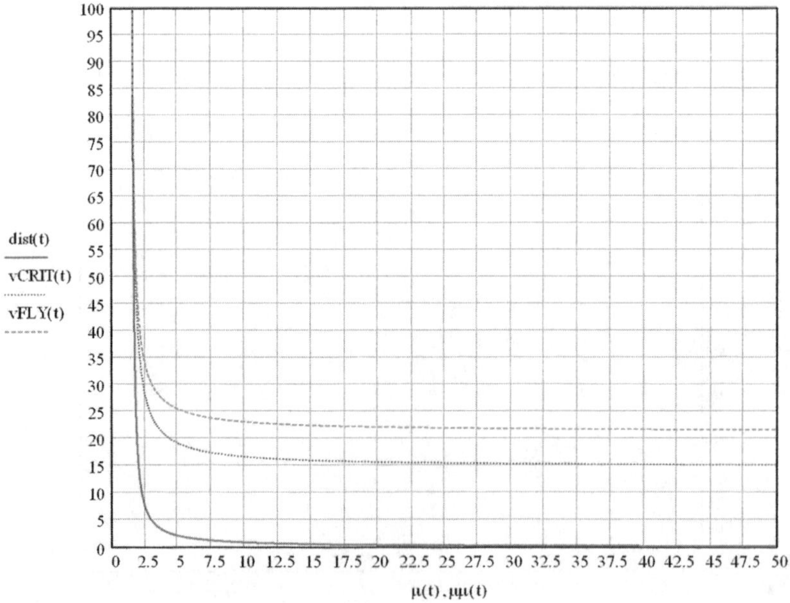

Slide dist(ance) (ft), and μ versus vCRIT (mph)

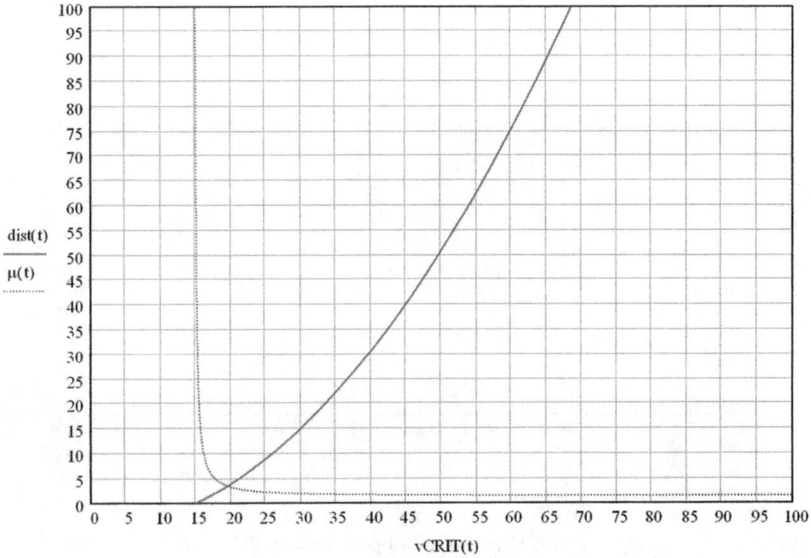

Slide Dist(ance) (ft) and μ versus vFLY (mph)

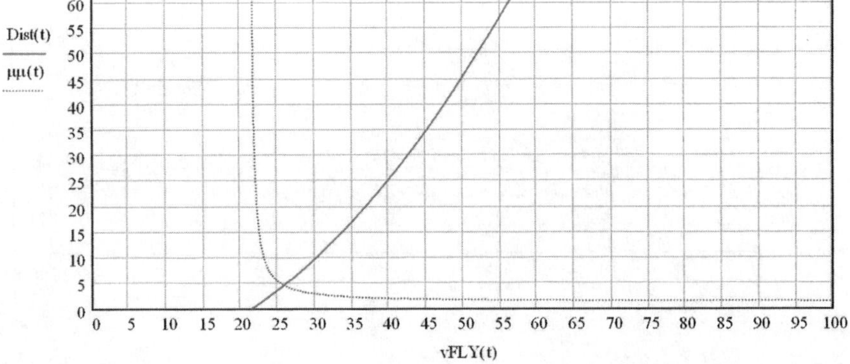

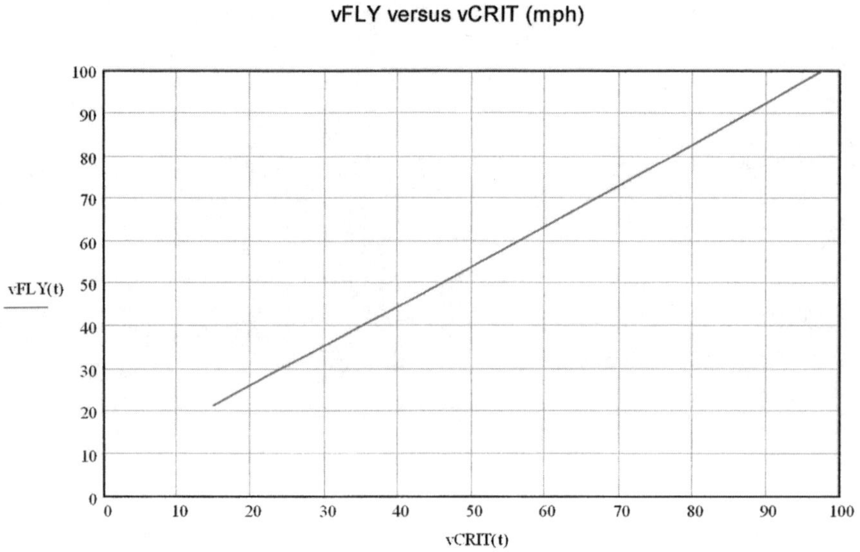
vFLY versus vCRIT (mph)
vFLY(t)
vCRIT(t)
0
10
20
30
40
50
60
70
80
90
100

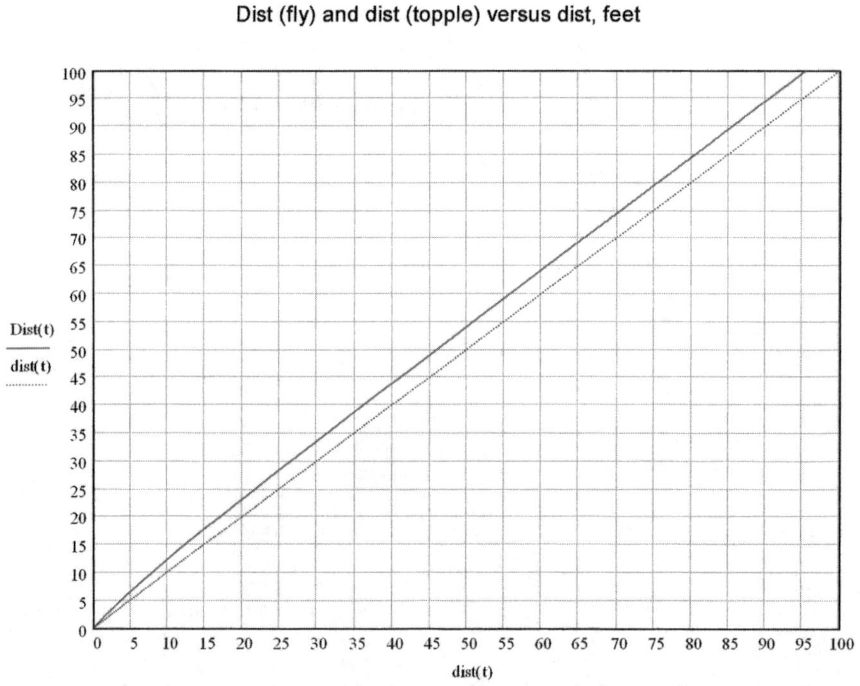
Dist (fly) and dist (topple) versus dist, feet
Dist(t)
dist(t)
dist(t)
0
5
10
15
20
25
30
35
40
45
50
55
60
65
70
75
80
85
90
95
100

Chapter 13

A Typical Mathcad Solution

Synopsis

13.1 Introduction

Here we illustrate the typical Mathcad approach to solving a two-vehicle collision. We define vehicle 1 as the *stronger* body (which is *usually* the heavier vehicle), 2 as the *weaker* one (usually the lighter vehicle). We use book-quoted values for $w1$, which is the curb weight, while $w3$ is the loaded weight (with occupants, cargo and any trailer(s)). Likewise, for vehicle 2 we use $w2$ and $w4$. Curb weight is needed because it typically determines the actual strength parameters of the vehicle. Using the POD model these are the R and a values. (Chapter 10 gives the relationship between the POD parameters and the more common CRASH3 parameters A, B and G.) Loaded weight is needed to determine total momentum and total energy. Ignoring special cases, such as a welded plate or strut, cargo does not affect the basic strength of a vehicle. In particular, for a frontal hit with a tractor-trailer unit the strength depends on the tractor. The loaded trailer merely adds to the total momentum and available energy. As an example, a large tractor (with sleeper cabin) can weigh about 18,000 lbs and would be used for $w1$. Adding the weight of the trailer and cargo then gives $w3$ (total loaded weight), which can be up to 80,000 lbs for typical inter-state commerce.

Conversely, for a rear-end hit into the trailer, $w1$ becomes the empty trailer weight, and we must estimate the equivalent "bumper capability" for any ICC rear bumper bar. We then add the tractor and cargo weight to get $w3$.

For bumper behavior we use full-width capability, since fractional width and angular effects are handled by the F and θ terms. Unless we have specific evidence to the contrary, we assume cars have 5 mph bumpers ($vL = 7.335$ ft/s) while pick-ups, vans, SUVs and heavy trucks have 2.5 mph bumpers (3.668 ft/s). For cases where there is no bumper (side hits into doors, or frontal hits for a car missing its front bumper etc.) we assume the equivalent bumper speed is very small at about 2 ft/s (about 1.4 mph).

In Chapter 6 we gave the relationship between bumper speed and the R term. Summarizing,

$$v_L^2 = Rgx \qquad 13.1$$
$$\text{or } x = v_L^2/(Rg)$$

where v_L is in ft/s, g is in ft/s^2 and x is in inches. For a 5 mph bumper and $R = 0.6$ the value of $x = 2.78$ inches, which is the "stroke" capability of the bumper before bottoming. On the other hand, if $v_L = 2$ ft/s we get $x = 0.21$ inches. This small value is typical of the very small deformation that non-bumper sections of the vehicle can withstand before permanent damage starts.

Most AR analyses are usually spot calculations. By this we mean the calculation(s) are done for a *specific* degree of crush for the vehicles. With the high speed capabilities of modern computers, we prefer to calculate *ranges* of possible crushes, starting with zero crush (the "incipient damage" condition) and extending to a crush known to be larger than actually occurred in a given collision. This approach has the immediate advantage of indicating the sensitivity of answers. Further, once the equations are written the code allows for very rapid changes (including temporary override values) in suggested parameter values so that overall sensitivity can be established.

The calculations are set up assuming a two-vehicle collision. To mimic a one-vehicle into a heavy rigid barrier case, we merely set vehicle 1 to have enormous weight (e.g., 1,000,000 lbs) and rigidity (large R value), so that the barrier's energy absorption due to induced motion and crush becomes negligible.

Having established the curb weights we perform an "off-code" (pen and paper or hand-calculator) estimate for the gamma terms, to handle any non-central impacts that cause vehicle spin. Note how the code allows a previously defined parameter, such as $w3$ and $w4$ to be redefined using these gamma factors. We also estimate the F values, which are the fractional width factors for damage regions, and the effective θ angular values to describe non-normal thrusts. We also establish the bumper speeds. These latter are the same as the "non-damage" estimates used by others. Note how we can define the bumper limits to account for angular thrusts.

We next use "scaling rules" to establish the R and a values. These can be overridden if the analyst prefers. These rules use the curb weights since they are used to establish strengths of the vehicles. This logic is similar to the one used by CRASH3 users who regularly choose A, B and G values based on "wheel-based groups" for vehicles that have not been individually tested.

The "built-in" scaling laws assume a "1/3 power law" for both the R and a terms. This is a simplification based on the logic that heavier vehicles are scaled-up versions of lighter ones with each dimension increasing with $w^{1/3}$, where w is the weight. In reality this assumption is rarely exact, but various alternative options have shown the overall results do not change very quickly. Since both the R, a, and v_L terms can be overridden the analyst can redefine these values using the CRASH3 A, B and G terms (if known and credible) by applying the following equations:

$$R = AW/12w \text{ (dimensionless)} \qquad 13.2$$

and

$$a = A/B \text{ (inches)} = A/12B \text{ (feet)}$$

where W is vehicle width (inches), and w is vehicle weight (lbs). The equivalent value for bumper speed is then given by

$$(1/2)(w/g)\,v_L^2 = (1/2)(A^2/B)(W/12) = GW/12 \text{ (ft-lbs)} \qquad 13.3$$

or

$$v_L^2 = (g/w)(A^2/B)(W/12) = (2g/w)(GW/12) \text{ (ft/s}^2\text{)} \qquad 13.4$$

Since the POD model is similar to CRASH3 (except for low speeds) this set of conversions essentially converts POD into the CRASH3 logic, for medium to high speeds.

Next, we compute the force levels to just-cause crush on the two vehicles. These forces are load values, $L1$ and $L2$. Since vehicle 1 is stronger (by definition), we use the force equations to determine the crush level for vehicle 2 (i.e., $x20$) that corresponds to the incipient crush of vehicle 1 (i.e., $x1 = 0$). For vehicle 2 the crush is $x2$ from zero up to the value $x20$. For greater crush, we redefine vehicle 2 crush as $x3$, while the strong vehicle is always $x1$. Note we always use *feet* rather than the more common *inches* for crush.

Thus, for $0 < x2 < x20$ we have $x1 = 0.0$, while for $x2$ $(= x3) > x20$ we have $x1$ finite.

Note how by computing $x1$ based on $x2$ (or $x3$) using the force equations we are automatically satisfying Newton's Third Law! This is a critical aspect of our technique.

We then use the quoted equation to calculate the critical speed, which is the maximum closing speed that just fails to produce permanent damage to the *weaker* vehicle (2). See Chapter 6 to understand the origin of this equation. This critical speed is useful for low-speed collisions, but it is also used to define the *mutual* coefficient of restitution for the *collision* (not just the individual barrier values). The coefficient of restitution ($ee(x2)$ and $ff(x3)$) values are automatically mutual answers since the coefficient is based on the critical speed (which is a mutual answer) and the calculated closing speed (which is also a mutual answer). Our logic is simplified to make restitution proportional to the critical speed (no permanent damage for either vehicle, so mostly "elastic" response) and inversely proportional to the computed final closing speed (which can involve vehicle crush(s) and be ever more strongly "plastic").

Initially, we compute for the range $0 < x2 < x20$ and establish absorbed energy and force for vehicle 2 as a function of increasing $x2$. In combination with the critical speed, this allows the closing speed to be established (a sum-of-squares calculation) and the restitution as well. Note that whereas the force-strength values are based on the *curb weights*, calculations for speeds (closing and delta-v's) are all computed using the *loaded weights,* which include any spin-related spin factors.

For $x2$ $(= x3) > x20$, we continue to calculate the increasing force and energy absorption for vehicle 2. But now we also compute the increasing values of $x1$, and the absorbed energy of vehicle 1. Consequently, as $x3$ increases so also $x1$ increases. Likewise the absorbed energies $E2(x3)$ and $E1(x1,x3)$ are also computed as a function of $x3$ and $x1$. This allows the closing speed to be established. This is based on the critical speed, the loaded weights and the *sum* of absorbed energies (again a sum-of-speeds calculation). Likewise, the (changing) value of mutual coefficient of restitution is also evaluated as a function of increasing crush.

Knowing the loaded weights (with spin corrections), the closing speed and the restitution, we can then compute the corresponding values of delta-v. These are the implied sudden changes in vehicle speeds. The initial values apply to the two *contact areas* of the vehicles. The second calculations are for the corresponding center-of-mass (CM or CG) motions. For central hits (gamma = 1.0 for a vehicle) the contact and CM answers are the same (there is no spin). Note that *which* vehicle experiences a positive or negative delta-v depends solely on the logic of which vehicle we consider to be the *bullet* and *target*. Physics states these terms are interchangeable! The code allows the appropriate + and – terms to be applied as required. Likewise, the plots can readily allow definition of zero and positive or negative limits to be defined.

Based on the rigidity of each vehicle we can compute the approximate implied timing of the collision. The timing is also a *mutual* answer. We compute the "quarter period" and "total contact time." The quarter period presupposes the response is similar to a mass-on-spring system, and describes the time during which the compressive phase occurs, whereas the total contact time includes the effects of restitution and rebound. These timings are seen to be functions of the crush of vehicle 2 (and of $x1$ where appropriate). For negligible crush the timings are determined by the stiffness of the vehicles in or near the bumper-only phase. The slope of the force-displacement curve is large for this phase. However, as vehicle crush increases, the slope of the force-displacement curve becomes that of the overall crush behavior of each vehicle (i.e., based on the *B* term for CRASH3 or the *a* term for POD). For this reason the quarter period starts as a small value for small crush but steadily increases (and then limits) as crush increases. Because the coefficient of restitution steadily decreases with increasing crush, the total contact time also steadily decreases towards the quarter period for large crush. But there can be a local maximum for small crush.

Finally, by knowing the mutual force between the vehicles we can also compute the peak acceleration experienced by each vehicle. Again, this can be given for the contact areas and the vehicle CM's, and also define + and – according to logic.

An estimate of the effect of vehicle braking *during* the collision can also be done. This is only an approximation since it is not based on a calculation that includes the time-dependent buildup of crush force versus the time-independent frictional forces. (Instead, we use the average crush force.) This logic is based on the one given in Chapter 11. This is mostly useful for low-speed collisions and is set up for the case of a moving bullet vehicle and a stationary target. The logic is simple: during a collision any braking by the bullet vehicle will *add* force to the mutual crush force, thereby increasing the deceleration (increasing the magnitude of bullet delta-v), while for the target braking force *subtracts* from the mutual crush force, thereby decreasing overall acceleration (and decreasing the target delta-v). Braking force is assumed to be a function of vehicle weight and friction and thus constant per vehicle. Crush force increases with the intensity of the collision.

The results are given as ratios of closing speed, and delta-v's in the form of *with friction or without friction,* and again are plotted versus *x*2 (*x*3). The largest deviations in the ratios from unity always occur for strong braking and very small crush, as expected. As crush increases for either or both vehicles, so braking forces become negligible versus the common crush force, and all ratios become unity. This, of course, is consistent with the usual "ignoring" of vehicle braking (during the crash) assumed for the analysis of most medium-to-high speed collisions.

A most interesting case is for a typical car rear-ending a stationary tractor-trailer unit which is fully applying its brakes. If we assume the 80,000 lb heavy truck has an overall drag factor of 0.5 we need a crush force of 40,000 lbs merely to start the truck moving. If the collision produces a mutual crush force of less than this the car will simply come to a halt but the delta-v for the truck will remain zero (the truck will merely undergo damped oscillation on its suspension). There will of course be crush damage to the front of the car and some to the rear of the trailer, but the truck motion is essentially zero. For this case the heavy truck acts as a barrier but with a crushable bumper. Because the rear end of the trailer absorbs energy (in addition to the car damage), the actual closing speed is *larger* than would occur for a true barrier hit, and likewise the car delta-v is also larger (even without including any restitution) for a given degree of crush for the car.

13.2 Code Output

Mathcad will give reams of tabular data if so desired. Such data is rarely of interest except for debugging efforts. Usually we suppress the tabular data to "short columns" merely to confirm that the code is giving meaningful results.

A far more useful output is the generation of 2D plots giving the response of one parameter versus another (3D plots are also possible, if appropriate). For overall consistency, and ease of comparison throughout the plots, we choose to use a common abscissa, which is the crush for the weaker vehicle $x2$ ($x3$). Using "internal interpolation" the code can plot any parameter versus any other, so we can plot delta-v versus crush $x1$ or versus closing speed, or any other paired combination.

As with other codes everything is read in a left-to-right and top-to-bottom fashion. The symbol ":=" implies a definition, whereas the symbol "=" implies an evaluation. The symbol ":= *a*, *b*,…*m*" gives a range and means "start with *a*, end with *m*, and use *b-a* as the interval."

With regard to angles the default is to assume radians. However, the code allows for degrees (e.g., sin45 with the angle in degrees is written sin(45*deg)). An alternative is to convert by using 1.0 radian = 57.3 degrees. We prefer the latter approach because it forces the user to think about the angles, rather than blindly assuming proper definition.

Note how a parameter can be instantly overridden by the simple act of redefinition so long as the new value is to the right or below the initial definition.

Having defined our inputs, we proceed to calculate the critical speed. Then we calculate force versus weak vehicle crush and calculate absorbed energy. We continue to do this as $x2$ ($x3$) increases, and include $x1$ values once the stronger vehicle begins to crush.

The first plot is of $x1$ versus $x2$ ($x3$). If this plot does *not* conform to the observed collision we must redefine the vehicle parameters (for strength) until a correct relationship is obtained. The logic here is the same as that proposed by Hull (ref 26). Assuming one vehicle has a reasonably understood crush behavior we adjust the other until the results are compatible.

The next plots are of the delta-v's for both the contact regions and the CMs. These delta-v plots are subsequently followed by plots giving closing velocity and implied restitution. Then we plot the relative absorbed vehicle energies and the implied timings. Finally, we plot the mutual contact force and the resulting peak accelerations for the contact regions and the vehicle CMs.

Chapter 14

Side-Swipe Collisions

Synopsis

14.1 Introduction

What exactly is a side-swipe collision? It is a collision in which the two contacting surfaces do *not* come to a common velocity. Remember, velocity is a vector and as such can be resolved into two components. One is perpendicular to a sliding surface and the other is tangential to the surface. While the perpendicular component (e.g., the *normal* component) may temporarily achieve a common velocity (before any rebound) the tangential component may not. Since the net velocity vector is the sum of the components, this means the net value does not reach the condition of commonality.

Be careful not to confuse this situation with the offset (or non-central) impact which induces spin for at least one vehicle. With the latter impact the two vehicle CM's (centers-of-mass) do not achieve a common velocity, but the two contacting surfaces may.

A side-swipe can usually be recognized by noting a disparity in the widths of damage. For instance, suppose a 5-foot wide car hits the side of a larger pick-up. The entire frontal width of the car suffers obvious impact damage, but the width of damage to the side of the pick-up is about 10 feet. Assuming this damage is not merely "induced crush" but is actual contact damage, then the pick-up must have been sliding across the front of the car during the collision, by the excess 5 feet.

Consider a mass, m, moving at velocity v_0 (which is the *closing velocity*) at an angle θ to the surface of a large, stationary, heavy, rigid wall. The angle is measured with respect to the normal. We choose a heavy wall (barrier) to force all velocity and energy changes to be those of the mass, m, only. We resolve the velocity into a normal component and a tangential component.

$$v_N = v_0 \cos(\theta) \quad \text{and} \quad v_T = v_0 \sin(\theta) \tag{14.1}$$

Now let the post-impact velocities be

$$v_N' = -e v_0 \cos(\theta) \quad \text{and} \quad v_T' = \mu v_0 \sin(\theta) \tag{14.2}$$

Here, e is the coefficient of restitution along the normal to the wall, and the negative sign occurs due to the usual rebound and reversal of direction. We assume $0 < e < 1.0$. The quantity μ is the "equivalent" factor describing the "pass-through" of velocity in the tangential direction. A positive value implies a continued component, whereas a value of zero implies the tangential component drops to zero. (Note, in theory the value of μ can actually become negative, but this implies a rebound in the tangential direction, and will only occur if the contact surfaces act like a "ratchet-and-pinion." For most cases we assume μ to be in the range $0 < \mu < 1.0$. Likewise, the value of e can also be negative, but this only applies if the bullet vehicle passes right through a target vehicle: the classic bullet-through-the-head case for weapons.

It can now be shown that $\mu = 1 - f(1 + e)/\tan(\theta)$ where f is the "operative" or "effective" value of friction between the surfaces. By this we mean it is rarely equal to the value quoted in standard tables. The latter values for friction assume the surfaces remain macroscopically flat, whereas with vehicle collisions a flat surface rarely occurs during impact.

We immediately see that we can define a critical value for the approach angle

$$\tan(\theta crit) = f(1+e) \text{ so we also have } \mu = \left(1 - \frac{\tan(\theta crit)}{\tan(\theta)}\right) \tag{14.3}$$

If $\theta < \theta\ crit$ we set $\mu = 0.0$

Now consider the changes in velocity. This will define the true direction of thrust (given by ϕ) and the true value of delta-v. We easily see that

$$\tan(\phi) = \frac{(1-\mu)v_0 \sin(\theta)}{(1+e)v_0 \cos(\theta)} = \frac{1-\mu}{1+e}\tan(\theta) \tag{14.4}$$

$$\text{And, } delta\text{-}v = v_0 \cos(\theta)\sqrt{1 + \left[\frac{1-\mu}{1+e}\right]^2 \tan(\theta)^2} \tag{14.5}$$

$$\text{i.e. } delta\text{-}v = v_0 \cos(\theta)\sqrt{1 + \tan(\phi)^2} = \frac{v_0 \cos(\theta)}{\cos(\phi)} \tag{14.6}$$

We see that $\phi < \theta$, which implies the direction of thrust is smaller than the direction of arrival, and is closer to the surface normal. Likewise the true delta-v is smaller than normally expected (e.g., using CRASH3 or the POD model). Because we are considering only a mass, *m*, this factor can be readily re-inserted to consider momentum effects.

For energy we note the input can be described by

$$\mathrm{E} = 0.5\ \mathrm{m}\ v_0^2 = 0.5\ \mathrm{m}\ v_0^2\ [\cos(\theta)^2 + \sin(\theta)^2] \tag{14.7}$$

Whereas, post-impact

$$\mathrm{E}' = 0.5\ \mathrm{m}\ v_0^2\ [e^2 \cos(\theta)^2 + \mu^2 \sin(\theta)^2]\ \text{giving} \tag{14.8}$$

$$\text{delta-E} = 0.5\ \mathrm{m}\ v_0^2\ [(1 - e^2)\ (\cos(\theta))^2 + (1 - \mu^2)\ \sin(\theta)^2] \tag{14.9}$$

$$\text{Or } delta\text{-}E = 0.5mv_0^2\left(1-e^2\right)\left(\cos(\theta)^2\right)\left[1+\frac{1-\mu^2}{1-e^2}\tan(\theta)^2\right] \tag{14.10}$$

Note carefully, the bracket term including μ and *e* is *not* the same for energy as for the velocity or momentum terms (we cannot convert into a tan(ϕ) term).

How do we use these equations for a two-vehicle case where one body is *not* considered a stationary barrier? This can be done by realizing that we must use the effective mass given by

$$m_{eff} = \frac{m_1 m_2}{m_1 + m_2} \tag{14.11}$$

which should also include any "gamma" factors describing non-central impacts that induce vehicle spin. Also, we must redefine the angles.

For the body that acts as the sliding surface, the angle θ is reduced to the angle ϕ. But this implies an angular swing of (θ *swing* = θ – ϕ) has occurred for the direction of thrust. Since Newton's Third Law states the angle of thrust must be equal (but opposite) for the other body, this implies any assumed initial angle of approach for this other body must also be swung around by the amount θ *swing*.

This process results in the same logic used by CRASH3 (or POD) but with modified angles of thrust for each body (and associated energy changes).

Note an interesting point: if we set *f* to a very large value and *e* to zero, the equations all revert back to those assumed by CRASH3 (or POD). Put another way, the methodology of CRASH3 *presupposes* very large friction and very small restitution, which is the same as saying it assumes the common velocity condition. This immediately allows for a simple modification of the CRASH3 equations. We merely introduce K factors (K for Korrect) which include *f* and *e*. This is shown below.

Also note that when (θ) > (θ *crit*) the value of

$$\frac{1-\mu}{1+e}\tan(\theta)=\tan(\phi)=f. \tag{14.12}$$

This merely means that for large enough values of θ the tangential thrust is directly determined by the effective friction.

An interesting consequence of these factors are given by the following two examples:

Example 1

Assume a car moves from left to right and also aims sideways (to its right) into a vertical bank of earth (dirt) which causes the right front corner (passenger side) to "dig into" the earth. For this case we assume a large friction and small restitution. The resulting thrust is parallel to the vehicle longitudinal axis (since $\phi = \theta$). But this thrust is along the passenger side of the vehicle, which constitutes a non-central hit. The result is to induce a clockwise spin and the car can swing around and end up facing the way it came.

Example 2

Now consider the same case except the earth is replaced by a "slippery" wall and restitution is finite. Now the thrust is much closer to the normal surface ($\phi << \theta$) of the wall. This thrust is now "across the bow" of the car and aims past the driver (to her left). The result is to induce a counterclockwise spin. Coupled with the finite restitution, the result is to redirect the car back into the traffic lane it came out of. This is more typical of what happens with a concrete (or metal) roadside barrier.

Finally, consider the resulting angle of reflection. This is defined in the same manner as used for optics where incidence and reflection angles are both defined relative to the normal to the surface. For incidence we have

$$\tan(\theta)=\frac{v_0\sin(\theta)}{v_0\cos(\theta)}=\tan(\theta), \text{ a trivial answer.} \tag{14.13}$$

But for reflection we have

$$\tan(\varepsilon)=\frac{\mu v_0\sin(\theta)}{ev_0\cos(\theta)}=\left(\frac{\mu}{e}\right)\tan(\theta) \tag{14.14}$$

For significant sliding (low friction) and moderate restitution we immediately see that $\varepsilon > \theta$. This is commonly seen in many roadside barrier hits where θ may be about 70 degrees (grazing angle of 20 degrees) while ε may be about

80 degrees (grazing angle of 10 degrees). Thus, without additional steering, the vehicle ricochets off the barrier with a small grazing angle. Sometimes the combination of rebound (restitution) and counterclockwise spin allows the rear of the vehicle to also impact the barrier before the vehicle "escapes" the barrier (a second "slap"). This causes a second clockwise spin and the vehicle stays close to the barrier, but still moving forward.

To help understand these effects consider the special case of an intersection collision, where the two vehicles are initially moving orthogonally (at 90 degrees) to each other. Assume the bullet (1) has velocity $v10$, while the target (2) has velocity $v20$. The closing velocity is given by the Pythagoras theorem:

$$v_{CLOSING} = \sqrt{v_{10}^2 + v_{20}^2} \tag{14.15}$$

Let the bullet run into the driver's side of the target. This makes the target side the sliding surface, while the hit on the bullet is frontal. Using the CRASH3 logic we would conclude that the two directions of thrust are parallel to the closing speed vector. Hence, relative to the normal of the target, the angle of thrust is $\tan(\theta_2) = v_{20} / v_{10}$. Likewise, for the bullet, the angle of thrust is $\tan(\theta_1) = v_{20} / v_{10}$. Thus for this *special case* the two angles are equal. This occurs because of the initial 90 degrees of motion.

However, the above logic assumes very high friction and very small restitution. When this is not true we must define μ and e and thus the new angle ϕ. Thus, the true angle of thrust to the side of the target is smaller than expected, and the angular swing is simply the difference between θ and ϕ. But this also causes the angle of thrust to swing around for the bullet. The new angle for the bullet is simply:

$$\theta_1 new = \theta_1 - (\theta_2 - \phi) = \phi, \text{ because } \theta_1 = \theta_2 \tag{14.16}$$

We see that both vehicles experience a smaller angle of thrust. This then alters the cosine and cosine^2 terms within CRASH3 and thus modifies the assumed energy-loss terms, the closing speed, and the two delta-v's for the vehicles, based on the crush observed *along the normal* for each vehicle surface.

Remember, crush is always measured along the normal to an impacted surface. When at an angle, CRASH3 (and POD) assume the effective crush is given by

$$X = \frac{x_{NORMAL}}{\cos(\theta)}, \text{ which also gives } thrust = \frac{thrust_{NORMAL}}{\cos(\theta)} \tag{14.17}$$

$$\text{Likewise, } E_{loss} = E_{normal}\left(1 + \tan(\theta)^2\right) = \frac{E_{normal}}{\cos(\theta)^2} \tag{14.18}$$

$$\text{Finally, } delta\text{-}v_1 = -\frac{w_2}{w_2 + w_1} v_{CLOSING} \tag{14.19}$$

$$\text{And, } delta\text{-}v_2 = +\frac{w_1}{w_1 + w_2} v_{CLOSING} \tag{14.20}$$

Where the w's are the effective vehicle weights (mass times gravity, g), taking into account any non-central spin effects. The latter are handled by *gamma* factors where

$$\gamma_1 = 1 + \left(\frac{r_1}{k_1}\right)^2 \quad \text{and} \quad \gamma_2 = 1 + \left(\frac{r_2}{k_2}\right)^2 \tag{14.21}$$

Where the r values are the torque-arms (or moment-arms) and the k values are the radii of gyration.

$$\text{Then } w_{EFF} = \frac{w_{TRUE}}{\gamma} \text{ for each vehicle.} \tag{14.22}$$

Note: some authors use the *inverse* of this definition for gamma. This merely means we multiply instead of divide (in either case effective mass, or weight, is reduced versus true values).

14.2 Small-Angle Effects

Many two-vehicle collisions inherently involve small angles of θ. These include near in-line crashes such as head-on and rear-end. Also an intersection crash can involve small angles if the target is stopped or slowly moving. For these cases the smaller value of ϕ *(versus* θ*)* will have very little effect. For example if θ is 10 degrees and ϕ is 5 degrees the ratio $\cos(\theta)/\cos(\phi)$ is only 0.9848/0.9962 = 0.9886. This is only a 1.0 percent difference. This explains why many CRASH3 analyses give credible answers. Only for large angles do the effects of surface sliding become significant.

How do we know the values of f and e *a priori*? Put bluntly this is always an issue in any analysis. The solution is to try multiple options and home in on values that appear best to fit the collision at hand. Of course, under ideal conditions we have access to both vehicles post-impact and can align them so as to help define the initial angles. We can also study the degree of entanglement of the bodies to decide if a high or low value of f is warranted. However, we frequently do not have that luxury. Far too often we are asked to solve a crash that occurred some time ago. The vehicles have been junked or repaired. At best someone took good photographs and we have supporting repair estimates, but all too often nobody actually measured the crush. Modern photogrammetry techniques can be useful here and help better define the crush.

14.3 The K Factors

CRASH3 and POD both assume that for a given depth of crush (x) the force involved is proportional to [1/cosine(θ)] where θ is measured from the normal to the surface. Likewise, both models assume the absorbed energy is proportional to $[1/\text{cosine}(\theta)]^2$. To maintain the overall formulation of CRASH3 and POD we rely on the following definition:

$$\frac{1}{\cos(\theta)^2} = 1 + \tan(\theta)^2 \tag{14.23}$$

This allows the definitions

$$K(1 \text{ or } 2) = \left(\frac{1+\tan(\phi)^2}{1+\tan(\theta)^2}\right)^{0.5} \tag{14.24}$$

$$\text{and so we use } F(x,\theta) = \frac{F(x,0)}{\cos(\theta)}K$$

$$KK(1 \text{ or } 2) = \frac{1+\dfrac{(1-\mu^2)}{(1-e^2)}\tan(\theta)^2}{1+\tan(\theta)^2} \tag{14.25}$$

$$\text{So that } E(x,\theta) = \frac{E(x,0)}{\cos(\theta)^2}KK$$

Finally, the delta-v values are multiplied by

$$KKK = \frac{\cos(\theta)}{\cos(\phi)}. \tag{14.26}$$

Because high friction (f) and low restitution (e) automatically reduce the K values to the value 1.0, this technique defaults to the usual CRASH3 or POD approach.

Note that for K(1 or 2) there are two possibilities, and the analyst must decide which is appropriate. Likewise for KK(1 or 2). Also, having decided that (θ1) has changed to (ϕ1) this then gives a swing in angles such that (θ2) becomes (θAS) for the second vehicle.

Analysts using CRASH3 are regularly advised not to use θ > 45 degrees because of potential sliding situations. However, using the above K factor logic, this limitation no longer applies. Indeed, if the values of f and e are large and small, respectively (so that all K become 1.0), the restriction disappears even for large angles.

Example

We give the first three pages of a Mathcad solution showing the application of these factors. The problem concerns a turning Toyota into the side of a Ford pick-up. Initial assumed approach angles (to the side of the Ford and to the front of the Toyota) are about 75 and 45 degrees, respectively. By assuming a friction of 1.0 and a restitution of 0.1 these angles become about 45 and 15 degrees, respectively. These two new angles are then used for the rest of the analysis.

Generic Sideswipe Case (sliding)

Initial Sliding Corrections

e is restitution normal to surface μ is out/in for transverse speed

θ is angle-of-approach for velocity vector (versus normal)

ϕ is angle-of-thrust (versus normal)

f is "effective friction" in the transverse direction

Then $\mu = [1 - f(1+e)/\tan\theta]$ or $\tan\theta = f(1+e)$ is limit to prevent sliding, so $\mu = 0$

NOTE: large f and small e gives the CRASH3 logic

$K = (1-\mu)/(1+e)$ $KK = (1-\mu.\mu)/(1-e.e)$

$KKK = (\cos\theta1/\cos\phi1)$

$p := 57.3$ $f := 1.0$ $e := 0.1$ $\text{Limit} := f\cdot(1 + e)$ $\text{Limit} = 1.1$

$\theta\text{crit} := p\cdot\text{atan}(\text{Limit})$ $\theta\text{crit} = 47.73$ $\delta := 0.1$ offset to prevent "overflow"

$$\theta1 := \frac{75 + \delta}{p} \qquad \theta2 := \frac{45 + \delta}{p} \qquad \cos(\theta1) = 0.257 \qquad \cos(\theta2) = 0.706$$

$$\mu1 := \left(1 - \frac{\tan\left(\frac{\theta\text{crit}}{p}\right)}{\tan(\theta1)}\right) \qquad \mu1 = 0.707 \qquad \mu1 := 0.707$$

Choose μ1

μ cannot be negative

$$\mu2 := \left(1 - \frac{\tan\left(\frac{\theta\text{crit}}{p}\right)}{\tan(\theta2)}\right) \qquad \mu2 = -0.096 \qquad \mu2 := 0.$$

Choose μ2

$$\text{Limit1} := \frac{(1 - \mu1)\cdot\tan(\theta1)}{(1 + e)} \qquad \text{Limit1} = 1.001$$

$$\phi1 := p\cdot\text{atan}(\text{Limit1}) \qquad \phi1 = 45.023 \qquad \cos\left(\frac{\phi1}{p}\right) = 0.707$$

$$\text{Limit2} := (1 - \mu2)\cdot\frac{\tan(\theta2)}{(1 + e)} \qquad \text{Limit2} = 0.912$$

$$\phi2 := p\cdot\text{atan}(\text{Limit2}) \qquad \phi2 = 42.373 \qquad \cos\left(\frac{\phi2}{p}\right) = 0.739$$

AS is angle swing θ-ϕ $\theta\text{swing} := \theta1\cdot p - \phi1$ $\theta\text{swing} = 30.077$

$$\theta\text{AS} := \theta2\cdot p - \theta1\cdot p + \phi1 \qquad \theta\text{AS} = 15.023$$

$$K1 := \sqrt{\frac{\left[1 + \left(\tan\left(\frac{\phi 1}{p}\right)\right)^2\right]}{\left[1 + (\tan(\theta 1))^2\right]}} \qquad K1 = 0.364$$

$$\text{or} \quad K1 := \sqrt{\frac{\left(1 + \tan\left(\frac{\theta AS}{p}\right)^2\right)}{\left(1 + \tan(\theta 1)^2\right)}} \qquad K1 = 0.266$$

Choose K1 $K1 := 0.364$

$$K2 := \sqrt{\frac{\left[1 + \left(\tan\left(\frac{\phi 2}{p}\right)\right)^2\right]}{\left[1 + (\tan(\theta 2))^2\right]}} \qquad K2 = 0.955$$

$$\text{or} \quad K2 := \sqrt{\frac{\left(1 + \tan\left(\frac{\theta AS}{p}\right)^2\right)}{\left(1 + \tan(\theta 2)^2\right)}} \qquad K2 = 0.731$$

Choose K2 $K2 := 0.731$

$$KK1 := \frac{\left[1 + \frac{\left(1 - \mu 1^2\right)\cdot(\tan(\theta 1))^2}{\left(1 - e^2\right)}\right]}{\left[1 + (\tan(\theta 1))^2\right]} \qquad KK1 = 0.538$$

$$\text{or} \quad KK1 := \frac{\left(1 + \tan\left(\frac{\theta AS}{p}\right)^2\right)}{\left(1 + \tan(\theta 1)^2\right)} \qquad KK1 = 0.071$$

Choose KK1 $KK1 := 0.538$

$$KK2 := \frac{\left[1 + \left(1 - \mu 2^2\right)\cdot\frac{(\tan(\theta 2))^2}{\left(1 - e^2\right)}\right]}{\left[1 + (\tan(\theta 2))^2\right]} \qquad KK2 = 1.005$$

or

$$KK2 := \frac{\left(1 + \tan\left(\frac{\theta AS}{p}\right)^2\right)}{\left(1 + \tan(\theta 2)^2\right)} \qquad KK2 = 0.534$$

Choose KK2 $KK2 := 0.534$

$$KKK := \frac{\cos(\theta 1)}{\cos\left(\frac{\phi 1}{p}\right)} \qquad KKK = 0.364$$

Notes: (a) '1' is *strongest* vehicle versus '2'. (b) W1 and W2 are true weights regardless of spin

(c) W3 and W4 are spin-dependent. (d) $\gamma = 1 + rr/kk$. r = torque-arm, k = rad of gyration

W1 is 2006 Ford Ranger empty weight lbs W2 is 2006 Toyota Corolla empty weight lbs

W3 is Ford with load lbs W4 is Toyota with occupant load lbs

γ3 is spin factor $\gamma 3 := 1.25$ γ4 is spin factor $\gamma 4 := 1.25$

$W1 := 3171$ $W2 := 2550$ $A1 := 2.5$ $A2 := 0.6$ $\theta 1 \cdot p = 75.1$ $\phi 1 = 45.023$

$W3 := 3351$ $W4 := 3090$ $F1 := 0.5$ $F2 := 1.0$ $\theta 2 \cdot p = 45.1$ $\theta AS = 15.023$

$vL1 := \frac{2.0 \cdot K1}{\cos(\theta 1)}$ $vL2 := \frac{7.335K2}{\cos(\theta 2)}$ $vL1 = 2.83$ $vL2 = 7.596$

$W3 := \frac{W3}{\gamma 3}$ $W4 := \frac{W4}{\gamma 4}$

$R1 := A1 \cdot \left(\frac{3000}{W1}\right)^{\frac{1}{3}}$ $R1 = 2.454$ $R2 := A2 \cdot \left(\frac{3000}{W2}\right)^{\frac{1}{3}}$ $R2 = 0.633$

$a1 := 0.5 \cdot \left(\frac{W1}{3000}\right)^{\frac{1}{3}}$ $a1 = 0.509$ $a2 := 0.5 \cdot \left(\frac{W2}{3000}\right)^{\frac{1}{3}}$ $a2 = 0.474$

x is crush feet L is load for given crush, lbs

$x2MAX := 5.0$ $L20 := 12 \cdot R2 \cdot W2 \cdot \frac{F2 \cdot K2}{\cos(\theta 2)}$ $L20 = 2.007 \times 10^4$

$x10 := 0$ $L1 := 12 \cdot R1 \cdot W1 \cdot F1 \cdot \left(1 + \frac{x10}{a1}\right) \cdot \frac{K1}{\cos(\theta 1)}$ $L1 = 6.608 \times 10^4$

$$x20 := a2 \cdot \left[R1 \cdot W1 \cdot F1 \cdot \frac{\left(1 + \frac{x10}{a1}\right) \cdot \cos(\theta 2) \cdot K1}{R2 \cdot W2 \cdot F2 \cdot \cos(\theta 1) \cdot K2} \right] - a2 \qquad ge := 32.2$$

$x20 = 1.086$ $L2 := 12 \cdot R2 \cdot W2 \cdot F2 \cdot \left(1 + \frac{x20}{a2}\right) \cdot \frac{K2}{\cos(\theta 2)}$ $L2 = 6.608 \times 10^4$

Chapter 15

Measuring the Crush

Synopsis

15.1 Introduction

What exactly is crush? As defined in the accident reconstruction (AR) profession it refers to the *changes in external dimensions* of a vehicle. In essence, how much a vehicle has permanently shortened in the direction of collision thrust. Strictly speaking this is incorrect. This merely describes the external changes.

During a collision (e.g., with a rigid massive barrier) two stress pulses are generated. The first is an *elastic* pulse whose amplitude is determined by the elastic limit (or yield point) of the structure. This pulse travels at a high speed (typically about 5×10^5 cm/s or about 16,000 ft/s) determined by the Young's Modulus of the material and its density. For a vehicle length of 16 feet this pulse takes only about 1.0 msec to reach the rear end of the vehicle, whereupon it reverberates back and forth along the vehicle length. Each time the pulse reaches the rear end it produces a small drop in vehicle speed. So the rear of the vehicle slows as a large number of small steps. The same process occurs for every other part of the vehicle that is beyond the plastically deforming portion, but with different timings. Each step can have similar magnitude but the timing between steps becomes progressively shorter since the vehicle is dynamically shortening. The result is an apparent increasing deceleration as per the response of a mass-on-spring.

The second pulse is a *plastic* wave. This has an amplitude superimposed on the elastic wave, but it propagates at a much slower speed dependent on the "plastic slope" of the stress-strain curve for the structure. This plastic wave involves permanent absorption of energy. This pulse is progressively "eaten into" by the reverberating elastic pulse until the entire vehicle comes to a stop. This description is highly simplified because a typical vehicle is not a uniform block of material, but nevertheless the description gives the gist of what happens. The plastic wave does not reverberate within the vehicle; it merely propagates backward until it subsides due to energy absorption.

When the vehicle finally stops (we ignore rebound) we have three zones. Let the initial length be 16 feet. Let the crush be 2 feet. The new length is thus 14 feet. However, there is a region beyond the new front surface that is twisted and compacted. Let this region be 2 feet. If we measure from the back of the vehicle we have three zones. There is a length of 12 feet which is essentially undisturbed and remains in its initial elastic state, followed by the compacted zone which extends to 14 feet, followed by a gap of 2 feet which is the missing material and gives the crush (we assume here that no significant material fell off the vehicle). From a *material scientist's* viewpoint, the *compacted* region constitutes the real crush.

We immediately see that there are *two* boundaries of interest. The first is the outer shortening of the vehicle (the measured crush). The second is the boundary between the compacted region and the undisturbed region. This second boundary is very important for considerations of intrusion of the bodywork into the safety cage for the occupants, and includes such effects as the rearward thrust on the foot wells, the dash and the steering column.

Unfortunately, all the emphasis in AR is inevitably on the outer crush, and it is rare to see quotes on the second boundary. Even IIHS (Insurance Institute for Highway Safety) rarely quotes this second boundary *unless* it is sufficient to start to cause problems for the instrumented dummies. The intrusion effects are even more important for side impacts (far less bodywork for protection), but most of the emphasis is on how well side airbags performed, and rarely is the actual second boundary position quoted. Indeed, one of the problems with IIHS tests is that emphasis is always placed on the *dollar cost* (they are an insurance group) with limited (if any) quotes of the crush damage. This is unfortunate, because their testing would be a valuable extra source of data.

15.2 Measuring the Crush

Vehicles are calibrated (speed versus crush) by performing barrier crash tests. The most common test is an impact across the entire frontal width of the vehicle at 90 degrees to the barrier. The barrier face is vertical, and the barrier has high mass relative to the vehicle. This ensures there is negligible energy transfer to the barrier in terms of kinetic energy. But the barrier is also very rigid, which ensures there is negligible energy absorption by the barrier since there is no crush (so no local deformation). This aspect of rigidity is very important, and explains why a collision with a heavy truck (18-wheeler) is *not* the same as a collision with a heavy barrier (for sufficient force the truck can yield whereas the barrier does not).

The offset frontal barrier tests performed by IIHS actually include a deformable front element for the barrier (an aluminum honeycomb) to roughly simulate the front of a pick-up or SUV. Since this deformable element absorbs energy, it becomes necessary to increase the initial vehicle speed in order to maintain the same level of vehicle crush as for a hit into concrete. This explains why the IIHS tests are done at 40 mph versus the 35 mph used for the NHTSA NCAP tests.

Because the vehicle is freely moving (no brake-induced nose diving) the arrangement guarantees that the strike is first into the bumper assembly of the vehicle, which in turn generates thrust into the two strong frame rails. As these rails collapse so other softer portions of the vehicle also become compressed or dragged along. This includes the outer fenders, the inner radiator region and the hood, and finally the (strong) engine. According to Huang (ref 112), about 65 percent of the energy is absorbed by the frame rail region and about 35 percent by the other soft parts of the vehicle.

But we immediately see a problem. What happens if the strike is *not* into or through the bumper, and instead is an underride situation, such as rear-ending a taller truck? The energy absorption is redistributed. Unfortunately, such tests are rare and there is little published data concerning the *A*, *B* and *G* parameters used in the CRASH3 algorithm, for such non-standard crash tests. The tests would require a barrier with a lower recess such that the contact was with the vehicle *above* the bumper.

Because the barrier is rigid the surface of the barrier does *not* conform to the damage surface of the vehicle. Instead, the reverse is true which means the damage contour of the vehicle attempts to give a flat crush. The barrier cannot reach the soft portions of the vehicle until after the strong parts start crushing. But this leads to an interesting effect for vehicle-to-vehicle collisions.

It is often stated that a barrier hit is the same as the mirror image collision for two identical vehicles each moving at the same velocity but in opposite directions. Thus a 35 mph barrier collision gives the same results as a collision of two identical vehicles with a closing speed of 70 mph. The doubled closing speed would (by itself) give four times the absorbed energy. But the two vehicles have an effective mass of only one-half of each vehicle, so the total absorbed energy is only twice that of the barrier hit. Since this total energy is shared equally between the vehicles then each vehicle absorbs the same energy as the barrier hit. This logic works provided the two vehicles really are identical and are aligned such that the strong frame rails of vehicle 1 match the strong frame rails of vehicle 2.

But now consider a small offset between the vehicles. The frame rails of vehicle 1 now engage the softer parts of vehicle 2, and vice versa. The resulting crush profile is no longer *identical* to the barrier hit, although the difference(s) may be small. This effect becomes more pronounced for hits between different vehicles (car into pick-up) *even if* the vehicles have similar weight and similar crush response, and the bumpers properly align (same height).

These effects have an important consequence for real vehicle-to-vehicle collisions: if we attempt to become smart and measure every little contour change, we run into a conundrum. For example, suppose the damage area on a vehicle has an overall lateral width of L and a *variable* degree of crush within this area. The usual approach is to break down the overall crush into *zones*. The most common case is to use five equal-width zones, and to measure the depth of crush per zone. To simplify the situation let us use only three zones, since this will still illustrate the nature of the problem.

According to the logic in the CRASH3 algorithm the force is given by

$$F = A + Bx \tag{15.1}$$

while the absorbed energy is given by

$$E = Ax + \tfrac{1}{2} Bx^2 + G \tag{15.2}$$

These values apply *per unit width* of the damage area. The units for A are lbs/inch, for B they are lbs/inch^2, while for G they are lbs-inches/inch width (since $G = A^2 / 2B$). For our three zones this gives:

$$F_1 = \frac{L}{3}(A_1 + B_1x_1),\ \ F_2 = \frac{L}{3}(A_2 + B_2x_2),\ \ F_3 = \frac{L}{3}(A_3 + B_3x_3) \tag{15.3}$$

Where $x1$, $x2$ and $x3$ are the three different *measured* crush depths for the three zones.

Thus the total force is given by

$$F_{total} = \frac{L}{3}\left[(A_1 + A_2 + A_3) + (B_1x_1 + B_2x_2 + B_3x_3)\right] \tag{15.4}$$

But we have six unknowns! There are essentially no experiments that define A or B for *separate* regions (or zones) across a given vehicle. The well-known solution to this problem is to assume the A value is a constant; likewise the B value (and G value) is also a constant. There have been various discussions of this problem, including arguments that cross-loading tends to give near-constant values (e.g., see Wood, ref 17).

We now obtain

$$F_{total} = \frac{L}{3}\left[3A + B(x_1 + x_2 + x_3)\right] = L\left[A + B\,x_{average}\right] \tag{15.5}$$

where

$$x_{average} = \frac{1}{3}(x_1 + x_2 + x_3). \quad (15.6)$$

We see an interesting fact: the total force is the *same* as simply using the average crush. This occurs because the force equation is *linear* with respect to crush. However, this *sameness* does not apply to the energy calculation. This is because the equation is *quadratic* with respect to crush.

For total energy absorption we obtain

$$E_{total} = L\left[A\frac{(x_1 + x_2 + x_3)}{3} + \frac{B}{2}\frac{(x_1^2 + x_2^2 + x_3^2)}{3} + G\right] \quad (15.7)$$

$$\text{Or } E_{total} = L\left[A\,x_{average} + \left(\frac{B}{2}x^{*2}\right) + G\right] \quad (15.8)$$

But note, x^{*2} is NOT the same as $xaverage^2$. In general the former term is larger than the latter. As a simple example, let $x1$ = 10 inches, $x2$ = 20 inches and $x3$ = 12 inches. This a significant non-uniform crush. Such a profile also demonstrates the variable stiffness across the damage region.

Then $xaverage$ = 14.00 inches and $xaverage^2$ = 196.00 inch^2. However, x^{*2} = $(10^2 + 20^2 + 12^2) / 3$ = 214.67 inch^2. This is an increase of about 9.5 percent. However, if we include the *A* and *G* terms we get a smaller overall difference.

For example, let us choose some representative values for a 3,000 lb. car. We choose $A = 300$, $B = 80$ and $G = 562.5$. Then using average crush we obtain

$$E = L\,[300x14 + 40x196 + 562.5] = L\,[12{,}603] \quad (15.9)$$

For the individual zone approach we obtain

$$E = L\,[300x14 + 40x214.67 + 562.5] = L\,[13{,}349] \quad (15.10)$$

We see the ratio of *E* values is only 5.9 percent. If this were the only energy term involved (as for a rigid barrier hit) this would give a difference of about 2.9 percent in implied collision speed. But for a two-vehicle collision there is a second energy term to include for this second vehicle. The result can be a further reduction in difference between a calculation using an average zone approach and the multiple-zone approach.

Use of the multiple-zone logic is good for properly defining the average crush. It is also useful for determining the centroid of thrust application (i.e., *where* the effective net thrust is being applied). But does it actually improve the energy-of-crush calculation? The situation is complicated by the following facts.

The improvement is really based on mathematics. But is it based on engineering or physics? Remember, we were forced to assume $A_1 = A_2 = A_3$, etc. Secondly, there has always been uncertainty with regard to the *vertical* aspect for crush measurements. When comparing barrier hits there is no problem: we simply perform the crush measurements at the same height (usually at the mid-height of the bumpers). But when bumper heights do not match we have uncertainty as to *where* to define the crush.

For these various reasons we have difficulty accepting the so-called improvement in energy calculations using the multiple-zone technique (*nice try, but no cigar, folks*). The problem is the same as occurs in mathematical equations. Even if one parameter is known to (say) 12 figures (like the value for π with a typical hand calculator) the other parameters may be known to only two significant figures. This immediately causes the overall calculated result to also be accurate only to the two significant figures. We cannot extract a better accuracy than the least-accurate parameter.

Perhaps the following helps to illustrate the situation. A typical table is frequently found in the *Accident Reconstruction Journal* (ARJ) describing the measured crash parameters for a 1988 Ford Taurus. This is given by the company 4N6XPRT Systems. Note there is nothing wrong with the quoted numbers (!): they are derived using standard techniques. We are merely indicating a problem with *use* of the quotes. The crash is a 35 mph full-width frontal NHTSA barrier test #1177.

The table indicates the vehicle weight (3,675 lbs), the crush width (71.2 inches) and then quotes three crush depths (18.7 inches for the left bumper corner, 21.4 inches for the center, and 19 inches for the right bumper corner). The table then breaks into three sections: values for minimum crush (18.7 inches), values for average crush (20.1 inches), and values for maximum crush (21.4 inches). For each section the analyst is invited to choose a no-damage speed (what we call the bumper speed) of either 2.5 mph, 5.0 mph, 7.5 mph or 10 mph. For each of these speeds the table then quotes the solved values of A, B and G for the vehicle.

Problem: we end up with a table of 36 values! There are twelve options for A, twelve for B and twelve for G! Yet we have only one test done at one impact speed! (Was the test repeated to demonstrate consistency?) Exactly how an analyst is supposed to use these values is far from obvious. Remember, the quotes are for a full-width crash into a barrier. How best should we handle a partial (offset) collision (such as damage across only 30 percent of the frontal width)? Should we assume an outer crush solution?

For all these various reasons we conclude that using average crush depth and average values of A, B and G are about as accurate as any other option.

Chapter 16

The Heavy Vehicle versus Light Vehicle Problem

Synopsis

16.1 Introduction

It is well-known that for a collision of a heavy vehicle into a light one the light vehicle invariably gets the worst of it. Consider a fixed closing speed (velocity). For a simple central impact (we ignore induced vehicle spin), the two different vehicle *delta-v*'s are dependent on the weight ratio, the closing speed and the coefficient of restitution—and nothing else! But restitution is usually small except for low speed impacts (as are any braking effects during the collision). Hence the relative *delta-v*'s depend on the weights via the terms (*w*3 / (*w*3 + *w*4)) and (*w*4 / (*w*3 + *w*4)) respectively, where *w*3 and *w*4 are the total (loaded) vehicle weights. This automatically states that (*delta-v*3 / *delta-v*4) = – (*w*4 / *w*3). This is true regardless of the individual vehicle crushes. The latter merely determine the overall timing of the crash, and influence the (small) changes in restitution. Stiff vehicles imply short timing, relatively large peak forces and thus large accelerations. But stiffness usually depends on vehicle weight (via the scaling laws). The result is that the lighter vehicle suffers the larger crush and thus absorbs the greater energy, while it also suffers the greater *delta-v*. The small car thus suffers a "double whammy"; there is a larger *delta-v and* a larger degree of crush, and *vice versa* for the heavy vehicle.

To understand these effects let us simplify the crush response of a vehicle and assume the behavior is similar to a mass-on-spring. This means we ignore the low-speed bumper responses and incipient crush force logic. For CRASH3 this is the same as setting $A = 0.0$ and thus $G = 0.0$. We also ignore restitution.

For two fixed weights, *w*3 and *w*4, and a fixed closing speed *vclose*, the energy lost during the collision is simply

$$E_{loss} = 0.5\left(\frac{w3w4}{w3 + w4}\right) v_{close}^2 = 0.5\, w_{eff}\, v_{close}^2 \tag{16.1}$$

But for each vehicle the absorbed energy is given by

$$E3 = 0.5\, k3\, x1^2 = \frac{F_{peak}^2}{2k3} \tag{16.2}$$

$$\text{and } E4 = 0.5\, k4\, x2^2 = F_{peak}^2 \,/\, 2k4$$

where $k3$ and $k4$ are the effective stiffness of each vehicle and *Fpeak* is the *mutual* peak force. This immediately tells us that the relative crush energies are inversely proportional to the individual stiffness factors.

$$\text{Summing, } E3 + E4 = E_{loss} = \frac{F_{peak}{}^2}{2k_{eff}} \tag{16.3}$$

$$\text{Here, } w_{eff} = \frac{w3w4}{w3 + w4} \text{ and } k_{eff} = \frac{k3k4}{k3 + k4} \tag{16.4}$$

We immediately obtain

$$Fpeak^2 = weff\; keff\; vclose^2$$

Thus the peak force is proportional to the square-root product of *weff* and *keff*, and directly to the closing speed. Of course, relative peak acceleration is proportional to peak force and inversely to the individual vehicle weight.

Note that the timing (quarter-period) is also given by

$$\text{Time} = \frac{\pi}{2}\sqrt{\frac{w_{eff}}{g\, k_{eff}}} \text{ where } g \text{ is gravity.}$$

16.2 Can We Build a Lightweight Car and Maintain Safety?

Small cars are usually also lightweight. As NHTSA and IIHS continually state the results of the NCAP 35 mph barrier crash test are the equivalent of the mirror image case of two similar vehicles impacting each other at +/- 35 mph (a closing speed of 70 mph). Even very small cars (the Smart Fortwo with a weight of only about 1,800 lbs) can achieve a good (5-star) rating. This would be meaningful if the average fleet of vehicles on the roads were all of similar low weight. But the reality is the present fleet is mixed, with some vehicles weighing considerably more, even above 6,000 lbs (large SUVs).

Consider a closing speed of 70 mph with one vehicle with weight 1,800 lbs and the other with weight 6,000 lbs. The *delta-v*'s become 53.8 mph for the small car and 16.2 mph for the large vehicle. This means the small car acts as if it suffered a barrier hit at 53.8 mph rather than at 35 mph.

In April 2009, IIHS had a video on its website showing a collision between the Mercedes-Benz Fortwo and a larger Mercedes-Benz C-type sedan. The result was horrendous for the little Fortwo: it was violently thrown-back and suffered a 450 degree spin and even underwent flight during the impact.

In his excellent book, *Traffic Safety* (ref 114), Leonard Evans points out that the tendency to suffer a fatality increases with $(delta\text{-}velocity/70)^{3.54}$, with speeds in mph. This is based on empirical data, since (to date) no one has given a scientific explanation for this exponent. However, the implication is that comparing a 53.8 mph case versus a 35 mph case gives a fatality ratio of about 4.58! Strictly speaking the ratio of probable fatality is about (0.39/0.086) = 4.58, and this applies to *unbelted* drivers. The equation also implies the 50 percent fatality point is for a *delta-v* of about 57.6 mph. Clearly, driving a small (lightweight) vehicle and colliding with a much heavier one is not good for your health.

The conundrum is easily seen. Based on simple physics we have

$$v^2 = (peakacell)\ x \qquad (16.5)$$

where *peakacell* is the peak acceleration and *x* is the equivalent stopping distance (again for a mass-on-spring situation). Note that this physics equation does not care *how* we achieve the acceleration and stopping distance. This means that it does not matter how we make the vehicle: whether high-strength steel (HSS), aluminum, magnesium, titanium or carbon-carbon fiber. It's the *response* that matters.

Assuming the requirements for occupant safety remain the same (seatbelts, airbags and safety-space within the cab) and humans continue to have the same vulnerabilities (neck, head, chest, pelvis etc.), we are stuck with the fact that we must limit the peak accelerations to values similar to today's well-behaved vehicles. But, to handle the larger *delta-v* we must significantly *increase* the effective stopping distance, which is the vehicle crush. Simultaneously, we must limit the overall real crush (not just the external dimensions) to prevent encroachment (intrusion) effects to prevent direct internal vehicle impact with the occupants. This leads to an unanticipated result (if you are not a scientist):

> To maintain safety while reducing weight (mass) we must increase (or at least maintain) the SIZE of the vehicle.

But this means we can no longer use small in order to ease inner-city parking, or fit more cars on a given road, or improve mpg. Indeed, if we want a safe small car, we must increase the weight! Add some lead, anyone? Worsen the mpg? Ironically the new electric cars have heavy batteries (frequently lithium-ion), so we actually *are* adding weight while the vehicle size stays roughly constant and we achieve better fuel mileage.

Fortunately, things are not quite as dire as the above logic states. The reason is simple: as the weight of the small car decreases so also does the effective weight for the collision. This effect then decreases the total absorbed energy and thus decreases the peak force and accelerations. For the case of a light vehicle the effective weight becomes similar to the low-weight vehicle. Thus, the absorbed total collision energy becomes almost that due to the low-weight vehicle but at the 70 mph closing velocity.

The above equation for peak force states the value is proportional to the square root of the effective weight. However, the peak acceleration then becomes inversely proportional to the square root of the weight of the lighter vehicle. The only other factor that can reduce the peak acceleration is the effective stiffness. But to reduce this factor we need to make the stiffness of the light vehicle noticeably smaller: hence the crush must increase, so the size of the vehicle cannot be made small! We are back to the same overall conclusion.

To help appreciate these effects we present the following Mathcad calculations.

16.3 Four Solutions

(1) The first is for the mirror image case of two 4,000 lbs cars, each with 5 mph bumpers, and full-width contact (so $F1 = F2$), and normal impact ($\theta = 0.0$). These conditions correspond to central thrusts and thus zero induced spin ($\gamma = 1.0$). We add 200 lbs to each vehicle for occupants. We guarantee there is no confusion over which vehicle is heavy by simply adjusting the curb weights by 1 lb (e.g., 4,000 lbs and 3,999 lbs).

The calculation gives the critical speed (no damage) of 10 mph. The first plot shows that the crush is the same for each vehicle over the range $0 < \text{crush} < 5$ feet. The plot showing closing speed versus crush then gives crush of 2.25 feet for a closing speed of 70 mph, while the calculated restitution is 0.1. The various *delta-v* plots show each vehicle undergoes a change of 38.5 mph.

The energy plot shows each vehicle absorbs the same energy of 1.75×10^5 ft-lbs while the total energy absorbed is twice this at about 3.5×10^5 ft-lbs.

The timing calculations give 0.055 secs (no damage) to 0.08 secs (significant damage) for the quarter period, and a range of 0.093 secs to about 0.086 secs (at 2.25 feet of crush) for the total contact time. Note the peak time of about 0.11 secs for a crush of about 0.1 feet.

For the 70 mph case (2.25 feet crush) the calculated peak mutual force is about

1.3×10^5 lbs, while the corresponding vehicle accelerations are about +/- 31 g.

Finally, we calculate the adjustments required if we assume the target is initially stopped with a braking friction of 0.7, while the bullet applies zero braking. We see that close to the no damage condition, the closing speed is really about 0.95 of our initial calculation, but rapidly approaches 1.0 as crush increases. Likewise, the *delta-v* of the target is about 0.88 near zero crush, but about 0.98 at 2.25 feet crush. Finally, for the *delta-v* of the bullet, the ratio is about 1.12 near zero crush but about 1.03 for the 2.25 feet crush (70 mph).

(2) For the second case everything remains the same as for the first case, *except* vehicle 2 has its weight reduced from 4,000 lbs to 2,000 lbs. The critical speed reduces to 8.35 mph. For a closing velocity of 70 mph the crush on the small car *increases* to about 2.35 feet, while that of the large car *decreases* to about 1.7 feet. The restitution is about 0.08.

The two *delta-v*'s are about 50 mph for the small car and about 26 mph for the large car. The energy plot gives about 1.35×10^5 ft-lbs for the small car and about 1×10^5 ft-lbs for the large car, for a total of about 2.35×10^5 ft-lbs. Note how these energy values are *less* than for the equal-weight case.

Timing is about 0.048 to 0.07 secs for the quarter period, and about 0.081 to 0.075 secs for the total contact time (with a local peak of about 0.095 secs near crush of 0.1 feet). Note how these timings are shorter than for case 1. This is a consequence of the changes in vehicle weight and stiffness for the small vehicle.

The peak mutual force is about 1.08×10^5 lbs, while the peak vehicle accelerations are about 48 g for the small car and about 25 g for the large one.

Finally, the adjusted closing speed ranges from about 0.95 to 1.0; *delta-v* of the target ranges from about 0.93 to 1.0, while the *delta-v* of the bullet ranges from 1.13 to about 1.02.

(3) This third case is again a mirror image case, but this time both vehicles weigh 2,000 lbs (curb weight) and 2,200 lbs with occupant. The critical speed is back to 10 mph. At the closing speed of 70 mph the vehicle crush *decreases* to about 1.8 feet (each vehicle), while the restitution is 0.1. The *delta-v* of each vehicle is about 38.5 mph.

The absorbed energy for each vehicle is about 8.6×10^4 ft-lbs while the total is about 1.75×10^5 ft-lbs.

Timing ranges from 0.043 to about 0.065 secs (quarter period) and from 0.074 to about 0.07 secs (total contact time). Peak accelerations are about +/- 40 g.

The adjusted values for closing speed, target *delta-v* and bullet *delta-v*, are similar to those for the previous cases.

(4) The fourth case replaces one car with a barrier, while the second car remains at 2,000 lbs (curb weight) and 2,200 loaded. To simulate a barrier we set the weight of car 1 at 1,000,000 lbs and increase the effective stiffness. Although we give a bumper speed of 5.0 mph to the barrier (?) we find it has negligible effect on the answers. As expected, the critical speed drops to 5.0 mph. Because the barrier is very rigid the corresponding crush $x1$ does not exceed zero until the crush on vehicle 2 exceeds about 274 ft! This absurd answer merely implies that car 2 would become "pulp" before the barrier started to crush. For these reasons $x1$ is always zero throughout the calculations, and all tables associated with vehicle 1 are suppressed.

Because this is a barrier hit we study the result for a closing speed of 35 mph, and see that the crush for the real car is about 1.8 ft, while restitution is again about 0.1. The *delta-v* is about 38.5 mph. Total absorbed energy is about 8.6×10^4 ft-lbs. The quarter period ranges from about 0.043 secs (zero crush) to about 0.065 secs, while the total contact time is from 0.074 to about 0.07 seconds. Peak force is about 86,000 lbs while the peak acceleration is about 39 g.

Note how all these values for a 35 mph barrier hit are essentially *identical* to the answers for the case 3 calculations—as they should be. Thus, we have demonstrated the equivalence between the one-car barrier hit and the two-car mirror image hit.

WeightCase1: 4200 lbs into 4199 lbs (loaded weights)

Notes: (a) '1' is *strongest* vehicle versus '2'. (b) W1 and W2 are true weights regardless of spin

(c) W3 and W4 are spin-dependent. (d) γ = 1+rr/kk. r = torque-arm, k = rad of gyration

W1 is Heavy Car empty weight lbs

W2 is Light Car empty weight lbs

W3 is Heavy Car with occupant load lbs

W4 is Light Car with occupant load lbs

γ3 is spin factor $\gamma 3 := 1.0$

γ4 is spin factor $\gamma 4 := 1.0$

$W1 := 4000 \quad W2 := 3999 \quad A1 := 0.6 \quad A2 := 0.6 \quad \theta 1 := \frac{0}{57.3}$

$W3 := 4200 \quad W4 := 4199 \quad F1 := 1.0 \quad F2 := 1.0 \quad \theta 2 := \frac{0}{57.3}$

$vL1 := \frac{7.335}{\cos(\theta 1)} \quad vL2 := \frac{7.335}{\cos(\theta 2)}$

$W3 := \frac{W3}{\gamma 3} \quad W4 := \frac{W4}{\gamma 4}$

$R1 := A1 \cdot \left(\frac{3000}{W1}\right)^{\frac{1}{3}} \quad R1 = 0.545 \quad R2 := A2 \cdot \left(\frac{3000}{W2}\right)^{\frac{1}{3}} \quad R2 = 0.545$

$a1 := 0.5 \cdot \left(\frac{W1}{3000}\right)^{\frac{1}{3}} \quad a1 = 0.55 \quad a2 := 0.5 \cdot \left(\frac{W2}{3000}\right)^{\frac{1}{3}} \quad a2 = 0.55$

x is crush feet

L is load for given crush, lbs

$x2MAX := 10.0$

$x10 := 0 \quad L1 := 12 \cdot R1 \cdot W1 \cdot F1 \cdot \left(1 + \frac{x10}{a1}\right) \cdot \frac{1}{\cos(\theta 1)} \quad L1 = 2.617 \times 10^{4}$

$$x20 := a2 \cdot \left[R1 \cdot W1 \cdot F1 \cdot \frac{\left(1 + \frac{x10}{a1}\right) \cdot \cos(\theta 2)}{R2 \cdot W2 \cdot F2 \cdot \cos(\theta 1)}\right] - a2 \qquad ge := 32.2$$

$x20 = 9.173 \times 10^{-5} \quad L2 := 12 \cdot R2 \cdot W2 \cdot F2 \cdot \left(1 + \frac{x20}{a2}\right) \cdot \frac{1}{\cos(\theta 2)} \quad L2 = 2.617 \times 10^{4}$

acell is acceleration (or deceleration) in g's

$accell1 := \frac{L1}{W1}$ $accell4 := \frac{L2}{W4}$ $accell1 = 6.542$ (g) $accell4 = 6.232$ g

$x2 := 0, 0.01 .. x20$ $accell3 := \frac{L1}{W3}$ $accell3 = 6.23$ (g)

Q's are crush- energy terms

$$Q2(x2) := \left(\frac{x2}{a2}\right)\cdot x2 + 2\cdot x2 + \frac{vL2^2}{12\cdot R2\cdot ge} \quad Q22(x2) := \left(\frac{vL2^2\cdot W2}{2\cdot ge}\right)\cdot\left(1 + \frac{x2}{a2}\right)$$

$$Q222(x2) := 6\cdot R2\cdot W2\cdot Q2(x2) - Q22(x2) \quad E2(x2) := F2\cdot\frac{Q222(x2)}{\cos(\theta 2)^2}$$

$$ETA(x2) := E2(x2)$$

vcritical is maximum closing speed to just avoid any crush, mph

$$vCRIT1 := \frac{(W3 + W4)\cdot\left[1 + \left(\frac{W4}{W3}\right)\cdot\left(F2\cdot\frac{R2}{F1\cdot R1}\right)^2\cdot\frac{\left(F1\cdot vL1^2\right)}{F2\cdot vL2^2}\right]\cdot F2\cdot vL2^2}{W3}$$

$ETA(x2) =$ $x2 =$

$ETA(x2)$	$x2$
$-4.547\cdot 10^{-13}$	0

$$vCRIT := \sqrt{vCRIT1}$$

$$vCRIT = 14.669$$

$$VCRIT := \frac{vCRIT}{1.467}$$

$VCRIT = 9.999$ (mph)

vclose is actual closing speed for total crush energy, mph

$$vCLOSE1(x2) := vCRIT1 + 2\cdot ge\cdot ETA(x2)\cdot\frac{(W3 + W4)}{W3\cdot W4}$$

$$vCLOSE(x2) := \sqrt{vCLOSE1(x2)}$$

ee and ff are coefficients of restitution (vehicle bounce)

$$ee(x2) := 0.7\cdot\frac{vCRIT}{vCLOSE(x2)} \qquad VCLOSE(x2) := \frac{vCLOSE(x2)}{1.467} \quad \text{(mph)}$$

vCLOSE1(x2) =	vCLOSE(x2) =	ee(x2) =	VCLOSE(x2) =	x2 =
215.176	14.669	0.7	9.999	0

Δv is sudden change in speed

$$\Delta v2(x2) := \left(\frac{W3}{W3 + W4}\right)\cdot(1 + ee(x2))\cdot vCLOSE(x2)$$

$$\Delta V2(x2) := \frac{\Delta v2(x2)}{1.467} \quad \text{(mph)}$$

$$\Delta v1(x2) := -\left(\frac{W4}{W3 + W4}\right)\cdot(1 + ee(x2))\cdot vCLOSE(x2)$$

$$\Delta V1(x2) := \frac{\Delta v1(x2)}{1.467} \quad \text{(mph)}$$

$$\Delta V2CM(x2) := \frac{\Delta V2(x2)}{\gamma 4} \qquad \Delta V1CM(x2) := \frac{\Delta V1(x2)}{\gamma 3}$$

$$VCLOSE(x2) := \frac{vCLOSE(x2)}{1.467} \quad \text{(mph)}$$

$\Delta v2(x2) =$	$\Delta v1(x2) =$	$\Delta V2(x2) =$	$\Delta V1(x2) =$	$x2 =$	$VCLOSE(x2) =$
12.47	-12.467	8.5	-8.498	0	9.999

$x3 := x20, (x20 + 0.01) .. x2MAX$ **continuation of crush x2**

$$Q3(x3) := \left(\frac{x3}{a2}\right) \cdot x3 + 2 \cdot x3 + \frac{vL2^2}{12 \cdot R2 \cdot ge} \qquad Q33(x3) := \left(\frac{vL2^2 \cdot W2}{2 \cdot ge}\right) \cdot \left(1 + \frac{x3}{a2}\right)$$

$$Q333(x3) := 6 \cdot R2 \cdot W2 \cdot Q3(x3) - Q33(x3)$$

$$E3(x3) := F2 \cdot Q333(x3) \cdot \frac{1}{\cos(\theta 2)^2}$$

crush E for vehicle 2

E3(x3) =	x3 =
1.843	$9.173 \cdot 10^{-5}$
205.172	0.01
413.256	0.02
626.093	0.03
843.685	0.04
$1.066 \cdot 10^3$	0.05
$1.293 \cdot 10^3$	0.06
$1.525 \cdot 10^3$	0.07
$1.762 \cdot 10^3$	0.08
$2.003 \cdot 10^3$	0.09
$2.249 \cdot 10^3$	0.1
$2.5 \cdot 10^3$	0.11
$2.756 \cdot 10^3$	0.12
$3.016 \cdot 10^3$	0.13
$3.281 \cdot 10^3$	0.14
$3.551 \cdot 10^3$	0.15

$x1 := 0$ **crush of vehicle 1**

$$x1(x3) := a1\cdot\left(R2\cdot W2\cdot\frac{F2\cdot\cos(\theta 1)}{R1\cdot W1\cdot F1\cdot\cos(\theta 2)}\right)\cdot\left(1+\frac{x3}{a2}\right) - a1$$

$$Q1(x1,x3) := \left(\frac{x1(x3)}{a1}\right)\cdot x1(x3) + 2\cdot x1(x3) + \frac{vL1^2}{12\cdot R1\cdot ge} \quad Q11(x1,x3) := \left(\frac{vL1^2\cdot W1}{2\cdot ge}\right)\cdot\left(1+\frac{x1(x3)}{a1}\right)$$

$$Q111(x1,x3) := 6\cdot R1\cdot W1\cdot Q1(x1,x3) - Q11(x1,x3)$$

$$E1(x1,x3) := F1\cdot Q111(x1,x3)\cdot\frac{1}{\cos(\theta 1)^2}$$ **crush E for vehicle 1**

$$ET(x1,x3) := E1(x1,x3) + E3(x3)$$ **sum of crush energies**

x1(x3) =	E3(x3) =	E1(x1,x3) =	ET(x1,x3) =
0	1.843	$-2.274\cdot 10^{-12}$	1.843
$9.999\cdot 10^{-3}$	205.172	203.302	408.474
0.02	413.256	411.358	824.613
0.03	626.093	624.168	$1.25\cdot 10^{3}$
0.04	843.685	841.732	$1.685\cdot 10^{3}$
0.05	$1.066\cdot 10^{3}$	$1.064\cdot 10^{3}$	$2.13\cdot 10^{3}$
0.06	$1.293\cdot 10^{3}$	$1.291\cdot 10^{3}$	$2.584\cdot 10^{3}$
0.07	$1.525\cdot 10^{3}$	$1.523\cdot 10^{3}$	$3.048\cdot 10^{3}$
0.08	$1.762\cdot 10^{3}$	$1.76\cdot 10^{3}$	$3.521\cdot 10^{3}$
0.09	$2.003\cdot 10^{3}$	$2.001\cdot 10^{3}$	$4.004\cdot 10^{3}$
0.1	$2.249\cdot 10^{3}$	$2.247\cdot 10^{3}$	$4.496\cdot 10^{3}$
0.11	$2.5\cdot 10^{3}$	$2.498\cdot 10^{3}$	$4.998\cdot 10^{3}$
0.12	$2.756\cdot 10^{3}$	$2.753\cdot 10^{3}$	$5.509\cdot 10^{3}$
0.13	$3.016\cdot 10^{3}$	$3.014\cdot 10^{3}$	$6.03\cdot 10^{3}$
0.14	$3.281\cdot 10^{3}$	$3.279\cdot 10^{3}$	$6.56\cdot 10^{3}$
0.15	$3.551\cdot 10^{3}$	$3.549\cdot 10^{3}$	$7.1\cdot 10^{3}$

$$vCLOSE3(x3) := vCRIT1 + 2 \cdot ge \cdot ET(x1, x3) \cdot \frac{(W3 + W4)}{W3 \cdot W4}$$

$$vCLOS(x3) := \sqrt{vCLOSE3(x3)} \qquad ff(x3) := 0.7 \cdot \frac{vCRIT}{vCLOS(x3)}$$

$$VCLOS(x3) := \frac{vCLOS(x3)}{1.467} \quad \text{(mph)}$$

$$\Delta v4(x3) := \left(\frac{W3}{W3 + W4}\right) \cdot (1 + ff(x3)) \cdot vCLOS(x3) \qquad \Delta V4(x3) := \frac{\Delta v4(x3)}{1.467} \quad \text{(mph)}$$

$$\Delta V4CM(x3) := \frac{\Delta V4(x3)}{\gamma 4}$$

$$\Delta v3(x3) := -\left(\frac{W4}{W3 + W4}\right) \cdot (1 + ff(x3)) \cdot vCLOS(x3) \qquad \Delta V3(x3) := \frac{\Delta v3(x3)}{1.467} \quad \text{(mph)}$$

$$\Delta V3CM(x3) := \frac{\Delta V3(x3)}{\gamma 3}$$

vCLOSE3(x3) =	VCLOS(x3) =	ff(x3) =	ΔV4(x3) =	ΔV3(x3) =
215.232	10.001	0.7	8.501	-8.499
227.704	10.286	0.68	8.644	-8.642
240.467	10.571	0.662	8.786	-8.784
253.521	10.854	0.645	8.928	-8.926
266.868	11.136	0.629	9.069	-9.067
280.506	11.417	0.613	9.209	-9.207
294.435	11.697	0.598	9.349	-9.347
308.657	11.976	0.584	9.489	-9.487
323.17	12.254	0.571	9.628	-9.626
337.974	12.532	0.559	9.767	-9.764
353.07	12.809	0.546	9.905	-9.903
368.458	13.085	0.535	10.043	-10.041
384.137	13.36	0.524	10.181	-10.179
400.108	13.635	0.513	10.319	-10.316
416.371	13.909	0.503	10.456	-10.453
432.925	14.183	0.494	10.593	-10.59

x3 =	x1(x3) =
$9.173 \cdot 10^{-5}$	0
0.01	$9.999 \cdot 10^{-3}$
0.02	0.02
0.03	0.03
0.04	0.04
0.05	0.05
0.06	0.06
0.07	0.07
0.08	0.08
0.09	0.09
0.1	0.1
0.11	0.11
0.12	0.12
0.13	0.13
0.14	0.14
0.15	0.15

Heavy Car (4200 lbs) Crush versus Light Car (4199 lbs) Crush in feet

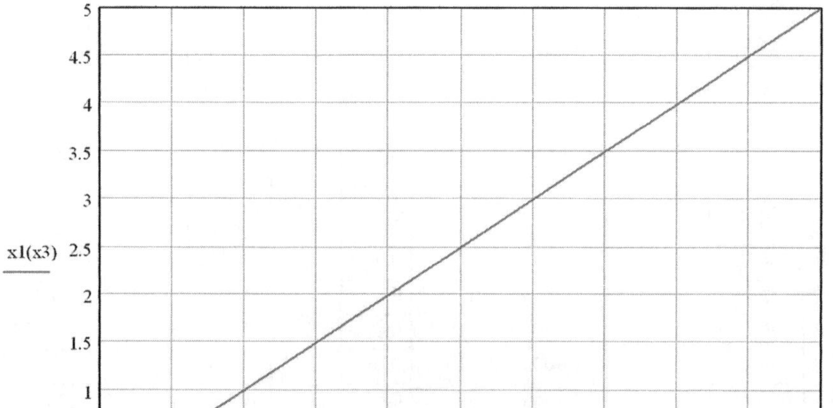

Light Car Speed Change (mph) at contact Point versus Light Car Crush (ft)

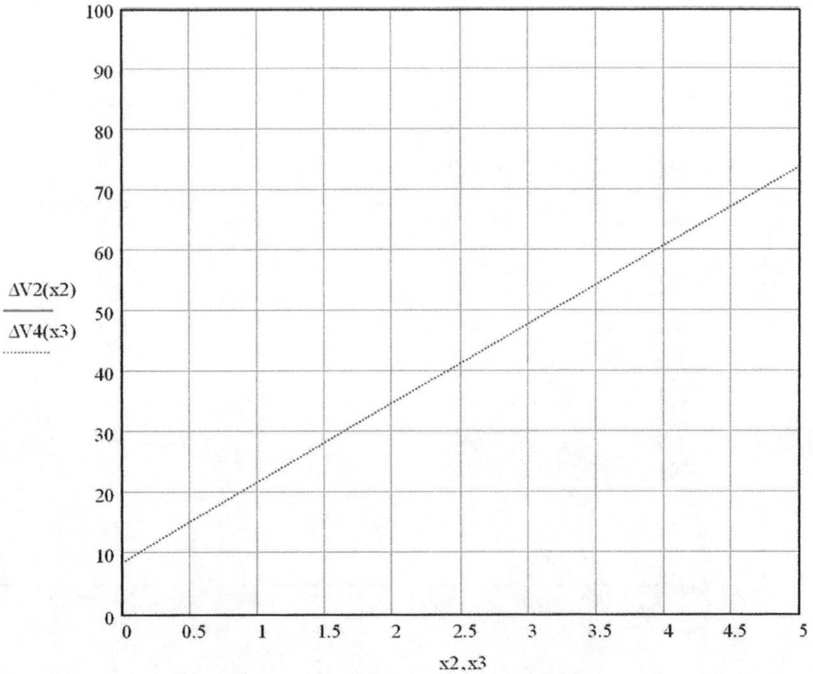

Light Car Speed Change (mph) at CM versus Light Car Crush (ft)

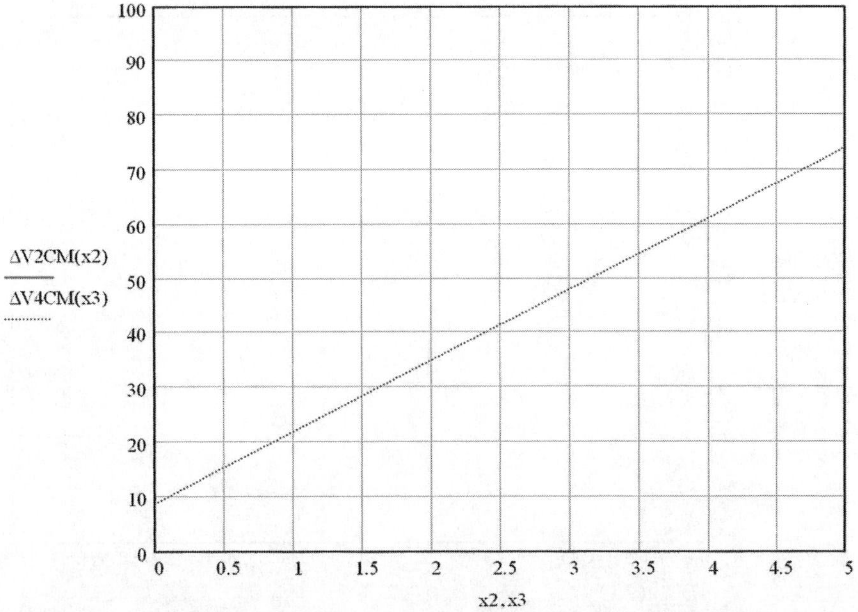

Heavy Car Speed Change (mph) at Contact Point vs. Light Car Crush (ft)

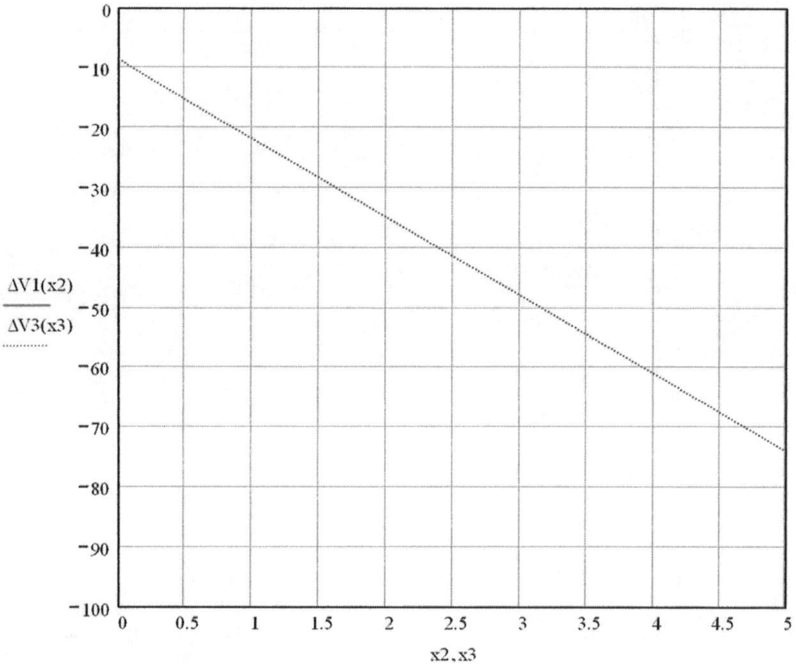

Heavy Car Speed Change (mph) at CM vs. Light Car Crush (ft)

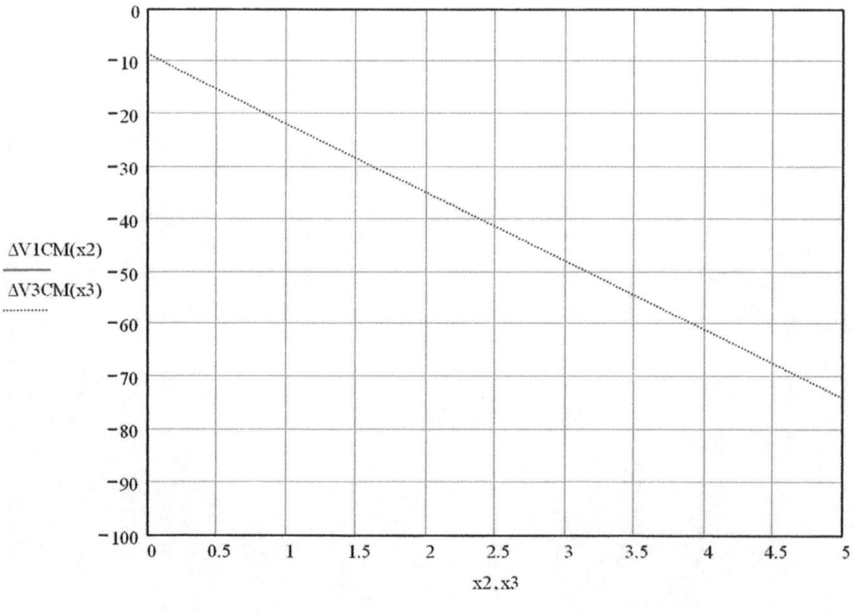

Closing Speed (mph) vs. Light Car Crush (ft)

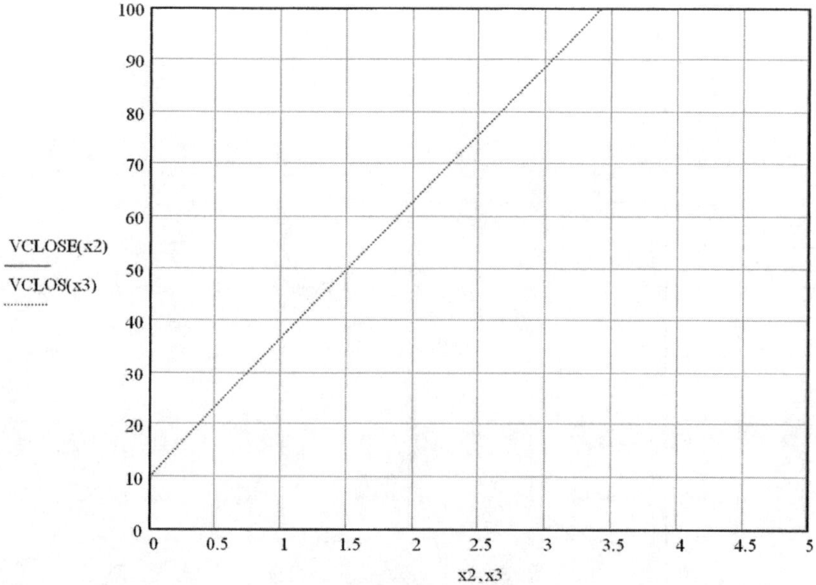

Restitution versus Light Car Crush (ft)

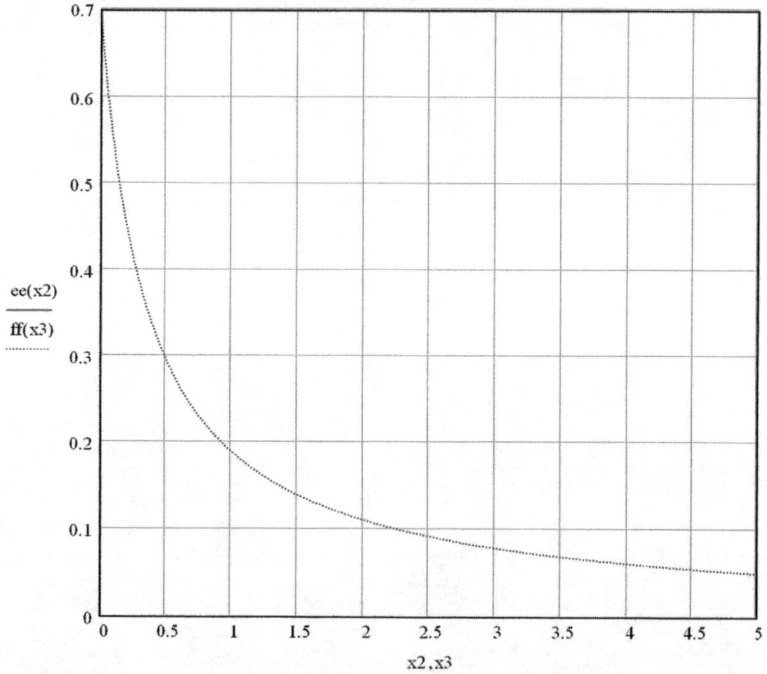

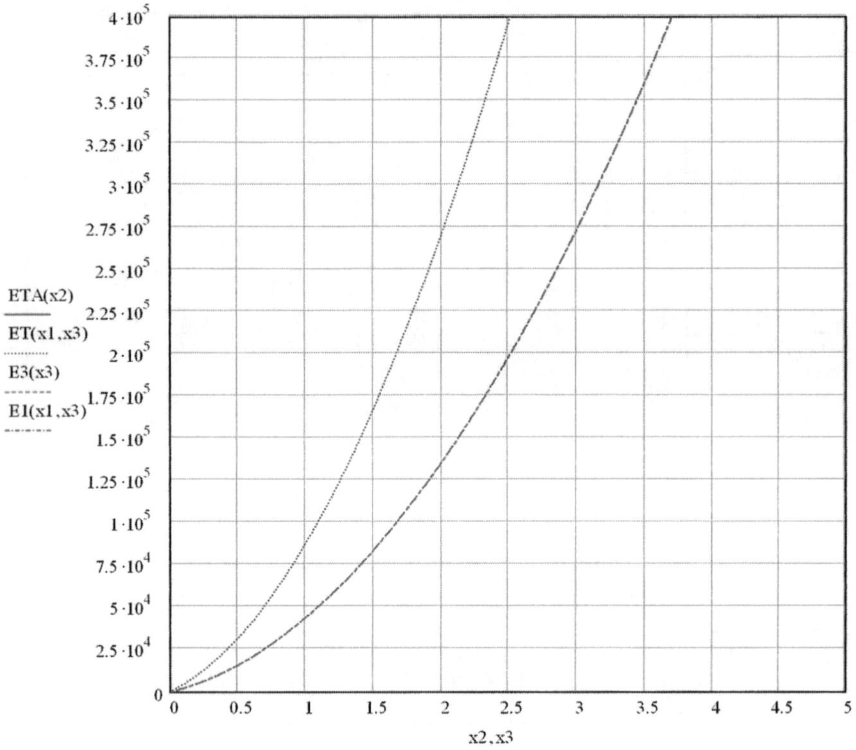
4·10^5
3.75·10^5
3.5·10^5
3.25·10^5
3·10^5
2.75·10^5
2.5·10^5
2.25·10^5
2·10^5
1.75·10^5
1.5·10^5
1.25·10^5
1·10^5
7.5·10^4
5·10^4
2.5·10^4
0
ETA(x2)
ET(x1,x3)
E3(x3)
E1(x1,x3)
0
0.5
1
1.5
2
2.5
3
3.5
4
4.5
5
x2,x3

$$TOPelast := R1^2 \cdot W3 \cdot F1 \cdot vL2^2 + R2^2 \cdot W4 \cdot F2 \cdot vL1^2$$

$$BOTTOMelast := 144 \cdot R1^2 \cdot R2^2 \cdot ge^2 \cdot (W3 + W4) \cdot F1 \cdot F2$$

$$Telastquart := \left(\frac{\pi}{2}\right) \cdot \sqrt{\frac{TOPelast}{BOTTOMelast}}$$

$$Tcontactelast := Telastquart \cdot 1.7$$

$$Telastquart = 0.055$$

$$Tcontactelast = 0.093$$

$$TOP := R1 \cdot W3 \cdot F1 \cdot a2 \cdot \cos(\theta 2) + R2 \cdot W4 \cdot F2 \cdot a1 \cdot \cos(\theta 1)$$

$$TOP = 2.52 \times 10^3$$

$$BOTTOM := 12 \cdot R1 \cdot R2 \cdot F1 \cdot F2 \cdot ge \cdot (W3 + W4)$$

$$BOTTOM = 9.645 \times 10^5$$

$$Tquarterp := \left(\frac{\pi}{2}\right) \cdot \sqrt{\frac{TOP}{BOTTOM}}$$

$$Tquarterp = 0.08$$

$$x2 := 0, 0.01 .. x20$$

$$x3 := x20, (x20 + 0.01) .. x2MAX$$

$$Frac(x2) := \sqrt{1 - \frac{VCRIT^2}{VCLOSE(x2)^2}}$$

$$frac(x3) := \sqrt{1 - \frac{VCRIT^2}{VCLOS(x3)^2}}$$

$$Tquart(x2) := (Telastquart) \cdot (1 - Frac(x2)) + Frac(x2) \cdot Tquarterp$$

$$Tquarter(x3) := (Telastquart) \cdot (1 - frac(x3)) + frac(x3) \cdot Tquarterp$$

$$Tcont(x2) := Tquart(x2) \cdot (1 + ee(x2))$$

$$Tcontact(x3) := Tquarter(x3) \cdot (1 + ff(x3))$$

Quarter Period for Collision (secs)

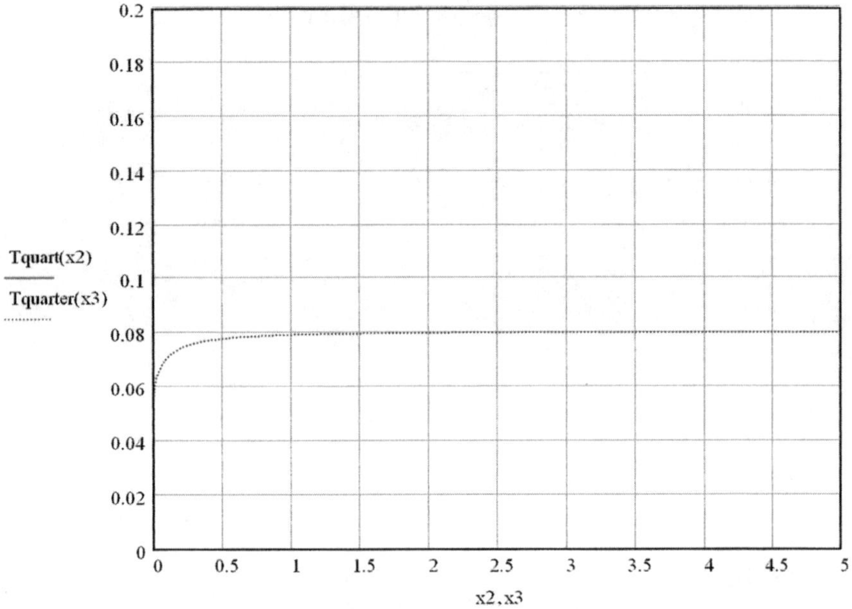

Total Contact Time for Collision (secs)

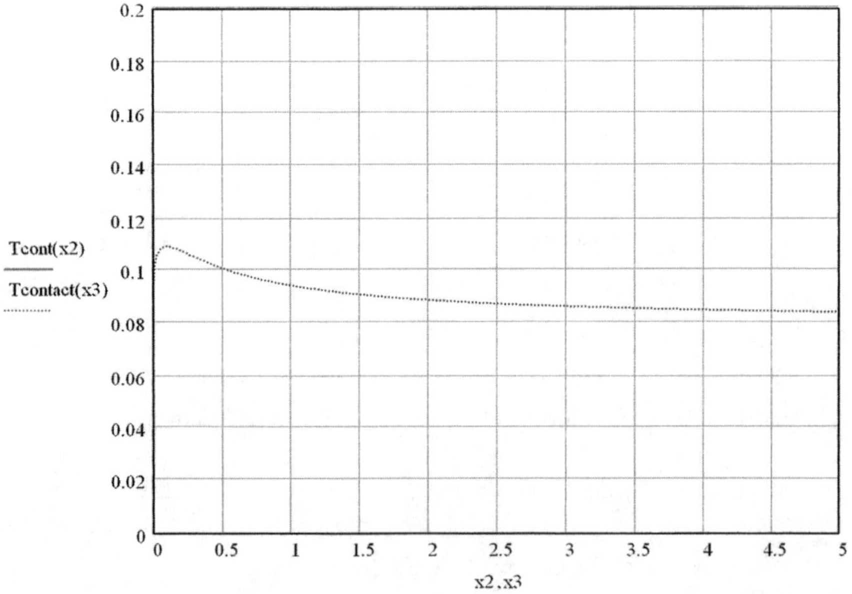

$$L2(x2) := 12 \cdot R2 \cdot W2 \cdot F2 \cdot \left(1 + \frac{x2}{a2}\right) \cdot \frac{1}{\cos(\theta 2)} \qquad L2(x3) := 12 \cdot R2 \cdot W2 \cdot F2 \cdot \left(1 + \frac{x3}{a2}\right) \cdot \frac{1}{\cos(\theta 2)}$$

$$Accel4(x2) := \frac{L2(x2)}{W4} \qquad Accel4(x3) := \frac{L2(x3)}{W4}$$

$$Accel3(x2) := \frac{-L2(x2)}{W3} \qquad Accel3(x3) := \frac{-L2(x3)}{W3}$$

Peak Mutual Force at Contact Point (lbs) versus Light Car Crush (ft)

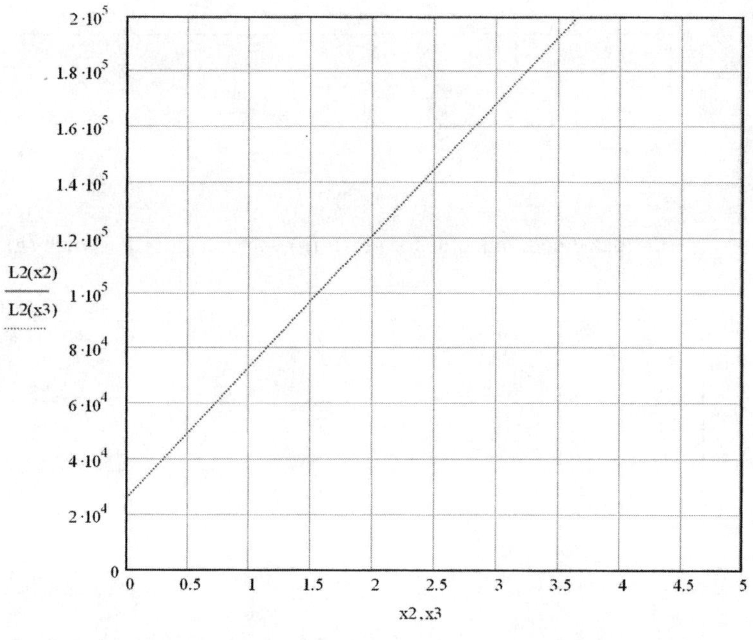

Peak Accel (Decel) of Heavy Car at CP (g) versus Light Car Crush (ft)

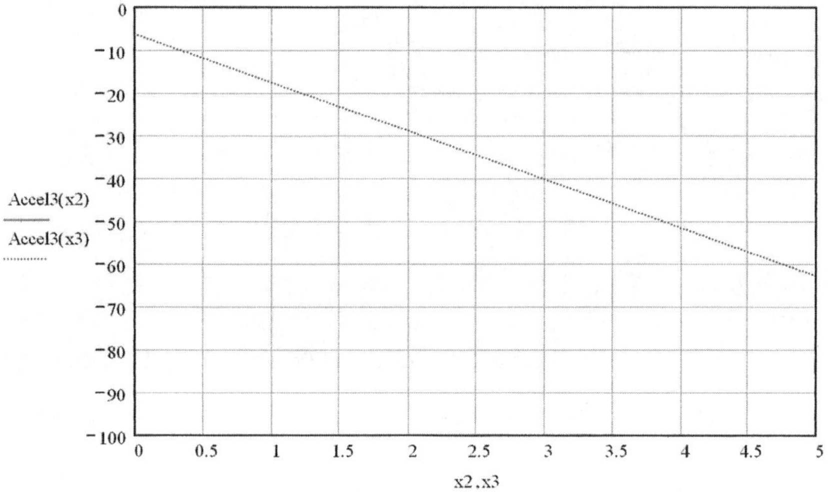

Peak Accel of Light Car at CP (g) versus Light Car Crush (ft)

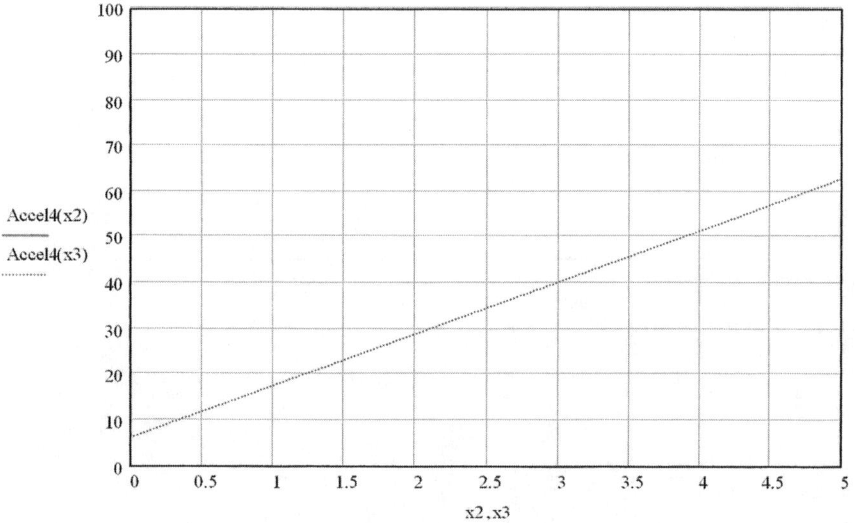

Peak Accel of Heavy Car CM (g) versus Light Car Crush (ft)

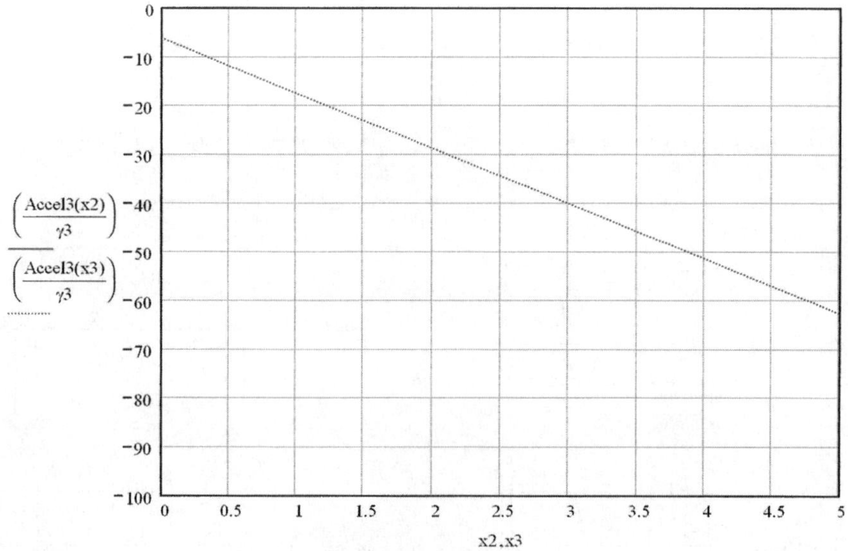

Peak Accel of Light Car CM (g) versus Light Car Crush (ft)

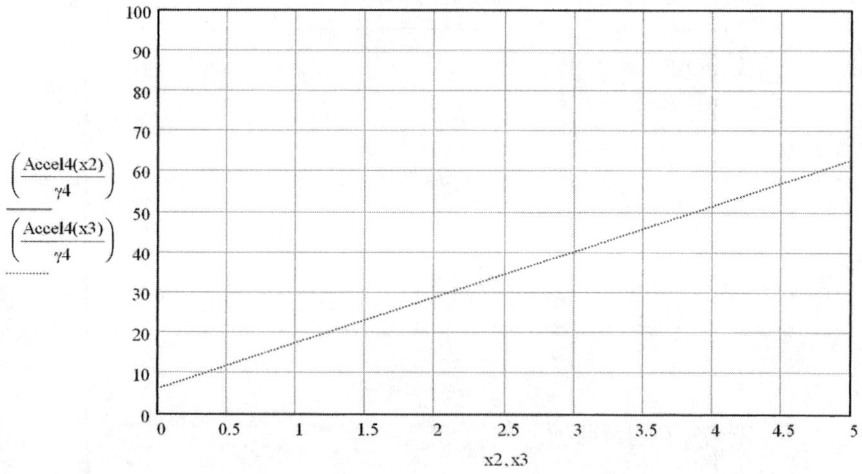

B is the bullet (W3), while T is the target (W4)

$$\mu B := 0.0 \qquad \mu T := 0.7 \qquad Wred := W3 \cdot \frac{W4}{(W3 + W4)}$$

$$Fclose(x2) := \sqrt{1 + (\mu B - \mu T) \cdot \frac{Wred}{\frac{L2(x2)}{2}}} \qquad Fclose(x3) := \sqrt{1 + (\mu B - \mu T) \cdot \frac{Wred}{\frac{L2(x3)}{2}}}$$

$$FdeltaT(x2) := \frac{\left[1 - \left(\mu T \cdot \frac{W4}{\frac{L2(x2)}{2}}\right)\right]}{\left[1 + Wred \cdot \frac{(\mu B - \mu T)}{\frac{L2(x2)}{2}}\right]} \qquad FdeltaT(x3) := \frac{\left[1 - \left(\mu T \cdot \frac{W4}{\frac{L2(x3)}{2}}\right)\right]}{\left[1 + Wred \cdot \frac{(\mu B - \mu T)}{\frac{L2(x3)}{2}}\right]}$$

$$FdeltaB(x2) := \frac{\left[1 + \left(\mu B \cdot \frac{W3}{\frac{L2(x2)}{2}}\right)\right]}{\left[1 + Wred \cdot \frac{(\mu B - \mu T)}{\frac{L2(x2)}{2}}\right]} \qquad FdeltaB(x3) := \frac{\left[1 + \left(\mu B \cdot \frac{W3}{\frac{L2(x3)}{2}}\right)\right]}{\left[1 + Wred \cdot \frac{(\mu B - \mu T)}{\frac{L2(x3)}{2}}\right]}$$

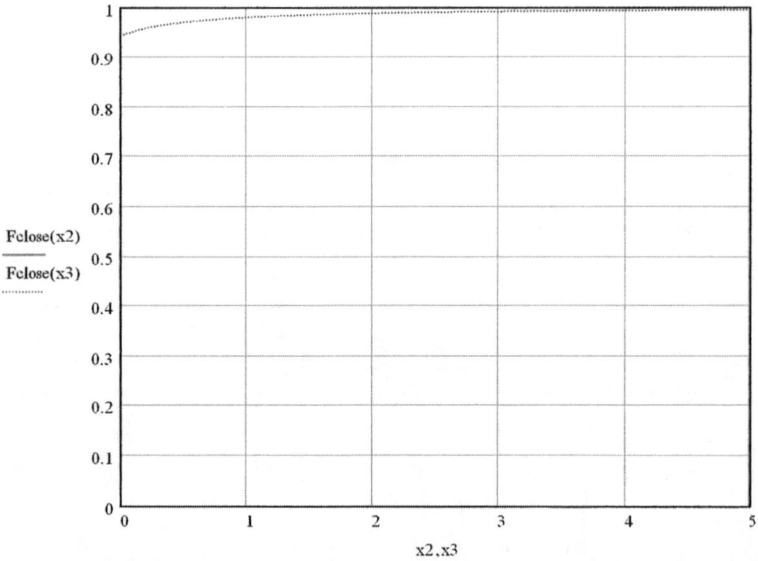

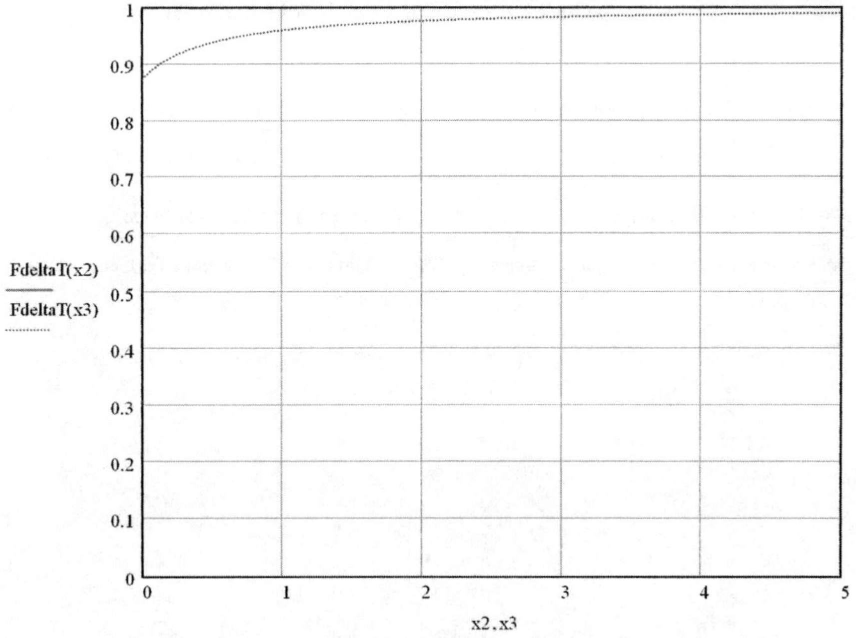
1
0.9
0.8
0.7
0.6
0.5
0.4
0.3
0.2
0.1
0
FdeltaT(x2)
FdeltaT(x3)
0
1
2
3
4
5
x2, x3

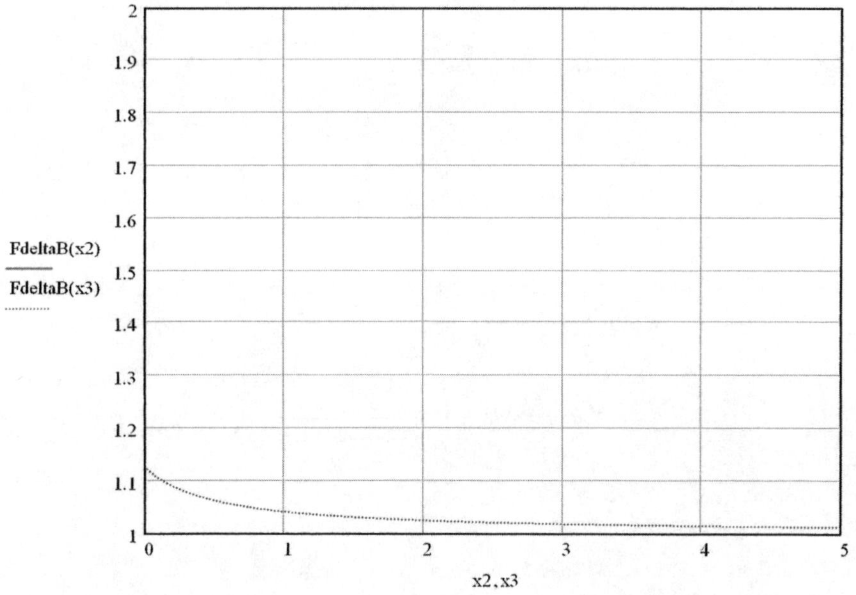
2
1.9
1.8
1.7
1.6
1.5
1.4
1.3
1.2
1.1
1
FdeltaB(x2)
FdeltaB(x3)
0
1
2
3
4
5
x2, x3

WeightCase2: 4200 lbs into 2200 lbs (loaded weights)

Notes: (a) '1' is *strongest* vehicle versus '2'. (b) W1 and W2 are true weights regardless of spin

(c) W3 and W4 are spin-dependent. (d) γ = 1+rr/kk. r = torque-arm, k = rad of gyration

W1 is Heavy Car empty weight lbs W2 is Light Car empty weight lbs

W3 is Heavy Car with occupant load lbs W4 is Light Car with occupant load lbs

γ3 is spin factor $\gamma 3 := 1.0$ γ4 is spin factor $\gamma 4 := 1.0$

$W1 := 4000$ $W2 := 2000$ $A1 := 0.6$ $A2 := 0.6$ $\theta 1 := \frac{0}{57.3}$

$W3 := 4200$ $W4 := 2200$ $F1 := 1.0$ $F2 := 1.0$ $\theta 2 := \frac{0}{57.3}$

$vL1 := \frac{7.335}{\cos(\theta 1)}$ $vL2 := \frac{7.335}{\cos(\theta 2)}$

$W3 := \frac{W3}{\gamma 3}$ $W4 := \frac{W4}{\gamma 4}$

$R1 := A1 \cdot \left(\frac{3000}{W1}\right)^{\frac{1}{3}}$ $R1 = 0.545$ $R2 := A2 \cdot \left(\frac{3000}{W2}\right)^{\frac{1}{3}}$ $R2 = 0.687$

$a1 := 0.5 \cdot \left(\frac{W1}{3000}\right)^{\frac{1}{3}}$ $a1 = 0.55$ $a2 := 0.5 \cdot \left(\frac{W2}{3000}\right)^{\frac{1}{3}}$ $a2 = 0.437$

x is crush feet L is load for given crush, lbs

$x2MAX := 10.0$

$x10 := 0$ $L1 := 12 \cdot R1 \cdot W1 \cdot F1 \cdot \left(1 + \frac{x10}{a1}\right) \cdot \frac{1}{\cos(\theta 1)}$ $L1 = 2.617 \times 10^4$

$$x20 := a2 \cdot \left[R1 \cdot W1 \cdot F1 \cdot \frac{\left(1 + \frac{x10}{a1}\right) \cdot \cos(\theta 2)}{R2 \cdot W2 \cdot F2 \cdot \cos(\theta 1)} \right] - a2 \qquad ge := 32.2$$

$x20 = 0.257$ $L2 := 12 \cdot R2 \cdot W2 \cdot F2 \cdot \left(1 + \frac{x20}{a2}\right) \cdot \frac{1}{\cos(\theta 2)}$ $L2 = 2.617 \times 10^4$

acell is acceleration (or deceleration) in g's

$accell1 := \frac{L1}{W1}$ $accell4 := \frac{L2}{W4}$ $accell1 = 6.542$ (g) $accell4 = 11.894$ g

$x2 := 0, 0.01 .. x20$ $accell3 := \frac{L1}{W3}$ $accell3 = 6.23$ (g)

Q's are crush- energy terms

$$Q2(x2) := \left(\frac{x2}{a2}\right)\cdot x2 + 2\cdot x2 + \frac{vL2^2}{12\cdot R2\cdot ge} \quad Q22(x2) := \left(\frac{vL2^2\cdot W2}{2\cdot ge}\right)\cdot\left(1 + \frac{x2}{a2}\right)$$

$$Q222(x2) := 6\cdot R2\cdot W2\cdot Q2(x2) - Q22(x2) \quad E2(x2) := F2\cdot\frac{Q222(x2)}{\cos(\theta 2)^2}$$

$$ETA(x2) := E2(x2)$$

vcritical is maximum closing speed to just avoid any crush, mph

$$vCRIT1 := \frac{(W3 + W4)\cdot\left[1 + \left(\frac{W4}{W3}\right)\cdot\left(F2\cdot\frac{R2}{F1\cdot R1}\right)^2\cdot\frac{\left(F1\cdot vL1^2\right)}{F2\cdot vL2^2}\right]\cdot F2\cdot vL2^2}{W3}$$

ETA(x2) =	x2 =
$2.274\cdot 10^{-13}$	0
128.472	0.01
260.718	0.02
396.738	0.03
536.532	0.04
680.1	0.05
827.442	0.06
978.557	0.07
$1.133\cdot 10^3$	0.08
$1.292\cdot 10^3$	0.09
$1.455\cdot 10^3$	0.1
$1.621\cdot 10^3$	0.11
$1.791\cdot 10^3$	0.12
$1.965\cdot 10^3$	0.13
$2.142\cdot 10^3$	0.14
$2.323\cdot 10^3$	0.15

$vCRIT := \sqrt{vCRIT1}$

$vCRIT = 12.254$

$VCRIT := \frac{vCRIT}{1.467}$

$VCRIT = 8.353$ (mph)

vclose is actual closing speed for total crush energy, mph

$$vCLOSE1(x2) := vCRIT1 + 2 \cdot ge \cdot ETA(x2) \cdot \frac{(W3 + W4)}{W3 \cdot W4}$$

$$vCLOSE(x2) := \sqrt{vCLOSE1(x2)}$$

ee and ff are coefficients of restitution (vehicle bounce)

$$ee(x2) := 0.7 \cdot \frac{vCRIT}{vCLOSE(x2)} \qquad VCLOSE(x2) := \frac{vCLOSE(x2)}{1.467} \quad \text{(mph)}$$

vCLOSE1(x2) =	vCLOSE(x2) =	ee(x2) =	VCLOSE(x2) =	x2 =
150.154	12.254	0.7	8.353	0
155.885	12.485	0.687	8.511	0.01
161.784	12.719	0.674	8.67	0.02
167.851	12.956	0.662	8.831	0.03
174.087	13.194	0.65	8.994	0.04
180.491	13.435	0.638	9.158	0.05
187.063	13.677	0.627	9.323	0.06
193.804	13.921	0.616	9.49	0.07
200.713	14.167	0.605	9.657	0.08
207.79	14.415	0.595	9.826	0.09
215.036	14.664	0.585	9.996	0.1
222.45	14.915	0.575	10.167	0.11
230.032	15.167	0.566	10.339	0.12
237.783	15.42	0.556	10.511	0.13
245.702	15.675	0.547	10.685	0.14
253.789	15.931	0.538	10.859	0.15

Δv is sudden change in speed

$$\Delta v2(x2) := \left(\frac{W3}{W3 + W4}\right)\cdot(1 + ee(x2))\cdot vCLOSE(x2) \qquad \Delta V2(x2) := \frac{\Delta v2(x2)}{1.467} \text{ (mph)}$$

$$\Delta v1(x2) := -\left(\frac{W4}{W3 + W4}\right)\cdot(1 + ee(x2))\cdot vCLOSE(x2) \qquad \Delta V1(x2) := \frac{\Delta v1(x2)}{1.467} \text{ (mph)}$$

$$\Delta V2CM(x2) := \frac{\Delta V2(x2)}{\gamma 4} \qquad \Delta V1CM(x2) := \frac{\Delta V1(x2)}{\gamma 3}$$

$$VCLOSE(x2) := \frac{vCLOSE(x2)}{1.467} \text{ (mph)}$$

Δv2(x2) =	Δv1(x2) =	ΔV2(x2) =	ΔV1(x2) =	x2 =	VCLOSE(x2) =
13.671	-7.161	9.319	-4.881	0	8.353
13.823	-7.24	9.422	-4.936	0.01	8.511
13.976	-7.321	9.527	-4.99	0.02	8.67
14.131	-7.402	9.633	-5.046	0.03	8.831
14.288	-7.484	9.739	-5.102	0.04	8.994
14.446	-7.567	9.847	-5.158	0.05	9.158
14.605	-7.65	9.955	-5.215	0.06	9.323
14.765	-7.734	10.065	-5.272	0.07	9.49
14.926	-7.819	10.175	-5.33	0.08	9.657
15.089	-7.904	10.286	-5.388	0.09	9.826
15.252	-7.989	10.397	-5.446	0.1	9.996
15.417	-8.075	10.509	-5.505	0.11	10.167
15.582	-8.162	10.622	-5.564	0.12	10.339
15.749	-8.249	10.735	-5.623	0.13	10.511
15.916	-8.337	10.849	-5.683	0.14	10.685
16.084	-8.425	10.964	-5.743	0.15	10.859

$x3 := x20, (x20 + 0.01) .. x2MAX$ **continuation of crush x2**

$$Q3(x3) := \left(\frac{x3}{a2}\right) \cdot x3 + 2 \cdot x3 + \frac{vL2^2}{12 \cdot R2 \cdot ge} \qquad Q33(x3) := \left(\frac{vL2^2 \cdot W2}{2 \cdot ge}\right) \cdot \left(1 + \frac{x3}{a2}\right)$$

$$Q333(x3) := 6 \cdot R2 \cdot W2 \cdot Q3(x3) - Q33(x3)$$

$$E3(x3) := F2 \cdot Q333(x3) \cdot \frac{1}{\cos(\theta 2)^2}$$

E3(x3) =	x3 =
$4.49 \cdot 10^3$	0.257
$4.715 \cdot 10^3$	0.267
$4.944 \cdot 10^3$	0.277
$5.177 \cdot 10^3$	0.287
$5.414 \cdot 10^3$	0.297
$5.654 \cdot 10^3$	0.307
$5.898 \cdot 10^3$	0.317
$6.146 \cdot 10^3$	0.327
$6.398 \cdot 10^3$	0.337
$6.654 \cdot 10^3$	0.347
$6.913 \cdot 10^3$	0.357
$7.176 \cdot 10^3$	0.367
$7.443 \cdot 10^3$	0.377
$7.713 \cdot 10^3$	0.387
$7.988 \cdot 10^3$	0.397
$8.266 \cdot 10^3$	0.407

crush E for vehicle 2

$x1 := 0$ crush of vehicle 1

$$x1(x3) := a1\cdot\left(R2\cdot W2\cdot\frac{F2\cdot\cos(\theta 1)}{R1\cdot W1\cdot F1\cdot\cos(\theta 2)}\right)\cdot\left(1+\frac{x3}{a2}\right) - a1$$

$$Q1(x1,x3) := \left(\frac{x1(x3)}{a1}\right)\cdot x1(x3) + 2\cdot x1(x3) + \frac{vL1^2}{12\cdot R1\cdot ge} \qquad Q11(x1,x3) := \left(\frac{vL1^2\cdot W1}{2\cdot ge}\right)\cdot\left(1+\frac{x1(x3)}{a1}\right)$$

$$Q111(x1,x3) := 6\cdot R1\cdot W1\cdot Q1(x1,x3) - Q11(x1,x3)$$

$$E1(x1,x3) := F1\cdot Q111(x1,x3)\cdot\frac{1}{\cos(\theta 1)^2}$$ crush E for vehicle 1

$$ET(x1,x3) := E1(x1,x3) + E3(x3)$$ sum of crush energies

x1(x3) =	E3(x3) =	E1(x1,x3) =	ET(x1,x3) =
0	$4.49\cdot10^{3}$	$1.819\cdot10^{-12}$	$4.49\cdot10^{3}$
$7.937\cdot10^{-3}$	$4.715\cdot10^{3}$	160.985	$4.876\cdot10^{3}$
0.016	$4.944\cdot10^{3}$	324.966	$5.269\cdot10^{3}$
0.024	$5.177\cdot10^{3}$	491.941	$5.669\cdot10^{3}$
0.032	$5.414\cdot10^{3}$	661.913	$6.076\cdot10^{3}$
0.04	$5.654\cdot10^{3}$	834.879	$6.489\cdot10^{3}$
0.048	$5.898\cdot10^{3}$	$1.011\cdot10^{3}$	$6.909\cdot10^{3}$
0.056	$6.146\cdot10^{3}$	$1.19\cdot10^{3}$	$7.336\cdot10^{3}$
0.063	$6.398\cdot10^{3}$	$1.372\cdot10^{3}$	$7.77\cdot10^{3}$
0.071	$6.654\cdot10^{3}$	$1.557\cdot10^{3}$	$8.21\cdot10^{3}$
0.079	$6.913\cdot10^{3}$	$1.745\cdot10^{3}$	$8.657\cdot10^{3}$
0.087	$7.176\cdot10^{3}$	$1.936\cdot10^{3}$	$9.111\cdot10^{3}$
0.095	$7.443\cdot10^{3}$	$2.13\cdot10^{3}$	$9.572\cdot10^{3}$
0.103	$7.713\cdot10^{3}$	$2.326\cdot10^{3}$	$1.004\cdot10^{4}$
0.111	$7.988\cdot10^{3}$	$2.526\cdot10^{3}$	$1.051\cdot10^{4}$
0.119	$8.266\cdot10^{3}$	$2.729\cdot10^{3}$	$1.099\cdot10^{4}$

$$\mathrm{vCLOSE3(x3)} := \mathrm{vCRIT1} + 2\cdot \mathrm{ge}\cdot \mathrm{ET(x1,x3)}\cdot \frac{(\mathrm{W3} + \mathrm{W4})}{\mathrm{W3}\cdot \mathrm{W4}}$$

$$\mathrm{vCLOS(x3)} := \sqrt{\mathrm{vCLOSE3(x3)}} \qquad \mathrm{ff(x3)} := 0.7\cdot \frac{\mathrm{vCRIT}}{\mathrm{vCLOS(x3)}}$$

$$\mathrm{VCLOS(x3)} := \frac{\mathrm{vCLOS(x3)}}{1.467} \quad \text{(mph)}$$

$$\Delta \mathrm{v4(x3)} := \left(\frac{\mathrm{W3}}{\mathrm{W3} + \mathrm{W4}}\right)\cdot (1 + \mathrm{ff(x3)})\cdot \mathrm{vCLOS(x3)} \qquad \Delta \mathrm{V4(x3)} := \frac{\Delta \mathrm{v4(x3)}}{1.467} \quad \text{(mph)}$$

$$\Delta \mathrm{V4CM(x3)} := \frac{\Delta \mathrm{V4(x3)}}{\gamma 4}$$

$$\Delta \mathrm{v3(x3)} := -\left(\frac{\mathrm{W4}}{\mathrm{W3} + \mathrm{W4}}\right)\cdot (1 + \mathrm{ff(x3)})\cdot \mathrm{vCLOS(x3)} \qquad \Delta \mathrm{V3(x3)} := \frac{\Delta \mathrm{v3(x3)}}{1.467} \quad \text{(mph)}$$

$$\Delta \mathrm{V3CM(x3)} := \frac{\Delta \mathrm{V3(x3)}}{\gamma 3}$$

vCLOSE3(x3) =	VCLOS(x3) =	ff(x3) =	ΔV4(x3) =	ΔV3(x3) =
350.433	12.761	0.458	12.211	-6.396
367.664	13.071	0.447	12.415	-6.503
385.196	13.379	0.437	12.617	-6.609
403.031	13.685	0.427	12.818	-6.714
421.167	13.989	0.418	13.018	-6.819
439.606	14.292	0.409	13.216	-6.923
458.346	14.594	0.401	13.414	-7.027
477.388	14.894	0.393	13.611	-7.13
496.733	15.193	0.385	13.807	-7.232
516.379	15.49	0.377	14.002	-7.335
536.327	15.786	0.37	14.197	-7.437
556.577	16.082	0.364	14.391	-7.538
577.129	16.376	0.357	14.584	-7.639
597.983	16.669	0.351	14.776	-7.74
619.139	16.961	0.345	14.968	-7.84
640.597	17.253	0.339	15.159	-7.941

x3 =	x1(x3) =
0.257	0
0.267	$7.937\cdot10^{-3}$
0.277	0.016
0.287	0.024
0.297	0.032
0.307	0.04
0.317	0.048
0.327	0.056
0.337	0.063
0.347	0.071
0.357	0.079
0.367	0.087
0.377	0.095
0.387	0.103
0.397	0.111
0.407	0.119

Heavy Car (4200 lbs) Crush versus Light Car (2200 lbs) Crush in feet

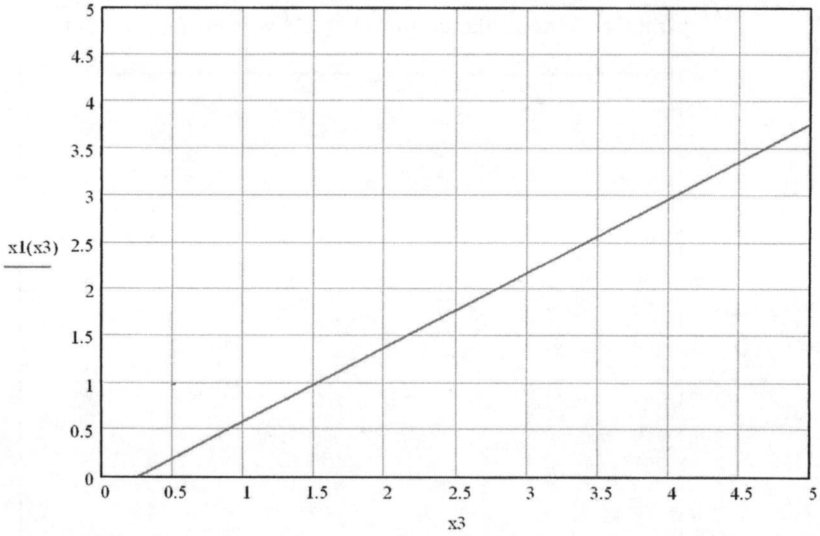

Light Car Speed Change (mph) at contact Point versus Light Car Crush (ft)

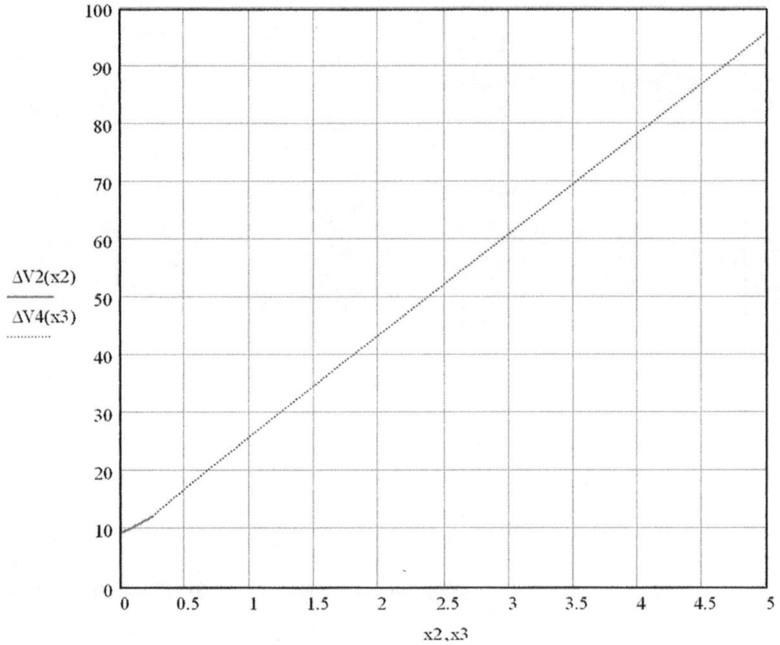

Light Car Speed Change (mph) at CM versus Light Car Crush (ft)

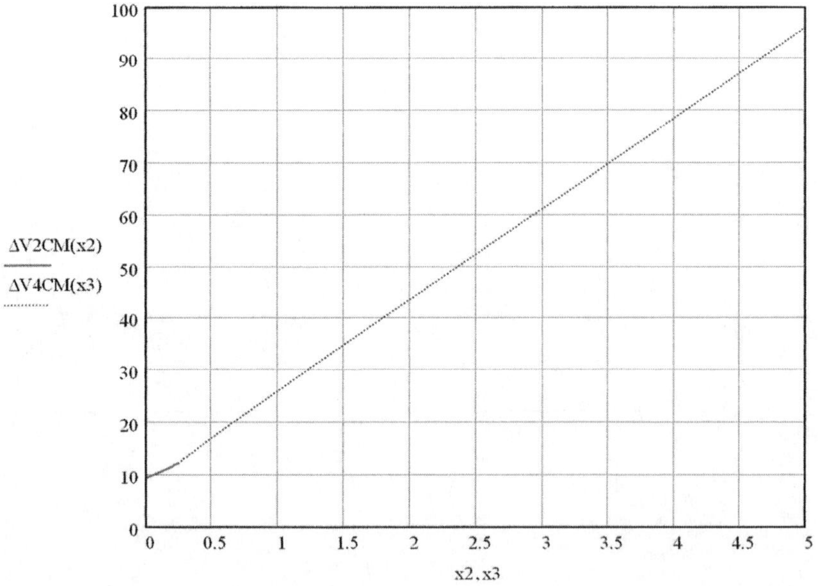

Heavy Car Speed Change (mph) at Contact Point vs. Light Car Crush (ft)

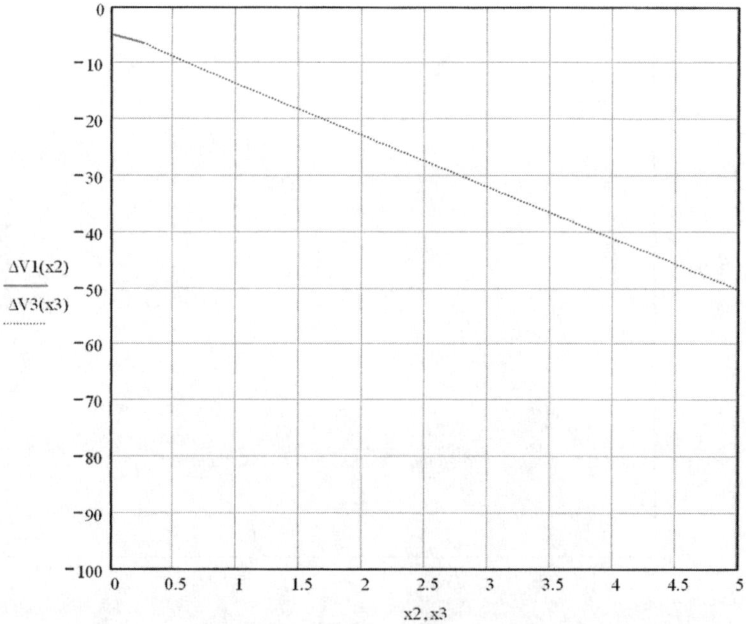

Heavy Car Speed Change (mph) at CM vs. Light Car Crush (ft)

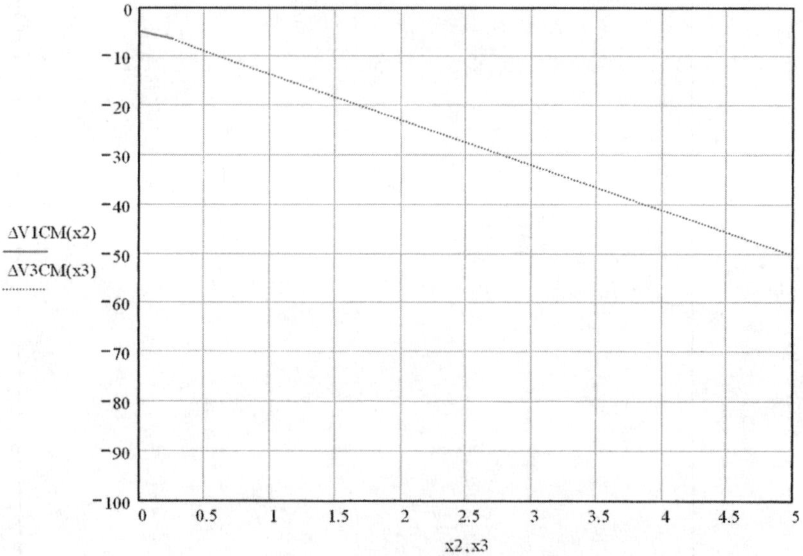

Closing Speed (mph) vs. Light Car Crush (ft)

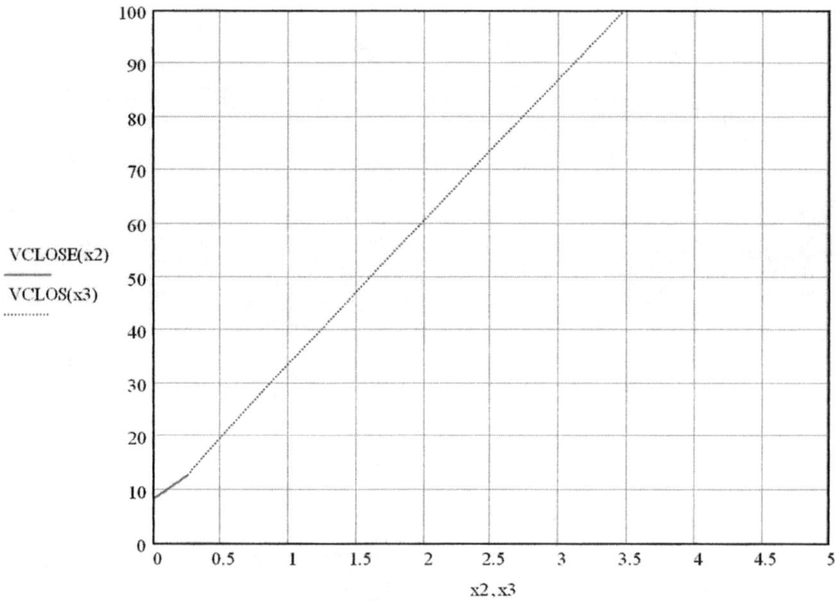

Restitution versus Light Car Crush (ft)

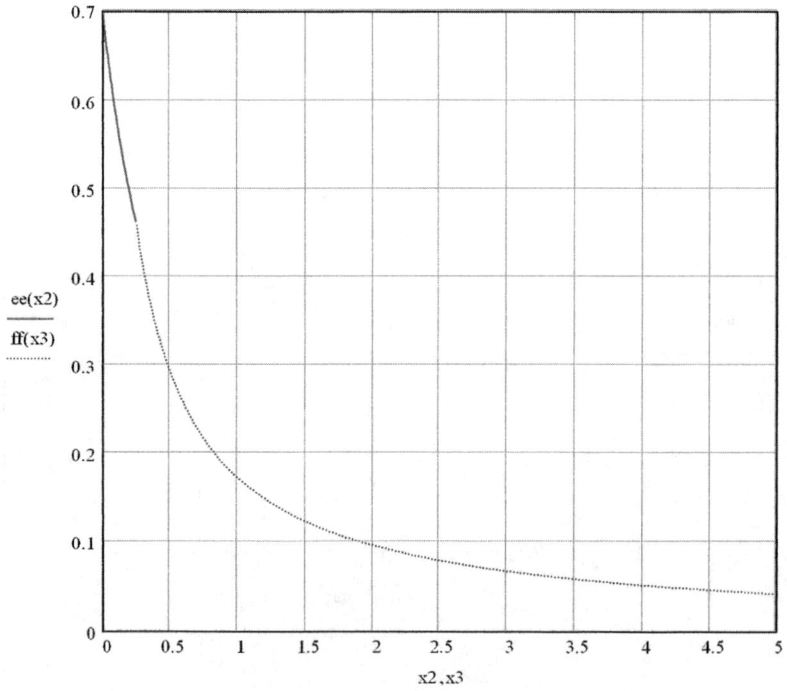

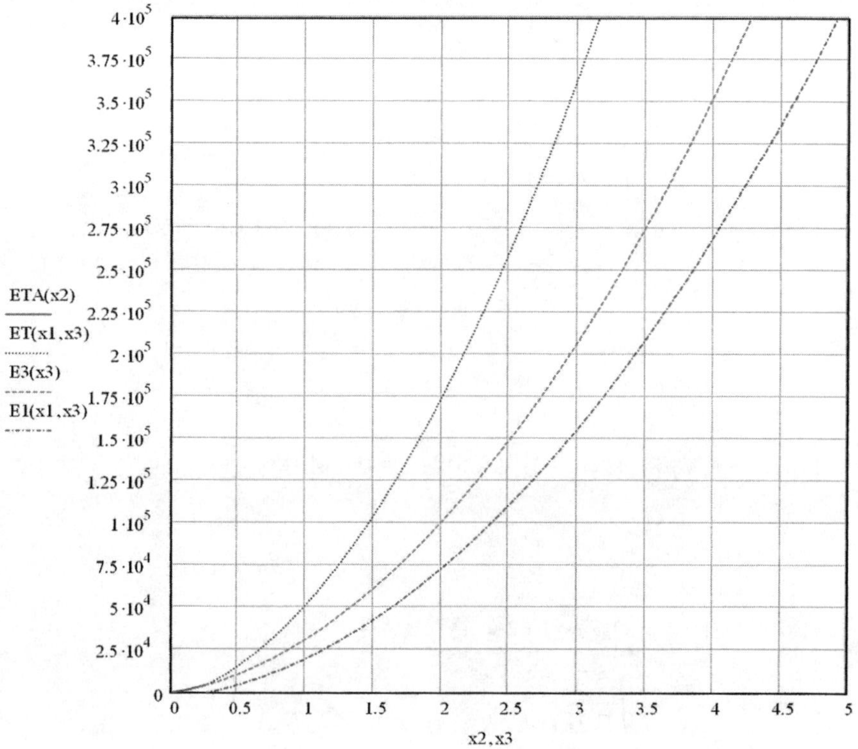

4·10^5
3.75·10^5
3.5·10^5
3.25·10^5
3·10^5
2.75·10^5
2.5·10^5
2.25·10^5
2·10^5
1.75·10^5
1.5·10^5
1.25·10^5
1·10^5
7.5·10^4
5·10^4
2.5·10^4
0
ETA(x2)
ET(x1,x3)
E3(x3)
E1(x1,x3)
0
0.5
1
1.5
2
2.5
3
3.5
4
4.5
5
x2,x3

$$TOPelast := R1^2 \cdot W3 \cdot F1 \cdot vL2^2 + R2^2 \cdot W4 \cdot F2 \cdot vL1^2$$

$$BOTTOMelast := 144 \cdot R1^2 \cdot R2^2 \cdot ge^2 \cdot (W3 + W4) \cdot F1 \cdot F2$$

$$Telastquart := \left(\frac{\pi}{2}\right) \cdot \sqrt{\frac{TOPelast}{BOTTOMelast}} \qquad Tcontactelast := Telastquart \cdot 1.7$$

$$Telastquart = 0.048 \qquad Tcontactelast = 0.081$$

$$TOP := R1 \cdot W3 \cdot F1 \cdot a2 \cdot \cos(\theta 2) + R2 \cdot W4 \cdot F2 \cdot a1 \cdot \cos(\theta 1)$$

$$TOP = 1.832 \times 10^3$$

$$BOTTOM := 12 \cdot R1 \cdot R2 \cdot F1 \cdot F2 \cdot ge \cdot (W3 + W4) \qquad BOTTOM = 9.259 \times 10^5$$

$$Tquarterp := \left(\frac{\pi}{2}\right) \cdot \sqrt{\frac{TOP}{BOTTOM}}$$

$$Tquarterp = 0.07$$

$$x2 := 0, 0.01 .. x20 \qquad x3 := x20, (x20 + 0.01) .. x2MAX$$

$$Frac(x2) := \sqrt{1 - \frac{VCRIT^2}{VCLOSE(x2)^2}} \qquad frac(x3) := \sqrt{1 - \frac{VCRIT^2}{VCLOS(x3)^2}}$$

$$Tquart(x2) := (Telastquart) \cdot (1 - Frac(x2)) + Frac(x2) \cdot Tquarterp$$

$$Tquarter(x3) := (Telastquart) \cdot (1 - frac(x3)) + frac(x3) \cdot Tquarterp$$

$$Tcont(x2) := Tquart(x2) \cdot (1 + ee(x2))$$

$$Tcontact(x3) := Tquarter(x3) \cdot (1 + ff(x3))$$

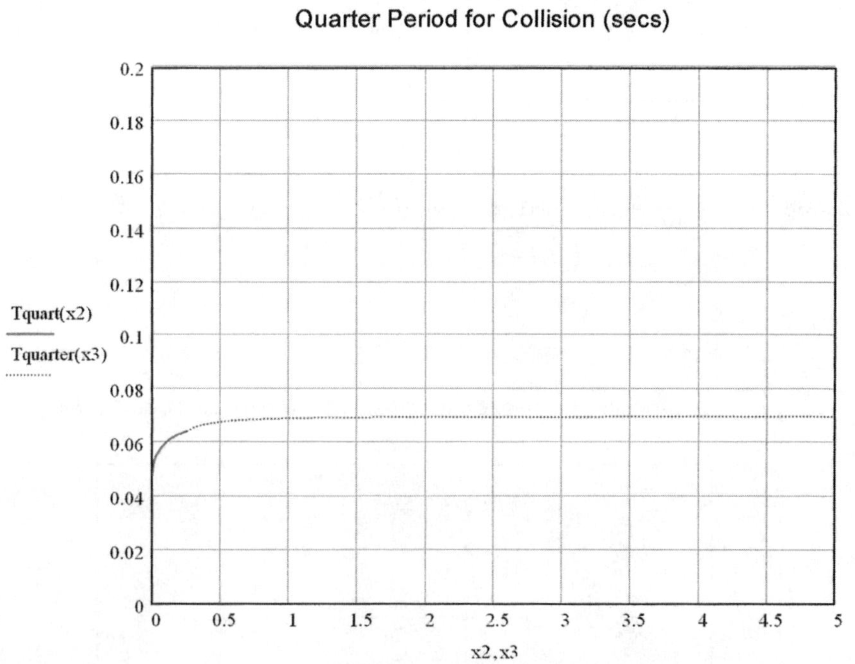
Quarter Period for Collision (secs)
Tquart(x2)
Tquarter(x3)
0.2
0.18
0.16
0.14
0.12
0.1
0.08
0.06
0.04
0.02
0
0
0.5
1
1.5
2
2.5
3
3.5
4
4.5
5
x2, x3

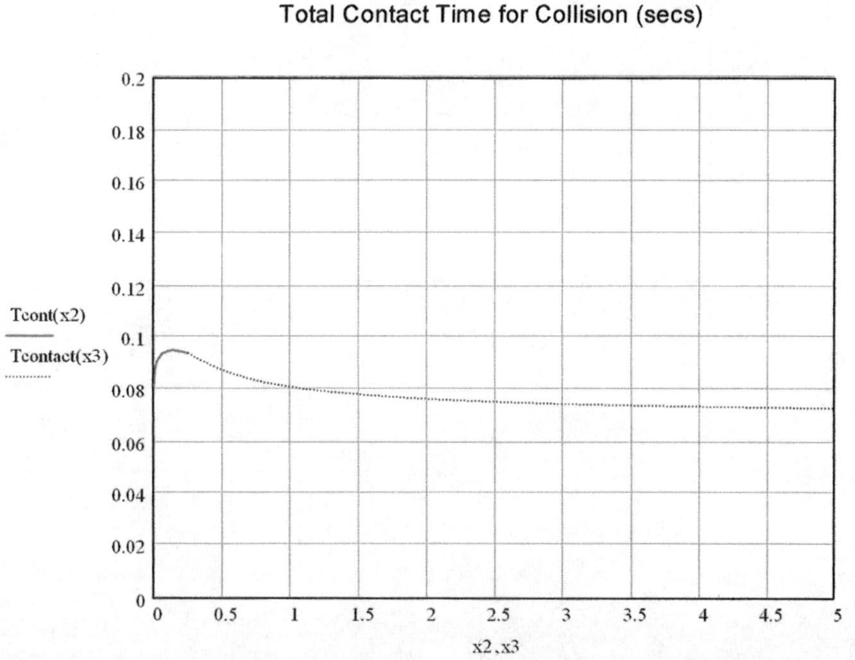
Total Contact Time for Collision (secs)
Tcont(x2)
Tcontact(x3)
0.2
0.18
0.16
0.14
0.12
0.1
0.08
0.06
0.04
0.02
0
0
0.5
1
1.5
2
2.5
3
3.5
4
4.5
5
x2, x3

$$L2(x2) := 12 \cdot R2 \cdot W2 \cdot F2 \cdot \left(1 + \frac{x2}{a2}\right) \cdot \frac{1}{\cos(\theta 2)} \qquad L2(x3) := 12 \cdot R2 \cdot W2 \cdot F2 \cdot \left(1 + \frac{x3}{a2}\right) \cdot \frac{1}{\cos(\theta 2)}$$

$$Accel4(x2) := \frac{L2(x2)}{W4} \qquad Accel4(x3) := \frac{L2(x3)}{W4}$$

$$Accel3(x2) := \frac{-L2(x2)}{W3} \qquad Accel3(x3) := \frac{-L2(x3)}{W3}$$

Peak Mutual Force at Contact Point (lbs) versus Light Car Crush (ft)

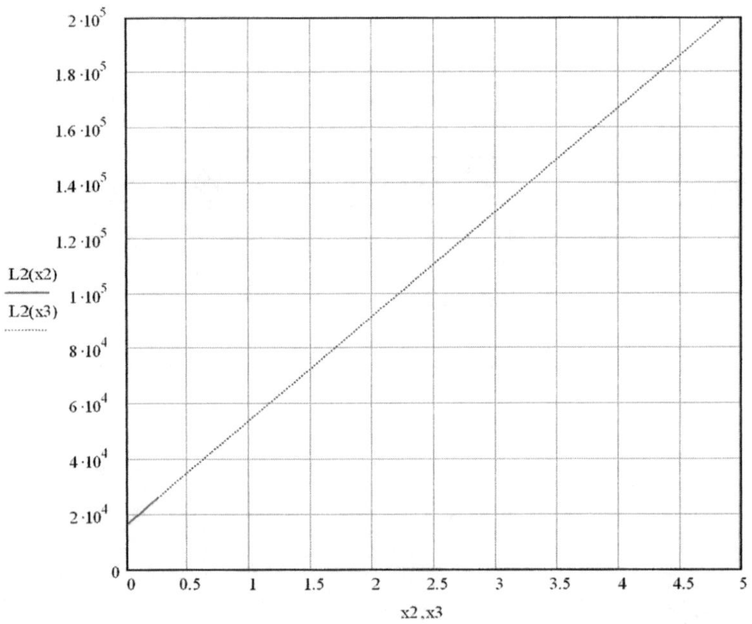

Peak Accel (Decel) of Heavy Car at CP (g) versus Light Car Crush (ft)

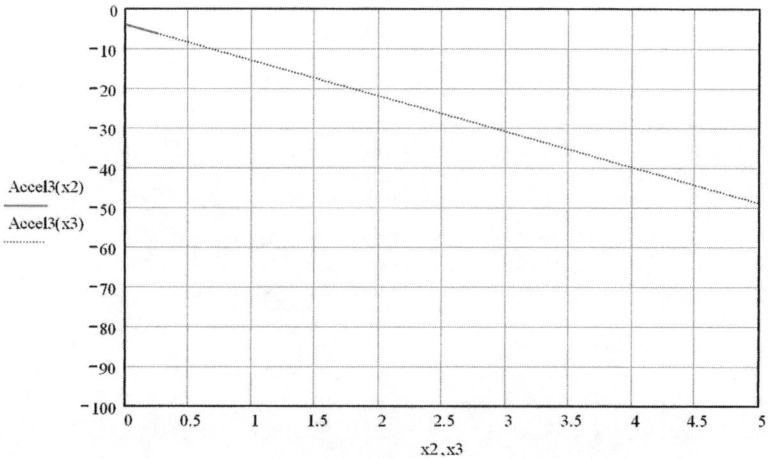

Peak Accel of Light Car at CP (g) versus Light Car Crush (ft)

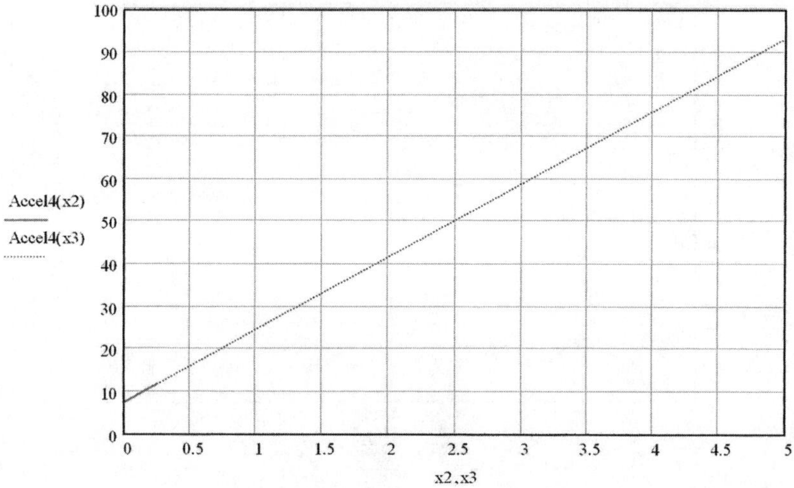

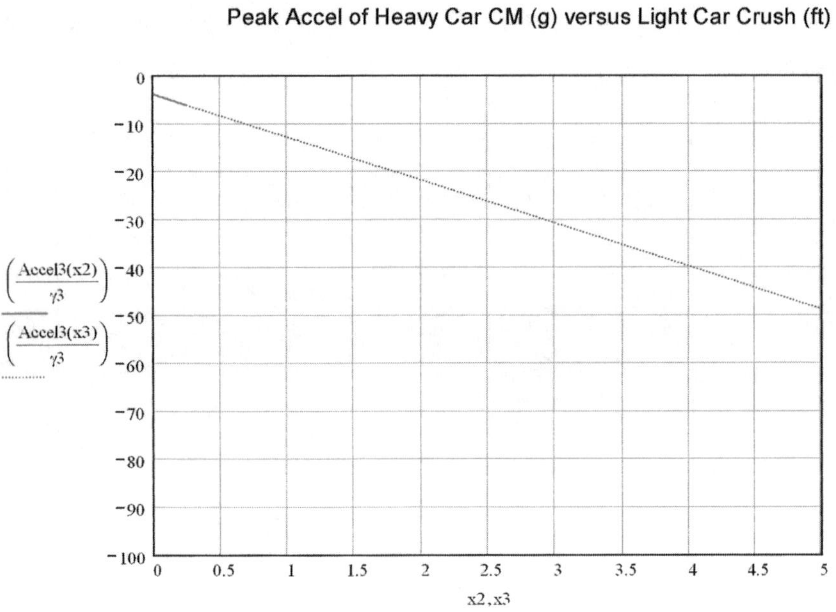
Peak Accel of Heavy Car CM (g) versus Light Car Crush (ft)
0
−10
−20
−30
−40
−50
−60
−70
−80
−90
−100
Accel3(x2) / γ3
Accel3(x3) / γ3
0
0.5
1
1.5
2
2.5
3
3.5
4
4.5
5
x2, x3

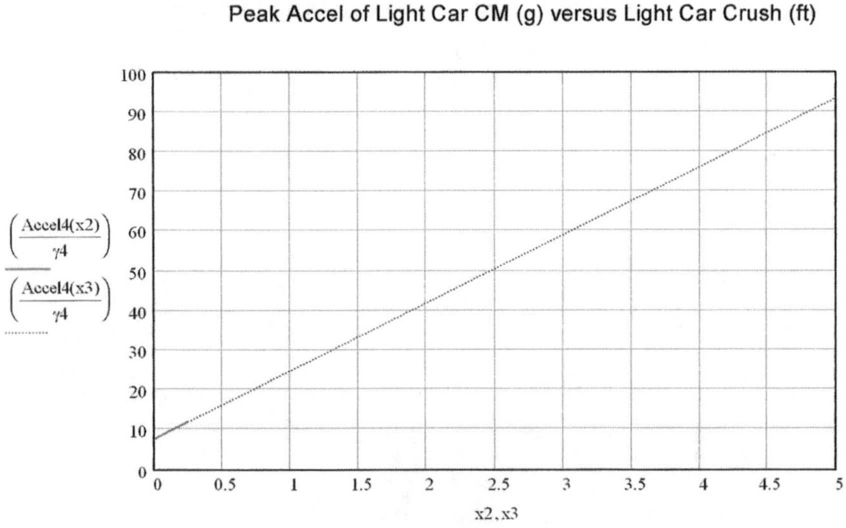
Peak Accel of Light Car CM (g) versus Light Car Crush (ft)
100
90
80
70
60
50
40
30
20
10
0
Accel4(x2) / γ4
Accel4(x3) / γ4
0
0.5
1
1.5
2
2.5
3
3.5
4
4.5
5
x2, x3

B is the bullet (W3), while T is the target (W4)

$$\mu B := 0.0 \qquad \mu T := 0.7 \qquad Wred := W3 \cdot \frac{W4}{(W3 + W4)}$$

$$Fclose(x2) := \sqrt{1 + (\mu B - \mu T) \cdot \frac{Wred}{\frac{L2(x2)}{2}}} \qquad Fclose(x3) := \sqrt{1 + (\mu B - \mu T) \cdot \frac{Wred}{\frac{L2(x3)}{2}}}$$

$$FdeltaT(x2) := \frac{\left[1 - \left(\mu T \cdot \frac{W4}{\frac{L2(x2)}{2}}\right)\right]}{\left[1 + Wred \cdot \frac{(\mu B - \mu T)}{\frac{L2(x2)}{2}}\right]} \qquad FdeltaT(x3) := \frac{\left[1 - \left(\mu T \cdot \frac{W4}{\frac{L2(x3)}{2}}\right)\right]}{\left[1 + Wred \cdot \frac{(\mu B - \mu T)}{\frac{L2(x3)}{2}}\right]}$$

$$FdeltaB(x2) := \frac{\left[1 + \left(\mu B \cdot \frac{W3}{\frac{L2(x2)}{2}}\right)\right]}{\left[1 + Wred \cdot \frac{(\mu B - \mu T)}{\frac{L2(x2)}{2}}\right]} \qquad FdeltaB(x3) := \frac{\left[1 + \left(\mu B \cdot \frac{W3}{\frac{L2(x3)}{2}}\right)\right]}{\left[1 + Wred \cdot \frac{(\mu B - \mu T)}{\frac{L2(x3)}{2}}\right]}$$

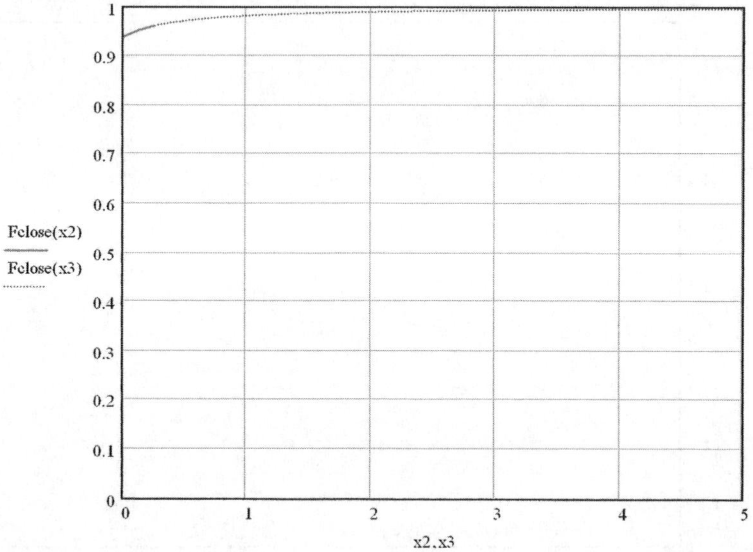

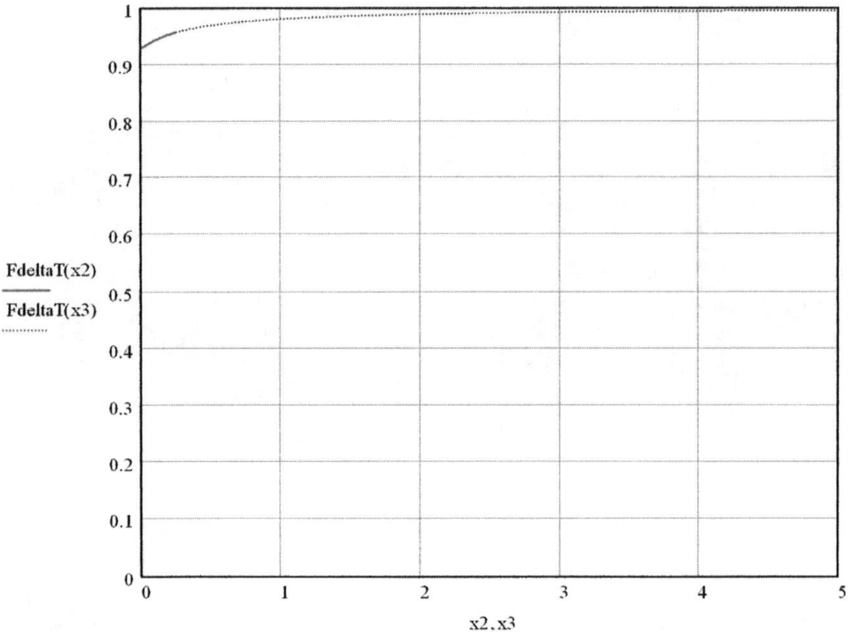
1
0.9
0.8
0.7
0.6
0.5
0.4
0.3
0.2
0.1
0
FdeltaT(x2)
FdeltaT(x3)
0
1
2
3
4
5
x2, x3

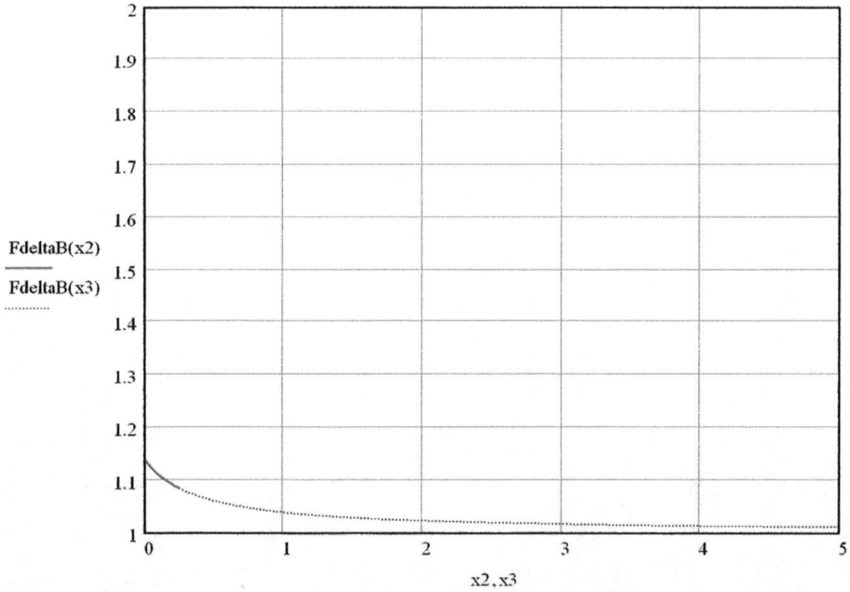
2
1.9
1.8
1.7
1.6
1.5
1.4
1.3
1.2
1.1
1
FdeltaB(x2)
FdeltaB(x3)
0
1
2
3
4
5
x2, x3

WeightCase3: 2201 lbs into 2200 lbs (loaded weights)

Notes: (a) '1' is *strongest* vehicle versus '2'. (b) W1 and W2 are true weights regardless of spin

(c) W3 and W4 are spin-dependent. (d) γ = 1+rr/kk. r = torque-arm, k = rad of gyration

W1 is Heavy Car empty weight lbs

W2 is Light Car empty weight lbs

W3 is Heavy Car with occupant load lbs

W4 is Light Car with occupant load lbs

γ3 is spin factor $\gamma 3 := 1.0$

γ4 is spin factor $\gamma 4 := 1.0$

$W1 := 2001$ $W2 := 2000$ $A1 := 0.6$ $A2 := 0.6$ $\theta 1 := \frac{0}{57.3}$

$W3 := 2201$ $W4 := 2200$ $F1 := 1.0$ $F2 := 1.0$ $\theta 2 := \frac{0}{57.3}$

$vL1 := \frac{7.335}{\cos(\theta 1)}$ $vL2 := \frac{7.335}{\cos(\theta 2)}$

$W3 := \frac{W3}{\gamma 3}$ $W4 := \frac{W4}{\gamma 4}$

$R1 := A1 \cdot \left(\frac{3000}{W1}\right)^{\frac{1}{3}}$ $R1 = 0.687$ $R2 := A2 \cdot \left(\frac{3000}{W2}\right)^{\frac{1}{3}}$ $R2 = 0.687$

$a1 := 0.5 \cdot \left(\frac{W1}{3000}\right)^{\frac{1}{3}}$ $a1 = 0.437$ $a2 := 0.5 \cdot \left(\frac{W2}{3000}\right)^{\frac{1}{3}}$ $a2 = 0.437$

x is crush feet

L is load for given crush, lbs

$x2MAX := 10.0$

$x10 := 0$ $L1 := 12 \cdot R1 \cdot W1 \cdot F1 \cdot \left(1 + \frac{x10}{a1}\right) \cdot \frac{1}{\cos(\theta 1)}$ $L1 = 1.649 \times 10^{4}$

$$x20 := a2 \cdot \left[R1 \cdot W1 \cdot F1 \cdot \frac{\left(1 + \frac{x10}{a1}\right) \cdot \cos(\theta 2)}{R2 \cdot W2 \cdot F2 \cdot \cos(\theta 1)}\right] - a2$$

$ge := 32.2$

$x20 = 1.456 \times 10^{-4}$ $L2 := 12 \cdot R2 \cdot W2 \cdot F2 \cdot \left(1 + \frac{x20}{a2}\right) \cdot \frac{1}{\cos(\theta 2)}$ $L2 = 1.649 \times 10^{4}$

acell is acceleration (or deceleration) in g's

$$accell1 := \frac{L1}{W1} \qquad accell4 := \frac{L2}{W4} \qquad accell1 = 8.241 \quad (g) \qquad accell4 = 7.495 \quad g$$

$$x2 := 0, 0.01 .. x20 \qquad accell3 := \frac{L1}{W3} \qquad accell3 = 7.492 \quad (g)$$

Q's are crush- energy terms

$$Q2(x2) := \left(\frac{x2}{a2}\right)\cdot x2 + 2\cdot x2 + \frac{vL2^2}{12\cdot R2\cdot ge} \qquad Q22(x2) := \left(\frac{vL2^2\cdot W2}{2\cdot ge}\right)\cdot\left(1 + \frac{x2}{a2}\right)$$

$$Q222(x2) := 6\cdot R2\cdot W2\cdot Q2(x2) - Q22(x2) \qquad E2(x2) := F2\cdot\frac{Q222(x2)}{\cos(\theta 2)^2}$$

$$ETA(x2) := E2(x2)$$

vcritical is maximum closing speed to just avoid any crush, mph

$$vCRIT1 := \frac{(W3 + W4)\cdot\left[1 + \left(\frac{W4}{W3}\right)\cdot\left(F2\cdot\frac{R2}{F1\cdot R1}\right)^2\cdot\frac{\left(F1\cdot vL1^2\right)}{F2\cdot vL2^2}\right]\cdot F2\cdot vL2^2}{W3}$$

$ETA(x2) =$ $\boxed{2.274\cdot 10^{-13}}$ $\qquad x2 =$ $\boxed{0}$

$$vCRIT := \sqrt{vCRIT1}$$

$$vCRIT = 14.668$$

$$VCRIT := \frac{vCRIT}{1.467}$$

$$VCRIT = 9.999 \quad \text{(mph)}$$

vclose is actual closing speed for total crush energy, mph

$$vCLOSE1(x2) := vCRIT1 + 2\cdot ge\cdot ETA(x2)\cdot\frac{(W3 + W4)}{W3\cdot W4}$$

$$vCLOSE(x2) := \sqrt{vCLOSE1(x2)}$$

ee and ff are coefficients of restitution (vehicle bounce)

$$ee(x2) := 0.7\cdot\frac{vCRIT}{vCLOSE(x2)} \qquad VCLOSE(x2) := \frac{vCLOSE(x2)}{1.467} \quad \text{(mph)}$$

vCLOSE1(x2) =	vCLOSE(x2) =	ee(x2) =	VCLOSE(x2) =	x2 =
215.147	14.668	0.7	9.999	0

Δv is sudden change in speed

$$\Delta v2(x2) := \left(\frac{W3}{W3 + W4}\right)\cdot(1 + ee(x2))\cdot vCLOSE(x2) \qquad \Delta V2(x2) := \frac{\Delta v2(x2)}{1.467} \ \text{(mph)}$$

$$\Delta v1(x2) := -\left(\frac{W4}{W3 + W4}\right)\cdot(1 + ee(x2))\cdot vCLOSE(x2) \qquad \Delta V1(x2) := \frac{\Delta v1(x2)}{1.467} \ \text{(mph)}$$

$$\Delta V2CM(x2) := \frac{\Delta V2(x2)}{\gamma 4} \qquad \Delta V1CM(x2) := \frac{\Delta V1(x2)}{\gamma 3}$$

$$VCLOSE(x2) := \frac{vCLOSE(x2)}{1.467} \ \text{(mph)}$$

$\Delta v2(x2) =$	$\Delta v1(x2) =$	$\Delta V2(x2) =$	$\Delta V1(x2) =$	$x2 =$	$VCLOSE(x2) =$
12.471	-12.465	8.501	-8.497	0	9.999

$x3 := x20, (x20 + 0.01) .. x2MAX$ **continuation of crush x2**

$$Q3(x3) := \left(\frac{x3}{a2}\right)\cdot x3 + 2\cdot x3 + \frac{vL2^2}{12\cdot R2\cdot ge} \qquad Q33(x3) := \left(\frac{vL2^2\cdot W2}{2\cdot ge}\right)\cdot\left(1 + \frac{x3}{a2}\right)$$

$$Q333(x3) := 6\cdot R2\cdot W2\cdot Q3(x3) - Q33(x3)$$

$$E3(x3) := F2\cdot Q333(x3)\cdot\frac{1}{\cos(\theta 2)^2}$$

crush E for vehicle 2

E3(x3) =	x3 =
1.843	$1.456\cdot 10^{-4}$
130.37	0.01
262.672	0.02
398.746	0.03
538.595	0.04
682.218	0.05
829.615	0.06
980.785	0.07
$1.136\cdot 10^3$	0.08
$1.294\cdot 10^3$	0.09
$1.457\cdot 10^3$	0.1
$1.623\cdot 10^3$	0.11
$1.793\cdot 10^3$	0.12
$1.967\cdot 10^3$	0.13
$2.145\cdot 10^3$	0.14
$2.326\cdot 10^3$	0.15

$x1 := 0$ crush of vehicle 1

$$x1(x3) := a1 \cdot \left(R2 \cdot W2 \cdot \frac{F2 \cdot \cos(\theta 1)}{R1 \cdot W1 \cdot F1 \cdot \cos(\theta 2)} \right) \cdot \left(1 + \frac{x3}{a2} \right) - a1$$

$$Q1(x1,x3) := \left(\frac{x1(x3)}{a1} \right) \cdot x1(x3) + 2 \cdot x1(x3) + \frac{vL1^2}{12 \cdot R1 \cdot ge} \quad Q11(x1,x3) := \left(\frac{vL1^2 \cdot W1}{2 \cdot ge} \right) \cdot \left(1 + \frac{x1(x3)}{a1} \right)$$

$$Q111(x1,x3) := 6 \cdot R1 \cdot W1 \cdot Q1(x1,x3) - Q11(x1,x3)$$

$$E1(x1,x3) := F1 \cdot Q111(x1,x3) \cdot \frac{1}{\cos(\theta 1)^2}$$ crush E for vehicle 1

$$ET(x1,x3) := E1(x1,x3) + E3(x3)$$ sum of crush energies

$x1(x3) =$	$E3(x3) =$	$E1(x1,x3) =$	$ET(x1,x3) =$
0	1.843	$-2.274 \cdot 10^{-13}$	1.843
$9.998 \cdot 10^{-3}$	130.37	128.493	258.864
0.02	262.672	260.759	523.431
0.03	398.746	396.799	795.545
0.04	538.595	536.612	$1.075 \cdot 10^3$
0.05	682.218	680.198	$1.362 \cdot 10^3$
0.06	829.615	827.557	$1.657 \cdot 10^3$
0.07	980.785	978.689	$1.959 \cdot 10^3$
0.08	$1.136 \cdot 10^3$	$1.134 \cdot 10^3$	$2.269 \cdot 10^3$
0.09	$1.294 \cdot 10^3$	$1.292 \cdot 10^3$	$2.587 \cdot 10^3$
0.1	$1.457 \cdot 10^3$	$1.455 \cdot 10^3$	$2.912 \cdot 10^3$
0.11	$1.623 \cdot 10^3$	$1.621 \cdot 10^3$	$3.244 \cdot 10^3$
0.12	$1.793 \cdot 10^3$	$1.791 \cdot 10^3$	$3.584 \cdot 10^3$
0.13	$1.967 \cdot 10^3$	$1.965 \cdot 10^3$	$3.932 \cdot 10^3$
0.14	$2.145 \cdot 10^3$	$2.142 \cdot 10^3$	$4.287 \cdot 10^3$
0.15	$2.326 \cdot 10^3$	$2.324 \cdot 10^3$	$4.65 \cdot 10^3$

$$vCLOSE3(x3) := vCRIT1 + 2 \cdot ge \cdot ET(x1,x3) \cdot \frac{(W3 + W4)}{W3 \cdot W4}$$

$$vCLOS(x3) := \sqrt{vCLOSE3(x3)} \qquad ff(x3) := 0.7 \cdot \frac{vCRIT}{vCLOS(x3)}$$

$$VCLOS(x3) := \frac{vCLOS(x3)}{1.467} \quad \text{(mph)}$$

$$\Delta v4(x3) := \left(\frac{W3}{W3 + W4}\right) \cdot (1 + ff(x3)) \cdot vCLOS(x3) \qquad \Delta V4(x3) := \frac{\Delta v4(x3)}{1.467} \quad \text{(mph)}$$

$$\Delta V4CM(x3) := \frac{\Delta V4(x3)}{\gamma 4}$$

$$\Delta v3(x3) := -\left(\frac{W4}{W3 + W4}\right) \cdot (1 + ff(x3)) \cdot vCLOS(x3) \qquad \Delta V3(x3) := \frac{\Delta v3(x3)}{1.467} \quad \text{(mph)}$$

$$\Delta V3CM(x3) := \frac{\Delta V3(x3)}{\gamma 3}$$

vCLOSE3(x3) =	VCLOS(x3) =	ff(x3) =	ΔV4(x3) =	ΔV3(x3) =
215.255	10.001	0.7	8.502	-8.498
230.299	10.345	0.677	8.674	-8.67
245.785	10.687	0.655	8.845	-8.841
261.712	11.028	0.635	9.015	-9.011
278.081	11.367	0.616	9.185	-9.181
294.892	11.706	0.598	9.355	-9.35
312.145	12.043	0.581	9.523	-9.519
329.839	12.38	0.565	9.692	-9.687
347.975	12.716	0.55	9.86	-9.855
366.553	13.051	0.536	10.027	-10.023
385.573	13.385	0.523	10.194	-10.19
405.034	13.719	0.51	10.361	-10.357
424.938	14.052	0.498	10.528	-10.523
445.283	14.384	0.487	10.694	-10.689
466.069	14.716	0.476	10.86	-10.855
487.298	15.048	0.465	11.026	-11.021

x3 =	x1(x3) =
$1.456 \cdot 10^{-4}$	0
0.01	$9.998 \cdot 10^{-3}$
0.02	0.02
0.03	0.03
0.04	0.04
0.05	0.05
0.06	0.06
0.07	0.07
0.08	0.08
0.09	0.09
0.1	0.1
0.11	0.11
0.12	0.12
0.13	0.13
0.14	0.14
0.15	0.15

Heavy Car (2201 lbs) Crush versus Light Car (2200 lbs) Crush in feet

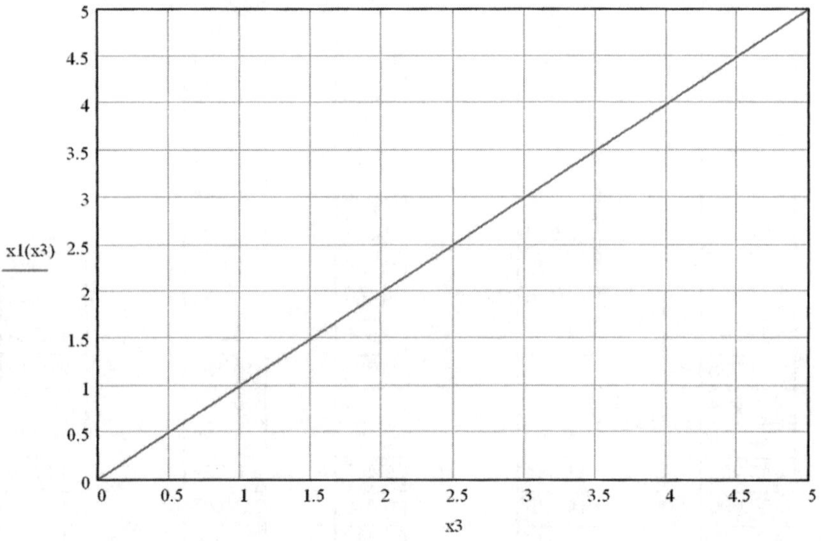

Light Car Speed Change (mph) at contact Point versus Light Car Crush (ft)

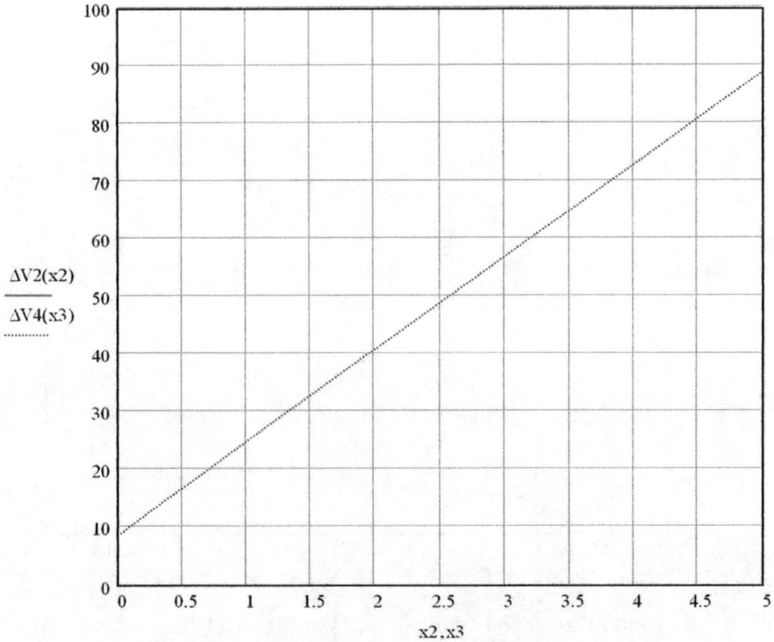

Light Car Speed Change (mph) at CM versus Light Car Crush (ft)

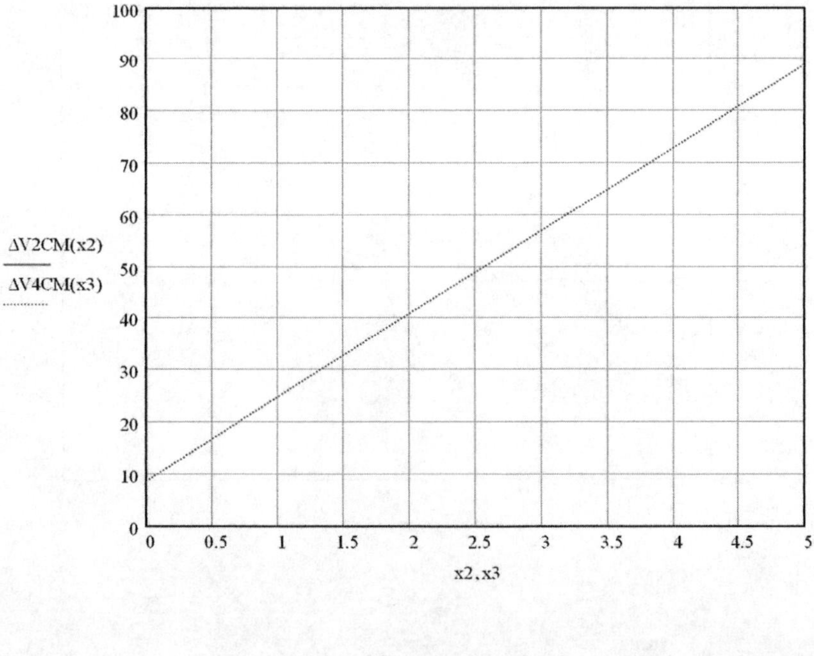

Heavy Car Speed Change (mph) at Contact Point vs. Light Car Crush (ft)

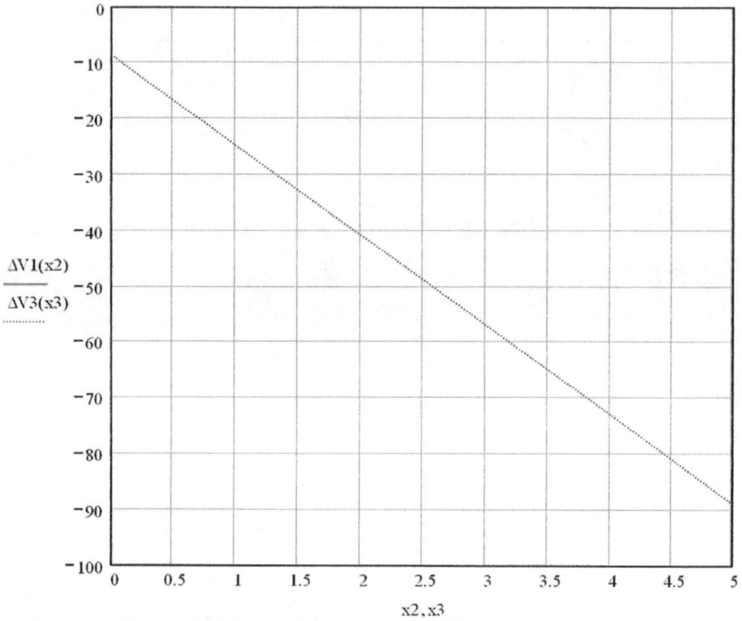

Heavy Car Speed Change (mph) at CM vs. Light Car Crush (ft)

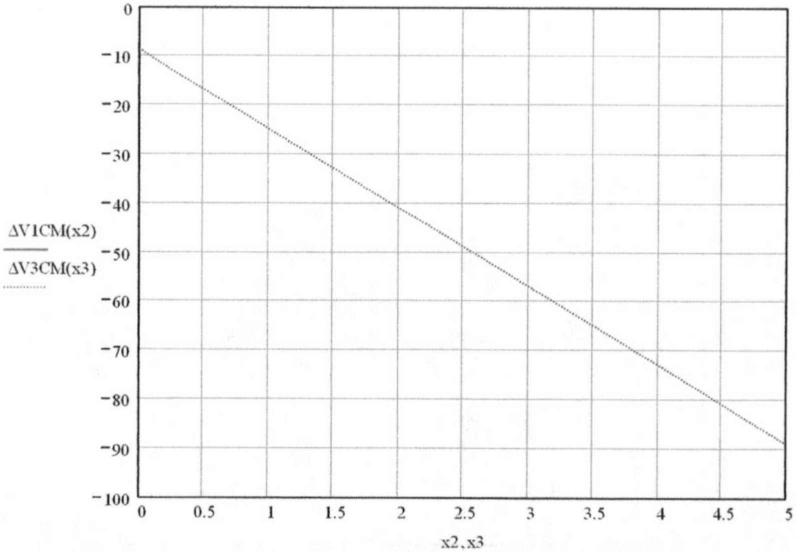

Closing Speed (mph) vs. Light Car Crush (ft)

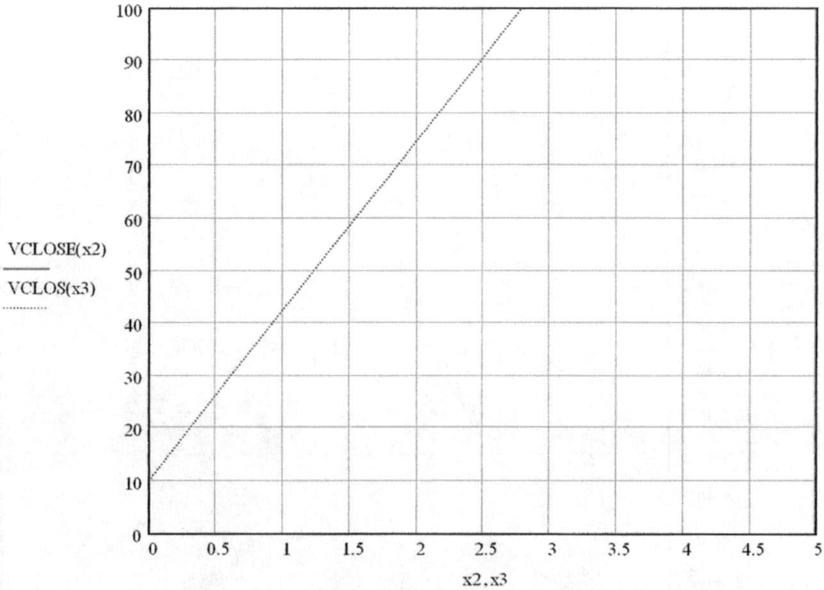

Restitution versus Light Car Crush (ft)

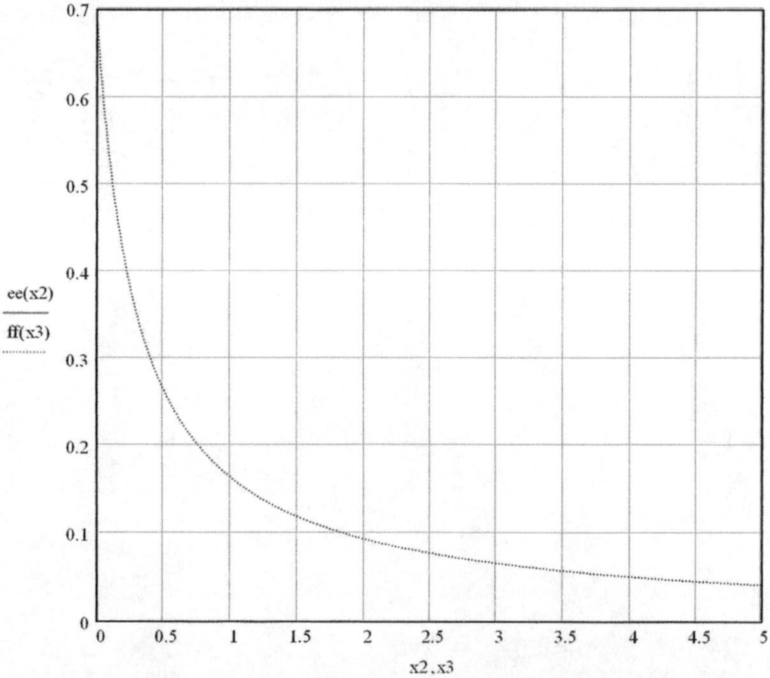

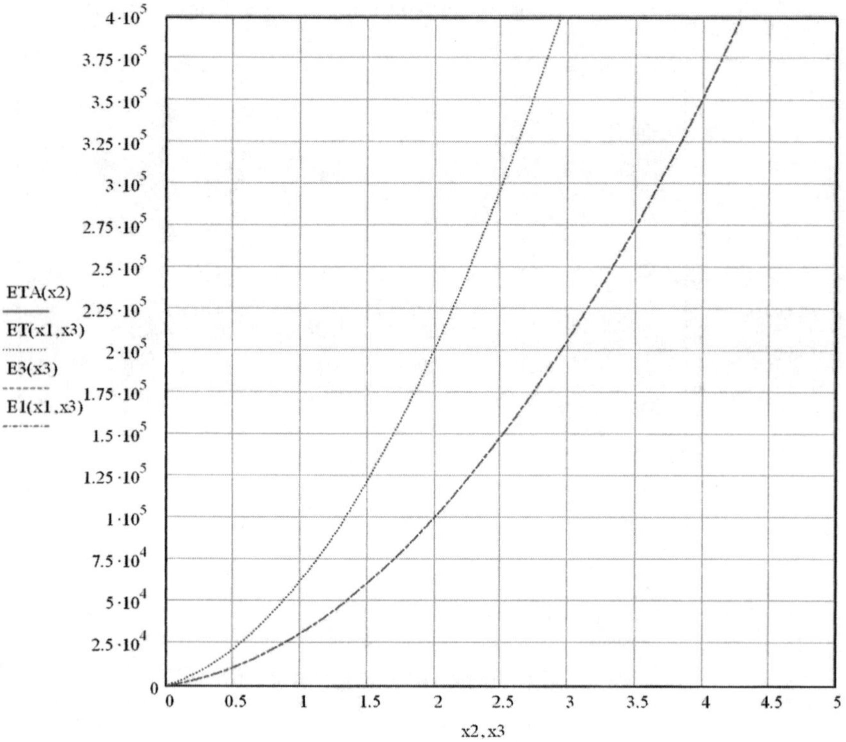
ETA(x2)
ET(x1,x3)
E3(x3)
E1(x1,x3)
4·10^5
3.75·10^5
3.5·10^5
3.25·10^5
3·10^5
2.75·10^5
2.5·10^5
2.25·10^5
2·10^5
1.75·10^5
1.5·10^5
1.25·10^5
1·10^5
7.5·10^4
5·10^4
2.5·10^4
0
0 0.5 1 1.5 2 2.5 3 3.5 4 4.5 5
x2, x3

$$\mathrm{TOPelast} := \mathrm{R1}^2 \cdot \mathrm{W3} \cdot \mathrm{F1} \cdot \mathrm{vL2}^2 + \mathrm{R2}^2 \cdot \mathrm{W4} \cdot \mathrm{F2} \cdot \mathrm{vL1}^2$$

$$\mathrm{BOTTOMelast} := 144 \cdot \mathrm{R1}^2 \cdot \mathrm{R2}^2 \cdot \mathrm{ge}^2 \cdot (\mathrm{W3} + \mathrm{W4}) \cdot \mathrm{F1} \cdot \mathrm{F2}$$

$$\mathrm{Telastquart} := \left(\frac{\pi}{2}\right) \cdot \sqrt{\frac{\mathrm{TOPelast}}{\mathrm{BOTTOMelast}}} \qquad \mathrm{Tcontactelast} := \mathrm{Telastquart} \cdot 1.7$$

$$\mathrm{Telastquart} = 0.043 \qquad \mathrm{Tcontactelast} = 0.074$$

$$\mathrm{TOP} := \mathrm{R1} \cdot \mathrm{W3} \cdot \mathrm{F1} \cdot \mathrm{a2} \cdot \cos(\theta 2) + \mathrm{R2} \cdot \mathrm{W4} \cdot \mathrm{F2} \cdot \mathrm{a1} \cdot \cos(\theta 1)$$

$$\mathrm{TOP} = 1.32 \times 10^3$$

$$\mathrm{BOTTOM} := 12 \cdot \mathrm{R1} \cdot \mathrm{R2} \cdot \mathrm{F1} \cdot \mathrm{F2} \cdot \mathrm{ge} \cdot (\mathrm{W3} + \mathrm{W4}) \qquad \mathrm{BOTTOM} = 8.021 \times 10^5$$

$$\mathrm{Tquarterp} := \left(\frac{\pi}{2}\right) \cdot \sqrt{\frac{\mathrm{TOP}}{\mathrm{BOTTOM}}}$$

$$\mathrm{Tquarterp} = 0.064$$

$$\mathrm{x2} := 0, 0.01 \,..\, \mathrm{x20} \qquad \mathrm{x3} := \mathrm{x20}, (\mathrm{x20} + 0.01) \,..\, \mathrm{x2MAX}$$

$$\mathrm{Frac}(\mathrm{x2}) := \sqrt{1 - \frac{\mathrm{VCRIT}^2}{\mathrm{VCLOSE}(\mathrm{x2})^2}} \qquad \mathrm{frac}(\mathrm{x3}) := \sqrt{1 - \frac{\mathrm{VCRIT}^2}{\mathrm{VCLOS}(\mathrm{x3})^2}}$$

$$\mathrm{Tquart}(\mathrm{x2}) := (\mathrm{Telastquart}) \cdot (1 - \mathrm{Frac}(\mathrm{x2})) + \mathrm{Frac}(\mathrm{x2}) \cdot \mathrm{Tquarterp}$$

$$\mathrm{Tquarter}(\mathrm{x3}) := (\mathrm{Telastquart}) \cdot (1 - \mathrm{frac}(\mathrm{x3})) + \mathrm{frac}(\mathrm{x3}) \cdot \mathrm{Tquarterp}$$

$$\mathrm{Tcont}(\mathrm{x2}) := \mathrm{Tquart}(\mathrm{x2}) \cdot (1 + \mathrm{ee}(\mathrm{x2}))$$

$$\mathrm{Tcontact}(\mathrm{x3}) := \mathrm{Tquarter}(\mathrm{x3}) \cdot (1 + \mathrm{ff}(\mathrm{x3}))$$

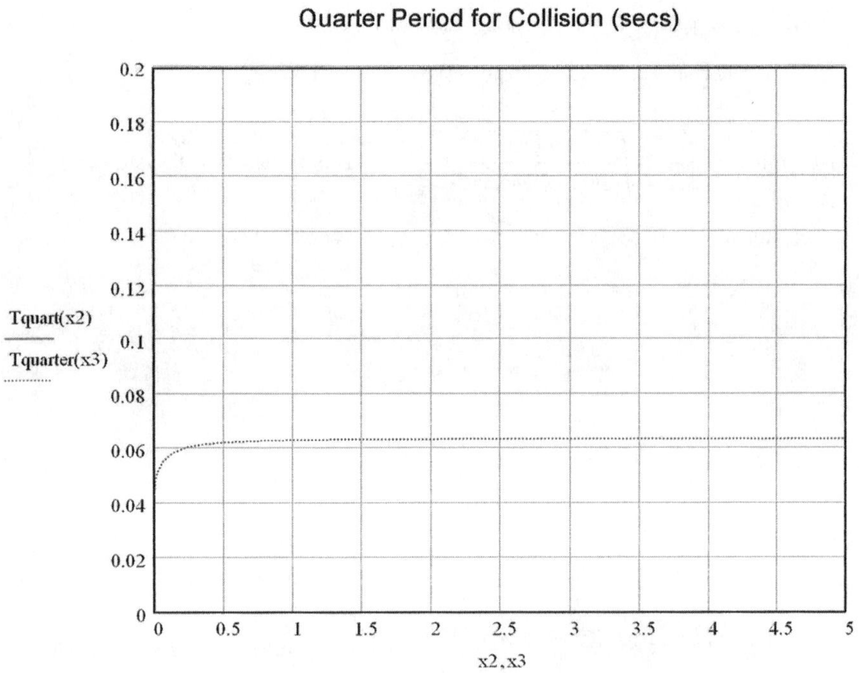
Quarter Period for Collision (secs)
0.2
0.18
0.16
0.14
0.12
0.1
0.08
0.06
0.04
0.02
0
Tquart(x2)
Tquarter(x3)
0
0.5
1
1.5
2
2.5
3
3.5
4
4.5
5
x2, x3

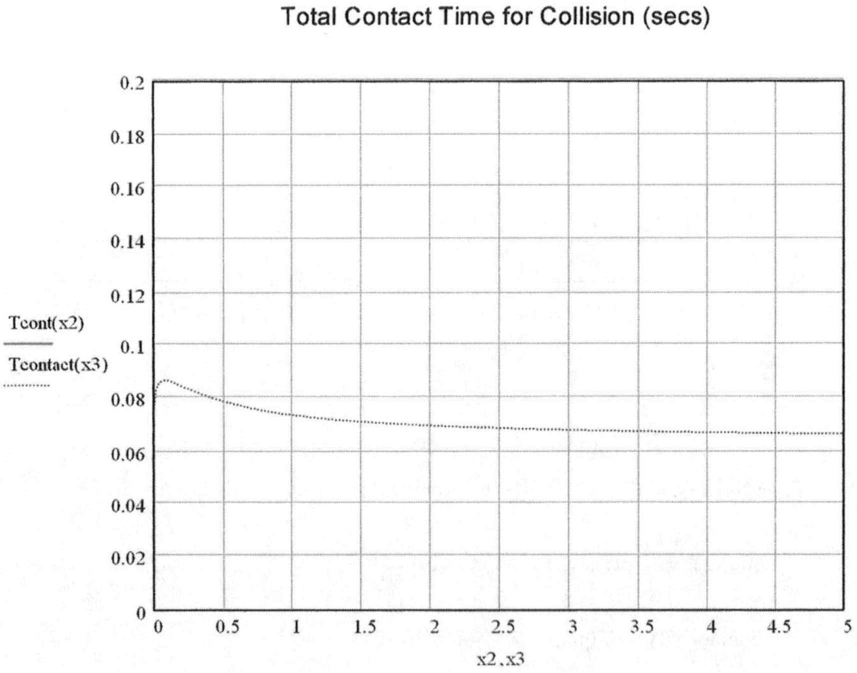
Total Contact Time for Collision (secs)
0.2
0.18
0.16
0.14
0.12
0.1
0.08
0.06
0.04
0.02
0
Tcont(x2)
Tcontact(x3)
0
0.5
1
1.5
2
2.5
3
3.5
4
4.5
5
x2, x3

$$L2(x2) := 12 \cdot R2 \cdot W2 \cdot F2 \cdot \left(1 + \frac{x2}{a2}\right) \cdot \frac{1}{\cos(\theta 2)} \qquad L2(x3) := 12 \cdot R2 \cdot W2 \cdot F2 \cdot \left(1 + \frac{x3}{a2}\right) \cdot \frac{1}{\cos(\theta 2)}$$

$$Accel4(x2) := \frac{L2(x2)}{W4} \qquad Accel4(x3) := \frac{L2(x3)}{W4}$$

$$Accel3(x2) := \frac{-L2(x2)}{W3} \qquad Accel3(x3) := \frac{-L2(x3)}{W3}$$

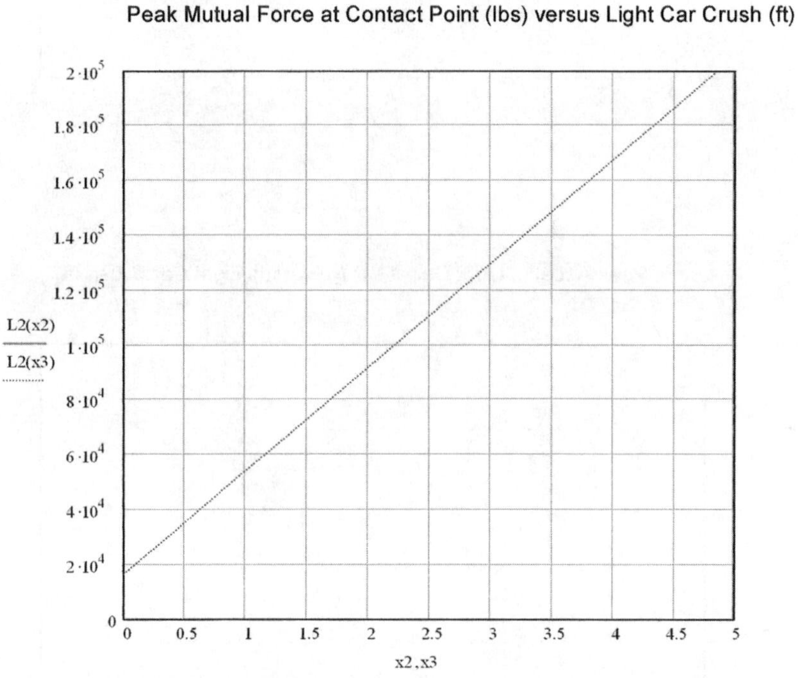

Peak Accel (Decel) of Heavy Car at CP (g) versus Light Car Crush (ft)

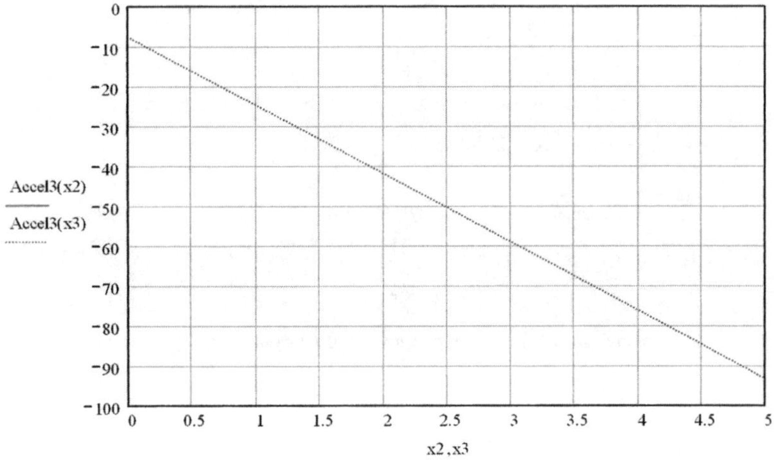

Peak Accel of Light Car at CP (g) versus Light Car Crush (ft)

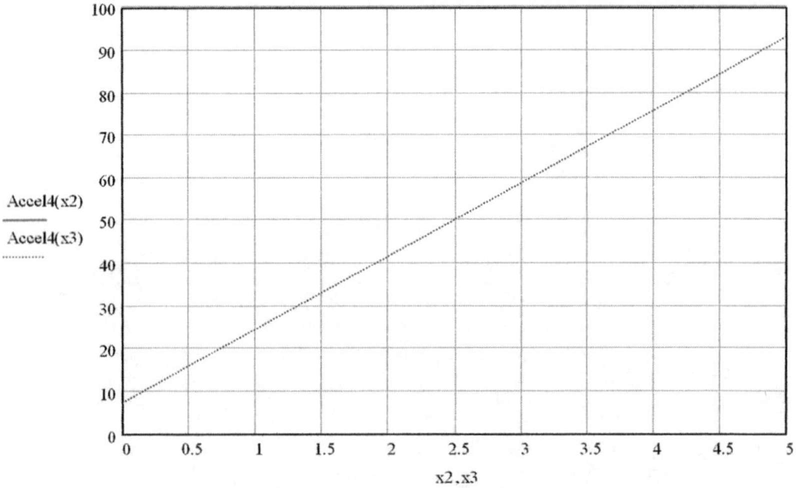

Peak Accel of Heavy Car CM (g) versus Light Car Crush (ft)

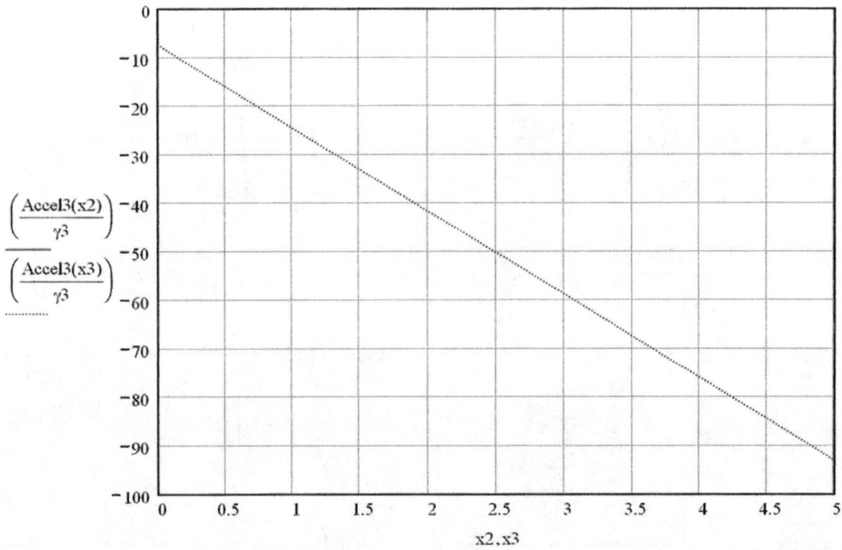

Peak Accel of Light Car CM (g) versus Light Car Crush (ft)

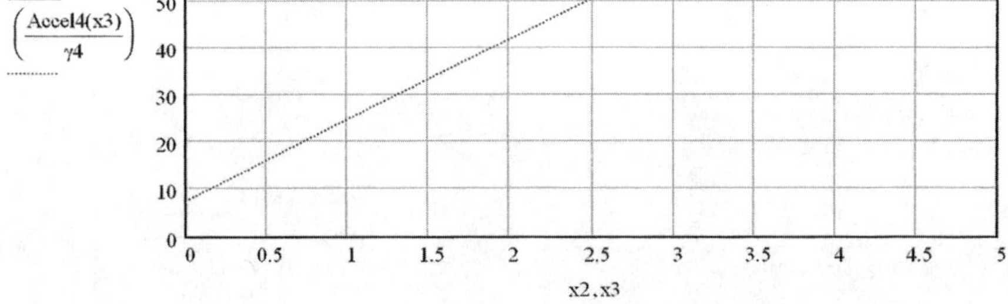

B is the bullet (W3), while T is the target (W4)

$$\mu B := 0.0 \qquad \mu T := 0.7 \qquad Wred := W3 \cdot \frac{W4}{(W3 + W4)}$$

$$Fclose(x2) := \sqrt{1 + (\mu B - \mu T) \cdot \frac{Wred}{\frac{L2(x2)}{2}}} \qquad Fclose(x3) := \sqrt{1 + (\mu B - \mu T) \cdot \frac{Wred}{\frac{L2(x3)}{2}}}$$

$$FdeltaT(x2) := \frac{\left[1 - \left(\mu T \cdot \frac{W4}{\frac{L2(x2)}{2}}\right)\right]}{\left[1 + Wred \cdot \frac{(\mu B - \mu T)}{\frac{L2(x2)}{2}}\right]} \qquad FdeltaT(x3) := \frac{\left[1 - \left(\mu T \cdot \frac{W4}{\frac{L2(x3)}{2}}\right)\right]}{\left[1 + Wred \cdot \frac{(\mu B - \mu T)}{\frac{L2(x3)}{2}}\right]}$$

$$FdeltaB(x2) := \frac{\left[1 + \left(\mu B \cdot \frac{W3}{\frac{L2(x2)}{2}}\right)\right]}{\left[1 + Wred \cdot \frac{(\mu B - \mu T)}{\frac{L2(x2)}{2}}\right]} \qquad FdeltaB(x3) := \frac{\left[1 + \left(\mu B \cdot \frac{W3}{\frac{L2(x3)}{2}}\right)\right]}{\left[1 + Wred \cdot \frac{(\mu B - \mu T)}{\frac{L2(x3)}{2}}\right]}$$

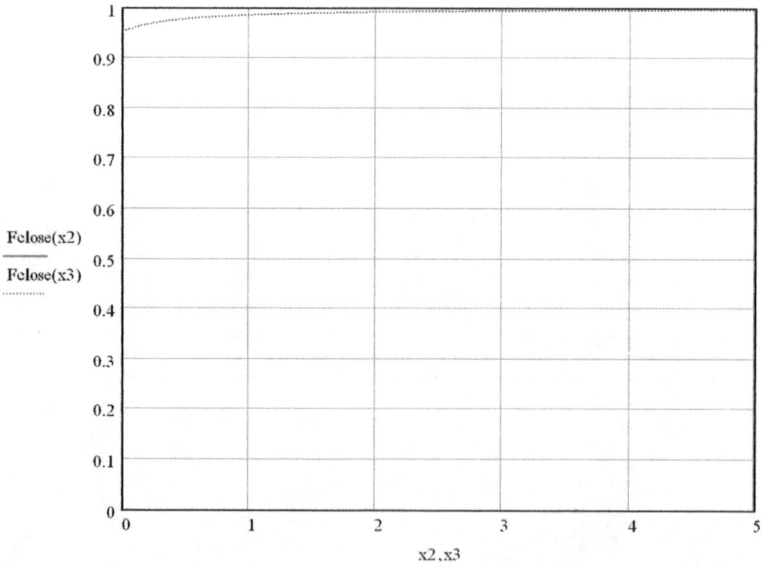

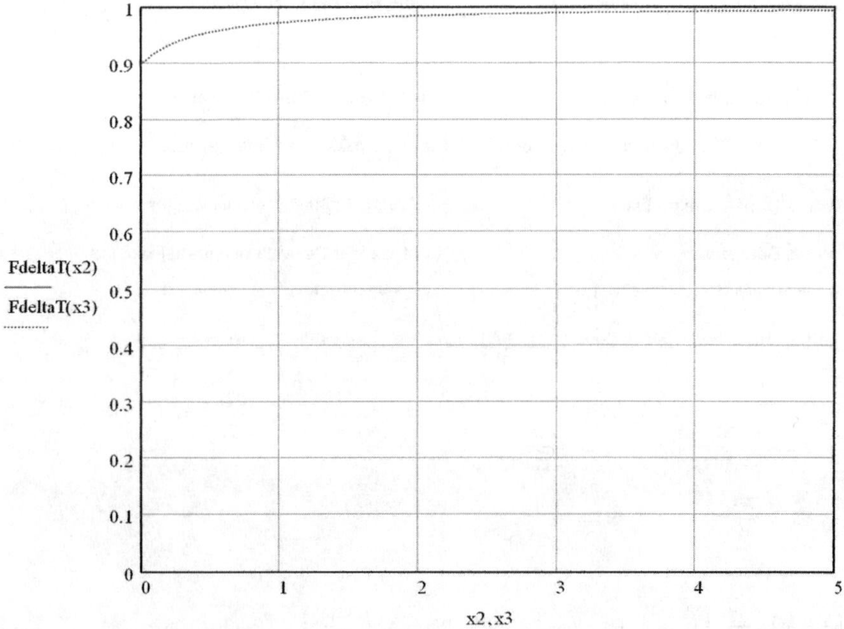
FdeltaT(x2)
FdeltaT(x3)
x2, x3
0
0.1
0.2
0.3
0.4
0.5
0.6
0.7
0.8
0.9
1
2
3
4
5

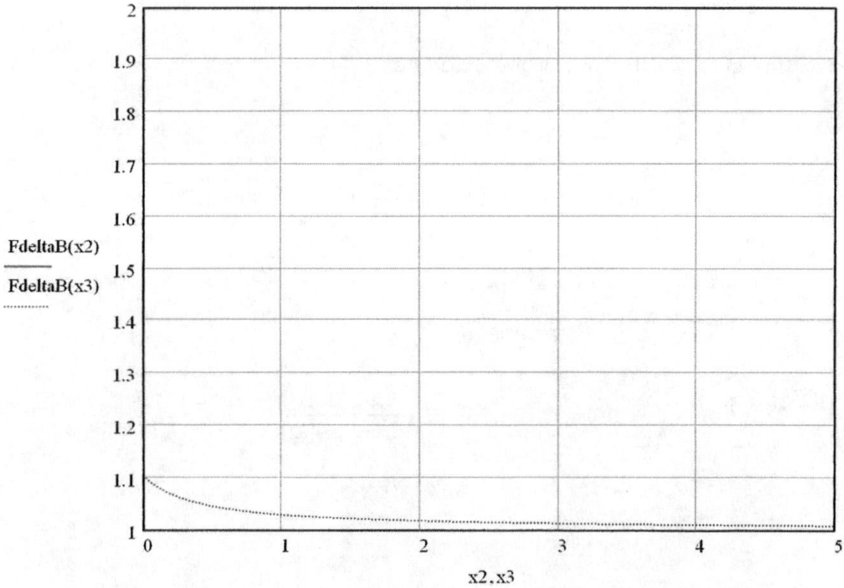
FdeltaB(x2)
FdeltaB(x3)
x2, x3
1
1.1
1.2
1.3
1.4
1.5
1.6
1.7
1.8
1.9
2
0
3
4
5

WeightCase4: 2201 lbs (loaded weight) into Barrier

Notes: (a) '1' is *strongest* vehicle versus '2'. (b) W1 and W2 are true weights regardless of spin

(c) W3 and W4 are spin-dependent. (d) γ = 1+rr/kk. r = torque-arm, k = rad of gyration

W1 is Barrier weight lbs

W2 is Light Car empty weight lbs

W3 is Barrier lbs

W4 is Light Car with occupant load lbs

γ3 is spin factor $\gamma 3 := 1.0$

γ4 is spin factor $\gamma 4 := 1.0$

$W1 := 1000000 \quad W2 := 2001 \quad A1 := 6.0 \quad A2 := 0.6 \quad \theta 1 := \frac{0}{57.3}$

$W3 := 1000000 \quad W4 := 2201 \quad F1 := 1.0 \quad F2 := 1.0 \quad \theta 2 := \frac{0}{57.3}$

$$vL1 := \frac{7.335}{\cos(\theta 1)} \qquad vL2 := \frac{7.335}{\cos(\theta 2)}$$

$$W3 := \frac{W3}{\gamma 3} \qquad W4 := \frac{W4}{\gamma 4}$$

$$R1 := A1 \cdot \left(\frac{3000}{W1}\right)^{\frac{1}{3}} \quad R1 = 0.865 \qquad R2 := A2 \cdot \left(\frac{3000}{W2}\right)^{\frac{1}{3}} \quad R2 = 0.687$$

$$a1 := 0.5 \cdot \left(\frac{W1}{3000}\right)^{\frac{1}{3}} \quad a1 = 3.467 \qquad a2 := 0.5 \cdot \left(\frac{W2}{3000}\right)^{\frac{1}{3}} \quad a2 = 0.437$$

x is crush feet

L is load for given crush, lbs

$x2MAX := 10.0$

$x10 := 0$

$$L1 := 12 \cdot R1 \cdot W1 \cdot F1 \cdot \left(1 + \frac{x10}{a1}\right) \cdot \frac{1}{\cos(\theta 1)} \qquad L1 = 1.038 \times 10^{7}$$

$$x20 := a2 \cdot \left[R1 \cdot W1 \cdot F1 \cdot \frac{\left(1 + \frac{x10}{a1}\right) \cdot \cos(\theta 2)}{R2 \cdot W2 \cdot F2 \cdot \cos(\theta 1)}\right] - a2 \qquad ge := 32.2$$

$x20 = 274.678$

$$L2 := 12 \cdot R2 \cdot W2 \cdot F2 \cdot \left(1 + \frac{x20}{a2}\right) \cdot \frac{1}{\cos(\theta 2)} \qquad L2 = 1.038 \times 10^{7}$$

acell is acceleration (or deceleration) in g's

$accell1 := \frac{L1}{W1}$ $accell4 := \frac{L2}{W4}$ $accell1 = 10.384$ (g) $accell4 = 4.718 \times 10^3$

$x2 := 0, 0.01 .. x20$ $accell3 := \frac{L1}{W3}$ $accell3 = 10.384$ (g)

Q's are crush- energy terms

$$Q2(x2) := \left(\frac{x2}{a2}\right) \cdot x2 + 2 \cdot x2 + \frac{vL2^2}{12 \cdot R2 \cdot ge} \quad Q22(x2) := \left(\frac{vL2^2 \cdot W2}{2 \cdot ge}\right) \cdot \left(1 + \frac{x2}{a2}\right)$$

$$Q222(x2) := 6 \cdot R2 \cdot W2 \cdot Q2(x2) - Q22(x2) \quad E2(x2) := F2 \cdot \frac{Q222(x2)}{\cos(\theta 2)^2}$$

$$ETA(x2) := E2(x2)$$

vcritical is maximum closing speed to just avoid any crush, mph

$$vCRIT1 := \frac{(W3 + W4) \cdot \left[1 + \left(\frac{W4}{W3}\right) \cdot \left(F2 \cdot \frac{R2}{F1 \cdot R1}\right)^2 \cdot \frac{\left(F1 \cdot vL1^2\right)}{F2 \cdot vL2^2}\right] \cdot F2 \cdot vL2^2}{W3}$$

ETA(x2) = x2 =

ETA(x2)	x2
$-2.274 \cdot 10^{-13}$	0
128.515	0.01
260.804	0.02
396.868	0.03
536.706	0.04
680.319	0.05
827.706	0.06
978.868	0.07
$1.134 \cdot 10^3$	0.08
$1.293 \cdot 10^3$	0.09
$1.455 \cdot 10^3$	0.1
$1.621 \cdot 10^3$	0.11
$1.791 \cdot 10^3$	0.12
$1.965 \cdot 10^3$	0.13
$2.143 \cdot 10^3$	0.14
$2.324 \cdot 10^3$	0.15

$vCRIT := \sqrt{vCRIT1}$

$vCRIT = 7.348$

$VCRIT := \frac{vCRIT}{1.467}$

$VCRIT = 5.009$ (mph)

vclose is actual closing speed for total crush energy, mph

$$vCLOSE1(x2) := vCRIT1 + 2\cdot ge\cdot ETA(x2)\cdot\frac{(W3 + W4)}{W3\cdot W4}$$

$$vCLOSE(x2) := \sqrt{vCLOSE1(x2)}$$

ee and ff are coefficients of restitution (vehicle bounce)

$$ee(x2) := 0.7\cdot\frac{vCRIT}{vCLOSE(x2)} \qquad VCLOSE(x2) := \frac{vCLOSE(x2)}{1.467} \quad \text{(mph)}$$

vCLOSE1(x2) =	vCLOSE(x2) =	ee(x2) =	VCLOSE(x2) =	x2 =
53.995	7.348	0.7	5.009	0
57.764	7.6	0.677	5.181	0.01
61.643	7.851	0.655	5.352	0.02
65.633	8.101	0.635	5.522	0.03
69.734	8.351	0.616	5.692	0.04
73.945	8.599	0.598	5.862	0.05
78.267	8.847	0.581	6.031	0.06
82.7	9.094	0.566	6.199	0.07
87.243	9.34	0.551	6.367	0.08
91.897	9.586	0.537	6.535	0.09
96.662	9.832	0.523	6.702	0.1
101.537	10.077	0.51	6.869	0.11
106.523	10.321	0.498	7.035	0.12
111.62	10.565	0.487	7.202	0.13
116.827	10.809	0.476	7.368	0.14
122.145	11.052	0.465	7.534	0.15

Δv is sudden change in speed

$$\Delta v2(x2) := \left(\frac{W3}{W3 + W4}\right)\cdot(1 + ee(x2))\cdot vCLOSE(x2) \qquad \Delta V2(x2) := \frac{\Delta v2(x2)}{1.467} \text{ (mph)}$$

$$\Delta v1(x2) := -\left(\frac{W4}{W3 + W4}\right)\cdot(1 + ee(x2))\cdot vCLOSE(x2) \qquad \Delta V1(x2) := \frac{\Delta v1(x2)}{1.467} \text{ (mph)}$$

$$\Delta V2CM(x2) := \frac{\Delta V2(x2)}{\gamma 4} \qquad \Delta V1CM(x2) := \frac{\Delta V1(x2)}{\gamma 3}$$

$$VCLOSE(x2) := \frac{vCLOSE(x2)}{1.467} \text{ (mph)}$$

Δv2(x2) =	Δv1(x2) =	ΔV2(x2) =	ΔV1(x2) =	x2 =	VCLOSE(x2) =
12.464	-0.027	8.497	-0.019	0	5.009
12.716	-0.028	8.668	-0.019	0.01	5.181
12.966	-0.029	8.839	-0.019	0.02	5.352
13.216	-0.029	9.009	-0.02	0.03	5.522
13.465	-0.03	9.178	-0.02	0.04	5.692
13.713	-0.03	9.347	-0.021	0.05	5.862
13.96	-0.031	9.516	-0.021	0.06	6.031
14.206	-0.031	9.684	-0.021	0.07	6.199
14.452	-0.032	9.852	-0.022	0.08	6.367
14.698	-0.032	10.019	-0.022	0.09	6.535
14.942	-0.033	10.186	-0.022	0.1	6.702
15.187	-0.033	10.352	-0.023	0.11	6.869
15.431	-0.034	10.519	-0.023	0.12	7.035
15.674	-0.034	10.685	-0.024	0.13	7.202
15.917	-0.035	10.85	-0.024	0.14	7.368
16.16	-0.036	11.016	-0.024	0.15	7.534

$x3 := x20, (x20 + 0.01) .. x2MAX$ **continuation of crush x2**

$$Q3(x3) := \left(\frac{x3}{a2}\right) \cdot x3 + 2 \cdot x3 + \frac{vL2^2}{12 \cdot R2 \cdot ge} \qquad Q33(x3) := \left(\frac{vL2^2 \cdot W2}{2 \cdot ge}\right) \cdot \left(1 + \frac{x3}{a2}\right)$$

$$Q333(x3) := 6 \cdot R2 \cdot W2 \cdot Q3(x3) - Q33(x3)$$

$$E3(x3) := F2 \cdot Q333(x3) \cdot \frac{1}{\cos(\theta 2)^2}$$

$E3(x3) =$ $x3 =$

crush E for vehicle 2

$x1 := 0$ **crush of vehicle 1**

$$x1(x3) := a1\cdot\left(R2\cdot W2\cdot\frac{F2\cdot\cos(\theta1)}{R1\cdot W1\cdot F1\cdot\cos(\theta2)}\right)\cdot\left(1+\frac{x3}{a2}\right) - a1$$

$$Q1(x1,x3) := \left(\frac{x1(x3)}{a1}\right)\cdot x1(x3) + 2\cdot x1(x3) + \frac{vL1^2}{12\cdot R1\cdot ge} \quad Q11(x1,x3) := \left(\frac{vL1^2\cdot W1}{2\cdot ge}\right)\cdot\left(1+\frac{x1(x3)}{a1}\right)$$

$$Q111(x1,x3) := 6\cdot R1\cdot W1\cdot Q1(x1,x3) - Q11(x1,x3)$$

$E1(x1,x3) := F1\cdot Q111(x1,x3)\cdot\frac{1}{\cos(\theta1)^2}$ **crush E for vehicle 1**

$ET(x1,x3) := E1(x1,x3) + E3(x3)$ **sum of crush energies**

$x1(x3) =$ $E3(x3) =$ $E1(x1,x3) =$ $ET(x1,x3) =$

$$vCLOSE3(x3) := vCRIT1 + 2\cdot ge\cdot ET(x1,x3)\cdot\frac{(W3 + W4)}{W3\cdot W4}$$

$$vCLOS(x3) := \sqrt{vCLOSE3(x3)} \qquad ff(x3) := 0.7\cdot\frac{vCRIT}{vCLOS(x3)}$$

$$VCLOS(x3) := \frac{vCLOS(x3)}{1.467} \quad \text{(mph)}$$

$$\Delta v4(x3) := \left(\frac{W3}{W3 + W4}\right)\cdot(1 + ff(x3))\cdot vCLOS(x3) \qquad \Delta V4(x3) := \frac{\Delta v4(x3)}{1.467} \quad \text{(mph)}$$

$$\Delta V4CM(x3) := \frac{\Delta V4(x3)}{\gamma 4}$$

$$\Delta v3(x3) := -\left(\frac{W4}{W3 + W4}\right)\cdot(1 + ff(x3))\cdot vCLOS(x3) \qquad \Delta V3(x3) := \frac{\Delta v3(x3)}{1.467} \quad \text{(mph)}$$

$$\Delta V3CM(x3) := \frac{\Delta V3(x3)}{\gamma 3}$$

vCLOSE3(x3) =	VCLOS(x3) =	ff(x3) =	ΔV4(x3) =	ΔV3(x3) =
▮	▮	▮	▮	▮

x3 = x1(x3) =

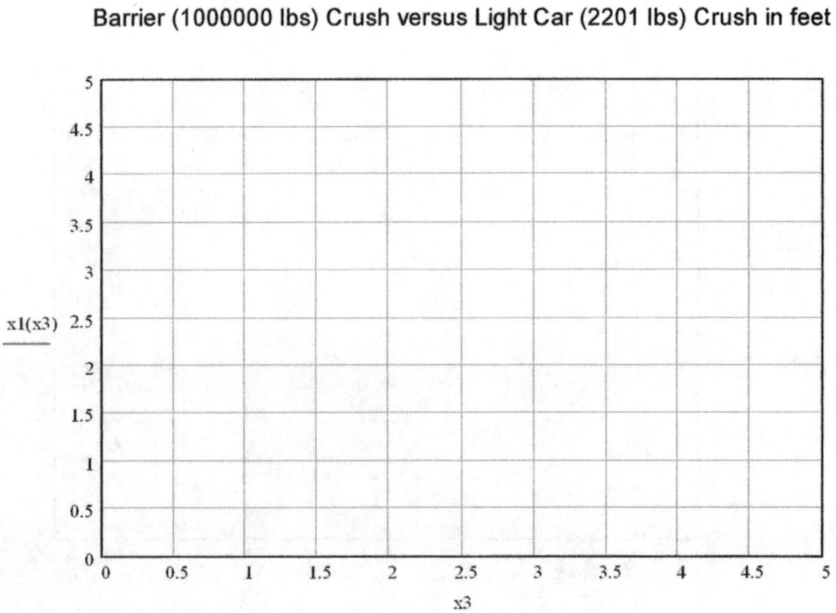
Barrier (1000000 lbs) Crush versus Light Car (2201 lbs) Crush in feet
x1(x3)
x3
0
0.5
1
1.5
2
2.5
3
3.5
4
4.5
5

Light Car Speed Change (mph) at contact Point versus Light Car Crush (ft)

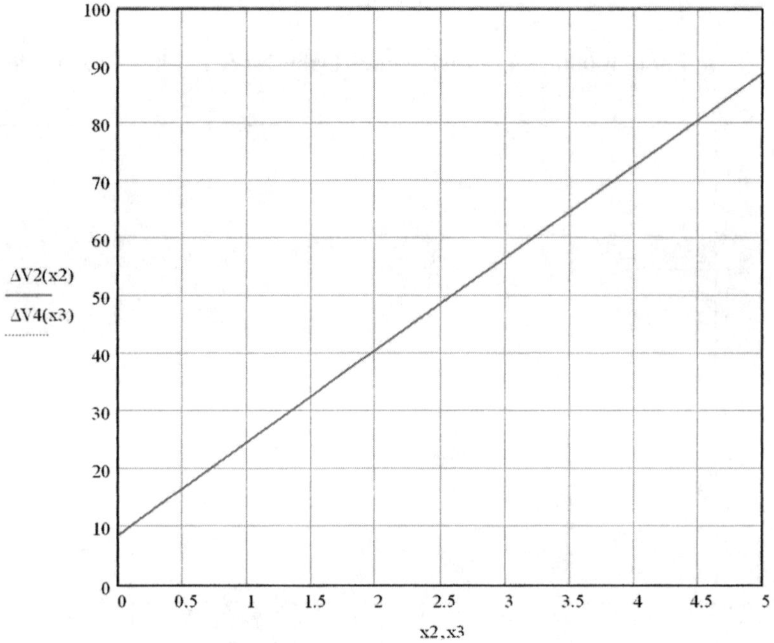

Light Car Speed Change (mph) at CM versus Light Car Crush (ft)

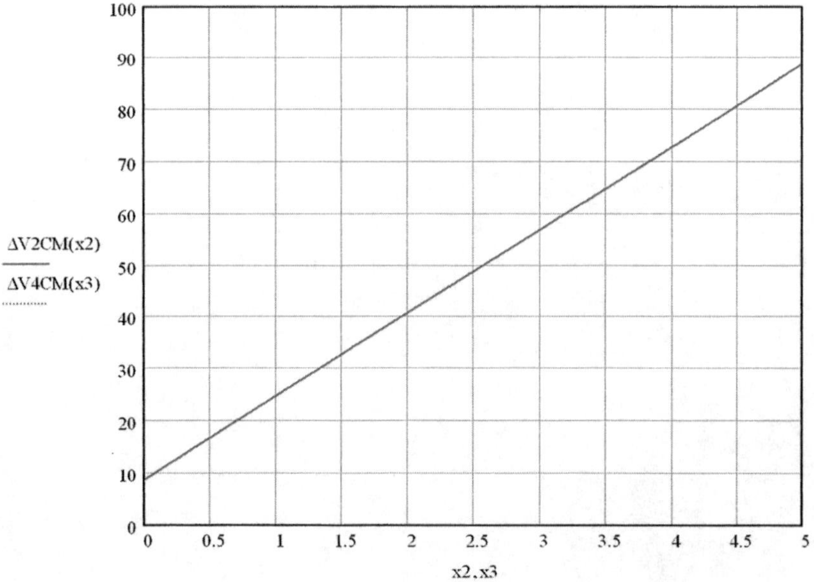

Barrier Speed Change (mph) at Contact Point vs. Light Car Crush (ft)

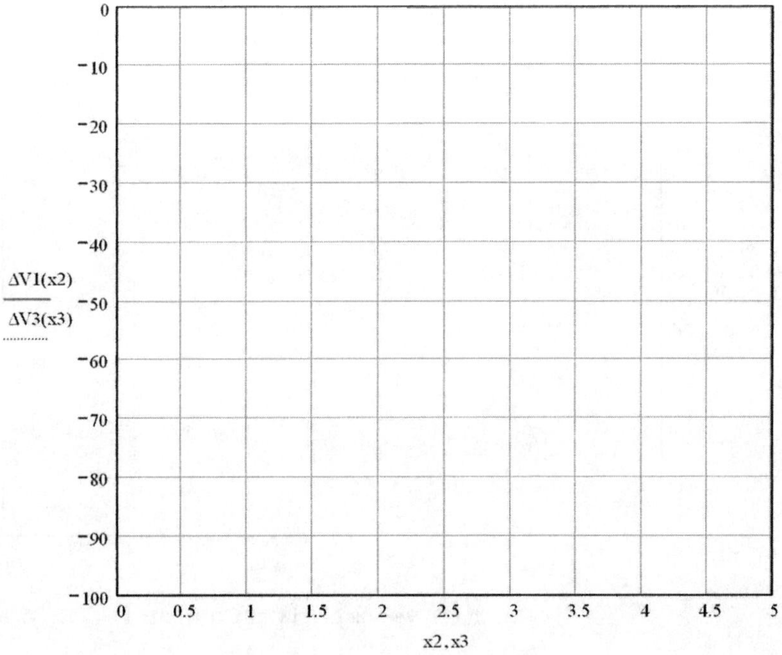

Barrier Speed Change (mph) at CM vs. Light Car Crush (ft)

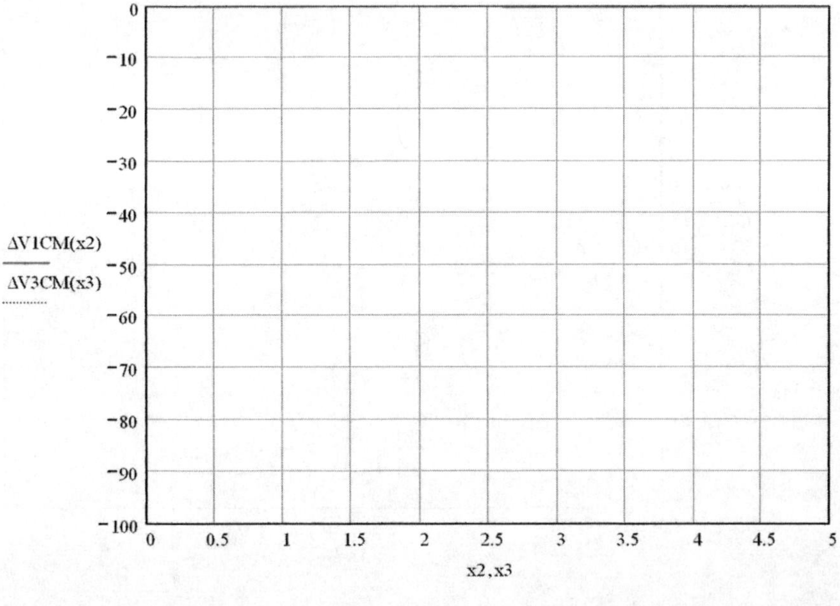

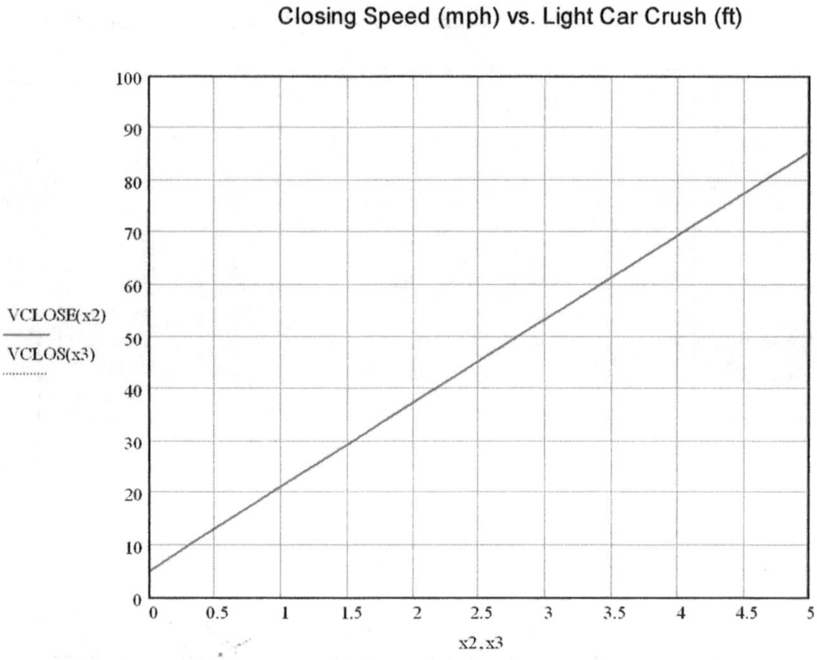
Closing Speed (mph) vs. Light Car Crush (ft)
VCLOSE(x2)
VCLOS(x3)
x2, x3

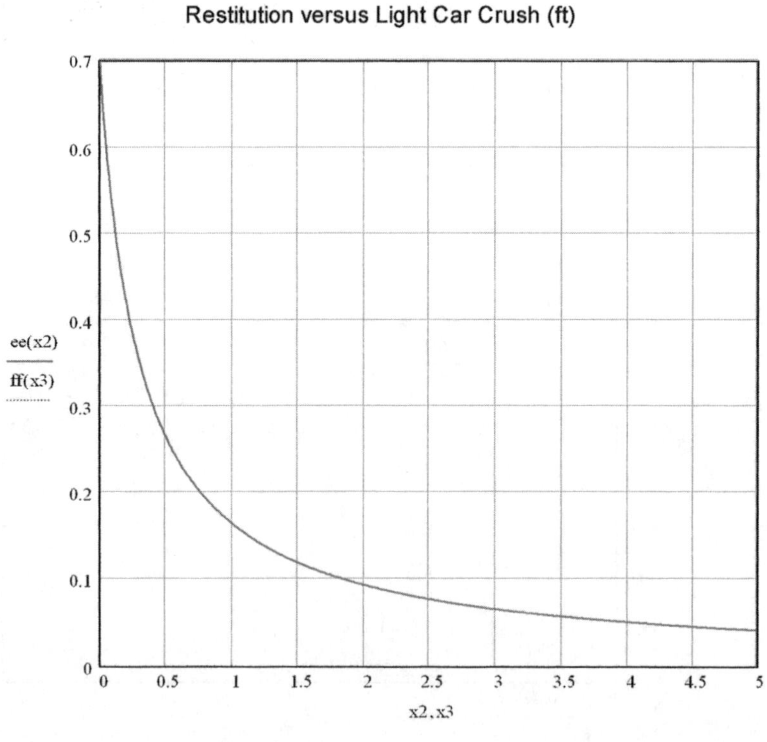
Restitution versus Light Car Crush (ft)
ee(x2)
ff(x3)
x2, x3

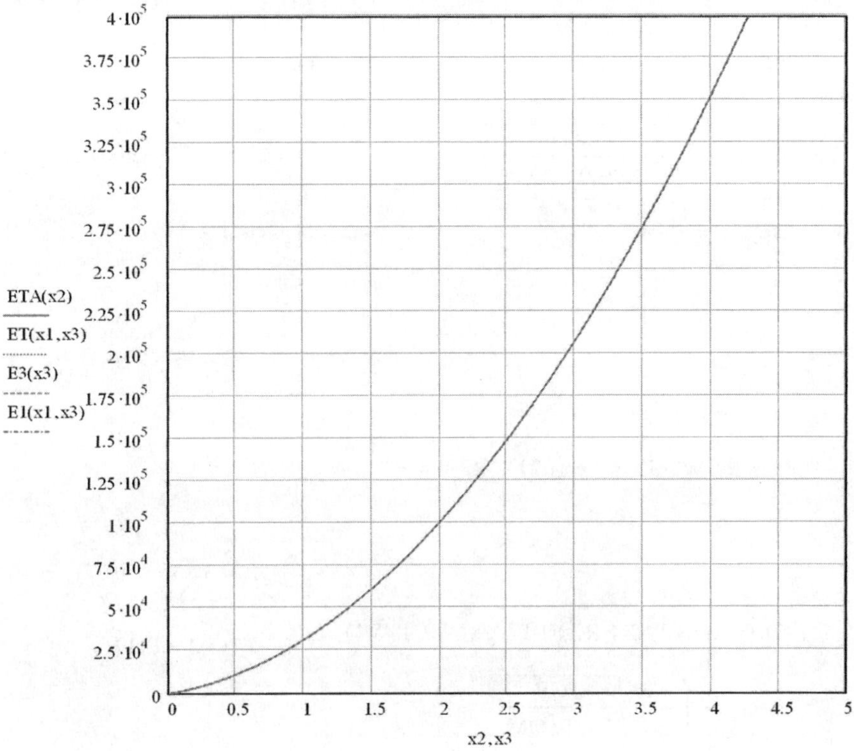

4·10^5
3.75·10^5
3.5·10^5
3.25·10^5
3·10^5
2.75·10^5
2.5·10^5
2.25·10^5
2·10^5
1.75·10^5
1.5·10^5
1.25·10^5
1·10^5
7.5·10^4
5·10^4
2.5·10^4
0
ETA(x2)
ET(x1,x3)
E3(x3)
E1(x1,x3)
0
0.5
1
1.5
2
2.5
3
3.5
4
4.5
5
x2,x3

$$TOPelast := R1^2 \cdot W3 \cdot F1 \cdot vL2^2 + R2^2 \cdot W4 \cdot F2 \cdot vL1^2$$

$$BOTTOMelast := 144 \cdot R1^2 \cdot R2^2 \cdot ge^2 \cdot (W3 + W4) \cdot F1 \cdot F2$$

$$Telastquart := \left(\frac{\pi}{2}\right) \cdot \sqrt{\frac{TOPelast}{BOTTOMelast}} \qquad Tcontactelast := Telastquart \cdot 1.7$$

$$Telastquart = 0.043 \qquad Tcontactelast = 0.074$$

$$TOP := R1 \cdot W3 \cdot F1 \cdot a2 \cdot \cos(\theta 2) + R2 \cdot W4 \cdot F2 \cdot a1 \cdot \cos(\theta 1)$$

$$TOP = 3.833 \times 10^5$$

$$BOTTOM := 12 \cdot R1 \cdot R2 \cdot F1 \cdot F2 \cdot ge \cdot (W3 + W4) \qquad BOTTOM = 2.301 \times 10^8$$

$$Tquarterp := \left(\frac{\pi}{2}\right) \cdot \sqrt{\frac{TOP}{BOTTOM}}$$

$$Tquarterp = 0.064$$

$$x2 := 0, 0.01 .. x20 \qquad x3 := x20, (x20 + 0.01) .. x2MAX$$

$$Frac(x2) := \sqrt{1 - \frac{VCRIT^2}{VCLOSE(x2)^2}} \qquad frac(x3) := \sqrt{1 - \frac{VCRIT^2}{VCLOS(x3)^2}}$$

$$Tquart(x2) := (Telastquart) \cdot (1 - Frac(x2)) + Frac(x2) \cdot Tquarterp$$

$$Tquarter(x3) := (Telastquart) \cdot (1 - frac(x3)) + frac(x3) \cdot Tquarterp$$

$$Tcont(x2) := Tquart(x2) \cdot (1 + ee(x2))$$

$$Tcontact(x3) := Tquarter(x3) \cdot (1 + ff(x3))$$

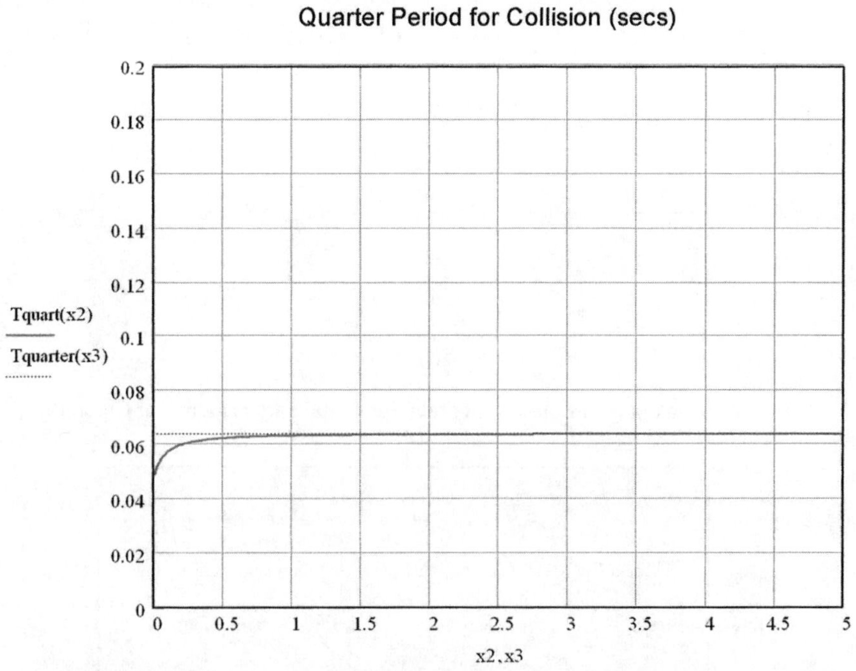
Quarter Period for Collision (secs)
Tquart(x2)
Tquarter(x3)
x2, x3
0
0.02
0.04
0.06
0.08
0.1
0.12
0.14
0.16
0.18
0.2
0.5
1
1.5
2
2.5
3
3.5
4
4.5
5

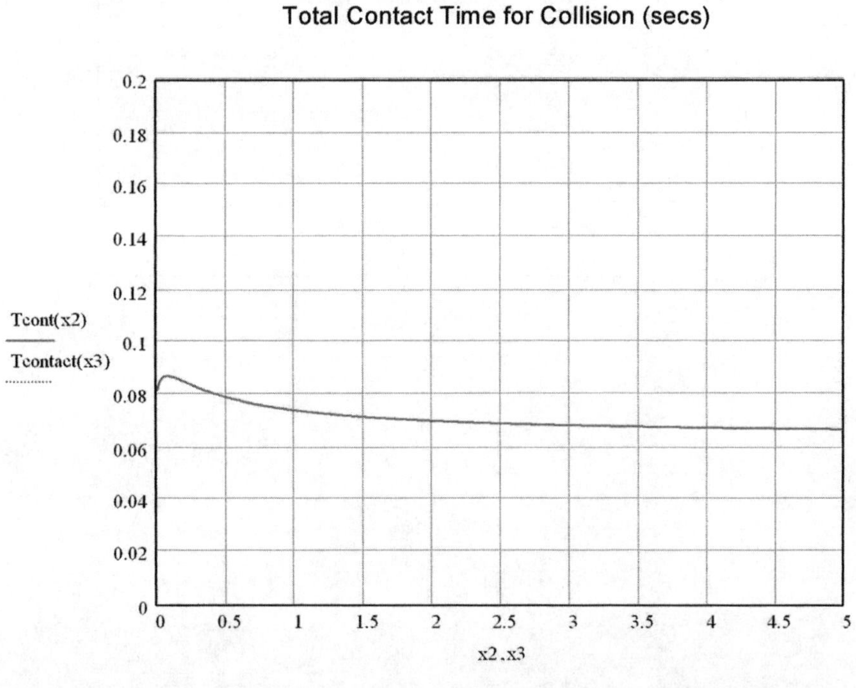
Total Contact Time for Collision (secs)
Tcont(x2)
Tcontact(x3)
x2, x3
0
0.02
0.04
0.06
0.08
0.1
0.12
0.14
0.16
0.18
0.2
0.5
1
1.5
2
2.5
3
3.5
4
4.5
5

$$L2(x2) := 12 \cdot R2 \cdot W2 \cdot F2 \cdot \left(1 + \frac{x2}{a2}\right) \cdot \frac{1}{\cos(\theta 2)} \qquad L2(x3) := 12 \cdot R2 \cdot W2 \cdot F2 \cdot \left(1 + \frac{x3}{a2}\right) \cdot \frac{1}{\cos(\theta 2)}$$

$$Accel4(x2) := \frac{L2(x2)}{W4} \qquad Accel4(x3) := \frac{L2(x3)}{W4}$$

$$Accel3(x2) := \frac{-L2(x2)}{W3} \qquad Accel3(x3) := \frac{-L2(x3)}{W3}$$

Peak Mutual Force at Contact Point (lbs) versus Light Car Crush (ft)

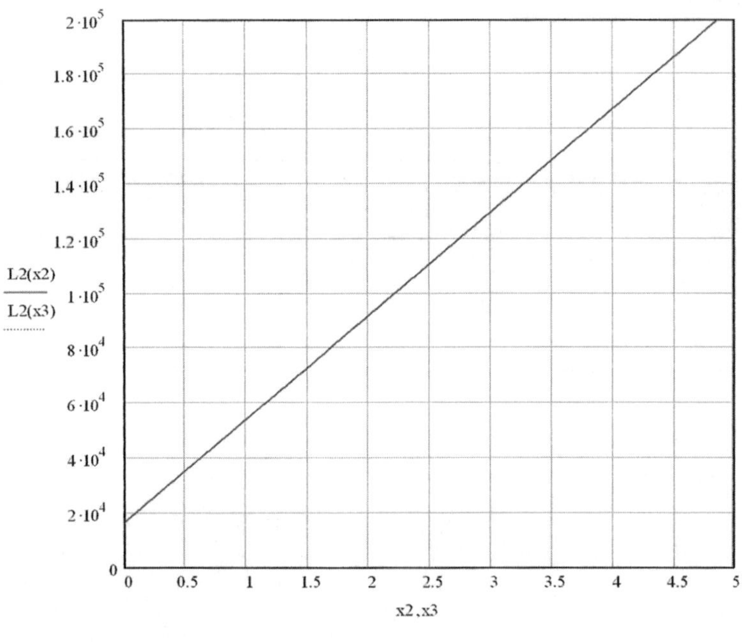

Peak Accel (Decel) of Barrier at CP (g) versus Light Car Crush (ft)

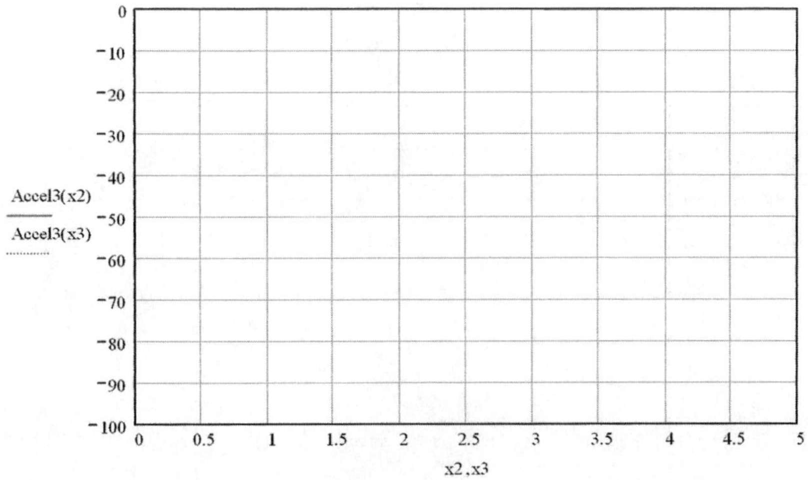

Peak Accel of Light Car at CP (g) versus Light Car Crush (ft)

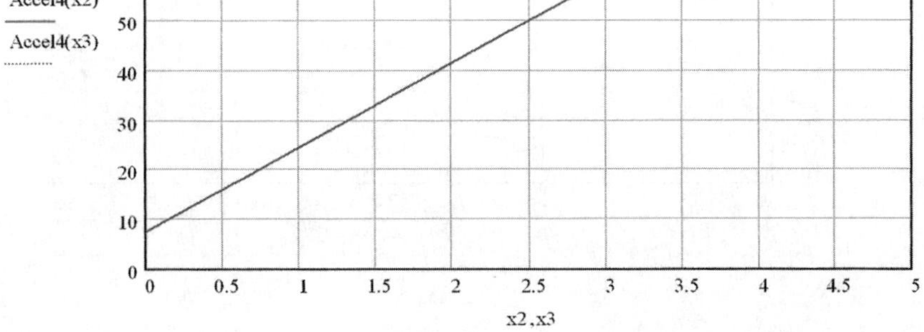

Peak Accel of Barrier CM (g) versus Light Car Crush (ft)

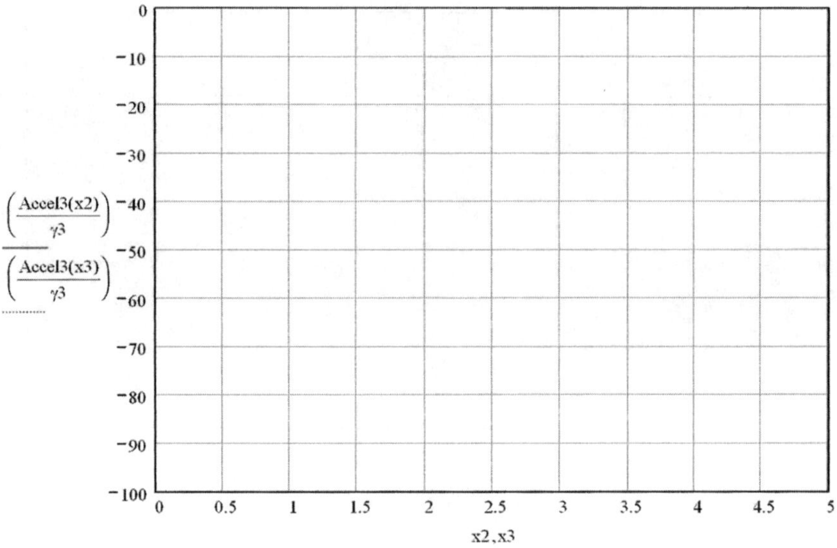

Peak Accel of Light Car CM (g) versus Light Car Crush (ft)

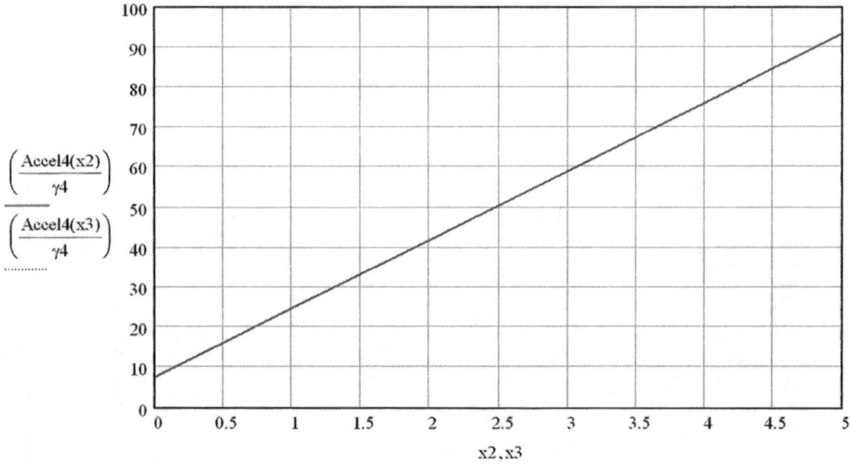

B is the bullet (W3), while T is the target (W4)

$\mu B := 0.0 \qquad \mu T := 0.7 \qquad Wred := W3 \cdot \frac{W4}{(W3 + W4)}$

$$Fclose(x2) := \sqrt{1 + (\mu B - \mu T) \cdot \frac{Wred}{\frac{L2(x2)}{2}}} \qquad Fclose(x3) := \sqrt{1 + (\mu B - \mu T) \cdot \frac{Wred}{\frac{L2(x3)}{2}}}$$

$$FdeltaT(x2) := \frac{\left[1 - \left(\mu T \cdot \frac{W4}{\frac{L2(x2)}{2}}\right)\right]}{\left[1 + Wred \cdot \frac{(\mu B - \mu T)}{\frac{L2(x2)}{2}}\right]} \qquad FdeltaT(x3) := \frac{\left[1 - \left(\mu T \cdot \frac{W4}{\frac{L2(x3)}{2}}\right)\right]}{\left[1 + Wred \cdot \frac{(\mu B - \mu T)}{\frac{L2(x3)}{2}}\right]}$$

$$FdeltaB(x2) := \frac{\left[1 + \left(\mu B \cdot \frac{W3}{\frac{L2(x2)}{2}}\right)\right]}{\left[1 + Wred \cdot \frac{(\mu B - \mu T)}{\frac{L2(x2)}{2}}\right]} \qquad FdeltaB(x3) := \frac{\left[1 + \left(\mu B \cdot \frac{W3}{\frac{L2(x3)}{2}}\right)\right]}{\left[1 + Wred \cdot \frac{(\mu B - \mu T)}{\frac{L2(x3)}{2}}\right]}$$

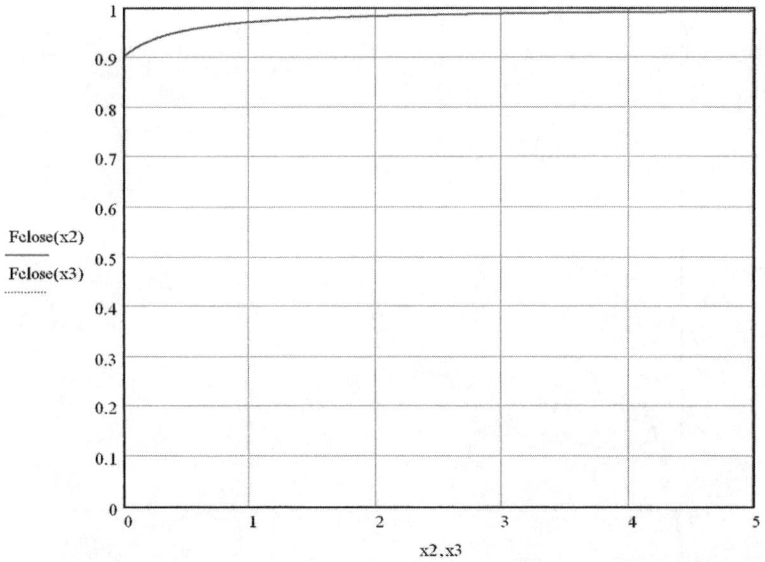

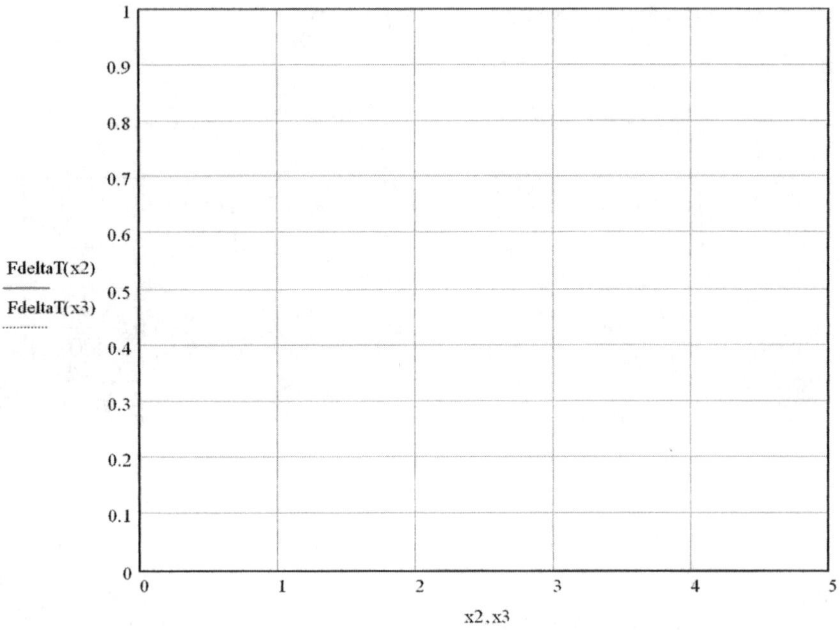

FdeltaT(x2)
FdeltaT(x3)
0
0.1
0.2
0.3
0.4
0.5
0.6
0.7
0.8
0.9
1
0
1
2
3
4
5
x2, x3

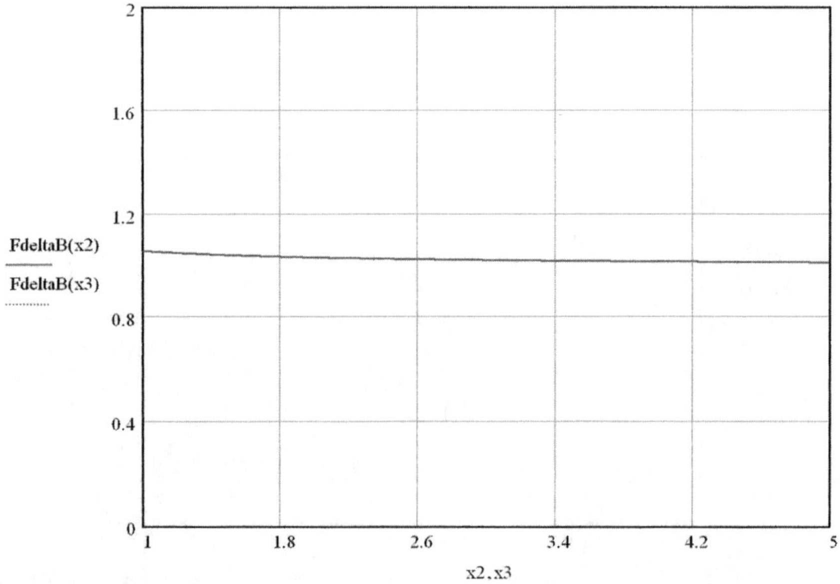

FdeltaB(x2)
FdeltaB(x3)
0
0.4
0.8
1.2
1.6
2
1
1.8
2.6
3.4
4.2
5
x2, x3

Chapter 17

Conservation of Linear Momentum

Introduction

There are two major methods for solving vehicle collisions. These are the "Conservation of Energy" technique (also known as the Crush-Energy approach) and the "Conservation of Linear Momentum" technique. Much of this book has concentrated on the Energy method. This is because this book originated with low-speed considerations, where it is common to have relatively little overall vehicle motion (so little in the way of skidmarks) and where many crashes involve almost in-line impacts, such as the typical rear-end collision.

We now discuss the Momentum approach. Linear Momentum is the product of mass (a scalar) and velocity (a vector) and is thus itself a vector (see Appendix A). Since most of the equations for momentum analysis include *mass* on both sides, a "global multiplication" by the term g (acceleration due to gravity) simply results in the ability to use *weights* instead (i.e., $w = mg$). Likewise, provided the units for velocity are consistent throughout the equations we may use any we choose. Thus we may use: mph, km/h, ft/s or m/s, or even (our favorite), "furlongs per fortnight": just kidding! Many analysts prefer to use weight (lb) and ft/s throughout.

Appendix A explains that speed is a scalar, whereas velocity is a vector. Speed represents distance per time but does *not* include any specific direction. Thus a car moving on a circular arc can maintain a speed of, say, 30 mph (as given by the speedometer) while changing its heading. However, velocity *does* include specific direction. This means that as a car moves from northbound to eastbound on a 90 degree arc we must assign the overall motion into components. Thus we may define the northbound velocity as $vN = v_0\cos(\theta)$ and eastbound as $vE = v_0\sin(\theta)$, where the angle is measured with respect to north. In practice, north is usually a graphical axis, such as y, while east is the x axis. We also see that for any given angle (using the Pythagoras theorem):

$$VNET = \sqrt{v0\cos(\theta)^2 + v0\sin(\theta)^2} = v0. \quad (17.1)$$

Thus we may think of v_0 as the speed (a scalar), while the inclusion of the sin and cos terms converts the components into velocities (vectors).

We have noticed that some analysts seem to have been taught that speed is quoted in mph while velocity is quoted in ft/s. This is utter nonsense! The distinction is between a scalar (no direction) and a vector (with direction). Any convenient set of units can be used for both entities (inches per year, anyone?).

Assuming negligible interaction during the collision with outside bodies (e.g., road friction, curbs etc.), the momentum immediately after the impact must equal that immediately before the impact. Because momentum is a vector, this means that *along any chosen direction, or axis*, the momentum must be conserved. Since a two-body collision can involve two different axes (one for the bullet and one for the target), we must also conserve momentum along each axis. But because vectors can be resolved along any two axes, this also means that we can *define* any axes we choose. The most common approach is to define the pre-impact motion of one vehicle as the x-axis, and to then define the other as the y-axis, with the axes orthogonal.

Linear momentum applies to the CM (center-of-mass, or CG, center-of-gravity) of each vehicle motion. It does *not* apply to rotations, which would involve Conservation of Rotational (or Angular) Momentum. Whereas conservation of rotational momentum can be considered, it is quite distinct from linear momentum, and usually far more complicated to solve. Note also, the fact that the two vehicles can have an angular difference in motion both pre- and post-impact does *not* convert a linear solution into an angular one. It is therefore incorrect to refer in-line collisions as linear momentum solutions and collisions with vehicles at an angle as angular momentum solutions.

The following gives an example of a linear momentum solution.

Let vehicle 1 travel along the positive x-axis at velocity $v10$, while vehicle 2 travels at the angle θ to the x-axis at velocity $v20$. If θ is less than 90 degrees the vehicles have a common positive x-component, while if greater than 90 degrees vehicle 2 has a counter (negative) x-component.

Let vehicle 1 leave the impact with velocity $v11$ and at the positive angle α with respect to the x-axis, while vehicle 2 leaves with velocity $v22$ at the positive angle β.

We solve by conserving momentum along the x-axis and y-axis independently.

$$\text{Along } x\text{: } W1v10 + W2v20\cos(\theta) = W1v11\cos(\alpha) + W2v22\cos(\beta) \quad (17.2)$$

$$\text{Along } y\text{: } W2v20\sin(\theta) = W1v11\sin(\alpha) + W2v22\sin(\beta) \tag{17.2}$$

Provided we can determine the angles and post-impact velocities correctly we can solve the second equation immediately. Indeed, this is why we choose the y-axis to be perpendicular to the x-axis because it forces one term ($W1.v10\sin(0)$) to reduce to zero along the y-axis. Then we have

$$v20 = \frac{W1v11\sin(\alpha) + W2v22\sin(\beta)}{W2.\sin(\theta)} \tag{17.3}$$

We now substitute the value of $v20$ into the first equation to get

$$v10 = \frac{W1v11\cos(\alpha) + W2v22\cos(\beta) - W2v20\cos(\theta)}{W1} \tag{17.4}$$

Thus, assuming we correctly know the vehicle weights, angles and post-impact velocities we see that we can derive the two input velocities. Note carefully, we must properly define the angles. The example above assumed positive angles because everything involved (both pre- and post-impact) was moving to the right. If there is a counter motion (one vehicle moving to the left) then some angles become negative. This effect is usually handled by measuring all angles with respect to a counterclockwise 360 degree circle. For example, in the example above we assumed θ to be positive such as 30 degrees. If instead vehicle 2 is moving leftward (along the $-x$ axis) the angle becomes 150 degrees. But $\cos(150) = -\cos(30)$, and this immediately provides the correct sign for the solution. It is always helpful to quickly draw a small diagram of the motions to check we are properly using the correct signs for the solution.

Having determined the input and output velocities for each vehicle we can now establish the individual *delta-v*'s (for the CMs) by employing the cosine law. Thus for vehicle 1 we write

$$(delta\text{-}v1)^2 = v10^2 + v11^2 - 2v10v11\cos(\alpha) \tag{17.5}$$

while for vehicle 2 we write

$$(delta\text{-}v2)^2 = v20^2 + v22^2 - 2v20v22\cos(\theta - \beta) \tag{17.6}$$

Unfortunately the solution is rarely this simple (!) for the following reasons.

1. The approach angle, θ, is frequently not known with precision. In fact most times it is based on the logic of the roadway (e.g., a 90 degree

intersection). In some cases one vehicle (rarely both) may leave pre-impact skidmarks that help define the initial vehicle relative motions, or we must ascribe one vehicle motion by assuming a pre-impact motion (such as making a turn within a given distance).

2. The output angles, α and β, can also be uncertain. This is especially true if the impact produces vehicle spin or the post-impact motions involve curved paths. The latter paths may be due to uneven tire or road forces or due to road cross-slope (camber). We need to extrapolate such motions back to the impact in order to obtain proper post-impact angles of departure. Also, the motions must refer to the CM of each vehicle which is not the same as the initial mutual contact regions.
3. The post-impact velocities can be uncertain since there may be little in the way of skidmarks. Also, the overall post-impact drag factor for a vehicle may be uncertain, especially for a spinning vehicle, since the drag factor varies with local orientation, and is different for a vehicle strongly applying braking versus one relying solely on sideways tire friction. Indeed, for any motion except a straight line the solution for post-impact motion is frequently a derivation of speed rather than velocity. This is because the post-impact motion is derived by applying the skid equation, which involves an integral of drag factor and overall (curved) path length. What is usually *not* allowed is to assume the post-impact motion is along the straight line between the APOI (approximate point of impact) and the final position.
4. The linear momentum solution can become very sensitive to the angle θ when the latter is small (or almost 180 degrees). This is seen by studying the second equation (for the y axis) where it can be seen that the solution for $v20$ is inversely proportional to the value of $\sin(\theta)$. For this reason linear momentum solutions are rarely reliable for near in-line collisions, such as rear-enders or head-on collisions (*unless* we know that one vehicle was stopped pre-impact). This is why energy solutions are much more reliable for such crashes. In fact, as a general rule, momentum solutions are best for large-angle crashes (90 degree intersections) while energy solutions are best for small-angle crashes (since it avoids the side-swipe complications).
5. The linear momentum solution can become sensitive to weight ratio when one vehicle is much heavier than the other. This is for the simple reason that the lighter vehicle has only a small effect on the heavy one. However, this does not mean a solution cannot be found; it simply means the accuracy may be lessened. Emphasis should be applied to solving for the low weight vehicle, because the heavy vehicle always

has lower induced changes in speed and angle. Conversely, solving for the heavy vehicle can result in absurdly large changes for the light vehicle.

6. Because of the uncertainties listed above it is always necessary to perform a series of sensitivity calculations. Simple examples include using a range for the angles α and β, and/or a range of possible effective drag factors. If the results change rapidly within such ranges the overall solutions are not very reliable, and some alternative approaches must be used, such as comparing the answers with energy solutions.

Why is the effective drag factor uncertain for spinning vehicles? Consider a vehicle moving at speed v_0 (CM velocity) along the y-axis, which we consider to be "up." Let the brakes be fully applied. Braking forces are *opposed* to the local velocity vector of a tire. Without vehicle spin the front and rear wheels can have a common velocity, so the drag forces are all anti-parallel to this velocity. On a flat and level road this results in a straight-line vehicle motion. This occurs because without spin ($\omega = 0.0$) the net tire forces are independent of the angle of the longitudinal axis versus the y-axis (θ). However, if spin becomes significant this is no longer true.

Let the distance from the front axle to the CM be a, while from the rear axle to the CM is b (so WB, the wheelbase = $a + b$). Let the rotation rate be ω (positive for a clockwise motion). Then the front axle has a sideways velocity $vS = a.\omega$ superimposed on the overall CM velocity of v_0 and the rear axle has $b.\omega$ superimposed. Unlike the CM velocity these sideways velocities can have opposing directions. As a simple example, suppose the longitudinal vehicle axis is initially parallel to v_0 (i.e., pointing up). With spin the net velocity for the front axle is partly to the right and up, while for the rear axle the motion is partly to the left and up. These net velocities change as the spin continues and the vehicle axis is no longer along the y-axis, because the sideways velocities are always perpendicular to the vehicle axis whereas the CM velocity is not. Since friction is anti-parallel to net velocity (per axle) we immediately see that the frictional forces are partly to the left and down, and partly to the right and down for the front and rear axles. These forces can be resolved into ones parallel to v_0 and ones perpendicular.

Because maximum friction is limited by the friction circle logic, this behavior results in a net *reduction* in drag along the direction of v_0 which is cyclic with vehicle rotation. Further, if the two sideways forces do not balance there can be a net sideways acceleration of the CM, which again is cyclic.

For small rotation rate these effects are also small. By "small" we mean the sideways velocities $a.\omega$ and $b.\omega$ are both much less than v_0. Indeed, if either side velocity exceeds v_0 we obtain the bizarre *looping* behavior for the skidmarks. This is because as the longitudinal vehicle axis approaches 90 degrees versus v_0 (i.e., the vehicle axis is along the x-axis) we can have the situation where the front axle is moving downward while the rear axle is moving upward. Ultimately, for very small v_0 the overall motion becomes a pure spin about the vehicle CM. But for this case the longitudinal forces (along the y-axis) will tend to cancel, and the net drag reduces to zero. The entire motion is now dominated by the *torque* exerted on the vehicle since the sideways forces tend to cancel along any axis while they add for the net torque.

Since all these effects are changing with time (friction is slowing the vehicle, both with regard to CM motion and the spin rate) the only true way of solving the problem is by forward tracking the behavior versus time, since there is no simple closed mathematical equation available. Various codes claim to do this including those produced by EDC (Engineering Dynamics Corporation).

We illustrate some of these effects by plotting the net drag along the y-axis (i.e., along the direction of v_0) for differing values of v_0 and ω. For cases with strong braking the resulting drag is called μ*eff*, whereas for negligible braking the term is μ*roll* (to recognize the fact that the wheels are actually free-rolling).

Case 1. Here we assume $a = b = 4.5$ feet (for simplicity only) which implies the vehicle has a 50/50 weight distribution for front/rear axles. This is the usual situation for sports cars, whereas many standard cars frequently have a weight ratio closer to 60/40. We assume $v_0 = 44$ ft/s (30 mph) along the y-axis. The angle θ is measured clockwise versus the y-axis. Thus θ = 90 degrees implies the front of the vehicle is pointing east (the + x-axis) and the vehicle is locally moving sideways versus v_0. We set ω = 5 radians/s clockwise. This gives a local rotation speed of 4.5 × 5 = 22.5 ft/s at both the front and rear axles. As θ changes so the net vector value of velocity changes for the two axles, which also modifies the direction of the frictional drag. At θ = 90 degrees we have the velocities of 44 – 22.5 = + 21.5 ft/s for the front axle, and 44 + 22.5 = + 66.5 ft/s, in the + y direction. Assuming tire/road friction is independent of local velocity (not strictly true) this case then gives the same frictional drag for both axles, and the friction is downward (along the – y-axis). For θ = 270 degrees the same situation occurs. But for all other angles the net drag becomes smaller. If we set peak friction to μ = 0.75, the effective net drag (μ*eff*) varies from a low of about 0.66 at θ = 0 and 180 degrees, but increases to the value 0.75 near θ = 90 and 270 degrees. The net drag thus modulates with angle, as shown in Figure 17.1.

Case 2. This is identical to case 1 except we reduce $v_0 = 10$ ft/s and increase ω = 10 radians/s. This gives local rotational velocities of 45 ft/s at the two axles.

Now we note a dramatic change in net drag versus angle. For θ at about 0 and 180 degrees the drag is a maximum of about 0.16. This low value is because the two velocity vectors have large components along the +/- x-axis but only small components along the +/- y-axis. For θ near 90 and 270 degrees the net drag (μ*eff*) becomes zero! This occurs because when the vehicle is moving sideways (at 90 degrees) to v_0 the net axle velocities become – 35 ft/s for the front axle and + 55 ft/s for the rear axle (both along the + y-axis). For speed-independent friction this means the two frictional drags oppose each other. These effects are given in Figure 17.2.

Case 3. This is the same as case 1, except we assume zero braking and have only side-forces acting on the wheels/tires. For zero spin the result is a simple sin(θ) modulation of friction. However, with finite spin the net velocities are changed which modifies the net drag (μ*roll*). See Figure 17.3.

Case 4. This case is the same as case 2, except again we have no braking. Now we find the effective drag (μ*roll*) is zero regardless of θ. The explanation is that the spin is now large enough to overcome v_0, and we are approaching the pure spin condition. See Figure 17.4.

Case 5. This is the situation where we have $v_0 = 44$, strong braking and negligible spin (ω = 0.5). Now we see that the effective drag (μ*eff*) is essentially constant at the value 0.75. See Figure 17.5.

Case 6. This is case 5 but with no braking. Now we see the net drag (μ*roll*) is almost purely sinusoidal versus θ. Why "almost"? We have included the fact that for side-slip friction there is a pseudo-linear increase in friction versus angle (usually for the first few degrees, e.g., 5 degrees) which then saturates. This effect explains the small curvature seen near θ = 0 and 180 degrees. (It also explains the odd kinks seen in Figure 17.3.) See Figure 17.6.

Note that the effects of combined spin and overall CM motion become even more bizarre if the vehicle does not have a 50/50 weight distribution. This is because the opposing forces condition is shifted away from the 90 and 270 degree positions.

Suppose our vehicle is initially facing along the + y-axis while v_0 is defined along the + x-axis. This corresponds to a side hit on a stationary vehicle. Then to interpret the graphical results we start at 90 degrees. Thus a finite value of v_0 with a finite value of ω corresponds to a non-central side hit ahead of the vehicle CM (e.g., towards the front).

V = 44 ft/s ω = 5 rad/s

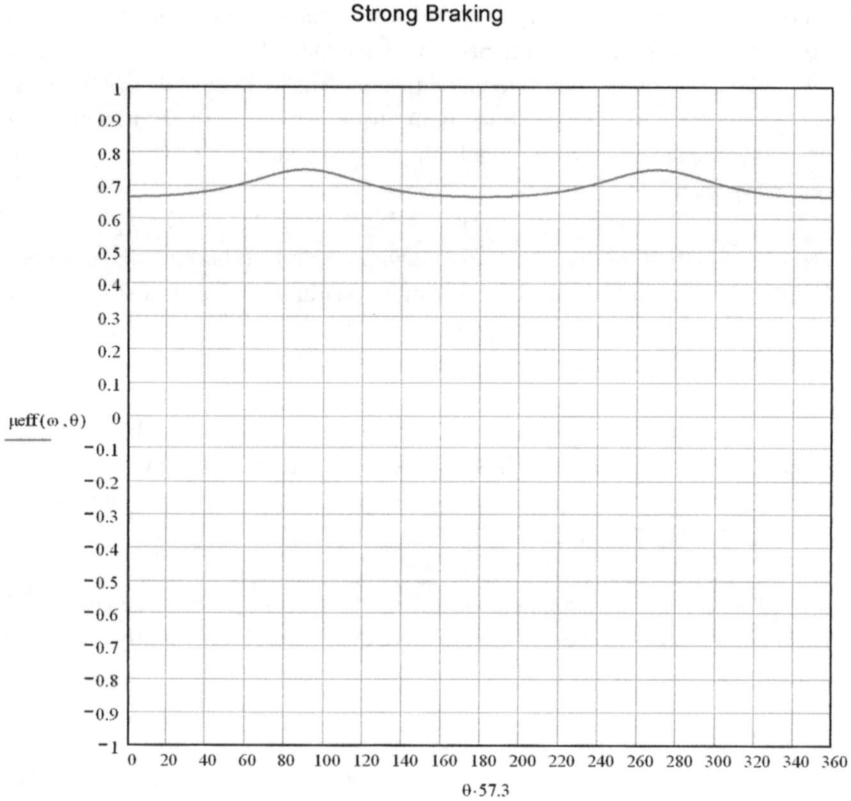

$V = 10$ ft/s $\omega = 10$ rad/s

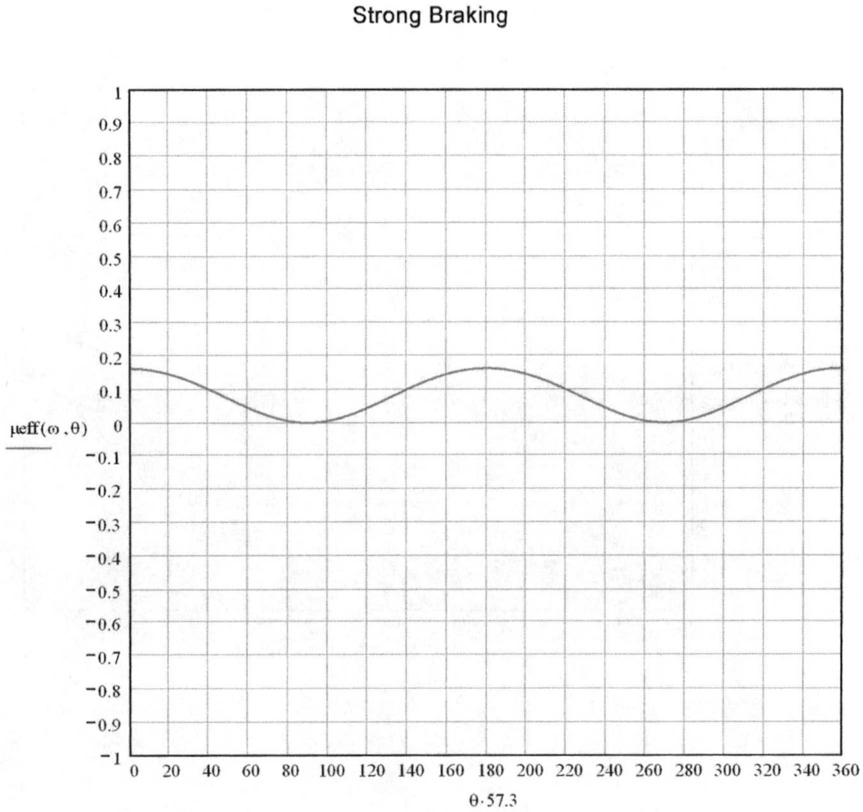

V = 44 ft/s   ω = 5 rad/s

No Braking

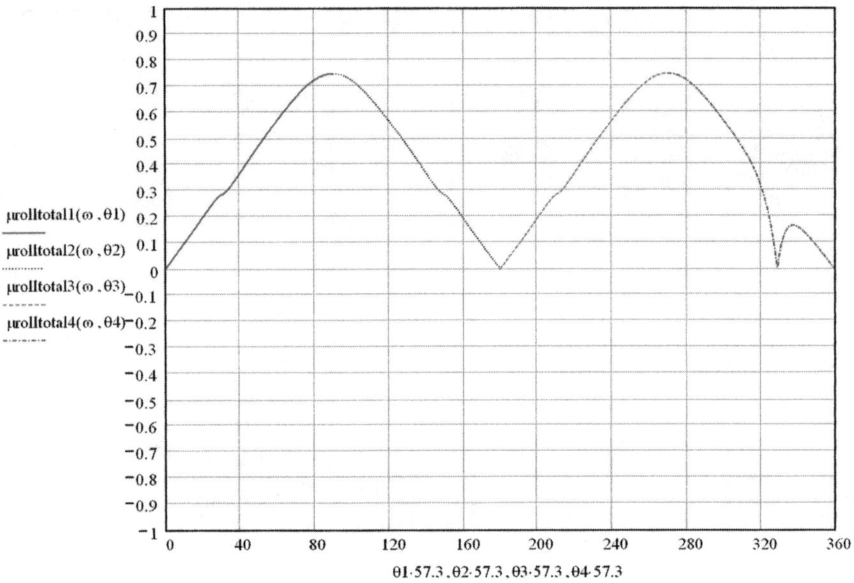

V = 10 ft/s   ω = 10 rad/s

No Braking

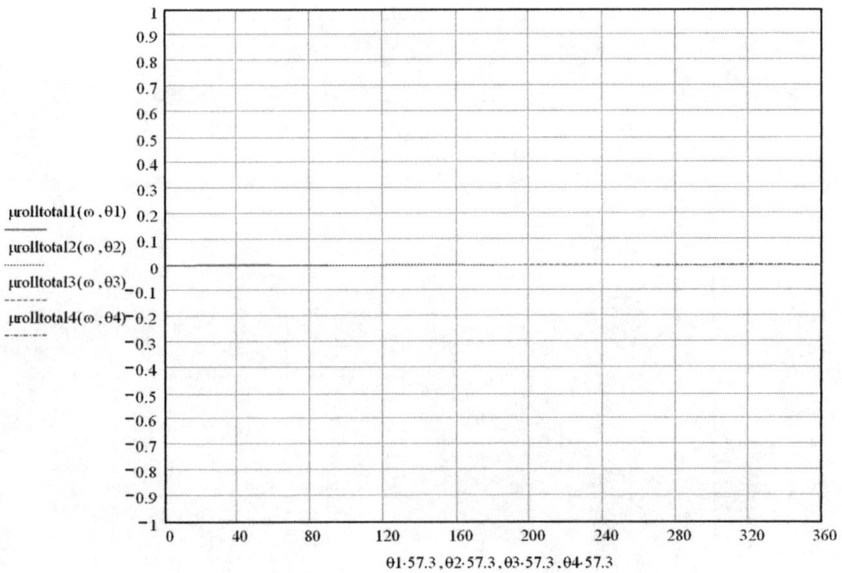

$V = 44$ **ft/s** $\omega = 0.5$ **rad/s**

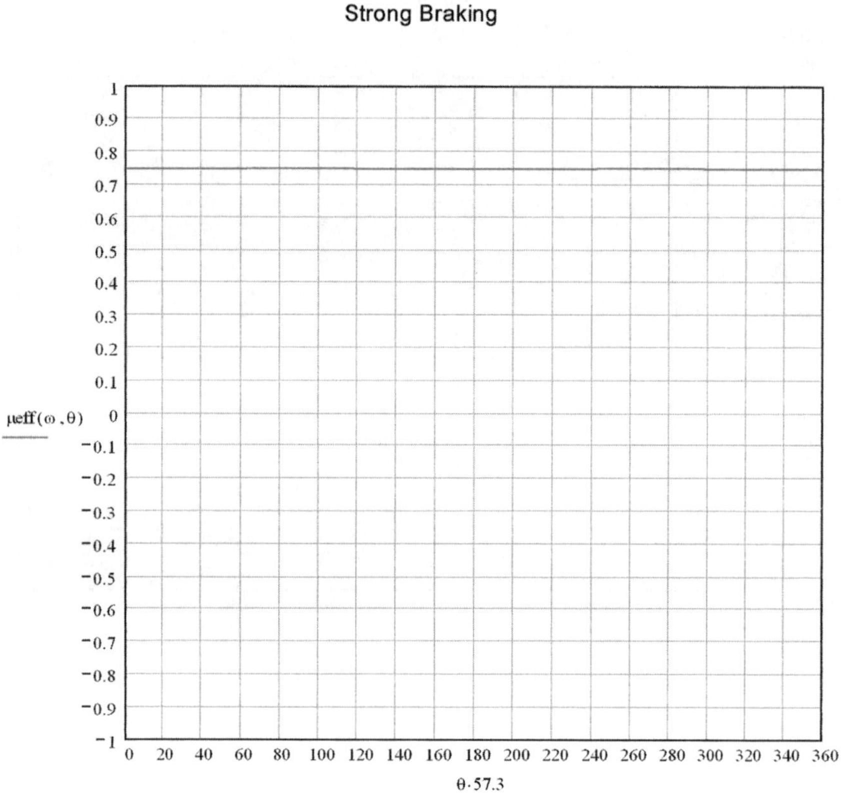

V = 44 ft/s   ω = 0.5 rad/s

No Braking

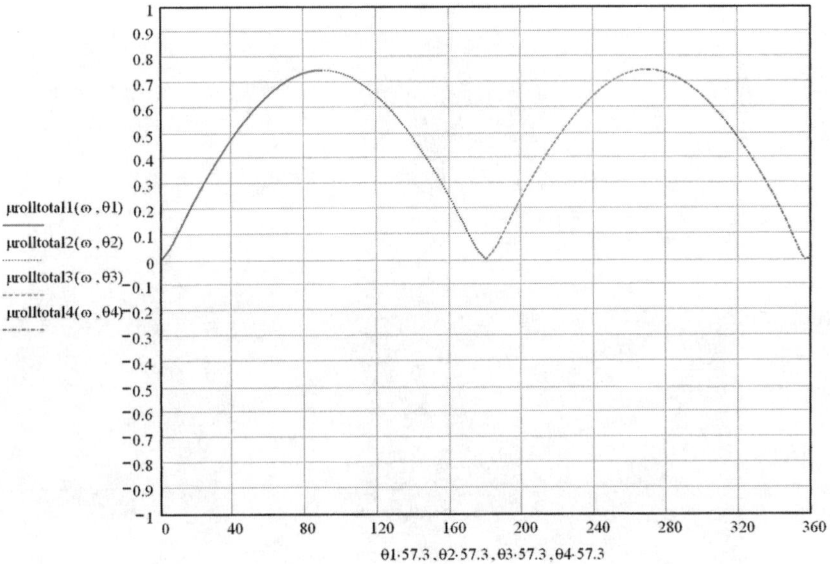

Chapter 18

Event Data Recorders (EDRs)

A relatively new phenomenon in the accident reconstruction world is the downloading of stored electronic data from a vehicle involved in an "event" (usually a crash or severe braking). The various sensors were originally mostly used to provide "feedback" data to the vehicle designers and manufacturers for diagnostic purposes. The data is stored in electronic memory that can be subsequently read with the use of appropriate cables and portable computers and programs. GM was the leader in the development of such systems, followed by Ford and Chrysler. Many foreign manufacturers are following suit. The equipment needed to download and interpret the data was initially provided by Vectonics, but more recently the Robert Bosch Company has taken over the task. Bosch now not only sells the necessary equipment but also gives many training courses for usage.

Much of the data is derived from the airbag control modules (ACM), with support from power-train modules (PCM) and engine control modules (ECM) and other sensors. The data devices are frequently called CDRs (crash data retrievers).

EDRs are frequently called "black boxes" by analogy with the aircraft equivalents. This is amusing because real aircraft "black boxes" are, in reality, bright orange to allow easy retrieval within a crash debris field.

As of 2011 EDRs are not a requirement, but NHTSA has decided all new passenger cars that provide them must provide a minimum set of data in a standardized form by 2013. NHTSA has also defined the minimum data that is to be recorded. These include:

1. Pre-event speed of the vehicle (usually for at least 5 seconds)
2. Change in speed (delta-v) along the x-axis (forward)
3. Time from start of delta-v until maximum delta-v
4. Percentage of throttle opening
5. Indication of braking
6. Indication of seatbelt usage
7. Indication of front airbag warning lamp status

8. Driver airbag deployment time
9. Front passenger airbag deployment timing
10. Ignition cycle at time of crash
11. Ignition cycle at time of downloading data
12. Number of crash events
13. Time between crash events, if appropriate
14. Whether or not the EDR completed recording

In addition the EDR should be capable of surviving intact an NCAP-like barrier impact. Some systems can provide additional data such as sideways delta-v (along the y-axis), engine speed, forward and reverse acceleration, driver steering input, seat track positions, and rollover initiation.

There are various potential problems with EDR data. For example, if a vehicle vaults before an impact the sudden removal of wheel loading may modify the apparent vehicle speed (suddenly speeding up from throttle response, or implying a sudden stop for braking that completely stops the wheel rotations during flight). Likewise, a recording of only the x-axis delta-v will only give part of the history that will need to be correlated with other accident reconstruction analysis. Even if the y-axis delta-v is also known the data is usually for the vehicle CM only and will not, by itself, give data concerning vehicle spin. Sometimes the reading time for the delta-v may not be long enough to guarantee recording the entire pulse, and it may not always be obvious that this is the case. And then we have the odd collisions that destroy the electrical power supply.

As with most automatic recorders, when the system works properly it can give very useful information. However there are occasions when the data could be miss-interpreted. Consequently, it would be dangerous to assume EDRs are going to replace standard accident reconstruction analysis. Presently, EDR data should be viewed as a *supplemental* set of information (rather like airbags are supplemental restraint systems to seatbelts).

An example of the usefulness of EDR was discovered in a crash between a car and a pick-up. Analysis indicated the truck suffered a delta-v of about 9 mph. But this value was for a PDOF acting at about 45 degrees to the longitudinal axis. The implied value for the x-axis was about 6 mph. The pick-up had its EDR downloaded (by the police) and gave a delta-v of about 5.9 mph for the x-axis. This was considered a good correlation.

We do not dwell on EDR usage for the simple reason that the practice of *reading* data is precisely that: it is reading data, it is not the act of reconstructing an accident, although the data may be usefully compared with the results of a proper reconstruction.

A very good history of EDR usage and development is given by Rusty Haight (ref 118).

Chapter 19

Going Round the Bend: Critical Yaw Velocity and Steering Logic

Synopsis

19.1 Introduction

In order to allow a vehicle to travel in a stable manner around a constant-radius curve a centripetal force must act upon the vehicle CM and "aim" at the geometric center of the curve. For a local speed, v, and a radius, R, this force is simply $m.v^2 / R = (w / g)v^2 / R$, where m is mass and w is weight. However, this force can only be derived from the tires-to-road surface frictions, none of which are at the position of the CM. Hence we must understand tire/road friction behavior, together with net forces and overall turning torques acting on the vehicle.

The true interactions of a typical tire and the road are highly complex: entire books are devoted to the issue (e.g., Pacejka—ref 115—and portions of Gillespie—ref 111), and are essential knowledge for understanding all the subtleties of vehicle dynamics. Fortunately, most of these intricacies are not needed for accident reconstruction. This is just as well, since many of the true parameters needed for an "exact" analysis are rarely available to the analyst. Consequently, we will attend to only the basics.

A free-rolling wheel/tire (no engine acceleration or braking or side slipping) exerts only a vertical force on the road (ignoring the normally very low drag due to tire-flexion hysteresis effects). The local speed of the tire at ground contact is zero. However, as braking is applied so the tire rotation slows and a longitudinal slip between the tire and the road develops. For full braking (wheel lockup) the tire develops 100 percent slip. The friction developed first increases quickly over the first 10–20 percent slip, then peaks and slowly decreases to a final value at 100 percent slip. For a dry asphalt surface the peak friction is typically about 0.8–0.9 while the locked wheel value is about 0.7–0.8. While the peak value is almost independent of speed the locked-wheel value usually decreases somewhat as speed increases. This latter behavior explains why pre-ABS braking systems tended to give lower overall drag factors as speeds increased.

One of the intended aspects of ABS brakes is to cause braking to momentarily cease as wheel lockup is approached and to immediately re-apply the brakes. The exact behavior is usually proprietary. The oscillation occurs at about 10–15 cycles/sec (Hertz) and explains the "noisy clatter" that is frequently heard coming from under the hood as the controlling hydraulic valves open and close. This process (hopefully) causes the slip to oscillate between a high value and a low value, which in turn causes the friction to oscillate near the peak. Because of the short "dead time" between brake applications the overall net friction is somewhat lower than the true peak value. The intention is that by preventing full wheel lockup some level of steering is still possible. A locked tire cannot provide steering because the "friction circle" has been reached (see later). The fact that the oscillating friction stays near the peak explains why modern vehicles do not display the obvious speed-dependence of non-ABS systems (at least on dry roads).

Reverting to the free-rolling wheel the effect of turning the wheel relative to the direction of motion develops a sideslip angle (difference between the local velocity vector and the "aim," or heading, of the wheel). This slip causes a friction to develop which is perpendicular to the wheel. With increasing slip angle the friction initially increases in a linear manner, but then starts to saturate and finally becomes a maximum for large slip angles. The exact behavior depends on tire design (radial versus cross-ply) and on the aspect ratio of the tire (tire wall height versus tread width). Radial tires with short wall heights give the steepest initial increase in friction versus slip angle. Typically, the linear region extends to about 5 degrees of slip and the tire essentially saturates above about 30 degrees. The peak frictional value is commonly similar to the ultimate longitudinal value, although some tires are designed to give larger side friction than longitudinal friction. The slope of the initial linear behavior is called the cornering stiffness and has units of lb/lb/degree (for friction) or is the cornering coefficient with units lb/degree (for actual force).

For a given longitudinal friction (along the direction of the tire heading) the side friction (perpendicular to the tire) can increase until the vector sum reaches the "friction circle," likewise for a given side friction the longitudinal value can increase until the vector sum again reaches the friction circle. If the tire develops significantly greater side friction than longitudinal friction, the circle becomes an ellipse. However, for either case when the vector sum of frictions equals the limit the net friction rapidly becomes a pure drag, meaning the net vector swings around and becomes anti-parallel to the local velocity vector of the tire regardless of the heading of the wheel. This explains why steering ability vanishes when the wheels starts to lock.

For varying combinations of longitudinal slip and sideslip the interactions are complex and depend on tire design. Application of sideslip tends to remove the peak in the longitudinal slip, while ever-increasing longitudinal slip lowers the side value and eventually gives a near-zero side friction as wheel lockup occurs.

19.2 Steering Effects

For cornering we need side forces. But parallel forces merely shift the vehicle sideways. We also need the forces to converge at a remote point, which is (initially) the center of the turn. At very low speeds the *required* centripetal forces are very small, which in turn means the required sideslip angles for the tires are also very small. As a result the side forces aim at the center of the turn along the perpendiculars to the wheels. For the typical two-wheel steering vehicles (front wheels only) this results in the center of the turn lying along the extension of the rear axle. The front wheels must therefore be rotated through an angle such that the perpendicular to each front wheel also aim at the center of the turn.

Since the front wheels are laterally separated by the track width, T, the wheels must rotate through two *different* angles. The inner wheel turns through a larger angle than the outer wheel. This is achieved by employing "Ackerman Steering" geometry. If the wheelbase is L and the radius of the turn is R (measured to the center of the rear axle) the two angles are given by

$$\tan(\text{angle outer}) = \frac{L}{R + \frac{T}{2}} \quad \text{and} \quad \tan(\text{angle inner}) = \frac{L}{R - \frac{T}{2}} \tag{19.1}$$

The average angle is known as the Ackerman Angle (AA) given by

$$\tan(AA) = \frac{L}{R} \tag{19.2}$$

A simple example of Ackerman geometry can be seen on a child's open-frame go-cart. From the vertical kingpins just inboard of each front wheel we have steering arms leading to the lateral steering rack bar. Typically, the steering rack is aft of the front wheels. These steering arms converge so that the corresponding distance between the two pivots at the steering rack is shorter than the lateral distance between the two kingpins, and the arrangement gives a trapezoidal configuration. How much shorter? Answer: with the front wheels parallel, draw lines between each kingpin to the center of the rear axle. Where these lines intercept the steering rack is where the pivots are placed. This arrangement gives a first-order approximation to the required condition that the front wheels are independently perpendicular to the radial lines aiming at the center of the turn, and prevents significant scuffing of the tires as the vehicle moves around the curve.

Does anyone remember the old record players? The turntables had a similar problem to solve. The groove on the record was cut using a radially-moving cutter, but the playing of the record most often used a tone-arm (holding the needle and cartridge) which swung on a circular arc. The problem was how to make the arc movement approximate the radial motion such that the cartridge "thought" it was always locally parallel to the groove. The solution was to actually make the cartridge "overhang" slightly (too long a tone arm) while simultaneously twisting the cartridge relative to the arm (inward towards the center of the record). This resulted in the "S-shaped" tone arms on many record player decks. Done properly there were two positions across the record where the cartridge was exactly perpendicular to the radius, while elsewhere the error was kept small.

19.3 Higher Speeds

At very low speed the description given above implies the center of turn lies perpendicular to the rear wheels and thus parallel to, and an extension of, the rear axle. Because the radius of the turn is usually much larger than the track width we may approximate the situation by "collapsing" the right and left wheels together, thus mimicking a two-wheel vehicle. This is known as the "bicycle model." We also consider the bicycle to act like a rigid barbell, with weights above the front and rear wheels. Let the radius to the rear wheels (center of the axle) be R1, while the radius to the vehicle CM is R0 and the radius to the front wheels is R2. It is immediately apparent that R2 > R0 > R1. Thus at low speeds the rear wheels track inboard of the front wheels, and also inboard of the CM. Note carefully, at low speeds the radius R0 is *not* perpendicular to the longitudinal axis of the vehicle. Consequently, the front of the axis leans "outward" relative to the tangent of the curve passing through the CM. This angle represents the overall side slip angle for the *vehicle* and is usually considered negative. It is also called the *float* angle.

Keeping R0 constant now consider increasing speeds. The required centripetal forces must increase which means both rear and front wheels need to develop sideslip. But the rear wheels do not (usually) steer. Thus the only way we can develop a sideslip angle is to rotate the vehicle longitudinal axis relative to the CM. This increases R1 and reduces R2. The rear end of the vehicle starts to swing out and the front swings in. Simultaneously the float angle becomes smaller in magnitude. Since the float angle starts as a negative quantity this merely means the angle is actually *increasing positively*. For a sufficiently large speed (and slip angle) the float angle passes through zero and becomes positive. Also, we reach the situation where R1 > R2, and the rear wheels now track outboard of the front wheels.

But this produces an interesting effect: the true side forces are perpendicular to the wheels and thus these forces converge at a point aft of the center of the turn. The higher the speed, the greater the needed side slip and the more the convergence point moves backward away from the true center of the turn. This means the actual forces that pass through the center of the turn are the components. If *muside* is the true side friction the component aiming at the center of the turn is *muside*.cos(sideslip angle). It is this component that provides the required centripetal force. The other component is *muside*.sin(sideslip angle). This second component acts along the local tangent to the wheel arc motion and provides a drag force. This explains why cornering vehicles naturally start slowing even without applying braking.

Because the side friction initially increases with side slip angle and then starts to saturate, the product *muside*.cos(sideslip angle) must pass through a maximum which can be at a side slip angle in the range 10–20 degrees. Beyond this peak increasing the sideslip angle *reduces* the available centripetal forces, and the vehicle can no longer follow the curve intended, and the radius of the turn must increase. But the true side friction (perpendicular to the wheel) is still increasing. Also note that when the peak in centripetal friction occurs the drag factor is usually around the value of 0.2. A similar drag value is frequently assumed by many analysts.

19.4 Yawing, Understeer and Oversteer

The term yaw originally came from the world of sailing ships. It is common for the combination of wind (acting on the sails) and water (acting on the hull and keel) to result in a ship moving "forward" but with its longitudinal axis "skewed" at an angle. This motion is called yawing and the angle is the yaw angle. Similar effects are regularly seen with aircraft.

For ground vehicles yaw means the vehicle has a heading that is at an angle to the overall velocity vector. Yawing involves rotation about the vertical axis through the vehicle CM.

Hopefully, it should be obvious that when a vehicle moves on a circular arc there are two types of rotation occurring. First we have the *orbital* motion that describes the CM motion about the center of the turn (by analogy with the earth-sun motion). This treats the vehicle as a point mass. Second we have the vehicle spinning about its vertical axis through the CM. This treats the change in heading of the vehicle. For stable cornering, the orbital rate (Ω) and the spin rate (ω) are the same (rates are in radians/sec). This situation occurs for the moon traveling around the earth, and explains why the moon always presents the same "face" as seen from the earth. For identical rates the vehicle simply develops a constant yaw angle, in accordance with the float angle mentioned above. Consequently, as speed increases so the yaw angle must also increase. Stable conditions imply a *neutral steer* condition whereby the yaw angle remains fixed along the circular arc, regardless of constant speed.

The net centripetal force acting on the vehicle CM is the sum of the front and rear wheel side forces. However, the front wheel forces act "ahead" of the CM. If the vehicle is making a turn to the right this produces a clockwise rotation about the CM. For the rear wheels the forces act "behind" the CM and we develop a counterclockwise rotation. Stable conditions imply these two counteracting torques cancel, yielding a zero rate rotational acceleration (ω remains steady). But if the torques do not cancel we develop a net rotational acceleration. *Over-steer* is the condition of increasing ω (clockwise) while *under-steer* is a reduction in spin. For over-steer the vehicle "tightens" into the curve with the front wheels rapidly moving inward and the rear wheels rapidly moving outward, both relative to the CM motion. For under-steer the vehicle front "plows out" and fails to keep its intended heading.

Most vehicles are either neutral steer (rare, sports cars) or under-steer (more common, typical cars). Small levels of under-steer are considered "safe." Why? Consider that a driver needs to "steer right" in order to corner to the right. Under-steer requires an increase in steering at higher speeds. The need to increase the steering "seems natural" to most drivers ("if a little is good, more must be better" logic). However, over-steer is not considered "natural" since at high speeds the driver must "unwind" the steering.

If we define delta as the required steering angle of the wheels it can be shown that

$$delta = 57.3\frac{L}{R} + \left[\text{sideslip angle}(\text{front}) - \text{sideslip angle}(\text{rear})\right] \ (\text{degrees}) \tag{19.3}$$

where the sideslip angles are given by

$$\text{sideslip angle}(\text{front}) = \frac{w(\text{front})}{g} \times \frac{v^2}{R} \times \frac{1}{\text{cornering stiffness}(\text{front})} \tag{19.4}$$

and similar for the rear. Here w(front) is the fraction of the vehicle weight on the front wheels. If the wheelbase is L, and the distances from the CM to the front and rear axles are a and b, respectively, and c is the cornering stiffness, then we have

$$w(front) = \left(\frac{b}{L}\right) w(total) \quad \text{and} \quad w(rear) = \left(\frac{a}{L}\right) w(total) \qquad (19.5)$$

and thus

$$delta = 57.3\frac{L}{R} + \left(\frac{w}{g}\right)\left(\frac{v^2}{R}\right)\left(\frac{1}{L}\right)\left[\frac{b}{c}(front) - \frac{a}{c}(rear)\right] \qquad (19.6)$$

where w is the total vehicle weight.

When the square bracket term [ ] is zero, delta = 57.3L/R regardless of velocity for a constant R, and is simply the Ackerman Angle. This is neutral steering.

If the term [ ] is positive, delta must be increased to maintain the constant radius curve. This is under-steer. If the term is negative we must decrease delta, and we have over-steer.

The cornering stiffness is also a function of the vertical load (weight) on each axle, and tends to decrease as the load increases. This effect helps explain why a vehicle that is neutral or slightly under-steering with small occupancy (e.g., driver only) can become over-steering with high occupancy. This has been observed with the 15-passenger vans. Adding more occupants moves the overall vehicle CM rearwards (due to the seating arrangement) but also increases the load on the rear tires more than on the front tires. Thus the term a increases while b decreases. Simultaneously the value of c (rear) decreases more than c (front). As a result the [ ] term given above can go from positive to negative. Since the addition of more occupants also raises the overall CM height, the vehicle becomes more prone to rollover.

19.5 The Yaw Critical Velocity

In its simplest form the condition for cornering is the balance of net side forces acting on the vehicle CM equating with the required centripetal force. But the side forces can only increase until the peak in the value *muside*.cos(sideslip angle) is reached. Thus we have

$$\left(\frac{w}{g}\right)\left(\frac{v^2}{R}\right) = w\,\mu side\,\cos(\text{sideslip angle}) \qquad (19.7)$$

or

$$v^2 = Rg\ \textit{muside}\ \cos(\text{sideslip angle}) \qquad (19.8)$$

where w is vehicle weight and we combine the front and rear tire forces. For a fixed radius of turn this limits the maximum speed that can be achieved. At, or near, this condition the tires are reaching the limit of friction, and we see tire marks (yaw marks) develop. These are recognized as curved marks with lateral striations. Note that this critical yaw condition assumes free-rolling wheels, with negligible traction or braking applied.

Surprisingly, there seem to be no published data on just *when* (what level of slip) tire marks will become "obvious." This applies to both longitudinal slipping and side slipping. Everyone knows that a fully locked tire can leave skid marks. This occurs because the energy absorbed and dissipated by the tire/road interaction is concentrated on a fixed patch of the tire which causes severe heating of the patch. But how much can we back away from 100 percent slippage to a lower value (which allows some wheel rotation and thus redistribution of heat around the tire circumference)? Is it 90 percent or 70 percent slippage? No one seems to know. This "backing off" effect explains why ABS brakes leave little (sometimes none) in the way of skid marks. Likewise there is no precise level of side slipping that defines when yaw marks are developed.

An interesting problem arises: although we know that lateral friction can be larger than longitudinal friction the "best" solution for defining the yaw limit speed is frequently found by using the longitudinal value. Why? A possible answer may be the "cosine effect" given above. Typically, if the saturation value for side friction is *mumax* the "effective value" is *mumax*.cos(sideslip angle), and this is always lower than the peak, and thus close to the longitudinal value for friction.

To correctly determine the yaw velocity we must check that the vehicle is truly yawing due to cornering. This check on cornering is usually done by observing *at least* two tire marks (the two outer wheels if possible). If both (or more) tire marks imply a near-common radius of motion (with the track width accounted for) we have a yaw condition. Also, a rear wheel must track outboard of a corresponding front wheel. Note that vehicle spin (due to a non-central impact) does not satisfy the logic of cornering. Individual tires can give yaw marks, but a check on multiple tires will reveal grossly differing radii of curvature. This is why we need at least two tire marks to analyze.

An interesting point is that at the sideslip angle that gives the peak in centripetal friction the outer front wheel (left for a right turn) is frequently at a similar radius to that of the CM of the vehicle. This means that analysis of the front outer tire mark tends to give the closest answer to that based on the CM motion.

As explained above, cornering automatically involves a drag component that causes vehicle slowing. This causes the critical radius to decrease with continued motion, and the yaw paths start to spiral inward. For this reason it is recommended that the first part of a yaw mark (e.g., the first one-third) be used to establish the initial vehicle speed.

19.6 High Rate Cornering and Electronic Stability Control

All the above logic applied to steady state cornering and/or the case of entering a corner at relative low rate (degrees/s). When the front wheels are steered the side forces cause the front of the vehicle to move sideways and also accelerate the CM sideways, but at a slower rate. The vehicle also rotates (spins) about its CM, and thus begins to produce a sideslip angle for the rear wheels. However, there is a time delay before the rear wheels develop sufficient sideslip to counteract the initial spin and cause a steady spin rate (radians/s). Typically a tire requires between one-half to a full wheel rotation in order to develop full sideslip force. If the initial buildup of spin is too large the vehicle can exceed the peak side force for the rear tires before reaching a stable state. When this happens the vehicle can lose control and the rear end swings out rapidly since the effective centripetal friction decreases beyond the peak with increasing sideslip angle for the rear wheels. This situation is an extreme case of over-steer.

Electronic Speed Control (ESC) is becoming common on many modern vehicles. Essentially, the vehicle's various sensors detect when an over-steer problem is developing, and the system then applies signals to either the brakes and/or the throttle. Early versions of ABS braking simply told all the front or rear brakes (or both sets) to apply the oscillation logic. However, the more refined versions of ABS can apply to *individual* wheels as appropriate. Hence for a vehicle making a right turn and which starts to over-steer, braking can be selectively applied to the left front outer wheel. The added drag produces a counterclockwise torque which stops (or minimizes) the over-steer. Simultaneously, the throttle can be closed causing the vehicle to slow. This combination can prevent many rollover situations. To cure under-steer braking can be applied to the inner (right) rear wheel.

IIHS now require vehicles to include ESC in order to receive their highest ratings for safety, and the government has decided all light vehicles (cars, vans, pick-ups and SUVs) must have ESC by model year 2012.

19.7 Mathcad Plots

Figures 19.1 and 19.2 show how the wheels vary their radii as a function of the sideslip angle (assumed the same for both rear and front wheels). The condition computed assumes a vehicle with a wheelbase of about 8 feet and a track width of 5 feet, undergoing a right turn. The true maximum side friction is assumed to be 0.7. However, the peak value (cosine effect) gives a value of about 0.65 at a sideslip angle of 18 degrees. For a friction of 0.65 the radius for the CM is about 41.1 feet for a speed of 20 mph. Note how for zero sideslip the rear wheels are inboard of the front wheels, but crossover occurs for an angle of about 6 degrees.

For an angle of 18 degrees the outer front wheel has a radius of about 42.8 feet versus the CM value of 41.1 feet. The float angle is about – 6 degrees for zero sideslip angle, becoming zero at the sideslip angle of 6 degrees and becoming 12 degrees at the sideslip angle of 18 degrees.

Note also how radii of the front left wheel and the rear right wheel crossover for an angle of about 35 degrees and at a value almost identical to the CM radius. Of course, this occurs beyond the yaw limit. The condition of sideslip angle = 90 degrees corresponds to a vehicle moving purely sideways.

Tire Forces versus Slip Angle

$p := 57.3$

Let δ be "build-up factor" for side friction

$\theta := \frac{0}{p}, \frac{0.01}{p} .. \frac{90}{p}$

$\delta := \frac{5}{p}$

$\mu 0 := 0.7$

$k(\theta) := \left(1 - e^{\frac{-\theta}{\delta}}\right)$

$\mathrm{Fric}(\theta) := \mu 0 \cdot k(\theta)$

$\mathrm{Fside}(\theta) := \cos(\theta) \cdot k(\theta) \cdot \mu 0$

$\mathrm{Fdrag}(\theta) := \sin(\theta) \cdot k(\theta) \cdot \mu 0$

$\mathrm{Ftotal}(\theta) := \sqrt{\left[\mathrm{Fside}(\theta)^2 + \left(\mathrm{Fdrag}(\theta)^2\right)\right]}$

$\mathrm{Fsidemax}(\theta) := \sqrt{\mu 0^2 - \mathrm{Fdrag}(\theta)^2}$

Tire forces versus slip angle

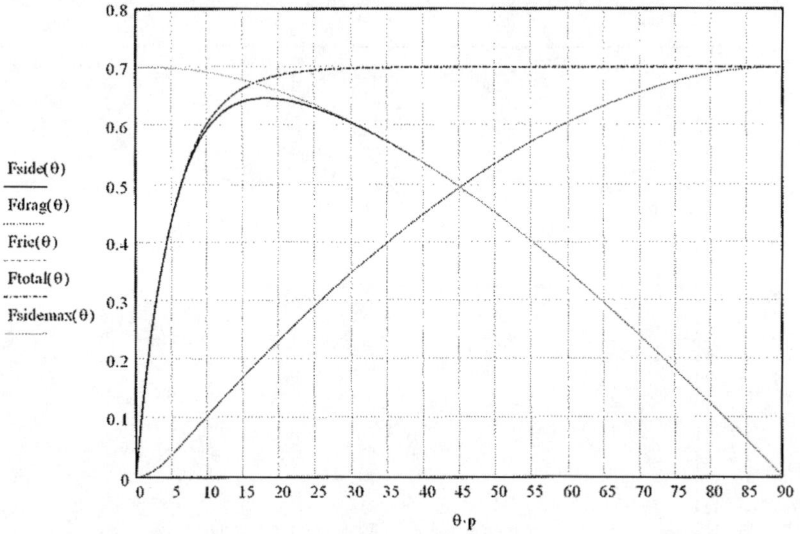

R0 = 41.129 ft μ = 0.65 v00 = 20 mph v0 = 29.34 ft/s

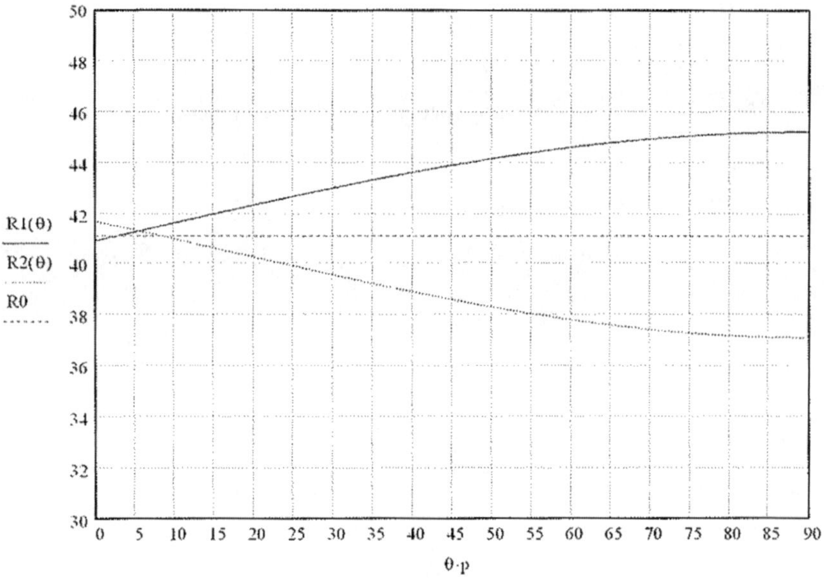

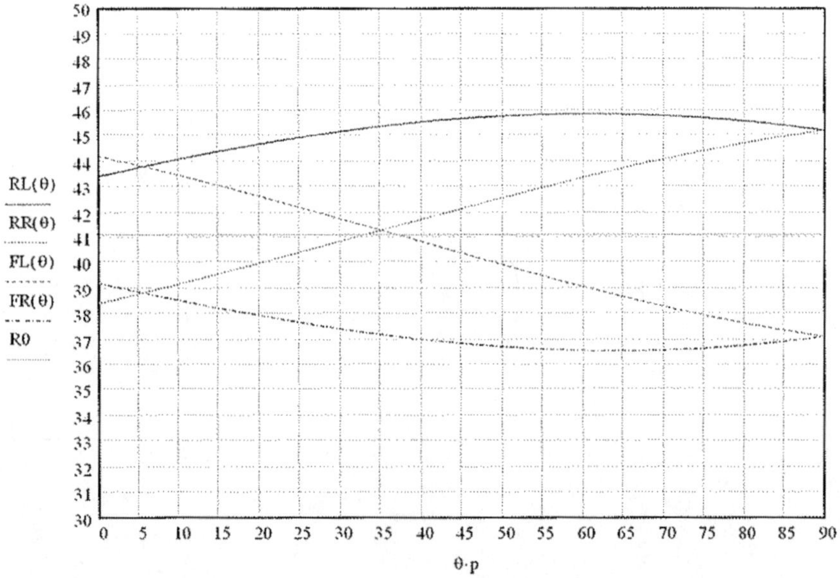

Appendix A

Accident Reconstruction Definitions and Other Notes

Unit Conversions

This book is written mostly in the old English customary units of pounds, feet and seconds. We have done this because most accident reconstructionists appear to still be using these units. Further, most police, attorneys, insurance adjusters, medics and even jurors seem more familiar with these units. However, the engineering professions (such as SAE) are trying to wean people onto the SI system (the metric system). The latter is used by all scientists and most engineers throughout the world. Accordingly, we give below some of the more important conversions.

mass:	1.0 kilogram = 2.2 pounds, or 1.0 lb = 0.454 kg
length:	1.0 meter = 100 cm = 1,000 mm = 39.37 inches = 3.28 feet, or 1.0 foot = 0.305 meter
speed:	1.0 km/h = 28.78 cm/s = 10.94 inches/s= 0.91 ft/s = 0.62 mph, or 1.0 mph = 1.61 km/h
	1.0 m/s = 39.37 inches/s = 3.28 ft/s = 2.236 mph, or 1.0 mph = 0.447 m/s
energy:	1.0 joule = 1.0 Nm = 0.2247 lb × 3.28 ft = 0.737 lb-ft, or 1.0 lb-ft = 1.36 Nm = 1.36 joules
power:	1.0 kilowatt = 1.34 hp, or 1.0 hp = 0.746 kilowatt
force:	1.0 newton = 0.2247 lb, or 1.0 lb = 4.45 newtons
acceleration:	1.0 g = 32.2 ft/s^2 = 9.81 m/s^2

Units and Dimensions

- *Mass* (m) is a measure of the quantity of matter, such as how many atoms, and is measured in *slugs* or *kilograms*.
- *Weight* (w) is a measure of the *force* acting on a mass due to *gravity*, and is measured in *lbsf* or *newtons* (N).

- *Gravity* (g) is the *acceleration* given to a body in free fall, and is *roughly constant* everywhere on Earth.
- $g = 32.2$ ft/s/s = 32.2 ft/s^2, or $g = 9.81$ m/s^2 = 981 cm/s^2
  w = lbsf or N
  1.0 lbf = 0.454 kg × 9.81 m/s^2 = 4.45 N, or 1.0 N = 0.225 lbf
  $m = w/g$ = slugs or kg
  1.0 slug = 1.0 lb/g = 1.0 lb/ 32.2 ft/s^2 = 0.031 lb × s^2/ft
  1.0 kilogram weight = 2.2 pounds weight
- One newton is the force required to accelerate one kg at 1.0 m/s^2.
  One lbf is the force required to accelerate one slug at one g.
  One poundal is the force to accelerate one slug at 1.0 ft/s^2.
- *Speed* is a *rate:* distance moved per time taken.
  Average speed is a finite distance moved divided by the finite time interval.
  Instantaneous speed is the local slope (or differential) of distance-time plot, (i.e., the speed at a given point in time, or a given position).
- *Velocity* is speed with a defined *direction.*
  If the speed remains constant, but the direction changes, the velocity changes.
- *Acceleration* is a *rate*: velocity changed per period of time.
  Thus, any change in velocity implies an acceleration, even if the speed is constant.
  Thus, moving along a curved arc always involves an acceleration, whether due to a change in speed or simply a change in direction.
- Speed or velocity are measured in ft/s or m/s or mph, and so on.
  Acceleration is measured in ft/s^2 or m/s^2 or mph/h, and so on.
  Deceleration is negative acceleration (slowing down instead of speeding up).
- *Linear momentum* is the product of *mass* times *velocity.*
- *Angular momentum* is the product of *mass* times *velocity* times a *fixed distance* perpendicular to the motion.
- *Impulse* is a rapid change in momentum.
- *Linear acceleration* is a change in velocity along a straight line path.
- *Angular (rotational) acceleration* is a change in velocity along a curved path.
- *Centrifugal force* is the *apparent* force that "pulls" a body "outward" when traveling along a curved path.
- *Centripetal force* is the *actual* force necessary to "pull" a body "inward" when traveling along a curved path (i.e., forcing the body to follow the path).

- *Kinetic energy* (KE) is the energy possessed by a body as a result of its motion.
  Linear KE is due to straight-line motion.
  Angular (rotational) KE is due to motion along a curved arc.
- *Potential energy* (PE) is energy *stored* by virtue of a body's position.
  This can be due to a change in height (falling off a cliff, running down a hill, etc.), or can be due to compression or tension (squeezing a spring, etc.) or both. This type of energy can be *recovered* by *reversing* the process.
- *Absorbed energy* (AE) is energy which is *permanently* converted into another form, such as skidding on a road, crushing a vehicle, generating heat, sound, light or any combination of those.
- Units for linear momentum are lb-s or Ns.
  Units for angular momentum are lb-s-ft or Nsm.
  Units for KE, PE and AE are ft-lb or Nm (or joules).
- *Dimensional analysis* is the process of verifying an equation by checking the "dimensions." These dimensions are M (for mass), L (for length) and T (for time). Speed or velocity are thus L/T, acceleration is L/T^2, Force is ML/T^2, Energy (all forms) is $M(L/T)^2$, linear momentum is M(L/T), angular momentum is $M(L^2/T)$.
  If the equation is correct then the dimensions on the left of the equals sign will match those on the right hand side (e.g., energy = force × distance). So $M(L/T)^2 = M(L/T^2)L$.

Newton's Three Laws

1. *Steady state* (*law of inertia*): Any body remains as it was unless an external force acts on it. Thus a stationary body remains at rest unless you push or pull it, and a moving body continues moving at constant velocity unless you push or pull on it.
2. If a force is applied to a body then the body will accelerate in proportion to the magnitude of the force and inversely according to the mass of the body.
   Thus, $a = F/m$, or $F = ma$, where F is the force, m is the mass and a is the acceleration. The acceleration is along the direction of the force, and vice versa.
3. For every action (force) there is an equal and opposite reaction. Thus, in order to push on a body, the body must "push back."

These three laws explain many effects. For example, if a force acts on a body the latter may accelerate (or decelerate). This means its speed increases (or decreases) and thus its KE increases (or decreases). Thus, the force must have done *work* on the body and the body gained (or lost) energy. The work done is given by the force *in the direction of the distance* times the distance. Forces which are perpendicular to the motion do not perform work.

The force is also the *net* force acting. If two equal forces act on a body but in opposite directions (on opposite sides) then the body does not accelerate. Instead, the body compresses (two pushes) or extends (two pulls). If two unequal forces are acting then the balanced portions compress (or extend) the body, while the remaining unbalanced portion provides the net acceleration. For example, if the force on one side is a push of 1,200 lbf, and on the other side is a push force of 900 lbf (acting in the opposite direction), then this can be considered as a compression of the body by two 900-lbf actions and an acceleration of the body by the "excess" 300 lbf on the first side.

The laws also explain why, when two bodies collide one must slow down while the other speeds up, until usually both bodies reach a common speed. If the impact involved the storage of some energy (as in compressing springs) then some of the energy is returned in the form of a bounce between the bodies. When this happens the "bullet" is slowed even more and the "target" is sped up even more. This happens because of the action/reaction (law 3). Since each body is in contact with the other for the *same* time, then the product of *Force* × *time* is equal and opposite for each. This product is the *impulse,* and numerically equal to the changes in momentum of each body. Thus momentum is conserved.

Conservation of Momentum and Energy

Linear Momentum

Whenever two bodies impact linear momentum must be conserved. This means that *along any straight line* (e.g., a defined axis) the momentum must remain constant. For an in-line (collinear) collision, only one axis is defined. For a collision at an angle (either incoming or outgoing, or both) two orthogonal axes (i.e., axes at 90 degrees) can be defined, and the momentum must remain constant along each axis independently. For the angled collision, the two momenta along the two orthogonal axes also define a *total* momentum for both vehicles (see vectors, later). This total momentum must also remain constant.

Momentum is mostly exchanged between the vehicles *during* the impact. However, some is also transferred to the ground during the impact, either because of braking or a side skid, or an impact with a rigid object attached to the ground. Usually the brake/skid ground effect is only important for low speeds *during* the impact, but can be very important after the impact.

Angular Momentum

During an impact the angular momentum must also be conserved. This simply means that if a reference point is chosen (this can be arbitrary, but is usually chosen to agree with a known center of rotation), then the product of momenta times the perpendicular distance to the reference point must remain constant.

Turning Torque

Torque is also known as "moment" or "couple." In all cases the torque is the product of a force times the perpendicular distance to a point of rotation. To remember, try this old physics joke: "Every *couple* has its *moments,* but we won't *torque* about that!" The effect of applying a torque to a body is to produce an angular acceleration. The angular acceleration is proportional to the magnitude of the torque and inversely proportional to the *moment of inertia* of the body (discussed later). This is the analog to a force producing linear acceleration for a mass.

Energy

All forms of energy must be conserved. However, the different forms can be exchanged with each other. Thus PE can be converted into KE (car runs down hill and increases its speed). KE can be converted into PE (spring is compressed). KE can be converted into AE (car crush, tire skid). See Figure A.1.

Scalars and Vectors

A scalar quantity is one which has magnitude *only,* such as speed, mass, time and all forms of energy. A vector has both magnitude *and* direction, such as weight, force, velocity, torque, momentum and angular momentum.

Basic Equations of Motion

Linear Acceleration

The fundamental equation relating force (F), mass (m) and accel (a) is

$$F = ma \quad \text{or} \quad F = \left(\frac{w}{g}\right)a \quad \text{or} \quad a = \frac{F}{m} \quad \text{or} \quad a = \frac{g}{w}F.$$

Whenever linear acceleration is involved the following applies

$$s_2 - s_1 = v_0\left(t_2 - t_1\right) + \frac{1}{2}a\left(t_2^2 - t_1^2\right)$$

where s_2 and s_1 are distances at times t_2 and t_1, v_0 is the initial speed and a is the accel.

$$v_2 - v_1 = a(t_2 - t_1)$$

$$v_2^2 - v_1^2 = 2a(s_2 - s_1)$$

where v_2 and v_1 are speeds corresponding to the distances and times. The value of a is (+) for increasing speed, and (–) for slowing down.

If the acceleration changes over either time ranges or distance ranges the equations are "ganged" to obtain the final result. Thus we may write

$$s_3 - s_1 = (s_3 - s_2) + (s_2 - s_1), \text{ etc.}$$

$$v_3 - v_1 = (v_3 - v_2) + (v_2 - v_1) = a_{3\text{-}2}(t_3 - t_2) + a_{2\text{-}1}(t_2 - t_1), \text{ etc.}$$

$$v_3^2 - v_1^2 = (v_3^2 - v_2^2) + (v_2^2 - v_1^2) = 2a_{3\text{-}2}(s_3 - s_2) + 2a_{2\text{-}1}(s_2 - s_1), \text{ etc.}$$

where a_{3-2} is the value of acceleration for step 3–2, and a_{2-1} is its value for step 2–1.

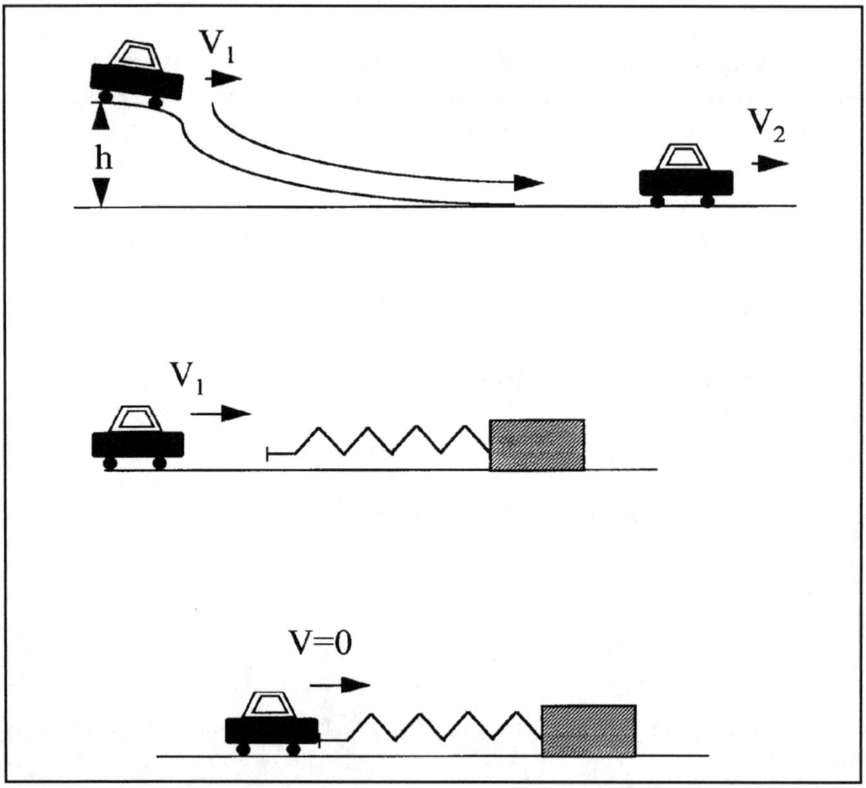

***Figure A.1** Energy conversions*

Angular Acceleration

The fundamental relationship for angular acceleration is

$$Fr = I\ddot{\theta} \quad \text{or} \quad \ddot{\theta} = F\frac{r}{1} = \dot{\omega}$$

where $\ddot{\theta}$ is the angular accel in radians/s² (one radian = 180°/π = 57.3°), r is the torque-arm, and I is the moment of inertia about the rotation point. The angular acceleration can also be defined as $\ddot{\theta} = \dot{\omega}$ where $\dot{\omega}$ is the value of radians/s. Note that the use of two dots (¨) over a symbol means per sec² (/s²), while one dot (˙) means per sec (/s).

Mass-Spring Response

For any system that behaves as a mass on a spring (occupant in the seat, bumper on a car), the equation for an *undamped* oscillation is

$$\omega^2 = \left(\frac{k}{m}\right) = \left(\frac{kg}{W}\right)$$

where ω is the angular oscillation rate (radians/s), k is the spring constant (change in force per unit distance of spring compression), m is the mass and W is the weight.

It is probably not obvious why the response is quoted in terms of angular *motion. To understand more clearly, consider the following.*

Imagine a mass rotating about a pivot at constant local speed with a fixed radial distance from the pivot. As seen "sideways" the body is simply moving in a circle. Now suppose you viewed the circular motion "edge-on" such that the circle collapses to a thin "line" (i.e., you draw the circle on paper and then view the paper edge-on). The rotating body will now appear to move "up and down" along this line. However, since we now see the edge motion the speed appears fastest when the mass is near the middle of the line and slowest when near the two ends. This is *identical* to the observed motion of a mass on a spring.

Going further, suppose two identical masses were *counter-rotating* about a pivot (one clockwise and one counterclockwise), but at the same speed. Let the positioning (known as the *phasing*) be such that the two masses meet each other at the top of the circle and again at the bottom of the circle. Once again, if viewed "edge-on" the two masses would look like *one* mass oscillating "up and down." The "edge view" is of the *components* of the motion, and involve sines and cosines of the true mass(es) positions. For example, when the masses are at the "top" or "bottom" of the circle, they are at either "end" of the straight-line.

At these points the radial lines are seen fully in profile and each "half line" has the length $r = r_0 \sin\theta = r_0$, since $\theta = 90$ degrees. At the center of the "line," however, $r = r_0 \sin\theta = 0$, since $\theta = 0$ degrees.

Thus any *circular* motion can be broken down into equivalent *angular* motion.

The apparent motion of the rotating mass(es) will be of the form

$$r(t) = r_0 \sin(\omega t) = \sin\theta \cdot r_0$$

where $r(t)$ means position from the center of the straight line as a function of time, t, r_0 is the constant true radial distance, ω is the corresponding angular rate (radians/s) and θ is the corresponding angle (radians) measured from the line pointing "at" the observer.

Now, since $\omega = 2\pi f$ where f is the frequency (cycles/s or Hertz), we get

$$f = \left(\frac{1}{2\pi}\right)\sqrt{\frac{kg}{W}}$$

or, since the period $T = 1/f$, we get

$$T = 2\pi\sqrt{\frac{w}{kg}}$$

where the period is in seconds, for a weight in pounds and a spring constant in lb/ft, and g in ft/s^2. Note that the period is for one complete cycle.

Thus, the period increases with the square-root of the weight and inversely with the square-root of the spring constant. So a rigid spring (high spring constant) and a small weight oscillate at a high frequency, and a soft spring and large weight oscillate at a low frequency. These effects are important for understanding how occupants can bounce in their seats. For example, with a rear-ender the person is driven forward with the vehicle *only* because the seat pushes on them. The result is to initially compress the seat. Eventually, the person catches up with the car, at which point the seat is at maximum compression. Then the seat continues to act like a spring and pushes the person forward *faster* than the car. If the seatbelt doesn't lock up quickly (and they frequently *don't* for rear-end collisions) then the occupant can actually hit the steering wheel. The typical time period for these motions is a small fraction of a second.

Compressing a bumper also acts like a spring, and even the crushing response of a car is somewhat spring-like (the car gets stiffer as it crushes). The high stiffness of bumpers and frame relative to the weight of the vehicle cause high frequency response. Consequently, the contact time for many crashes is only about 0.1 to 0.2 second. Because there is nearly always some relaxation of the bumper or frame, the two vehicles nearly always bounce to some extent, causing gaps between them after the collision. Note that unless there is some form of sticking between the vehicles, such as interlocked bumpers, or between the occupant and the seat (tight belt), these motions are really half-cycle oscillations, because the second half does not exist because the bodies come apart after the first half cycle.

Braking Effects

General Factors

If no wheels lock up, a vehicle can be steered provided the lateral forces needed to cause the car to follow a path (curved or otherwise) do not exceed the maximum possible for the tire/road combination. However, once the frictional limit is exceeded then no steering is possible for that tire. This means that the tire in question wants to travel in the direction governed by the rest of the car's motion. If an axle locks up then the axle wants to travel in a direction which either depends on the motion of the rest of the car or on the initial motion of that axle. When all tires lock the entire vehicle travels with its center of mass (CM) moving according to any external forces. Thus, on a flat level road, the CM travels in a straight line, whereas, on a cambered surface the CM follows a path governed by gravity, which usually means the vehicle slides off to the side of the road.

Speed-from-skid analysis can be done based on considerations of the basic equations of motion, or based on energy arguments. Note that energy arguments are the more basic and fundamental.

The standard equation of motion approach is to use

$$v = \sqrt{2fgs}$$

where s is the observed skidmark distance and f is the *net coefficient of friction* or, more properly, the *drag factor*. The drag factor is the overall effective friction between the vehicle and the road. Each individual tire may have a different coefficient of friction, μ, and each wheel may have a differing weight on it of w. Then the total drag on the vehicle is

$$(f\,W) = \Sigma(w\mu) = (w_1\mu_1) + (w_2\mu_2) + (w_3\mu_3) + (w_4\mu_4),$$

where

$$W = w_1 + w_2 + w_3 + w_4.$$

The energy approach is to equate the lost KE with the frictional energy given to the road surface, (i.e., with the product of the drag force and the skid distance).

Thus,

$$KE = \frac{W}{2g}v^2 = fWs$$

which can be rewritten as

$$v^2 = 2fgs$$

which is the same as the equation above. The major advantage of the energy method is that it immediately allows for other energy terms to be included, such as those resulting from crush or change in elevation. For example, if a car first skids and then strikes a rigid barrier to lose crush energy E_c, then we write

$$KE = \frac{W}{2g}v^2 = (fWs)E_c$$

$$v^2 = (2fgs) + \left(\frac{2g}{W}\right)E_c.$$

Thus, by knowing both the skid behavior and the crush energy, the initial speed can be obtained directly.

Number of Tire Tracks

When a car skids there may be anywhere from one to four skidmarks (i.e., up to one per wheel). What does this imply for the net drag factor? Assuming no definite proof of brake failure, or knowledge that an axle does not have brakes, the usual assumption is that those wheels not giving skids are providing at least as much friction as those wheels that are giving skidmarks (but this should be checked).

The logic behind this is that tires will first climb to a maximum in friction, and will then drop in friction as the slip between tire and road increases. Those wheels with the lowest ratio of friction to vertical load will skid first. Thus the assumption is that the tires giving the skidmarks have already passed the limit, whereas, the other tires are just about to reach their limit. This logic then suggests that the longest skidmark is the one to use to establish the pre-skid speed.

Differing Surfaces

Of course, sometimes the various wheels may be on different surfaces known to give different friction. In this case the appropriate value of friction should be applied to each wheel in turn, using the fractional weight of the vehicle on each wheel. An example is when a car is half-off a road with two wheels running on dirt. Another example is when the car sequentially skids across several in-line surfaces. For this case, the energy loss per surface must be computed. Thus

$$E = \frac{W}{2g} v^2 = f_1 W s_1 + f_2 W s_2 + f_3 W s_3 \text{ etc.}$$

$$v^2 = \frac{2g}{W}\left(f_1 W s_1 + f_2 W s_2 + f_3 W s_3\right)$$

$$= 2g\left(f_1 s_1 + f_2 s_2 + f_3 s_3\right)$$

where the f values represent the mean drag factors over the various s distances.

Linear Skids and Yaw Marks

True skidmarks are essentially straight and show striations parallel to the skid. They are caused by the nonrotating tire leaving rubber on the road according to the tread design, or scraping on the asphalt or dirt. When a tire slides sideways with a nonrotating wheel, a skidmark is also left, but the treads are usually less distinct (they can overlap). However, if the tire is rotating and sliding sideways the result is not a true skid but rather a yaw mark.

For a yaw, the mark will show side lines which run *across* the skid. If the wheel is undergoing free rotation (no acceleration or deceleration) these marks are essentially perpendicular to the major longitudinal mark. For a wheel undergoing acceleration along its motion, the side-marks are observed to lean backward relative to the major mark, whereas, for a wheel undergoing deceleration, the side marks lean forward. The reason for these side marks is that the slipping/rotating tire is really screwing its way along the road, and thus the marks are those of a corkscrew. See Figure A.2.

The Friction Circle

As a first approximation it can be assumed that the maximum friction possible between a tire and the road is the *same* regardless of the direction of motion of the tire versus the road (i.e., along the rolling direction or perpendicular to it). This leads to the concept of the *friction circle*. This states that the *net* maximum friction can never exceed an upper limit for a given tire/surface combination, defined as a *radial* vector (see vectors, later). Thus, if the *vector sum* of the longitudinal and transverse frictional forces equal or exceed this radial value, no further increase in friction is possible, regardless of tire direction. This means that if the tire is almost at the longitudinal limit of skidding then any additional side slipping will immediately cause a true skid of the tire in the direction of motion of the vehicle. Likewise, if the side slip force is almost at its limit, then any additional braking effort will also cause a true skid to occur. This is the reason why it can be dangerous to try to sharply steer *and* brake hard at the same time. See Figure A.2.

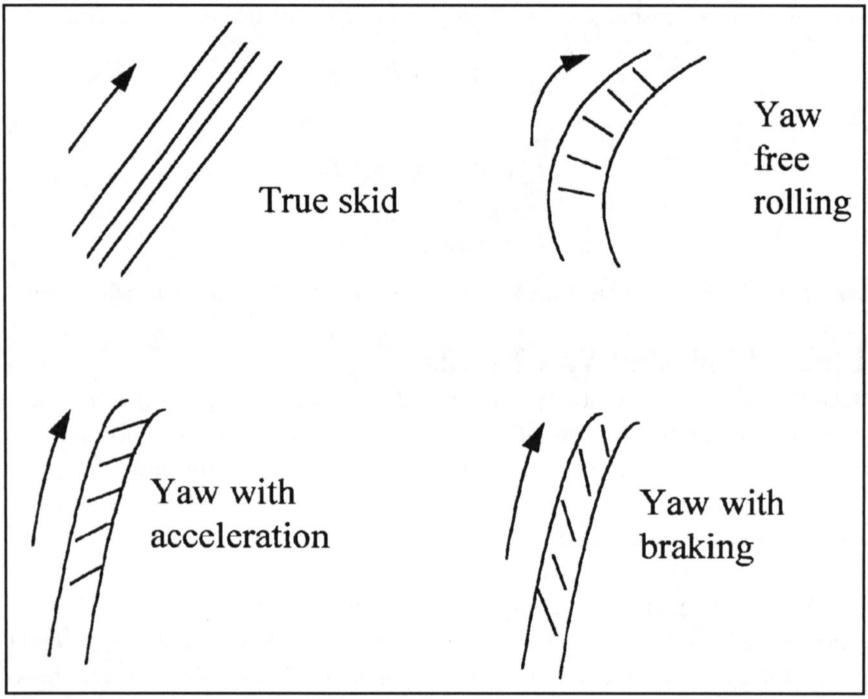

Figure A.2 *Tire marks*

Tracking the Arc

If a car both skids and rotates, the true definition of the skidmark length is that *along* the individual arcs, not merely that along the CM motion of the vehicle. This is because, for a true skid the energy consumed is due to forces which act along the local arc direction. However, frequently the degree of rotation is small relative to the CM distance, and can thus be ignored as a first approximation. If the rotation dominates the total motion, the true arc lengths must be used.

Road Grade and Camber

Usually, most roads have quite low grades such that the latter can be ignored for many cases of skidding. However, when significant the grade can be included by using

$$f_{net} = \frac{\mu - G}{\sqrt{1+G^2}}$$

where f_{net} is the net drag, μ is the true friction and G is the grade. If the vehicle is skidding uphill the value of G is (+), whereas, for skidding downhill G is (–). If

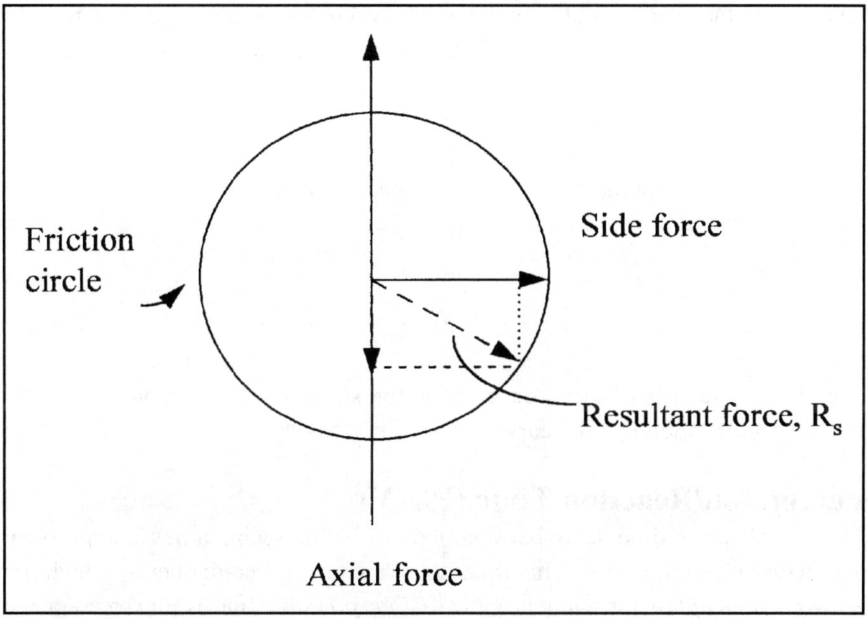

Figure A.3 *Tire/road friction circle*

the road additionally has a significant side camber the result for a skidding car is to produce a gravitational trajectory causing the vehicle to slowly slide sideways off the road, with a path which describes a parabolic section. This parabolic path is really the same as that for a body which falls at the same time as it moves horizontally (see **Flips and Vaults**, later), except that it occurs on a flatter surface rather than involving a truly vertical fall. This simply reduces the effective value of gravity (g) ($g' = g\sin\theta$, where θ is the slope relative to the horizontal).

Critical Yaw Speeds

When a vehicle follows a curved path it does so only because there are side forces acting on the tires which force the vehicle to make the turn (the centripetal forces). These necessary forces will eventually exceed the local maximum value of friction, at which point sideslip yawing will occur. The corresponding maximum speed when this occurs is known as the *critical yaw speed*. Because a force is really a product of mass and acceleration, the critical speed can be understood by considering the lateral accelerations.

When turning a curve at speed v and radius R, it can be shown that the corresponding radial acceleration (centripetal) is given by

$$accel = \frac{v^2}{R} = R\omega^2$$

where ω is the corresponding angular rate of change (radians per second). To cause the tire to follow this curved path, the corresponding side tire force is

$$F = f\,W$$

where ω is the weight and *f* the friction. Then, equating accelerations

$$accel = \frac{v^2}{R} = \frac{F}{m} = \frac{gF}{W}\,gF \text{ and thus}$$

$$v_{crit}^2 = gfR \quad \text{or} \quad v_{crit}^2 = \sqrt{gfR}.$$

Hence, the critical speed depends on the square-root of the product of the friction and the radius of the curve.

Perception/Reaction Time (PIEV)

There is always a time delay between a driver's first seeing a possible problem and actually reacting to it. This time delay has several components, which are known as *perception* (an event is noticed), *interpretation* (the event is recognized as a threat), *evaluation* (the appropriate response is decided) and *volition* (the action is taken, such as applying the brakes). Hence: *PIEV.*

The actual components take differing times, depending on the individual and the circumstances of the situation. Typically, *perception* lasts for about 0.1–0.2 second, whereas *interpretation* takes about 0.2–0.4 second. *Evaluation* can last from 0.2–1.0 second, and depends strongly on the complexity of the situation (e.g., how many options may exist for a solution). *Volition* is the actual act of motion (applying the brakes, or turning the steering wheel) and can take from 0.2–0.5 second. Thus, for a simple reaction (brake or no-brake) the total PIEV is from 0.7–2.1 seconds, with a frequently quoted average of about 1.0 second. All the above quotes assume a reasonably alert driver who is sober. Alcohol can increase these times up to 3–4 seconds. For road design purposes (AASHTO) a response time of 2.5 seconds is frequently used. However, this "long" time is intended to include even slow-witted or partially impaired drivers, and is *not* a true definition of typical response time. See Figure A.4.

Skidmarks at Low Speed

It is frequently assumed that for strongly applied brakes skidmarks can always be created regardless of speed. However, this ignores the timing issues in PIEV. In reality, once the decision to brake is made, the foot is removed from the accelerator and then moved to the brake. As this happens the car begins to slow merely because it is suffering engine drag. Further, even when the foot reaches

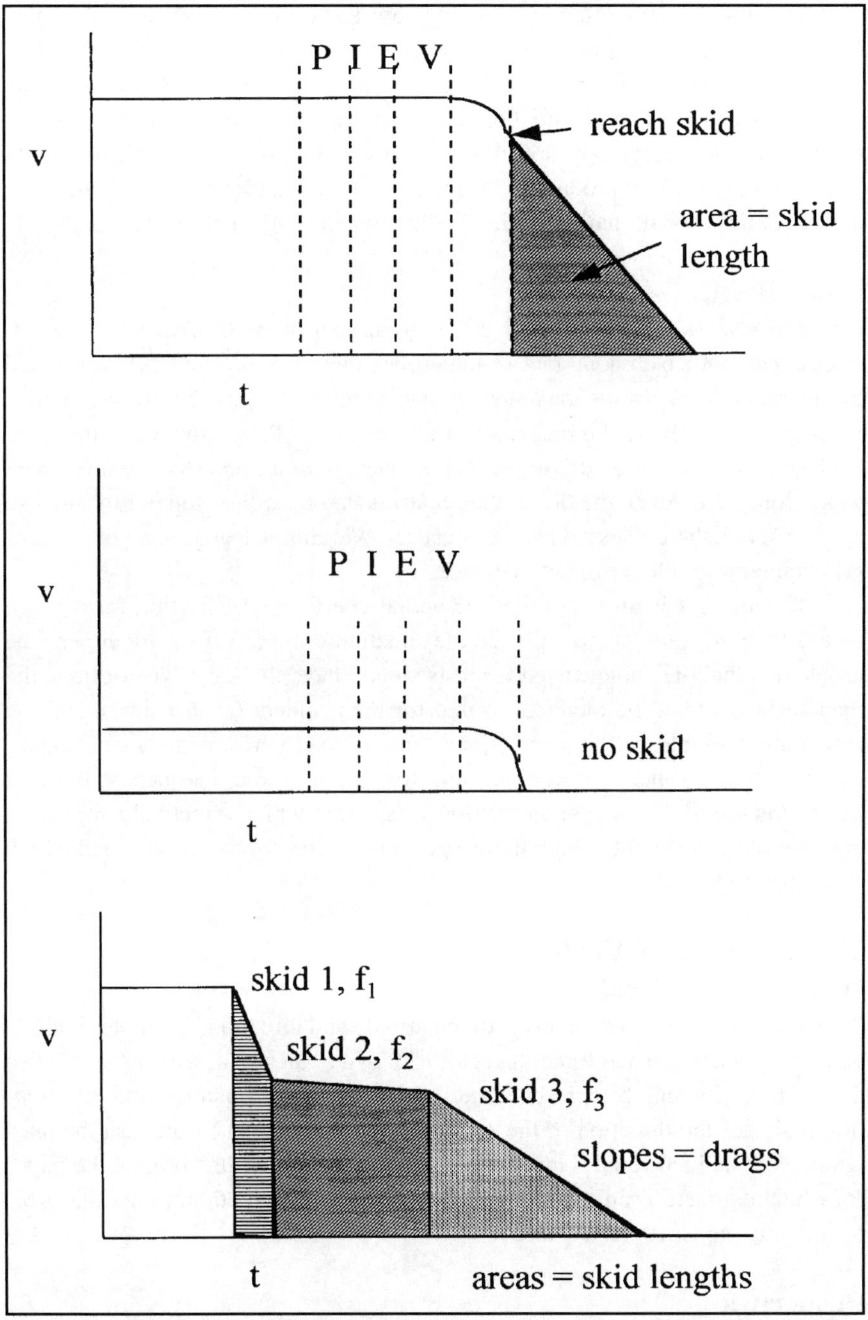

Figure A.4 *Reaction timing and skidding*

the brake, there is still a finite time delay before maximum braking effort can be applied. During these times the car is decelerating. Consequentially, for a slow enough initial speed, it is possible for the car to effectively stop *before* skidding can be induced. To complicate the matter, tire/road friction is usually highest at low speeds. Hence, for slow speeds (below about 3 mph) it is possible to rapidly stop a vehicle *without* producing skidmarks even for attempted very hard braking. Also, tire/asphalt marks require heating which is small at low speeds.

Final Point

It should always be remembered that braking can occur *without* leaving skidmarks. This rather obvious fact is sometimes overlooked. The speed estimated from skidmarks is always the *lowest* possible, since it is possible for the vehicle to have been applying the brakes prior to actual skidding without leaving clear evidence. For example, a driver perceives a need to brake and starts to do so with gentle force. However, the driver then realizes that he won't stop in time, and so then he slams the brakes on hard and causes skidding. Clearly, *none* of the pre-skid behavior will leave direct evidence.

Of course, it is also rare that the actual coefficient of friction for a given case is known. Attempts to replicate the situation don't always work either. The problem is that the vehicle used for tests should have the same type of tires, the road surface should be identical to that for the accident (at that time), and the temperature should be the same (since tire and road performance can change). Lastly, a trial test may wrongly account for reaction time. Frequently, the trial test yields *too high* an apparent friction versus that which effectively applied at the time of the accident, which in turn gives estimates for the crash speed which err on the high side.

The Concept of Vectors

Definition of a Vector

A vector is a quantity which has both magnitude and direction. Examples include velocity, momentum and force. A vector is drawn as an arrow, with a "head" (tip) and a "tail." Its length represents the magnitude of the quantity, and its direction indicates the direction of the quantity. Any convenient "scale" can be used (example: one inch equal 5 lb-s for momentum), and any direction on the paper (or whiteboard, etc.) can represent the initially desired direction (rather like arbitrarily drawing North on a sketch).

Properties

Any vector can be redrawn as a pair of other vectors which are then called *components* of the original vector. The most common use for this is to draw these components as two vectors which are at 90° to each other (i.e., orthogonal), and which have the two components along required orthogonal axes. The converse of this is that any two initial vectors can be drawn to give either the *sum* or the *difference* of the two vectors.

Vector Sum

Two vectors can be summed in the following way. First draw the two vectors with their "tails" joining. Now complete the parallelogram by drawing two "ghost" vectors from the "heads" of the first two vectors such that the two "ghosts" are parallel and equal to the initial two vectors. The result is a parallelogram. The "diagonal" which joins the two mutual "tails" of the first two vectors and the new "head" of the parallelogram gives the *sum* of the two vectors.

Vector Difference

For the same parallelogram, the diagonal which extends between the two heads of the initial vectors gives the *difference* of the two vectors.

Uses of Vectors

Vectors are used whenever directional quantities need to be added or subtracted. Examples include adding forces to find the equivalent net force, adding momenta to establish the net momentum and subtracting velocities to find the effective closing velocity between two moving bodies. In all cases the new information gives both the magnitude and direction. Adding is simply finding the *sum,* whereas subtracting is finding the *difference.*

The most common use for vectors in accident reconstruction is to establish total momentum for a two body collision, and from this, establish the initial speeds and directions of each body before impact.

The Two-Car Crash Using Vectors

Whenever a two-car crash is to be solved there are generally *seven momentum* vectors to be drawn. These are: The two *output momentum* vectors (one per car), the two *input momentum* vectors, the common *total momentum* vector, and the two *difference momentum* vectors. See Figure A.5.

The problem is solved in reverse. From a knowledge of the post-impact vehicle speeds (e.g., based on skidmarks, etc.), vehicle masses and initial directions *leaving* the crash (note: *not* necessarily the same as the overall final directions), the two *output momentum* vectors can be drawn. From these two vectors the *total momentum* vector can be derived (completing the parallelogram).

This *total momentum* vector must remain the same as the one for the *two input momentum* vectors. Thus any choice for these input vectors *must* give the

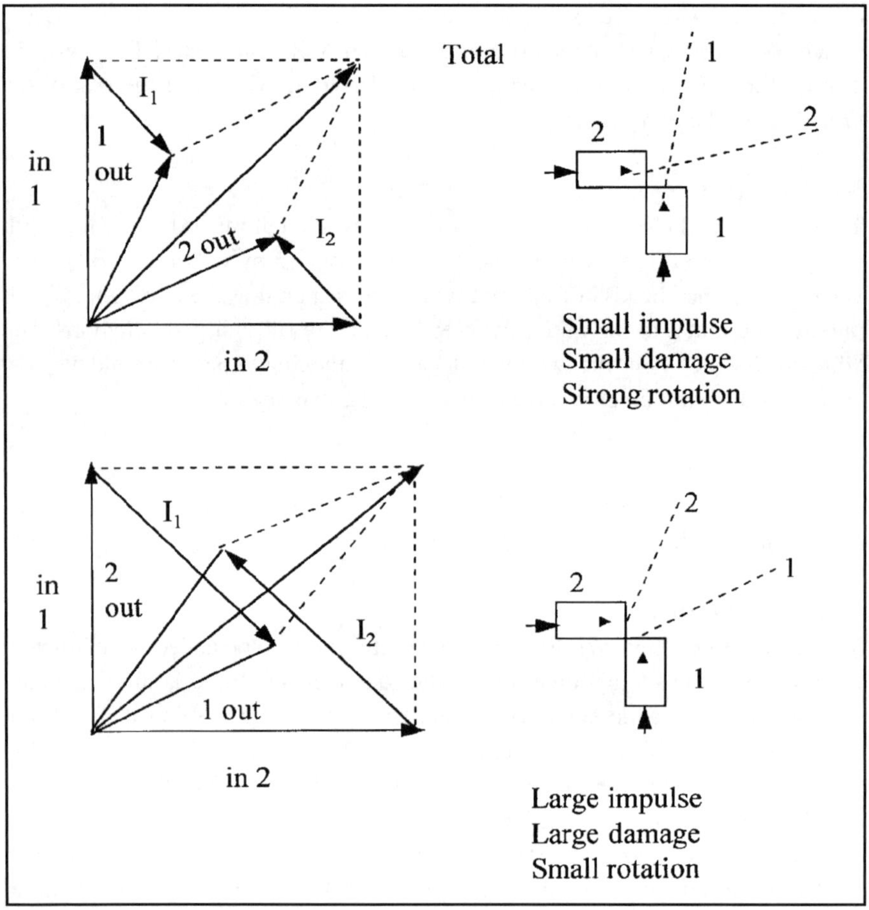

Figure A.5 *Two-vehicle vector-momentum logic*

same final total momentum vector. Usually, at least one of the vehicle's pre-crash motions are known (speed and direction). Thus, for this vehicle an *input momentum* vector can be drawn. Then completing the parallelogram based on the total momentum vector allows deduction of the missing input momentum vector for the other vehicle. Since the vehicle mass is known, the speed and direction are known.

Once the input and output momentum vectors are known, then the *difference* vectors can be derived. These are the vectors that stretch between the "heads" of the "input" and "output" momentum vectors for each vehicle independently. If done properly, it will be found that these two difference vectors are equal in magnitude and opposite in direction (and parallel to each other but not usually collinear). These two difference momentum vectors describe the two *impulses* seen by each vehicle. The direction of these difference vectors defines the principal direction of force (PDOF).

Sometimes, the exact input vector is not known for either vehicle. In this case, an estimate of the PDOF gives details of the direction of the difference vectors. Thus knowing the PDOF can allow estimation of the input conditions since the overall reconstruction must give the difference vectors in accordance with the PDOF, while the total momentum vector also constrains the options.

Trips, Flips, Vaults and Rollovers

Definitions

A *trip* is any general process whereby a vehicle is rapidly decelerated at the contact point between the wheels and ground, such that the vehicle proceeds to start a spin. If the resulting spin involves little lift off the ground then it is usually a form of *rollover*, especially for sideways rotation. If the result is to launch significantly into the air then for a side rotation it is called a *flip*, whereas, for an end-over-end rotation it is called a *vault*.

Side Rolls (Rollovers)

A vehicle can only roll over sideways (about its longitudinal axis) if the rotational turning torque is greater than the restoring gravitational torque. For a side-slip motion on a road the side force is that caused by the tire friction and equal to $F = f\,W$. This force acts as one through the CM together with a torque of $Fh = fWh$, where h is the height above the ground of the CM. The restoring gravitational torque is $W \times T/2$, where T is the track width. Thus, to cause rolling we need

$$fWh \geq W\frac{T}{2} \quad \text{or} \quad f \geq \frac{T}{2h}.$$

For *most* cars $T > 2h$, and so the vehicle *cannot* roll simply because of side friction, because f is almost always *less* than 1.0. However, some sport utility vehicles have unusually high CMs and small wheel tracks. For these vehicles a high value of side friction *can* initiate a roll. Once a roll starts the situation rapidly becomes uncontrollable. This is because, as the vehicle tips over (balancing on only one set of wheels on one side) the CM rises which increases the turning torque, while the effective track width decreases owing to the inclination of the vehicle. Thus, for a rotation about the side wheels we have

$$R^2 = h_0^2 + \left(\frac{T_0}{2}\right)^2$$

where R is the diagonal between the side wheel/road and the CM. This defines an initial angle for this diagonal relative to the road surface. See Figure A.6.

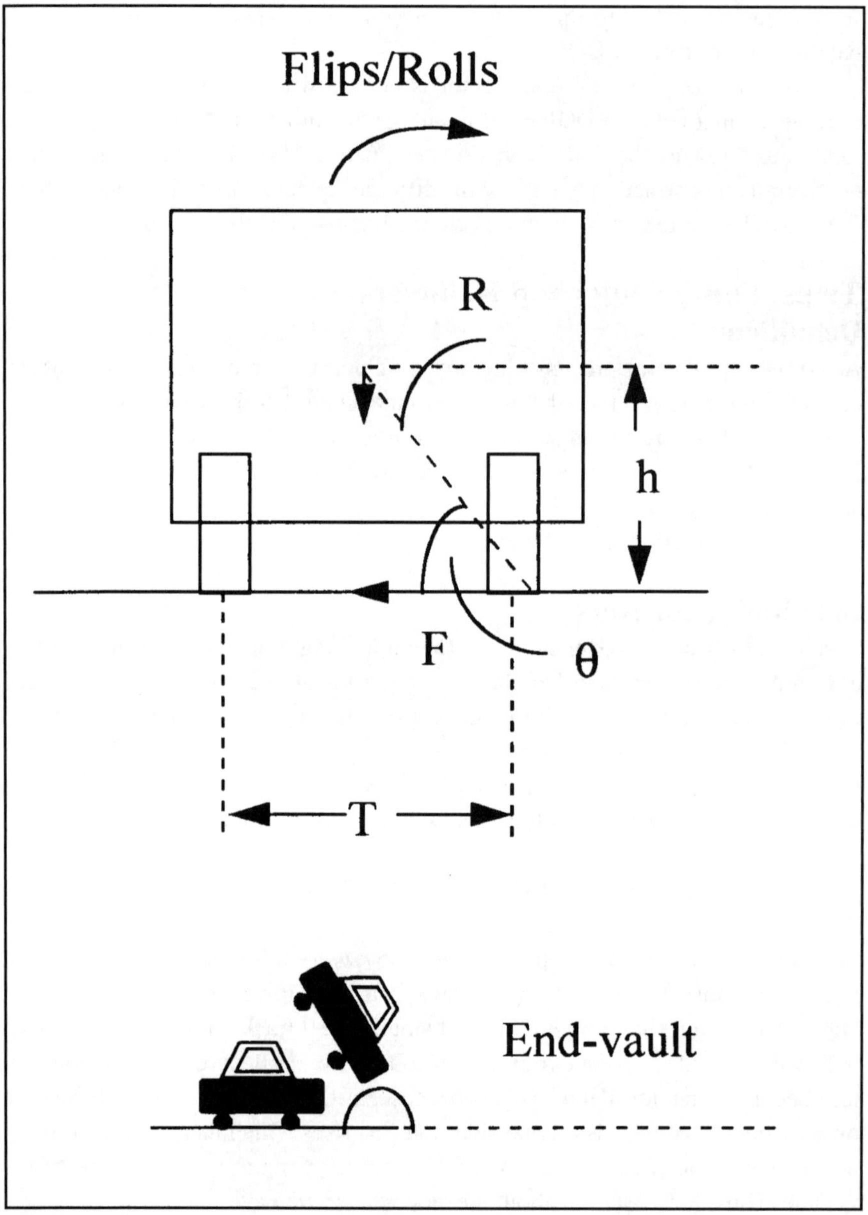

Figure A.6 *Roll logic*

$$\sin\theta = \frac{h_0}{R} \quad \text{or} \quad h_0 = R\sin\theta_0 \quad \text{and} \quad \frac{T_0}{2} = R\cos\theta_0$$

where h_0 and $T_0/2$ are the true initial values before rolling. As rolling progresses, the value of θ increases causing the local value of *h* to increase while the local value of *T*/2 decreases. Therefore, the situation becomes ever less stable, and can only be corrected by *very fast countermeasures,* such as a quick counter-steer.

However, if the vehicle impacts a *rigid low object* (e.g., a curb) then the effective value of *f* is much larger than simple friction. For this case a roll can easily be induced. The limit to cause a complete roll is given by the condition that the vehicle's KE sideways be greater than the energy needed to lift the CM to a vertical position above the side wheels. This "lift" is simply $H = R - h_0$, and the corresponding change in PE is *WH.* Thus, the car can roll if

$$\frac{W}{2g}v_{CM}^2 \geq WH = W(R - h_0) = W\left[\sqrt{h_0^2 + \frac{T_0^2}{4}} - h_0\right]$$

$$v_{CM}^2 \geq 2g\left[\sqrt{h_0^2 + \frac{T_0^2}{4}} - h_0\right].$$

If this condition is not reached the car will start to rise but will not complete the roll. The velocity is the one perpendicular to the curb. Similar effects occur if the curb is replaced with a rut, or with anything which can suddenly stop the wheel side motion.

Ordinarily, merely steering a vehicle around a curve will not induce a roll because the maximum side force is still limited by tire friction. However, the situation can occur if the vehicle turns in an uphill direction when on a sloped road. For example, let a vehicle be traveling north on a road which leans down toward the east. The vehicle makes a sharp left turn to the west. The vehicle will transfer weight to the right-hand wheels. However, because of the initial lean, the CM will be higher than normal with respect to these RH wheels, while the effective track width will also be shorter than normal. This is equivalent to altering the initial value of the angle θ. Thus a vehicle which is normally stable on a horizontal road may become unstable on a sloped road. This effect is quite common for off-road driving where a vehicle may try to go sideways up a dirt hill and then turn sharply in the up direction.

Vaults

A similar forward flip can occur if the front of the vehicle is suddenly stopped by a low rigid object (a high curb or large rock). This object must be sufficiently high to prevent the front wheels from simply riding up over the obstacle. For such a forward flip the half-wheel base is involved instead of the half-track width. Since the wheel base is usually significantly longer than the track width, the ability to flip is less than for a side flip.

For sufficiently high impact speed these flips may cause the vehicle to become airborne, in which case we have a *vault*. Except for very high speeds where air-drag must be included (usually above 50 mph) the trajectory is governed by gravity. The path followed by the vehicle is a *ballistic trajectory.* Let the motion involve an initial speed of v_0 at an angle θ to the horizontal. The velocity vector has two components, namely, a vertical velocity of $v_v = v_0 \sin\theta$ and a horizontal velocity of $v_h = v_0 \cos\theta$. The vertical velocity will be reduced to zero by gravity in the time $t = v_v/g$. During this time the vehicle CM will rise a distance given by the energy balance equation

$$\frac{W}{2g}(v_0 \sin\theta)^2 = WH \quad \text{or} \quad H = \frac{v_0^2 \sin\theta}{2g}$$

while the horizontal distance moved is given by

$$D = v_0 \cos\theta \frac{v_0}{g} \sin\theta = \frac{v_0}{g} \sin\theta \cos\theta.$$

For a flat horizontal ground this will describe the half-trajectory. Thus, the time to return to the ground is the same as the rise time, and the total horizontal distance moved before re-impacting the ground is $2D$. Thus the total distance is

$$D_{total} = \frac{2v_0^2}{g} \sin\theta \cos\theta.$$

It is easily shown that the product sinθcosθ is a maximum when θ = 45°, with a value

$$\sqrt{\frac{1}{2}} \times \sqrt{\frac{1}{2}} = \frac{1}{2}$$

Thus,

$$D_{total,Max} = \frac{v_0^2}{g}$$

This equation then gives the *lowest* speed necessary to produce a given total horizontal motion. For any other launch angle the speed must increase. In the absence of a known launch angle the value of 45° is frequently assumed in order to obtain conservative speeds.

If the ground is not level, such that the launch point is above the fall point by an amount Δ, then the two half-trajectories must be calculated separately. For example, if the fall point is lower than the launch point the time taken to fall is

$$H + \Delta = \frac{g}{2} t_{fall} \quad \text{or} \quad t_{fall} = \sqrt{\frac{2(H + \Delta)}{g}}$$

and during this time the horizontal motion is $v_0\, t_{fall} \cos \theta$, etc. If the fall point is higher than the launch point we simply use $H - \Delta$ instead.

All the above treats the motion of the vehicle CM (i.e., we treat the vehicle as if it were a "point-mass"). This works fine provided the vertical motions are large compared to the vehicle's dimensions. If not, then we should include the effects of any vehicle rotation (especially forward pitching), since the impact point may be on the nose instead of the wheels. In this case the CM is higher off the ground at impact. Some form of forward pitching always occurs, whether a result of impacting a low rigid obstacle before launch or simply because the front wheels leave the ground before the back wheels do. Once the front wheels leave the ground the vehicle is balanced only on its back axle. Hence, gravity starts a forward pitch about the rear axle, and an angular acceleration (nose-down) occurs. This acceleration stops when the rear axle leaves the ground, at which point the vehicle has developed a steady angular rotation rate. The total angle seen by the vehicle before re-striking the ground is simply the product of this rotation rate and the time taken to reach the ground. Thus,

$$\ddot{\theta} = W \frac{L}{I}$$

where L is the torque-arm equal to the distance between the CM and the back axle, and I is the moment of inertia for a *pitch motion about the rear axle*. Then

$$\dot{\theta} = \ddot{\theta} t = W \left(\frac{L}{I} \right) \left(\frac{WB}{v} \right)$$

where WB is the wheel base and v is the road velocity, and t_{rot} is the time between the front axle leaving the ground and the rear axle doing so. To this we must also add the angle achieved during the acceleration, which is

$$\theta = \left(\frac{W}{2} \right) \left(\frac{L}{I} \right) \left(\frac{WB}{v} \right) \left(\frac{WB}{v} \right).$$

Finally,

$$\theta = \dot{\theta} t_{fall}$$

where t_{fall} is the total fall time, and is the total rotation.

Combined Flight and Skid

Sometimes a body suffers a flight followed by a skid. An example is when a pedestrian is knocked forward by a car. The body first flies in an airborne trajectory and then finally comes to a halt by skidding. Let the drop height for the pedestrian's CM be H, and the friction on the ground be *f*, and the induced initial horizontal velocity be *v*. Then we first compute the fall time and then the horizontal motion during the fall. Upon hitting the ground the body still has the same horizontal velocity. We next compute the resulting skid. The flight plus skid then give the total horizontal motion from the point of impact (POI). Thus,

$$t_{fall} = \sqrt{\frac{2H}{g}}, \quad D_{Horiz} = v\sqrt{\frac{2H}{g}}, \quad D_{skid} = \frac{v^2}{2gf}, \quad D_{total} = D_{Horiz} + D_{skid}.$$

Thus,

$$\left(\frac{v^2}{2gf}\right) + \left(\sqrt{\frac{2H}{g}}v\right) - D_{Total} = 0.$$

Compare with

$$Av^2 + Bv + C = 0.$$

This is a *quadratic* equation, with the solution

$$v = -\frac{B}{2A} \pm \frac{\sqrt{B^2 - 4AC}}{2A}$$

where

$$A = \frac{1}{2gf} \quad \text{and} \quad B = \sqrt{\frac{2H}{g}} \quad \text{and} \quad C = -D_{total}.$$

In reality, since we need a positive solution, the term is always +.

Sun Position

Sometimes a crash occurs in which a driver claims he was blinded by the sun. Consequently, it is necessary to verify the sun's position. A site visit will allow knowledge of such factors as direction and inclination of the road(s). This visit can be done whenever convenient. However, unless the visit is made on the anniversary of the accident (or at least within a few days) it will not be possible to *directly* determine the position of the sun. The latter such visit is very inconvenient, and thus frequently there is a need to compute the appropriate sun position. The following equations allow this to be done with an accuracy of a few degrees (or a time of a few minutes), which is more than sufficient for most practical purposes.

First we define three axes, X, Y and Z. These represent the local axes of north-south, east-west and vertical (the local zenith). Next the position on the earth's surface is needed. The latter requires the value of local latitude (LAT) and local longitude. The latter is defined in terms of time, in particular the time before or after local true noon. Lastly, the inclination of the earth's axis needs to be known. Because of the tilt of the earth's axis of about 23.5 degrees to the plane of the earth's orbit, this declination (DEL) varies sinusoidally throughout the year, with the sun's maximum altitude climbing to a peak in summer, when it apparently stops (or stands), and then decreasing again to apparently stop at a minimum. In summer (northern hemisphere) the north pole leans toward the sun such that the sun is highest in the sky on the summer solstice (about June 21). The reverse is true for winter, and the sun is lowest on the winter solstice (about December 21). Midway between these solstices ("sun standing") we have the eqinoxes ("equal nights") where the axis is perpendicular to the orbit and each night equals 12 hours, the same as each daylight period.

Latitude can be read from any good map or obtained from various almanacs (better still a GPS system can be used at the site: Global Positioning System receivers are rapidly becoming much cheaper, with simple ones about $100). Longitude can be obtained similarly. However, two "corrections" must be made for longitude in terms of local noon timing. The first is a correction for Daylight Savings Time, whereby local time is shifted by one hour relative to true time during the summer months (April though October) in most (but not all; e.g., Arizona) of the states. Thus during summer local noon would be a clock time of 1:00 P.M. The second more subtle correction concerns true longitude versus the local time zone.

In reality there are even more subtle corrections. For example, the earth's axis undergoes a *nutational wobble* (rather like a child's spinning top is observed to wobble). Likewise, the leap year is ignored in this set of calculations. Also, because a day is not truly 24 hours, local time can be fast or slow relative to clock time. Lastly, there is even an odd correction because of the earth's atmosphere (see below). While these corrections are very important for astronomical purposes, they have no significance for our purpose of working out roughly where the sun is.

Since the earth rotates 360 degrees in 24 hours each hour represents 15 degrees of longitude, and each degree of longitude represents 4 minutes. Within the U.S., time zones are usually based on "chunks" of 15-degree widths relative to the zero meridian (the longitude through Greenwich in London, U.K.). For example, Albuquerque is in the Mountain Time Zone. This zone is 7 hours behind London. Thus local noon would correspond to $7 \times 15 = 105$ degrees west longitude. However, since each time zone has a finite width very few places within the zone are exactly at 105 degrees W. The official center of Albuquerque is at about 35° 05' N (which is 35.083° N) and 106° 38' W (which is 106.63° W). Thus

Albuquerque is 1.63 degrees farther W than true local clock time. This means that the true local noon really occurs about $1.63 \times 4 = 6.52$ minutes *later* than the clock time.

For example, if the clock reads 2:30 P.M. in summer (DST), the real time is 1:30 P.M. and the true *local time* is [1:30 P.M. – 0:06.52 P.M.] = 1:23.48 P.M. Thus we are [60 + 23.48] = 83.48 minutes post local true noon. This time relative to true local noon will be called MINUTES.

To compute the sun's position we now use

$$\text{TIM} = \text{MINUTES}/4$$

$$\text{DEL} = 23.5 \times \sin(0.986 \times (\text{DAY} - 81.25))$$

where DAY is the day of the year starting on January 1 = DAY 1. (Any calendar or almanac can give this).

$$\text{ZA} = \cos(\text{LAT}) \times \cos(\text{DEL}) \times \cos(\text{TIM}) + \sin(\text{LAT}) \times \sin(\text{DEL})$$

$$\text{YA} = -\cos(\text{DEL}) \times \sin(\text{TIM})$$

$$\text{XA} = \sin(\text{LAT}) \times \cos(\text{DEL}) \times \cos(\text{TIM}) - \cos(\text{LAT}) \times \sin(\text{DEL})$$

Then

$$\text{AZI} = \alpha\text{tan}(\text{XA}/\text{YA})$$

$$\text{ALT} = \alpha\text{tan}(\text{ZA}/(\text{XA}^2 + \text{YA}^2)^{1/2})$$

Here, AZI is the local azimuthal angle, which is the angle of the sun, north (+) or south (–), relative to the local east-west axis. ALT is the local altitude of the sun measured up from the horizon (here we mean the nautical or geometric horizon, such as seen at sea from sea level, and we ignore local perturbations due to mountains, trees, etc.). The nautical horizon is really an extension of the local tangent to the earth's curvature.

However, a subtle correction is necessistated by the atmosphere. Without any atmosphere the sun would indeed set at the nautical horizon. But the atmosphere behaves like a lens and causes refraction of the sunlight (the same effect causes mirages). The result is that the sun can still be seen even though it is actually below the horizon. This bending of light is greatest just near sunset or sunrise (the light travels through a large distance in the atmosphere) and minimal near noon (the light is passing down through a thinner path of atmosphere). These effects are also linked to light scatter (Rayleigh scattering). Since short wavelengths (blue) are scattered more than long wavelengths (red) the sky looks blue (side scatter of light) and the setting (or rising) sun looks red (minimal scatter of sunlight along the long path of the light). This light bending means that the apparent sunset occurs a few minutes after/before geometrical sunset/sunrise. This effect is only important very close to sunset/sunrise. It is also more important at low elevations than for high elevations (the setting sun looks much more red at sea level than in Albuquerque, which is at about 5,000 feet). It has very little effect on the azimuth angle, but it does shift (delay) the apparent time for sunset and the altitude angle. Note also that this lens effect explains why the sun (and moon) look larger when very close to sunrise and sunset (moonrise and moonset).

To illustrate these equations consider the calculation of sunset in Albuquerque on midsummer's day. At sunset we clearly have ALT = 0.0 degrees. From the previous equations we then get

$$\cos(\text{TIM}) = -\tan(\text{LAT}) \times \tan(\text{DEL})$$

For Albuquerque this gives

$$\cos(\text{TIM}) = -\tan(35.083) \times \tan(23.5) = -0.3054$$

Hence, TIM = 107.8 and so MINUTES = 4 × TIM = 431.1 minutes past noon.

This is 7 hours 11.1 minutes past noon. However, in June Albuquerque is on DST, so the clock will read 8 hours 11.1 minutes. Finally, the longitude correction adds a further 6.52 minutes to give a final clock time of about 8.18 P.M. The atmosphere delays apparent sunset by a few more minutes.

However, substitution into the equations now gives the azimuthal angle of about 29.16 degrees north of west. By sequential substitution into the equations we get the sun positions as a function of time *pre-sunset* on the summer solstice in Albuquerque, NM, as shown in Table A.1.

We see that near sunset the azimuthal angle changes slowly, as does the altitude. This explains the observation that the sun appears to "home in" to the horizon at almost 45 degrees on Midsummer Day (June 24th). Also note how the sun is in the northern hemisphere for about 3.5 hours before sunset. With sunset at clock time of 8.18 P.M. DST, the sun is due west at about 4.51 P.M. DST. True Local Noon is at 1.065 P.M. DST.

"Blinding" of a driver depends on exactly where he is looking, and also on how clean his windshield is. A dirty windshield will cause light scatter. Such

Table A.1

Time Pre-sunset (mins)	Altitude (°)	Azimuth (°)	
0.0	0.0	+29.16	N of W
2.0	0.36	+28.87	
7.0	1.26	+28.16	
12.0	2.17	+27.45	
16.0	2.89	+26.90	
60.0 (1 hr)	11.12	+21.01	
120.0 (2 hrs)	22.84	+13.47	
180.0 (3 hrs)	34.92	+5.96	N of W
207.0 (3 hrs 27 m)	43.93	0.00	Due W
240.0 (4 hrs)	47.18	–2.34	S of W
300.0 (5 hrs)	59.33	–13.25	
noon	78.50	–90.0	Due S

scatter causes the direct view to dim while the background apparently lights up. The result is a much poorer contrast and resolution. This effect is well known for night driving, such as when staring into the bright headlights of an oncoming car. A dim object (such as a darkly clothed pedestrian) off to the side of the car will frequently appear to vanish into the glowing windshield, a potentially dangerous situation. Since such scatter effects are rarely known with any precision it is rare that we need to know the exact position of the sun within better than a few degrees. The equations given here will suffice for most such needs.

The Transition from a Rollover to a Flip

We previously indicated how a sudden stop (or slowing) of the wheels for sideways motion can lead to a rollover. To merely roll the lateral speed needs to be

$$v_0^2 \geq 2g\left[\sqrt{\left(h_0^2 + \frac{T_0^2}{4}\right)} - h_0\right]$$

where h_0 is the CM height above the ground (assumed horizontal), T_0 is the track width and v_0 is the initial horizontal speed. These parameters also define an initial angle, θ, given by $\sin\theta = h_0/R$ and $\cos\theta = T_0/2R$, where R is the diagonal distance between the rotation point and the vehicle CM. Thus,

$$R = \sqrt{\left(h_0^2 + \frac{T_0^2}{4}\right)}.$$

This critical speed is quite low. For example, if $h_0 = 2.0$ feet and $T_0 = 6.0$ feet, the speed is about 10.2 ft/s = 6.93 mph. The value of $R = 3.606$ feet, and $\theta = 33.7$ degrees. This roll speed assumes sudden stopping of the sideways wheel motion enough to just cause the vehicle CM to rise vertically over the leading wheel/ground contact point. Clearly, for this case of "just toppling" the kinetic energy of the vehicle drops to roughly zero when the CM is at maximum height, and the initial kinetic energy simply trades with the potential energy involved in lifting the CM.

Conversely, for much higher speeds the vehicle develops an airborne flight known as a flip. However, many rollovers involve speeds greater than the simple roll case yet still low enough to prevent significant flight. This is the transition region.

To understand the transition consider that the initial horizontal motion is converted into rotational energy via the equation

$$\frac{wv_0^2}{2g} = \frac{I\omega^2}{2} \text{ where } I_{contact} = \frac{w}{g}k^2$$

is the moment of inertia of the vehicle about the contact point, and ω is the induced spin rate (radians/s), and k is the radius of gyration about the rotation point. This ignores local energy losses due to bent wheels and the like. The inertia relative to the rotational contact point is approximately

$$I_{contact} = \frac{w}{g}\left(W^2 + H^2\right)/3$$

where W is the width (roughly the same as the track, at least within the accuracy of this analysis) and H is the height. Thus we get

$$\omega^2 = \frac{3v_0^2}{\left(W^2 + H^2\right)}.$$

The corresponding local tangential CM speed is now $v_{CM} = R\omega$ and is on a path directed upward at the angle θ versus the vertical. This combination of CM speed and angled motion imply that the vehicle has the potential to undergo airborne flight. For example, let $W = 6.0$ feet and $H = 5.5$ feet. Then $R = 3.606$ feet, and $\omega = 0.213v$, so $v_{CM} = 0.767v_0$.

The corresponding vertical and horizontal components of the CM speed are given by the product of v_{CM} and the cosine and sine of the angle, respectively. These values are $v_{vert} = v_{CM}\cos\theta = 0.767\, v_0 \cos\theta = 0.638v_0$ and $v_{hor} = 0.767v_0 \sin\theta = 0.425v_0$. If these motions were applied to a *point mass* they would immediately imply the possibility of the parabolic flight path. However, because a real vehicle has finite lateral dimensions true flight can only occur if no part of the vehicle contacts the ground. In essence we need to compare the two possible motions of the vehicle CM. Whereas the flight involves the parabolic path the simple roll involves a path which is just part of a circle. At low speed the parabola drops under the circle, and the CM does not "fly." At greater speeds the parabola rises above the circle and "flight" starts.

For a true roll the vehicle will first impact the ground on its leading roof edge and then can proceed to roll onto its roof, and beyond. However, when in the transition region it becomes possible for the vehicle to lift sufficiently for this leading edge to rotate under the CM without ground contact. For this case it is common for the trailing roof edge to contact first. Since the vehicle simultaneously has greater energy such a hit is also more dramatic. Indeed, such impacts are the most common for moderate speeds. Of course, if the speed is much higher then the lift can allow significant angular rotation while in the air. Precisely which surface then first impacts depends on the details of timing for the spin versus the parabolic trajectory and the geometry of the vehicle.

In the same way as we defined R to be the diagonal between the initial rotation point (wheel on ground) and the CM, so we can define Q as the corresponding diagonal from the roof edge to the CM. This is given by

$$Q = \sqrt{(H - h_0)^2 + \frac{W^2}{4}}.$$

For our previous quoted geometry this gives $Q = 4.61$ feet. This distance allows us to consider a circumscribed circle about the CM which includes both the leading and trailing roof edges versus the CM. To avoid the first hit being on the leading edge the CM must lift by the amount $\Delta = (Q - h_0)$. To achieve this the energy balance must account for the vertical flight of the CM, the horizontal flight of the CM *and* the rotational kinetic energy of the body. The latter is due to rotation about the CM rather than about the contact point. This is because once the vehicle starts its flight there are no external forces acting which can alter the rotation (ignoring air-drag problems). So immediately upon "stopping" the lateral wheel motion the vehicle suffers an induced spin (ω) and then starts to lift, but maintains this spin rate. But spinning about the CM reduces the moment of inertia versus the spin about the contact point. Now the inertia is approximated by

$$I_{CM} = \frac{w}{g}\frac{\left(W^2 + H^2\right)}{12}$$

and thus the associated kinetic energy decreases. The energy balance becomes

$$\frac{w}{2g}v_0^2 = KE_{vertical} + KE_{horizontal} + KE_{spin}.$$

To reach the maximum vertical height which exceeds Δ we then get

$$\frac{w}{2g}v_0^2 \geq 2g\Delta + \frac{w}{2g}v_{horizontal}^2 + \frac{1}{2}I_{CM}\omega^2.$$

Substituting for the CM horizontal speed, the inertia about the CM and the initial induced spin rate we obtain

$$v_0^2 \geq \frac{8}{3}g\Delta\left(\frac{W^2+H^2}{H^2}\right).$$

Hence, for our given geometry we get $v_0^2 = 2.667 \times 32.2 \times (4.61 - 2.0) \times (2.19) = 490.8\ (\text{ft/s})^2$. Thus, $v_0 = 22.16$ ft/s = 15.1 mph. This is the minimum speed to guarantee that the leading roof edge does not contact first and instead the trailing roof edge hits first. It also assumes a horizontal ground surface. We see that there is a "speed window" between just rolling and partial flight with first landing on the trailing roof edge. For a tall narrow vehicle (e.g., an eighteen-wheeler) the probability of a simple roll can be high, but the probability of the trailing roof hit is low. Large trucks simply crash onto their leading edges. Conversely, for a short wide vehicle (e.g., a racing car) the probability of a roll is low, but, once started, the probability of the trailing roof hit is high. Indeed, NASCAR races regularly demonstrate this. Although these cars rarely roll, once they do it is common for them to spin in the air, and the "speed window" between roll and spin is quite narrow.

The Break-Away Pole Problem

An interesting problem is that of a car impact into a tall pole (such as a lamppost). Modern poles are designed to break away at the base once the exerted force climbs past a relatively low value. Clearly, the designer must ensure the pole can survive forces and bending moments due to high-speed winds. However, once the contact force increases the pole shears off its base and becomes free. The result is to knock the pole forward and to simultaneously cause a vertical spin, with the base rising and the top falling. The CM of the pole will also move on a parabolic arc, since the CM is moving forward and also dropping under gravity. Usually the top of the pole hits the ground first, and then the pole reverses its spin and falls to the ground. However, this takes time, and during this time the car can often continue to move forward. The result can be that the car "escapes" from the falling pole.

To analyze this assume the pole has a length L and a true weight w_P. Assume the pole is of uniform mass/length, and that the hit-point is very low so that the torque-arm (r) is effectively $r = L/2$ from the pole CM. For the free pole the radius of gyration is given by $k_P^2 = L^2/12$. For this offset hit the apparent pole weight is

$$w'_P = \frac{w_P}{1+\dfrac{r^2}{k_P^2}} = \frac{w_P}{4}$$

and the common-speed at the hit-point is given by

$$v_{HIT} = \frac{w_c}{w_c + w'_P} v_0$$

where w_C is the car weight and v_0 is the car speed.

Then the pole CM speed is

$$v_{CM} = \frac{v_{HIT}}{1+\dfrac{r^2}{k_P^2}} = \frac{v_{HIT}}{4}$$

and the spin-rate of the pole is

$$\omega = \frac{v_{HIT} - v_{CM}}{r} = \frac{3v_{HIT}}{4}\frac{2}{L}.$$

However, as the pole spins its top drops by

$$x_1 = \left(\frac{L}{2}\right)(1 - \cos\omega\theta)$$

above the pole CM, while the CM itself drops by $x_2 = 0.5gt^2$.

So the top of the rod hits the ground when $L = x_1 + x_2$. To solve for time we have

$$L = 0.5gt^2 + \left(\frac{L}{2}\right)(1 - \cos\omega t).$$

During this time (t) the car moves forward by the distance $x_C = v_{HIT}t$, while the foot of the pole moves forward by $x_{P,FOOT} = v_{CM}\, t + (L/2)\sin(\omega t)$.

Example

Let the car weigh 3,000 pounds and be moving at 44 ft/s (30 mph). Let the pole weigh 400 pounds and have a length of 30 feet. Then the apparent pole weight is 400/4 = 100 pounds. The common hit-point speed now becomes 42.58 ft/s (29.06 mph), so the car only slows slightly, and will thus suffer only moderate damage. Treating this problem as a two-car crash (3,000 pounds into 100 pounds, and setting the "bumper speed" of the pole to zero, the change in energy is about 2,909 ft-lbs which gives about 3.1 inches of crush if the damage area is about 50 percent (= F) of the frontal width of the car, with $R = 0.6$ and $a = 0.5$ foot. If $F = 1.0$ (full-width hit) the crush would be about 1.8 inches, while for $F = 0.25$ (narrow pole hit) the crush would be about 5.3 inches. The CM forward speed of the pole becomes 10.65 ft/s (7.26 mph). The induced spin-rate is now given as ω = 2.129 radians/s = 122 degrees/s.

The time for the top of the pole to reach the ground is t = 0.847 second, during which the spin-angle becomes 103.3 degrees, and the CM of the pole has dropped by 11.55 feet. So the total drop of the top of the pole is 18.45 feet from rotation and 11.55 feet from gravitational fall, which is 30 feet, equal to the initial height. At this same time the foot of the pole has risen by 18.45 feet due to rotation but also dropped by 11.55 feet due to the fall. So the net height of the foot of the pole is 6.9 feet.

During this same time the car has moved about 36.07 feet. The foot of the pole has moved forward by 9.02 feet due to the induced hit and a further 14.6 feet due to the rotation, giving a total forward motion of 23.62 feet. Thus, for this case the car is 12.45 feet ahead of the pole, and has thus escaped being hit by the pole on its roof. This escape is actually even better, since some additional time is needed before the pole finally completely falls to the ground.

Rear-End Impact Calculations

Let the front vehicle (target) be 1, while the one behind (bullet) is 2. At time t = 0.0, let the speeds be v_1 and v_2 (ft/s), let the gap between the vehicles be Δ (feet), and let the perception/reaction time (P/R) for driver 2 be τ (seconds). At t = 0.0 the first driver brakes at the rate a_1 (ft/s^2), while driver 2 subsequently brakes at a_2 but only after his P/R time (if at all). At impact, the two vehicle speeds are v_1' and v_2', respectively, and $v_{impact} = (v_2' - v_1')$.

There are two optional equations describing the collision. These are:

$$\text{Option A.}\quad v_{impact} = \sqrt{\left(v_1 - v_2 - a_2\tau\right)^2 - 2\left(a_2 - a_1\right)\left(\frac{1}{2}a_2\tau^2 + \Delta\right)}$$

$$\text{Option B.}\quad v_2' = \sqrt{2a_2\left(v_2\tau - \Delta\right) + v_2^2 - \left(\frac{a_2}{a_1}\right)v_1^2 + \left(\frac{a_2}{a_1}\right)v_1'^2}$$

Option A is the more generic version and should be used for cases where the first vehicle is still moving when hit (thus it should be used for higher-speed rearenders). Option B requires knowledge of v_1' (the first vehicle speed when hit). Frequently this is not always known in advance. However, if the first vehicle is known to have stopped (or almost stopped) we can set v_1' = 0.0. This then gives $v_2' = v_{impact}$.

To use either equation some degree of common sense is required. For example, if both vehicles are at high speed and very close the *wrong* approach would be to use a large value for P/R (= τ) in option A. Instead, the *correct* approach is to set a_2 = 0.0. This is because while the proper value of τ may not be known we do know that the driver of the second vehicle is unable to apply his brakes before the hit.

Several special cases arise:

Case (a): Here we have $v_1 = v_2$ and no braking by driver 2, hence $a_2 = 0.0$. Here we assume that τ is greater than the time to hit.

The result is

$$v_{impact} = \sqrt{2a_1\Delta}$$

This result says that the *smaller* the initial gap the *safer* the situation! Clearly, this goes against the "common wisdom" of always leaving the largest gap, and seems counter-intuitive. However, this result is *exactly* what is regularly seen in NASCAR races. Here we often have cars traveling at about 120 to 190 mph with a gap of only a few feet. Yet when they hit (because the first driver suddenly brakes) we frequently observe very limited damage. Of course, this describes the first collision. If either driver subsequently "loses it" the *second (and third)* collision (such as with the wall) may be much worse. A little thought reveals that the "same speed, small gap" condition is the one that applies to the carriages and engine of a train. When the train stops the carriages do not all collide significantly with the rear of the engine. If a series of cars were initially "glued" to each other there would likewise be no effective collisions between them when the first car tried to brake.

Case (b): Here driver 2 does start to brake, and $a_2 = a_1$, while $v_2 = v_1$. This situation corresponds to the case where τ is less than the time to hit.

The result is

$$v_{impact} = a_2\tau = a_1\tau$$

This result applies provided the front vehicle is still moving when hit. Note how this result does not depend on the initial gap. The gap becomes important *only* for cases where the two braking decelerations are *not* equal (i.e., the term $[a_2 - a_1]$ is finite).

Option B regularly applies to the more common low-speed case where the front vehicle actually stops (or almost stops) before the second car hits.

Case (c): If $v_2 = v_1$, $a_2 = a_1$ and $v_1' = 0.0$, we get

$$v_{impact} = \sqrt{2a_2\left(v_2\tau - \Delta\right)}$$

This *is* the "large gap is safer" rule. In particular, this explains the "1-second" (or "2-seconds," etc.) rule for safe driving. In reality, the equation merely states that the resulting impact speed drops to zero if the "bracket" becomes zero. Thus, if the distance traveled by vehicle 2 during the P/R time of driver 2 is *less* than the initial inter-vehicle gap there will be no collision, *provided* both vehicles can brake at similar rates. If the P/R time is 1.0 seconds this becomes the "1-second" rule, and so on. At 10 mph = 14.67 ft/s a 1.0 second P/R implies a distance of about 1 car length. Hence the "1-second" rule is also "one car-length for every 10 mph," and so forth.

To help decide which equations to use, compare the brake-stop time for vehicle 1 versus the P/R time for driver 2. If the former is equal to or less than the P/R time then (usually) the target stops before the bullet reaches it. Typical P/R times (for simple brake/no-brake decisions) are in the range 1.0 to 1.5 seconds. Typical hard braking is about $0.7g$. Hence initial speeds below about $0.7g \times 1.5 =$ 34 ft/s = 23 mph will usually imply the use of option B. Conversely, if the initial speeds are highway values (e.g., 75 mph = 110 ft/s) the brake-stopping time is about 4.9 seconds. Since this time is much longer than typical P/R times the usual result is that the bullet catches the target before the latter has stopped. Hence, option A usually applies. These effects should always be confirmed by a few quick "optional calculations" to confirm the correct choice.

Part of the attempt to design "intelligent cars" involves suggested transmitter/receiver systems (usually microwave radar) which "take over the driving" of the bullet car should the system decide the bullet is dangerously close to the target ahead. However, as seen in the equations above, this decision is more complicated than might at first be suspected, since some degree of logic must be employed. Otherwise, the wrong equation might be used.

Some More Statistical Comments

As explained in Chapter 19, if we know the number of tests (n) and the probability of injury (p) we can calculate the expected mean number of injuries ($m = np$) and the standard deviation ($s^2 = np(1 - p)$). This information then allows the lower and upper ranges to be calculated. Thus, for 95 percent confidence the lower range is $m - 2s$, while the upper range is $m + 2s$. However, when performing experiments we do *not* know, *a priori*, whether a measurement is at the low end of an upper probability, or at the high end of a lower probability. Our measurement could be to the low side of the Gaussian curve or to the high side of the curve (or any point in between). Thus, we must compute the lower and upper possibilities.

Let R be the number of actually observed injuries. Let N be the number of occupants tested in a given scenario (fixed vehicle, seat, seatback, headrest, delta-v, etc.). Let P_L be the lower probability, and P_U be the upper probability. Then we have, for 95 percent confidence,

$$R = NP_u - 2\sqrt{NP_u(1-P_u)}$$

or

$$R = NP_L - 2\sqrt{NP_L(1-P_L)}$$

This implies there are two limits for the probabilities. Table A.2 shows the results

Table A.2

N	R	P_L	P_U
5	0	0.000	0.444
10	0	0.000	0.286
20	0	0.000	0.167
30	0	0.000	0.118
40	0	0.000	0.091
50	0	0.000	0.074
100	0	0.000	0.038
200	0	0.000	0.020
300	0	0.000	0.013
500	0	0.000	0.008

for the case of $R = 0.0$ (no observed injuries) for varying N (number tested).

What Table A.2 illustrates is that even if no injuries are observed this is still consistent with either a lower probability of zero or a higher probability of P_U. Thus, testing only five subjects still allows a 44.4 percent chance of injury for the overall population. Testing fifty subjects reduces the possible upper value to 7.4 percent, while testing 500 subjects reduces the upper value to 0.8 percent.

This merely demonstrates that to really know the upper probability of injury for the general population it is necessary to test large numbers of subjects. Furthermore, *each* of these groups of N must apply to *only one specific set of testing conditions*. It is *not* scientific to perform a mix and match such that variations in occupant's sex, weight, height, headrest position, prior medical problems, and so on, are within any group.

To illustrate the problem, suppose "Aunt Daisy" is fifty-five years old and has had prior neck problems. Suppose she is rear-ended when looking left and is out-of-position (twisted torso). Let her experience a delta-v of 5 mph with an offset hit that spins her vehicle clockwise through 10 degrees.

Question: what low-speed volunteer tests exist that

1. test someone like "Aunt Daisy" (sex, age, size, weight, prior injury)

and

2. test someone looking left and out-of-position

and

3. involve a delta-v of 5 mph

and

4. involve an offset impact that produces a clockwise spin of 10 degrees?

Answer: Absolutely none! Thus, there is no data for *this* case, despite all the "many" low-speed experiments. So there is no relevant experimental data that can be cited.

Likewise, little meaning can be ascribed to tests which use the *same* subject and multiple delta-v's.

If a *given* person is tested at 2 mph, 4 mph and 6 mph and suffers no injury, how many test points do we have?

There are two options. Option A is that we subscribe to *cumulative* injury (but most experts don't seem to assume this). For example, if the cumulative injury is based on energy we could use

$$v_{effective} = \sqrt{2^2 + 4^2 + 6^2} = 7.48 \text{ mph}.$$

But, we immediately see that our three data points are reduced to only one point. This will be true regardless of which cumulative law we invoke. Multiple tests will always be reduced to *one* equivalent test.

Option B: However, if we do *not* assume cumulative injury, we are forced to admit that our "three tests" only give *one* datum point, *anyway*. If there is no injury for 6 mph then there was clearly no expectation of injury at any lower speed either! To illustrate the absurdity of including all the lower speed tests as part of the "impressive" number of total low-speed tests, note that we could logically include all *zero-speed* tests! It would be absurd (and totally non-scientific) to include the hundreds (or thousands) of non-impacts as part of our data base for "no injury."

It should also be noted that practically all such testing *specifically removes* potential problems, such as volunteers with previous neck injuries. Thus, in reality, the tests are useful studies of the kinematic motions of the individuals (but for limited conditions), but are *not* studies of *injury thresholds*.

When the foregoing factors are considered we rapidly discover that the existing data base for low-speed volunteer testing is very small, and frequently does not apply to a specific case in hand.

The Angular Momentum Approach for Tripped Rollovers

We previously explained that to allow a sideways curb hit to just cause a rollover the initial horizontal kinetic energy of the vehicle must be at least as large as the energy required to lift the vehicle CM from its initial height above the road to the position directly above the trip point. This modeling approach gives the lower bound to the velocity because it assumes negligible energy loss during the collision with the curb. Thus this approach relies on the conservation of energy, and assumes

$$\frac{1}{2}mv_0^2 = mg(R-h)$$

where m is mass, v_0 is the initial horizontal velocity, R is the diagonal between the trip point and the vehicle CM, and h is the initial height of the CM above the trip point.

However, there is a second modeling technique which relies on the conservation of angular momentum (AM). This model is described by Huang (ref 112), and appears to be the one adopted by NHTSA. For this model we first allow the horizontal vehicle motion to define an angular momentum relative to the trip point. Thus:

Step 1

$$mv_{00}h = I_x\omega$$

where v_{00} is the initial horizontal velocity, I_x is the momentum of inertia about the trip point and ω is the induced rotation rate immediately after the curb hit.

We now compute the corresponding rotational energy and equate this with the energy needed to cause the CM to rise to above the trip point. Thus:

Step 2

$$\frac{1}{2}I_x\omega^2 = mg(R-h)$$

The local CM velocity immediately after the trip is given by $v = \omega R$ and is perpendicular to R.

If we compare the AM technique with the energy one we find that the AM method immediately implies a significant loss of energy, and fails to account for this loss.

To show this, consider a square-section vehicle of uniform density such that $H = W$, where H is the height and W is the width. Then $h = H/2$, and $I_x = m(H^2 + W^2)/3 = 2mH^2/3$. If we now compute the angular kinetic energy and compare with the initial linear kinetic energy we obtain

$$\frac{1}{2}I_x w^2 = \frac{1}{2}mv_{00}^2\left(\frac{h}{k_{rot}}\right) = \frac{1}{2}mv_{00}^2\left[\frac{3}{4}\frac{H^2}{\left(H^2+w^2\right)}\right] = \frac{1}{2}mv_{00}^2\left(\frac{3}{8}\right)$$

Thus, KE(rotational) = (3/8)KE(linear).

Over one-half of the original energy is missing! Comparing the equations for the energy model with those for the AM model we see that v_{00} will need to be larger than v_0 by the factor $\sqrt{8/3} = 1.63$.

Although vehicles do lose energy during a collision we normally account for this by allowing some to be lost permanently during crush and allowing some to be regained due to elastic rebound. The AM technique assumes all the loss to be some form of plastic crush, because there is no other explanation for the energy loss. Further, the AM technique also ignores conservation of linear momentum. When the vehicle is first tripped and starts to rotate there is a reduction in the horizontal speed. Simultaneously, there is an increase in the vertical speed. Both effects imply that we have both a horizontal and vertical impulse. Because these impulses are with the earth, which is assumed rigid and infinitely massive, there can be no energy loss to the earth. So the entire energy loss must be within the vehicle (as with a rigid barrier hit). Yet the critical velocity for a tripped rollover is small, so we would not ordinarily expect a purely plastic vehicle response.

Thus, whereas the energy model gives a lower bound for just rolling (negligible energy loss), the AM model gives an upper bound for the roll (maximum energy loss), in terms of the necessary initial horizontal speed. Only an experiment can determine which of the two options is closest to reality.

Note that after the rotation starts the remainder of the logic is essentially the same regardless of the model used. Hence the major difference is in the definitions of v_0 and v_{00}.

Pole-Vaulting

It may not be obvious, but the athletic sport of pole-vaulting is merely a variant on the tripped rollover. During athletic pole-vaulting the distinction between the energy model and the AM model becomes more obvious. For this case the energy model is closest to reality. The pole used is very elastic and is designed to flex during the jump, thereby storing elastic energy. As the jumper leaves the ground it will be observed that the pole bends. Further, the jumper's horizontal motion is slowed by virtue of the reaction through the pole. Because the pole is angled with respect to the horizontal this reaction force also causes a vertical motion of the jumper. Then as the jumper rises the pole is observed to re-straighten. By the time the jumper is about to clear the bar the pole is once again straight and has returned its stored elastic energy to the jumper. Thus, the pole-vaulter relies on this elastic response to help achieve the high jump.

The trajectory of the jumper is also non-circular, and is close to an ellipse. The reason is simple; initially as the jumper starts to rise the bending of the pole puts the jumper closer to the pivot point than the original pole length, but when the jumper is about to reach the bar the pole has straightened. Consequently, the trajectory is more of an ellipse with the major axis vertical and the minor axis horizontal.

Restitution with Rotating Bodies

Restitution is usually defined with regard to the velocities of the CM motions of the bullet and target. (Strictly speaking, it refers to momentum.) For a near-inline collision the bullet does not (usually) go through the target, hence the bullet slows and the target speeds up and any finite bounce (restitution) results in the target moving faster than the bullet. Here, there is no confusion between "bounce" and "restitution." However, consider the strongly off-set impact, such as the bullet hitting a stationary target perpendicularly at the extreme front of the bullet (see Chapters 4 and 11). Similar considerations also apply for the "glancing blow."

When hit in this off-set manner the apparent weight of the target reduces and acts as if it is w/γ where w is the true weight and $\gamma = 1 + (r/k)^2$ where r is the torque-arm (or moment-arm) and k is the radius of gyration about the CM for the target. The bullet slows down but continues along its original straight-line path if the impact force on the bullet is itself central (along the longitudinal axis). The front of the target rapidly speeds up in the direction of the bullet. Simultaneously, the CM of the target also speeds up in this direction but is slower than the front (by the same factor, γ). This is due to the induced spin of the target. More importantly, *without material bounce at the regions of contact,* the new target CM velocity is less than the new bullet CM velocity.

Since restitution is usually defined with regard to the CM velocities, we see that this results in a coefficient of restitution which has the opposite sign to the normal value. If we define the in line case as a *positive* quantity we are forced to admit that the off-set hit gives a *negative* quantity.

Now allow there to be some form of "bounce" at the regions of material contact. This will reduce the CM velocity of the bullet even more, but it will also increase the new spin rate of the target. Simultaneously, the new velocity of the front of the target will increase as will the new CM velocity of the target. For sufficient bounce the new target CM velocity can become larger than the new CM velocity of the bullet. Voila! The restitution suddenly becomes *positive* again! Thus, the whole notion that we can have positive restitution, negative restitution, or both, reveals itself.

Specifically, consider a bullet of weight w_1 hitting a target of weight w_2 in the nose-hit off set manner. If we define e_B as the "material bounce" and e_{CM} as the "CM restitution" it can then be shown that

$$e_{CM} = \left(\frac{w_1 + w_2}{\gamma_2 w_1 + w_2} \right) (1 + e_B) - 1$$

where we define e_B as positive (as most people do). For $\gamma_2 = 1.0$ (a central hit on the target) we obtain the "trivial" result $e_{CM} = e_B$. However, for a larger γ_2 (this can range from 1.0 to about 4.0) we see that e_{CM} can be less than e_B. For small e_B and large γ_2, e_{CM} becomes negative.

Because energy changes relate to the square of velocities, the sign of the restitution does not matter. Hence, the overall lost energy is still related to the maximum energy loss (which occurs for maximum material deformations before rebound) by $\Delta E_{net} = (1 - e^2)\, E_{max}$.

As a simple example, let the two vehicles have identical weights and let $\gamma_2 =$ 4.0, then we obtain

$$e_{CM} = 0.4 e_B - 0.6$$

If $e_B = 0.0$ (no material bounce at the contact region) $e_{CM} = -0.6$. This merely means that the new bullet CM velocity is $0.8v_0$ where v_0 is the original bullet velocity. This is also the new "nose" velocity for the target. But the new target CM velocity is only $0.2v_0$. Hence restitution for the CM velocities is $-(0.8 - 0.2)\, v_0/1.0v_0 = -0.6$.

However, if $e_B = 0.5$, then $e_{CM} = -0.4$. Hence the two CM velocities have "closed up" on each other. For smaller torque-arms (hence smaller γ_2) the value of e_{CM} can "pass through" zero as e_B increases, and ultimately become positive.

References

1. "Vehicular Occupant Restraint Systems and Components Standards Manual." SAE HS-13, 1993.

2. Limpert, R. *Motor Vehicle Accident Reconstruction and Cause Analysis*, 3rd ed. Michie Company, 1989.

3. Hollings, E.F. and Bryan, R.H. "Highway Safety: Reliability and Validity of DOT Crash Tests," United States General Accounting Office, Report to Congressional Requesters, GAO/PEMD-95-5.

4. NHTSA Memorandum 79-17-N01-709, "1994 NCAP Final Report."

5. *Accident Reconstruction Journal,* Volume 7, No. 4, July/August,1995, Victor Craig ed.

6. Medical School for Lawyers (three videos): "The Complete Orthopedic Examination," "Medical Evidence of Soft Tissue Injury" and "The Complete Neurological Examination," SEAK, Inc., 1995.

7. Fung. *Biomechanics: Mechanical Properties of Living Tissues*, 2nd ed., Springer Verlag, 1993. [This describes much of the physical workings of the body, with emphasis on elasto-viscous behavior].

8. Mertz and Patrick. "Strength and Response of the Human Neck," SAE 710855, 1971.

9. Gurdjian, Lange, Patrick and Thomas. *Impact Injury and Crash Protection.* Charles C. Thomas, publisher, Springfield, Illinois, 1970.

10. Damask, A.C., Damask and Damask. *Injury Causation Analyses* (two vols.). The Michie Company, 1990 and 1993. (Note: these books quote much data from Yamada, *The Strength of Biological Materials.* Williams & Wilkins, Baltimore, MD, 1970)

11. McConnell et al. "Analysis of Human Test Subject Kinematic Responses to Low Velocity Rear End Impacts," SAE 930889, 1993.

12. West et al. "Low Speed Rear-End Collision Testing Using Human Subjects," *Accident Reconstruction Journal*, May/June 1993.

13. Siegmund et al. "Speed Change (delta-V) of Amusement Park Bumper Cars," Proceedings of the Canadian Multidisciplinary Road Safety Conference VIII; Saskatoon, Saskatchewan, June 14–16, 1993.

14. Ommaya and Hirsch. "Tolerances of Cerebral Concussion from Head Impact and Whiplash in Primates," *Journal of Biomechanics*, Vol 4, Pergamon Press, Inc, 1971.

15. Siegmund et al. "Characteristics of Specific Automobile Bumpers in Low-Velocity Impacts," SAE 940916, 1994.

16. Woolley R.L. et al. "Rear Stiffness Coefficients Derived from Barrier Test Data," SAE 910120, in SAE SP-853, 1991.

17. Bohan, T.L. and Damask, A.C., eds. *Forensic Accident Investigation: Motor Vehicles*, Michie, 1995. (Wood, D.P., Chapter 7.)

18. Szabo et al. "Human Occupant Kinetic Response to Low Speed Rear-End Impacts," SAE 940532, 1994.

19. "Expert AutoStats™," a computer program from 4N6XPRT Systems™, Forensic Expert Software, La Mesa, CA, 1994.

20. Noon. *Introduction to Forensic Engineering*, CRC Press, 1992.

21. Baker and Fricke. *The Traffic Accident Investigation Manual*, Northwestern University Traffic Institute, 1986, and *Traffic Accident Reconstruction*, Northwestern University Traffic Institute, 1990.

22. Noga and Oppenheim. "CRASH3 User's Guide and Technical Manual," U.S. Department of Transportation, 1981.

23. Harris. *The Shock and Vibration Handbook*, 3rd ed., McGraw-Hill, 1988. (Chapter 44)

24. Lundstrom. "The Safety Factor in Automotive Design," SAE West Coast Meeting, August 1966.

25. *Crush Stiffness Coefficients for Vehicle Model Years 1960–1994,* Neptune Engineering, P.O. Box 1597, Clovis, CA.

26. Hull and Newton."Estimating Crush Stiffness when Reconstructing Vehicle Accidents," SAE 930898, 1993.

27. Eubanks and Hill. *Pedestrian Accident Reconstruction and Litigation,* 2d ed. (with videotape), Lawyers & Judges Publishing Co., 1998.

28. McConnell, W. et al. "Human Head and Neck Kinematics After Low Velocity Rear-End Impacts—Understanding 'Whiplash'," SAE 952724, in 39th Stapp Car Crash Conference Proceedings, SAE P-299, 1995.

29. Campbell. "Energy Basis for Collisional Severity," SAE 740565, 1974.

30. Nystrom, G.A. et al. "Stiffness Parameters for Vehicle Collision Analysis," SAE 910119 in SAE SP-853, 1991.

31. Nielsen, G. et al. "Human Subject Responses to Repeated Low Speed Impacts Using Utility Vehicles," SAE 970394, in SAE SP-1231.

32. Malmsbury, M. and Eubanks, J., "Damage and/or Impact Absorber (Isolator) Movements Observed in Low Speed Crash Tests Involving Ford Escorts," SAE 940912, in SAE SP-1030.

33. Ishikawa, H. "Impact Center and Restitution Coefficients for Accident Reconstruction," SAE 940564, in SAE SP-1030.

34. Lee, W. "Performance Consistency of Thermoplastics," *Automotive Engineering*, November 1994.

35. Siegmund, G., Bailey, M. and King, D., "Characteristics of Specific Automobile Bumpers in Low-Velocity Impacts," SAE 940916, in SAE SP-1030.

36. Siegmund, G. and King, D. "Low-Speed Impacts," Chapter 1 in *Forensic Accident Investigation: Motor Vehicles—2*, ed. Bohan T., Lexis Law Publishing, 1998.

37. "An Improved MPV Bumper System," *Automobile Engineering*, SAE May 1995, page 53.

38. IIHS Status Report, Vol. 28, No. 3, March 1993.

39. "Low Speed Crash Test Program of 1991 Model Vehicles," National Technical Systems, Hartwood, VA, Report No. 533-2802, Rev. A, February 20, 1991. Performed for IIHS.

40. Cornille, H. Jr. "A Front Rail Design for Efficient Crush Energy Absorption," Ford Motor Company, International Body Engineering Conference, IBEC Ltd., Publications, 1995, page 88.

41. Neptune, J. and Flynn, J. "A Method for Determining Accident Specific Crush Stiffness Coefficients," SAE 940913, in SAE SP-1030.

42. "An Analysis of Trends of Vehicle Frontal Impact Stiffness," Varat, M., Husher, S. and Kerkhoff, J. SAE 940914, in SAE SP-1030.

43. "Effects of Restitution in the Application of Crush Coefficients," McHenry, R. and McHenry, B. SAE 970960, in SAE SP-1237.

44. Alexander, R.M. *Exploring Biomechanics: Animals in Motion*, Scientific American Library, 1992.

45. Carola, R., Harley J.P. and Noback C.R. *Human Anatomy and Physiology*, 2nd ed., McGraw-Hill, Inc., 1992.

46. Crowe, H. "Medical Symposium," 1928 (unpublished). Also Davis, A.G. "Injuries of the Cervical Spine," *JAMA*, 127: 149-156, 1945.

47. Kroemer, Kroemer and Kroemer-Elbert. *Ergonomics*, Prentice-Hall, 1994.

48. Weimer. *Handbook of Ergonomic and Human Factors Tables*, PTR Prentice-Hall, 1993.

49. Backaitis, S.H., ed. "Biomechanics of Impact Injury and Injury Tolerances of the Head-Neck Complex," SAE PT-43, 1993. Specifically: Foust D. R., et al., "Cervical Range of Motion and Dynamic Response and Strength of Cervical Muscles," SAE 730975, 1973.

50. "Shopping for a Safer Car," IIHS Report, 1995.

51. Backaitis, S.H., ed. "Biomechanics of Impact Injury and Injury Tolerances of the Head-Neck Complex," SAE PT-43, 1993. Specifically: Mertz H.J. and Patrick L.M. "Investigation of the Kinematics and Kinetics of Whiplash," SAE 670919, 1967.

52. Gray. *Gray's Anatomy*, Running Press, 1974.

53. Netter. *Atlas of Human Anatomy*, Ciba-Geigy Corporation, 1993.

54. Miller, C.E. *How Insurance Companies Settle Cases*, James Publishing, 1995.

55. Ruan, J.S., Khalil, T. and King, A.I."Dynamic Response of the Human Head to Impact by Three-Dimensional Finite Element Analysis," Transactions of the ASME, Journal of Biomechanical Engineering, Feb 1994, Vol. 116.

56. Backaitis, S.H., ed. "Biomechanics of Impact Injury and Injury Tolerances of the Thorax-Shoulder Complex," SAE PT-45, 1994. Specifically: Lau I. V., and Viano D. C., "The Viscous Criterion-Bases and Applications of an Injury Severity Index for Soft Tissues," SAE 861882, 1986.

57. Backaitis, S.H., ed. "Biomechanics of Impact Injury and Injury Tolerances of the Thorax-Shoulder Complex," SAE PT-45, 1994. Specifically: Patrick L. M., "Frontal Force Impact Tolerance of the Human Thorax," SAE P-67, 1967.

58. Tallarida, R.J. *Pocket Book of Integrals and Mathematical Formulas*, CRC Press, 1991.

59. Pope, M. et al. "Electromyographic Changes Under Whiplash Loading," in *Frontiers in Head and Neck Trauma: Clinical and Biomechanical*, Yoganandon, N. et al., IOS Press, 1998.

60. Data provided by attorney Nicholas Vakula, of Dasse and Vakula, P.C., Scottsdale, Arizona. This package includes various affadavits, including those by Professor (Dr.) Reiser, Arizona State University. Professor Reiser is a statistician and discusses the inadequacy of the existing "volunteer database," illustrating how the limited data, and methods of performing the tests can *not* presently lead to anything other than an "illustrative overview," and certainly does *not* allow specific assessment of individuals suffering injury.

61. Brault, J. et al. "Clinical Response of Human Subjects to Rear-End Automobile Collisions," Arch Phys Med Rehabil, Vol. 79, January 1998.

62. Cesarani, A. et al. *Whiplash Injuries: Diagnosis and Treatment*, Springer-Verlag, 1996. Chapter 3 by P. L. Ardoino (FIAT Motor Works).

63. Benson, B. et al. "Effect of Seat Stiffness in Out-of-Position Occupant Response in Rear-End Collisions," 388SAE 962434, Stapp 40th Conference, 1996.

64. Allen M. et al. "Acceleration Perturbations of Daily Living—A Comparison to 'Whiplash'," *Spine,* Vol. 19, number 11, 1994, pp. 1285–1290.

65. Nahum, A.M. and Melvin, J.W., eds. *Accidental Injury: Biomechanics and Prevention,* Springer Verlag, 1993.

66. Anderson. J. et al. *Materials Science*, 4th ed., Chapman and Hall Publishers, 1990. "Miners Law" in chapter 9, pp. 226 and 227.

67. Di Maio, D.J. and Di Maio, V.J.M. *Forensic Pathology*, CRC Press, 1993.

68. "Science," May 20, 1994, page 1102, published by the American Association for the Advancement for Science (AAAS). This article discussed the Phineas Gage case.

69. Ommaya, A. "Biomechanics of Head Injury: Experimental Aspects," *The Biomechanics of Trauma* (Nahum and Melvin eds.) pp. 245–269, 1985. Also, Gennarelli. T. and Thibeault, L. "Clinical Rationale for a Head Injury Angular Acceleration Criterion," in *Head Injury Mechanisms: The Need for an Angular Acceleration Criterion,* AAAM, 1989.

70. Evans, L. *Traffic Safety and the Driver*, Van Nostrand Reinhold, 1991.

71. *Automotive Handbook*, 3rd ed., Robert Bosch GmbH, 1993.

General Bibliography

Engineering/Mechanics/Reconstruction Texts

72. Backaitis, S.H., ed. "Accident Reconstruction Technologies: Pedestrians & Motorcyclists in Automotive Collisions," SAE PT-35, 1990.

73. Grimes, W.D. and Day, T.D. "Accident Reconstruction: Technology and Animation IV," SAE SP-1030, 1994.

74. "Automobile Safety: Present and Future Technology," SAE SP-925, 1992.

75. "Occupant Containment and Methods of Assessing Occupant Protection in the Crash Environment," SAE SP-1045, 1994.

76. "Accident Reconstruction: Technology and Animation," SAE SP-853, 1991.

77. "Seat Safety: Comfort and Safety," SAE SP-963, 1993.

78. "Accident Reconstruction: Technology and Animation V," SAE SP-1083, 1995.

79. "Reconstruction of Motor Vehicle Accidents: A Technical Compendium," S.H. Backaitis, ed. SAE PT-34, 1989.

80. Johnson, W. and Mamalis, A.G. *Crashworthiness of Vehicles*, Mechanical Engineering Publications (MEP), Ltd., London, 1978.

81. Carvill, J. *Mechanical Engineer's Data Handbook*, CRC Press, 1993.

82. Bolton, W. *Engineering Materials Pocket Book*, CRC Press, 1989.

83. Barrett, C.R., Nix, W.D. and Tetelman, A.S. *The Principles of Engineering Materials*, Prentice-Hall, Inc., 1973.

84. MacInnis, D., Williamson, P. and Nielsen, G. "Sun Position and Twilight Times for Driver Visibility," SAE 950359 in SP-1083.

85. Kornhauser, M. "Delta-V Thresholds for Cervical Spine Injury," SAE 960093.

86. Griffith, *Complete Guide to Sports Injuries*, The Body Press, 1986. [This indicates the correlations between many contact sports injuries and those which occur in auto accidents].

87. Orner, P.A. "A Physician-Engineer's View of Low Velocity Rearend Collisions," SAE 921574.

88. Lim G. et al. "Normalization of Head Impact Test Data to 24 km/hr (15 mph)," SAE 970389 in SP-1231.

89. Nusholtz, G., Glascoe, L. and Wylie. E. "Cavitation During Head Impact," SAE 970390.

90. Levine, R.S., ed. "Head and Neck Injury," SAE P-276, 1994.

91. Rothenberg, M.A. *Anatomy and Physiology for Lawyers*, John Wiley & Sons, 1994.

92. Goodman, H.F., ed. *Orthopedic Disability and Expert Testimony*, 4th ed., John Wiley & Sons, 1993.

93. Backaitis, S.H., ed. "Biomechanics of Impact Injury and Injury Tolerances of the Abdomen, Spine and Pelvis," SAE PT-47, 1995.

94. Doege, T.C. and Houston, T.P., eds. *Guides to the Evaluation of Permanent Impairment*, 4th ed., American Medical Association.

95. Pascarelli, E. and Quilter, D. *Repetitive Strain Injury*, John Wiley & Sons, Inc., 1994.

96. Roberts, A.C. et al. *Litigating Head Trauma Cases,* John Wiley & Sons, Inc., 1994.

97. Carroll, C., McAfee, P.C. and Riley, L.H. "Whiplash Injuries and How to Treat Them," *Journal of Musculoskeletal Medicine*, June, 1992.

98. Youdas, J.W. et al. "Normal Range of Motion of the Cervical Spine: An Initial Goniometric Study," *Physical Therapy*, Vol.72, No. 11, November 1992.

99. Clark, C.R. "Common Neck Problems," Chapter 23 in *Orthopaedics: Essentials of Diagnosis and Treatment*, pp. 285–294, 1992.

100. Evans, R.W. "Some Observations on Whiplash Injuries," *Neurological Clinics*, Vol. 10, No. 4, pp. 975–997, November 1992.

101. Hirsch, S.A. et al. "Whiplash Syndrome: Fact or Fiction?," *Orthopedic Clinics of North America*, Vol. 19, No. 4, pp. 791–795, 1988.

102. Maimaris, C., Barnes, M.R. and Allen, M.J. "Whiplash Injuries of the Neck: A Retrospective Study," *Injury: The British Journal of Accident Surgery* (1988), Vol. 19, No. 5.

103. MacNab, I. "Acceleration Injuries of the Cervical Spine," *The Journal of Bone and Joint Surgery*, Vol. 46-A, No. 8, December 1964.

104. Aubrey, J.B., Dobbs, A.R. and Rule, B.G. "Layperson's Knowledge about the Sequelae of Minor Head Injury and Whiplash," *Journal of Neurology, Neurosurgery, and Psychiatry* 1989; 52: 842–846.

105. Radonov, B.P. et al., "Role of Psychosocial Stress in Recovery from Common Whiplash," *The Lancet*, Vol. 338: September 1991.

106. Norris, S.H. and Watt, I. "The Prognosis of Neck Injuries Resulting from Rearend Vehicle Collisions," *The Journal of Bone and Joint Surgery*, Vol. 65-B, No. 5, November 1983.

107. Yoganandon, N. et al., eds. *Frontiers in Head and Neck Trauma: Clinical and Biomechanical*, IOS Press, 1998. See especially Chapter 6: "Whiplash Injury Biomechanics" (six papers).

108. Stern, B. "Putting the Brakes on Defense Experts in Low-Impact Collision Cases," Chapter 6 in 1999 *Wiley Expert Witness Update: New Developments in Personal Injury Litigation*, Pierson, ed. Apen Law & Business, 1999.

109. Rothenberg, M. "Chiropractic Terms and Literature," Chapter 2 in *Preparing Orthopedic Disability Cases*, Aspen Law & Business, 1999.

110. Rothenberg, M. "Neck and Back Pain," Chapter 3 in *Preparing Orthopedic Disability Cases,* Aspen Law & Business, 1999. This describes the fact that discs *do* have nerves.

New References

111. Gillespie, T.D."Fundamentals of Vehicle Dynamics," published by SAE, 1992.

112. Huang, M. *Vehicle Crash Mechanics*, published by CRC, 2002.

113. Brach, Raymond M. and Matthew R. Brach. *Vehicle Accident Analysis and Reconstruction Methods,* published by SAE, 2005.

114. Evans, Leonard. *Traffic Safety,* Science Serving Society, 2004.

115. Pacejka, Hans B., *Tire and Vehicle Dynamics,* Second Edition, published by SAE, 2006.

116. Rose, N. and Beauchamp, G. *A Variable Deceleration Rate Approach to Rollover Crash Reconstruction,* Collision Magazine, Volume 5, Issue 1 (Spring 2010).

117. Cooperrider, N. K. et al. *Testing and Analysis of Vehicle Rollover Behavior,* SAE paper 900366, 1990.

118. Haight, R. *An Abbreviated History of CDR TECHNOLOGY,* Collision Magazine, Volume 5, Issue 1, (Spring 2010).

About the Author

Alan J. Watts, Ph.D., is presently a consultant on accident reconstruction and biomechanics and the owner of Watts-Co in Albuquerque, NM, which he started in 2000. From April 2000 to September 2001 he also worked (by invitation of the owner) as the chief scientist for Permacharge Corporation in Rio Rancho, NM, a company that specializes in electrostatic charging of various materials, where his job was to explain how their existing system was actually working and to suggest improvements and options. Prior to that he was the chief scientist at POD Associates, Inc., in Albuquerque, NM, a company that initially performed defense-related U.S. government contract work before concentrating on computer programming/information systems. Prior to that he was the senior staff scientist at Ktech Corporation in Albuquerque, NM, another U.S. government contractor working on defense issues. He has also been recently appointed to be an adjunct professor at the Union Institute and University (based in Cincinnati, Ohio), overseeing a Ph.D. course in biomechanics.

He received his B.Sc. (1965) and Ph.D. (1969) in physics from Exeter University, England. His Ph.D. included studies of metals using ESR (electron spin resonance) and NMR (nuclear magnetic resonance—the forerunner of the medical MRI). He performed research for the British government at the Atomic Weapons Research Establishment, where he studied the effects of dynamic impacts, the use of high explosives, and the effects of rapid, very strong energy deposition in materials (due to x-rays, electrons and protons), which automatically involved the studies of shockwave behavior, and material failure modes (plastic flow, rupture, material spallation, melting, vaporization and ionization). His studies ranged from the design of low-impulse momentum gauges to the use of high-pressure stress gauges, and the synergistic effects of thermal-mechanical material responses, including aspects of nuclear weapon designs. Diagnostic techniques used included very powerful "flash x-ray" machines, capable of taking x-rays of rapidly moving opaque objects on time scales of microseconds.

He emigrated to the U.S. in 1979 to Albuquerque, NM, where he has since performed research on behalf of the U.S. Government, primarily in the defense arena (Department of Defense, Department of Energy and the Defense Nuclear Agency), and also for civilian agencies (NASA). His studies have emphasized the effects of material responses to various stress-strain loadings, whether weapon-related or impact-related. This has included producing complex computer codes (for USAF, Phillips Laboratory) to evaluate the synergistic effects of thermomechanical responses, and the use of two-stage "gas guns" to evaluate the shock response and equation-of-state of various materials. He has previously made use of three-dimensional finite element codes (3D FE) such as DYNA-3D (using a Cray computer), which is now used by the car industry to assess car crush behavior. Recently he formulated scaling laws for NASA allowing predictions of cratering and perforations for satellite structures due to hypervelocity impacts (space debris and micrometeoroids with impact speeds of several miles per second), with results comparing favorably to large hydrodynamics codes such as CTH from Sandia National Laboratory (SNLA). Some of this work has been used to help design shielding requirements for the International Space Station. Materials studied have ranged from metals through various plastics and composites to elastomers and glasses, with response modes ranging from simple elastoplastic through elastoviscous to phase change effects.

He has worked under contract for the Phillips Laboratory (Albuquerque, NM), Wright Patterson Laboratory (Dayton, OH), Defense Nuclear Agency (Washington, DC), Sandia National Laboratories (Albuquerque, NM), Los Alamos Laboratory (NM) and Lawrence Livermore Laboratory (CA). His work has ranged from studies of x-ray material interactions to the phenomenon of material fragmentation and the behavior of small liquid droplets.

Dr. Watts has been qualified in several state courts and in federal court to do both accident analysis and biomechanics. He has performed accident analyses on behalf of both plaintiffs and defendants, and has worked for both the U.S. Attorney's and the Public Defender's offices. He has also represented the City of Albuquerque (including a SWAT officer and the previous police chief) in federal court where he was qualified to discuss gunshot wounds to the head, the resulting victim's body motion and the resulting blood flow and spatter. While most of his litigation involvement has been in low-speed car crashes he has also handled higher-speed cases (including DWI), some slip-and-fall cases and several murder cases.

He is a member of the American Association for the Advancement of Science (AAAS), a member of the National Association of Professional Accident Reconstruction Specialists (NAPARS), a member of the ARC Network, and a member of the Society of Automotive Engineers (SAE). He has authored over one hundred refereed technical publications and presentations on behalf of government, and has acted as a peer reviewer on several publications of others. He has given talks concerning low-speed accidents to both the Defense Lawyers Association and the Trial Lawyers Association. He has also given similar talks at the Institute for Police and Technology Management (IPTM) in Jacksonville, Florida, and to the Institute of Law Enforcement Education, Pennsylvania.

Index

D

E

F

N

O

P

R

S

Forensic Vision with Application to Highway Safety with CD-Rom 3rd Edition

By Marc Green, Merrill J. Allen,
Bernard S. Abrams, and Leslie Weintraub

Written for attorneys, law enforcement personnel, optometrists, highway engineers, automobile manufacturers, legislators, expert witnesses, and other related professionals, Forensic Vision: with Application to Highway Safety is your reference for accident cases with a vision component. While it does have a focus on the roadway environment, it is primarily about vision and the visual science that applies to analyzing all types of transportation accidents and non-transportation accidents such as auto accidents, pedestrian accidents, falls, medical errors, warnings, eyewitness identification, and more.

When reconstructing the accident, vision is always a component. You need to know what questions are vital to ask, when to call the expert, what evidence will be needed, what kind of help can be expected, and how to structure testimony. Forensic Vision: With Application to Highway Safety provides you with a basic reference in the vision area as well as a starting point for more advanced research.

Produce Code: 5244 • ISBN: 978-1-933264-54-7
Pages: 496 • Casebound • 7″ x 10″

Commercial Vehicle Accident Reconstruction and Investigation, Second Edition

By Rick W. Varner and Roy Sutphen, Sr.

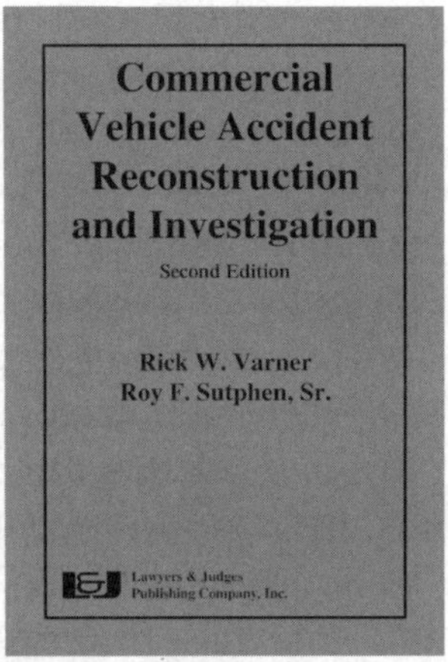

Is it safe to drive with these large trucks? What happens when the small car in front of the commercial vehicle slams on its brakes? Reconstructing commercial vehicle accidents is a complex task that is often misunderstood or misinterpreted. Frequently, mistakes are made in determining the vehicle's ability to brake efficiently, the engine speeds and the loading condition. This reference book identifies the proper techniques you should use in order to correctly assess a commercial vehicle accident scene.

The authors of this text discuss in great detail the unique aspects of commercial vehicle operation, performance and regulations. Chapters are dedicated to the various operating systems of these vehicles such as the electrical systems, tires, steering, suspension and much more. You will also learn about the human factors in commercial vehicle operations and accidents. The drivers of these trucks must drive at 100 percent of their ability in all situations and must meet certain requirements before they are allowed behind the wheel. Even so, accidents do occur and are sometimes caused by the driver's response.

New to this expanded second edition are chapters on vehicle headlamps, terminology, Automatic On-Board Recording Devices (AOBRD), wireless communications equipment, collision warning systems and smart cruise, vehicle speed sensor, and testimony questions, among others.

If you are interested in reconstructing or investigating commercial vehicle accidents, or if you are already involved in this but would like a better understanding of the issues, this book will prove to be valuable tool.

Produce Code: 6478 • ISBN: 978-1-933264-83-7
Pages: 448 • Casebound • 6″ x 9″

Human Factors in Traffic Safety, Second Edition

Edited by Robert E. Dewar and Paul L. Olson

There are more than 175 million licensed drivers in the United States. Combined with the many pedestrians, bicyclists, motorcyclists, and other road users, this creates an interesting mix of elements with very different characteristics. Moving these elements efficiently and safely to their destinations presents a major challenge, particularly in densely populated areas. This book will provide guidance in how to identify these elements in your collision investigations. The authors introduce you to the ways in which designers of vehicles and roadways historically often did not take into account the full range of road user characteristics. The book discusses the substantial improvements in design principles and standards achieved over the years due to the concerted effort by concerned individuals interested in roadway and vehicle design and its impact on traffic safety.

Most importantly, this book introduces you to the behavior of the road user. Driver limitations and driver or pedestrian error are the major factors in traffic accidents, contributing to about 90% of roadway crashes. Driver behavior, however, is often the most complex and yet least understood element in the roadway system. A wide variety of perspectives on human factors and driver behavior are covered ranging from the design of roads, vehicles and traffic control devices to emotional and motivational determinants of driver behavior. Many traffic safety experts have contributed to this book in order to give you a comprehensive introduction to human factors as it pertains to driver and pedestrian behavior and traffic safety. This new edition has been extensively revised, and contains new chapters on driver education and driver distraction. If you are involved with accident investigation or the promotion of traffic safety in any capacity, this book is an essential part of your library.

Produce Code: 5473 • ISBN: 978-1-933264-24-0
Pages: 549 • Softbound • 8.5″ x 11″

Vehicle Speed and Stopping Distance Calculator

By Steve Weintraub

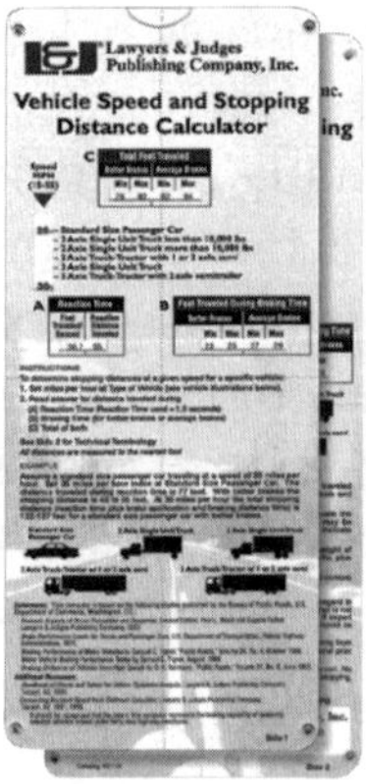

You will use this essential calculator during interviews, investigations, depositions, and trials in determining the speed and stopping distance of automobiles or small or large trucks. One side gives you the stopping distance of cars, and two truck types; the back side shows the stopping distance for three truck tractors and semitrailers.

Example: Assume a standard passenger car traveling at a speed of 35 miles per hour. Dial the calculator to 35 miles per hour and read the section for standard size passenger cars. The distance traveled during reaction time is 37.5 feet. With better brakes the stopping distance is 46 to 47 feet. At 35 miles per hour the total stopping distance (reaction time plus brake application and braking distance time) is 83.5 to 84.5 feet for a standard size passenger car with better brakes.

Produce Code: 0115 • Slide Calculator • 4″ x 9″